INTRODUCTION

Congratulations! Your decision to pursue a career in real estate in Florida is an exciting one. You probably have many questions about real estate as a career, requirements for becoming licensed, and real estate in general. We have made every attempt to address your questions. The material is concise, yet presented in sufficient detail to facilitate your understanding. The content conforms to the Florida Division of Real Estate's prescribed Florida Real Estate Commission (FREC) Course I Syllabus for the prelicense course for sales associates.

As with any profession, the real estate profession has an abundance of terms unique to the industry. Key terms are presented at the beginning of each unit. Learn what these terms mean, and apply them in your real estate discussions. To aid your learning process, each term presented in a key term section is defined in the corresponding unit. You should master these definitions in preparation for your licensing examination.

There are literally hundreds of real estate terms that you will use and apply in your professional career. However, only a limited number of these terms appear in the key term sections. This is because a priority system has been used to help you plan your preparation. Bolded key terms are top priority terms. Throughout the units, you will also find italicized terms. These are important real estate terms that you should understand and be able to apply in your real estate discussions. However, it is not necessary to be able to "recite" a precise definition for italicized terms.

We have also included learning objectives for each unit. The objectives have been carefully selected to coordinate with the key concepts in the course syllabus. Think of the learning objectives as a "road map" to help guide your journey toward licensure. As you proceed through each unit, be sure to complete the Practice Questions and the Unit Exams at the end of each unit so that you can see how well you have mastered the content presented in the unit.

You will note also that each line of the text is numbered for easy reference. In the left margins, you will find shaded boxes with Florida Statute and Administrative Rule numbers. You should read the actual laws and rules in preparation for the license exam. Web links and QR codes to important rules, statutes, and key documents for studying are presented throughout this textbook. During your state exam preparation, referring to the actual real estate license law and FREC rules is important because the state exam law questions often use the wording as it is written in the statute.

Text boxes are featured in your textbook. These boxes contain valuable information. The To Remember boxes contain learning crutches called acronyms to help you recall certain information. Be sure to study these. Other text boxes feature excerpts of Florida statutes and rules for easy reference. The Formula text boxes feature arithmetic formulas that you must be able to apply. You will find all these special features very valuable as you delve into this book.

To be successful, you need to be prepared to devote considerable time to study. There is a large amount of material to master and the end-of-course exam is challenging. This course covers all of the topics that are tested on the state license exam. But alas, there is no magic bullet. You must study and master the material to do well on the end-of-course and state exam. This is the beginning of a new career. A career in real estate requires real estate knowledge, but it also requires being able to be organized, punctual, focused, and to possess good listening skills. All of these characteristics make up the successful real estate student and real estate professional. We are excited for you and wish you the very best as you embark on your new career.

I want to take a moment to thank my co-author, my mentor, my cheerleader, and my dear friend, Linda L. Crawford. Linda has been the word behind this book for over 30 years, and I can only hope that I'm able to continue her legacy for many years to come. She has been available to me every step, guiding my fingers in the right direction and giving me room to offer new ideas. Linda's contributions to this industry are priceless and will continue for many years. She has been a pioneer in the education community, offering her wisdom to the Florida Real Estate Commission with suggested rule updates that will benefit all licensees. She has ensured that education remains at the forefront for Florida real estate licensees. Linda, thank you for your support and constant belief in my abilities; it is truly an honor to walk in your footsteps — Denise.

Before developing this edition, we received specific comments and suggestions that we incorporated into this edition to ensure you the textbook with the absolute best quality. Special thanks are extended to this edition's textbook reviewers: Robert Gordon, GRI, Instructor for Bob Hogue School of Real Estate, and broker owner of Gordon & Associates, and our second reviewer is a valued industry member who wishes to stay anonymous. The reviewers are extremely valuable to ensuring the textbook has the most up to date information to help you become a successful real estate licensee. We genuinely appreciate their hard work and dedication to helping us.

We also want to thank all the instructors who reached out to us to let us know of items that may require clarification in the next edition or errors missed during a review. Their feedback is essential to ensure we supply the best product to you.

This book is coordinated with additional study tools designed to assist you with mastery of the material. Many students choose the *Florida Sales Associate Prelicensing Key Point Review Audio MP3*, which is designed to aid aspiring real estate sales associates in successfully completing the prelicensing course, end-of-course exam, and state licensing exam.

If you are concerned or even panicky about taking the end-of-unit practice quizzes and the practice exam, as well as the state licensing examination, obtain in advance a personal copy of the *Florida Real Estate Exam Manual for Sales Associates and Brokers*. It contains, among other valuable sections, a section titled "Successful Exam-Taking Strategies" and two sample exams, both designed and proven to improve your test-taking ability and scores.

We wish you the very best in your endeavor and would like to hear from you.

Linda L. Crawford
Denise Stolar Johnson
November 2023

FLORIDA

Real Estate Principles, Practices & Law

47th Edition | Linda L. Crawford with Denise Stolar Johnson

FLORIDA REAL ESTATE PRINCIPLES, PRACTICES & LAW 47TH EDITION

Published by DF Institute, LLC, d/b/a Dearborn Real Estate Education and Kaplan Real Estate Education
1515 West Cypress Creek Road
Fort Lauderdale, Florida 33309

ISBN: 978-1-0788-4157-3

10 9 8 7 6 5 4 3 2 1

ISBN: 978-1-0788-4160-3 (custom)

10 9 8 7 6 5 4 3 2 1

ISBN: 978-1-0788-4158-0 (custom)

10 9 8 7 6 5 4 3 2 1

ISBN: 978-1-0788-4159-7 (custom cover)

10 9 8 7 6 5 4 3 2 1

CONTENTS

UNIT

1 THE REAL ESTATE BUSINESS

LEARNING OBJECTIVES

When you have completed this unit, you will be able to accomplish the following.

- Describe the various activities of real estate brokerage.
- Distinguish among the five major sales specialties.
- Identify the role of property managers and situations that require a CAM license.
- Describe activities that require appraiser services, *USPAP*, state regulation of appraisers, and distinguish among a CMA, a BPO, and an appraisal.
- Understand the mortgage process and the role of the mortgage loan originator.
- Explain the three phases of development and construction.
- Distinguish among the three categories of residential construction.
- Describe the National Association of REALTORS®, how a licensee is different from a REALTOR®, and the purpose of an MLS.

KEY TERMS

absentee owner
appraisal
appraiser
broker's price opinion (BPO)
business broker
business opportunity
community association manager (CAM)
comparative market analysis (CMA)
dedication
farm area
follow-up
multiple listing service (MLS)
property management
property manager
real estate brokerage
REALTOR®
rental agent
subdivision plat map
target market

INTRODUCTION

The purpose of this unit is to introduce the reader to the real estate business. The unit discusses real estate brokerage, development, and construction.

1.1 AN INTRODUCTION TO THE REAL ESTATE BUSINESS

Overview of the Real Estate Industry

Real estate is a significant part of the U.S. economy. Jobs in real estate and construction are important contributors to the nation's total employment. Complex real estate transactions demand the services of licensed real estate associates, appraisers, attorneys, mortgage lenders, title insurance agents, architects, surveyors, and accountants. Residential real estate is often the greatest source of wealth and savings for individuals. Commercial real estate addresses the need for retail, office, and manufacturing space.

Real Estate Professionals Possess Expert Information

Real estate brokers provide specialized service for others in return for compensation in the form of a commission, fee, or other valuable consideration. Today, a real estate licensee is paid to handle other people's properties because the licensee is a professional who provides specialized service and expertise. The product that real estate licensees market is expert information. A property handled by a broker normally will be sold more quickly and with less reduction in the desired sale price than if an owner handles the sale without professional assistance. Real estate professionals provide expert information in three areas:

1. *Knowledge of property transfer.* A competent licensed real estate professional must know the economic and legal intricacies associated with transfers of title, property taxes, financing, and local zoning ordinances. Real estate professionals must be intimately familiar with the real estate purchase and sale contract used in their locale.
2. *Knowledge of market conditions*. Property values are affected by changing market conditions. Changes in market conditions are due to changes in income tax laws, building moratoriums, and fluctuations in supply and demand. Changes in market conditions and their effect on valuation must be understood in order to competently assist sellers with listing their property and buyers with purchasing decisions.
3. *Knowledge of how to market real estate and businesses*. To be successful, licensees must know how to market real estate and businesses. The sale presentation that is most effective when working with a physician relocating to a new city may be completely different from the approach used to assist the owner of an expanding gourmet coffee bar in choosing an additional location.

Practice Questions

1. The product that a real estate sales associate must market is ________ ___________.

2. List the three areas of expertise that real estate licensees bring to the transaction.

    1. Knowledge of ____
    2. Knowledge of ____
    3. Knowledge of ____

1.2 REAL ESTATE BROKERAGE

Real estate brokerage is the business of bringing together buyers and sellers, owners and renters, and completing real estate transactions. There are many components of real estate brokerage, including sales and leasing, property management, appraising, financing, and counseling.

A real estate brokerage company legally can be involved with all types of property and provide all types of real estate services. However, this is usually not practical—as the saying goes, "a jack of all trades, a master of none." Companies and licensed real estate professionals usually specialize in the type of services provided, as well as the type of real estate handled, insuring that the company's associates have a competitive advantage in their chosen area of expertise.

Sales and Leasing

Sales and leasing involves real estate license–related activities performed under the authority of a real estate broker. The broker acts as an agent or an intermediary between two or more people in the negotiation of the sale, purchase, or rental of real estate. Sales associates work for a broker, providing services to prospective buyers and sellers.

Understanding sale and lease transactions requires expert knowledge that the average layperson does not possess. Therefore, buyers and sellers and renters and landlords find it more efficient to acquire real estate information through a licensed professional.

Sales Specialties

Real estate sales associates involved in sales and leasing often specialize in one of five major sales specialties:

1. *Residential.* Residential sales associates need to know the best access routes and locations of schools, shopping facilities, and recreation facilities. They must be able to explain property taxes, homestead exemptions, restrictive covenants, and approximate utility costs in the area. One of the more important aspects of residential sales is knowing how to help prospective buyers obtain financing. Most real estate licensees specialize in the sale and purchase of owner-occupied residential property.
2. *Commercial.* Real estate professionals who specialize in commercial sales need expertise regarding income-producing properties, investment analysis, and the various techniques for increasing after-tax cash flow. Improved residential property of more than four units, retail stores, office buildings, and shopping centers are examples of income-producing commercial properties.
3. *Industrial.* Real estate licensees who provide real estate expertise of industrial real estate must have technical knowledge of the needs of different industries, such as transportation requirements, industrial construction methods, and local land-use restrictions affecting industrial properties. Many industrial brokers are developing and marketing industrial subdivisions.

4. *Agricultural*. Professionals who specialize in the sale of farms and agricultural land must be familiar with the operation of farms and the economic problems associated with the various types of farming. Real estate licensees who specialize in agricultural real estate are knowledgeable about farm operations and the federal programs affecting farm operations.
5. *Businesses*. Real estate licensees who engage in the sale, purchase, or lease of businesses are called **business brokers**. A **business opportunity** involves the sale or lease of an existing business, including the sale of tangible and intangible assets. In most states, if real property is an asset of the business, a real estate broker's license is required to sell the business. There is a presumption in Florida law that businesses will have some sort of real property involved, either land with physical improvements (such as a building) or a long-term lease. For this reason, in Florida, an active current real estate license is required to sell or lease business opportunities.

Target Marketing

Real estate professionals have found that advertising money is more efficiently spent and produces better outcomes if efforts are focused on a **target market**. Target marketing involves expertise in locating prospects for property listings and sales. For example, a real estate professional who specializes in listing and finding homes for physicians who are relocating out of state or moving to Florida will develop contacts with the personnel in various local hospitals who work as liaisons with hospital staff.

Effective real estate marketing starts with a strong database of potential customers. Real estate professionals use the database of leads to send targeted advertising. For example, a real estate licensee who specializes in residential leasing might target students moving to a college town. Understanding the demographic, financial, and lifestyle characteristics of a target market helps real estate professionals choose personalized messaging and appropriate advertising media.

Many brokers and sales associates prefer to select one specific portion of a city and become an expert in that particular portion, called a **farm area**. This method of target marketing is called *farming*. Licensees get to know almost every lot, house, and business in their farm areas. Farming involves maintaining data on each property, including when it was built, the sale history, typical marketing time, assessed value, the amount of property taxes, and so forth. Real estate professionals meet the people in the area and make it known that they specialize in that section of town. The farm area soon begins to produce a harvest in the form of listings and sales. Licensees create a reputation for expertise through hard work. When residents in the farm area move or decide to sell, they call on the area expert who knows what price their property will bring in the current market.

Sales associates often contact buyers and sellers within a reasonable time after the title closing. One of the best ways to ensure satisfied buyers and sellers is through **follow-up**. Follow-up is what a sales associate does for buyers and sellers after the sale. The follow-up is important to all aspects of real estate sales because it results in a good reputation, future referrals, and word-of-mouth advertising.

Practice Questions

3. List the five major sales specialties.
    1. ______________________________
    2. ______________________________
    3. ______________________________
    4. ______________________________
    5. ______________________________

4. Real estate sales associates often specialize in a particular geographic area or property type called a ____________ ____________.

5. ____________ ____________ involves developing a database of prospects to direct a specific message.

1.3 PROPERTY MANAGEMENT

Property management is a professional service conducted by a person or company hired to maintain and manage property on behalf of property owners. The scope of the work the property manager performs is detailed in the management agreement. Property management typically involves leasing, managing, marketing, and maintenance of property. A **property manager** is the property owner's local representative. The property manager is responsible for maintaining the property and managing the expenses. The property manager's primary charge is to protect the owner's investment and to maximize the owner's return on the investment. Property management is much more involved than being a rental agent. **Rental agents** typically find a tenant for property and collect a fee. Rental agents (or leasing agents) act as intermediaries between a potential tenant and the property owner seeking to acquire a tenant. Property managers continue to manage the property once a tenant is secured.

Many investors desiring to participate in the growth of income-producing property are absentee owners. An **absentee owner** is a property owner who does not reside on the property and who often relies on a professional property manager to manage the investment. The field of property management has experienced rapid growth and specialization, primarily because of the increase in absentee ownership. As agents of absentee owners, property managers are typically responsible for rent collection, improving tenant relations, and advertising and merchandising the space. Investors usually hire qualified property managers because the investors have neither the time nor the desire to become involved in the complexities of property management.

Compensation and Licensure Requirements

Property managers are compensated in a number of ways. Some work for a guaranteed base amount plus a small percentage of effective gross income (total income collected after taking vacancies into account). A property manager who is paid by commission or on a transactional basis must be licensed as an active real estate broker. A broker's license is not required if the property manager is paid a salary. The compensation arrangement is detailed in the management agreement. Sales associates work under the direction of their broker; licensed sales associates cannot work independently as property managers.

468, Part VIII, F.S.
61-20, F.A.C.
61E14, F.A.C.

Community Association Manager (CAM)

Community association management is applicable to mobile home parks, planned unit developments, homeowners associations, cooperatives, time-shares, condominiums, and other residential units. A **community association manager (CAM)** must hold a CAM license when the community association consists of more than 10 units or has an annual budget in excess of $100,000. A CAM license is not required to manage apartment buildings, commercial property, or single-family dwellings.

Practice Questions

6. An ____________ ____________ is a property owner who does not reside on the property and who often relies on a professional property manager to manage the investment.
7. ____________ ____________ typically find a tenant for property and collect a fee; however, ____________ ____________ continue to manage the property once a tenant is secured.
8. A property manager's duty is to protect the owner's ____________ on the ____________.
9. The scope of work a property manager performs is detailed in the ____________ ____________.

1.4 APPRAISING

475.611(1)(a), F.S.

An **appraisal** is the process of developing and communicating an estimate of a property's value. Appraisals are needed for many types of real estate activities. Lenders most often require the property to be appraised before approving a mortgage loan. Local city and county governments hire appraisers to assist with tax assessments. Appraisers are hired to determine value when property is taken by eminent domain. Insurance companies employ appraisers to assist with insurance adjusting. Individual investors have learned the value of obtaining an appraisal before investing.

475.611, F.S.

The Florida Real Estate Appraisal Board (FREAB) regulates state-certified and licensed appraisers. Only a state-certified or licensed **appraiser** can prepare an appraisal that involves a federally related transaction (federally related transactions are explained in detail in Unit 16).

WEBLINK @

The *USPAP* is available at www.appraisalfoundation.org. Select "USPAP (Standards)."

Appraisers charge a fee based on the time and difficulty of the appraisal assignment. Appraisers are not paid a commission to reduce the possibility of a conflict of interest. The ethics rule of the *Uniform Standards of Professional Appraisal Practice (USPAP)* states that it is unethical for an appraiser to accept compensation that is contingent on the value of the property.

Valuation and Real Estate Licensees

Real estate brokers and sales associates may appraise real property for compensation (certain exceptions exist). However, they may not represent themselves as state-certified or licensed appraisers unless they also hold those licenses and certifications (see Figure 1.1).

FIGURE 1.1 ■ Valuation Chart

Type of Valuation Product	Conform to *USPAP*	Certified or Licensed Appraiser Required
Appraisal assignment to originate a federally related loan	Yes	Yes
Appraisal assignment that does not involve a federally related transaction	Yes	No
Broker's price opinion (BPO)	No	No
Comparative market analysis (CMA)	No	No

475.25(1)(t), F.S.

61J2-24.001(3)(t), F.A.C.

Florida law requires appraisers, real estate brokers, and sales associates to abide by the *USPAP* when conducting appraisals of real property. The *USPAP* is a set of guidelines (standards of practice) to follow when providing appraisal services. A real estate licensee who fails to abide by the *USPAP* when conducting appraisal services may be subject to disciplinary proceedings and sanctions.

Comparative Market Analysis and Broker's Price Opinion

Sellers often ask real estate brokers and sales associates what buyers are likely to pay for their properties. Real estate licensees may help potential sellers determine an asking price by preparing a **comparative market analysis (CMA)**. Also, sales associates and brokers prepare CMAs for buyers to help them make informed decisions when offering to purchase real property. CMAs are developed by collecting information concerning real estate activity in the area, including recent sales of similar properties, properties currently offered for sale, and recently expired listings. A CMA is a marketing tool and may not be referred to or represented as an appraisal; therefore, CMAs do not have to conform to the *USPAP* standards. Licensees may charge a fee or otherwise be compensated for preparing a CMA, either as a part of or in addition to the normal sale commission. If a sales associate or broker associate charges for a CMA, the compensation must be paid to the employing broker and not directly to the sales associate or broker associate who prepared the CMA. However, licensees typically prepare CMAs for sellers for free as a courtesy to the sellers and to solicit new business.

A **broker's price opinion (BPO)** is a written opinion of the value of real property. Florida real estate licensees are allowed to prepare and charge for BPOs, provided the BPO is not called an appraisal. Price opinions are often requested by relocation companies and lenders involved in short sales of distressed properties (a *short sale* produces less money than what is owed the lender; the lender releases its mortgage so that the property can be sold free and clear to the new purchaser). A licensed or certified appraiser must conduct an appraisal when the valuation assignment involves originating a federally related mortgage loan.

475.25(1)(t), F.S.

Sales associates may perform BPOs only at the direction and under the control and management of the associate's employing broker. If a sales associate or broker associate performs a BPO, the compensation must be paid to the broker and not directly to the sales associate or broker associate who prepared the BPO. The broker directly compensates the associate. The *USPAP* standards of practice do not apply to brokers, broker associates, and sales associates who, in the ordinary course of business, prepare BPOs.

Practice Questions

10. A state-certified or licensed appraiser must conduct an appraisal when the valuation assignment involves originating a ____________ ____________ mortgage loan.

11. If a sales associate performs a BPO, the compensation must be paid to the ____________ and not ____________ to the sales associate who prepared the BPO.

12. ________ is a set of guidelines to follow when providing appraisal services.

1.5 FINANCING

Financing is the business of providing the funds that make real estate transactions possible. Sources of financing include commercial banks, savings associations, credit unions, and mortgage lenders. Financing can be regarded as the lifeblood of real estate sales. Knowledge of how to arrange financing and how to solve financing problems is essential to success in real estate. The licensee who can prequalify a prospective buyer and demonstrate how a prospective buyer can afford to buy has a tremendous advantage over the individual who only can show houses.

Anyone who processes residential mortgage loan applications or offers to negotiate the terms of residential mortgage loan applications for compensation must be licensed as a *mortgage loan originator (MLO)*. A real estate licensee may not operate as a mortgage loan originator unless the real estate licensee also holds a mortgage loan originator license.

COUNSELING

Counseling is the real estate service of analyzing existing or potential projects and providing advice to individuals and firms regarding the purchase and use of real estate investments. The services of counselors are in demand by developers, investors, corporations, and large-scale buyers and sellers.

Practice Questions

13. Anyone who takes residential mortgage loan applications or offers to negotiate the terms of residential mortgage loan applications for compensation must be licensed as a ____________ ________ ____________.

14. The real estate service of analyzing existing or potential projects is called ____________.

1.6 DEVELOPMENT AND CONSTRUCTION

Real estate development involves dividing larger parcels of land into lots and constructing roads and other offsite improvements. There are three general phases of development and construction:

1. *Land acquisition*. Developers and builders acquire raw land and then prepare the site for construction. They must carefully study zoning and land-use plans to determine what type of development is permissible. During this phase, the developer seeks approval for the proposed project from the local municipality. The

developer incurs costs for engineering plans, attorney fees, surveys, and application fees.

2. *Subdividing and development. Subdividing* is the process of converting parcels of land into smaller units or lots. *Development* is the process of improving raw land so that it can be put to productive use.

177.081, F.S.

3. *Recording the subdivision plat map*. Before work can begin, most local governments require that developers submit a **subdivision plat map** of a new development for review by the applicable government planning board (commission). A subdivision plat map is an engineer's plan for land use superimposed on a map of the land to be developed (see Figure 10.8 on page 240). The subdivision plat map indicates the proposed size and location of individual building lots, streets, and public utilities, including water and sewer lines, and other clarifying information.

The developer is responsible for improving the raw land with paved streets, curbs, storm drains, and so forth. Typically, the streets, curbs, and other public area improvements are dedicated to the local city or county. **Dedication** is the gift of land by an owner, in this case a developer, to a government body for a public use. A valid dedication of land from the owner to the municipality requires both an offer to dedicate (donate) the land and an acceptance by the municipality. To accomplish this, the developer typically indicates on the plat map that the streets, sidewalks, park areas, and other improvements that will not be sold to private individuals will be dedicated to the local municipality. Plat approval and recording of the plat into the public records serves as an acceptance of the dedicated streets and public areas and obligates the local government to maintain them once they are installed. County subdivision ordinances, in effect, have combined subdividing the land into individual lots with the development phase to provide greater protection to the public.

Practice Questions

15. List the three general phases of development and construction.

    1. ______________________________

    2. ______________________________

    3. ______________________________

16. ______________ is a gift of land by an owner to a local government to be used for a public use.

1.7 RESIDENTIAL CONSTRUCTION

There are three general categories of residential construction:

1. *Speculative (spec) homes*. Building "on speculation" involves purchasing one or more lots and constructing a home (or homes) without a buyer in advance of construction (no presale).
2. *Custom homes*. A custom builder constructs homes under contract with a buyer, often using building plans provided by architects or buyers.
3. *Tract homes*. Tract building involves construction of model homes in a new subdivision so that buyers can see the builder's product and choose a floor plan. The buyer then has a home built on a lot in the subdivision.

THE ROLE OF GOVERNMENT

The real estate business is regulated or influenced by the federal, state, and local governments:

- *Local government* impacts the real estate business through property taxation and regulatory activities such as occupational licensing, business tax receipts, building permits, building moratoriums, zoning, and building codes.
- *State government* owns and manages a large amount of land and identifies coastal regions and other areas that are protected from development. State documentary and intangible taxes are required when ownership to real property is transferred or pledged as collateral for a mortgage.
- The *federal government* impacts the real estate business through its fiscal and monetary policies. Various agencies influencing the real estate field include the Department of Housing and Urban Development (HUD), the Federal Housing Administration (FHA), the Department of Veterans Affairs (VA), the Environmental Protection Agency (EPA), and the Internal Revenue Service (IRS). Subsequent units will cover in greater detail the role of the various units of government in the real estate business.

Practice Questions

17. List the three general categories of residential construction.

    1. ______________________________
    2. ______________________________
    3. ______________________________

18. Purchasing one or more residential lots and constructing homes on the lots without first finding a ______________ for the new construction is called building on ______________.

1.8 PROFESSIONAL ORGANIZATIONS

There is a variety of professional organizations in existence. Membership in professional trade organizations is voluntary. The largest trade organization in the world is the National Association of REALTORS® (NAR). NAR promotes ethics and education in the real estate industry.

NAR created the REALTOR® Code of Ethics and Standards of Practice. The Code emphasizes fair dealings in three major areas: (1) with clients, (2) with other real estate brokers, and (3) with the general public. NAR's fundamental strength is the local association of REALTORS®.

Real Estate Licensees vs. REALTORS®

Real estate licensees are individuals who are licensed by the Florida Department of Business and Professional Regulation (DBPR). A **REALTOR®** is a real estate licensee who is a member of NAR. The Florida Realtors® and NAR are privately run professional organizations. The DBPR does not set the rules, fees, or membership requirements of NAR. Therefore, the terms REALTOR® and real estate licensee are not synonymous.

Not all real estate licensees are REALTORS®. REALTORS® must subscribe to the REALTORS® Code of Ethics.

Multiple Listing Service (MLS)

An important service created by NAR is the **multiple listing service (MLS)**. The MLS is a database that allows real estate brokers representing sellers under a listing agreement to share information about properties with real estate brokers who may represent potential buyers. The MLS compiles the listings of all member brokers, making the property information available to all brokers and their associates.

Buyers working with licensees who are members of their local MLS have access to information about all listed properties, regardless of which brokerage actually has the property listed.

To participate in an MLS, brokers agree to cooperate with each other in a sharing of the commission between the listing broker and the selling broker. The terms for division of commission can vary from broker to broker. Depending on the population of an area, a broker may be a member of more than one MLS. The MLS is not a registered trademark of NAR. Anyone can create an MLS.

Practice Questions

19. A real estate licensee who is a member of the National Association of REALTORS® is referred to as a ________________.

20. The ________ ________ service is a database for brokers representing sellers to share information with brokers representing buyers.

1.9 SUMMARY OF IMPORTANT POINTS

- Real estate brokers provide specialized service for others in return for compensation in the form of a commission, fee, or other valuable consideration.
- Real estate professionals provide expert knowledge of property transfer, market conditions, and how to market real estate and businesses.
- The five major sales specialties are (1) residential, (2) commercial, (3) industrial, (4) agricultural, and (5) businesses.
- *Farm area* refers to a selected and limited geographic area to which a sales associate devotes special attention and study. *Target marketing* involves expertise in locating prospects.
- Business opportunity brokerage involves the sale or lease of an existing business. A real estate license is required to sell and lease business opportunities for others.
- Property management is a professional service conducted by a person or company hired to maintain and manage property on behalf of property owners. Absentee owners are property owners who do not reside on the property and who often rely on a professional property manager to manage the investment.
- Federal and state laws require appraisals that involve a federally related transaction to be prepared by a state-certified or licensed appraiser.
- When preparing appraisals, Florida law requires appraisers and real estate licensees to abide by the *Uniform Standards of Professional Appraisal Practice (USPAP)*.

The *USPAP* is a set of guidelines (standards of practice) to follow when conducting appraisal services. Real estate licensees may not represent themselves as state-certified, registered, or licensed appraisers unless they also hold those licenses.

- A *comparative market analysis (CMA)* is a marketing tool that is prepared for a potential buyer or seller based on recent sales of similar properties, properties currently on the market, and recent expired listings. A CMA may not be referred to or represented as an appraisal.
- A broker's price opinion (BPO) is a broker's written opinion of the value of real property. A broker may charge a separate fee for a BPO, provided it is not used in connection with originating a federally related loan and it is not labeled as an appraisal.
- A mortgage loan originator (MLO) must be licensed to receive compensation for taking a residential mortgage application or negotiating the terms of a residential mortgage loan.
- Dedication is the gift of land by an owner to a government body for public use. The developer installs the improvements and the local municipality agrees to maintain the improvements as part of the subdivision plat approval process.
- The three categories of residential construction are (1) speculative (spec) homes, (2) custom homes, and (3) tract homes.
- A REALTOR® is a real estate licensee who is a member of the National Association of REALTORS® (NAR). Real estate licensees are individuals licensed by the Florida Department of Business and Professional Regulation (DBPR). Not all real estate licensees are REALTORS®.

UNIT 1 EXAM

1. Which statement is TRUE regarding the use of the term REALTOR®?
   a. All real estate licensees are REALTORS®.
   b. All REALTORS® are members of the National Association of REALTORS® (NAR).
   c. The terms real estate licensee and REALTOR® may be used interchangeably.
   d. The Florida DBPR authorizes the use of the term REALTOR®.
2. The term *follow-up* refers to
   a. returning calls in a timely manner.
   b. completing instructions given by one's broker.
   c. following through on listing calls made to for sale by owners.
   d. what a sales associate does for buyers and sellers after the sale.
3. Even though certain exceptions apply, an active real estate licensee is legally entitled to appraise real property for compensation concerning a nonfederally related transaction
   a. as long as she does not represent herself as a state-certified or licensed appraiser and complies with the *USPAP*.
   b. only if the appraisal is called a comparative market analysis.
   c. provided the compensation is based on a commission agreed on before the appraisal work is done.
   d. provided a licensed or certified appraiser signs the appraisal report.
4. The field of property management has experienced growth and specialization primarily because of
   a. the deregulation of the real estate industry.
   b. the increase in the number of licensees specializing in property management.
   c. the increase in the number of absentee owners.
   d. higher construction costs that have caused an increase in the number of renters.
5. Real estate licensees must comply with the *Uniform Standards of Professional Appraisal Practice (USPAP)* when conducting which value estimates?
   a. Appraisals
   b. Broker price opinions
   c. Comparative market analyses
   d. Real estate licensees are exempt from the provisions of *USPAP*
6. Appraisers are paid a fee because
   a. to accept compensation based on the appraised value is a conflict of interest.
   b. custom dictates the method of compensation.
   c. the fee would be too high if it were based on a percentage of property value.
   d. only brokers and sales associates are paid commissions for their services.
7. The five major sales specialties do NOT include
   a. agricultural.
   b. special use.
   c. commercial.
   d. businesses.
8. An owner of a Florida property has decided to hire someone to handle the property's leasing, managing, marketing, and maintenance. This person is someone in
   a. commercial sales.
   b. property management.
   c. counseling.
   d. rental agency.
9. Which type of construction involves building to a buyer's specifications?
   a. Tract homes
   b. Spec homes
   c. Custom homes
   d. Model homes

10. The term *dedication* as it applies to development and construction refers to
    a. a gift of land by the owner to the local government for a public use.
    b. the builder's careful attention to construction details.
    c. recording a subdivision plat map in the public records.
    d. preparing raw land for site improvements.

11. What type of license is required to sell or lease business opportunities for another person?
    a. Business broker license
    b. Business opportunity broker license
    c. Real estate license
    d. None required, unless a building is being sold with the business

12. Selecting a limited geographical area in which a real estate professional develops special expertise is
    a. dedicating land.
    b. subdividing.
    c. farming.
    d. follow-up.

13. Managing which type of property of more than 10 units requires a CAM license?
    a. Apartment building
    b. Commercial property
    c. Business complex
    d. Condominium complex

14. Effective advertising involving developing a database of prospects to direct a specific message is called
    a. institutional advertising.
    b. computer efficiency.
    c. target marketing.
    d. merchandizing.

15. A broker charges a prospective seller $50 for a comparative market analysis (CMA). Which statement applies?
    a. Brokers are not permitted to charge for CMAs.
    b. This is permissible, provided the broker does not represent the CMA as an appraisal.
    c. The broker must be a state-certified or licensed appraiser to do this.
    d. The CMA must be signed by a state-certified or licensed appraiser.

UNIT

2 REAL ESTATE LICENSE LAW AND QUALIFICATIONS FOR LICENSURE

LEARNING OBJECTIVES

When you have completed this unit, you will be able to accomplish the following.

- Distinguish among the federal and state laws and administrative rules important to real estate.
- Distinguish among the three license categories.
- Describe license application requirements.
- Describe nonresident application requirements and explain mutual recognition agreements.
- Identify the qualifications for a sales associate license.
- Describe the education requirements for post-license education and continuing education.
- Identify the qualifications for a broker license.
- Distinguish between registration and licensure.
- Identify real estate services that require a real estate license and exemptions for licensure.

KEY TERMS

broker
broker associate
compensation
expungement
Florida resident
license
license by endorsement
mutual recognition agreement
nolo contendere/no contest
owner-developer
prima facie evidence
real estate services
reciprocity
registration
sales associate
sealed
withhold adjudication

INTRODUCTION

The purpose of this unit is to give the reader a historical perspective of real estate license law in Florida and to describe in detail the requirements for obtaining a real estate license. The unit discusses real estate services that require a license and exemptions from licensure.

2.1 A HISTORICAL PERSPECTIVE OF FLORIDA REAL ESTATE LICENSE LAW

475.001, F.S.

20.03, F.S.

Before the latter part of the 19th century, the real estate business was unorganized and extremely competitive. In 1923, the Florida Legislature passed the Real Estate License Law, Chapter 475 of the Florida Statutes.

In 1925, the Florida Legislature created the Florida Real Estate Commission to administer and enforce the license law. The Legislature granted the Commission authority to keep records and conduct investigations, as well as the power to grant, deny, suspend, and revoke licenses. The Florida Real Estate Commission is also called the *Commission* or the *FREC*.

Today, the Division of Real Estate (DRE) provides support services to the Commission. The DRE is under the Department of Business and Professional Regulation (DBPR).

STATUTES AND RULES IMPORTANT TO REAL ESTATE

Applicants must meet certain application and academic requirements and demonstrate minimal competence with regard to the real estate business. Prospective licensees must demonstrate knowledge of real estate business practices and knowledge of Florida real estate license law and certain federal laws pertaining to real estate. To be prepared for the licensure examination and to competently perform real estate practices, the licensee must be familiar with the laws regulating the real estate business (scan QR code).

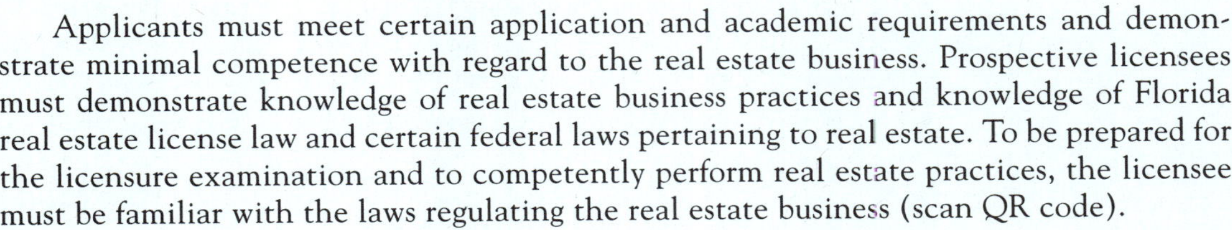

A brief description of the laws and rules that applicants must be familiar with are described as follows:

- *Florida Statute Chapter 20*. Chapter 20, Organizational Structure, establishes the structure of the executive branch of Florida's government. The Florida Constitution provides for the legislative, executive, and judicial branches of government. The executive branch executes the programs and policies adopted by the Legislature. The policies are implemented by the departments of the executive branch, including the Department of Business and Professional Regulation (DBPR).
- *Florida Statute Chapter 475*. This law is often called the Real Estate Professional Practice Act. Chapter 475 was created by the Florida Legislature to establish the legal rights and responsibilities of real estate licensees and real estate appraisers. Chapter 475 is divided into four parts. Part I pertains to real estate brokerage. Real estate licensees are responsible for knowing the provisions of this chapter. The Florida Real Estate Commission (FREC) implements, interprets, and enforces the regulatory provisions of Chapter 475.

  Part II of Chapter 475 pertains to real estate appraisers and sets forth the requirements for licensed and certified appraisers according to federal statute. The Florida Real Estate Appraisal Board (FREAB) regulates state-certified, licensed, and registered trainee appraisers. The FREAB functions very similarly to the Florida Real Estate Commission (FREC). Both quasi-judicial bodies follow the same procedures for disciplining licensees.

  Part III of Chapter 475, the Commercial Real Estate Sales Commission Lien Act, gives a broker lien rights for earned commission. This act applies only to commercial property (not residential property). The lien is only against the owner's net proceeds (personal property) from the sale and does not attach to the commercial real property (see "Liens on Real Property," Unit 5).

Part IV of Chapter 475, the Commercial Real Estate Leasing Commission Lien Act, gives a broker lien rights for earned commission associated with a brokerage agreement to lease commercial real estate (see "Liens on Real Property," Unit 5).

- *Florida Statute Chapter 455.* Chapter 455, Business and Professional Regulation: General Provisions, defines the general legal practice and procedure for the DBPR and the licensees of all professions regulated by the DBPR, including real estate. For example, Section 455.10 of the statute provides that an individual cannot be disqualified from practicing an occupation or profession regulated by the State of Florida solely because the person is not a U.S. citizen. Another section of this statute sets forth laws regarding Commission and board organization, meetings, compensation, and so forth. This statute also concerns the unlicensed practice of a profession, including real estate. Requirements concerning license examinations and the use of professional testing services are set forth in Chapter 455. This law also mandates what actions the DBPR may take in regulating licensees. Licensees who fail to comply with the provisions of this chapter can be disciplined by the FREC.
- *Florida Statute Chapter 120.* The Administrative Procedure Act defines the procedural process by which regulatory agencies decide and implement agency action. The licensing and disciplinary process for real estate licensees is outlined in this chapter.
- *Chapter 61J2, F.A.C.* (scan QR code). Chapter 61J2 is the rules of the Florida Real Estate Commission. It is a set of administrative rules developed by the Florida Real Estate Commission, pursuant to the rulemaking process outlined in Chapter 120, Florida Statutes. Administrative rules are published in the Florida Administrative Code (FAC). (Appraisal rules are in Chapter 61J1 of the FAC.).

Figure 2.1 summarizes the information in this list.

FIGURE 2.1 ■ Governing Powers

Statutes and Rule	Governs
Chapter 20, Florida Statute	Executive branch of Florida government
Chapter 475, Part I, Florida Statute	Real estate brokers, sales associates, and schools
Chapter 455, Florida Statute	Department of Business and Professional Regulation and the professions under the Department
Chapter 120, Florida Statute	Procedural process for all governmental entities authorized under the Florida Constitution
Chapter 61J2, Florida Administrative Code	Florida Real Estate Commission rules

Important Federal and State Laws

The Bureau of Education and Testing's *Candidate Information Booklet for Sales Associates Examination* lists 38 Florida statutes and one rule of the Florida Administrative Code that are tested on the state license exam. Students are also responsible for knowing the main points associated with eight Federal regulations. The *Candidate Information Booklet* lists the applicable federal and state laws.

WEBLINK

The best way to access the Florida statutes is to use the official Online Sunshine website (www.leg.state.fl.us/statutes/).

For the most up-to-date version of the administrative rules of the Florida Real Estate Commission, go to www.flrules.org/gateway/Division.asp?DivID=283.

Download a copy of the *Candidate Information Booklet* at http://www.myfloridalicense.com/DBPR/examination-information/candidate-information-booklets/. The booklet includes important information regarding taking the state license exam (scan QR code).

Practice Questions

1. Chapter ______________ is a set of administrative rules developed by the Florida Real Estate Commission.

2. Chapter ______________ of the Florida statutes establishes the structure of the executive branch of Florida's government.

2.2 GENERAL LICENSING PROVISIONS

475.01, F.S.

The three categories of real estate licenses are as follows:

1. *Sales associate*—A person who performs real estate services for compensation but who does so under the direction, control, or management of a broker or an owner-developer.
2. *Broker*—A person who, for another and for compensation or other consideration (or anticipation of compensation or other consideration), performs real estate services.
3. *Broker associate*—A person who holds a broker's license but chooses to register and work in real estate under the direction of another broker.

An individual typically begins a real estate career in Florida as a licensed **sales associate**. Applicants who have completed the required education and passed the license exam are initially licensed as voluntary inactive sales associates. Inactive sales associates can become active by finding an employer and filing the information with the DBPR.

475.011(2), F.S.

Sales associates and broker associates are employed by and work under the direction and control of a broker or an owner-developer. An **owner-developer** is an unlicensed entity that sells, exchanges, or leases its own property. An example of an owner-developer is a real estate development company that develops raw land into subdivisions and then builds and sells homes on newly developed homesites. An owner-developer may hire unlicensed salespeople and licensed associates to sell its properties. Unlicensed salespeople must be paid strictly on a salaried basis. If the owner-developer wishes to pay its sales staff a commission or other compensation based on actual sales (that is, on a transactional basis), the sales staff must hold active real estate licenses. In such cases, the name and address of the owner-developer is registered with the DBPR. Once the owner-developer information is registered into the DBPR database, sales associates and broker associates may be registered with the owner-developer.

Becoming a **broker** requires additional education, experience, and passing the broker license exam. While many sales associates want the prestige of a broker's license, they are not interested in opening their own real estate brokerage business. A **broker associate** is an individual who holds a broker's license but chooses to register and work in real estate under the direction of another broker.

Practice Questions

3. A licensed real estate broker who chooses to register under an employing broker is referred to as a ______________ ______________.

4. Unlicensed sales staff employed by an owner-developer must be paid a ________________ and not ____________________ or other forms of compensation based on actual sales.

2.3 APPLICATION REQUIREMENTS

475.175, F.S.

475.181(2); F.S.

A person desiring to be licensed must submit a DBPR license application. The application is available on the internet at the DBPR's Form Center (see the web link that follows). Applicants may download, print, and mail the application, or they may apply online. The license application expires two years after the date the DBPR receives the appropriate signed or electronically authenticated application.

You can apply for a Florida real estate license online at www.myfloridalicense.com/dbpr/ (scan QR code) and select "Apply For/Update Licenses."

Application Fees

475.125, F.S.

61J2-1.011, F.A.C.

New applicants for licensure are assessed an application fee in addition to the biennial license fee. Applicants for initial licensure and for subsequent license renewal also pay an unlicensed activity fee and may be required to pay a Real Estate Recovery Fund fee, if applicable (see "Real Estate Recovery Fund," Unit 6). Applicants submit the license exam fee and the fingerprint processing fee directly to the vendor that is providing the service.

Initial License Fee Exemptions

The DBPR exempts three categories of applicants from the initial licensing fee for a professional license:

455.219(7)(a), F.S.

1. Low-income applicants
2. Military personnel and their spouses
3. Military veterans and their spouses

The fee waiver applies to all professional licenses issued by the DBPR, not just real estate licenses. Each category of exemption has specific qualification requirements. In all cases, license applicants are required to submit a license application, submit fingerprints, complete prelicense education, and pass the state exam. All applicants pay the license examination fee and the fingerprint processing fee to the vendor that is providing the service. The fee waiver does not include the examination fee and the fingerprint processing fee, because these fees are paid to outside vendors rather than to the DBPR. The DBPR can only waive fees paid directly to it. If applicable during the current biennial license period, all applicants pay the unlicensed activity fee and the Real Estate Recovery Fund fee ("Real Estate Recovery Fund" is explained in Unit 6).

Fee Waiver for Low-Income Applicants. The DBPR is required by Florida law to waive the initial biennial license fee for qualifying low-income applicants. Eligibility is based on the applicant's before-tax household income (see Figure 2.2).

Fee Waiver for Military Personnel and Their Spouses. The DBPR is required by law to waive the initial biennial license fee for a member of the U.S. armed services that has served on active duty. The fee waiver also applies to a spouse who was married to the active duty member during a period of active duty, and to a surviving spouse of a member of the U.S. armed services who at the time of death was serving on active duty (see Figure 2.2).

455.213(12), F.S.

DBPR Veterans Fee Waiver Program. The DBPR is required to waive the initial biennial license fee, the application fee, and the unlicensed activity fee for military veterans and their spouses who apply for a license issued by the DBPR. Note that this group is exempt from three types of fees. The application *must* be made within 60 months after honorable discharge from the U.S. armed services. If a veteran submits a license application after the 60 months has lapsed, the veteran applicant and spouse would be entitled only to the initial biennial license fee exemption (see Figure 2.2).

FIGURE 2.2 ■ **DBPR Fee Waivers Per Applicant Category**

Applicant Category	Application Fee	Initial Biennial License Fee	Unlicensed Activity Fee
Low-income		✓	
Military personnel and spouses		✓	
Military veterans and spouses*	✓	✓	✓

*The applicant or applicant's spouse must have been honorably discharged within the last 60 months before the date of application.

Fingerprints

Applicants must submit their fingerprints as part of the license application process. An applicant's fingerprints are scanned and electronically submitted to the Florida Department of Law Enforcement (FDLE) and the Federal Bureau of Investigation (FBI). The purpose of the fingerprinting process is to determine whether an applicant has a criminal history. It typically takes up to five days for the fingerprint process to be completed and the results to be forwarded to the DBPR for evaluation. The evaluation process will not begin until the DBPR has received the fingerprint report and the application.

The DBPR accepts electronic fingerprinting services offered by Livescan device vendors that are approved by the FDLE and listed at its site. To view the vendor options and contact information at Livescan Device Vendors List go to http://www.fdle.state.fl.us/cms/Criminal-History-Records/Documents/ApplicantLivescanService-ProvidersVendors.aspx. Applicants can also contact Pearson VUE at https://pearson.ibtfingerprint.com.

WEBLINK

For additional facts regarding the fingerprinting process and for instructions regarding how to submit fingerprint information, download and print the DBPR's "Electronic Fingerprinting Frequently Asked Questions" at www.myfloridalicense.com/dbpr/servop/testing/documents/finger_faq.pdf.

BACKGROUND CHECK OF CRIMINAL HISTORY

On the license application, applicants are asked whether they are currently under criminal investigation in any jurisdiction or have ever been convicted of a crime, found guilty, or entered a plea of guilty or nolo contendere (no contest) to a criminal charge, even if the applicant received a withhold of adjudication.

When the court determines that a defendant is not likely to again engage in a criminal act and that the ends of justice and the welfare of society do not require that the defendant suffer the penalty imposed by law, the court may **withhold adjudication** of guilt, stay (stop) the imposition of the sentence, and place the defendant on probation. A withhold of adjudication must be disclosed on the application.

Nolo contendere is a plea of no contest entered in a criminal court of law. The defendant does not admit or deny the charges, though a fine or a sentence may be imposed by the court.

Background Check Questions

Applicants are cautioned to complete the application carefully, particularly with respect to past history concerning felonies, misdemeanors, and certain traffic offenses. On the license application are four questions concerning the applicant's criminal history. The questions are summarized as follows:

1. Have you ever been convicted or found guilty of, or entered a plea of nolo contendere or guilty to, regardless of adjudication, a crime in any jurisdiction, or are you currently under criminal investigation? This question applies to any criminal violation of the laws of any county, state, or nation, including felony, misdemeanor, and traffic offenses (other than parking, speeding, inspection, or traffic signal violations), without regard to whether you were placed on probation, had adjudication withheld, were paroled, or pardoned. If you intend to answer no because you believe those records have been expunged or sealed by court order pursuant to Florida statute or an applicable law of another state, you are responsible for verifying the expungement or sealing prior to answering no. Your answer to this question may be checked against local, state, and federal records. Failure to answer this question accurately may result in the denial or revocation of your license.
2. Has any judgment or decree of a court been entered against you in this or any other state or nation, related to the practice or profession for which you are applying, or is there any such case or investigation pending?
3. Have you ever had an application for registration, certification, or licensure in Florida or in any other jurisdiction denied, or is there now pending a proceeding or investigation to deny such an application?
4. Has any license, registration, or permit to practice any regulated profession, occupation, vocation, or business been revoked, annulled, suspended, relinquished, surrendered, or otherwise disciplined in Florida or in any other jurisdiction, or is any such proceeding or investigation now pending?

Applicants' background questions concern criminal matters. Applicants are not asked to disclose personal financial information such as bankruptcy, foreclosures, credit information, and so forth. Applicants who answered yes to question 1 who have been convicted of a crime, found guilty, or entered a plea of guilty or nolo contendere, even if court action (*adjudication*) was withheld, are instructed to attach full details of all cases with dates and outcomes, including any sentence and conditions imposed. Applicants are required to provide a copy of the arrest report, disposition or final order(s), and documentation providing all sanctions that have been served or satisfied. Applicants must provide documentation for each occurrence.

If the applicant was unable to secure documentation, the applicant should attach to the application proof that the applicant sent a certified letter to the clerk of court of the relevant jurisdiction stating the status of criminal records has been requested and that the information is required for license application purposes. If an applicant is currently on probation, the applicant should attach a letter from the probation officer, on an official letterhead, stating the status of the probation.

It is recommended that applicants who have a criminal history submit character letters with the application. The Commission has indicated that it would like such applicants to submit at least three letters. One of the letters may be from a family member and the other two letters should be from people who are not related to the applicant and that can attest to the applicant's character.

Applicants should never assume that a past crime has been expunged and does not require disclosure. **Expungement** is a process by which the record of a criminal conviction is destroyed or sealed after expiration of time. Expungement is not automatic. Attorneys charge extra for this process, and applicants should confirm that the matter no longer appears on one's criminal history. If the applicant's attorney indicated that the criminal conviction would be expunged, contact the attorney who handled the case to confirm that the criminal matter was, indeed, expunged. Statutes in some states permit a person's criminal record to be **sealed**. State statutes that provide for sealing of records usually pertain to juvenile offenders. If an applicant does not confirm the past crime was expunged or sealed, and in reality, it was not, the DBPR will consider the error a nondisclosure of a past crime that required disclosure.

For out-of-state criminal history, an applicant should first contact the attorney who handled the matter. The applicant should also contact the court where the matter took place. An applicant who is not sure or cannot confirm the expungement of a criminal matter should disclose it. It is better to disclose only to find out that the matter did not have to be disclosed than to not disclose and be charged with obtaining a license by fraud. Failure to truthfully disclose criminal history information may result in the Commission deciding to deny the applicant a real estate license. In cases where a license has already been issued and a criminal offense is later discovered, revocation of the license may result.

Applicants who responded yes to question 2 are instructed to provide a copy of the judgment or decree. The applicant must also supply documentation providing all sanctions that have been served and satisfied or, if not, stating the current status of any proceedings. If an applicant responded yes to question 3 regarding denial or a pending proceeding or investigation to deny an application, the applicant must supply copies of documentation explaining the denial or pending action. Applicants who responded yes to question 4 must supply copies of the order(s) showing the disciplinary action taken against the license or permit to practice a regulated profession. If the investigation to discipline the license to practice a regulated profession is pending, the applicant must provide documentation showing the status of the pending action.

WEBLINK

For information regarding Florida's seal and expunge process, visit the Florida Department of Law Enforcement's Seal and Expunge home page at https://www.fdle.state.fl.us/Seal-and-Expunge-Process/Seal-and-Expunge-Home.aspx.

Applicants can file their applications online. However, for study purposes, the sales associate license application can be downloaded at http://www.myfloridalicense.com/DBPR/real-estate-commission/ (scan QR code).

Applicant Agendas

475.17, F.S.

Applicants who have answered yes to the background questions on the license application and disclosed one or more crimes and applicants whose fingerprint results disclose issues in the applicant's background are flagged by the Division of Real Estate (DRE). A list of flagged applicants is prepared each month and placed on a nonappearance agenda called a *Consent Agenda*. The applications and all supporting documentation are sent to the FREC for its review. The FREC will either approve the application or the Commission will determine that they have additional questions for the applicant and request the applicant appear at a future FREC meeting called a *Summary of Applicant (SOA)*.

The DRE sends a letter to each applicant on the SOA agenda. The letter details the date, time, and location of the FREC meeting. Applicants are strongly encouraged to appear at the meeting. The letter also outlines the applicant's rights to hire an attorney if desired, bring character witnesses, and submit letters of good character. After the applicant appears on an SOA agenda, the FREC will make a decision to approve or deny the applicant for licensure.

Time Periods

Period to Check for Errors and Omissions. A 30-day period is allowed after receipt of the application for the DBPR to check for errors and omissions and to send the applicant a *notice of insufficiency* concerning any additional information required. An applicant's failure to supply additional information may not be grounds for denial of a license application unless the applicant was notified within the 30-day period.

WEBLINK

To check the status of your application, go to www.myfloridalicense.com/dbpr/. Select Check Your Application Status.

120.60(1), F.S.

Period to Inform Applicant of Approval or Denial. Any application for licensure that is not processed within the legislated time periods must be considered approved. An applicant must be informed of approval or denial of the application within 90 days after receipt of the last correctly submitted application. When the Commission denies an application, it sends a copy of the denial to the applicant, lists the reasons for the denial, and advises that the applicant has 21 days from the date of receipt of the order to request a hearing in accordance with Chapter 120, F.S.

61J2-3.015, F.A.C.

Exam Eligible

When the application processing is complete and the applicant is considered qualified, the DBPR notifies the national testing vendor. The vendor then sends a notice informing the candidate of eligibility to take the state license examination.

Applicants schedule examination appointments directly through the testing vendor. License examinations for sales associate and broker applicants are given in person at a testing center or online proctor through the testing vendor. Examinees must show sufficient identification before being allowed to take the test. Sufficient identification is defined as two forms of signature identification, one of which must contain a photograph and the applicant's signature. Student and employment identification cards are not accepted. Examinees must also provide a copy of the course completion certificate issued by the school at the scheduled examination (in-person or proctored) as proof that they have completed the Commission-prescribed course satisfactorily. (The school issues a course completion certificate directly to the student only.)

License by Endorsement for U.S. Armed Service Members and Their Spouses

455.02(3)(a), F.S.

The Occupational Opportunity Act provides license reciprocity to active duty and former active duty members of the U.S. armed forces and their spouses, including surviving spouses. Former active duty members must have been honorably discharged. In the case of a surviving spouse, the member of the armed forces must have been serving on active duty at the time of death.

License by endorsement are qualifications from another state that will be accepted by another state regardless if an agreement between states exists. The law applies to all professional licenses issued by the DBPR, including real estate licenses. The applicant must, at the time of application to the DBPR, currently hold a valid license for the corresponding profession in another state, U.S. territory, or a foreign jurisdiction. Applicants must submit fingerprints for a background check as part of the application process. The initial fees are waived except for the fingerprint fee.

To qualify for a real estate license by endorsement, the eligible military applicant, spouse, or surviving spouse must currently hold a valid real estate license issued in another state, U.S. territory, or foreign jurisdiction. After a satisfactory background check is completed and the license application is approved, the DBPR must issue a real estate license without requiring the applicant to complete prelicense education or take the state license exam. Once the license is issued, the licensee is responsible for complying with license renewal requirements, including applicable renewal fees.

WEBLINK

Information concerning professional licensure for military personnel, veterans, and military spouses is available on the DBPR website at: http://www.myfloridalicense.com/DBPR/military-services/military-on-active-duty/.

Practice Questions

5. Which fees are charged to a veteran applicant who applies for a real estate license within 60 months after honorable discharge? Choose all that apply.
   a. Application fee
   b. Initial licensing fee
   c. License exam fee (paid to vendor providing the service)
   d. Fingerprint processing fee (paid to vendor providing the service)
   e. Unlicensed activity fee (if applicable)

6. The time period for the DBPR to check for errors and omissions is ______________ days.

7. The time period for the DBPR to inform the applicant of approval or denial of the license application is ______________ days.

2.4 NONRESIDENT APPLICANT REQUIREMENTS

Applicants are not required to be residents of Florida.

Florida Resident Defined. For application and licensing purposes, the FREC rules define a **Florida resident** as a person who has resided in Florida continuously for a period of four calendar months or more within the preceding year, regardless of whether the person resided in a recreational vehicle, hotel, rental unit, or other temporary or permanent location. Any person who presently resides in Florida in any of the previously described accommodations with the intention of residing continuously in Florida for four months or longer, beginning on the date the person established the current period of residence, is also considered a legal Florida resident. This is the test used to determine whether an applicant for licensure qualifies as a nonresident under mutual recognition.

61J2-26.001, F.A.C.

Mutual Recognition Agreements. The intent of **mutual recognition agreements** is to recognize the education and experience of individuals licensed in another state or nation when the other jurisdiction has education and experience requirements comparable to Florida's requirements. A person who is licensed in a mutual recognition state and who wants to obtain a Florida license through mutual recognition must complete the process of Florida licensure *before* becoming a resident of Florida. The agreements apply exclusively to *nonresidents* who are licensed in other jurisdictions. A resident of Florida who is licensed in a mutual recognition state cannot apply for a Florida real estate license under mutual recognition.

A nonresident applicant requests mutual recognition on the Florida real estate license application and indicates from which state mutual recognition is being requested. An applicant applying for mutual recognition must obtain a *certification of license history* from the real estate commission in the state where the applicant is licensed. A certification of license history must contain the applicant's initial license exam information, current license status, the number of active months of licensure within the preceding five years, and whether any disciplinary action has been taken against the licensee. The certification is submitted with the application.

Real estate applicants approved for licensure under mutual recognition are exempt from the prelicense education course. However, the mutual recognition applicant must demonstrate mastery of Florida's real estate license law by passing a written Florida-specific real estate law license exam. The exam consists of 40 questions worth 1 point each. A grade of 30 points (75%) or higher is required to pass the exam. After demonstrating knowledge of Florida license law, the applicant is issued a Florida real estate license. Individuals who receive a Florida real estate license under mutual recognition must fulfill the same post-license and continuing education requirements as all other Florida real estate licensees (post-license education and continuing education requirements are explained later in this unit).

Mutual recognition agreements also ensure that Florida licensees have an opportunity for licensure in mutual recognition states. The agreements are state specific, and what is required of Florida licensees varies among mutual recognition states depending on how another state's license law compares with Florida's license law. A Florida real estate licensee interested in obtaining a license from a mutual recognition state should contact that state's real estate commission for information regarding application procedures.

MUTUAL RECOGNITION IS NOT RECIPROCITY

Reciprocity is an agreement between two states that allows a real estate licensee with a valid license in one of the states to obtain a real estate license in the other state. Florida does not have reciprocity with other states.

Florida instead has entered into contractual agreements, called **mutual recognition agreements**, with some other states. The Florida Real Estate Commission and another state's licensing agency enter into a contract to recognize each other's real estate license education. Mutual recognition applicants must demonstrate knowledge of Florida's real estate laws by passing a license law exam that consists of 40 questions concerning Florida-specific real estate law. After demonstrating knowledge of Florida license law, the applicant is issued a Florida real estate license. Only nonresidents of Florida may use education obtained in a mutually recognized state to obtain a Florida real estate license.

Practice Questions

8. An applicant is considered to be a Florida resident for licensure purposes if the applicant has resided in Florida for ______________ consecutive calendar months within the preceding year.

9. Mutual recognition applicants must pass a ________ question real estate law license exam with a grade of ________ or higher.

2.5 SALES ASSOCIATE QUALIFICATIONS FOR LICENSURE

455.10, F.S.
475.17, F.S.
61J2-2.027

U.S. citizenship is not required to become licensed. Qualifications for a real estate license are as follows:

- Be 18 years of age or older
- Have a high school diploma or its equivalent

- Possess a U.S. Social Security number
- Be honest, truthful, trustworthy, of good character, and possessing a reputation for fair dealing
- Be competent and qualified to make real estate transactions and conduct negotiations with safety to investors and others with whom the applicant may undertake a relation of trust and confidence

When completing an application for licensure, the applicant must disclose:

- regardless of adjudication, whether the applicant has ever been convicted or found guilty of a crime, has ever entered a plea of guilty or *nolo contendere* (no contest) to a crime, or is currently under criminal investigation;
- whether the applicant has ever done business under any name ("also known as" [A/K/A] or alias) other than the name signed on the application (this includes maiden names);
- whether in Florida or in any other state or jurisdiction, the applicant has had disciplinary action against a license (registration or permit) to practice a regulated profession (disciplinary action includes revocation, annulment, suspension, relinquishment, surrender, or a pending investigation against a professional license); and
- whether in Florida or in any other state or jurisdiction, the applicant has had an application for a real estate license denied or there is a pending proceeding to deny an application.

LICENSE APPLICATION

A U.S. Social Security number is required to apply for a real estate license. In the Full Legal Name section of the license application, applicants must enter their names as they appear on their Social Security cards. Florida law requires that an applicant's Social Security number be disclosed on all professional license applications. The Social Security number is used to determine whether applicants are in compliance with child support obligations.

A real estate license application is valid for two years from the date the complete application is received by the DBPR.

Reference: Section 475.181(2), 455.213, F.S., and 559.79, F.S.

Education Requirements

475.17(2), F.S.

61J2-3.008, F.A.C.

Sales associate candidates must successfully complete the Commission-prescribed prelicense course for sales associates (Course I) or an equivalent FREC-approved prelicense course. The course is based on understanding and applying the fundamentals of real estate principles and practices, real estate law, real estate license law, and real estate mathematics.

Course I consists of 60 hours of instruction plus 3 hours for an end-of-course examination. The end-of-course examination consists of 100 questions worth 1 point each and is usually organized with 45 questions on principles and practices, 45 questions on real estate law, and 10 math questions. A passing score of at least 70 is required on the end-of-course exam.

REGULATIONS PERTAINING TO PRELICENSE COURSES

A student may not miss more than eight hours of instruction. An instructional hour is considered to be 50 minutes (Section 475.17, F.S.).

A student may attend makeup classes to take the end-of-course exam or a makeup exam if absences were due to student or family illness, if done within 30 days of the regularly scheduled exam time, or later with Commission approval. Makeup classes must consist of the original course material that the student missed (61J2-3.008, F.A.C.).

The school or institution provides each student passing the end-of-course exam with a FREC-prescribed grade report of successful completion of the course (Section 475.175, F.S.).

The student must pass the school-administered end-of-course exam with a grade of 70 or higher (61J2-3.008, F.A.C.).

A student failing the end-of-course exam must wait at least 30 days from the date of the original examination to retest. Within one year of the original examination, a student may retest a maximum of one time. Otherwise, a student failing the end-of-course exam must repeat the course before being eligible to retake the end-of-course examination. Schools must administer a different form of the end-of-course exam to a student who is retaking the exam or repeating the course (61J2-3.008, F.A.C.).

Students may choose to complete a distance-learning course and satisfactorily complete a timed, distance learning course examination (Section 475.17, F.S.).

The prelicense course may be taken by correspondence or other suitable means by anyone who, because of individual physical hardship, cannot attend the course where it is regularly conducted or who does not have access to distance learning courses (Section 475.17, F.S.).

Exemptions to the Prelicense Course Requirement. Attorneys who are active members of The Florida Bar are exempt from Course I. Additionally, individuals who have received a four-year degree or higher in real estate from an accredited institution of higher education are exempt from the prelicense course (see Figure 2.3). Individuals who qualify for the education exemptions must complete the license application and fingerprint requirements.

FIGURE 2.3 ■ **Summary of Education Exemptions**

61J2-3.008(8), F.A.C.

475.17(6), F.S.

61J2-3.012(2), F.A.C.

	FREC Course I (Sales)	FREC Course II (Broker)	Post-License	Continuing Education	License Exam
4-year or higher real estate degree	Exempt	Exempt	Exempt	Not exempt	Not exempt
Florida-licensed attorney*	Exempt	Not exempt	Not exempt	Exempt	Not exempt

* Must be an active member of The Florida Bar. Exempt from Course I only, but must pass the license exam.

TIME LIMIT FOR PRELICENSE EDUCATION

If an applicant does not pass the state license exam within two years after the course completion date, the course completion expires and the applicant must again complete the prelicense education course.

The completion date is the date the student passed the prelicense end-of-course exam.

Reference: Section 475.181(2), F.S.

License Examinations

61J2-2.029, F.A.C.

61J2-3.015, F.A.C.

The license examination consists of multiple-choice questions and is administered as a computerized test. The license exam is offered in English and Spanish. Students who want the Spanish version must request the Spanish language examination when making the test reservation. Students who elect to take the license exam in Spanish may toggle between the Spanish and English translation of each question while taking the exam. The passing score on the license exam is a grade of 75 or higher.

Examinees' answers are graded by the testing vendor. Examinees receive a photo-bearing exam report immediately following completion of the exam. The testing vendor uploads the grade information to the DBPR system, and the DBPR issues a license number to examinees with grades of 75 or higher. The DBPR sends an email to the applicants who passed the exam with instructions to access their online accounts and print the real estate license.

475.17(5)(a), F.S.

61J2-3.013, F.A.C.

New sales associates must change their license to active status before legally operating as a sales associate. A change from inactive to active status is accomplished by submitting DBPR form RE 11: Change of Status for Sales Associates and Broker Associates. The form is signed by the broker or owner-developer and the sales associate. Florida brokers may also register new licensees online at the DBPR's website. New licensees must not begin working until the DBPR website indicates that the license has been changed to active status under the proper broker or brokerage entity.

WEBLINK

To download and print the Change of Status for Sales Associates and Broker Sales Associates form, go to www.myfloridalicense.com/dbpr/re/documents/DBPR_RE_11_Change_of_Status_Associates.pdf.

To monitor the progress of a request for change of status, go to www.myfloridalicense.com. Select "Check Your Application Status" and follow the prompts.

455.217, F.S.

120.57, F.S.

120.569, F.S.

61-11.017(2)(a), F.A.C.

61-11.010(4), F.A.C.

Failure Notice and Examinee Rights. Examinees who fail the license exam are entitled to review the questions they answered incorrectly. Examinees are entitled to review only their most recently administered exam. Requests to review the exam must be received within 21 days after the date of the examination (release date on the original exam report). Review appointments are scheduled with the test vendor.

Applicants who fail the license exam have the right, at their own expense, to have an attorney review the exam with them. If the examination review results in a corrected score, the new score will apply only to the applicant who challenged the examination questions.

61J2-2.030, F.A.C.

An applicant also has the right to petition for a formal hearing before the Division of Administrative Hearings. A request for a hearing before an administrative law judge must be filed within 21 days from the date of the onsite grade notice, or 21 days from the date of the letter notifying the student of the DBPR evaluation decision regarding the student's challenges. The request for a hearing is filed with the Chief, Bureau of Education and Testing, DBPR.

455.11, F.S.

61-11, F.A.C.

Qualifications for Reexamination in a Foreign Language. Florida statute provides for the right to have a license examination translated into a foreign language. This section does not apply to the Spanish language because the license exam is already provided in Spanish. A group of 15 or more license applicants who have failed the license exam may request that the license exam be translated into the applicants' native language. The cost of translating and administering the state license examine in a group's native language (other than Spanish) must be paid by the applicants.

WEBLINK

The Department's administrative rule regarding examinations is available at www.flrules.org/gateway/ChapterHome.asp?Chapter=61-11.

Practice Questions

10. Circle the corresponding letter(s) to indicate which qualifications are required for a Florida real estate license.
    a. U.S. citizenship
    b. Florida resident
    c. High school diploma or its equivalent
    d. Social Security number
    e. Age 18 or older

11. __________ who are active members of The __________ ________ are exempt from the sales associate prelicense course.

12. Circle the corresponding letter(s) to indicate which sales associate requirements are NOT required of individuals who have received a four-year degree or higher in real estate.
    a. Prelicense course
    b. State license exam
    c. Post-license course

13. A real estate license application is valid for ____________ years.

14. A real estate applicant must pass the license exam within ____________ years after the course completion date.

15. A real estate license applicant must file a request to review the MOST recent license exam within ____________ days.

2.6 POST-LICENSING EDUCATION

475.17, F.S.

61J2-3.020, F.A.C.

Sales associates are required to successfully complete a prescribed post-licensing education requirement before the first renewal of their licenses. This requirement has the effect of placing all initial licenses in a conditional (probationary) status because failure to complete the post-licensing education requirement will cause the initial license to become null and void by operation of law. Sales associates who do not complete the 45-hour post-licensing requirement and want to continue in the real estate business are required to requalify for licensure by repeating the prelicense course and end-of-course exam and by again passing the state licensing exam.

Students must pass the 45-hour end-of-course exam with a score of 75% or higher. Students who fail the end-of-course exam may retest only one time using a different form of the end-of-course examination. If the student fails the alternate exam, the course becomes invalid and the student must retake the post-license course. Florida-licensed attorneys who are also licensed real estate sales associates must complete the post-licensing education requirement. A licensed sales associate who has received a four-year degree or higher in real estate from an accredited institution of higher education is exempt from the sales post-license education requirement (see Figure 2.3).

475.183(4), F.S.

61J2-3.013, F.A.C.

Hardship Cases

The Commission may allow real estate licensees an additional six-month period following the initial license expiration to complete the post-license education requirement if, due to individual physical hardship, as defined by rule, they could not complete the education requirement before the license expiration date. A physical hardship is defined as a licensee's long-term illness or an illness involving a close relative or person for whom the licensee has caregiving responsibilities; the required course was not reasonably available, or the licensee had an economic or technological hardship that substantially relates to the ability to complete education requirements. An economic hardship is defined as the inability to meet reasonable basic living expenses. Licensees must request the post-license hardship extension in writing to the Commission, setting forth the basis of the alleged hardship. The Commission may request documentation to support the request. There is no legislative authority to extend the post-license requirement beyond the six-month period.

TIPS REGARDING POST-LICENSE EDUCATION

Students should not enroll in a post-license course until first becoming licensed. If you take your post-license course before becoming licensed, the course will not count.

Students are encouraged to take their post-license education soon after becoming licensed. Do not wait until the last minute. It is wise to allow yourself ample time so that if you need to retake the exam, you can do so before the expiration date on your license. If you are taking the course by distance education, your school will need time to grade your exam and electronically submit the results to the state before your expiration date. Furthermore, you need to allow for unexpected events, such as computer problems, sickness, and emergencies.

CONTINUING EDUCATION

61J2-3.009, F.A.C.

After completing the post-licensing education requirement during the initial license period, active and inactive licensees must complete at least 14 hours of continuing education during every 2-year license period after that. Three of the 14 hours must consist of core law, which includes updates to applicable rules and statutes. Real estate licensees must also take a 3-hour business ethics course once during each license renewal period. Licensees who complete the core law course and the business ethics course will receive 6 credit hours toward the 14-hour requirement.

While only 3 hours of core law are required in the two-year, 14-hour renewal cycle, the Florida legislature encourages licensees to take three hours of core law in each year of the renewal cycle to stay current on changes in the Florida real estate laws. A licensee who takes the three-hour core law course in each year of the renewal period receives three hours of core law credit and three hours of specialty credit toward the 14-hour continuing education requirement. A licensee who takes the 3-hour business ethics course in each year of the renewal period receives 3 hours of business ethics and 3 hours of specialty education toward the 14-hour requirement.

475.182, F.S.

A licensee may substitute attendance at one legal agenda session of the FREC for three classroom hours of specialty continuing education (CE) credit. A licensee may substitute three CE credits only one time per renewal cycle. To obtain the credit, the licensee must notify the DRE at least seven days in advance of the licensee's intent to attend the FREC's legal agenda session. A licensee may not earn CE credit for attending a legal agenda session if the licensee is a party to a disciplinary action slated for that FREC legal agenda.

Active members in good standing with The Florida Bar are exempt from the continuing education requirements for real estate licensees (see Figure 2.3).

Practice Questions

16. After the initial license period, licensees must complete 14 hours of continuing education every ______________ years.
17. The 14-hour continuing education requirement includes a 3-hour business ethics course and a 3-hour __________ __________ requirement.
18. Licensees who attend one legal agenda session for the FREC may substitute ______________ specialty continuing education credits per renewal cycle.
19. Sales associates must successfully complete ______________ hours of post-licensing education before the first renewal of their licenses.

2.7 BROKER REQUIREMENTS

475.17(2)(c), F.S.

Applicants who hold a Florida sales associate license must fulfill the 45-hour post-licensing education requirement first. This is true even if the Florida broker applicant is submitting real estate experience from another state. If the applicant does not hold a Florida sales associate license, the 45-hour post-licensing education requirement does not apply.

Broker applicants must successfully complete Course II or an equivalent FREC-approved course (unless qualifying as a broker under the mutual recognition provision). Course II consists of 69 hours of instruction plus three hours for the end-of-course examination.

Broker Experience Requirements

475.17(2)(b), F.S.

61J2-2.027, F.A.C.

Broker applicants must fulfill an experience requirement in addition to the education requirement. To fulfill the experience requirement, a broker applicant must have held an active real estate license for at least 24 months during the five-year period preceding application to become a Florida real estate broker. A broker applicant can fulfill the experience requirement in one of three ways:

1. The applicant has held an active sales associate license under one or more real estate brokers for at least 24 months during the five-year period preceding application to become a Florida real estate broker. The experience cannot be earned by working for an owner-developer unless the owner-developer is also registered as a real estate brokerage with a qualifying broker. The employment can be under a Florida real estate broker or a broker licensed in another state or in any foreign jurisdiction.
2. The applicant held an active sales associate license while working as a salaried employee of a governmental agency and performing the duties authorized in Chapter 475, F.S., for at least 24 months during the five-year period preceding application to become a Florida real estate broker.
3. The applicant held an active broker license in another state or in any foreign jurisdiction for at least 24 months during the five-year period preceding application to become a Florida real estate broker.

Broker Post-Licensing Education

475.17, F.S.
61J2-3.020, F.A.C.

Broker licensees are required to successfully complete post-licensing education before the first renewal of their licenses. If a broker does not complete the 60-hour post-licensing requirement, the broker's license becomes null and void by operation of law. However, the broker may revert to a sales associate's license after completing 14 hours of continuing education within the six months following expiration of the broker's license—and provided the broker has complied with all requirements for renewal.

A licensee who has received a four-year degree or higher in real estate from an accredited institution of higher education is exempt from the broker prelicense and post-license education requirements to become initially licensed (see Figure 2.3).

Broker Continuing Education

Broker licensees must complete the same continuing education requirements required for sales associates (see "Continuing Education," earlier in this unit).

Practice Questions

20. A broker applicant must have held an active real estate license for at LEAST __________ __________ during the preceding __________ __________.

21. A broker must complete ______________ hours of post-licensing education before the __________ __________ of the initial broker license.

2.8 REGISTRATION AND LICENSURE

475.215(2), F.S.

Registration is the process of submitting information to the DBPR that is entered into the Department's records. Information placed on record with the DBPR includes the name and address of each licensed broker and sales associate; the name and business address of each sales associate's employer; the sales associate's and broker's license status (active or inactive); and the person's involvement as an officer, director, or partner of a real estate business. Sales associates and broker associates licensed in Florida must be registered under their employing broker (or owner-developer, if applicable). Sales associates and broker associates may have only one registered employer at any given time. Florida licensees may also hold active licenses in other states. Individuals who do not intend to engage actively in the real estate business, such as a director of a real estate corporation, simply register this information with the DBPR so that the information can be entered into the database. However, an individual who wishes to actively engage in the real estate industry must be licensed and registered as active with the DBPR.

Licensure is obtained when an applicant has met all the qualifications for practice that are specified in Florida statute and has passed the state license exam. Passing the license examination gives the applicant the right to request and be issued a real estate **license**. The license is a written document that serves as **prima facie evidence** that the licensee (holder) possesses a current and valid license. The license indicates the licensee's full name and address, type of license, license number, effective date, expiration date, the name of the governor, and the DBPR secretary. The two-letter prefix before the license number indicates the license type: BK signifies broker; SL, sales associate; BO, branch office; CQ, corporations and LLCs; and PR, partnerships and LLPs.

PRIMA FACIE EVIDENCE

Prima facie evidence is a legal term used to refer to evidence that is good and sufficient on its face (at first view) to be accepted by the court as a fact. Unless it is refuted by evidence to the contrary, prima facie evidence will prove a case (presumptive evidence).

Official Commission documents become prima facie evidence once they are signed by the FREC chairperson or the chairperson's designee and affixed with the Commission's seal (see "Commission General Powers and Duties," Unit 3).

Practice Questions

22. A real estate license serves as __________ __________ evidence that the person named on the license possesses a current and valid license.

23. Circle the corresponding letter(s) to indicate which information is included on the face of the real estate license.
    a. Florida governor's name
    b. Name of the secretary of the DBPR
    c. Licensee's name and address
    d. License type
    e. Expiration date
    f. Licensee's email address
    g. License number

2.9 REAL ESTATE SERVICES

475.01, F.S.

Florida real estate license law identifies real estate–related activities called **real estate services** that require a Florida real estate license. Real estate services include any real estate activity involving compensation for performing the service for another.

TO REMEMBER: REAL ESTATE SERVICES	
A	Advertise real estate services
B	Buy
A	Appraise (non-federally related transactions)
R	Rent or provide rental information or lists
S	Sell
A	Auction
L	Lease
E	Exchange

Real estate services are further defined in license law to include the following activities in the sale, exchange, or lease of real property, including mineral rights, business enterprises, or business opportunities:

- Offer to, agree to, or attempt to perform real estate activities
- Advertise or otherwise indicate to the public that one is in the business of performing real estate services
- Direct or assist in the procurement of sellers, buyers, lessors, or lessees
- Negotiate or close a real estate transaction (note that case law has determined that the intention to close a real estate transaction is sufficient)

Anyone who performs real estate services for another person for compensation of any type must be licensed, unless specifically exempted by law. **Compensation** is defined as anything of value or a valuable consideration, directly or indirectly paid, promised, or expected to be paid or received. Compensation includes money in the form of a salary, bonuses, commissions, and gratuities. Compensation is also things of value such as dinner, flowers, wine, gift certificates, event tickets, and so forth.

It is a violation of license law to share a commission with or to pay a fee or other compensation to an unlicensed person for the referral of real estate business clients, prospects, or customers. However, a Florida broker may pay a referral fee to a broker licensed in another state so long as the foreign broker does not violate Florida law.

Presumption of Acting as a Real Estate Broker

475.43, F.S.

If an individual performs services of real estate for another person and a disciplinary case is filed as a result of that activity, there is a presumption that the individual is acting as a real estate licensee. Even if the individual attempts to perform a service of real estate for another person without being compensated for the service, the individual may be held liable. If an individual has sold or leased real estate that is not titled in his name, or has maintained an office bearing signs that real estate is for sale or lease, or has advertised real estate for sale or lease, there is a presumption that the individual was acting or attempting to act as a real estate broker. The burden of proof is upon the individual to show that he was not acting or attempting to act as a broker or sales associate. Unlicensed individuals may find themselves facing charges of unlicensed activity. Licensed sales associates beware—don't find yourself defending real estate activities conducted for friends or relatives. Any real estate activities must be with your broker's knowledge and consent.

EXEMPTIONS FROM A REAL ESTATE LICENSE

475.011, F.S.

A person who performs real estate services for others must be licensed, unless specifically exempted by law. The Florida statutes identify specific exemptions from the requirement to be licensed as a real estate broker or sales associate. The exemptions have been organized into five groups for study purposes. The five groups are:

1. Owner exemptions
2. Exemptions based on career
3. Salaried employee exemptions
4. Court and legally appointed persons
5. Miscellaneous exemptions

Owner Exemptions. This group includes individuals and business entities that are exempt from licensure because they are selling their own property.

- Property owners may buy, sell, exchange, and lease their own property.
- Officers and directors of corporations (and owners of other business entities) may buy, sell, exchange, and lease the property of the business entity.
- Partners in a real estate partnership are exempt from licensure if selling property owned by the partnership provided the partner receives a share of the profits in proportion to their interest in the partnership. For example, a 40% partner may receive 40% of the profits of the business. A real estate license is required if the 40% partner received more than 40% of the profits.
- Owners of time-share periods who own the time-share for their own use and occupancy may later sell their interest.

Exemptions Based on Career. Florida statute exempts certain individuals from real estate licensure because of their career (or occupation).

- Attorneys-at-law, when acting within the scope of their professional duties in the attorney-client relationship, are exempt from real estate licensure. However, holding a Florida attorney license does *not* entitle an attorney to compensation for performing real estate services. For example, an attorney must be a real estate licensee if the attorney wants to charge a fee for referring a commercial client to a broker.
- Certified public accountants (CPAs) are exempt from real estate licensure when performing accounting duties within the scope of their professional duties.
- State-certified and licensed real estate appraisers licensed under Chapter 475, Part II, are exempt from a real estate license when conducting appraisals.

Salaried Employee Exemptions. Salaried employees are individuals who receive a salary and do not receive compensation based on the actual real estate transaction. Florida Statute 475 exempts salaried employees in specific situations:

- Salaried employees of a business entity may buy, sell, exchange, and lease property for their employers. However, the employees may not be paid on a transactional basis. (The employees may not receive a fee, commission, or other compensation based on the transaction.)
- Salaried employees of an apartment community who work in an onsite rental office are exempt from licensure. The employees cannot be compensated based on transactions completed. Salaried employees may complete leases regardless of the length of tenancy. (Note: Real estate licensees are prohibited from completing leases that are more than one year in duration [see "Leases," Unit 9].)
- Salaried managers of a condominium or cooperative apartment complex who rent individual units for periods *no longer than one year*, and do not receive compensation based on transactions. (Note: The salaried rental apartment agent [in the previous bullet] has no restriction on the duration of the leases. However, managers of condominiums and cooperative units are limited to leases of one year or less.) See also the Web link at the end of this section.

468, Part VIII, F.S.

- Salaried employees of an owner-developer (real estate developer), are exempt from real estate licensure, provided the employees do not receive compensation based on transactions.

Court and Legally Appointed Persons. Sometimes, a court of law will require an unlicensed individual to liquidate real estate. In some situations, an individual may authorize another person to sign legal documents on one's behalf.

- Court-appointed individuals acting within the limitations of their duties are exempt from licensure. For example, a personal representative designated in a will or an executor of an estate of a deceased person is exempt from a real estate license.
- An *attorney-in-fact* is a person who has been authorized by another person to act in his place. For example, a seller who is stationed overseas in the armed services may choose to give a power of attorney to a trusted relative to sign legal documents, such as a sale contract or a deed, on the seller's behalf. A real estate license is not required to act as an attorney-in-fact. (However, a power of attorney cannot be used to authorize an individual to conduct real estate services—to do so would be unlicensed activity.)

Miscellaneous Exemptions There are several other diverse groups that are exempt from licensure when they perform services related to real estate.

- Individuals who rent lots in a mobile home park or recreational travel park. (Rentals in mobile home parks and recreational vehicle lot rentals are not considered real property.)
- Persons who sell cemetery lots. (Cemetery lots are not considered real property.)
- Dealers who are registered with the Securities and Exchange Commission (SEC) selling business enterprises to accredited investors.
- Hotel and motel clerks who rent transient occupancy of public lodging establishments.
- Tenants of an apartment community may receive a fee up to $50 for the referral of a new tenant to the same apartment community.

WEBLINK

Property managers of residential community associations are required to obtain a community association manager (CAM) license from the Department of Business and Professional Regulation (DBPR) for communities of more than 10 units or when the annual budget exceeds $100,000. For more information visit the Division of Professions, Regulatory Council of Community Association Managers at http://www.myfloridalicense.com/DBPR/community-association-managers-and-firms/.

Practice Questions

24. Using the memory tool A BAR SALE, list the services of real estate.
    1. ______________________________
    2. ______________________________
    3. ______________________________
    4. ______________________________
    5. ______________________________
    6. ______________________________
    7. ______________________________
    8. ______________________________

25. Circle the corresponding letter(s) to indicate which individuals listed are exempt from real estate licensure.
    a. A person who has been given a power of attorney for the purpose of signing a contract on another person's behalf
    b. A salesperson for a real estate developer who receives commission for each lot the salesperson sells
    c. Owners of a time-share period who offer their time-share period for resale
    d. A salaried employee of a corporation who sells property owned by the corporation solely as part of the employee's responsibilities as an employee

2.10 SUMMARY OF IMPORTANT POINTS

- A *sales associate* is a person who performs real estate services for compensation or other consideration but does so under the direction, control, and management of an active broker or owner-developer.
- A *broker* is a person who, for another and for compensation or other consideration, performs real estate services.
- A *broker associate* is an individual who meets the requirements of a broker but who chooses to work in real estate under the direction (employ) of another broker.
- An *owner-developer* is an unlicensed entity that sells, exchanges, or leases its own property. Sales staff must hold active real estate licenses to be paid commission. The sales staff is exempt from licensure if paid strictly on a salaried basis.
- The DBPR is required to waive the initial license fee for eligible low-income applicants.
- The DBPR waives the initial licensing fee for a member of the armed services that has served on active duty. The fee waiver also applies to a spouse who was married to the active duty member during a period of active duty, and to a surviving spouse of a member of the armed services who at the time of death was serving on active duty.
- The DBPR waives the application fee, the initial license fee, and the unlicensed activity fee for military veterans and their spouses who apply for a real estate license within 60 months after honorable discharge from the armed services.

- The DBPR issues a license by endorsement to eligible military applicants, spouses, or surviving spouses who currently hold a valid real estate license issued in another state, U.S. territory, or foreign jurisdiction at the time of application. The initial fees are waived except for fingerprinting. The applicants are exempt from taking prelicense education and the state exam.
- To become a sales associate, applicants must complete (1) a 63-hour prelicense course with a score of at least 70 and (2) the application process, including the DBPR license application, fingerprints submission, background check information, affidavit of honesty (attest statement), initial license and application fee payment, and passage of the state license exam with a score of at least 75.
- Applicants must be at least 18 years of age and have earned a high school diploma or its equivalent. U.S. citizenship is not required, and applicants do not have to be Florida residents. Applicants must possess a U.S. Social Security number.
- Sales associates must complete a 45-hour post-licensing course before the expiration of their initial license. Brokers must complete a 60-hour post-licensing course during the initial license period. Failure to complete the post-license education before the expiration of the initial license will cause the license to become null and void.
- Fourteen hours of continuing education each license period is required for all real estate licensees following the initial license period. The continuing education requirement includes a three-hour core law course and a three-hour business ethics course.
- Individuals who have earned a four-year degree or higher in real estate are exempt from the sales associate and broker prelicense courses, as well as the post-license requirement. They are not exempt from the continuing education requirement.
- Florida-licensed attorneys who are active members of The Florida Bar are exempt from the sales associate prelicense course and from continuing education. They are not exempt from the broker prelicense education and the post-license requirement.
- To become a broker, applicants must complete a 72-hour prelicense course with a score of at least 70; have at least 24 months of active real estate licensure during the previous five years, and successfully pass the state broker exam. Applicants who hold a Florida sales associate license must also complete the sales associate post-licensing education before being eligible for a broker license.
- Real estate services include any real estate activities involving compensation for performing the service for another. Compensation is anything of value paid or promised to be paid to an individual for performing any service of real estate.

Note to Readers

The same FREC rule may appear in several different forms: "Rule 61J2-1.011, Florida Administrative Code"; "Chapter 61J2-1.011, F.A.C."; "Commission Rule 61J2-1.011"; simply as "61J2-1.011"; et cetera. Similar variations apply to the same Florida law: "Chapter 475.01, Florida Statutes"; "Florida Statute 475.01"; "Section 475.01"; "s. 475.01"; "475.01, F.S."; et cetera.

Practice Exercise: When a Real Estate License Is (or Is Not) Required

Instructions: In each of the following scenarios, an individual is performing an activity that may or may not require a real estate license. Determine if a real estate license is required or not required and give a brief description of your answer. *(For answers, see the Unit 2 answer key.)*

1. Chris works as an administrative assistant in a brokerage office. He is a salaried employee who does not have a real estate license. Last week, Chris showed a listing to a customer because the broker was too busy to show the property to the customer. Chris walked the customer through the property, pointing out its features and discussing the homeowners association clubhouse, pool, and annual dues.

   Was Chris required to be licensed to show the property to the customer?

2. A court of law appoints Matthew, who is unlicensed, to sell property in an estate.

   Is Matthew required to be licensed in order to be compensated for selling the property?

3. Mariah and John have agreed to sell a parcel of land that they both own. They each own a 50% share of the property. Mariah has a broker's license; John is not licensed.

   Is John required to be licensed in order to receive 50% of the proceeds from the sale of the land?

4. An owner-developer pays a commission to employee Sally for selling a lot in the development. Sally has an inactive real estate license, and the developer is not a broker.

   Did Sally need her license to get paid for selling the lot?

5. Teresa is a sales associate who is registered under the broker for Complete Real Estate Services, Inc. Teresa also works on the weekends as a leasing agent for College Town Apartments. College Town Apartments pays Teresa a salary.

   Is Teresa in violation of Chapter 475, F.S.?

UNIT 2 EXAM

1. A licensed sales associate may operate
   a. for any registered broker.
   b. for the broker registered as the sales associate's employer.
   c. independently if registered with the DBPR.
   d. as a broker associate.

2. A sales associate applicant is NOT required to comply with which requirement?
   a. Submit an application fee
   b. Be 18 years of age or older
   c. Be a bona fide Florida resident
   d. Possess a Social Security number

3. Which person does NOT meet the experience requirements to obtain a Florida broker's license?
   a. An applicant who has held an active California broker's license for the preceding three years
   b. An applicant who has held an active Ohio sales associate license during four of the preceding five years while employed by an Ohio broker
   c. An applicant who has held an active Florida sales associate license for the preceding two years while employed by a Florida broker
   d. An applicant who has held an active Florida sales associate license during two of the preceding five years while employed by an owner-developer

4. What information appears on the face of a real estate license?
   a. Governor's signature
   b. Secretary of the DBPR's signature
   c. License number
   d. Licensee's email address

5. A sales associate applicant is NOT required to disclose which information on the license application?
   a. Convicted of a crime
   b. Proof of U.S. citizenship
   c. Maiden name, if applicable
   d. A finding of guilt in conduct that would have resulted in disciplinary action if the applicant had been licensed to practice real estate

6. A real estate licensee works on a commission basis for two separate brokerage companies. Which statement is TRUE?
   a. Sales associates may have only one registered employer at any given time.
   b. The sales associate may work for both companies as long as the associate is registered under both employers.
   c. This is legal as long as the associate only works part time for each company.
   d. The sales associate must be registered as a broker associate for this to be legal.

7. What is the Latin term for a plea of "no contest"?
   a. Prima facie
   b. Caveat emptor
   c. Writ of mandamus
   d. Nolo contendere

8. John is an active Marine ordered to relocate to Florida. His spouse, a valid real estate broker in Tennessee, where they currently live, wants to continue their career as a real estate broker in Florida. The spouse may get a license by
   a. completing a license by mutual agreement application, providing proof of spouse's military status, submitting fingerprints for a background check, and passing the state's law exam.
   b. completing a license by exam for a broker application, providing proof of spouse's military status, submitting fingerprints for a background check, passing prelicense education for a broker, and passing the state's broker exam.
   c. completing a license by endorsement application for a real estate broker, providing proof of spouse's military status, and submitting fingerprints for a background check.
   d. completing a license by exam for a sales associate application, providing proof of spouse's military status, submitting fingerprints for a background check, passing prelicense education for a sales associate, and passing the state's sales exam.

9. Which event may cause the FREC to refuse to certify an individual as qualified for licensure?
   a. Dropped out of high school and later earned a GED
   b. Was convicted of fraud in an insurance scam
   c. Changed residency to a state other than Florida
   d. Lost a lot of one's own money in a bad real estate investment

10. An applicant has held a real estate license in good standing in another state since 2019. The applicant is licensed in a state that has a mutual recognition agreement with Florida. Five months ago, the license applicant moved to Orlando, Florida. Is this licensee eligible to apply for a Florida real estate license under mutual recognition?
    a. No, the applicant is now considered a Florida resident.
    b. No, Florida does not have reciprocity with other states.
    c. Yes, the applicant may apply for a Florida license under mutual recognition.
    d. Yes, the applicant may exchange the out-of-state license for a Florida license.

11. A woman received her Florida sales associate's license last year. Which requirement must she complete to become a licensed real estate broker?
    a. Successfully complete the 45-hour post-licensing course
    b. Complete 14 hours of continuing education for sales associates
    c. Document at least three closed real estate transactions
    d. Complete at least three years' experience as a sales associate before taking the broker license exam

12. A man has a North Carolina broker's license, but he is not licensed in Florida. He sells a parcel of land he owns in Florida. Assuming all else is proper, this is a legal transaction because
    a. mutual recognition agreements allow this.
    b. Florida law exempts from licensure individual owners selling their own real property.
    c. Florida has honored his nonresident broker's license.
    d. he has the knowledge and qualifications necessary to handle the transaction.

13. A sales associate applicant who has submitted a correctly completed application for the state license examination and who successfully passes the state exam may legally begin to operate as a licensee when the
    a. application and proper fees are received by the state.
    b. applicant receives a return receipt acknowledging acceptance of the application.
    c. applicant receives the canceled check as evidence of payment followed by an assigned date for the state exam.
    d. applicant is notified of having passed the state exam, has filed the appropriate form to become registered as active with the DBPR, and the DBPR website indicates the applicant's license status is active.

14. If the post-licensing requirement is not fulfilled before the first renewal and a sales associate licensee wishes to continue in the real estate business, the licensee
    a. must retake the state exam within one year.
    b. must requalify for licensure.
    c. is allowed a six-month grace period to meet the requirement but must hold an inactive license during that period.
    d. must retake the prelicense course within one year.

15. Services of real estate do NOT include
    a. advertising rental property lists.
    b. appraising real property.
    c. selling cemetery lots for compensation.
    d. conducting an auction of real property.

16. Which statement BEST describes who must be licensed to practice real estate in Florida?
    a. Anyone who performs any of the services of real estate
    b. Anyone who performs any of the services of real estate for another
    c. Anyone who performs any of the services of real estate for another for compensation
    d. Anyone who performs any of the services of real estate for another for compensation, unless specifically exempted by law

17. Which individual is NOT exempt from licensure under F.S. 475?
    a. A salaried employee of a governmental agency who performs real estate services for the state and does not receive commission
    b. Individual dealing in personal property only
    c. Individual serving as a personal representative and acting within the statutory limits of that designated role
    d. An employee of a real estate developer who receives a salary plus bonuses based on sales quotas

18. A salaried individual manages a condominium building and rents units for three-month to six-month periods. The manager
    a. must be licensed under F.S. 475 because leasing is one of the real estate services.
    b. must be licensed under F.S. 475 because she rents condominium units for compensation.
    c. must be licensed by the Division of Condominiums and Time Share Sales.
    d. is exempt from licensure under F.S. 475.

19. A developer purchased a tract of land and subdivided the property into individual lots. The developer hired his son, who was not licensed to sell the lots. The father agreed to pay his son a salary of $200 per week. After two weeks, the son had sold only two lots, so the father decided to add an incentive. The father promised his son that after every fifth lot was sold, he would give his son a lot free and clear. After one more week, the son had sold only one more lot. The son quit his job to go work for another developer who paid a higher weekly salary. Which statement applies to this arrangement?
    a. There is no violation of F.S. 475.
    b. The son alone has violated F.S. 475.
    c. Only the father has violated F.S. 475.
    d. Both the father and the son have violated F.S. 475.

20. FBI files reveal that six months ago a man worked as a real estate broker in Georgia, where he was charged with arson related to a large insurance claim. To avoid a long court fight without pleading guilty, the man agreed to revocation of his real estate license and entered a plea of nolo contendere. The FREC has just received the man's application for licensure as a sales associate disclosing the previously stated information. The application shows that all academic requirements have been met. The FREC will
    a. use its discretion to determine the applicant's qualification for licensure based on the facts in the criminal background check and an interview with the applicant.
    b. approve the application because the applicant was not convicted of a crime.
    c. deny the application because the applicant agreed to revocation of the Georgia license.
    d. refer the case to the Florida Department of Justice because of the serious nature of the offense.

UNIT 3

REAL ESTATE LICENSE LAW AND COMMISSION RULES

LEARNING OBJECTIVES

When you have completed this unit, you will be able to accomplish the following.

- Describe the scope and function of the DBPR and the DRE.
- Describe the composition and member qualifications of the Florida Real Estate Commission.
- Describe the Commission's general powers and duties.
- Distinguish between active and inactive license status and describe the regulations regarding involuntary inactive status.
- Distinguish between multiple and group licenses.

KEY TERMS

active license
cancel
cease to be in force
current mailing address
current status
executive powers
group license
involuntary inactive
ministerial duties
multiple licenses
null and void
promulgates
quasi-judicial
quasi-legislative
voluntary inactive
voluntary relinquish

INTRODUCTION

The purpose of this unit is to discuss in detail the Florida Real Estate Commission and its composition and powers. The unit also explains license requirements, including active and inactive status, license activation, and void and ineffective licenses.

20.165, F.S.

455.201, F.S.

455.223–455.225, F.S.

61J2-20.048, F.A.C.

3.1 DEPARTMENT OF BUSINESS AND PROFESSIONAL REGULATION (DBPR)

The Department of Business and Professional Regulation (DBPR) is the agency charged with licensing and regulating businesses and professionals in Florida. It is the intent of the Florida Legislature that individuals desiring to engage in a licensed profession be allowed to do so. Regulation of the real estate industry is necessary to protect the health, safety, and welfare of the public (consumer protection); however, the Legislature has mandated that it does not want extraordinary or unreasonable restrictions created that would deter qualified persons from entering their chosen profession. The Legislature believes professions under the DBPR should be regulated when:

- the unregulated practice can harm the public, the potential harm is recognizable, and the danger outweighs any anticompetitive impact that might result from regulation;
- the public is not adequately protected by other state statutes, local ordinances, or federal laws; or
- less restrictive means of regulation are not available.

The DBPR is under the executive branch of the governor, and it is governed by Chapter 120, F.S. The agency is structured according to the requirements of Chapter 20.165, F.S. The Legislature, under Chapter 455, F.S., granted authority to the DBPR to investigate consumer complaints, issue subpoenas when conducting investigations, issue cease and desist orders to unlicensed individuals, and issue citations to individuals licensed by the DBPR.

The chief administrator of the DBPR is the secretary of the DBPR, who is appointed by the governor, subject to confirmation by the state senate (see Figure 3.1). The main DBPR office is located in Tallahassee, Florida. The divisions under the Department of Business and Professional Regulation that are most relevant to real estate are presented in the following paragraphs.

FIGURE 3.1 ■ Organizational Chart

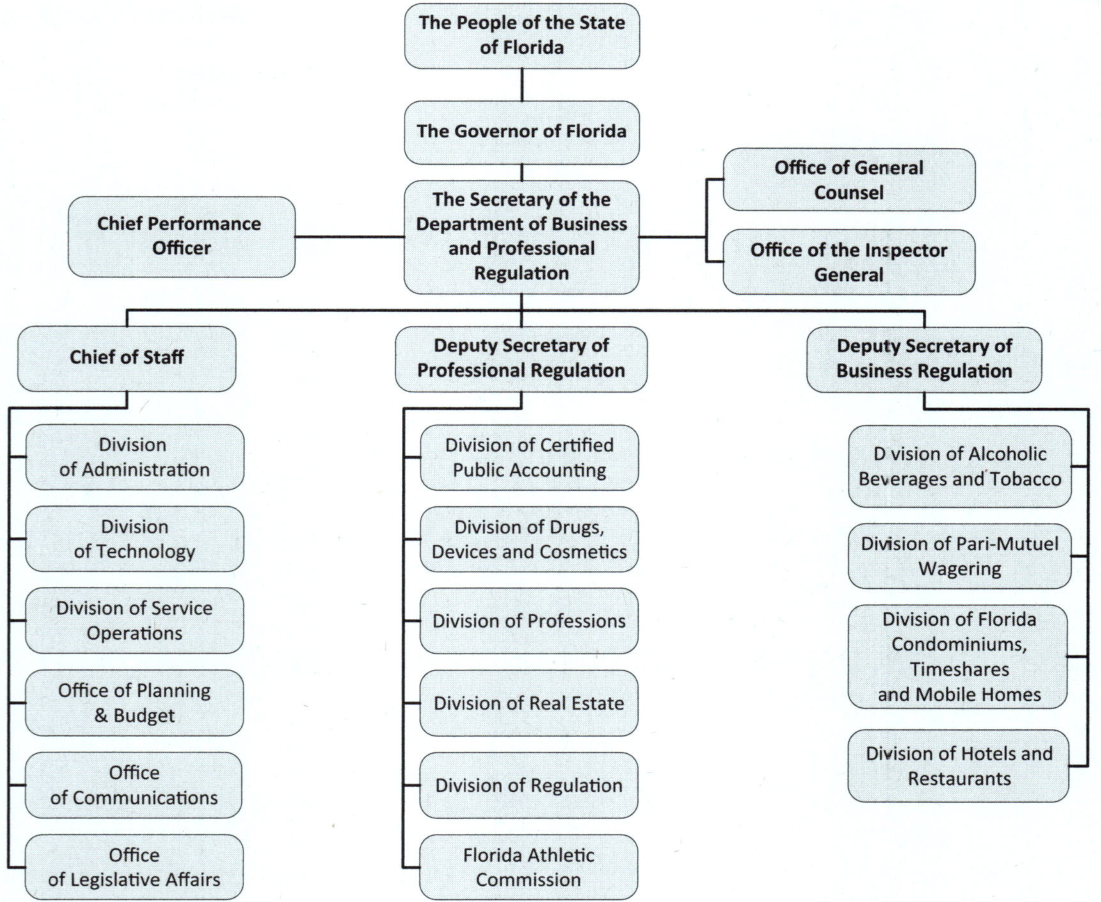

Source: http://www.myfloridalicense.com/dbpr/os/documents/DBPROrgChart_000.pdf.

Division of Professions

The Division of Professions administers numerous professional boards. Because of the magnitude of the real estate profession, it is organized as a separate division under the DBPR. The Division of Professions regulates education courses and license examinations for each profession under the DBPR.

455.217, F.S.

455.2171, F.S.

The Division of Professions contracts with a professional testing service for exam services. The DBPR, acting with its Division of Professions and the Division of Real Estate, must ensure that the license examinations adequately and reliably measure an applicant's ability to practice real estate.

Florida law requires that an accurate record of each applicant's examination questions, answers, papers, grades, and grading key be stored for two years. Examinees' grades and the state examination questions are confidential.

Division of Service Operations

There are two important units under the Division of Service Operations:

- The Customer Contact Center handles all incoming telephone, postal, and email inquiries from licensees and the general public.
- The Central Intake Unit processes all the license applications and license fees that come into the DBPR. The Central Intake Unit is also responsible for the issuance of all licenses and license renewal notifications for the Department.

Division of Florida Condominiums, Timeshares, and Mobile Homes

718, F.S.

719, F.S.

720, F.S.

721, F.S.

This Division provides consumer protection for Florida residents through education, complaint resolution, mediation and arbitration, and developer disclosure. It regulates condominiums, cooperatives, time-shares, and mobile home parks. The Division of Florida Condominiums, Timeshares, and Mobile Homes is also charged with providing an arbitration program to handle recall and election disputes for homeowners associations (HOAs).

Division of Real Estate (DRE)

20.165, F.S.

475.021, F.S.

The Division of Real Estate (DRE) provides all services required to administer the Florida real estate license law. The duties of the DRE are essentially administrative and ministerial. The administrative duties include routine duties and clerical functions on behalf of the FREC. The DRE's **ministerial duties** involve recordkeeping.

Important facts concerning the DRE are as follows:

- Florida statute mandates that the DRE offices and the principal office of the Commission be located in Orlando, Florida.
- The director of the DRE is appointed by the secretary of the DBPR, subject to approval by majority vote of the FREC. The director is a senior employee charged with the direct service assistance to the Commission.
- The DBPR employs all DRE personnel to support FREC activities.

Practice Questions

1. The DBPR offices are located in ______________, Florida.
2. The secretary of the DBPR is appointed by the ________________, subject to confirmation by the state ______________.
3. The DRE offices are located in ______________, Florida.
4. The DRE ministerial duties involve ______________________.
5. The director of the DRE is appointed by the DBPR ______________.
6. The appointment of the director of the DRE is subject to approval by the ______________.

3.2 FLORIDA REAL ESTATE COMMISSION

475.451, F.S.
475.04, F.S.
475.001, F.S.
455.201(1), F.S.

The Florida Real Estate Commission (FREC) is the regulatory body charged by the Florida Legislature with protecting the general public by regulating real estate brokers and brokerage firms, broker associates, sales associates, and real estate schools and instructors. The FREC is also charged with fostering the education of real estate licensees and permit holders. This includes the regulation of proprietary real estate schools and all noncredit, FREC-approved courses offered by colleges, universities, community colleges, and area technical centers. The objective of such regulation is to protect the public (consumer protection) by ensuring that real estate licensees have at least a minimal degree of competence.

Composition and Qualifications

475.02, F.S.
455.209, F.S.
20.052, F.S.

The Florida Real Estate Commission (FREC) consists of seven members (see Figure 3.2):

- Five of the members are *professional* (licensed) members, of which:
  - four must be Florida real estate brokers who have held active licenses during the five years preceding appointment; and
  - one must be either a Florida real estate broker or sales associate who has held an active license during the two years preceding appointment.
- The two remaining members are *consumer* (unlicensed or lay) members who have never been real estate brokers or sales associates.
- At least one of the seven members must be 60 years of age or older.

FIGURE 3.2 ■ Composition of the Florida Real Estate Commission

Four Active Brokers	One Active Broker or Sales Associate	Two Consumer Members	One 60 years of age or older
Licensed for at least Five Years	Licensed for at least Two Years	Never Been Licensed	Any of the Seven Members

Term of Office and Compensation

The governor, subject to confirmation by the Florida Senate, appoints Commission members to four-year staggered terms. There is no legislated maximum number of years

Commissioners may serve, though Commissioners may not serve more than two consecutive terms. Each member of the Commission is accountable to the governor, not the DBPR, for proper performance. All FREC members are exempt from civil liability while performing in their official capacity.

455.207, F.S.
61J2-20.049, F.A.C.

Commission members do not receive a salary. In lieu of salary, they are paid $50 per day for each day they attend an official meeting and for each day they participate in other Commission business. Commissioners also are reimbursed for out-of-pocket travel expenses, including mileage, meals, and hotel charges associated with their official duties.

Legal Counsel, Meetings, and Minutes

455.207, F.S.
61J2-20.040, F.A.C.

The FREC meetings are held each month at the Division of Real Estate (DRE) headquarters in Orlando, Florida. There must be a quorum (majority) consisting of four Commission members to conduct official business. One of the meetings is designated the annual meeting when the Commission elects from its members a chairperson and vice-chairperson.

Legal counsel is provided to the Commission through the Office of the State Attorney General of the Department of Legal Affairs. An Assistant Attorney General is assigned to the Division of Real Estate.

Practice Questions

7. Four FREC members must be licensed brokers who have held active licenses for ________ years preceding appointment.
8. One Commission member must be licensed as a broker or a sales associate who has held an active license for ________ years preceding appointment.
9. At least ______________ Commissioner must be 60 years of age or older.
10. Two members of the FREC are consumer members who are ______________.

3.3 COMMISSION GENERAL POWERS AND DUTIES

475.04, F.S.
475.125, F.S.
475.10, F.S.

The FREC makes decisions and sets policies that are carried out by the Division of Real Estate. The powers and duties of the FREC fall into three general areas of responsibility:

1. **Executive powers** to regulate and enforce the license law are delegated to the Commission by the legislature.
   - *Foster the education of applicants and licensees.* The Commission fosters the education of licensees and instructors in ethical, legal, and business principles. It also prescribes post-licensing education requirements and continuing education requirements to qualify for license renewal. Executive powers include publication of educational materials.
   - *Adopt a seal.* The seal, when affixed to rules, regulations, or other official documents, properly signed, becomes *prima facie evidence* that the document is authentic (see "Prima Facie Evidence," Unit 2).
   - *Establish fees.* The Commission uses the DBPR estimates of required revenue to determine the amount of licensing fees needed to implement the real estate license law and other laws and regulations relating to the regulation of real estate practitioners.

475.05, F.S.

2. **Quasi-legislative** responsibilities include the power to enact and revise administrative rules and bylaws and decide questions regarding the practice of real estate. The Florida Legislature is an elected body that enacts statutes, whereas the Commission is an appointed body with quasi-legislative powers. *Quasi* means almost or nearly.
   - *Create and pass rules and bylaws.* The Commission **promulgates** (adopts) rules that provide details as to how the statutes are to be administered.
   - *Regulate professional practices.* For example, when requested and deemed appropriate, the Commission may issue an escrow disbursement order (EDO) to determine the disposition of escrow (earnest money) deposits in the case of a dispute when requested by the broker holding the escrowed funds. The Commission also establishes rules to support regulations requiring that records be maintained by brokers and the manner in which deposits of money, funds, checks, or drafts are to be made in escrow, pending disbursement.

475.25, F.S.

475.181, F.S.

475.455, F.S.

3. **Quasi-judicial** responsibilities include the power to grant or deny license applications, to determine license law violations, and to administer penalties.
   - *Grant or deny applications for licensure.* The Commission certifies an applicant as qualified before a license is issued.
   - *Suspend or revoke licenses and impose administrative fines.* The Commission adopts, by rule, guidelines for the disciplinary actions that it imposes.
   - *Make determinations of violations.* The Commission is obligated to report any criminal violation of Chapter 475, when it knows of such violations, to the state's attorney having jurisdiction. Furthermore, the FREC must inform the Division of Florida Condominiums, Timeshares, and Mobile Homes when any disciplinary action is taken by the FREC against any of its licensees.

Practice Questions

11. List the three general areas of responsibility that encompass the FREC's powers and duties.
    1. ______________________________
    2. ______________________________
    3. ______________________________

12. The Commission's power to enact rules and regulations is an exercise of its ______________ power.

13. The Commission's power to determine violations of license law and to administer penalties is an exercise of its ______________ power.

14. Fostering education of real estate licensees is an exercise of the FREC's ________ power.

15. The seal, when affixed to official documents, becomes ________ ________ evidence that the document is authentic.

16. The Commission ________ rules and regulations.

3.4 LICENSE RENEWAL AND LICENSE STATUSES

License Renewal Periods

455.203, F.S.

475.182, F.S.

The initial effective date of a real estate license is the date DBPR issues the license. All real estate licenses are issued with an expiration date of either March 31 or September 30. The expiration date assigned to a particular license is the date that will give the licensee as close to 24 months of licensure as possible, without exceeding 24 months. License law mandates that the initial license period must provide the licensee at least 18 months of licensure but not more than 24 months.

EXAMPLE: Assume the initial effective date of a sales associate license was July 25, 2023. What expiration date will give the licensee at least 18 months of licensure but not more than a 24-month license period?

Hint: 24 months from the initial effective date is July 25, 2025.

To answer this question, ask yourself which expiration date in 2025 is closest to July 25, 2025, but not after July 25, 2025?

March comes before July, so the expiration date closest to July 25, 2025, but not past July 25 must be March 31, 2025. (September 30, 2025, is after July 25, 2025.) March is four months before July, so this licensee will have approximately 20 months of licensure (24 months minus 4 months). Thereafter, this license will always expire every two years (biennially) on March 31.

If a real estate sales associate later decides to become a broker, the effective date of the broker license will be the issue date of the broker license. The broker license may have a different expiration date than was on the sales associate license. Assume the sales associate's license expired biennially on March 31. Depending on the effective date of the broker license, the new broker license may have a September 30 expiration date.

License Renewal

455.273, F.S.

Ninety days before the end of a license cycle, the DBPR sends a renewal notice to licensees. The DBPR either mails the notice to the licensee's last known address of record or electronically sends the notice to the licensee's email address of record. It is the licensee's responsibility to keep track of renewal dates and license requirements. Failure to receive the notice will not excuse the licensee from completing the renewal requirements. Sales associates and brokers must complete their post-license education before the first renewal of their initial licenses. After the post-license education is satisfied and the initial license is renewed, licensees must complete 14 hours of continuing education during each renewal period.

475.182, F.S.

61J2-3.020, F.A.C.

To renew a real estate license, the licensee submits the renewal notice and the biennial license fee. By submitting the renewal notice to the DBPR, the licensee is attesting to having completed the education requirement (see "Post-licensing Education and Continuing Education," Unit 2).

If licensees renew after the expiration date, a late fee is charged. If a licensee does not renew a license by the expiration date, the license reverts automatically to involuntary inactive status (involuntary inactive status is discussed later in this unit). An active licensee who fails to renew a license following the expiration date has 24 months in which to renew the license. A real estate licensee must not practice real estate following the expiration date of the license. It is also unlawful for a licensee holding a current inactive license to perform the services of real estate for compensation.

455.02, F.S.

Armed Forces Renewal Exemption. A licensee in good standing who is a member of the U.S. armed forces is exempt from the renewal provisions during the licensee's period of active duty and two years after discharge from active duty. If the military duty is out of state, the exemption also applies to a licensed spouse, or a licensed surviving spouse provided the member of the armed forces was serving on active duty at the time of death. The armed forces exemption applies, provided the licensee is not engaged in real estate brokerage activity in the private sector for profit.

If a servicemember (or the servicemember's spouse) is actively engaged in real estate in the private sector, for profit, during active duty and for the two years following discharge, the servicemember must complete the required license renewal provisions. However, the DBPR will waive the license renewal fee.

Active vs. Inactive Status

475.183, F.S.

475.182, F.S.

An **active license** is required to engage in real estate brokerage services. Sales associates achieve active status by finding an employer and registering with the DBPR under the employing broker or owner-developer. Licensees who choose not to engage in the real estate business may place their licenses on inactive status. There are two types of inactive status: (1) voluntary inactive and (2) involuntary inactive.

61J2-1.014, F.A.C.

Voluntary Inactive. A licensee who has qualified for a real estate license but who voluntarily chooses not to engage in the real estate business during a given period and requests such a change is placed on **voluntary inactive** status. A licensee cannot legally perform any real estate services for compensation while holding a voluntary inactive license. A licensee may change an active license to a voluntary inactive license status by submitting the proper form to the DBPR. Such licensees hold a current inactive license.

Voluntary inactive sales associates and broker associates who subsequently wish to activate their licenses may do so at any time simply by completing the proper form requesting an active license with an active broker or owner-developer. (To be active, sales associates must be registered with an employer.) As with an active license, a licensee may renew a current voluntary inactive license indefinitely. Voluntary inactive licensees who satisfactorily complete the prescribed continuing education courses every two years must pay the appropriate fees to qualify for renewal of a voluntary inactive license. A license that is not renewed at the end of the license period reverts automatically to involuntary inactive status, except for initial licenses when post-licensing education requirements have not been completed satisfactorily. In this case, the license becomes null and void.

475.01(1)(g), F.S.

61J2-3.010, F.A.C.

Involuntary Inactive. If a licensee fails to renew an active or voluntary inactive license before the expiration date (other than the first renewal), the license reverts automatically to **involuntary inactive** status. The licensee must complete continuing education and renew the license to either active or voluntary inactive status within the next two years.

475.183, F.S.

455.271(6), F.S.

61J2-3.010, F.A.C.

61J2-1.014, F.A.C.

Involuntary inactive licensees may activate their license during the two-year period following expiration of a valid current license only after satisfactorily completing FREC-prescribed courses of instruction. When a licensee has been involuntary inactive for:

- 12 months or less, they may satisfy the education requirement by completing 14 hours of FREC-approved continuing education; or
- more than 12 months but less than 24 months, they are required to complete 28 hours of a Commission-prescribed reactivation education course.

Reinstatement of a Null and Void License. A license can only remain in an involuntary inactive status for up to two years. After two years, the license automatically expires (becomes null and void) by operation of law without further FREC or DBPR action. Once their license becomes void, individuals who want to practice real estate again must reapply and requalify for licensure, and retake and pass the state license exam.

475.183 (4), F.S.

61J2-3.013, F.A.C.

The FREC may reinstate the license of an individual whose license has become null and void if the Commission determines that the former licensee failed to comply with the statute because of physical hardship or economic hardship. The former licensee must apply to the FREC for reinstatement within six months after the date that the license became null and void. There is no legislative authority to extend the renewal requirement beyond the six-month period (see "Hardship Cases," Unit 2 for additional information regarding physical hardship and economic hardship).

Other License Classifications

475.183(2)(b), F.S.

Null and Void. When a license is **null and void**, it no longer exists. A license becomes null and void when the following situations occur:

- When a license has been involuntary inactive for more than two years, the license becomes null and void without any further action by the DBPR or FREC.
- A license that has been revoked after a disciplinary proceeding becomes null and void. Revocation of a license is a permanent penalty.
- Failure to complete the post-license education requirement before the expiration of the initial license will cause the license to become null and void.
- A person who no longer wants to engage in the real estate business can **voluntarily relinquish** or **cancel** the license, provided there is no investigation or disciplinary proceeding pending against the licensee. The licensee sends written communication to the DBPR indicating that the licensee is retiring or no longer desires to be licensed. When a license is canceled, it becomes null and void. Cancellation of a license is effective on the date the Commission accepts the voluntary relinquishment. Cancellation does not involve disciplinary action.

455.227(5), F.S.

475.23, F.S.

Cease to Be in Force. The DBPR must be notified within 10 days when the following occurs:

- A broker changes business address
- A real estate school changes business address
- A sales associate changes employer
- An instructor changes employer

475.42(1)(b), F.S.

The purpose of timely notifying the DBPR of the change in business address and change of employer is so that the DBPR database can be updated. All official DBPR communications will be mailed to the address of record or emailed to the email address of record, so it is very important that the DBPR has up-to-date contact information. License law requires that sales associates and broker associates be registered under their employing broker.

EXAMPLE: If a sales associate leaves one brokerage firm and wants to work for another brokerage firm, the DBPR must be informed of the associate's new employer. Until the sales associate is registered under the new employer, the sales associate cannot work. The license ceases to be in force until the sales associate has registered under the new broker. Otherwise, the sales associate would be acting as a broker (performing real estate services without being registered under an employing broker). The DBPR may issue a $1,000 citation to a sales associate who works in the capacity as a sales associate without being properly registered under the employing broker.

When a license **ceases to be in force** it means that under Florida law, the associate is not authorized to perform real estate services that require a real estate license, because the associate is not properly registered. The DBPR database would indicate that the associate's license is active and registered under the previous employer, when in fact, the associate is working for the new employer. The DBPR database is not updated until the change of employer information is submitted to the DBPR.

EXAMPLE: If a broker changes his or her business address, the new location must be registered and a fee paid. New brokerage business may not be conducted (the license ceases to be in force) until the DBPR is notified of the new business location and it is properly registered. To avoid a gap in brokerage service the broker can register the new brokerage office in advance. The DBPR may issue a $1,000 citation for failure to timely notify the DBPR of the change in business address.

The most efficient way to notify the Commission of a change of address or employer is through the DBPR's online portal. (When making changes online, it is recommended that the licensee print the change and preserve the documentation.) At the time of filing the change of business address notification, the broker or real estate school must inform the Commission of the names of any sales associates or instructors who are no longer employed by the brokerage or the school. The DBPR updates its database by removing sales associates and instructors who should no longer be registered under the brokerage or the school. Sales associates who are no longer employed with the broker of record are placed on inactive status. When a broker changes business address, the licenses of the sales associates employed by the broker remain in force. The same is true for instructors employed by a real estate school that changes business address.

455.275(1) and (2), F.S.

475.22(1), F.S.

61J2-10.038, F.A.C.

61J2-24.002(aa), F.A.C.

Current Mailing Address. Licensees are responsible for notifying the DBPR in writing of their current mailing address, email address, and place of practice. **Current mailing address** is the current residential address a licensee uses to receive mail through the U.S. Postal Service. A post office box is an acceptable mailing address. The DBPR sends official communication to a licensee at the last known mailing address or email address, referred to by the DBPR as the address of record.

Change of Address. Licensees must notify the DBPR in writing within 10 calendar days of a change in current mailing address or email address. Licensees may mail or fax the appropriate form to the DBPR, or licensees may submit a change of address or email address online at the DBPR Online Service website. The DBPR may issue a $1,000 citation for a first-time failure to timely notify the Commission (DBPR) of the current mailing address or a change in the current mailing address. Second or subsequent violations of failure to notify the DBPR of a change in either the mailing address or email address will result in disciplinary proceedings against the licensee. Licensees who do not keep their address up to date with the DBPR may miss important notices. If a notice requires action on the part of the licensee, the licensee's failure of timely action may lead to administrative discipline.

475.180(2), F.S.

Rules Pertaining to Nonresident Licensees. A Florida real estate licensee who moves out of state and becomes a nonresident of Florida is required by law to notify the Commission within 60 days of the change in residency. The licensee agrees to keep the licensee's mailing address current. Nonresident licensees must satisfactorily complete the post-licensing and continuing education required of all Florida real estate licensees. Nonresident applicants and licensees must comply with all other F.S. 475 requirements and FREC rules. Licensees must always notify the FREC within 10 days of their change in mailing address or email address; however, licensees have up to 60 days to comply with nonresident requirements.

NONRESIDENT LICENSEE REQUIREMENTS

Any resident licensee who becomes a nonresident must notify the Commission within 60 days of the change in residency and comply with all nonresident requirements.

A Florida resident licensee who fails to notify the Commission of becoming a nonresident as prescribed in Section 475.180 may be issued a citation and fined $600.

Reference: Section 475.180, F.S., and 61J2-24.002, F.A.C.

Eligibility for Receiving Commission

475.25(1)(h), F.S.

A real estate licensee may not share compensation with an unlicensed person for performing real estate services or for referral of real estate business, prospects, or customers. A real estate licensee whose license is inactive at the time of performing real estate services may not receive compensation. Prior to paying a referral fee or a commission to another brokerage office, the broker should verify that the brokerage to receive the compensation is properly licensed. Sharing commission or paying a fee to a person who is not properly licensed may subject the licensee to disciplinary action.

DISCIPLINARY GUIDELINES

Sharing a commission with or paying a fee to a person not properly licensed under Chapter 475, F.S., is a violation of section 475.25(1)(h), F.S. For a first violation, the licensee may be issued a $1,000 to $2,500 administrative fine and be subject to a 30-day suspension to possible revocation of the license, depending on the details of the case.

Reference: 61J2-24.001(3)(i), F.S.

DBPR License Portal. The license status of individuals who are licensed in Florida can be verified using the Department's license portal online service. The DBPR maintains a database of all professional licenses issued by the Department. An individual may search the license status of anyone who possesses a license issued by the DBPR (see the web link that follows). Two terms are used to describe the status of DBPR applications and real estate licenses: *primary status* and *secondary status*. Primary status is the first status, followed by the secondary status.

To access the DBPR's online license portal, visit www.myfloridalicense.com/dbpr/online-services (scan QR code).

EXAMPLE 1: A search of Jane Doe, licensed sales associate, revealed the following license status: Current/Active.

Current is the primary status. A **current status** indicates that the licensee is up to date with respect to the DBPR's requirements for licensure (e.g., timely renewal). Active is the secondary status. Active indicates that the licensed sales associate is allowed to operate under the associated license. Sales associates must have a registered broker or be registered with an owner-developer (the associated license). It is prudent for sales associates and other licensees who are required to have their license associated with another licensee to verify the association by selecting "View Related License Information" when conducting a license search. Licensees should not assume their license is registered with the appropriate broker/brokerage. Errors do happen, so when becoming initially licensed or changing employers, verify your license status and that your license is associated with your registered broker.

EXAMPLE 2: A search of John Jones, licensed real estate sales associate, indicated the following license status: Probation/Active.

The primary status is probation. This status allows the licensee to continue to practice real estate while completing conditions imposed by the FREC as a condition of discipline, such as to complete education courses and pay fines. The secondary status is active. This indicates a licensee has been disciplined but is able to continue to operate under the associated license.

PRIMARY STATUS ELIGIBILITY

To perform real estate services for another for compensation, the primary status must state either *current* or *probation* and the secondary status must state *active*. Any other primary status (such as involuntary inactive or null and void) indicates that the licensee may not operate.

EXAMPLE 3: A licensee's status is Involuntary Inactive/Active.

The primary status is involuntary inactive, indicating that the licensee has not completed a timely renewal of the license (the license is past the expiration date). However, the secondary status is active. The secondary status does not change automatically in the database system when someone fails to renew the license. The secondary status indicated is whatever status existed before the license expiration until the information in the database is manually updated. Therefore, a licensee should always refer to the primary status first and then look to the secondary status. If a license is involuntary inactive in the primary status, the licensee has failed to comply with the renewal requirements and may not operate regardless of what the secondary status indicates.

Change of Employer

When sales associates choose to work for a different brokerage firm, the associates have certain responsibilities to their former employer.

Listings. Duplication of records from a previous employer constitutes breach of trust, even if the person copying the records originated them, when done for the purpose of taking listings to a new employer. Furthermore, the removal of records from a previous employer's office constitutes theft.

Fiduciary Duties. A sales associate represents the broker when working with buyers and sellers, or tenants and landlords. A sales associate is obligated by what is known as *fiduciary* duties to the employing broker. The associate must work with the broker's customers and clients with the same trust and professionalism as if the broker were working directly with the customer. Additionally, sales associates must represent their broker with trust and confidence. Because of this *fiduciary* relationship, after leaving an employer, sales associates must not divert buyers and sellers of the former broker/employer from completion of a transaction. To do so would expose the associate to liability for breach of the fiduciary allegiance to the former employer. Sales associates and broker associates represent their employing broker (principal) and, as such, a fiduciary duty exists. To divert buyers or sellers or to use confidential information is both unethical and illegal in Florida. Additionally, a sales associate may have agreed contractually to a noncompete agreement.

Because of the fiduciary relationship between sales associates and their employers, the obligations of sales associates do not end with termination of employment. Sales associates are prohibited from disclosing confidential information learned as a result of employment. Licensees are further prohibited from doing anything that might discredit a former employer or damage the goodwill of the employer's business.

Practice Questions

17. If a licensee does not renew a license by the expiration date, the license reverts automatically to ____________ ____________ status.

18. A real estate licensee must not perform real estate services following the ____________ date on the license.

19. A licensee who is a member of the U.S. armed forces is exempt from the renewal provisions during active duty and ________ ____________ after discharge.

20. A license that has been involuntary inactive for more than ________ ________ becomes ____________ and ____________ without further action by the DBPR or FREC.

21. A licensee who has been involuntary inactive for more than ________ months but less than ________ months must complete ________ hours of reactivation education.

22. Licensees must notify the DBPR within ________ days of a change in current mailing address.

23. The only broker of a real estate brokerage retires and changes his license status to voluntary inactive. The sales associates' licenses ________ ______ ______ ______ ________ until the associates are registered under a new broker-employer.

24. A sales associate who is registered under the retiring broker in the previous question has been working with several prospective buyers. The associate wants to continue showing property to the prospects. The associate must register under a new broker-employer ____________ to continue to perform real estate services.

25. A licensed sales associate who moves from Florida to another state must comply with nonresident licensee requirements within ____________ days.

3.5 MULTIPLE LICENSES AND GROUP LICENSE

Multiple Licenses

475.215(2), F.S.

Multiple licenses are issued to a broker who qualifies as the broker for more than one business entity. A separate broker license must be obtained for each business. Additional (multiple) broker licenses may be issued by the DBPR when it is shown to the Commission's satisfaction that the additional licenses are necessary and that the licenses will not be used in a manner that is prejudicial or harmful to another person. A broker who holds more than one Florida broker license is said to hold multiple licenses. Multiple licenses allow a broker to legally act as a broker for more than one brokerage firm. Because sales associates and broker associates may have only one registered employer at a time, sales associates and broker associates may not hold multiple licenses.

EXAMPLE 1: Jane Doe is the broker for both Extra-Fine Real Estate Services and Extra-Fine Property Management. One company handles only sales, while the other handles only rentals. Jane must register both real estate companies with the DBPR. Therefore, she needs multiple broker licenses to qualify both brokerage entities.

EXAMPLE 2: Ray Jones is a sales associate registered under Extra-Fine Real Estate Services. Ray would like to try representing a few landlords that purchased his listings. He is wondering if he can work for both Extra-Fine Real Estate Services and Extra-Fine Property Management since Jane Doe is the broker of both companies. Sales associates and broker associates may engage in real estate activities that require a real estate license only on behalf of the brokerage company where the associate is registered. It is true that Jane is the broker of both companies; however, the associate is registered under Extra-Fine Real Estate Services, and sales associates may have only one registered employer at any one time.

Group License

61J2-6.006, F.A.C.

A **group license** is sometimes issued to sales associates or broker associates who are registered under an owner-developer. An owner-developer may own properties in the names of various entities. If the entities are all connected so that ownership and control is with the same individual(s), sales associates and broker associates employed by the owner-developer may be issued a group license.

The owner-developer sends an affidavit to the DBPR with a list of all the legal company names used by the owner-developer. This allows the associate to sell for all the affiliated entities owned by the owner-developer. Owner-developers are not required to hold real estate licenses if they only sell their own properties. The owner-developer is registered with the DBPR under a pseudo number (not a real estate license) that is entered into the DBPR records. The pseudo number becomes a placeholder under which sales associates and broker associates register. To activate a sales associate license under an owner-developer, the sales associate and the developer complete the appropriate DBPR form. The sales associate's name and license number are entered on the form. The owner-developer's name, business location address, and pseudo number are entered on the form. In actual practice, the sales associate (or broker associate) is issued a real estate license and no distinction regarding group license is made on the associate's license.

EXAMPLE: Joseph Jones is an owner-developer. He owns and controls two development companies, Happy Estates and Excellent Homes. A sales associate is employed by Jones to sell properties for both development companies. The associate is registered as active under the owner-developer's pseudo number. The associate is said to have a group license so that she can work for both Happy Estates and Excellent Homes. The licensee has one sales associate license and one employer (Jones).

Practice Questions

26. A ________________ license is sometimes issued to sales associates or broker associates who are registered under an owner-developer.

27. ________________ ________________ are issued to a broker who qualifies as the broker for more than one business entity.

3.6 SUMMARY OF IMPORTANT POINTS

- The DBPR is under the executive branch of the governor. Chapter 455, F.S., grants authority to the DBPR to investigate consumer complaints, issue subpoenas when conducting investigations, issue cease and desist orders to unlicensed individuals, and issue citations to individuals licensed by the DBPR.
- The chief administrator of the DBPR is the secretary of the DBPR, who is appointed by the governor, subject to confirmation by the state senate.
- The Commission consists of seven members: five professional members and two consumer members. Four of the professional members must have held active broker licenses during the five years preceding appointment. The fifth professional member must have been licensed as an active broker or sales associate for the two years preceding appointment.
- Members of the Commission are appointed by the governor, subject to senate confirmation, and are not employees of the DBPR.
- The Commission's powers are primarily quasi-judicial and quasi-legislative. The FREC exercises its quasi-legislative powers when it adopts rules. It exercises its quasi-judicial powers when it hears complaints, disciplines licensees, and grants or denies recovery fund claims.
- There are two types of inactive status: voluntary and involuntary. A licensee who has qualified for a real estate license but who voluntarily chooses not to engage in the real estate business may request voluntary inactive status. Involuntary inactive status occurs when a licensee fails to renew an active or voluntary inactive license before the expiration date.
- A null and void license no longer exists. When an individual performs real estate services with a void license, that activity is considered unlicensed activity. A license becomes null and void when an involuntary inactive status has continued more than two years. When the FREC revokes a real estate license, the license becomes null and void. A license that is voluntarily relinquished by the licensee is canceled by the FREC without the involvement of disciplinary action. Once canceled, the license is null and void.
- A licensee in good standing who is a member of the U.S. armed forces is exempt from license renewal provisions during active duty and for two years after discharge from active duty. The armed forces exemption is valid, assuming the service member is not actively engaging in real estate practices during the exemption period. This is another example of an ineffective license.
- Licensees must notify the DBPR within 10 days of a change in mailing address or email address.
- Resident licensees who move out of the state must notify the Commission within 60 days of the change in residency.
- "Multiple licenses" refers to those cases in which a broker holds more than one broker's license.
- A group license is issued to a sales associate or a broker associate employed by an owner-developer (real estate developer) who owns properties in the name of various entities. A group license entitles the licensee to work for the separate sales projects owned by the owner-developer.

UNIT 3 EXAM

1. The following statements are true with respect to the members of the Florida Real Estate Commission EXCEPT that they
   a. are a mix of real estate practitioners and consumer members.
   b. are accountable to the governor for proper performance.
   c. are DBPR employees.
   d. depend on the DRE for their administrative assistance.
2. Members of the FREC are appointed by the
   a. governor and confirmed by the secretary of state.
   b. governor and confirmed by the DBPR secretary.
   c. DBPR Secretary and confirmed by the governor.
   d. governor and confirmed by the state senate.
3. Which duty is an exercise of the FREC's quasi-legislative power?
   a. Adopt a seal
   b. Make determinations of violations
   c. Promulgate rules
   d. Grant or deny applications for licensure
4. Real estate licensees on active duty with the U.S. Army are required to renew their licenses
   a. every two years.
   b. on discharge.
   c. within one year after discharge.
   d. within two years after discharge.
5. The term of office for each Commission member is
   a. two years.
   b. four years.
   c. five years.
   d. seven years.
6. The members of the Commission receive
   a. no compensation for their services.
   b. only a per diem fee when on official business.
   c. $50 per day when on official business, plus out-of-pocket travel expenses.
   d. an annual salary equal to a state legislator's annual salary.
7. Which Commission responsibility is an exercise of its quasi-judicial power?
   a. Adopt a seal
   b. Create and pass rules
   c. Regulate professional practices
   d. Grant or deny license applications
8. The Commission is NOT empowered to
   a. make determinations of violations.
   b. impose administrative fines.
   c. levy fines and imprisonment as penalties for certain crimes.
   d. adopt an official seal that, when used on a document, certificate, proceeding, or act of the Commission, is prima facie evidence of its authenticity in all matters of law in this state.
9. Specific responsibilities of the FREC do NOT include
   a. determining the amount of licensing fees needed to operate the Commission.
   b. reporting criminal violations to the state's attorney.
   c. informing the Division of Florida Condominiums, Timeshares, and Mobile Homes of disciplinary action against any of its licensees.
   d. providing the services necessary for the preparation and administration of licensing examinations.
10. Which power is NOT granted to the DBPR under Florida Statute 455?
    a. Issue citations
    b. Investigate consumer complaints
    c. Appoint FREC members
    d. Issue subpoenas

11. Which statement regarding the Department of Business and Professional Regulation (DBPR) is TRUE?
    a. The DBPR Secretary is appointed by the Commission.
    b. The DBPR is under the executive branch of the state government.
    c. The main DBPR office is located in Orlando.
    d. The DBPR does not have the legal authority to issue citations.

12. FREC may reinstate a null and void license when
    a. it is determined that the licensee failed to comply with the statute because of physical hardship or economic hardship.
    b. the licensee timely pays the renewal fee and completes the education requirement the next day after the license is null and void.
    c. the licensee timely completes the education but fails to pay the renewal fee prior to the license becoming null and void due to a busy work schedule.
    d. the licensee apologizes for the oversight and promises to timely renew in the future.

13. How many members of the FREC may hold a current active sales associate license?
    a. One
    b. Two
    c. Four
    d. Five

14. If an active licensee fails to renew her third two-year license before the expiration date on the license, the license will
    a. revert automatically to involuntary inactive status at the end of the license period.
    b. be suspended automatically.
    c. be canceled, and the licensee will have to retake both the course and the licensing exams.
    d. be canceled, and the licensee will have to retake the licensing exam only.

15. An involuntary inactive license will automatically become void without further action by the FREC or the DBPR after
    a. 2 years.
    b. 4 years.
    c. 5 years.
    d. 10 years.

16. Who may NOT reactivate a license to active status?
    a. A voluntary inactive sales associate
    b. A licensed corporate director of a real estate company
    c. An involuntary inactive broker
    d. A sales associate who did not complete post-licensing education before the expiration of the initial license

17. An owner-developer owns several properties with different names, but all are business entities closely connected and controlled by the owner-developer. A sales associate working for that owner-developer may legally obtain
    a. a group license.
    b. multiple licenses.
    c. either a group license or multiple licenses, but not both.
    d. neither a group license nor multiple licenses.

18. A broker moves his real estate office to a new, trendy location. He is so busy coordinating the move that he forgets to notify the DBPR. The broker's license
    a. will cease to be in force.
    b. is null and void.
    c. is automatically suspended.
    d. is canceled.

19. Which statement is TRUE regarding multiple licenses?
    a. A broker associate may hold multiple licenses.
    b. A broker who qualifies as the broker for more than one brokerage company holds multiple licenses.
    c. Sales associates may be registered under more than one brokerage company provided the companies are owned by the same broker.
    d. Unlicensed owner-developers are issued multiple licenses if they own more than one real estate development.

20. A broker decides to relocate her real estate brokerage office. She notifies the DBPR of the change in business address. She also informs the DBPR of the names of two sales associates who are no longer associated with her brokerage. The sales associates' licenses will be
    a. suspended until they find new employment.
    b. canceled.
    c. null and void.
    d. placed on inactive status.

UNIT

4 AUTHORIZED RELATIONSHIPS, DUTIES, AND DISCLOSURE

LEARNING OBJECTIVES

When you have completed this unit, you will be able to accomplish the following.

- Distinguish among agency relationships in general business dealings.
- Describe the three brokerage relationship options.
- Describe the duties owed in a no brokerage relationship (nonrepresentation).
- Describe the duties that single agents have to their principals.
- Describe the duties owed in a transaction broker relationship.
- Describe the process of transition from a single agent to a transaction broker.
- Describe the disclosure procedures and the required content and format of the disclosure notices.
- Describe the disclosure requirements for nonresidential transactions where the buyer and seller have assets of $1 million or more.
- List the events that will cause a brokerage relationship to be terminated.

KEY TERMS

agent
caveat emptor
consent to transition
customer
designated sales associates
dual agent
fiduciary
general agent
limited representation
no brokerage relationship
principal
residential sale transactions
single agent
special agent
subagent
transaction broker

INTRODUCTION

This unit begins with a general explanation of the law of agency and then details the various types of brokerage relationships practiced in Florida. The unit also explains the licensee's duties and obligations to principals and customers.

4.1 LAW OF AGENCY

When a person delegates authority to someone to act on his behalf, an agency relationship has been created. Agency relationships fall within the body of law called *law of agency*.

There are three types of law that society looks to for guidance regarding agency relationships: common law, statutory law, and administrative law.

2.01, F.S.
775.01, F.S.

Common law (sometimes called unwritten law or case law) is judge-made law manifested in decrees and judgments of the courts as opposed to statutory law. It originated in England, where it was used in the kings' courts as one of the earliest legal systems and is still used today in the English legal system and the U.S. legal system. When statutory law is missing or ambiguous, it leaves room for a judicial written opinion known as common law to take precedence due to local practice or acceptance.

Statutory law is written statutes enacted by a legislature. Chapters 455 and 475 are two Florida statutes enacted by the Florida Legislature pertaining to license law (see "Statutes and Rules Important to Real Estate," Unit 2).

Administrative law is a body of law created by administrative agencies in the form of rules, regulations, orders, and decisions. Florida Statute 475 empowers the Florida Real Estate Commission to govern real estate practice in Florida.

In addition to the statutory laws of agency, real estate license law and the Florida Real Estate Commission (FREC) rules directly affect and regulate the brokerage relationships among real estate licensees, buyers and sellers, and the public.

Agency Relationships in General Business Dealings

A person who delegates authority to another is called the **principal**. A person who accepts the authority (and the responsibilities, duties, and obligations associated with that authority) is called the *agent*. An **agent** is the person entrusted with another's business. An agent is authorized to represent and act for the principal.

EXAMPLE: The broker is the *principal* in dealings with the sales associates and broker associates because the broker delegates to the associates the responsibility of representing the broker's interests. Sales associates and broker associates are *agents* of their broker or owner-developer (if registered with the DBPR under an owner-developer). The broker's associates (sales and broker associates) are authorized and consent to represent the broker in dealings with buyers and sellers, and landlords and tenants.

SALES ASSOCIATES AND BROKER ASSOCIATES ARE AGENTS OF THE BROKER

Broker (principal) → Sales associates and broker associates (agent of the broker in dealings with buyers and sellers)

Fiduciary Relationships. The agency relationship creates a *fiduciary relationship* with the principal. A **fiduciary** acts in a position of trust and confidence for another. The fiduciary owes complete allegiance to the principal. A fiduciary relationship contrasts with the common public relationship that exists in normal trading transactions where people with adverse interests deal *at arm's length* with one another. People dealing at arm's length conduct negotiations on their own behalf without trusting the other's fairness or integrity and without being subject to the other's control or influence. In such cases, the legal doctrine of **caveat emptor** (a Latin term meaning "let the buyer beware") applies. Agency relationships exist in many business transactions such as between an attorney (agent) and client (principal). An agency relationship may exist in certain real estate transactions (this will be explained in detail in the following section).

Two types of agents are characterized by the extent of authority delegated to an agent in general business dealings: (1) general agent, and (2) special agent.

A **general agent** is authorized by the principal to perform acts associated with the continued operations of a particular job or a certain business of the principal. A general agent may represent the principal in a broad range of matters related to a particular business.

EXAMPLE 1: A property manager is a *general agent* if authorized by the principal to show and rent apartments, collect rents, supervise maintenance of the property, handle tenant relations, and perform bookkeeping duties. A property manager is a general agent because the manager is authorized to perform on a continued basis a broad range of services associated with management of rental property on behalf of the principal.

EXAMPLE 2: Sales associates and broker associates are *general agents* of the broker with whom they are registered. Associates solicit listings and buyers, negotiate contracts, attend closings, and perform other real estate services on behalf of their broker. Therefore, in general business dealings, sales associates and broker associates are general agents of the employing broker.

A **special agent** is authorized by the principal (broker or owner-developer) to handle a specific business transaction or to perform a specific act.

EXAMPLE: A broker enters into an agreement with a seller to represent the seller in negotiations to find a buyer for the seller's property. The broker is a *special agent* of the seller. The broker represents the seller to sell a specific property (a single business transaction) and the broker has been given authority to accomplish only this task.

Practice Questions

1. A person who delegates authority to another is called the ______________.
2. An ______________ is the person entrusted with another's business.
3. People who deal ______ __________ __________ conduct negotiations on their own behalf without trusting the other's fairness or integrity.
4. Common law is sometimes called ___________ ________.
5. Laws created by the Florida Legislature are called _____________ ________.
6. A sales associate is a ____________ agent of the employing broker.

4.2 BROKERAGE RELATIONSHIPS IN FLORIDA

475.255, F.S.

475.01, F.S.

Historically, there has been confusion among buyers and sellers regarding what role real estate licensees have in real estate negotiations. Sellers assumed that real estate licensees represented their interests because sellers traditionally paid the commission. However, the payment of commission or the promise of compensation alone is not what determines whether a brokerage relationship exists. A brokerage relationship can be accidently (inadvertently) created by a licensee's actions and words. For example, referring to a prospective purchaser as "my buyer" or "my client" may imply that the licensee is representing the buyer when in actuality the brokerage is representing the seller. Because of this confusion, the Florida legislature passed the *Brokerage Relationship Disclosure Act*. The Brokerage Relationship Disclosure Act is intended to inform and educate the public regarding the types of authority (brokerage relationships) that can be granted to a broker and the duties brokers have in each type of brokerage relationship.

475.278, F.S.

Brokerage Relationship Options

In a residential transaction, there are three brokerage relationship options that a real estate broker will assume for buyers and sellers:

1. No brokerage relationship
2. Single agent
3. Transaction broker

The appropriate type of brokerage relationship is determined by the broker. Associates should consult with their employing broker regarding what type of brokerage relationships the brokerage practices. Florida law mandates certain duties and obligations for each type of brokerage relationship. We begin our overview of the types of relationships authorized by Florida Statutes with the relationship that has the fewest duties and obligations.

Practice Questions

7. List the three brokerage relationship options in Florida.

   1. ____________________
   2. ____________________
   3. ____________________

4.3 NO BROKERAGE RELATIONSHIP (NONREPRESENTATION)

Florida law allows prospective buyers and sellers to opt out of representation. A broker working in a no brokerage relationship is not an agent of either party in a transaction. A broker working in a no brokerage relationship capacity with a seller can enter into a listing agreement with the seller and be paid compensation. Similarly, a brokerage firm working in a no brokerage relationship capacity can work with a buyer. The broker may only relay information to the parties and may not negotiate on behalf of either party. The parties in a no brokerage relationship are referred to as customers. Chapter 475 defines **customer** as a member of the public who is or may be a buyer or a seller of real property and may or may not be represented by a real estate licensee in an authorized brokerage relationship. Therefore, the seller (or the buyer) who chooses nonrepresentation is a customer under the no brokerage relationship.

A broker (and the broker's associates) working in a no brokerage relationship with the parties to a transaction, owe three duties to customers:

1. *Account for all funds*. Brokers must account for all funds entrusted to them in a real estate transaction. (Unit 5 explains in detail the procedures associated with holding trust funds.)

2. *Deal honestly and fairly*. Real estate licensees owe a duty of good faith and honesty to customers. A broker's customers are entitled to rely on material statements related to a real estate transaction.
3. *Disclose all known facts that materially affect the value of residential real property and are not readily observable to the buyer*. Real estate licensees have a duty to disclose to buyers all known facts (such as defects) that materially affect the value of residential property. *Material defects* have to do with the property, the structure, and issues not readily observable to a buyer (such as mold that was not remediated but covered with drywall, a pending change in zoning, and so forth). It does not concern information about previous occupants. For example, if it is known to a licensee that there is a rotting wood floor under the wall-to-wall carpeting, the licensee is obligated to inform the buyer of the condition of the wood floor.

The three duties listed previously are fundamental to honest, fair business dealings—so much so that real estate licensees are bound to these three duties in all three types of brokerage relationships (see Figure 4.1).

FIGURE 4.1 ■ Brokerage Relationship Duties

Duty	No Brokerage	Transaction Broker	Single Agent
Account for all funds	✔	✔	✔
Deal honestly and fairly	✔	✔	✔
Disclose all known facts that affect value of residential property	✔	✔	✔
Use skill, care, and diligence		✔	✔
Present all offers and counteroffers		✔	✔
Exercise limited confidentiality		✔	
Perform additional duties that are mutually agreed to		✔	
Confidentiality			✔
Obedience			✔
Loyalty			✔
Disclosure (full)			✔

TO REMEMBER: THREE DUTIES REQUIRED IN ALL BROKERAGE RELATIONSHIPS

A	Account for all funds
D	Deal honestly and fairly
D	Disclose all known facts that affect value of residential property

The degree of guidance and representation the buyer desires and the broker provides determines which of the next two brokerage relationships is used.

Practice Questions

8. List the three duties in a no brokerage relationship.

    1. ______________________________
    2. ______________________________
    3. ______________________________

9. The buyer or the seller who chooses a no brokerage relationship with the broker is called the ______________.

4.4 SINGLE AGENT RELATIONSHIP

475.278(3), F.S.

475.01, F.S.

Florida license law defines a **single agent** as a broker who represents, as a fiduciary, either the buyer or the seller, but *not both*, in the same transaction. Recall that the broker does not represent either party in a no brokerage relationship. What makes a single agent relationship unique is that only one party in a transaction may be represented by the brokerage in a fiduciary capacity. A fiduciary relationship is a relationship of trust and confidence between the broker as agent and the person who delegated the authority to the broker (the principal). A fiduciary relationship between a broker and a buyer or a seller exists only when a single agent relationship is chosen. The terms *principal* and *client* should only be used when referring to a single agent relationship.

FIDUCIARY AND NONFIDUCIARY RELATIONSHIPS

Type of Authorized Relationship	Fiduciary Relationship	Works With
Transaction Broker	No	Customer
No brokerage relationship	No	Customer
Single Agent	Yes	Principal/Client

475.01, F.S.

475.272, F.S.

Dual Agency. A brokerage firm may represent as a single agent either the buyer or the seller in a real estate transaction, but never both. A **dual agent** relationship occurs when a brokerage firm represents as a fiduciary (single agent) both the buyer and the seller in the same real estate transaction. It is illegal in Florida for real estate licensees to operate as dual agents. Because the relationship is established with the brokerage firm, it is still dual agency if two different licensees in the same brokerage entity represent the seller as a single agent and the buyer as a single agent.

Subagents. Because a broker can only represent either the buyer or the seller in a real estate transaction as a fiduciary, there is one of two scenarios possible:

1. The seller lists property with the broker and the broker is an agent (represents in a fiduciary capacity) of the seller. The broker's sales associates and broker associates are **subagents** of their broker in dealings with the seller who is the principal in a single agency relationship.
2. The broker enters into a single agency relationship with the buyer who has a buyer representation agreement with the broker. The broker is an agent (represents in a fiduciary capacity) of the buyer. The broker's sales associates and broker associates are subagents of their broker in dealings with the buyer who is the principal.

When a broker enters into a single agent relationship with either a seller or a buyer in a real estate transaction, the broker is an agent of the principal (buyer or seller, but not both). The sales associates and broker associates who work with the principal on behalf of their broker are subagents of the broker's principals. Subagents (the broker's associates) have the same duties as the agent (broker). Therefore, sales associates and broker associates owe the same fiduciary obligations to the broker's principals as does their broker. This is true regardless of whether the associates, for tax purposes, are employees or independent contractors of the broker.

SUBAGENTS IN SINGLE AGENT RELATIONSHIPS

Seller as principal:

Seller is the principal → Broker is the agent of the seller → Sales associates and broker associates are the subagents of the seller/principal

Buyer as principal:

Buyer is the principal → Broker is the agent of the buyer → Sales associates and broker associates are the subagents of the buyer/principal

Single Agent Duties. A single agent is bound to the three duties required in all brokerage relationships (duties 1–3 in the following list). There are two duties owed by both single agent brokers and transaction brokers (duties 4–5). The transaction broker relationship is discussed in the next section of this unit. Four duties are required of single agents only (duties 6–9). These four unique duties owed only in a single agent relationship define the duties of a fiduciary (see text box and Figure 4.1).

1. *Account for all funds.*
2. *Deal honestly and fairly.*
3. *Disclose all known facts that materially affect the value of residential real property and are not readily observable to the buyer.*
4. *Use skill, care, and diligence.* Licensees must keep informed of developments that may affect the value of the property.
5. *Present all offers and counteroffers.* Unless a party has previously directed the licensee otherwise in writing, the licensee must present all oral and written offers and counteroffers in a timely manner even if a valid contract exists.
6. *Confidentiality.* Much of the information a broker gains while employed by the principal is confidential. An agent may not reveal to a third party, without the principal's permission, personal or private information that might lessen the principal's bargaining position. For example, a licensee may not tell a buyer that a seller is forced to sell owing to poor health or loss of a job without the principal's permission. A broker may not divulge confidential information learned during the course of the single agency even after the transaction is concluded and the agent-principal relationship is ended. A broker is never free to use confidential information to the disadvantage of or reveal any harmful or unfavorable information about a former principal.
7. *Obedience.* An agent is obligated to act in good faith according to the principal's lawful instructions. The broker-agent is at all times obligated to act in conformity with the principal's instructions, as long as those instructions are legal and relevant to the contractual relationship. If a broker feels that carrying out

the principal's legal directions will harm the principal, then the broker must promptly inform the principal of all known facts, along with the broker's opinion. However, if the principal will not change the instructions, the broker must either carry them out or withdraw from the relationship.

Brokers may not violate the law. For example, if a principal instructs a listing broker not to show the property or sell to a member of a particular minority or ethnic group, the broker may not obey the principal's instructions because doing so would violate the law. In such an instance, the broker must inform the principal that to restrict certain groups of people from seeing or purchasing a listed property is a violation of the fair housing laws.

8. *Loyalty*. The agent as fiduciary in a real estate transaction must avoid any situation that might breach the duty of undivided loyalty to the principal. The overriding rule is that brokers may not adopt an attitude that is adverse to the interests of their principals or act for themselves or some other person whose interests are contrary to those of the principal. Loyalty (faithfulness) requires brokers to always place the principal's interests above those of other persons with whom the brokers deal. Courts have ruled (case law) that for brokers to be loyal to their principals, they cannot exercise duties in such a manner as to profit themselves or anyone else at the expense of the principal. The duty of loyalty includes, for example:
   - obtaining the most favorable price and terms for the principal,
   - acting on behalf of the principal,
   - not acting for parties with adverse interest in the same transaction,
   - never concealing the identity of the purchaser to induce the principal to sell,
   - disclosing to the principal if the agent becomes personally interested in the principal's property, and
   - never advancing the agent's or another person's interest at the expense of the principal.
9. *Full disclosure*. It is a broker-agent's duty to keep the principal fully informed at all times of all the facts or information that might affect the transaction or the value of the property. An agent is obligated to disclose facts regarding a property's true worth. Agents may be held responsible for material facts they should have known and communicated to their principal but did not. Also, broker-agents must inform their seller principals, for example, of the buyer's financial condition, the status of the earnest money deposit, or if a personal relationship exists between the agent and the buyer. All material facts must be revealed to the principal even if the disclosure of such facts might cause the transaction to fail.

   Full, fair, and prompt disclosure also includes notifying the principal if the broker is personally interested in buying the listed property. In such an event, the broker must clearly terminate the agent-principal relationship and inform the principal of all facts regarding the property that the broker has learned while in an agent's capacity. Otherwise, the broker could buy from the principal and subsequently sell at a higher price and keep the profit ("overage," "secret profit," or "secret commission"). To do so could be construed as fraud, misrepresentation, concealment, and/or dishonest dealing and could expose the broker to liability to both seller and buyer for the full amount of the secret profit. It might further give rise to disciplinary proceedings against the licensee.

The nine duties just listed apply to *all* real estate transactions (residential and otherwise) when the parties have agreed to a single agent relationship.

TO REMEMBER: FOUR UNIQUE DUTIES OF A SINGLE AGENT

A single agent owes nine duties to the principal. Four of the duties apply only to single agent relationships.

C	Confidentiality
O	Obedience
L	Loyalty
D	Disclosure (full)

Practice Questions

10. The duty of _______________ prevents an agent from revealing to a third party, without the principal's permission, personal or private information that might lessen the principal's bargaining position.

11. The duty of _______________ obligates an agent to act in good faith according to the principal's lawful instructions.

12. The duty of _______________ requires the broker to place the principal's interests above those of other persons with whom the broker deals.

13. _________ _______________ is a broker-agent's duty to keep the principal fully informed at all times of all the facts or information that might affect the transaction or the property value.

4.5 TRANSACTION BROKER RELATIONSHIP

475.278(2), F.S.

Recall that in a no brokerage relationship, the broker (and the broker's sales associates) simply facilitated the transaction process without representing or negotiating on behalf of the parties. In the single agent relationship, the broker is the agent of the principal and the broker's associates are subagents of the principal. The broker and the broker's associates are bound to a fiduciary relationship with the principal. The single agent broker (and subagent associates) represents only one party in a transaction because to represent both the buyer and the seller as a fiduciary in a transaction would be a conflict of interest and create dual agency, which is prohibited under Chapter 475. Therefore, for both the buyer and the seller to be represented in the same transaction within the same brokerage, a different type of brokerage relationship was created. To avoid the issue of an illegal dual agency, this third type of brokerage relationship was developed to give both buyers and sellers limited representation (rather than full fiduciary representation). This brokerage relationship has proved to be so useful that Florida law has deemed the transaction broker relationship to be the presumed relationship in dealings with buyers and sellers.

Under Florida law, it is presumed that all licensees are operating as transaction brokers unless one of the other two brokerage relationships is established, in writing, with the customer. A **transaction broker** is a broker who provides **limited representation** to a buyer, a seller, or to both parties in a real estate transaction. Transaction brokers do not represent either party in a fiduciary capacity. Recall that a fiduciary owes complete allegiance (undivided loyalty) to the principal. It is not possible to give undivided loyalty to both the buyer and the seller.

In a transaction broker relationship, the parties to a real estate transaction are giving up their rights to the undivided loyalty of a licensee. *Limited representation* allows a broker (and the broker's associates) to facilitate a real estate transaction by assisting a buyer and a seller who are both parties to the same transaction within that brokerage. In this case, a broker will not work to represent one party to the detriment of the other party. Because associates represent buyers and sellers in the same brokerage relationship as that of their broker, it doesn't matter if one associate is working with both the buyer and the seller or one associate is working with the buyer and another associate is working with the seller. All licensees are providing limited representation to both parties. Because a transaction broker does not represent the seller (or the buyer, or both parties) in a fiduciary capacity, Florida law refers to the parties as customers.

In a transaction broker relationship, the broker and the broker's associates are bound to the three duties required in all brokerage relationships (duties 1–3) and two duties also required of single agent brokers (duties 4–5). The sixth and seventh duties enable the broker to provide a nonfiduciary limited representation (see Figure 4.1).

1. *Account for all funds.*
2. *Deal honestly and fairly.*
3. *Disclose all known facts that materially affect the value of residential property and are not readily observable to the buyer.*
4. *Use skill, care, and diligence in the transaction.*
5. *Present all offers and counteroffers in a timely manner.*
6. *Exercise limited confidentiality, unless waived in writing by a party.*
7. *Perform any additional duties that are mutually agreed to with a party.* However, a real estate licensee must be careful not to accept duties beyond the scope of limited representation.

Distinct Features of a Transaction Broker Relationship

A transaction broker must exercise limited confidentiality. This limited confidentiality prevents disclosure of the following information:

- That the seller will accept a price less than the asking or listed price
- That the buyer will pay a price greater than the price submitted in a written offer
- The motivation of the parties for selling (if the seller) and/or buying (if the buyer) of the property
- That a seller or a buyer will agree to financing terms other than those previously disclosed in writing (for example, in the original listing or during the contract negotiations)
- Any other information requested by a party to remain confidential

Another distinct feature is the customer in a transaction broker relationship is not responsible for the acts of a licensee, as a principal might be in a single agent relationship.

KEY POINTS OF A TRANSACTION BROKER RELATIONSHIP

- Transaction broker relationship is presumed in all residential and nonresidential transactions
- Limited representation to a buyer, a seller, or both the buyer and the seller (in the same transaction within the same brokerage)
- No fiduciary relationship with the buyer or the seller
- Parties are represented as customers

Practice Questions

14. In Florida, there is a presumption that the brokerage is working in a ________________ ____________ relationship.

15. A transaction broker is a broker who provides ________________ representation to a buyer, a seller, or both the buyer and the seller in the same real estate transaction.

16. In a transaction broker relationship, the brokerage does not represent the buyer or the seller in a ________________ capacity.

4.6 TRANSITION FROM SINGLE AGENT TO TRANSACTION BROKER

When a broker enters into a single agent relationship with a buyer or a seller, the broker and the broker's associates are bound to a fiduciary relationship with the principal. A broker who has a single agent relationship with a seller cannot also be a single agent for a buyer interested in the seller's property.

EXAMPLE: Assume that a broker represents seller Rebecca as a single agent. The same broker has a single agent relationship with buyer Mike. Because Mike has a single agent relationship with the broker, the broker's sales associates and broker associates may not show Rebecca's home to Mike. A broker may not be a single agent of the buyer and a single agent of the seller in the same transaction. This is true even if seller Rebecca and buyer Mike use different sales associates within the same brokerage. If a real estate broker represents both parties in a transaction in a fiduciary capacity, an illegal dual agency is created. To manage such situations, the buyer and seller would have to consent in writing to allow the broker to transition (change) to transaction broker relationships before the broker can show Rebecca's home to Mike.

A single agent relationship may be changed to a transaction broker relationship at any time during the relationship between the agent and principal, provided the agent first obtains the principal's written consent to the change in relationship. To gain the principal's written consent to a change in relationship, the buyer or the seller (or both) must sign the **consent to transition** to transaction broker notice set forth in Chapter 475. Note that this disclosure notice requires the buyer's or the seller's signature before the licensee may change from one brokerage relationship to another. If the principal refuses to sign the consent to transition notice, the broker must continue to act as a single agent.

Brokerage Relationship Limitations

- If the brokerage firm has a transaction broker relationship with the seller, the brokerage firm can also work with the buyer, in the same transaction, as a transaction broker or in a no brokerage relationship capacity. The brokerage firm *cannot* represent the buyer as a single agent if the firm has a transaction broker relationship with the seller.
- If the brokerage firm is representing the seller as a single agent, the brokerage firm can work with the buyer, in the same transaction, in a no brokerage relationship capacity. The brokerage firm *cannot* represent the buyer as a single agent or work with the buyer as a transaction broker if the firm is also representing the seller as a single agent.

The brokerage relationship limitations described previously apply even if the buyer and the seller are working with different sales associates in the same brokerage firm (see Figure 4.2).

FIGURE 4.2 ■ Authorized Relationships in One Brokerage Firm in the Same Transaction

Relationship with the Seller		Authorized Relationship with the Buyer
If a Transaction Broker for the seller	→	Transaction Broker *or* No Brokerage Relationship *with the buyer*
If a Single Agent for the seller	→	No Brokerage Relationship *with the buyer*

Practice Questions

17. A single agent relationship may be changed to a transaction broker relationship, provided the agent first obtains the principal's signature on the ____________ to ____________ notice.

18. Michael was transferred to Seattle, so he wanted to sell his Florida residence. Harbor Realty entered into a single agent relationship with Michael. Harbor Realty later transitioned to a transaction broker relationship with Michael. Sales associate Merissa was working with Michael on behalf of Harbor Realty. Michael told Merissa that the air-conditioning compressor would run for about an hour and then overheat and stop running. Merissa knew that Michael was anxious to sell, so she did not mention the air-conditioning compressor to the buyer.

    a. Does the fact that Michael had a transaction broker relationship with Harbor Realty excuse nondisclosure of the air-conditioning compressor's condition?

    ____

    ____

    b. Can the sales associate be disciplined for failing to inform the buyer that the compressor would overheat?

    ____

    ____

    c. Can Merissa's broker be held accountable for not disclosing the air conditioning compressor's condition to the buyer?

    ____

    ____

4.7 DISCLOSURE REQUIREMENTS

Brokerage Relationship Disclosure Act

475.278(5)(a), F.S.

Residential Transactions. The Brokerage Relationship Disclosure Act (BRDA) mandates that the duties and obligations that have been detailed in this unit apply to *all* real estate transactions (residential and nonresidential). However, written disclosures are required *only* for residential sale transactions when the brokerage firm acts in the capacity of a single agent or in a no brokerage relationship. Written disclosures are not required when the brokerage firm acts in the capacity of transaction broker because this relationship is presumed under Florida law. **Residential sale transactions** are defined as:

- improved property of four or fewer residential units;
- unimproved property zoned for four or fewer residential units; and
- agricultural property of 10 or fewer acres.

Residential transactions include single-family homes, single condominium units, duplexes (two-unit residential structure), triplexes (three-unit residential), and quadruplexes (four-unit residential). A large apartment complex is not considered to be residential real estate under the BRDA. Residential transactions include vacant land that is zoned for four or fewer residential units. A 5-acre property zoned agricultural falls within the definition of a residential transaction under the BRDA; however, a 50-acre farm, even if an individual lives on the property, is not considered to be a residential transaction for disclosure purposes under the BRDA.

Brokerage relationship disclosure requirements do not apply to transactions involving nonresidential real estate, business opportunities, and lease agreements (see the following text box). Furthermore, brokerage relationship disclosure documents are not required for the auction or appraisal of real estate.

TYPES OF TRANSACTIONS THAT DO NOT REQUIRE BROKERAGE RELATIONSHIP DISCLOSURES

- Nonresidential transactions
- Rent or lease agreements (except when there is an option to purchase residential property)
- Business opportunities (except for property with four or fewer residential units)
- Auctions
- Appraisals

475.278, F.S.

Disclosure Format. The duties of the single agent relationship and nonrepresentation must be fully described and disclosed in writing to a buyer or a seller, either as a separate and distinct disclosure document or included as part of another document, such as a listing agreement or buyer broker agreement. If the disclosure document is incorporated into a listing or buyer broker agreement, a signature line must be inserted immediately following the disclosure information. It is not sufficient to only have a signature line at the bottom of the listing or buyer broker agreement.

When incorporated into other documents, the required disclosure notice must be of the same size as, or larger type than, other provisions of the document and must be conspicuous in its placement to advise customers (or principals in a single agent relationship) of the brokerage duties. The first sentence must be printed in uppercase and bold type. The list of duties must be presented on the disclosure in the same order as listed in the statute. The disclosure notice may include information concerning the real estate brokerage, such as the company name and logo, address, phone number, email address, et cetera.

Nonrepresentation. The no brokerage relationship notice must be disclosed in writing before the showing of property (see Figure 4.3).

Single Agent. The single agent disclosure must be made before, or at the time of, entering into a listing agreement or an agreement for representation, or before the showing of property, whichever occurs first (see Figure 4.4).

Transaction Broker. Recall that under Florida law, it is presumed that all licensees are operating as transaction brokers unless another brokerage relationship is established. Therefore, there is no requirement to give a written transaction broker disclosure to the buyer and/or the seller. However, licensees must fulfill the duties of a transaction broker when that form of representation is selected.

Consent to Transition to Transaction Broker. The consent to transition to transaction broker notice includes wording regarding the principal's permission to allow the single agent to transition to a transaction broker. The notice also includes a list of the duties that a transaction broker owes to the customer. The consent to transition to transaction broker notice can either be a separate document or be included as part of another document—for example, in the listing agreement. See "Disclosure Format" earlier in this unit for information concerning the required format of the disclosure notice (see Figure 4.5).

475.5015, F.S.

Recordkeeping and Retention of Disclosure Documents. Brokers must retain brokerage relationship disclosure documents for five years for all residential transactions that result in a written contract to purchase and sell real property. Documents may be stored in a digital format as long as they are readily accessible by the broker. Files of properties that have failed to close must also be retained. If a transaction fails to close, the broker should retain the brokerage relationship disclosure documents with the purchase and sale contract and other documents associated with the property and place them in the "dead" (failed to close) file. The Commission may discipline a licensee for failure to abide by any provision in Section 475.278, F.S., including the duties owed to customers and principals, disclosure requirements, and recordkeeping requirements set forth in the law.

FIGURE 4.3 ■ No Brokerage Relationship Disclosure Form

NO BROKERAGE RELATIONSHIP NOTICE

FLORIDA LAW REQUIRES THAT REAL ESTATE LICENSEES WHO HAVE NO BROKERAGE RELATIONSHIP WITH A POTENTIAL SELLER OR BUYER DISCLOSE THEIR DUTIES TO SELLERS AND BUYERS.

As a real estate licensee who has no brokerage relationship with you, (insert name of Real Estate Entity and its Associates) owe to you the following duties:

1. Dealing honestly and fairly;
2. Disclosing all known facts that materially affect the value of residential real property which are not readily observable to the buyer; and
3. Accounting for all funds entrusted to the licensee.

Seller or (buyer)__________ __________

Signature Date

__________ __________

Signature Date

FIGURE 4.4 ■ Single Agent Disclosure Form

SINGLE AGENT NOTICE

FLORIDA LAW REQUIRES THAT REAL ESTATE LICENSEES OPERATING AS SINGLE AGENTS DISCLOSE TO BUYERS AND SELLERS THEIR DUTIES.

As a single agent, (insert name of Real Estate Entity and its Associates) owe to you the following duties:

1. Dealing honestly and fairly;
2. Loyalty;
3. Confidentiality;
4. Obedience;
5. Full disclosure;
6. Accounting for all funds;
7. Skill, care, and diligence in the transaction;
8. Presenting all offers and counteroffers in a timely manner, unless a party has previously directed the licensee otherwise in writing; and
9. Disclosing all known facts that materially affect the value of residential real property and are not readily observable.

Seller or (buyer)__________ __________

Signature Date

__________ __________

Signature Date

FIGURE 4.5 ■ Consent to Transition to Transaction Broker

FLORIDA LAW ALLOWS REAL ESTATE LICENSEES WHO REPRESENT A BUYER OR SELLER AS A SINGLE AGENT TO CHANGE FROM A SINGLE AGENT RELATIONSHIP TO A TRANSACTION BROKERAGE RELATIONSHIP IN ORDER FOR THE LICENSEE TO ASSIST BOTH PARTIES IN A REAL ESTATE TRANSACTION BY PROVIDING A LIMITED FORM OF REPRESENTATION TO BOTH THE BUYER AND THE SELLER. THIS CHANGE IN RELATIONSHIP CANNOT OCCUR WITHOUT YOUR PRIOR WRITTEN CONSENT.

As a transaction broker, ______________________________ (insert name of Real Estate Firm and its Associates) provides to you a limited form of representation that includes the following duties:

1. Dealing honestly and fairly;
2. Accounting for all funds;
3. Using skill, care, and diligence in the transaction;
4. Disclosing all known facts that materially affect the value of residential real property and are not readily observable to the buyer;
5. Presenting all offers and counteroffers in a timely manner, unless a party has previously directed the licensee otherwise in writing;
6. Limited confidentiality, unless waived by a party. This limited confidentiality will prevent disclosure that the seller will accept a price less than the asking or listed price, that the buyer will pay a price greater than the price submitted in a written offer, of the motivation of any party for selling or buying property, that a seller or buyer will agree to financing terms other than those offered, or of any other information requested by a party to remain confidential; and
7. Any additional duties that are entered into by this or by separate written agreement.

Limited representation means that a buyer or seller is not responsible for the acts of the licensee. Additionally, parties are giving up their rights to the undivided loyalty of the licensee. This aspect of limited representation allows a licensee to facilitate a real estate transaction by assisting both the buyer and the seller, but a licensee will not work to represent one party to the detriment of the other party when acting as a transaction broker to both parties.

___________________________ I agree that my agent may assume the role and duties of a transaction broker. [must be signed]

Exceptions to Disclosure Requirements

475.278(5)(b), F.S.

Certain interactions a licensee has with buyers and sellers do not constitute a brokerage relationship. These situations are described in the real estate license law. When a licensee has an encounter with a buyer or a seller under these specific situations, the licensee is not required to give a prospective buyer or a prospective seller a disclosure notice. The six situations that do not create a brokerage relationship are as follows:

1. When the licensee knows that a single agent or a transaction broker represents a prospective seller or a prospective buyer
2. At a bona fide "open house" or model home showing that does not involve eliciting confidential information; the execution of a contractual offer or an agreement for representation; or negotiations concerning price, terms, or conditions of potential sale
3. During unanticipated casual encounters between a licensee and a prospective seller or a prospective buyer that do not involve eliciting confidential information; the execution of a contractual offer or an agreement for representation; or negotiations concerning price, terms, or conditions of a potential sale
4. When responding to general factual questions from a prospective seller or a prospective buyer concerning properties that have been advertised for sale

5. Situations in which a licensee's communications with a prospective buyer or a prospective seller are limited to providing either written or oral communication that is general, factual information about the qualifications, background, and services of the licensee or the licensee's brokerage firm
6. When an owner is selling new residential units built by the owner and the circumstances or setting should reasonably inform the potential buyer that the owner's employee or single agent is acting on behalf of the owner, whether because of the location of the sales office or because of office signage or placards or identification badges worn by the owner's employee or single agent

If, during any of these situations, a member of the public begins to provide confidential information or begins to negotiate concerning price, terms, and so forth, the licensee would at that point present the person with the appropriate disclosure notice depending on the circumstances and desire of the parties.

Practice Questions

19. A residential sales transaction is defined as the sale of improved residential property of ______________ or fewer units.

20. Circle each example of a residential sale transaction.
    a. Medical office condo listing
    b. Condo unit listing in a 20-unit condominium complex of residential dwellings
    c. Sales contract of a fourplex zoned multifamily residential
    d. Lease agreement for a single-family dwelling

21. The no brokerage relationship notice must be given before the ____________ ______ ____________.

22. The consent to transition to transaction broker notice includes a list of the ______________ that a transaction broker owes to the ______________.

23. The single agent disclosure must be made before, or at the time of entering into a ______________ ___________ or before the ______________ of property, whichever occurs first.

24. Real estate brokers are required to retain buyer brokerage agreements for a period of ______________ years.

4.8 NONRESIDENTIAL TRANSACTIONS

Recall that the disclosure notice requirements discussed in this unit only apply to residential sale transactions. However, brokers who deal in nonresidential transactions, such as commercial and industrial property, are bound by Chapter 475 regarding the brokerage relationship *duties* of nonrepresentation, single agent, and transaction broker relationships.

475.2755, F.S.

Designated Sales Associates. In a nonresidential real estate transaction where the buyer and seller each have assets of $1 million or more, the broker at the request of the buyer and the seller may designate two sales associates to act as single agents for the buyer and the seller in the same transaction. The two sales associates in such an arrangement are called **designated sales associates.** (In a residential transaction, dual agency is illegal.) However, the designated sales associate form of representation in nonresidential transactions is *not* considered to be dual agency.

The broker serves as an advisor to each designated sales associate—not to the buyer or the seller. The broker serves as a neutral party helping to facilitate the process without giving guidance or representation to the parties in the transaction. Designated sales associates have the duties of a single agent.

Disclosure Requirements. The buyer and the seller must sign a disclosure notice stating that their assets meet the $1 million threshold and requesting that the broker use the designated sales associate form of representation. The disclosure notice includes special language regarding confidential information and also includes duties of a single agent (see Figure 4.6). Brokers must retain brokerage relationship disclosure documents for five years for all nonresidential transactions that use designated sales associates.

FIGURE 4.6 ■ Designated Sales Associate

I have assets of one million dollars or more. I request that (*Insert Name of Broker*) use the designated sales associate form of representation.

____

Signature of Buyer or Seller (circle one)

FLORIDA LAW PROHIBITS A DESIGNATED SALES ASSOCIATE FROM DISCLOSING, EXCEPT TO THE BROKER OR PERSONS SPECIFIED BY THE BROKER, INFORMATION MADE CONFIDENTIAL BY REQUEST OR AT THE INSTRUCTION OF THE CUSTOMER THE DESIGNATED SALES ASSOCIATE IS REPRESENTING. HOWEVER, FLORIDA LAW ALLOWS A DESIGNATED SALES ASSOCIATE TO DISCLOSE INFORMATION ALLOWED TO BE DISCLOSED OR REQUIRED TO BE DISCLOSED BY LAW AND ALSO ALLOWS A DESIGNATED SALES ASSOCIATE TO DISCLOSE TO HIS OR HER BROKER, OR PERSONS SPECIFIED BY THE BROKER, CONFIDENTIAL INFORMATION OF A CUSTOMER FOR THE PURPOSE OF SEEKING ADVICE OR ASSISTANCE FOR THE BENEFIT OF THE CUSTOMER IN REGARD TO A TRANSACTION. FLORIDA LAW REQUIRES THAT THE BROKER MUST HOLD THIS INFORMATION CONFIDENTIAL AND MAY NOT USE SUCH INFORMATION TO THE DETRIMENT OF THE OTHER PARTY.

SINGLE AGENT NOTICE

FLORIDA LAW REQUIRES THAT REAL ESTATE LICENSEES OPERATING AS SINGLE AGENTS DISCLOSE TO BUYERS AND SELLERS THEIR DUTIES. As a single agent, (Insert name of Real Estate Entity) and its Associates owe to you the following duties:

1. Dealing honestly and fairly;
2. Loyalty;
3. Confidentiality;
4. Obedience;
5. Full disclosure;
6. Accounting for all funds;
7. Skill, care, and diligence in the transaction;
8. Presenting all offers and counteroffers in a timely manner, unless a party has previously directed the licensee otherwise in writing; and
9. Disclosing all known facts that materially affect the value of residential real property and are not readily observable.

____________________________	____________________________
Seller or (buyer)	Signature Date

Practice Questions

25. Designated sales associates are used only in ______________ transactions.

26. The broker serves as an advisor to the ___________ ___________ ___________.

27. The designated sales associates act as ____________ ____________ for the buyer and the seller in the same transaction.

28. Designated sales associates have the duties of a ____________ ____________.

4.9 TERMINATING A BROKERAGE RELATIONSHIP

Generally speaking, a transaction broker relationship or a single agent relationship is terminated when the objectives have been accomplished according to the terms of the contract that created the brokerage relationship and notice is given to the other party. A principal is justified in revoking a single agent relationship with the broker if the broker-agent breaches any of the fiduciary duties.

A brokerage relationship between a principal (or a customer) and a broker may be terminated for any one of the following reasons:

- Fulfillment of the brokerage relationship's purpose (for example, finding a ready, willing, and able buyer).
- Mutual agreement to terminate the brokerage relationship.
- Expiration of the terms of the agreement. (If no term is specified, the courts have ruled that a brokerage relationship may be terminated after a "reasonable" time.)
- Broker renounces the single agent relationship by giving notice to the principal or the broker renounces the transaction broker relationship by giving notice to the customer.
- Principal revokes a single agent relationship or the customer revokes a transaction broker relationship, by giving notice. (In this case, the principal or the customer may be liable for damages, such as advertising expenses, incurred by revoking the brokerage relationship before the termination date of the listing agreement or exclusive buyer agreement.)
- Death of a seller's broker or the seller before the broker finds a ready, willing, and able buyer.
- Death of the buyer's broker or the buyer before the broker finds a suitable property for the buyer.
- Destruction of the property or condemnation by eminent domain.
- Bankruptcy of the principal or the customer.

Practice Questions

29. Fill in the blanks to complete the list of reasons that a brokerage relationship may be terminated:
    ______________ of the brokerage relationship's purpose.
    __________ ______________ to terminate.
    ______________ of the seller's property.
    ______________ of a seller's broker or the seller before the broker finds a ready, willing, and able buyer.
    ______________ of the principal or the customer.

4.10 SUMMARY OF IMPORTANT POINTS

- A person who delegates authority to another is the *principal*. A person who accepts the authority is the *agent*. An agent is authorized to represent and act for the principal. The agency relationship creates a *fiduciary* relationship with the principal. A fiduciary acts in a position of trust and confidence with the principal.
- A real estate licensee may act as a special agent with buyers or sellers. This occurs when the buyer or the seller, but not both, and the brokerage firm enter into a single agent relationship. In this relationship, the buyer or the seller is the principal and the broker is the agent.
- In all real estate transactions, there are three options concerning the role the real estate brokerage firm will assume: (1) nonrepresentation (or no brokerage relationship) for the buyer and/or the seller, (2) single agent of either the buyer or the seller, and (3) transaction broker for the buyer and/or the seller.
- Licensees may not operate as dual agents. A dual agent is a broker who represents both the buyer and the seller as a fiduciary in the same transaction.
- The duties and obligations in each type of brokerage relationship apply to all real estate transactions.
- License law mandates that a real estate broker working in a no brokerage relationship capacity has three duties: (1) deal honest and fairly, (2) disclose all known facts that materially affect the value of residential real property that are not readily observable to the buyer, and (3) account for all funds entrusted to the licensee.
- F.S. 475 mandates that a real estate broker working as a single agent has the duties required in a no brokerage relationship plus the first two additional duties required in a transaction broker relationship. Four duties apply exclusively to a broker working as a single agent: (1) confidentiality, (2) obedience, (3) loyalty, and (4) full disclosure.
- License law mandates that a real estate broker working as a transaction broker has the duties required in a no brokerage relationship plus four additional duties: (1) use skill, care, and diligence; (2) present all offers and counteroffers; (3) exercise limited confidentiality; and (4) perform additional duties that are mutually agreed to.
- A written disclosure is required for residential transactions when a single agent relationship or nonrepresentation is chosen. The single agency disclosure must be made before, or at the time of, entering into a listing agreement or an agreement for representation, or before the showing of property, whichever occurs first. The no brokerage relationship disclosure must be made before the showing of property.
- A *residential sale transaction* is defined as the sale of improved property of four or fewer residential units, the sale of unimproved property intended for use as four or fewer residential units, or the sale of agricultural property of 10 or fewer acres.
- Under Florida law, it is presumed that all licensees are operating as transaction brokers unless another brokerage relationship is chosen. A transaction broker provides limited representation to a buyer, a seller, or both, but does not represent either in a fiduciary capacity or as a single agent.

- A real estate broker may change from a single agent relationship to a transaction broker relationship only with the express written permission of the principal. The principal must sign or initial the Consent to Transition to Transaction Broker disclosure before the change can occur.
- Brokers must retain brokerage relationship disclosure documents for five years for all residential transactions that result in a written offer to purchase and sell real property and all nonresidential transactions that use designated sales associates.
- In a nonresidential transaction and where the buyer and the seller each have assets of $1 million or more, the broker, at the request of the buyer and the seller, may designate two sales associates to be *designated sales associates*. Each designated sales associate has a fiduciary responsibility to their client (buyer or seller). The broker acts as a neutral party advising the designated sales associates to help facilitate the process. The buyer and the seller must sign the Designated Sales Associate disclosure form attesting to the duties of the agents and their assets meeting the minimum of $1 million.

UNIT 4 EXAM

1. A real estate brokerage company has entered into a single agent buyer broker relationship with the buyer. In order to show this buyer property that is listed with the same brokerage company for which it is a single agent, in what brokerage capacity may the company work with this buyer and seller?
   a. Single agent for the seller and transaction broker for the buyer
   b. Single agent for the seller and single agent for the buyer
   c. Any relationship that is agreed to by both the buyer and the seller
   d. Both the seller and the buyer must transition to a transaction broker relationship before the buyer can be shown the seller's property

2. The brokerage relationship disclosure requirements in Chapter 475, F.S., apply to the
   a. sale of a 20-unit apartment complex.
   b. sale of a condominium unit.
   c. residential lease agreement in a duplex.
   d. sale of a bookstore business and real property.

3. Which statement BEST describes the duty of loyalty in a single agent relationship?
   a. The broker must act in the best interest of the principal.
   b. The broker must disclose all latent defects to prospective buyers.
   c. The broker is held to a standard of care that requires knowledge concerning the land and physical characteristics of the property.
   d. The broker must be able to account for all funds received on behalf of the principal.

4. A real estate broker who works in a limited capacity for both the buyer and the seller in the same transaction is
   a. a dual agent.
   b. a transaction broker.
   c. bound to fiduciary duties to both the buyer and the seller.
   d. a single agent of both the buyer and the seller.

5. A licensee of ABC Realty must give the no brokerage relationship notice to
   a. a buyer who has a single agent relationship with XYZ Realty.
   b. every prospective buyer and prospective seller in all cases.
   c. a for-sale-by-owner (FSBO) seller before showing the FSBO home to a buyer customer of ABC Realty.
   d. every prospective buyer who walks through an open house listed by ABC Realty.

6. A broker has listed a seller's property. The seller has disclosed to the broker that the ceramic tile is loose in the dining room because the cement did not adhere to the tile. The loose tile is not readily visible because it is covered with an area rug to protect the seller's toddler. The broker has satisfied his legal obligation if he tells the buyer
   a. that the floor appears to be in good condition.
   b. that ceramic tiles in the dining room are loose.
   c. that the buyer can order an inspection at his own expense if he is concerned about the floor.
   d. nothing unless he is asked specifically about the tile floor's condition.

7. A transaction broker has all the duties listed EXCEPT
   a. limited confidentiality.
   b. to use skill, care, and diligence.
   c. to disclose all known facts that materially affect the value of residential real property and are not readily observable to the buyer.
   d. obedience.

8. A seller lists her home for $216,900. The seller tells the sales associate that she needs to get at least $212,000 for the home. After Sunday's open house, the sales associate receives two offers on the home. The first offer for $216,900 is contingent on the seller's financing a portion of the down payment. The second offer is for $209,000, with the prequalified buyer to secure her own financing. The sales associate should
   a. seek his broker's advice regarding which offer to present.
   b. present the full-price offer to the seller.
   c. present the second offer to the seller.
   d. present both offers, explaining the details of each to the seller.

9. In the common public relationship that exists in a typical real estate transaction, buyers and sellers are said to be dealing
   a. in a fiduciary capacity.
   b. at arm's length with each other.
   c. in an agency status with each other.
   d. under the doctrine of ethical confidentiality.

10. If a principal gives the broker instructions that will result in loss or harm to the principal, the broker
    a. is justified in not carrying out such instructions.
    b. should carry out such instructions without question.
    c. should carry out only that portion of the instructions that will not cause loss or harm to the principal.
    d. should inform the principal of possible harm inherent in the instructions, and then either do as instructed or withdraw from the relationship.

11. A broker's obligations to consumers with whom the brokerage firm has no brokerage relationship include the duty of
    a. full disclosure.
    b. accounting for all funds.
    c. loyalty.
    d. limited confidentiality.

12. Designated sales associates are BEST described as
    a. single agents for the buyer and the seller in nonresidential transactions where the buyer and the seller meet certain asset thresholds.
    b. the sales associates designated to represent the buyer and the seller in a transaction broker relationship.
    c. undisclosed dual agents.
    d. the sales associates in charge of the required brokerage disclosure forms for the brokerage office.

13. Which relationship is a general agency relationship?
    a. Brokerage company employed under a listing agreement
    b. Relationship between the employing broker and a broker associate
    c. Sales associate working with a prospective buyer
    d. Relationship between a sales associate and the seller who has listed property with the brokerage

14. Which action will terminate a single agent relationship with the principal who has listed a home for sale with the brokerage?
    a. Death of a customer interested in the listing
    b. Buyer's offer not accepted by the seller
    c. Decision of sales associate who acquired the listing for the brokerage to leave the company
    d. Destruction of the listed property by a large sinkhole

15. A real estate broker (and the broker's associates) are obligated to which duty in all three brokerage relationships?
    a. Loyalty
    b. Full disclosure
    c. Deal honestly and fairly
    d. Perform additional duties that are mutually agreed to

UNIT

5 REAL ESTATE BROKERAGE ACTIVITIES AND PROCEDURES

LEARNING OBJECTIVES

When you have completed this unit, you will be able to accomplish the following.

- Identify the requirements for a broker's office(s) and explain what determines whether a temporary shelter must be registered as a branch office.
- List the requirements related to sign regulation.
- List the requirements related to the regulation of advertising by real estate brokers.
- Explain the term *immediately* as it applies to earnest money deposits.
- Describe the four settlement procedures available to a broker who has received conflicting demands or who has a good-faith doubt as to who is entitled to disputed funds.
- Describe the regulations regarding lien rights for unpaid sales commission.
- Contrast the features and requirements of the various types of business organizations.

KEY TERMS

arbitration
blind advertisement
commingle
conflicting demands
conversion
corporation
deposit
earnest money
escrow account
escrow disbursement order (EDO)
failure to account or deliver
general partnership
good-faith doubt
immediately
interpleader
kickback
limited liability company (LLC)
limited liability partnership (LLP)
limited partnership
litigation
mediation
ostensible partnership
personal assistant
point of contact information
professional association (PA)
sole proprietorship
team advertising
trade name

INTRODUCTION

This unit concerns the day-to-day operations of a real estate brokerage office, including principal office and branch office regulations, rules governing signs, advertising, recordkeeping, and conduct. The broker's role as an expert and the proper handling of escrow funds, rental lists, and compensation are discussed. The unit also describes the various forms of business entities that may be encountered and that are permitted to engage in real estate brokerage activities in Florida.

5.1 BROKERAGE OFFICES

475.22, F.S.
61J2-10.022, F.A.C.

All active Florida real estate brokers are required to have an office and to register the office with the Department of Business and Professional Regulation (DBPR). A broker's office must consist of at least one enclosed room in a building of stationary construction that will provide privacy to conduct negotiations and closings of real estate transactions. Florida law does not regulate the specifics of a broker's office. For example, Florida law does not require brokers to have a telephone, desk, business checking account, or an escrow account. The tools needed to conduct business are the broker's decision. Florida law, however, does require that the broker's accounting books, records, and real estate transaction files are to be kept in the office. Brokers may store the files in an electronic format that can be readily accessible by the broker.

If local zoning allows, the broker's office may be located in the broker's residence. However, the broker must comply with all office and brokerage signage requirements. The broker should also consult applicable homeowners association rules or restrictive covenants and rules. A broker may have an office or offices in another state, provided the broker agrees in writing to cooperate with any investigation initiated under Chapter 475, F.S.

Sales associates are not permitted to open offices of their own. They must be registered from and work out of an office maintained and registered in the name of their employer.

Branch Offices

A broker who desires to conduct business from additional locations must register each additional location as a branch office and pay the appropriate registration fees.

Branch Office Registrations. The Florida Real Estate Commission (FREC) may insist that a broker open and register a branch office whenever the FREC decides that the business conducted at a place other than the principal office is of such a nature that the public interest requires registration of a branch office. Further, any office will be considered a branch office if the advertising of a broker, who has a principal office elsewhere, is such that it leads the public to believe that the office of concern is owned or operated by the broker in question.

Registrations Issued to Branch Offices Are Not Transferable. If a broker decides to close one branch office and open a new branch office at a different location, the registration of the closed office may not be transferred to the new location. This is true even though these actions may take place at the same time. The new branch office location must be registered with the DBPR and the branch office registration fee paid before business is conducted there. A broker may reopen a branch office in the same location during the same license period by requesting a reissue of the branch office license without paying an additional fee.

Temporary Shelters. A *temporary shelter* in a subdivision being sold by a broker is not a branch office if the shelter is intended only for the protection of customers and sales associates. But if sales associates are permanently assigned there and sale transactions are closed there, then the temporary structure must be registered as a branch office. The permanence, use, and character of activities customarily conducted at the office or shelter determine whether it must be registered.

Practice Questions

1. A brokerage office must be at least _______________ enclosed room that will provide _______________ to conduct negotiations and close real estate transactions.
2. A broker may have an office in the broker's residence provided local _______________ allows such activity and the broker's _______________ is displayed at the entrance to the office.
3. Registrations issued to branch offices are _______________ transferable to a different _______________.
4. Sales associates are ______ permitted to open offices of their own. They must be registered from and work out of an office maintained and registered in the name of their _______________.

5.2 OFFICE SIGNS

475.22, F.S.

61J2-10.022, F.A.C.

Active real estate brokers must display an official sign on either the exterior or the interior of the entrance to their principal office and all branch offices. The sign(s) must be easily observed and read by anyone entering the office. The sign must contain the following information:

- Trade name (if one is used)
- Broker's name
- The words "Licensed Real Estate Broker" or "Lic. Real Estate Broker"

Refer to the example of an office sign in Figure 5.1. The registered trade name is Little Mo Realty, the broker's name is Murl H. Crawford, and the required wording "Licensed Real Estate Broker" appears on the sign.

FIGURE 5.1 ■ Example of a Sole Proprietor With a Trade Name Sign

61J2-10.025, F.A.C.

The names of the sales associates and broker associates are not required on the entrance sign. However, if the associates' names appear on the sign, the names must not appear misleading, false, deceptive, or fraudulent. In Figure 5.1, the office sign clearly identifies Carl Stoufer as the broker associate.

If the brokerage entity is a partnership, corporation, limited liability company (LLC), or limited liability partnership, the sign must contain the following information (see Figure 5.2):

- Name of the firm or corporation (or trade name, if one is used)
- Name of at least one active broker
- The words "Licensed Real Estate Broker" or "Lic. Real Estate Broker"

FIGURE 5.2 ■ Example of a Brokerage Corporation Sign

Practice Questions

5. List three items that must be on all real estate office entrance signs.
    1. ______________________________
    2. ______________________________
    3. ______________________________

6. Active brokers must display an official sign on either the ______________ or the ____________ of the entrance to all of their registered offices.

5.3 ADVERTISING

475.01(1), F.S.

61J2-10.025, F.A.C.

Anyone who advertises or claims to be providing real estate services is acting as a real estate broker. Therefore, under Florida law, advertising is considered a broker activity. All advertising must be in the name of the brokerage and under the supervision of the broker. Sales associates may not advertise real estate services in their own names. If sales associates create promotional materials, such as refrigerator magnets and notepads, they must include the licensed name of the brokerage firm on them. The broker is accountable for all advertising, regardless of who actually prepares the advertisement. Advertising includes letterhead stationery and flyers, business cards, yard signs and billboards, newspaper and magazine ads, internet, radio and television, promotional materials, and so forth.

61J2-10.026, F.A.C.

Team (Group) Advertising

It has become popular in recent years for associates within a brokerage firm to form a team. **Team advertising** (also known as group advertising) is the name or logo used by one or more licensees who represent themselves to the public as a team or group. The concept of teams allows broker associates and sales associates to specialize in their area of expertise and to join forces to serve a wider group of customers more efficiently. Teams must perform licensed activities under the supervision of their registered broker.

Each team must file with their employing broker the name of the licensee whom the team designates to be responsible for ensuring that the team advertising complies with

Florida license law and administrative rules. At least monthly, the registered broker must maintain a current written record of each team's members. Teams must advertise in the name of the brokerage. All advertising must be in a manner in which reasonable persons would know they are dealing with a team. The team name in advertisements may be no larger than the name of the registered broker.

Real estate team names may include the word *team* or *group* as part of the name. Real estate team names must not include words in their name suggesting that the team is a separate real estate brokerage. The team advertising rule includes a list of words (see Figure 5.3) that may not be included in team names. The rule regarding team advertising applies to all forms of advertising used by the team.

FIGURE 5.3 ■ Words That May Not Be Used in Team Names

Agency	Brokers	LP, LLP, or Partnership
Associates	Company	Properties or Property
Brokerage	Corporation, Corp., Inc., or LLC	Real Estate or Realty

ADVERTISING KEY CONCEPTS

All advertisements must include the name of the brokerage firm.

If a licensee inserts a personal name in the ad, the licensee's last name as registered with the DBPR must also be included.

Licensees may use their nickname in advertisements provided they also include their last name as registered with the DBPR.

The brokerage firm's address and phone number are not required to be included in the advertisement (note the exception regarding internet advertisement, as discussed later).

Blind Advertisements

61J2-10.025, F.A.C.

All advertising must be worded so that reasonable people will know that they are dealing with a real estate licensee. A licensee may not advertise real estate services in such a way as to mislead the public that the offer is being made by a private individual rather than a real estate licensee. Advertisements must clearly reveal the licensed name of the brokerage firm. Advertisements that fail to disclose the license name of the brokerage firm are **blind advertisements**. For example, an advertisement that provides only a post office box number, telephone number, and/or street address is a blind ad and is prohibited.

Including Personal Information

61J2-10.025(2), F.A.C.

Licensees may insert their personal names in ads, provided the advertisement includes the name of the brokerage and the licensees include their last name as registered with the DBPR. Advertisements created by associates must be supervised directly by their broker. Licensees may use their nickname in combination with their last name on business cards and in advertisements, but must be mindful that the advertising rule states that advertisements must not be misleading. Sales associates should get their broker's approval of the advertisement to ensure that the ad meets current advertising rules. Sales associates and their brokers should review advertisements for accuracy and also make certain the ad is canceled when, due to sale or listing expiration, the property is no longer on the market. Sales associates may indicate their cell phone number or other alternate number and/or address on their business cards, provided the card also includes the name of the brokerage firm. FREC does not require that the brokerage firm's phone number or address be included in ads.

False Advertising

Publication of false or misleading information by means of radio, television, or written matter for the purpose of inducing someone to buy, lease, rent, or acquire an interest in title to real property is illegal. If a sales associate prepares a misleading ad, both the broker and the sales associate can be disciplined. False advertising is a misdemeanor of the second degree.

FALSE ADVERTISING

A person may not disseminate or cause to be disseminated by any means any false or misleading information for the purpose of offering for sale, or for the purpose of causing or inducing any other person to purchase, lease, or rent, real estate located in the state or for the purpose of causing or inducing any other person to acquire an interest in the title to real estate located in the state.

Reference: 475.42(1)(n), F.S.

475.42(1)(n), F.S.

475.25(1)(c), F.S.

61J2-10.025, F.A.C.

FREC rules mandate that real estate advertisements must not be fraudulent, false, deceptive, or misleading. For example, it would be considered false and misleading advertising for a broker associate to use the title, "broker" on the associate's business card. Even though the broker associate is qualified to operate as a broker, the broker associate is not working in a broker capacity with the brokerage firm.

Licensees must take care when constructing real estate advertisements to make certain they are not misleading. Take a look at these examples and consider if they are misleading.

EXAMPLE 1: Spacious 4BR, 3BA home in Crystal Pines Subdivision. New roof July 2016. Home is on wooded lot. Call Alfonzo "Fonzie" Lombardi, Excellent Realty, 333-222-4444.

Is the phone number Alfonzo's direct number or that of the brokerage firm? If the phone number of the licensee appears directly below the company name (or directly next to it), it gives the appearance that it is the brokerage phone number. To prevent someone from considering this ad to be misleading, the licensee, after identifying the brokerage, should make clear that the phone number is the licensee's personal number and not the brokerage firm's main business number. It is recommended that when using only the licensee's phone number in the ad that the word *direct, cell,* or something similar be inserted adjacent to the phone number. Doing so informs the public that the number is not the brokerage phone number, but that of the licensee. Therefore, a better constructed advertisement follows:

EXAMPLE 2: Spacious 4BR, 3BA home in Crystal Pines Subdivision. New roof July 2016. Home is on wooded lot. Excellent Realty. Call Alfonzo "Fonzie" Lombardi, (mobile) 333-222-4444.

Internet Sites

61J2-10.025, F.A.C.

When advertising on an internet site, the name of the brokerage firm must appear adjacent to or immediately above or below the point of contact information. **Point of contact information** refers to any means by which to contact the brokerage firm or individual licensee, including mailing address(es), physical street address(es), email address(es), telephone number(s), or facsimile (fax) telephone number(s).

Unauthorized Use of Association Names

61J2-24.002(2)(x), F.A.C.

61J2-10.027, F.A.C.

A licensee cannot use an association's name or an organization's designation unless the licensee is currently a member in good standing of the association (dues are up-to-date). Active and inactive real estate licensees can be disciplined by FREC for false advertising for using the name or designation of an association (such as on business cards) to lead people to believe the licensee is a member of the association.

Licensee Selling Property By Owner

The rules regarding advertising real property do not prevent real estate licensees from selling their own property. Real estate licensees who own property and are selling the property "by owner" may place their own classified advertisements. Licensees may include their personal contact information in the ads, such as the home phone number and street address of the property. It is not necessary for a licensee to indicate in the advertisement that the seller is a real estate licensee. However, because a licensee has superior knowledge and expertise in real estate, to reduce liability the "by owner" licensee-seller should disclose before entering into serious negotiations that the seller is a real estate licensee. Disclosure of this fact should also be documented in the sale contract. Such disclosure is mandated in the National Association of REALTORS® Standards of Practice. NAR requires that member REALTORS® who advertise unlisted real property for sale or lease in which they have an ownership interest disclose their status as owners (or landlords) and as REALTORS®. Licensees considering selling property that they own "by owner" should first consult with their broker and review the office policy manual. Some brokers expect the licensee to list the property through the brokerage office.

Telephone Solicitation

A **telephone solicitation** is the initiation of a telephone call for the purpose of encouraging the purchase of, or investment in, property, goods, or services. Telemarketing is regulated at the federal and state level. The Telephone Consumer Protection Act (TCPA) established a National Do Not Call Registry for consumers who wish to avoid telemarketing calls. The Federal Trade Commission (FTC) maintains the registry. Consumers at no charge may request to have their residential and mobile phone numbers added to the registry. Telemarketers must first search the national registry before making telemarketing calls. Calls are restricted to the hours between 8:00 am and 9:00 pm. Violators of the federal law may be fined for each illegal call.

Prerecorded Telemarketing Calls. *Robocalls* are unsolicited, prerecorded telemarketing calls to landline home telephones and all autodialed or prerecorded calls or text messages to wireless numbers. FCC rules ban text messages sent to mobile phones using an auto dialer unless the consumer previously gave consent to receive the message. The ban applies even if the consumer has not placed the mobile phone number on the National Do-Not-Call List. FCC rules require a business to obtain written consent, on paper or through electronic means, before it may make a prerecorded telemarketing call to a residential phone number or make an autodialed or prerecorded telemarketing call or text to a wireless number.

Cold Calls. Oftentimes, real estate sales associates will make unsolicited calls to prospective buyers or sellers to introduce themselves and solicit listings. Real estate associates should follow the FTC rules and regulations closely when making cold calls. Violations of FTC rules and regulations could result in the FTC fining the sales associate and the associate's registered broker.

501.604 (25), F.S.

501.059, F.S.

State Regulation. Florida's telemarketing law is administered through the Department of Agriculture and Consumer Services (FDACS). The FDACS maintains a "no sales solicitation calls" registry for consumers who do not wish to receive telephone solicitation calls on their residential and mobile telephones. Consumers may apply online to be included on the state registry. The Florida statute mandates that the FDACS include in the Florida registry listings from the national registry that relate to Florida. Violators of Florida's Telemarketing Act may be fined for each illegal call.

A major difference between the state and federal telemarketing laws is that the Florida law exempts real estate licensees who solicit listings in response to a "For Sale" yard sign (see Figure 5.4). However, the federal law does not exempt calls to for sale by owners (FSBOs) whose numbers are on the national registry. If a phone number is on both the national and the state registry, the FCC ruled that real estate licensees must comply with the national registry, regardless of the Florida exemption. Florida's law which provides an exemption for real estate licensees who wish to solicit listings from FSBOs is considered less restrictive and is therefore preempted by the federal law. The federal law provides the following exceptions:

- A sales associate representing a potential buyer may call the FSBO seller, but only if the associate has an actual buyer interested in the property and for purposes of negotiating a sale.
- A sales associate may contact individuals with whom the associate has had an established business relationship, even if those customers' numbers are on the national registry. For example, the company that previously listed a property may contact the former customer to solicit new business for up to 18 months after the business transaction has been concluded.
- Sales associates may contact a customer for three months after a business inquiry or application (such as a customer who registered at an open house or a FSBO seller who requested information from a sales associate).

FIGURE 5.4 ■ Telephone Solicitation

Florida Law	Federal Law
No solicitation calls registry	National Do Not Call Registry
Calls restricted to 8:00 am to 9:00 pm	Calls restricted to 8:00 am to 9:00 pm
FSBO exception	No FSBO exception—must check registry (federal law supersedes state law)

If a sales associate calls a FSBO or an expired listing under the exceptions listed previously and the homeowner requests not to be called, the sales associate must comply. Telemarketers must state their names, the business name, and the business telephone number. Telemarketers may not block their phone numbers. Businesses that use telemarketing must develop and adhere to written procedures regarding the firms' calling policies.

Businesses must advise and train their personnel and independent contractors engaged in telephone solicitation regarding do-not-call list maintenance and procedures. Real estate companies that wish to use telemarketing in their business strategy must obtain the list of phone numbers in the registry. Licensees must search the national registry at least quarterly and delete from their call lists the phone numbers of consumers who have registered.

Electronic Mail Advertising

The CAN-SPAM Act is a federal law that sets national standards for commercial electronic mail messages. The law applies to any business that uses electronic mail messaging in its marketing program. FCC rules restrict sending unwanted commercial electronic mail messages (spam) to computers and wireless devices, including cell phones. All commercial electronic messages must allow the consumer to opt out of receiving future messages. Senders have 10 business days to honor requests to opt out. To be CAN-SPAM compliant when sending electronic messages, the sender must do the following:

1. Provide no false or misleading header information
2. Ensure that subject lines are not deceptive
3. Include a valid physical postal address in every message
4. Provide a clear and obvious way to opt out on every electronic message sent and honor the unsubscribe request within 10 business days
5. Use clear "From," "To," and "Reply to" language that accurately reflects the person or business sending the message, as well as the domain name and email address
6. Identify the message as an advertisement or solicitation

WEBLINK

To learn more about the National Do Not Call Registry, visit the FCC website at www.donotcall.gov.

To find out more regarding the Florida Do Not Call Program, visit https://www.fdacs.gov/Consumer-Resources/Florida-Do-Not-Call. A CAN-SPAM compliance guide for businesses is available at https://www.ftc.gov/business-guidance/resources/can-spam-act-compliance-guide-business.

Practice Questions

7. Kimberly is a sales associate with Fast Results Realty. Kimberly is bilingual and she wants to use her language skills to attract international customers. Kimberly decides to form an international team within her broker's company. She and two other sales associates refer to themselves as Your International Team. Your International Team has business cards designed with the team member's names, contact information, and the name Your International Team. Open house signs are designed with the name Your International Team and the team member's contact information. A disgruntled sales associate who was not invited into the team files a complaint with the DBPR. What is the likely result of the complaint?

   The DBPR will agree that the advertising by Your International Team is a violation of the team advertising rule because the name of the ______________ ________ is not included on the business cards and open house signs.

8. Circle the corresponding letter(s) to indicate which information must be included in an advertisement for a listed property.
   a. Name of the listing agent
   b. Address of the brokerage office
   c. Name of the brokerage firm

9. Jed Smith is a member of the Results Team at ABC Realty. Jed is a licensed sales associate who is registered with the DBPR under his legal name, Jedidiah Smith; however, he uses the name Jed. Jed's cell phone number is 444-111-2222. The Results Team's phone number is 444-123-4567. ABC Realty's phone number is 444-222-3333. Jed is writing a classified ad and he wants prospects to either call him or the team directly. Circle the corresponding letter(s) to indicate which information Jed must include in the classified advertisement.
   a. Call Jed Smith
   b. 444-123-4567 (The Results Team's direct line)
   c. 444-111-2222
   d. 444-111-2222 (cell)
   e. ABC Realty
   f. The Results Team

10. False advertising is a misdemeanor of the _______________ degree.

11. When advertising on an internet site, the __________ of the brokerage firm must appear adjacent to or immediately above or below the __________ _______ ___________ information.

12. A sales associate licensee chooses NOT to become a member of the NAR. The licensee uses the designation REALTOR® on her business cards. The FREC can discipline the licensee for _____________ _______________.

13. The law that prohibits real estate licensees from soliciting listings from prospects whose numbers are listed in the national registry in response to For Sale yard signs is the __________________ _______________ _______________ Act.

14. Telephone solicitation calls are restricted to the hours between _______________ and _______________.

5.4 ESCROW OR TRUST ACCOUNTS

475.25(1)(k), F.S.

61J2-14.008, F.A.C.

Typically, when a buyer makes an offer on real property, the buyer includes with the offer a deposit to show good faith that the buyer is serious about purchasing the property. A **deposit** is a sum of money, or its equivalent, delivered to a real estate licensee as **earnest money** or a payment, or partial payment in connection with a real estate transaction. Earnest money deposits are also called *good-faith deposits* or *binder deposits*.

An **escrow account** is an account for the deposit of money a disinterested third party (i.e., not a party to the contract) holds in trust for others; hence the term *trust funds*. Trust funds include cash, checks, money orders, and items that can be converted into cash, such as deeds and personal property. In addition to earnest money deposits associated with sale transactions, some brokers hold in trust for others money associated with leasing property, such as rent deposits and security deposits. Brokers are not required to keep earnest money deposits separate from rental deposits. However, tracking trust funds is easier when separate escrow accounts are established for funds associated with sales and funds associated with rentals.

61J2-14.010(1)

Acceptable Depositories

Brokers may maintain their escrow accounts in a Florida commercial bank, credit union, or savings association. Florida law does not require brokers to open an escrow account. However, without an escrow account, a broker cannot hold funds belonging to customers and clients. A broker who does not want the responsibility and liability of maintaining escrow accounts may choose to have a Florida-based title company with trust powers to maintain the escrow funds, or alternatively, if designated in the sale contract, a Florida attorney may escrow the funds.

61J2-14.009, F.A.C.

Immediately Defined

Florida law mandates the time frame for depositing escrow funds. Sales associates and broker associates who receive a binder deposit from a buyer or a rental deposit from a tenant must deliver it to their broker-employer no later than the end of the next business day. Saturdays, Sundays, and legal holidays are not counted as business days. When a sales associate or an employee (such as a receptionist) of the brokerage company accepts funds on behalf of the broker, the broker is liable for those funds. Therefore, it is extremely important that brokers train their personnel regarding the importance of turning over all earnest money in a timely manner.

61J2-14.008, F.A.C.

Brokers must place trust funds into an escrow account **immediately**, which is defined in administrative rule as no later than the end of the third business day following receipt by the brokerage (such as an associate or a receptionist) of the item to be deposited. The first day of the three-business-day period is the day that the sales associate must deliver the deposit to the broker.

EXAMPLE: A sales associate receives a deposit from a buyer on Tuesday (no legal holidays are involved).

- The sales associate has until the end of the next business day (Wednesday) to deliver the deposit to the broker.
- The broker has until the end of the third business day following receipt of the item to be deposited (Friday).

FIGURE 5.5 ■ Time Line to Deposit Escrow Funds

Tuesday (Day 0)	Wednesday (Day 1)	Thursday (Day 2)	Friday (Day 3)
Sales associate receives escrow deposit	Sales associate must deliver deposit to broker by end of day		Broker must deposit funds by end of the day

EXAMPLE: A sales associate receives a rental deposit from a tenant on Saturday (no legal holidays are involved).

- The sales associate has until the end of the next business day (Monday) to deliver the deposit to the broker.
- The broker has until the end of the third business day following receipt of the item to be deposited (Wednesday).

FIGURE 5.6 ■ Time Line to Deposit Rent Funds

Saturday (Day 0)	Monday (Day 1)	Tuesday (Day 2)	Wednesday (Day 3)
Sales associate receives rent deposit	Sales associate must deliver deposit to broker by end of day		Broker must deposit funds by end of the day

When computing the deadline for the broker to deposit the funds, it must start with the next business day after the sales associate receives the funds from the buyer (or tenant), even if the sales associate fails to deliver the funds timely to the broker. A broker does not have to wait until the third business day to deposit the funds; rather, this is the deadline for making the deposit. The broker can make the deposit earlier.

Brokers are required to keep records of all transactions and escrow and property management funds as well as to make available to the Department of Business and Professional Regulation (DBPR) such books, accounts, and records as will enable the DBPR to determine whether the broker is in compliance with Chapter 475. If requested, the broker must make all ledgers, bank statements, and other records available for inspection to the DBPR.

KEY CONCEPTS REGARDING ESCROW ACCOUNTS

- Brokers may open an escrow account in a Florida bank, savings association, or credit union.
- If a broker chooses not to maintain an escrow account, the funds may be held by a title company or in a Florida-licensed attorney's trust account.
- Sales associates (and broker associates) must deliver escrow deposits to their broker by the end of the next business day following receipt of the funds.
- Brokers must deposit escrow funds by the end of the third business day following the day that the funds are accepted by the brokerage.

Personal Checks, Postdated Checks, and Insufficient Funds

If an escrow check is made out to the sales associate personally, the best course of action is to ask the prospective buyer to write a new check payable to the broker's escrow account. However, if this is not practical, the sales associate should immediately endorse the check and include the words, "For Deposit Only to the (name of the escrow account)" and turn it over to the broker.

673.1131, F.S.

61J2-14.008(1), F.A.C.

Postdated Checks and Insufficient Funds. Occasionally, a licensee may be given a postdated check (considered a promissory note) as an earnest money deposit. Extreme caution should be taken in handling such deposits. The seller's approval must be obtained before accepting the postdated check. Once accepted, the broker should secure the instrument in a proper place, such as an office safe, until the date on the check becomes current, and then immediately deposit the check into the broker's escrow account. A broker will not be held responsible for the nonpayment of an escrow check, provided the broker timely deposits the check into the escrow account and the broker's own carelessness (culpable negligence) did not cause the check not to be honored.

Management of Escrow Accounts

61J2-14.010(1), F.A.C.

Signatory on Escrow Account. FREC rules require brokers to be a signatory on all their brokerage escrow accounts. The escrow accounts must be properly reconciled each month, and the broker must review, sign, and date the monthly bank reconciliations. The broker may designate another person, such as a bookkeeper, to sign checks on the account in the ordinary course of business. Brokers should use caution when delegating escrow responsibilities to another person. Florida law holds the broker accountable for reviewing the brokerage firm's escrow accounting procedures to ensure compliance with Florida license law.

61J2-14.014, F.A.C.

Interest-Bearing Escrow Accounts. A broker's escrow account may be an interest-bearing or a non-interest-bearing account. If the broker's escrow account is an interest-bearing account, the broker must get written permission from all parties before placing the funds in this type of account. The written authorization must specify who is entitled to the interest earned. The broker may receive the interest earned, but only if it is specifically agreed to by all parties. A broker can be disciplined by the FREC for failure to secure the written permission of all interested parties prior to placing trust (escrow) funds in an interest-bearing escrow account.

61J2-14.010(2), F.A.C.

475.5015, F.S.

Money to Maintain Escrow Account. Commission rules allow a broker to have up to $1,000 of personal money or business operating funds in an escrow account for sales transactions. You may ask, isn't that commingling? The Commission realized that if you have only trust funds in an escrow account and you do not have any sales pending at a particular time during a month, the escrow account balance would be zero and the bank could potentially close the account or charge low-balance fees. Therefore, the Commission decided that it was prudent to allow a broker to keep up to $1,000 of the broker's personal funds or business operating funds in a sales escrow account for maintenance purposes, such as check printing, bank fees, and so forth. The money to maintain the account is not considered to be commingling and must be accounted for in the broker's monthly accounting records.

The FREC rules also allow brokers to keep up to $5,000 of their own monies in an escrow account for property management. The Commission allows a larger amount of funds for maintenance purposes in a property management escrow account because many tenants' monthly rent checks are deposited each month. If a tenant's rent check were to be returned for nonsufficient funds, the broker cannot use the funds of another property owner to pay repairs on the property that had the rent check returned for NSF.

It is advisable that brokers keep sales escrow funds separate from property management escrow funds to simplify the accounting process. However, Florida law does not require separate sales escrow accounts and property management escrow accounts. If a broker maintains sales escrow funds and property management escrow funds in a single escrow account, the amount of personal funds or brokerage funds in the account cannot exceed $5,000.

Recordkeeping and Retention. Brokers must keep business records, books, and accounts in compliance with Florida law and Commission rules and make them available for audit or spot checks by the DBPR at any reasonable time. Records must be preserved for at least five years from the date of receipt of money, funds, deposits, or checks entrusted to the broker. Furthermore, records must be retained for at least five years from the date of any executed agreement, including buyer brokerage agreements, listing agreements, offers to purchase, rental property management agreements, rental or lease agreements, or any other written or verbal agreement that engages the services of the broker. If a broker's records have been the subject of litigation or have served as evidence for litigation, the relevant records must be preserved for two years beyond the conclusion of the civil action or the conclusion of an appellate proceeding, but in no case for less than five years.

KEY CONCEPTS REGARDING ESCROW ACCOUNT MANAGEMENT

Brokers must be a signatory on their escrow account.

Brokers must review, sign, and date the monthly reconciliation statements.

Brokers must review the brokerage's escrow accounting procedures.

Brokers must maintain records of real estate transactions for five years, regardless of whether escrow funds were pledged or who was the escrow agent (two years after the completion of litigation if beyond the five-year period).

Mishandling of Escrow Funds

Conversion. All trust funds deposited in an escrow account must be kept in the escrow account until the transaction is closed or other fulfillment of an escrow condition occurs or until otherwise disposed of legally. An escrow account is an account where deposits are held in trust for the owner until the transaction is closed. Brokers may not use earnest money funds for their personal or business expenses, even if they intend to pay the money back. A violation has occurred at the moment of a withdrawal for these purposes. Misappropriation of another's property will expose the broker to charges of conversion, dishonest dealing, and fraud. **Conversion** is the unauthorized use of another person's funds or property for one's own use.

> **EXAMPLE:** Broker Bob has $50,000 in the escrow account. Broker Bob has a separate business operating account with a current balance of $500. He had an unexpected bill to pay because of the need to install plexiglass partitions and hand-sanitizing areas; $1,100 is due upon completion of the work. Bob has a closing next week, at which time the brokerage will receive a $10,000 commission check. Bob transfers "an advance" of $1,000 from the escrow account to the business operating account. When the closing occurs next week, Bob will reimburse the escrow account for the $1,000 advance.
>
> Bob committed conversion because he used trust funds that belonged to a customer to pay for a business expense.

Commingling. Brokers may not mix escrow deposits with other types of funds. To **commingle** funds means to mix the money or other personal property of a buyer or a seller, or a tenant or landlord, with the broker's own money or property or to combine escrow money with the broker's personal funds or business operating funds, except for funds allowed by law to maintain the account (see "Money to Maintain an Escrow Account").

> **EXAMPLE:** A broker received a deposit in the amount of $5,000 for a pending transaction on a listing. The broker's procedure was to deposit all funds received into her general operating account. The broker would always enter into her ledger the amount of each deposit and confirm she had the funds available to transfer at closing. The broker also used the account to pay brokerage expenses, commissions, and miscellaneous items that would occur unexpectedly at the brokerage. Three days before closing the pending

transaction, the broker wrote a check from her general operating account payable to the title company.

The broker commingled the trust funds with her operating account. The trust funds should have immediately been deposited and held in the escrow account until the closing.

475.25(1)(d), F.S.

Failure to Account or Deliver. A licensee who fails to deliver any personal property, such as money, legal documents, or real estate commission, to a person entitled to receive it can be disciplined for **failure to account or deliver**. A broker who fails to pay an earnest money deposit at the title closing, in accordance with the contract for sale and purchase, may be charged with failure to account or deliver trust funds.

EXAMPLE: A broker received an earnest money check for $5,000 payable to John Stetson, Attorney Trust Account. The broker placed the check in his desk drawer with the intent to take it to the attorney's office the next day. When the broker received a copy of the Closing Disclosure before the closing, the buyer noticed that the earnest money was not mentioned. The attorney had no record of an earnest money deposit.

Because the broker did not deliver the check to the attorney, the broker can be disciplined by the FREC for failing to account for or deliver escrowed property.

61J2-14.008(2)(b), F.A.C.

Title Company and Attorney Escrow Accounts

A broker may choose to avoid the paperwork and accounting responsibilities of handling escrow funds associated with sale contracts. To do so, the broker must have someone else act as the escrow agent. If the broker does not have an escrow account, the broker must place escrow funds with a title company or an attorney who will serve as the escrow agent. The broker is required under Chapter 475, F.S., to deliver the funds to the escrow agent within the same time frame required for depositing the funds into the broker's escrow account. Therefore, brokers who choose to use a title company or an attorney as escrow agent must turn the funds over to the escrow agent no later than the end of the third business day following the day the funds are accepted on behalf of the brokerage.

When a deposit is placed with a title company or with an attorney, the following procedure must be used:

- The real estate licensee who prepared or presented the sale contract must indicate on the purchase and sale agreement the title company's name (or attorney's name, if applicable), address, and telephone number.
- No later than 10 business days after each deposit is due under the terms of the sale contract, the licensee's broker must request a written verification of receipt of the deposit. The broker's request to the title company (or to the attorney) must be in writing. If the deposit is held by a title company or by an attorney nominated in writing by the seller or the seller's agent, the verification is waived.
- No later than 10 business days after the date the broker made the written request for verification of the deposit, the broker must provide the seller's broker with a copy of the written verification. If the title company (or attorney) failed to provide the broker with a written verification, this information must be given to the seller's broker no later than 10 business days after the request for verification of the deposit. If the seller is not represented by a broker, the licensee's broker must notify the seller directly.

Sometimes, the purchase and sale contract will require the buyer to make more than one earnest money deposit. For example, the contract may state that the buyer is to make a $5,000 earnest money deposit at the time the contract is accepted by the seller and then a $15,000 second deposit 30 days after the date the contract is signed by the seller. When the contract requires more than one earnest money deposit, the procedure described earlier must be employed for every deposit specified in the purchase and sale agreement.

Real estate license law governs only broker's escrow accounts. A broker may be subject to administrative discipline for failing to follow the procedure described in this section. However, because real estate license law governs only broker escrow accounts, the FREC has no jurisdiction over the title company or the attorney used as an escrow agent.

Many brokers view having an attorney or title company maintain escrow funds as a benefit. However, if the broker is not the escrow agent and the transaction fails to close and both the seller and buyer claim the escrow funds, the FREC will not issue an Escrow Disbursement Order (EDO). The buyer and seller will need to take their concerns to the holder of the escrowed monies (title company or attorney) and will likely be left with the financial expense of going to court to resolve the dispute (see "Notice and Settlement Procedures," in this unit).

KEY PROVISIONS PERTAINING TO TITLE COMPANY AND ATTORNEY ESCROW ACCOUNTS

- Indicate the name, address, and telephone number of the title company or attorney on sale contract
- Buyer's broker must make a written request within 10 business days to the title company (or attorney) to provide written verification of the deposit (unless the deposit is held by a title company or by an attorney nominated in writing by a seller or seller's agent)
- Within 10 business days after the written request, buyer's broker must provide seller's broker with either a copy of the verification or written notice that no verification was received

Reference: Section 61J2-14.008(2)(b), F.A.C.

Practice Questions

15. A sales associate receives a deposit from a buyer on Thursday (no legal holidays are involved). The contract states that the escrow deposit will be held by ABC Title Company.
    a. The sales associate has until the end of business on ____________ to deliver the deposit to the broker.
    b. The broker has until the end of business on ____________ to deliver the funds to ABC Title Company.

16. The broker must be a ______________ on the escrow acccount.

17. If the broker chooses not to open an escrow account, the funds may be held by a __________ ______________ or in an ______________ __________ ___________.

18. Sales associates must deliver escrow deposits to their broker by end of the ________ ________________ __________.

19. Brokers must deposit escrow funds by the end of the ________ ____________ _____.

20. On Monday afternoon, a buyer gave XYZ Brokerage $1,000 in cash as a binder deposit with an offer. The broker made the nightly deposit by placing all the funds collected for the day, including the binder deposits, in the broker's operating account. The FREC can discipline this broker for ________________.

21. A broker is the property manager for a duplex that rents $1,000 per unit. Last month, he collected the rent from each tenant at the beginning of the month. Because the broker was having trouble making his mortgage payments, he used the $2,000 from rent collections to pay his lender instead of sending the funds to the absentee owner. The broker can be disciplined by the Commission for failure to ____________ or ____________.

5.5 NOTICE AND SETTLEMENT PROCEDURES

When a broker holds escrow funds in the broker's trust account (the escrow agent) in a real estate transaction, the deposit belongs to and is under the control of the depositor (for example, a prospective buyer) until another party (for example, the seller) accepts the offer and acquires some interest or equity in the deposited funds. At this point, both the buyer and the seller have an interest in the deposit. The broker must not deliver the deposit to the other party until the transaction is closed, except as otherwise directed and agreed to in writing by all parties to the transaction. Chapter 475, F.S., provides a dispute resolution process when there are conflicting demands between the parties or a broker has a good-faith doubt as to who is entitled to receive the escrowed funds.

Good-Faith Doubt

If a broker has a **good-faith doubt** as to which party should receive the escrowed property, the broker must notify the FREC, in writing, within 15 business days after having such doubt and institute one of the settlement procedures (described earlier) within 30 business days after having such doubt. The term *good faith* is used to describe a party's honest intent to transact business, free from any intent to defraud the other party, and generally speaking, each party's faithfulness to the duties or obligations set forth by contract. Therefore, if the broker doubts the parties' good faith, the law requires that the broker abide by the notice requirement and initiate one of the settlement procedures in a timely manner. Individuals must look to case law for interpretations of what specific circumstances constitute a good-faith doubt. Situations that may constitute good-faith doubt by the broker include the following:

- The transaction closing date has passed, and the broker has not received identical instructions from both the buyer and the seller regarding how to disburse escrowed funds.
- The transaction closing date has not passed, but one or more parties have expressed the intention not to close and the broker has not received identical instructions from the buyer and the seller regarding how to disburse escrowed funds.
- One party to a failed transaction does not respond to a broker's inquiry about escrow disbursement. In this situation, the broker may send a certified notice letter, return receipt requested, to that nonresponding party stating that a demand has been made on the escrowed funds and that failure to respond by a designated date will be regarded as authority for the broker to release the funds to the demanding party. (*Note*: Although not required by law, to limit the broker's potential liability, it is advisable before releasing the trust funds to secure the postal return receipt as proof the notice was delivered.)

61J2-10.032(1)(c), F.A.C.

475.25(1)(d)1, F.S.

61J2-10.032(1)(a), F.A.C.

Conflicting Demands

Conflicting demands occur when the buyer and the seller make demands regarding the disbursing of escrowed property that are inconsistent with the other party's request and cannot be resolved. If a broker who maintains an escrow account receives conflicting demands on escrowed property, the broker must notify the FREC, in writing, within 15 business days of receiving the conflicting demands unless specifically exempted.

Settlement Procedures

The broker must institute one of the four settlement (or escape) procedures within 30 business days from the time the broker received the conflicting demands. For example, if a broker waits 10 business days to report the conflicting demands, the broker has just 20 business days remaining to implement one of the settlement procedures.

The four settlement procedures are as follows:

455.2235, F.S.

1. *Mediation*. If all parties give written consent, the dispute may be mediated. **Mediation** is an informal, nonadversarial process intended to reach a negotiated settlement. An independent third party works with the disputing parties to help them resolve their differences. If an agreement is reached between the parties, the mediation is reduced to an enforceable written agreement. If the mediation process is not successfully completed within 90 days following the party's last demand for the disputed funds, the licensee must employ one of the other three settlement procedures.
2. *Arbitration*. **Arbitration** is a process whereby, with the prior written consent of all parties to the dispute, the matter is submitted to a disinterested third party. Each side presents its case to a third party, who makes a *binding* judgment in favor of one side or the other. The parties must agree in advance to abide by the arbitrator's final decision.
3. *Litigation*. If the disputing parties cannot agree, a disputing party may file a lawsuit so that the matter can be resolved in a court of law. Such a legal process is called **litigation**. The litigation can involve either of two court procedures:

475.25(1)(d), F.S.

61J2-10.032(2), F.A.C.

   a) *Interpleader*. If the broker does not have a financial claim to the disputed escrow funds, the funds can be deposited with the court registry. The broker is then excused from the case, and the disputing parties argue their case in court. This court procedure is called **interpleader**.
   b) *Declaratory judgment*. Brokers who believe they are entitled to a portion of disputed funds can file a court action called a declaratory judgment. In this court procedure, the judge declares each party's rights to the disputed escrow funds.
4. *Escrow disbursement order (EDO)*. The broker may request that the Commission issue an **escrow disbursement order (EDO)**, a determination of who is entitled to the disputed funds. Because real estate license law governs only broker escrow accounts, the Commission has no jurisdiction over the title company or the attorney used as an escrow agent. The FREC will not issue an EDO if the funds are held in an attorney's escrow account or by a title company. An EDO procedure is only available if the disputed deposit does not exceed $50,000 and the funds are held in a brokerage escrow account. In the event the broker is informed in writing that the Commission will not issue an EDO, the broker must use one of the other settlement procedures. The broker must notify the Commission which settlement procedure will be used. In the event the broker has requested an EDO and the dispute is subsequently settled or goes to court before the EDO is issued, the broker must notify the FREC within 10 business days that the dispute has been settled or that litigation is being commenced.

TO REMEMBER: FOUR SETTLEMENT PROCEDURES

M	**M**ediation (negotiated settlement)
A	**A**rbitration (binding)
L	**L**itigation
E	**E**scrow disbursement order

If the real estate broker promptly employs one of the four settlement procedures and abides by the resulting order or judgment, a complaint may not be filed against the broker for failure to account or deliver escrowed property (the broker has immunity from disciplinary action).

KEY REPORTING DEADLINES REGARDING ESCROW ACCOUNTS

- Brokers must notify the FREC in writing of receiving conflicting demands or of having a good-faith doubt within 15 business days.
- Brokers must institute one of the settlement procedures within 30 business days of receiving conflicting demands or of having a good-faith doubt.
- If a broker requests an EDO and the escrow dispute is either settled or goes to court before the EDO is issued, the broker must notify the FREC within 10 business days that the dispute has been settled or that litigation is being commenced.

718.503, F.S.

475.25(1)(d), F.S.

61J2-10.032(4), F.A.C.

Exceptions to Notice and Settlement Procedures

Chapter 475, F.S., and FREC 61J2, F.A.C., provide three specific exceptions to the notice and settlement procedures for sales escrow accounts. Under these three situations, the broker holding the escrow deposit is not required to notify the FREC of conflicting demands and does not need to institute a settlement procedure.

1. Brokers who are entrusted with an earnest money deposit concerning a residential sale contract used by HUD in the sale of HUD-owned property are required to comply with the earnest money deposit requirements for the specific HUD contract.
2. If a buyer of a residential condominium unit timely delivers to a licensee written notice of the buyer's intent to cancel the contract as authorized by the Condominium Act, the broker may return the escrowed property to the purchaser (see "Disclosures and Cancellation Period" and Figure 8.7, Unit 8).
3. If a buyer of real property in good faith fails to satisfy the terms specified in the financing clause of a contract for sale and purchase, the broker may return the escrowed funds to the purchaser. Although not required by law, licensees are cautioned that they may be exposing themselves to civil liability if they release escrowed funds without first getting the parties to agree as to who is entitled to the funds. Florida Realtors® has developed preprinted forms that can be used to obtain the written permission of all parties to release escrowed funds.

In all other situations, where a buyer and seller or a landlord and tenant make demands for escrowed funds that cannot be resolved between the parties and the broker, it is prudent for the broker to consult an attorney. If the parties are still unable to resolve the conflicting demands, the broker should timely notify the Commission of the conflicting demands.

Title Company or Attorney as Escrow Agent. If a title company or an attorney is the escrow agent, the broker has no obligation to report an escrow dispute to the FREC or to institute a settlement procedure. Generally, a title company or the attorney will not disburse funds without authorization from the parties to the transaction. Usually, if the parties cannot come to an agreement regarding the funds, the matter is submitted to a court of law for resolution.

Monies Paid in Advance for Performing Real Estate Services

721.20(6), F.S.

Sometimes a broker will receive commission or partial compensation before completing the real estate service. When this occurs, the broker is entrusted with funds that must be placed into the broker's escrow or trust until the services are completed. Once the service is completed, the broker has earned the compensation and may at that time transfer the funds into the broker's operating account. However, the Florida Vacation Plan and Timesharing Act (721 F.S.) prohibits a real estate licensee from collecting an advance fee for the listing of a time-share unit.

Practice Questions

22. List the four settlement procedures.

    1. ______________________________
    2. ______________________________
    3. ______________________________
    4. ______________________________

23. Brokers must notify the Commission in ______________ of conflicting demands or of a good-faith doubt within ______ ______________ days.

24. A broker must institute one of the settlement procedures within _______ ______________ days from the time the broker ______________ the conflicting demands.

5.6 BROKER'S COMMISSION

Sales Associate's Commission

Sales associates (and broker associates) must work under the supervision of a broker or an owner-developer. Sales associates may not operate as a broker or operate independently. Sales associates may not open their own offices. All customers, clients, commissions, referral fees, listing contracts, rental management agreements, and sale contracts are property of the broker. The amount of commission to be paid is negotiable, and it is arrived at by agreement between the broker and the buyer or the seller. Florida law does not establish or regulate the amount of commission paid.

The sales associate's share of the total commission is determined by agreement with the associate's employer. Sales associates are compensated by receiving a share of the commission paid to their employer. The amount that is retained by a broker and the amount that is received by a sales associate is agreed upon in the sales associate's independent contractor agreement. The details of the various commission structures offered by the broker should be part of a broker's policy manual.

All monies earned by sales associates for real estate services must be paid to the sales associates by their employer and not directly by the buyer or the seller. Sometimes a buyer or seller may want to thank the sales associate with extra compensation. In such cases, a sales associate should never accept extra compensation directly from the buyer or the seller. The better course of action would be to ask the customer or client to send a letter to the broker commending the associate and sending the extra compensation to the broker on behalf of the associate. Even gift cards and theater tickets should only be accepted with the broker's knowledge and consent.

61J2-10.028(2), F.A.C.

Sharing Commission with a Party to the Transaction. Generally, brokers may only share real estate compensation with another broker. However, the FREC provides an exception for sharing brokerage compensation with a party to the real estate transaction, with full disclosure to all interested parties. The transaction may involve residential or commercial real estate and be either a contract for sale or a lease. The key to compliance with FREC rules and license law is that the arrangement is disclosed in writing to all interested parties in the lease or the sale contract.

EXAMPLE: A sales associate wants to give the associate's split of the commission to the buyer because the buyer is the associate's nephew. The commission rebate must be disclosed to the seller and to the buyer's lender (the rebate could impact the lender's loan calculations).

Antitrust Laws

542, F.S.

Antitrust laws protect competition. Brokers risk their assets and their careers by attempting to get other brokers to fix commissions. The Sherman Antitrust Act, the Clayton Antitrust Act, and the Federal Trade Commission deal with preserving competition and ensuring against restraint of trade. It is illegal for real estate brokers to conspire to fix commissions or fees for the services they perform. Local real estate boards and multiple listing services may not fix commission rates or splits between cooperating brokers. A violation of antitrust laws is a criminal offense. Two prohibited acts are the following:

- *Price-fixing* occurs when competing brokers conspire to establish a standard commission rate rather than letting the rate be set by the open market. Even if a price fix is lower it is still a violation of the law. A broker's office can establish a commission rate, but it must do so independently of any other brokerage. Licensees should never make statements such as "the going rate" or a "normal commission rate" to avoid even the impression of price fixing.
- *Market allocation* occurs when brokers agree to split up competitive market areas among themselves and not compete in each other's areas.

Liens on Real Property for Unpaid Sales Commission

Recall that listing agreements and sales commission are the property of the broker. Therefore, only the broker can initiate an action for unpaid commission. Sales associates cannot sue a customer or client for unpaid commission. Sales associates can seek compensation only from their broker. Rules regarding sales commission due but not paid to the broker depend on whether the real estate involved in the transaction is residential or commercial.

475.42(1)(i), F.S.

61J2-24.001(3)(dd), F.A.C.

Residential Property. A broker may place a lien on residential real property for nonpayment of commission only if the broker is expressly authorized to do so in the listing agreement, the buyer representation agreement, or the sale contract. Otherwise, when a buyer or a seller refuses to pay a broker's commission after the commission has been earned, the broker must file a lawsuit and obtain a judgment for the commission owed. The FREC is authorized to suspend or revoke a real estate license for the unauthorized recording of a lis pendens or a lien or other instrument that affects the title of real property or that encumbers real property.

Brokers and their associates may not place on the public records false or unauthorized information that affects the title to real property. For example, a lis pendens (notice of pending legal action) or a lien for unpaid commission is unauthorized information that encumbers the title to real property, unless the seller had previously agreed in writing to give the broker such authority. A licensee found guilty of placing a lis pendens or lien on real property without authorization, may be issued an administrative fine and be subject to license suspension or revocation.

475, Part III, F.S.

Commercial Real Estate Sales. Chapter 475, Part III, called the Commercial Real Estate Sales Commission Lien Act, gives a broker lien rights for nonpayment of earned commission. This act applies only to commercial property. Commercial real estate is any real estate that is not defined as residential property in Chapter 475, Part I.

The Commercial Real Estate Sales Commission Lien Act gives the broker lien rights to the seller's net proceeds for the commission earned by the broker in accordance with the listing agreement to sell commercial property. The lien is against the owner's net proceeds (personal property) from the sale and in contrast with a residential sale, does not attach to the real property. The broker must disclose to the owner (seller) at the time executing the listing agreement (referred to as brokerage agreement in the statute) and the subsequent sale of the property, that the agreement creates lien rights for commission earned and that the owner (seller) cannot waive the lien rights once the owner has agreed to the broker's lien right (see the following text box).

475, Part IV, F.S.

Commercial Real Estate Leasing Commission Lien Act. Chapter 475, Part IV, called the Commercial Real Estate Leasing Commission Lien Act, gives a broker lien rights for earned commission associated with a brokerage agreement to lease commercial real estate. If the landlord is the person obligated to pay the leasing commission, the broker's lien attaches to the landlord's interest in the commercial real estate. If the tenant is the person obligated to pay the leasing commission, the broker's lien attaches to the tenant's leasehold estate.

REQUIRED COMMERCIAL REAL ESTATE SALES COMMISSION DISCLOSURE

The Florida Commercial Real Estate Sales Commission Lien Act provides that when a broker has earned a commission by performing licensed services under a brokerage agreement with you, the broker may claim a lien against your net sales proceeds for the broker's commission. The broker's lien rights under the act cannot be waived before the commission is earned.

Reference: 475.703(5)

FIGURE 5.7 ■ Key Points Regarding Residential and Commercial Lien Rights

Residential	Commercial
Broker cannot place a lien on real property unless owner gives express authority in the listing agreement, buyer representation agreement, or sale contract	Broker must include in the brokerage agreement the required disclosure regarding the broker's lien rights at or before the time the owner (seller) enters into the brokerage agreement
Unless a lien right is authorized, the broker must seek relief in a court of law and obtain a judgment for the amount owed	If the disclosure is included in the brokerage agreement and signed by the owner, the broker has a lien right on owner's net sale proceeds for any unpaid commission
It is a violation of law to place a lien or lis pendens on property unless the broker is expressly authorized to do so	The owner cannot waive the broker's lien right once agreed to

Kickbacks

475.25(1)(h), F.S.

61J2-10.028(1), F.A.C.

A **kickback** (or *rebate*) is an unearned fee paid to a licensee associated with a real estate transaction for non-real-estate services (payment for something other than one of the eight services of real estate). Kickbacks are legal only under limited conditions. Here is a list of important facts regarding kickbacks and rebates:

- *The parties to the transaction must be fully informed of the kickback.* Before payment and receipt of the kickback, the buyer and the seller must be fully informed of all facts regarding the kickback. For example, assume a broker refers buyers to Nifty Blinds and receives $25 for each buyer who purchases window treatments from Nifty. The broker, before payment and receipt of the $25, must fully advise all parties in the transaction of the arrangement the broker has with Nifty Blinds.
- *The kickback must not be prohibited by other law.* The Real Estate Settlement Procedures Act (RESPA) prohibits the payment of a kickback or unearned fee associated with a settlement (closing) service, including title searches, title insurance, attorney services, surveys, credit reports, and appraisals. A person paid a fee regarding settlement services must have actually rendered (performed) the service (see "Real Estate Settlement Procedures Act [RESPA]," Unit 13).
- *It is unlawful to share a commission with an unlicensed person other than the seller or the buyer in the transaction.* Florida law allows the sharing of the commission with the buyer or the seller in a real estate transaction, provided the rebate is disclosed to all interested parties. Sharing a portion of the commission with a party to the transaction is an example of a legal (permissible) kickback or rebate.
- *It is unlawful for a licensee to pay an unlicensed person for performing real estate services.* Florida law prohibits a real estate licensee from paying an unlicensed person money for the referral of real estate business. However, Florida license law does provide that a property management firm or the owner of an apartment complex may pay a finder's fee (or referral fee) of no more than $50 to an unlicensed person who is a tenant of the apartment complex for the referral of a prospect who becomes a tenant of the apartment complex.

Practice Questions

25. A sales associate wants to pay for an FHA-required repair to the property which neither party to the transaction is willing to cover. The shared commission with a non-real estate licensee must be ____________ to the buyer, the seller, and the lender.

26. The Commercial Real Estate Sales Commission Lien Act gives the broker lien rights to the seller's __________ ____________ for the commission earned by the broker in accordance with the listing agreement to sell _____________ property.

5.7 TYPES OF BUSINESS ENTITIES THAT MAY REGISTER AS BROKERAGE ENTITIES

475.161, F.S.

475.15, F.S.

475.01(1)(a), F.S.

A broker may choose from a variety of business entities (see Figure 5.8). Sole proprietorships, partnerships (both general and limited), limited liability partnerships, corporations, and limited liability companies may be registered as real estate brokers and/or brokerage entities. Chapter 475.01, F.S., defines the term *broker* to include any person who is a general partner of a partnership or an officer or a director of a corporation that acts as a real estate broker.

FIGURE 5.8 ■ Business Entities

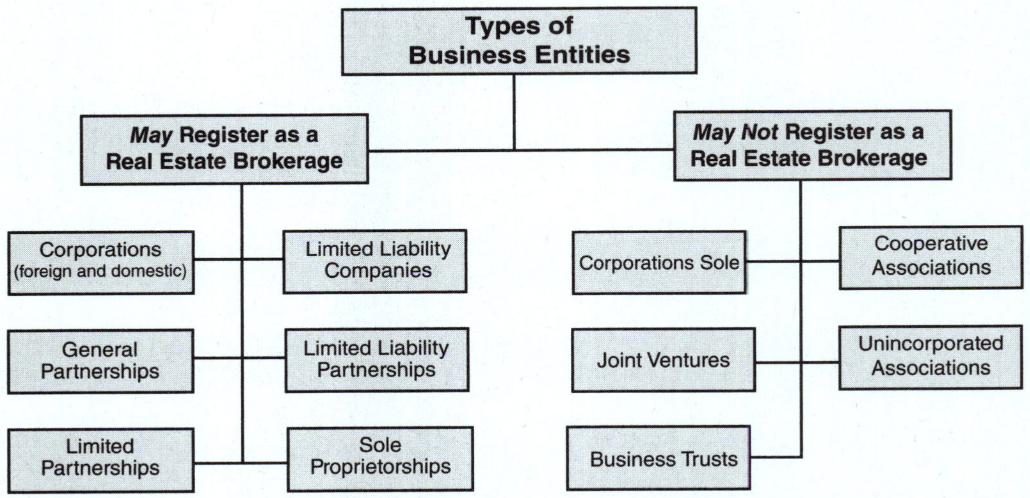

All real estate brokerage entities must register with the DBPR. Registration includes the names of every licensed and unlicensed general partner of a real estate brokerage general partnership or limited partnership and every officer and director of a real estate brokerage corporation. Every member of a member-managed real estate brokerage limited liability company must also register. A person licensed as a sales associate or broker associate may not register as a general partner of a brokerage partnership, a member of a member-managed real estate limited liability company, a member or a manager of a manager-managed real estate limited liability company, or an officer or a director of a brokerage corporation.

Sole Proprietorships

A **sole proprietorship** is a business owned by an individual. Sole proprietorships are the simplest form of business organization; however, they provide no legal protection for the broker's personal assets. Sole proprietors are personally liable not only for their own actions but also for the actions of any employees acting within the scope of their employment. For this reason, many brokers choose a business structure that reduces personal liability. A sole proprietorship can be formed without a written document, and it does not require filing with the Florida Department of State (DOS).

Sole Proprietor Real Estate Brokerage. A sole proprietor who holds a current active and valid broker's license can operate a real estate brokerage business. The broker must register the business address with the DBPR. Brokers may use their own name or a trade name. A sole proprietorship may be dissolved by ceasing business activities and notifying the DBPR, or by expiration of the license, court order, or death of the owner.

Partnerships

620, F.S.

475.15, F.S.

A **general partnership** is an association of two or more persons for the purpose of jointly conducting a business. Every general partner equally shares in the profits and losses of the business (unless a different share is specified in a written agreement). Each general partner has unlimited personal liability because each is responsible for all the debts incurred in conducting that business and each has the power to bind the other(s). All general partners are joint and severally liable for damages resulting from lawsuits. General partners are agents for one another. If one partner enters into an agreement, the other partners are also bound to the agreement. A general partnership is created by a contract that may be written, oral, or implied from the conduct of the parties.

Real Estate Brokerage General Partnerships. Brokers may choose to form a general partnership. In addition to complying with all laws governing general partnerships, requirements regarding real estate brokerage partnerships include the following:

- The partnership must register with the DBPR under the partnership name.
- At least one partner must be licensed as an active broker.
- Partners who will deal with the public and perform services of real estate must be licensed as active brokers.
- Sales associates and broker associates may not be general partners in a real estate brokerage partnership.

61J2-5.019, F.A.C.

61J2-4.009, F.A.C.

It is the responsibility of every active broker in the real estate brokerage partnership to see that the partnership and all of its partners and associates have current and appropriate registration and licenses. Only one partner must be licensed as an active broker. (See "Vacancies of Office" later in this unit for the procedure in the event of a vacancy of the only active broker.)

Limited Partnerships. A **limited partnership** is created by a written instrument filed with the Florida DOS. There must be one or more general partners and one or more limited partners to qualify under the law. The limited partners have no managerial control; they make an investment of cash or of property, but not of services (limited partners are investors only).

620, F.S.

475.15, F.S.

The liability of the general partner(s) is nearly the same as in a general partnership. Limited partners are not liable for debts of the partnership unless the limited partners' names appear in the partnership name (with certain exceptions) or the limited partners take part in the management of the business. Limited partners are liable only for any unpaid part of their pledged contribution, any assets of the partnership in their hands, and any distribution made to them while the partnership is insolvent.

Real Estate Brokerage Limited Partnerships. In addition to complying with all the laws governing any limited partnership, requirements regarding real estate brokerage limited partnerships include the following:

- The limited partnership must register with the DBPR under the limited partnership name.
- General partners who will deal with the public and perform services of real estate must be licensed as active brokers.
- At least one general partner must be licensed as an active broker.

- All other general partners must register (names and addresses are disclosed) with the DBPR for identification purposes.
- Sales associates and broker associates may not be general partners in a real estate brokerage limited partnership; however, they may be limited partners. (Limited partners are investors and are regarded in the same light as stockholders in a corporation.)
- Limited partners are not required to register with the DBPR.

Limited Liability Partnerships (LLPs)

The partners in a **limited liability partnership (LLP)** enjoy protection from personal liability in much the same way as limited partners in a limited partnership. Limited liability partners are not liable for obligations or liabilities of the partnership arising from contract, errors or omissions, negligence, malpractice, or wrongful acts committed by another partner or by an employee, agent, or representative of the partnership. A limited liability partner is liable for any errors, omissions, negligence, malpractice, or wrongful acts committed by that partner, or any person under the partner's direct supervision and control in any activity in which the wrongful act occurred, or for any debts for which the partner agreed in writing to be liable. The partners in a limited liability partnership are not subject to the limitations imposed on limited partners in a traditional limited partnership. Registered limited liability partnerships must file with the Florida Department of State. The name of a registered limited liability partnership must include the words "Registered Limited Liability Partnership" or the abbreviation "L.L.P." or the designation "LLP" as the last words or letters of its name.

Corporations

607, F.S.

475.15, F.S.

61J2-24.002(2)(s–t), F.A.C.

61J2-5.012-5.020, F.A.C.

A **corporation** is a legal entity created by law and consists of one or more persons. The corporation is an artificial person considered to have an existence of its own, separate from the corporation's officers and directors. A corporation is formed by filing articles of incorporation with the Florida DOS. The abbreviation *Inc.* is often used to mean an incorporated legal entity. A corporation has the legal capacity to make contracts and incur debts when an officer signs documents on behalf of the corporation.

Both foreign and domestic corporations may register as brokerage entities. A *foreign corporation* is organized under the laws of another state but does business in Florida. *Domestic corporations* are incorporated in Florida and do business in Florida. The owners of the corporation are the stockholders. The stockholders elect the board of directors to manage the corporation. The officers—president, vice president, secretary, and treasurer—carry out the directives of the board.

In Florida, a corporation may be formed as a real estate brokerage firm after providing proof of legal corporate existence. Requirements regarding real estate brokerage corporations include the following:

- The corporation must register with the DBPR under the corporation name; this is accomplished by completing the brokerage corporation application. (If the brokerage is going to operate under a trade name, that information is also entered on the application.)
- At least one of the officers or directors must be licensed as an active Florida broker (the *principal broker* or *qualifying broker*).
- Active Florida brokers, inactive Florida brokers, and unlicensed people may serve as officers and directors of a real estate brokerage; however, officers and directors who will deal with the public and perform services of real estate must be licensed as active brokers.

- All officers and directors who are not licensed must be registered with the DBPR for identification purposes; this is accomplished by submitting each individual's name, residence address, office held, and percentage of ownership when completing the management information section of the brokerage corporation application.
- Inactive brokers and unlicensed individuals may perform managerial functions for the brokerage corporation that do not involve real estate functions, such as administrative matters, bookkeeping, and accounting duties.
- Sales associates and broker associates may not be an officer or a director in a real estate brokerage corporation; a sales associate or broker associate may be issued a citation and fined for serving as an officer or a director of a brokerage corporation.
- Sales associates and broker associates may be shareholders of a real estate brokerage corporation.

617, F.S.

61J2-5.012-.020, F.A.C.

Nonprofit Corporations. A *nonprofit* (or *not for profit*) *corporation* is organized in substantially the same manner as a corporation for profit. Chapter 475, F.S., does not make a distinction between profit and nonprofit corporations. However, any broker who is considering forming a nonprofit corporation for real estate brokerage activity should consult a tax advisor before proceeding.

Limited Liability Companies

605, F.S.

A **limited liability company (LLC)** is a business structure allowed by state statute. An LLC offers the best features of a corporation and a partnership. It provides the owners protection from personal liability for business debts in the same way a corporation does. Income is taxed only once, as in a partnership. An LLC has great flexibility in how it passes income and deductions to its members. Limited liability companies are formed in Florida under Chapter 605, F.S.

Vacancies of Office

61J2-5.018 (2), F.A.C.

61J2-4.009, F.A.C.

61J2-5.019, F.A.C.

Recall that every brokerage company and partnership (brokerage entity) must be registered with the DBPR and have at least one active broker qualifying the brokerage entity. The brokerage entity must immediately notify the FREC if the only active broker of a brokerage entity dies, resigns, or is unexpectedly unable to remain in the position as active broker. In such a case, the vacancy must be filled within 14 calendar days. The vacancy may be filled with either a permanent or temporary broker. Failure to appoint another permanent or temporary broker within the 14-day deadline will result in the automatic cancellation of the brokerage registration, and the licenses of all people associated with the brokerage will become inactive. New brokerage business may not be performed by the brokerage or by a licensee registered with the brokerage until a new permanent broker or a temporary broker is appointed and registered with the DBPR. However, business that is currently in progress (such as existing listings) can continue to be managed during the 14-day period. A temporary broker may be registered with the DBPR for up to 60 days without the need to comply with the Florida DOS registration requirements. No later than 60 days after the DBPR registration of the temporary broker, the brokerage must file with the DBPR proof that a new permanent broker is properly registered with the Florida DOS.

If the brokerage entity has more than one active broker and one of the brokers dies, resigns, or is unexpectedly unable to remain in the position as an active broker, the brokerage registration and the licenses of the broker associates and sales associates are not affected by the vacancy.

BUSINESS ARRANGEMENTS AND ENTITIES THAT MAY NOT REGISTER AS A BROKERAGE

Ostensible Partnerships

An **ostensible partnership** (or quasi partnership) is not intentionally created. Rather, the conduct of two or more persons creates the "appearance" that a partnership exists. It is considered fraudulent and deceitful if the public is led to believe that those with whom they are working are partners when they are not. In such a situation, the courts may consider that a partnership exists. Under the law, the parties can be held liable for each other's debts and torts (wrongful acts). Real estate licensees who operate as ostensible partners may be subject to license suspension.

Brokers sometimes do business in the same office building. This is permissible provided each broker displays their own office sign and sets up each brokerage so that it is clear to the public that the brokers are separate businesses. If such is the case, they cannot operate under the same name or use their joint names or the same trade name. Brokers should indicate their true statuses by using separate telephone listings, letterheads, business cards, and so forth. Advertisements reflecting that a properly registered broker is a franchisee do not fall under the definition of ostensible partnership.

Corporation Sole

A *corporation sole* is a nonprofit entity that is designed to ensure continuity of ownership of property dedicated to the benefit of a legitimate religious organization. A corporation sole should not be confused with a sole proprietorship or a corporation. A broker should consult an experienced attorney with knowledge of a corporation sole's structure and title. A corporation sole cannot be registered as a real estate brokerage.

Joint Venture

A *joint venture* (or joint adventure) is a temporary form of business arrangement often encountered in the real estate business. The joint venture structure is normally used when two or more parties combine their efforts to complete a single business transaction or a fixed number of business transactions. No written agreements are required for the formation of a joint venture. The rights, duties, and obligations of joint venturers are similar to those of partners in a partnership, except that they are restricted to the transaction for which the joint venture was formed.

609, F.S.

475.011(2), F.S.

Real estate brokers often combine their efforts in real estate transactions to create a joint venture. A joint venture, when composed of separate real estate brokers, can provide real estate services. In such a case, the joint venture would not be required to register with the DBPR because each of the individuals is registered and licensed. If two parties form a joint venture to provide real estate services for compensation, both parties must be licensed real estate brokers.

Business Trust

A *business trust* is a form of business entity that may be created to engage in transactions involving its own real property. A business trust is formed by any number of persons who make an investment at a stipulated amount per unit. The monies collected in this manner are then used to buy, develop, and/or sell real estate. Title to real property acquired by a business trust is taken in the name of a trustee or group of trustees. Although brokerage activities take place within the trust, a business trust cannot be registered with the DBPR as a real estate broker. However, any employee who buys or sells real property for a trust and is compensated on a transaction basis must be licensed.

Cooperative Association

A *cooperative association* is permitted to conduct commercial business and to convey, sell, or buy its own property, but it cannot be registered as a real estate broker.

Unincorporated Association

Unincorporated associations are generally recognized as groups of people associated for some noncommercial common purpose. They are not regarded as partners and are not incorporated. An example is a group of property owners in a subdivision who organize for such purposes as beautification, planning, maintenance, or even the performance of services such as garbage removal. Such associations can incur liabilities, and members are liable for debts to creditors in the same manner as partners. For example, each member is liable for all the debts, but as to one another, the members are liable only for their individual proportionate share. Unincorporated associations sometimes buy or sell their own real property through a trustee or board of trustees. Unincorporated associations may not be registered as real estate brokers.

TRADE NAMES

865.09, F.S.

475.42(1)(j), F.S.

61J2-10.034, F.A.C.

61J2-9.007, F.A.C.

A **trade name** (or fictitious name) is a business name other than the legal name of a person or a business entity. For example, if a broker is a sole proprietor and the broker operates under a name other than the broker's personal name, the broker is operating under a trade name. The DBPR uses the term *trade name* in rule and statute. *Fictitious name* refers to the name registered with the Florida Department of State (DOS). The letters *T/A* are used to indicate *trading as*. The letters *D/B/A* refer to *doing business as*. Sole proprietorships and business entities may choose to operate under these designations.

DBPR Registration of a Trade Name

An individual broker or brokerage entity who desires to use a trade name must register the trade name with the DBPR. The DBPR will not allow a broker or a brokerage entity to register a trade name if another business entity has previously registered the same trade name with the DOS or the DBPR. An individual broker or brokerage entity may register only one trade name. Sales associates and brokerage associates may not use a trade name. Associates must register under their legal name.

EXAMPLE 1: If Broker Julia Moy desires to do business as Orange Park Realty, Julia must register with the DBPR the fictitious name Orange Park Realty.

EXAMPLE 2: If New Towne Realty, Inc., desires to do business as Towne Realty, then the business New Towne Realty, Inc., must register with the DBPR the D/B/A Towne Realty as a fictitious name.

DOS Registration of a Fictitious Name

621.12, F.S.

475.161, F.S.

Individuals licensed by the DBPR are exempt under the Fictitious Name Act from registering a fictitious name with the DOS. In Example 1, Broker Moy does not have to register the name "Orange Park Realty" with the DOS. Brokerage corporations, limited partnerships, limited liability companies, and limited liability partnerships that have registered the business entity with the DOS and are in good standing with the DOS are considered to have met the requirements for fictitious name registration, provided they do not transact business under any other name. Additionally, if an owner's first and last names are included in the business name, the business is exempt from filing a fictitious name.

TRADE NAMES

No person shall operate as a broker under a trade name without causing the trade name to be noted in the records of the Commission and placed on his license, or so operate as a member of a partnership or as a corporation or as an officer or manager thereof, unless such partnership or corporation is the holder of a valid current registration.

Reference: Section 475.42, F.S.

FORMING A PROFESSIONAL ASSOCIATION IN ASSOCIATE'S LEGAL NAME

475.161, F.S.

621.12 (2) (b), F.S.

Florida license law provides that broker associates and sales associates may be licensed in only their legal name or in their legal name as a professional corporation, limited liability company, or professional limited liability company. Becoming licensed as one of these professional associations makes it possible for one's employing broker to pay a commission to the professional association rather than to the individual licensee. Florida license law further requires that the associate's license be issued in the licensee's legal name and may include the entity designation. Forming a professional association for income tax purposes (after consultation with a CPA or an attorney) should not be confused with forming a brokerage business entity to conduct real estate services. Recall that broker associates and sales associates must work under a broker or an owner-developer.

Florida Statute 621 designates the term *professional association* to mean a professional corporation (PA), limited liability company (LLC), or a professional limited liability company (PLLC). In the case of a professional corporation, F.S. 621 designates that the abbreviation P.A. is to be used. For the purposes of this text, we will use the term *professional association* to refer to any of the three legal entities mentioned here. To register one's legal name with a professional association, a licensed broker associate or sales associate must first register a professional association with the Florida DOS.

EXAMPLE: A sales associate's legal name is Jane Doe. Jane forms a professional association with the DOS and requests that her real estate license be issued in the name Jane Doe, PA. Jane would be required to provide the DBPR proof of the creation of a professional association that is registered with the Florida DOS. Jane's broker could then make her commission checks payable to Jane Doe, PA.

475.161, F.S.

Florida license law requires that an associate's professional association be made up of only one individual. Therefore, a married couple (both licensed real estate sales associates) would not be allowed to form a professional corporation. Each spouse would be required to form a separate professional corporation.

PERSONAL ASSISTANTS

Personal assistants are hired by licensees to perform administrative tasks associated with real estate transactions. Whether a personal assistant must be a real estate licensee is determined by the tasks the assistant performs. Unlicensed personal assistants help with routine office activities, such as mass mailings, writing ads, and preparing market analyses. Licensees who use personal assistants do so to increase their customer base and improve service.

A sales associate who employs an unlicensed personal assistant must be certain that the assistant only performs tasks that do not require a real estate license. Unlicensed personal assistants may not be paid commission or compensated on a transactional basis. Unlicensed personal assistants are considered employees of the sales associate. They are under the control of their employer (the sales associate). Employing sales associates must comply with all state and federal employment laws.

Some sales associates prefer to use licensed personal assistants because licensed assistants can perform services of real estate, including showing listed property. A licensed personal assistant must be registered under the employing broker, and the broker must pay the assistant for brokerage activities. A sales associate may pay the licensed personal assistant for nonbrokerage activities on a salaried or an hourly basis. A sales associate may not compensate a personal assistant for brokerage activities that require a license.

Practice Questions

27. Circle the types of business entities that may register as a real estate brokerage.
    a. Limited liability company
    b. Corporation sole
    c. Business trust
    d. Sole proprietorship
    e. Limited partnership

28. In the event a brokerage has only one active broker, and the broker is unable to remain the active broker of the corporation, the vacancy must be filled within _____ calendar days. The corporation may appoint a _____________ broker for up to ______ days.

29. Circle the activities for which a personal assistant would need a real estate license.
    a. Present an offer to the seller.
    b. Place a phone call to a tenant who is late in paying monthly rent.
    c. Negotiate and prepare a listing agreement with a property owner.
    d. Update social media sites with approved promotional information.

5.8 SUMMARY OF IMPORTANT POINTS

- To have active status, a real estate broker is required to open an office and register it with the DBPR.
- The brokerage office sign must contain (1) the trade name (if applicable), (2) the broker's name, and (3) the words "Licensed (or Lic.) Real Estate Broker." If desired, the names of the sales associates and broker associates may be added below the broker's name(s), provided the appropriate title (sales associate or broker associate) appears after their name. A line or a space must separate the brokers' names from the associates' names.
- Blind advertising fails to disclose the license name of the brokerage firm and provides only a post office box number, telephone number, and/or street address.
- *Point of contact information* refers to the information provided on the internet for contacting a brokerage firm or individual licensee, including mailing addresses, physical street addresses, email addresses, telephone numbers, and FAX telephone numbers. The brokerage firm name must be above, below, or adjacent to point of contact information.
- Licensees who include their personal name in advertisements must use their last name as registered with the DBPR.
- A *telephone solicitation* is a telephone call placed for the purpose of encouraging the purchase of, or investment in, property goods, or services. Telemarketers (including real estate licensees) must search the National Do Not Call Registry before making telemarketing calls.
- An *escrow account* is an account for the deposit of money held by a third party in trust for another for safekeeping. Brokers may open escrow accounts in a Florida bank, a savings association, or a credit union. The broker must be a signatory on the escrow account. If the broker chooses not to open an escrow account, the funds may be held by a title company or in a Florida-licensed attorney's trust account.
- Sales associates must deliver binder deposits to their broker-employer no later than the end of the next business day. Brokers must deposit the funds into their escrow account no later than the end of the third business day after the brokerage received the funds.
- If the broker's escrow account is an interest-bearing account, the broker must get written permission from all parties before depositing the funds. The written authorization must specify who is entitled to the interest earned. The broker may receive the interest.
- Brokers must maintain records of real estate transactions for five years, regardless of whether escrow funds were pledged (or two years after litigation, if beyond the five-year period).
- *Commingling* is the illegal practice of mixing a buyer's, seller's, tenant's, or landlord's funds with the broker's own money or mixing escrow money with the broker's personal funds or brokerage funds.
- *Conversion* is the unauthorized control or use of another person's personal property.
- Brokers are allowed to place up to $1,000 of personal or brokerage funds in a sales escrow account or up to $5,000 of personal or brokerage funds in a property management escrow account.

- Brokers must notify the FREC in writing of conflicting demands or of a good-faith doubt within 15 business days. Brokers must institute one of the settlement procedures within 30 business days of receiving conflicting demands or of having a good-faith doubt. The four settlement procedures are (1) mediation, (2) arbitration, (3) litigation, and (4) escrow disbursement order.
- The penalty for a first-degree misdemeanor is a fine of not more than $1,000 and/or up to one year in jail.
- A *kickback* occurs when a broker receives money from someone other than the buyer or the seller, such as for referring a buyer or a seller to a particular vendor for services. Buyers and sellers must be fully informed before the payment.
- Florida law prohibits a real estate licensee from paying money to an unlicensed person for the referral of real estate business.
- Florida law allows the sharing of part of the commission with the buyer or the seller in a real estate transaction, provided the rebate is disclosed to all interested parties.
- Types of business entities that may register as a brokerage entity include the following: sole proprietorship, general partnership, limited partnership, limited liability partnership, corporation, and limited liability company.
- An *ostensible partnership* (or quasi-partnership) is created when the actions of two or more persons create the appearance that a partnership exists. Licensees who operate as ostensible partners may be subject to license suspension.
- Sales associates and broker associates may not be members of the board of directors or officers of a real estate brokerage corporation.
- Sales associates and broker associates are not allowed to register as general partners of a real estate brokerage general or limited partnership.

UNIT 5 EXAM

1. John Anderson is a licensed real estate sales associate. Under which name may he register and be licensed?
   a. Complete Real Estate Sales Services
   b. John Anderson Brokerage
   c. John Anderson, LLC
   d. John Anderson and Partners

2. A sales associate receives a binder deposit from a buyer on Monday. By the end of business on what day of the week must the broker deposit the funds into the escrow account?
   a. Tuesday
   b. Wednesday
   c. Thursday
   d. Friday

3. Real estate sales associates who receive checks payable to them as deposits on the purchase of real property must
   a. endorse the checks, deposit them in their employers' accounts, and maintain good records.
   b. endorse the checks and immediately turn them over to their employers.
   c. deposit the checks immediately in their own accounts and notify their employers of the transactions.
   d. deposit the checks immediately and give their employers the equivalent amounts in the form of checks or cash.

4. Which statement is FALSE regarding escrow accounts?
   a. The escrow account may be either interest-bearing or non-interest-bearing.
   b. A broker may choose to have an attorney or a Florida title company maintain the escrow account.
   c. It is illegal for the broker to keep any earned interest even if the buyer and the seller give written permission.
   d. A broker must get written authorization from the buyer and the seller before placing escrow funds in an interest-bearing escrow account.

5. A dispute arises between the buyer and the seller as to which one is entitled to escrowed property. The broker should first
   a. mediate the matter.
   b. arbitrate the matter with the consent of both parties.
   c. notify the FREC in writing, unless exempted from the notice requirements.
   d. submit the matter to a court of law for adjudication.

6. When a deposit is placed with a title company, what information regarding the title company must be included on the purchase and sale agreement?
   a. Telephone number
   b. Name of the title company
   c. Address of the title company
   d. All of these

7. An active broker associate wants to form an entity to be paid commissions. Which is the broker associate NOT legally allowed to form?
   a. Sandy Jones, LLC
   b. Sandy Jones, PLLC
   c. Sandy Jones, Inc.
   d. Sandy Jones, PA

8. The Excellence Team is ordering For Sale signs. The team works for broker Bob Sloane at Sunshine Realty. Which statement is FALSE regarding the team advertising requirements?
   a. The advertisement must include the name Sunshine Realty.
   b. The brokerage office phone number must be included in the ad.
   c. The name Excellence Team may be no larger than the name of the brokerage.
   d. The Excellence Team must file with Sloane a designated licensee to be responsible for ensuring that the team advertising complies with Florida license law and administrative rules.

9. A sales associate employs an unlicensed personal assistant to help with real estate property management. The unlicensed assistant may NOT
   a. collect rent payments from tenants.
   b. deposit rent payments in the bank.
   c. place For Rent signs on properties.
   d. show a rental property to a potential tenant.

10. Which statement is TRUE regarding a lien filed by a broker under the Commercial Real Estate Sales Commission Lien Act?
    a. The lien applies to commission only and does not include other fees the owner agrees to pay in the brokerage agreement.
    b. The lien is filed against the real property covered in the brokerage agreement.
    c. The lien takes priority as of the date of the brokerage agreement.
    d. The broker must disclose to the owner at the time of signing, or before the owner signs the brokerage agreement, that Chapter 475, Part III, creates lien rights for commission earned by the broker.

11. One difference between a general partnership and a limited partnership is that
    a. only a general partnership may be registered as a real estate broker.
    b. limited partners must make a cash or property investment.
    c. while both have general partners, there must be two or more general partners in a limited partnership.
    d. limited partners must be licensed as either active or inactive sales associates.

12. Which business entity may be registered as a real estate broker?
    a. Corporation sole
    b. Cooperative association
    c. Limited partnership
    d. Business trust

13. A broker is preparing to open Sunnyside Realty as a sole proprietorship and is placing an order to have an entrance sign made. Which wording does NOT need to be included on the sign?
    a. Sunnyside Realty
    b. The broker's legal name
    c. Licensed real estate broker
    d. 1000 Sunset Blvd.

14. A licensed real estate broker and an attorney who specializes in contract law form a joint venture for the purpose of locating and selling to investors raw land that is suitable for commercial development. Which statement is TRUE regarding this arrangement?
    a. The attorney is exempt from the requirement to hold a broker's license because she is an attorney.
    b. They have formed an illegal ostensible partnership.
    c. Because they are performing real estate services for compensation, both must be licensed real estate brokers.
    d. A joint venture is not required to register with the DBPR; therefore, there is no need for both parties to hold real estate licenses.

15. A broker receives conflicting demands concerning a roof inspection report. Both the buyer and the seller claim the earnest money deposit. The broker must
    a. provide written notification to the FREC within 10 business days.
    b. follow the written instructions of the broker's buyer or seller.
    c. institute one of the statutory settlement procedures within 30 business days from the time the broker received conflicting demands.
    d. request an escrow disbursement order from the DBPR.

16. The sales commission rates applicable to the various types of property sold in Florida are determined by
    a. FREC rules and regulations.
    b. agreement between each broker and buyer or seller.
    c. the local board of REALTORS®.
    d. agreement between each seller and buyer.

17. A real estate brokerage has one active broker who resigns unexpectedly due to a cancer diagnosis. Which statement regarding the vacancy of the only active broker is FALSE?
    a. The vacancy must be filled within 14 calendar days.
    b. A temporary broker may be registered with the DBPR for up to 90 days without the need to comply with the Secretary of State registration requirements.
    c. New brokerage business may not be performed by a sales associate registered with the brokerage until a new active or temporary broker is registered with the DBPR.
    d. Failure to appoint another active or temporary broker within the required deadline will cause the automatic cancellation of the brokerage entity's registration.

18. In Florida, listings obtained and any commissions paid by the buyer or the seller are
    a. legally the sales associate's property.
    b. jointly owned by the sales associate and the sales associate's employer.
    c. legally classified as the property of the employing property owner.
    d. legally the property of the sales associate's employer.

19. Which statement is FALSE concerning the payment of an unearned fee or kickback?
    a. A real estate licensee may be paid a fee for referring buyers to a title company, provided the buyer is informed in advance of the facts concerning the fee.
    b. A real estate licensee may share part of the commission with the buyer or the seller in a real estate transaction.
    c. A real estate licensee must also be licensed as a mortgage loan originator to be legally paid a fee for referring buyers to a mortgage lender.
    d. The payment of a kickback must not violate RESPA.

20. Two brokers from different brokerages agree to work with one another to market a prestigious marina in Naples, Florida. One broker is particularly knowledgeable regarding marinas and the other is an expert on the Naples real estate market, so they decide to combine their expertise on this particular listing. This business arrangement is called
    a. an ostensible partnership.
    b. a general partnership.
    c. a joint venture.
    d. a limited partnership.

UNIT 6

VIOLATIONS OF LICENSE LAW, PENALTIES, AND PROCEDURES

LEARNING OBJECTIVES

When you have completed this unit, you will be able to accomplish the following.

- Distinguish among the legal terms presented in this unit.
- Explain the procedures involved in the reporting of violations, the elements of a valid complaint, and the investigation of complaints.
- Describe the composition of the probable-cause panel.
- Describe the hearing process.
- Recognize events that would cause a license application to be denied.
- Distinguish among the various violations and administrative penalties.
- Distinguish among the various penalties that may be issued by a court of law.
- Explain the provisions of the Real Estate Recovery Fund.

KEY TERMS

breach of trust
citation
complaint
concealment
culpable negligence
final order
formal (administrative) complaint
fraud
legally sufficient
material fact
misrepresentation
moral turpitude
notice of noncompliance
probable cause
probation
recommended order
reprimand
stipulation
subpoena
summary (emergency) suspension order
voluntary relinquishment for permanent revocation

INTRODUCTION

This unit details the procedures for investigations and hearings via the complaint process. The unit describes many types of violations of the laws and rules governing real estate activities and the possible consequences that may result. Finally, the Real Estate Recovery Fund is explained regarding its function when damages are suffered in a real estate transaction due to a wrongful act of a Florida licensee.

6.1 LEGAL TERMS TO KNOW

To assist you in learning important but often difficult-to-understand real estate terms in the legal realm, the following definitions and examples are presented.

Breach of Trust

Section 475.25(1)(b), F.S.

A **breach of trust** is defined as any violation or omission of a legal or moral duty. It is the breaking of a promise or obligation, either by an act of commission or omission, default, or nonperformance.

EXAMPLE 1: A sales associate signed a contract for sale in the name of the buyers without the buyers' permission or knowledge. The sales associate indicated that the buyers were busy, and so the associate signed the contract to save time. According to the associate, time was an issue because the bank wanted a signed contract right away.

The DBPR served the real estate sales associate with an administrative complaint. Section 475.25(1)(b), F.S., subjects a real estate licensee to discipline for committing "fraud, misrepresentation, concealment, false promises, false pretenses, dishonest dealings by trick, scheme, or devise, culpable negligence, or *breach of trust* [italics added for emphasis] in any business transaction."

The sales associate violated the statute by signing a contract for sale in the name of the buyers for the purchase of subject property. The sales associate was fined $1,000 and investigative costs of $700. The sales associate's real estate license was suspended for 60 days. The licensee was further ordered to attend a 45-hour post-license course and a 3-hour ethics course. The education ordered is in addition to any course requirement to maintain the real estate license.

Reference: DBPR Case Number 2011005450

Concealment

Concealment is the withholding of information or a material fact. In a fiduciary relationship, for example, the broker has a duty to speak, unless the principal knows the information or fact.

Culpable Negligence

Culpable negligence involves negligent conduct that, while not intentional, involves a disregard of the consequences likely to result for one's actions. Brokers may be charged with culpable negligence if they do not give ordinary, careful attention to their brokerage and do not exercise reasonable control over the brokerage's agents.

Fraud

Fraud is intentional deceit and reliance on the deception for the purpose of inducing another person to rely on the deceitful information and for the injured person to part with something of value or to surrender a legal right. A broker may be charged with fraud when the broker does not disclose known defects or remains "silent" when the defect is not readily observable. (See "Misrepresentation and Fraud," Unit 11).

Material Fact

A **material fact** is information that is relevant to a person making a decision and that affects the value of the real property. Information about the condition of a property, such as known defects or code violations are material facts.

Misrepresentation

Misrepresentation is an untrue statement of fact or an incorrect or false representation of the facts. A licensee may be charged with misrepresentation for failing to indicate in a newspaper that a listed property is advertised by a real estate licensee.

Moral Turpitude

Moral turpitude involves conduct contrary to honesty, good morals, justice, or accepted custom. Case law has further defined moral turpitude to mean a depravity against society. Felonies such as embezzlement, larceny, and robbery are generally considered moral turpitude.

EXAMPLE 2: A man's elderly mother died of cancer at home. In her last days, the elderly woman was prescribed controlled drugs including morphine and hydrocodone. The man was a close friend of a real estate sales associate. The friend explained to the licensee that he had drugs in his home left over from his mother's care. According to the licensee, the friend was at a loss regarding what to do with the drugs. The friend asked the licensee if he would place the drugs in the licensee's storage unit so that he could get them out of his house. The licensee agreed and placed a box of drugs in the storage unit.

Sometime later the storage unit was burglarized. The police were sent to the unit. The police found the drugs during their investigation. In circuit court, the licensee was found guilty of possession and trafficking in morphine, hydrocodone, and other controlled substances.

The licensee timely notified the FREC of the felony conviction. The DBPR served the real estate sales associate with an administrative complaint. Section 475.25(1)(f), F.S., subjects a real estate licensee to discipline for being convicted or found guilty of "a crime in any jurisdiction which...involves *moral turpitude* [italics added for emphasis] or fraudulent or dishonest dealing."

The sales associate violated Section 475.25(1)(f), F.S., for being convicted or found guilty of a crime in any jurisdiction that involves moral turpitude. The sales associate was fined $1,000 and investigative costs of $396. The sales associate was given one year of probation. The licensee was further ordered to attend one two-day FREC meeting.

Reference: DBPR Case Number 2011059856

Practice Questions

1. In Example 1, the licensee was charged with concealment. What did the licensee conceal?

2. A seller covered several areas of permanently stained wood plank flooring with area rugs and did not mention the damaged wood planks to the listing sales associate. The buyer does not discover the damaged wood flooring until after the closing when the house is vacated and the rugs are removed. The buyer files a complaint with the DBPR against the listing company and sues the seller and the broker. The seller's failure to disclose the permanently stained flooring is considered to be a __________ fact.

THE COMPLAINT PROCESS

Seven steps are involved in the process of dealing with complaints of alleged violations:

1. A complaint is filed with the DBPR.
2. The complaint is investigated.
3. A determination is made as to probable cause.
4. A formal complaint is issued if probable cause is found.
5. An informal hearing or a formal hearing is conducted.
6. The final order is issued.
7. The final order may be appealed to the district court.

6.2 FILING THE COMPLAINT

475.25, F.S.

455.225, F.S.

The complaint process begins when a **complaint** (an alleged violation of a law or rule) is filed with the DBPR's Division of Real Estate (DRE). The complaint process is consumer driven, meaning the process is initiated when a written complaint is submitted by a consumer, licensee, or another agency. Complaints are submitted on the Uniform Complaint Form for Real Estate. The form may be downloaded from the DRE website, or the *complainant* (person filing a complaint) can file the complaint online through the online complaint portal (see the following web link). A complaint that is filed in writing and is legally sufficient will be investigated. A complaint is **legally sufficient** if it contains facts indicating that a violation of any of the following has occurred:

- Florida Statute 455 (DBPR and the professions under the Department)
- Florida Statute 475 (real estate license law)
- DBPR rule
- FREC rule

455.225, F.S.

Anyone may file a complaint against a licensee, an applicant, or an unlicensed person for actions believed to violate Chapter 455, F.S.; Chapter 475, F.S.; or any existing DBPR or FREC administrative rule. The DRE has its own enforcement section. The DRE's authority to process and investigate complaints is granted by the DBPR's Section 455.225 of the Florida statutes. The DRE's enforcement section oversees the complaint process for both licensed and unlicensed individuals.

EXAMPLE 1: A consumer filed a complaint against an unlicensed person who was showing rental units, procuring tenants, and collecting tenant rent and deposits for a fee. The unlicensed person can be charged with unlicensed activity.

A person may also file a complaint for an alleged violation that does not pertain to a real estate transaction or an incident that took place in another state.

EXAMPLE 2: A consumer filed a complaint against a real estate licensee who was convicted of a DUI in Alabama.

Anonymous Complaints The DRE may investigate an unsigned (anonymous) complaint, or one made by a confidential informant, provided the complaint is in writing and is legally sufficient; the alleged violation of law or rule is substantial; and the DRE has reason to believe, after preliminary inquiry, that the alleged violations in the complaint are true. An anonymous complaint is confidential (even to the unknown complainant that filed it) until 10 days after probable cause has been found to exist or the subject of the investigation waives the privilege of confidentiality, whichever occurs first.

WEBLINK

You can download the Uniform Complaint Form and instructions at www.myfloridalicense.com/dbpr/re/documents/re-2200-1.pdf.

Consumers may also file a complaint online. Go to http://www.myfloridalicense.com/DBPR/file-a-complaint/.

Investigation

The DBPR has granted authority to the DRE enforcement section to initiate an investigation on its own if it has reasonable cause to believe that a licensee has violated Chapter 455, F.S.; Chapter 475, F.S.; DBPR rule; or FREC rule. Although most investigations result from a complaint being filed, an investigation may be initiated as a result of an inspection of a brokerage office (including an audit of the broker's escrow account) or because a licensee self-reported a criminal matter. If the act under investigation is a criminal offense, the DRE is authorized to conduct its investigation without notifying the subject(s) to the investigation.

455.225, F.S.

If the original complainant decides to withdraw the complaint or otherwise indicates a desire not to continue with the investigative process, the DRE may continue with the investigation and the Commission may take the appropriate final action once the case is prosecuted to completion.

The DRE forwards a copy of the complaint to the subject of the investigation or to the subject's attorney. The subject may submit a written response to the complaint. The complaint and all information obtained during any resulting investigation must be treated as confidential until 10 days after probable cause has been found to exist or the subject of the investigation waives the privilege of confidentiality, whichever occurs first (except for a criminal violation). If probable cause is not found to exist, the investigative report and supporting documents never are released to the public. Once a legally sufficient complaint has been investigated, an investigative report with all supporting documentation is forwarded to the Department's legal section located in the Division of the General Counsel to determine what type of violation may have occurred, if any.

120.60(6), F.S.

455.225(8), F.S.

Summary Suspension. In rare situations, during the investigative process, the DBPR may uncover something so serious that it cannot allow the licensee to continue to endanger the public welfare. For example, the investigator may discover that a broker is stealing thousands of dollars from the escrow account. In such extreme circumstances, the DBPR may decide that the licensee cannot be allowed to continue to practice real estate during the normal disciplinary process. Such situations require emergency action. The DBPR secretary (or a legally appointed designee) has the authority to issue a **summary (emergency) suspension order**.

When it has been demonstrated that a summary suspension is necessary, due process does not require a hearing before the emergency suspension, provided a formal proceeding for suspension or revocation is promptly instituted.

Practice Questions

3. A complaint is __________ ______________ if it contains facts indicating that a violation of Florida Statute 475, Florida Statute 455, or administrative rule has occurred.

4. A complaint and the information obtained during the investigation is treated as ________________ until _______ days after probable cause is found to exist.

6.3 PROBABLE CAUSE

455.225(4), F.S.

61J2-20.009, F.A.C.

Reasonable grounds for prosecution is called **probable cause**. The determination as to whether probable cause exists is made by majority vote of FREC's probable-cause panel. The sole responsibility of the probable-cause panel is to determine whether probable cause exists.

Composition

The FREC may convene multiple probable-cause panels to handle the volume of investigative reports. Each probable-cause panel is composed of two individuals. One of the panel members must currently serve on the Commission. Various combinations of current and former commissioners are used on the probable-cause panels:

- At least one of the panel members must be a former or current professional Commission member. If the probable-cause board member is a former professional member of the FREC, the former commissioner must currently hold an active valid real estate license (see "Composition and Qualifications," Unit 3).
- The second panel member may be a former or current professional FREC member, or a former or current consumer member of the Commission.

EXAMPLE: A probable-cause panel may consist of the following:

1. One current professional member of the FREC and one former consumer FREC member
2. One current consumer member of the FREC and one former professional FREC member who holds an active valid real estate license
3. One current professional member of the FREC and one former professional FREC member who holds an active valid real estate license

455.225(4), F.S.

Probable Cause Determination

Probable-cause proceedings are not open to the public, and the remaining FREC members are prohibited from attending. The segregation of Commission members allows the probable-cause panel to serve in a "grand jury" type of arrangement. Because the remaining commissioners do not participate in the probable-cause proceedings, they are able to maintain objectivity in the matter if it comes before the Commission in an informal hearing.

The probable-cause panel reviews the investigative report and the staff attorney's recommendations. The probable-cause panel must make a decision within 30 days after receipt of the final investigative report, unless an extension is granted by the secretary of the Department. After a complete review of the record, the probable-cause panel makes a determination as to whether probable cause exists.

If the panel finds that probable cause does not exist, it may simply dismiss the case, or it may dismiss the case with a *letter of guidance* to the subject. A confidential report is placed in the licensee's DBPR file describing a minor incidence of misconduct that resulted in no disciplinary action. If probable cause is found, a formal complaint is filed. Once the probable-cause proceeding has been concluded, the complainant and the subject of the investigation are sent written notification of the outcome. The DBPR must give timely written notice to a licensee's broker or employer when a formal complaint has been filed against a sales associate or a broker associate.

Practice Questions

5. At least _______ of the probable cause panel members must be a __________ member of the Commission.
6. If probable cause is found, a _________ ___________ is filed.
7. Probable cause proceedings are _______ open to the public, and the remaining FREC members are ______________ from attending the proceedings.

6.4 FORMAL COMPLAINT

455.225(5), F.S.

If probable cause is found to exist, the probable-cause panel will direct the Department to file a formal complaint against the subject of the investigation (respondent). A **formal (administrative) complaint** consists of allegations of facts and charges against the licensee.

Address of Record

455.275, F.S.

120.60(5), F.S.

Administrative complaints are sent by email, regular U.S. mail, and certified mail to the licensee's address of record. Service by regular mail or email to a licensee's last known mailing address or email address of record constitutes adequate and sufficient notice to the licensee for most other official DBPR communication to a licensee. For example, final orders are sent by regular mail. Licensees are solely responsible for notifying the DBPR in writing of the licensee's current mailing address, email address, and place of practice. Licensees should regularly check the email address on record.

Election of Rights

An Election of Rights form is sent with the administrative complaint. The licensee is instructed to select one of three options in the Election of Rights and return the completed Election of Rights form to the DBPR on or before the 21st day after receipt of the administrative complaint. The licensee may choose to:

1. not dispute the allegations of fact and request an informal hearing,
2. dispute the allegations of fact and request a formal hearing, or
3. not dispute the allegations of fact and waive the right to be heard.

Settlement Stipulation

Sometimes a licensee-respondent and the licensee's attorney (if the licensee has legal counsel) will meet with an attorney from the DBPR General Counsel before a hearing to discuss a possible settlement and enter into a stipulation. A **stipulation** is an agreement as to the facts of the case and the penalty reached between the attorneys for the General Counsel and the licensee or licensee's attorney. The stipulation must be approved by the FREC for it to be effective. The licensee and the licensee's legal counsel, where there is one, are encouraged to appear before the FREC to defend the stipulation. The FREC will approve or deny the stipulation during a Commission meeting. If the FREC denies the stipulation, it usually provides guidance or a counteroffer to the General Counsel concerning additional penalties it believes appropriate in order for it to support a revised stipulation.

Voluntary Relinquishment for Permanent Revocation

Sometimes a licensee-respondent will choose to avoid a disciplinary hearing and relinquish the real estate license in lieu of discipline. **Voluntary relinquishment for permanent revocation** is an affidavit signed by the licensee relinquishing the license from further discipline while agreeing the license status will show revoked. A revocation is a permanent action against the license.

Case Presented in Either an Informal Hearing or a Formal Hearing

455.225(5), F.S.
120.57(2), F.S.
120.569, F.S.

If the licensee-respondent's case was not resolved with a stipulation, the respondent's case will either be heard by the FREC in an informal hearing or the case may be heard before an administrative law judge in a formal hearing. If there is no dispute of material fact, the case is presented in an informal hearing before the FREC. If the licensee-respondent disputes the alleged facts noted in the complaint, the licensee-respondent's case must be heard by an administrative law judge in a formal hearing. The licensee-respondent must be given at least 14 days' notice of a hearing.

120.57(3), F.S.
455.2273(5), F.S.
120.52, F.S.

Informal Hearing. An informal hearing is an expedited way of resolving the disciplinary case provided the licensee does not dispute the alleged facts stated in the complaint. During an *informal hearing*, normally held at a regular Commission meeting, the licensee-respondent is given an opportunity to explain the details of the case with supporting evidence and/or witnesses. Any Commissioners who served on the probable-cause panel for the particular complaint may not participate in this informal hearing. If any party raises an issue of disputed fact during an informal hearing, the hearing is terminated and a formal hearing will be scheduled before an administrative law judge. The FREC will determine, based on the admitted facts, whether the licensee is guilty of the charges alleged in the complaint. If the licensee is found guilty of the charges, the FREC will determine which penalties are appropriate based on the details of the case, taking into consideration any *mitigating* circumstances (reasons to reduce the impact of the violation), and it will issue a final order (see "Final Order," later in this unit).

455.225, F.S.
120.60(5), F.S.
120.57(1), F.S.
Ch 28, Sections 101–110, DOAH Rules, F.A.C.
120.57(1), F.S.

Waiver Hearing. If the subject of an administrative complaint fails to timely respond to the Election of Rights, the licensee-respondent is considered to have waived the election of rights. The case proceeds and is heard by the FREC in an informal hearing.

Formal Hearing. If the licensee-respondent requests a *formal hearing* or if the licensee-respondent disputes the allegations, the DBPR requests that the case be prosecuted under Chapter 120, F.S. Hearings under Chapter 120 are conducted by full-time Florida administrative law judges who are employed by the *Division of Administrative Hearings (DOAH)*. The DOAH may legally employ only those persons who have been members of The Florida

Bar in good standing for the preceding five years. Administrative law judges are not subject to control, supervision, or direction by any party, commission, or department of state government. Once an administrative law judge is assigned, the DBPR may take no further action except as a litigating party.

The administrative law judge has the power to swear witnesses, to take their testimony under oath, and to issue subpoenas. A **subpoena** is a command to appear at a certain time and place to give testimony or to produce records. Failure to comply with a subpoena could result in a finding of contempt of court.

455.2273(5), F.S.

120.57(3), F.S.

120.52, F.S.

The administrative law judge prepares and submits to FREC a **recommended order** that includes the administrative law judge's findings of fact and conclusions of law and the recommended penalty, if any, in accordance with the Commission's range of penalties as set forth in rule. Any party of record in the case may submit (within the statutory time limit) written exceptions to the administrative law judge's recommended order.

WEBLINK

To learn more about the formal hearing process, visit the Florida Division of Administrative Hearings website at www.doah.state.fl.us/ALJ/. Click on "Statutes and Rules."

Final Order

475.31, F.S.

455.225, F.S.

120.57, F.S.

61J2-24.001, F.A.C.

The FREC (with the members who served on the probable-cause panel excused) issues the final order in each disciplinary case. The **final order** is FREC's final decision as to innocence or guilt and the determination of the appropriate penalty. The FREC issues a final order at the conclusion of an informal hearing. If the matter was heard by an administrative law judge in a formal hearing, the FREC must review and consider the administrative law judge's findings and recommended order before issuing its final order.

The Commission members who did not serve on the probable-cause panel consider the administrative law judge's report and recommended order, plus any filed exceptions to the report and the accused party's final arguments, if any. After all final arguments are heard, the Commission members make a determination and issue the final order, concluding the quasi-judicial process.

A copy of the final order is mailed to each party in the case. The notice must inform the recipient of the appeal process. The final order becomes effective 30 days after it has been entered. A licensee has the right to practice real estate during the complaint process and up until the final order becomes effective.

Judicial Review (Appeal)

475.37, F.S.

120.68, F.S.

The licensee-respondent may challenge the final order within 30 days by filing an appeal. The petition of judicial review (notice of appeal) must be filed with the DBPR and with the appropriate district court. The licensee may request a *stay of enforcement*. A stay of enforcement, if granted, stops the enforcement of the final order pending the outcome of the appeal process. To obtain a stay of the final order, the district court of appeals must issue a *writ of supersedeas*. The writ is an order issued by a court that supersedes the action of the Commission and allows the licensee to continue to practice until the case can be heard on appeal.

If the reviewing court finds that a material error in procedure by the FREC has affected the fairness of the hearing or the correctness of the action taken, the case will be sent back to the FREC for corrective action. Unless the court finds legitimate grounds to set aside, modify, remand for further FREC proceeding, order additional action by the FREC, or order some auxiliary relief under Florida Statute 120.68, the court is required to affirm (support) the action taken by the Commission.

If a FREC final order is affirmed, reversed, or set aside, a mandate (copy) is filed with the Commission attesting to that event. The respondent's rights and privileges as a licensee will be restored as of the date of filing, if the final order is reversed. When the inquiry or proceeding is in reference to an application to become licensed, the application must be approved and processed. If a court reverses or sets aside a final order, the court may award attorney's fees and costs to the aggrieved prevailing party.

CASE STUDY

STIPULATION CASE

Florida DBPR v. R. G. Hansen, Respondent

What follows is information concerning an actual case (DBPR 2009006963). This case was resolved in a stipulation. The information has been summarized for education purposes.

Stipulation:

Petitioner, Florida DBPR, Division of Real Estate (DBPR), and Respondent, R. G. Hansen, hereby stipulate and agree that the Florida Real Estate Commission issue a Final Order adopting and incorporating the provision of this Stipulation as final agency action in this case.

Stipulated Facts and Conclusions of Law:

1. Respondent at all times held a valid active sales associate license.
2. Respondent admits that the DBPR served the Respondent with an Administrative Complaint charging Respondent with violation of provisions of Chapter 455 and 475, Florida Statutes.
3. Respondent neither admits nor denies the factual allegations in all counts of the Administrative Complaint.
4. Respondent was found guilty of having failed to advertise property or services in a manner in which reasonable persons would know they are dealing with a real estate licensee. Respondent failed to include the licensed name of the brokerage firm in an advertisement, and having placed or caused to be placed an advertisement that is fraudulent, false, deceptive, or misleading in form or content, in violation of Rule 61J2-10.025, Florida Administrative Code, and Section 475.25(1)(c), Florida Statute.

Stipulated Disposition:

1. Respondent shall pay a fine of $500 and $650 in costs.
2. Respondent shall attend one two-day FREC general meeting. Respondent is placed under probation for a period of two years. Respondent must pass the 28-hour reactivation course. The education herein is in addition to any requirement for respondent to maintain his real estate license.
3. Noncompliance with the terms of this Stipulation shall result in the suspension of Respondent's license without notice to Respondent or further hearing, until Respondent submits satisfactory proof of compliance to the DBPR. The suspension period shall not exceed 10 years.

4. A summary of the action of Final Order shall be published in the FREC News and Report.
5. The parties understand that this Stipulation is subject to the approval of the DBPR and of the FREC.
6. Respondent executes this Stipulation to avoid further administrative action with respect to these causes.

The FREC has not taken prior disciplinary action against Respondent.

Practice Questions

8. A __________________ is a possible settlement between a licensee-respondent and the DBPR General Counsel that is reached before a hearing.
9. If a licensee-respondent does not dispute the material facts of the case, the case is heard in an ________________________ hearing.
10. An _______________ ________ ___________ presides over formal hearings.
11. The administrative law judge prepares and submits to the FREC a __________________ ____________.
12. The licensee-respondent may challenge the final order within __________ days by filing an appeal.

6.5 ADMINISTRATIVE PENALTIES

Three types of penalties may be imposed for violations of the real estate license law: administrative, civil, and criminal. The powers of the FREC are limited to administrative matters and do not extend to criminal actions. The Commission may impose administrative penalties for violations of Florida statute and administrative rules and regulations.

The primary purpose of the administrative jurisdiction granted to the Commission is to enforce duties and obligations as they apply to individuals and firms actively engaged in the real estate business. Thus, the FREC may not impose imprisonment as a penalty. Imprisonment is a criminal punishment that must be ordered by a court. Furthermore, the FREC does not have the authority to order restitution to an injured party. If the acts of a licensee harm a consumer, the injured party may seek damages in a court of law.

Denial of a License Application and Refusal to Recertify a License for Renewal

475.17, F.S.

Some application denials are the result of a deficient application. When an application is deficient, the applicant may correct the deficiency and submit an amended application or file a new application. Examples of a deficient application are:

- neglecting to answer completely all questions on the application;
- neglecting to forward the proper fees with the application request; and
- neglecting to correct errors or omissions on applications returned.

Grounds for denial of a license application are more serious and result in an applicant being denied licensure. A denied application requires a decision by the FREC during a Commission meeting. Examples of cause for license denial are that the applicant:

- lacked minimum qualifications;
- did not possess the character required by the provisions of Florida Statutes 455 and 475;
- did not possess the general competence to deal with the public or complaints against the applicant were received by the FREC or the DBPR;
- was guilty of acts that would have resulted in revocation or suspension of a license had the applicant already been licensed;
- acted in violation of any provision of F.S. 475.42 or was at the time subject to discipline under F.S. 475.25; and
- received assistance or cheated while taking a state license exam.

Practice Questions

13. Circle the actions which are cause for an application to be denied.
    a. Cheated on the state license exam
    b. Applied for a license online
    c. Failed the prelicense end-of-course exam
    d. Was guilty of acts that would have resulted in license suspension if the applicant had already been licensed

14. An application for licensure may be denied if the applicant is guilty of acts that would have resulted in the license being ______________ or suspended if the applicant were already a Florida licensee.

6.6 VIOLATIONS AND ADMINISTRATIVE PENALTIES

455.2273, F.S.

61J2-24.001(1), F.A.C.

455.225(3), F.S.

The Commission has set forth administrative rule guidelines that apply to each specific disciplinary action that it may impose. The purpose of these disciplinary guidelines is to inform licensees of the range of penalties that normally will be imposed for each count (offense) during a formal or informal hearing. A finding of *mitigating* (less severe) circumstances or *aggravating* (more severe) circumstances allows the Commission to impose a penalty other than those provided. Two types of administrative penalties are issued by the DBPR/DRE: (1) a notice of noncompliance and (2) citations. A summary suspension (discussed earlier in this unit) is issued by the DBPR secretary. There are a variety of administrative penalties that the Commission may impose. Combinations of administrative penalties may be imposed. For example, the Commission may impose attendance at a FREC meeting or completion of an educational course, in addition to a fine and costs of the investigation. The various types of penalties that may be imposed by the DRE and the Commission are summarized in Figure 6.1.

120.695, F.S.

61J2-24.003, F.A.C.

Notice of Noncompliance. The FREC has set forth in administrative rule a list of violations that are considered to be minor violations. The DRE may only issue a **notice of noncompliance** for a first offense of a minor violation listed in the rule. A *minor violation* is defined in rule as one that does not create a significant threat of harm; result in economic or physical harm to a person; or adversely affect public health, safety, or welfare. The licensee must take corrective action within 15 calendar days of being issued a notice of noncompliance. A notice of noncompliance does not involve a fine. Failure to comply with a notice of noncompliance may result in a citation. A notice of noncompliance does not appear on the licensee's public records (see Figure 6.1).

WEBLINK

The administrative rule, Notification of Noncompliance, can be downloaded at https://www.flrules.org/gateway/RuleNo.asp?id=61J2-24.003.

455.228(3), F.S.

455.224, F.S.

61J2-24.002, F.A.C.

Citation. The FREC has set forth in administrative rule a list of violations that are of no substantial threat to the public health, safety, and welfare. Each violation listed in rule indicates the fine that is imposed. Licensees receiving a citation have 30 days to accept or reject the alleged violation(s), as specified in the citation. If the licensee accepts the alleged violation, the licensee must pay the fine within 30 calendar days from the date the citation becomes a final order. For licensees who do not dispute the matter, the citation penalty will become effective (a final order) and the case will be closed. Licensees who dispute the alleged violation(s) must file a written objection. An investigation is opened for licensees who dispute the allegations and for licensees who fail to respond to the citation. After the investigation is complete, the investigative report and supporting documents will go to the DBPR General Counsel so that the documents can be presented to the probable cause panel. A citation is considered public discipline and will appear on public records against the licensee (see Figure 6.1).

EXAMPLE: A licensee who fails to timely notify the DBPR of their current mailing address or email address or any change in the current mailing address or email address may be issued a citation and fined $1,000 for a first-time offense [Rule 61J2-10.038, F.A.C.].

WEBLINK

The administrative rule, Citation Authority, can be downloaded at https://www.flrules.org/gateway/RuleNo.asp?id=61J2-24.002.

FIGURE 6.1 ■ Types of Administrative Penalties

TYPES OF ADMINISTRATIVE PENALTIES

Penalty	Severity Level	Who Issues	Action Required by Licensee	Example
Notice of Noncompliance	First offense only of a minor violation that did not cause economic or physical harm or affect the public health, safety, or welfare	DBPR/DRE	Corrective, show proof action corrected within 15 calendar days	A sales associate was serving as an officer of a registered brokerage corporation. He must remove himself as an officer and show proof of removal.
Citation	No substantial threat to the public	DBPR/DRE	Pay a fine, corrective action of the violation, show proof action was corrected (fines range from $250 to $1,000), 30 calendar days to accept or reject the allegations specified in citation.	A licensee failed to timely notify the DBPR of the current mailing address or any change in the current mailing address or email address. The licensee was fined $1,000 for a first-time failure to notify.
Reprimand	Violation found but not cause to affect economic or physical harm to the public health, safety, and welfare of another	FREC	Stay out of trouble and do not repeat offense. Take corrective action if not already done so. May mandate additional education outside of normal CE.	A broker failed to register a branch office.

FIGURE 6.1 ■ Types of Administrative Penalties (Cont.)

TYPES OF ADMINISTRATIVE PENALTIES				
Penalty	**Severity Level**	**Who Issues**	**Action Required by Licensee**	**Example**
Denial	Administrative action	FREC	Loss of license, must start initial licensing procedures and take and pass the state exam	An applicant is denied an application for licensure due to attempting to cheat on the state exam.
Probation	Violation found that may have caused economic or physical harm or affected the public health, safety, and welfare of another	FREC	Complete the terms of the discipline. Probation issued with penalties such as fines, costs, and education. Once the fines and other terms are completed, the probation period ends.	A licensee uses false advertising to entice prospective tenants. The licensee is placed on probation until all fines, attendance at FREC meetings, suspension, and costs are satisfied.
Fine	May have caused economic or physical harm or affected the public health, safety, and welfare of another	FREC	Complete the terms of their discipline, pay fine within time period. Maximum fine of $5,000 per offense.	A licensee advertised in a false, deceptive, or misleading manner.
Suspension	May have caused economic or physical harm or affected the public health, safety, and welfare of another	FREC	Not to practice real estate during suspension period. The maximum suspension period is 10 years. Keep renewal requirements current; timely complete all other terms of discipline.	A broker failed to deposit escrow funds timely or did not deposit them in a trust account.
Revocation	Economic or physical harm to public health, safety, and welfare has been affected	FREC	Stop practicing real estate; no longer licensed. May also be assessed fine and costs.	A broker failed to account for or deliver an escrow check.

Reprimand. The least severe penalty that the FREC can issue is a **reprimand**. A legally sufficient complaint is received by the DRE and an investigation is conducted. The DBPR General Counsel will present to the probable-cause panel the charging documents with the investigation report and supporting documents. Probable cause is found to exist, and a formal complaint is issued against the licensee. The case is heard in an informal hearing. Sometimes, the evidence indicates that the licensee's actions did not harm the public; however, the violation of law does not fall within the guidelines in administrative rule that would allow for a notice of noncompliance or a citation. In such situations, the FREC hears the case and may decide that a reprimand is an appropriate penalty. A reprimand appears in public records as a violation of license law. The reprimand generally does not come with a fine; however, the licensee could be ordered to complete education or attend Commission meetings and would be required to pay the investigative costs (see Figure 6.1).

Denial. In the event an applicant commits a license law violation prior to being licensed, FREC has the authority to issue a denial of an application for licensure. The DBPR has the authority to initiate an investigation on its own if it has reasonable cause to believe that the applicant has violated license law. Once legal sufficiency is determined, the DBPR opens an investigation. The DRE investigator would follow the same procedures for investigating a licensed complaint (see Figure 6.1).

EXAMPLE: An individual submitted his application for a real estate sales associate license that met all of the requirements for licensure. During the state exam, the applicant is caught cheating by having answers written on the inside of his shirt. The applicant is subject to all license laws as is a current holder of a license. The actions were a violation under Chapter 455, F.S., relating to examination.

61J2-24.001, F.A.C.

Administrative Fine. The FREC may impose a maximum fine of $5,000 per violation of Chapter 455, F.S., and Chapter 475, F.S. The Commission has established by rule a list of violations and a range of recommended fines for each violation (see the following web link).

WEBLINK @

The administrative rule 61J2-24.001, Disciplinary Guidelines, can be downloaded at https://www.flrules.org/gateway/ruleNo.asp?id=61J2-24.001.

475.42, F.S.

475.25, F.S.

Suspension. The maximum period for which the FREC may suspend a license is 10 years. Florida statutes refer to many acts that are unlawful, any one of which may result in license suspension. Each unlawful act constitutes grounds for suspension or revocation of licensure, depending on the seriousness attached to the offense by the Commission. A second suspension for the same or a different violation may result in revocation of the license. Licensees must continue all renewal requirements during the period of suspension.

475.31, F.S.

475.25, F.S.

455.227, F.S.

Revocation. The most severe type of administrative penalty that the FREC is authorized to impose is revocation of a license. The FREC treats revocation of a license as permanent. At its discretion, the FREC is empowered to revoke a licensee's license for any of the causes that constitute grounds for suspension or denial.

When a real estate broker's license is suspended or revoked, all licenses issued to sales associates and broker associates who work for the penalized broker are in jeopardy of becoming inactive. Sales associates and broker associates have the options to go inactive, move their licenses to another registered broker, or remain with the current brokerage if another qualifying broker is registered. If the revoked or suspended broker is a qualifying broker for a partnership or corporation, affected sales and broker associates may not be affected if the brokerage has another qualifying broker in place (see "Vacancies of Office" in unit 5).

475.25(2), F.S.

Revoke without prejudice. A license may be revoked or canceled if it was issued through the mistake or inadvertence of the Commission. Such revocation or cancellation shall not prejudice any subsequent application for licensure filed by the person against whom such action was taken.

Probation. The FREC may, in addition to other disciplinary penalties, place a licensee on probation. **Probation** is an administrative penalty imposed by the FREC that allows the licensee to continue to practice real estate while completing conditions specified in a final order and while being monitored by the FREC for a specified period of time. The Commission is empowered to set the time period and conditions of probation. Probationary conditions may include, for example, requiring the licensee to attend a prelicense or post-license course or other educational offering, attend one or more Commission meetings, submit to and successfully complete the state-administered examination, or to be subject to periodic inspections by a DBPR/DRE investigator.

LICENSURE REISSUE

The Department shall reissue the license of a licensee against whom disciplinary action was taken upon certification by the Commission that the licensee has complied with all of the terms and conditions of the final order imposing discipline.

Reference: Section 475.25(3), F.S.

Practice Questions

15. If a license is issued by mistake, the license will be revoked without __________________.
16. The FREC may suspend a real estate license for up to __________ years.
17. The LEAST severe administrative penalty that the FREC can impose is a ________________.
18. Revocation of a license is ________________.
19. A notice of noncompliance may be issued for a minor ________________ offense.
20. A ________________ may be issued for a licensee's first-time failure to timely notify the DBPR of a change in current mailing address or email address.

6.7 CIVIL AND CRIMINAL PENALTIES

Civil Penalties

In civil court, one person files a case against another person because of a dispute between two parties. If a person is sued in civil court and loses the case, that person may be ordered to pay money to the other party. Civil cases generally have to do with disputes over money or property. The results of a court ruling in favor of the plaintiff (the person bringing a suit) could allow the individual to file a complaint with the DRE against the licensee, leading to possible discipline of the real estate licensee.

EXAMPLE: A buyer sues their broker for culpable negligence (carelessness) and misrepresentation in a residential real estate transaction because the broker failed to inform them that a new extension of a major highway would take a portion of their property. The buyer claimed the broker lives in the same subdivision as the property in dispute and the broker was sent a letter from the city months earlier informing the broker of the highway extension. The court ruled in favor of the buyer, ordering the broker to pay monetary damages and court costs to the buyer. The buyer may file an administrative complaint with the Division of Real Estate stating the broker violated license law per the court order.

Criminal Penalties

775.083, F.S.

455.2277, F.S.

Criminal penalties are issued by criminal courts. All imprisonment penalties or fines (except administrative fines) must be obtained in a court of law because the Commission lacks the authority to assess such penalties. The DBPR must refer any criminal matters to the state attorney general's office for investigation and possible prosecution. If a licensee gets arrested for a criminal violation that is not related to real estate, in most situations, the Commission cannot take disciplinary action against the licensee until the case has gone to court and a court decision has been entered. Figure 6.2 shows common criminal penalties.

775.082, F.S.

775.083, F.S.

455.2277, F.S.

Second-Degree Misdemeanor. Misdemeanors of the second degree are the least serious misdemeanor crimes in Florida. If the Florida legislature fails to classify a misdemeanor, then it is punishable as a misdemeanor of the second degree. Therefore, a criminal violation of real estate license law (Chapter 475) is a misdemeanor of the second degree unless specifically deemed in statute to be a more severe violation. For example, it is a misdemeanor of the second degree to advertise property or services in a fraudulent, false, deceptive, or misleading manner. The maximum criminal penalty for a second-degree misdemeanor is a fine of $500 and/or imprisonment for 60 days (see Figure 6.2).

475.453(3)(a), F.S.

First-Degree Misdemeanor. A first-degree misdemeanor is the most serious type of misdemeanor crime in Florida and, therefore, has harsher penalties. For example, Florida Statute 475.453, F.S., specifically states that it is a first-degree misdemeanor to fail to provide accurate and current rental information for a fee. The maximum penalty for a first-degree misdemeanor is a fine of $1,000 and/or one year in jail (see Figure 6.2).

475.42(1)(a), F.S.

455.228, F.S.

455.2175, F.S.

455.2275, F.S.

Third-Degree Felony. Felonies are the most serious type of crimes. A first-degree felony is a more serious type of felony crime than a second-degree felony or a third-degree felony. If the Florida legislature does not designate the degree of felony, the crime is a third-degree felony. The maximum penalty for a third-degree felony is a fine of $5,000 and/or five years in jail. Three third-degree felonies associated with license law are listed as follows:

1. Making misleading statements or giving false information on a DBPR license application
2. Conducting unlicensed activity, including providing real estate services for compensation without a real estate license
3. Theft or reproduction of a DBPR license exam

WEBLINK

The DBPR maintains a website dedicated to unlicensed activity at http://www.myfloridalicense.com/DBPR/unlicensed-activity/. Consumers may call 866-532-1440 to report unlicensed activity.

FIGURE 6.2 ■ **Maximum Criminal Penalties**

Criminal Penalty	Fine	Incarceration
Second-degree misdemeanor	$500	60 days
First-degree misdemeanor	$1,000	1 year
Third-degree felony	$5,000	5 years

Requirement to Self-Report

455.227(1)(t), F.S.

Florida Statute requires licensees to inform the Commission, in writing, within 30 days of being convicted or found guilty of a crime. The requirement for written notification also applies to licensees who have entered a plea of nolo contendere (no contest) or a plea of guilty, regardless of adjudication, to a crime, regardless of where the event occurred. Crimes that must be reported include misdemeanor offenses and felonies. To report the crime, the licensee should download and print the Criminal Self-Reporting Document, and mail the completed form to the Division of Real Estate.

CASE STUDY

FAILURE TO NOTIFY THE COMMISSION OF A CRIME

What follows is information concerning an actual disciplinary proceeding (Case No. 2015-017374). The information has been summarized for education purposes.

Facts:

A real estate sales associate was convicted in 2014 of three separate counts: criminal mischief (misdemeanor), battery (misdemeanor), and domestic battery (felony). The sales associate did not report the crimes to the DBPR.

Another licensee who received uninvited sexual advances from the sales associate conducted a background check of the sales associate and discovered the criminal offenses. A complaint was filed against the sales associate (herein referred to as Respondent).

The DBPR investigated and the FREC panel found probable cause. The Respondent appeared before the Commission in an informal hearing in February 2016.

Order:

Administrative fine of $1,500 and investigative costs of $172.

License was suspended for six months, beginning 30 days after the filing date of the final order.

Licensee was placed on probation for six months, during which time the Respondent must complete the 28-hour Reactivation course and attend two 2-day Commission meetings.

WEBLINK

The DBPR's Criminal Self Reporting Document can be downloaded from the Department's website at http://www.myfloridalicense.com/DBPR/criminal-self-reporting/.

Practice Questions

21. List three real estate violations that are third-degree felonies.
    1. ______________________________
    2. ______________________________
    3. ______________________________

22. Failing to provide accurate and current rental information for a fee is a misdemeanor of the __________ degree.

23. False and misleading advertising is a misdemeanor of the __________ degree.

6.8 REAL ESTATE RECOVERY FUND

475.482, F.S.

215.37, F.S.

The Real Estate Recovery Fund reimburses consumers who have been financially injured by a licensee. The recovery fund is available as a last resort to individuals who have been found by a Florida court to have suffered monetary damages from an act committed by a Florida real estate licensee.

Licensee Requirements. A licensee who has violated real estate license law and whose actions cause a consumer to seek reimbursement from the recovery fund must:

- have a current, valid, active real estate license at the time the real estate activity occurred;
- not have been a buyer, seller, landlord, or tenant in the transaction (nor an officer, director, member, or partner of a business entity that was the seller, buyer, landlord, or tenant); and
- have acted solely in the capacity of a real estate licensee in the transaction.

475.483, F.S.

Claimant Requirements. The injured consumer (claimant) seeking reimbursement from the recovery fund must meet certain specific requirements.

- The claimant must have filed a civil suit and received a judgment against the individual licensee (not against a real estate brokerage entity) based on a real estate transaction (real estate sale contract or lease agreement).
- The claimant must secure a *writ of execution* issued on the judgment and make a diligent attempt to satisfy the judgment from the assets of the licensee by conducting an asset search and showing that there were insufficient assets available to satisfy the judgment.
- If the licensee files bankruptcy and the bankruptcy court obstructs obtaining a judgment, the Commission may waive the requirement for a final judgment.
- The claimant must execute an affidavit stating the final judgment is not on appeal. (In the event the judgment was appealed, the claimant must state in an affidavit that the appellate proceedings have concluded and provide the outcome of the appeal.)
- The claimant cannot be the spouse of the offending licensee (the judgment debtor).

A real estate licensee who was the buyer or the seller (lessor or lessee) in a real estate transaction may also make a claim against the fund, provided the licensee did not act in the capacity of a real estate agent. In other words, if a licensed person is the buyer or the seller of real property and suffers monetary damages as a result of an act committed by another licensed broker or sales associate who acted in the capacity of an agent, the fact that the victim is licensed will not prevent the victim from seeking reimbursement from the fund.

Time Limit to File a Claim. A claim must be made within two years of either the alleged violation or discovery of the alleged violation. However, in no case may a claim for recovery be made more than four years after the date of the alleged violation.

475.484, F.S.

Maximum Payment from the Fund. Florida Statute sets limits on the maximum payment per real estate transaction and the maximum payment against a real estate licensee for multiple claims for recovery from the fund.

- Payment from the fund may not exceed $50,000 for a claim resulting from a real estate transaction, or the unsatisfied portion of the judgment claim, whichever is less, regardless of the number of claimants.
- Total payments for claims based on judgments against one real estate licensee may not exceed, in the aggregate, $150,000.

475.482(3) and (4), F.S.

Recovery Fund Fee. Recovery claim funds are accumulated by charging active and inactive licensees a recovery fund fee when a new license is issued or an existing license is renewed. A fee of $3.50 per year for brokers and $1.50 per year for sales associates is added to the license fee for both new and renewed licenses. The collection of these special fees stops when the fund reaches $1 million. Collection of fees begins again when the fund drops below $500,000. Disciplinary fines imposed by the FREC and collected by the DBPR are also transferred into the fund. The chief financial officer makes all payments from the fund following receipt of a voucher signed by the DBPR secretary.

475.484(1)(a), F.S.

Compensatory Damages Only. The recovery fund will reimburse a claimant for compensatory damages. Compensatory damages are actual monetary damages incurred by the claimant as opposed to punitive damages, which are awarded as punishment by the court. The fund will not reimburse a claimant for attorney's fees, court costs, interest, treble (triple) damages, or punitive damages.

475.484(7), F.S.

Mandatory Suspension. Suspension of a licensee's license is mandatory on payment of any amount from the Real Estate Recovery Fund in settlement of a claim to satisfy a judgment against any licensee as described in 475.482(1), F.S. The license is automatically suspended on the date of payment from the recovery fund and will not be restored until the licensee has repaid the amount paid from the fund in full (plus interest).

Recovery Fund Claims Resulting From an EDO

475.482(2), F.S.

475.483(3), F.S.

Recall from Unit 5 that when the parties to a real estate transaction make conflicting demands for escrowed funds that cannot be resolved, the broker must initiate one of four settlement procedures. One of the settlement procedures is to request an escrow disbursement order (EDO). In this settlement procedure, the Commission determines who is entitled to the disputed funds.

If a broker who complied with an escrow disbursement order (EDO) is later sued by the buyer or the seller, and as a result is required by a court of law to pay damages, the FREC is authorized to order reimbursement for the amount of the judgment against the broker up to $50,000. Furthermore, in cases involving compliance with an EDO, Florida statute provides for the Commission to pay the broker-defendant's reasonable attorneys' fees and court costs and, if the plaintiff prevails in court, the plaintiff's (person who filed the lawsuit) reasonable attorney's fees and court costs. However, punitive damages and interest are never paid by the recovery fund.

To be eligible for reimbursement, the broker must notify the FREC of the court case and the broker-defendant must diligently defend in court the disputed actions concerning the transaction. No disciplinary action will be taken against a broker who previously requested an EDO and followed its instructions. The broker's license will not be suspended, and no repayment to the fund is required.

EXAMPLE: A broker complied with an escrow disbursement order (EDO). The buyer was awarded the earnest money deposit of $12,000. The seller in the transaction sued the broker. The seller prevailed, and a judgment was filed against the broker that resulted in $12,000 actual monetary damages (earnest money deposit), $2,500 court costs, and seller's attorney fees of $3,500. The broker incurred attorney fees totaling $5,000. How much can the Commission authorize to disburse from the recovery fund?

$12,000 monetary damages + $2,500 court costs + $5,000 attorney fees + $3,500 seller's attorney fees = $23,000.

A broker who complies with an EDO may be reimbursed the amount of the EDO ($12,000 monetary damages), attorney fees ($5,000), and court costs ($2,500). Because the plaintiff (seller) prevailed in court, the fund is also authorized to pay the plaintiff's attorney fees of $3,500.

KEY CONCEPTS OF RECOVERY FUND CLAIMS

- The maximum payment from the fund for a single transaction is $50,000.
- The maximum payment in aggregate against one licensee is $150,000.
- The fund can never reimburse for punitive damages, treble damages, or interest.
- License suspension is mandatory upon payment from the fund (EDO exception).
- A broker who complies with an EDO may be reimbursed the amount of the EDO, attorney fees, and court costs; if the plaintiff prevails in court, the fund will reimburse the plaintiff's attorney fees and court costs.

CASE STUDY

REAL ESTATE RECOVERY FUND CASE

P. Warner, Claimant v. D. Hughes, Licensee

What follows is information concerning an actual Real Estate Recovery Fund Claim (RFC 2010018090). The information has been summarized for education purposes.

Findings of Fact:

1. Claimant is a nonlicensee and is unrelated to the licensee.
2. Licensee held a valid real estate license at the time of the transaction.
3. Hughes acted solely as a broker in accepting earnest money deposits totaling $44,800 related to claimant's purchase of three parcels of Florida real property.
4. None of the transactions closed, and the licensee failed to account for or return the deposits upon claimant's demand, and converted said sums to licensee's own use.
5. Claimant notified the FREC of his intention to make a claim against the licensee and the recovery fund, within two years of the date the claimant became aware of the licensee's misappropriation of escrow funds.
6. A final judgment against the individual licensee arising from the violation of his duties as a real estate licensee was entered in circuit court and the time for appeal of the judgment has passed.
7. Claimant has attempted to execute on the judgment but after reasonable inquiry has been unable to locate assets of the licensee.
8. The claim does not exceed the $50,000 cap imposed by Florida statute and total claims paid based on judgments against licensee do not exceed, in total, $150,000.

Order:

1. The FREC ordered payment from the recovery fund in the amount of $44,800 be made to the claimant.

2. The license of the licensee shall be automatically suspended upon the date of payment from the recovery fund and may not be reinstated until the licensee has repaid in full, plus interest, the amount paid from the recovery fund.
3. Within 30 days of the filing date of this order, the licensee may institute a review proceeding by filing the Notice of Appeal with the appropriate district court of appeals.

Practice Questions

24. List the types of costs that may be reimbursed to a broker who complies with an EDO and is later sued in court.

    1. ______________________________
    2. ______________________________
    3. ______________________________

25. The maximum payment from the fund for a single transaction is ______________.

26. The maximum payment based on multiple transactions against a single licensee is ______________.

27. The recovery fund can never reimburse for ___________ damages or ___________.

28. At the time of payment from the Real Estate Recovery Fund resulting from a licensee's misconduct, the license is ____________ until the licensee ____________ the fund for the claim (plus interest).

29. A claimant has obtained a judgment against a licensee in the amount of $30,500. The judgment includes a $10,000 escrow deposit (liquidated damages) and $10,000 in punitive damages. The remaining balance of the judgment is for the claimant's attorney fees and court costs. The claimant can be awarded __________ from the recovery fund.

30. A broker complied with an EDO. The buyer later sued the broker and was awarded a judgment of $25,000. Actual compensatory damages totaled $20,000. The judgment also included the buyer's attorney fees and court costs totaling $5,000. The real estate broker incurred attorney fees of $3,000. The FREC can authorize payment of __________ from the recovery fund.

6.9 SUMMARY OF IMPORTANT POINTS

- Seven steps comprise the complaint process:

1. A complaint (an alleged violation of a law or rule) is filed with the DBPR's Division of Real Estate (DRE).
2. If the complaint is legally sufficient, the DRE conducts an investigation and notifies the licensee-respondent. The complaint and the information obtained during the investigation are kept confidential until 10 days after probable cause has been found to exist. The investigative report is forwarded to the probable-cause panel. In rare situations deemed to be too serious to allow the licensee to continue to practice real estate while the complaint process proceeds, the DBPR secretary may issue a summary (emergency) suspension.

3. The probable-cause panel consists of two FREC members. The probable-cause panel determines whether probable cause exists.
4. If probable cause is found, the DBPR issues a formal (administrative) complaint. An Election of Rights is mailed with the complaint to the licensee. The licensee has 21 days to (1) not dispute the allegations of fact and request an informal hearing, (2) dispute the allegations of fact and request a formal hearing, or (3) not dispute the allegations of fact and waive the right to be heard. The licensee-respondent may enter into a stipulation (an agreement as to the facts of the case and the penalty reached between the attorneys for the DRE and the licensee). Stipulations must be approved by the FREC for them to become effective.
5. If there are no disputed facts, the Commission (probable-cause panel members are excused) decides the case and imposes the penalty in an informal hearing held during a regular FREC meeting. If the licensee-respondent requests a formal hearing or if the respondent disputes the allegations, the case is heard by a Florida administrative law judge in a formal hearing. The administrative law judge prepares a recommended order.
6. The FREC imposes the final order (members of the probable-cause panel do not participate). The final order becomes effective 30 days after it has been entered.
7. The licensee-respondent may appeal the final order.

- The FREC may impose an administrative penalty for violations of law or rules and regulations. The DRE may issue a citation for violations that are of no substantial threat to the public. Such citations carry fines ranging from $100 to $500. The DRE may issue a notice of noncompliance as a first response to a minor violation. The FREC may punish more serious offenses by issuing fines of up to $5,000 for each violation of Chapters 455 and 475 and/or a suspension of up to 10 years. In extreme cases, the FREC may revoke a license.
- Failing to provide accurate and current rental information for a fee is a misdemeanor of the first degree, punishable in a court of law by a fine of up to $1,000 and/or by imprisonment of up to one year.
- Misdemeanors of the second degree are punishable by a fine of up to $500 and/or by imprisonment of up to 60 days.
- Falsifying a license application, unlicensed activity, and theft or reproduction of a license exam are felonies of the third degree. The penalty, per offense, is a fine of up to $5,000, up to five years in jail, or both.
- Individuals can be reimbursed from the Real Estate Recovery Fund for monetary damages as a result of license law violations by a licensee. Claims are limited to $50,000 per transaction or the unsatisfied portion of a judgment claim, whichever is less, and no more than $150,000 in the aggregate against one licensee involving multiple transactions. The license is automatically suspended upon payment from the fund until the fund is reimbursed (unless EDO exception).

UNIT 6 EXAM

1. A person is eligible to seek recovery from the Real Estate Recovery Fund if that
   a. person received a final judgment against a licensee in a legal action and the case was based on a real estate brokerage transaction (assuming no specific exceptions apply).
   b. person is a licensed broker who acted as the agent in the transaction that is the subject of the claim.
   c. person's claim is based on a real estate transaction in which the broker did not hold a valid, current, and active license at the time of the transaction.
   d. person's claim is based on a licensee who was the seller of the property.

2. The decision as to whether probable cause exists is made by a majority vote of the
   a. Commission.
   b. Commission or the Department, as appropriate.
   c. administrative law judges.
   d. probable-cause panel.

3. Which action would cause a license to be revoked without prejudice?
   a. A licensee accepted an earnest money deposit on a property that he knew was encumbered by an undisclosed lien.
   b. The broker obtained his license by means of fraud, misrepresentation, or concealment.
   c. A sales associate received her license as a result of an administrative error by the Division of Real Estate.
   d. For the referral of real estate business, a licensee shared a commission with a person (not party to the transaction) who did not have a real estate license.

4. Which offense is a misdemeanor of the first degree?
   a. Failing to provide current and accurate rental information for a fee
   b. Publishing false or misleading information to induce a buyer to purchase real property
   c. Failing to timely deposit earnest money into the escrow account
   d. Failing to timely notify the FREC of conflicting demands

5. Who prepares and submits a recommended order of findings and conclusions in a complaint case?
   a. Court of law
   b. Administrative law judge
   c. Probable-cause panel
   d. The DBPR

6. Any order issued by the DBPR secretary or a legally appointed designee that results from circumstances posing an immediate danger to the public's health, safety, or welfare is called a
   a. petition for review.
   b. stay of enforcement.
   c. summary or emergency suspension.
   d. license revocation.

7. A buyer gives the broker a $47,500 earnest money deposit. The broker defrauds the buyer of the $47,500. The buyer sues the broker and is awarded a judgment in the amount of $62,500 for the original $47,500 deposit plus $15,000 for punitive damages. Because the buyer was unable to collect the judgment from the broker, the buyer requests relief from the Florida Real Estate Recovery Fund. How much can the buyer receive from the recovery fund?
   a. $15,000
   b. $47,500
   c. $50,000
   d. $62,500

8. The DRE is authorized to investigate a written complaint filed against a licensee
   a. if the alleged complaint is legally sufficient.
   b. only if the claimant has been harmed by the actions of the licensee.
   c. only if the alleged violation was committed in the state of Florida.
   d. only if all of these conditions have been met.

9. Which administrative penalty is issued by the Division of Real Estate?
   a. Citation
   b. Probation
   c. Suspension
   d. Reprimand

10. A sales associate was issued a formal administrative complaint following a probable-cause determination. The associate was frightened after receiving the complaint and chose to avoid responding to the Election of Rights form. What is the likely outcome of failing to respond to the Election of Rights form?
    a. The case will be heard in a formal hearing before an administrative law judge.
    b. The case will proceed in an informal waiver hearing before the Commission.
    c. A subpoena will be issued by the DBPR to require the licensee to appear before the Commission.
    d. The DRE will send a notice of noncompliance to the licensee's address of record.

11. A licensee received a citation for $1,000 for operating as a sales associate without a registered employer. The sales associate feels the citation was issued in error. How should the sales associate proceed?
    a. File a written objection within 30 days
    b. File a written objection within 15 days
    c. Request a hearing before the FREC within 30 days
    d. Request a civil court hearing within 15 days

12. When payment from the Real Estate Recovery Fund is made to satisfy a claim against a licensee and the claim was not the result of the broker complying with an escrow disbursement order, the Commission's action against the licensee must be
    a. a citation.
    b. probation.
    c. mandatory suspension.
    d. emergency suspension.

13. Florida Statute 455 requires real estate licensees to notify the DBPR of a conviction, plea, or adjudication of a crime within how many days?
    a. 10
    b. 15
    c. 30
    d. 60

14. The Florida Real Estate Commission may NOT impose which disciplinary penalty?
    a. Imprisonment
    b. Probation
    c. Administrative fine
    d. Denial of a license application

15. The collective amount to be paid from the Real Estate Recovery Fund as a result of any one real estate transaction may NOT exceed
    a. $25,000.
    b. $50,000.
    c. $75,000.
    d. $150,000.

UNIT 7

FEDERAL AND STATE LAWS PERTAINING TO REAL ESTATE

LEARNING OBJECTIVES

When you have completed this unit, you will be able to accomplish the following.

- Describe the features of the Civil Rights Acts of 1866, 1964, and 1968 and explain the significance of the *Jones v. Mayer* court case.
- List the property exempt from the 1968 Fair Housing Act and describe the types of discriminatory acts that are prohibited under the Fair Housing Act.
- Describe the objectives and major provisions of the Americans with Disabilities Act.
- Describe the major provisions of the Interstate Land Sales Full Disclosure Act.
- Describe the provisions of the Florida Residential Landlord and Tenant Act.

KEY TERMS

blockbusting	Fair Housing Act	public accommodations
Civil Rights Act of 1866	familial status	redlining
disability	property report	steering

INTRODUCTION

For many families, the purchase of a home is the largest single investment they will make during their lifetime. The federal government and all state governments have enacted laws to ensure that the public interest in real estate is adequately protected. This unit highlights some of the laws most important to Florida real estate practitioners. Licensees should study these laws to make certain they comply with these laws in order to better serve the public.

7.1 FEDERAL FAIR HOUSING LAW

Civil Rights Act of 1866

The **Civil Rights Act of 1866** prohibits any type of discrimination based on race in any real estate transaction (sale or rental) without exception (see Figure 7.1). This law is still in force today. A suit can be filed in a federal court under the 1866 Civil Rights Act. The court may award actual (monetary) damages and punitive damages for racial discrimination.

FIGURE 7.1 ■ Protections Under Civil Rights Acts and Fair Housing Act

Law	Type of Real Estate	Protected Class
Civil Rights Act of 1866	All real estate (residential and commercial)	Race only
Civil Rights Act of 1964	Public accommodations and public facilities	Race, color, religion, and national origin; Ended racial segregation
Fair Housing Act (as amended)	Sale or rental of single-family and multifamily residential property, including advertising sales and rentals, financing, and brokerage services	Race, color, religion, sex, national origin, familial status, and disability

42 U.S.C. § 1982 states that "all citizens of the United States shall have the same right, in every State and Territory, as is enjoyed by white citizens thereof to inherit, purchase, lease, sell, hold, and convey real and personal property."

WEBLINK

To read about the Civil Rights Act of 1866, visit http://law.cornell.edu/uscode/text/42/1982.

Jones v. Mayer. Joseph Lee Jones filed a complaint in 1965 in district court alleging that Alfred H. Mayer Company had refused to sell him a home because he was black. The famous legal case *Jones v. Alfred H. Mayer Company* reached the U.S. Supreme Court in 1968. The court upheld the Civil Rights Act of 1866, which prohibits all racial discrimination without exception. The Supreme Court declared that the 1866 act still applies today and that it prohibits all racial discrimination (public and private) in the sale of all real property (residential and commercial). Remember, when race is involved, no exemptions apply. This court decision allows a person who has experienced discrimination on the basis of race to sue the individuals who committed the alleged discrimination despite certain exemptions in the Civil Rights Act of 1968 (discussed later) when the discrimination is based on race.

Civil Rights Act of 1964 (Titles II and III)

The Civil Rights Act of 1964 was landmark legislation that ended racial segregation in schools, workplaces, and public accommodations. Title II of the 1964 act prohibits discrimination on the basis of race, color, religion, and national origin in places of public accommodation engaged in interstate commerce, including hotels, motels, restaurants, gas stations, and places of entertainment. Title III prohibits state and municipal governments from denying access to public facilities on the grounds of race, color, religion, or national origin (see Figure 7.1).

Civil Rights Act of 1968: The Fair Housing Act

The **Fair Housing Act** (Act) is contained in Title VIII of the Civil Rights Act of 1968. The Fair Housing Act of 1968, including amendments, prohibits discrimination on the basis of race, color, religion, sex, and national origin when selling or renting residential property. This law covers residential dwellings and apartments (single-family and multifamily), as well as vacant land acquired for the purpose of constructing residential dwellings. The act prohibits discrimination in sales, leasing, advertising sales or rentals, financing, and brokerage services.

WEBLINK

Title VIII of the Civil Rights Act of 1968 (Fair Housing Act) is published in the United States Code and is available at https://www.law.cornell.edu/uscode/text/42/chapter-45/subchapter-I.

Fair Housing Amendments Act. In 1988, Congress amended the Fair Housing Act of 1968 to include two additional protected classes: **familial status** and **disability**. The Fair Housing Act, as amended, prohibits discrimination in sales, leasing, the advertising of sales and rentals, financing, and brokerage services. Today, the Fair Housing Act includes seven protected classes: race, color, religion, sex, disability, familial status, and national origin. The protected classes are described in detail in Figure 7.2.

Sexual Orientation and Gender Identity. In 2021, President Biden signed an executive order requiring the Department of Housing and Urban Development (HUD) to enforce the Fair Housing Act to prohibit discrimination based on sexual orientation and gender identity. HUD extended the protections based on sex discrimination to include sexual orientation and gender identity.

FIGURE 7.2 ■ **Fair Housing Protected Classes**

Protected Class	Description
Race	A family, tribe, or group of people coming from the same common ancestors. For example, a seller instructs the real estate associate to find another buyer because the buyer making an offer to purchase is African American.
Color	Pigmentation or shade of a person's skin. For example, a person is discriminated against because of albinism.
Religion	One's spiritual beliefs. For example, discrimination against a person of Islamic faith.
Sex	Sexual orientation, gender, gender identity, and sexual harassment. A landlord may not take into account one's gender identity as a condition of renting an apartment.
Disability	Physical or mental impairments that limit major life activities. For example, refusing to allow a disabled individual to have a service animal live in the apartment.
Familial status	Families with one or more children under 18 and pregnant women. For example, requiring families with young children to rent apartments only on the first floor of a midrise building.
National origin	The country of birth or from which a person's ancestors came. For example, discrimination against an individual because the individual's last name is of Greek origin.

Discrimination in General. Legal forms of discrimination are present in everyday society. Some property owners may discriminate against smokers by refusing to rent to tenants who smoke. To refuse to rent to smokers is not illegal. However, when discrimination is directed at a "protected class" that is designated under law, it is illegal. There are many characteristics and behaviors that have no protection. For example, pet ownership is not a protected class.

State and local governments may expand the classes afforded fair housing protection in their jurisdiction. Provided a state includes the seven protected classes of the federal Fair Housing Act, the state may include additional categories. If a county or a city decides to pass a fair housing ordinance, it must include the protected classes designated under its state's fair housing statute. Because protected classes for fair housing vary from jurisdiction to jurisdiction, it is important that the licensee be familiar with the laws enacted at each level of government.

There are some categories of people that in some situations are considered protected classes and in other settings are not. For example, no protection is given under the Fair Housing Act to individuals based on age, occupation, and marital status. However, there are federal laws that protect people based on age and marital status when seeking credit (see "Equal Credit Opportunity Act," Unit 13).

Equal Housing Opportunity Poster. The 1988 amendment also created the equal housing opportunity poster. The poster features the equal housing logo and a statement pledging adherence to the Fair Housing Act. The poster is available without charge from the Department of Housing and Urban Development (HUD). The poster must be displayed at real estate offices and other businesses involved in the housing industry. In the event a discrimination complaint is made against a broker, HUD considers failure to prominently display the equal housing opportunity poster in the broker's place of business as evidence of discrimination.

For additional information regarding the Fair Housing poster and other outreach materials offered by HUD, visit https://www.hud.gov/program_offices/fair_housing_equal_opp/outreachtools (scan QR code).

Practice Questions

1. Circle the corresponding letter to indicate the protected classes under the Fair Housing Act, as amended.
   a. Familial status
   b. Age
   c. Religion
   d. Marital status
   e. National origin

2. The equal housing opportunity poster must be displayed at real estate ____________ and other businesses involved in the ____________ industry.

3. When ____________ is involved in ____________ real estate transaction, there are no exceptions.

4. The Civil Rights Act of 1866 prohibits discrimination based on ______________ in both ______________ and ______________ real estate.

5. The Fair Housing Act is contained in the __________ __________ __________ of __________.

7.2 PROVISIONS OF THE FAIR HOUSING ACT AS AMENDED

The Fair Housing Act applies to single-family residential property and multifamily housing. Commercial property is not covered under the Fair Housing Act.

Residential Real Estate Transactions Covered Under the Fair Housing Act

The Fair Housing Act, as amended, covers the following residential real estate:

- Government owned residential property
- Privately owned residential property if a broker is employed to sell or rent the property
- Single-family homes owned by a business entity (such as a development corporation or partnership)
- Sale or rental of single-family property by an individual who owns four or more houses
- Multifamily housing of five or more units
- Multifamily housing of four or fewer units, if the owner does not reside in one of the units

Residential Real Estate Transactions Exempted Under the Fair Housing Act

Certain residential real estate transactions are exempted under Fair Housing Act provided a real estate brokerage was not involved in the transaction and no discriminatory advertising was used to market the property:

1. The sale or rental of a single-family residential property, provided the seller does not own more than three dwellings, and no more than one house is sold during a two-year period in which the owner was not the most recent resident.
2. Rental of multifamily residential property of four or fewer units and the owner resides in one of the units.

Discriminatory advertising includes print ads, billboards, direct mail, and promotional materials such as flyers and handouts. Remember, even though the previous transactions are exempted under the Fair Housing Act, discriminatory advertising may not be used. Any advertising that implies preference against one of the protected classes is a violation of the Fair Housing Act. Furthermore, if racial discrimination occurs in any real estate transaction, the individual may be liable under the Civil Rights Act of 1866.

> **EXAMPLE:** A property owner owns a four-unit multifamily dwelling. The owner lives in one of the units. The owner advertises a vacant unit for rent, stating that no children are allowed because the existing residents are all couples with no children.
>
> The owner resides in one of the units in a four-unit multifamily dwelling. The rental transaction would be exempt from the Fair Housing Act, *provided* the owner did not use discriminatory advertising to market the unit. Advertising that no children are allowed is discriminatory advertising against a protected class (familial status).

Housing for Older Persons. Certain housing for older persons is exempt from the familial status protection under the Fair Housing Act, provided:

- all units are occupied by persons 62 years of age or older; or
- at least 80% of the units are occupied by one or more persons 55 years of age or older, and housing policies are published and followed that demonstrate an intent to be housing for persons 55 and older.

Special Exemptions Under the Act. Housing operated by religious organizations and private clubs is exempt from the Fair Housing Act, provided the housing is not operated for commercial purposes:

- Religious organizations may restrict dwelling units they own or operate to members of their religion if the organization does not otherwise discriminate in accepting its membership.
- Private clubs may restrict rental or occupancy of its units to its members.

Prohibited Activities. Discrimination against any of the protected classes in the sale or rental of housing, financing of housing, or the provision of brokerage services is illegal. It is a violation of the Fair Housing Act to do any of the following activities:

- Channel homeseekers to or away from particular neighborhoods because they are members of a protected class (commonly called **steering**)
- Use the entry, or rumor of the entry, of a protected class into a neighborhood to persuade owners to sell (commonly called **blockbusting**)

- Deny loans or insurance coverage by a lender or an insurer that present different terms or conditions for homes in certain neighborhoods (commonly called **redlining**)
- Refuse to rent to, sell to, negotiate with, or deal with a member of a protected class
- Quote different terms, conditions, or privileges for buying or renting
- Advertise that housing is available only to people of a certain race, color, religion, sex, national origin, disability, or familial status
- Deny membership in or use of any real estate service, broker's organization, or multiple listing service
- Make false statements concerning the availability of housing for inspection, rent, or sale

WEBLINK

Visit the FHEO website for housing discrimination examples https://www.hud.gov/program_offices/fair_housing_equal_opp/examples_housing_discrimination.

Enforcement of the Fair Housing Act

Federal fair housing laws are enforced by the Department of Housing and Urban Development (HUD) and the Department of Justice (DOJ). HUD's Office of Fair Housing and Equal Opportunity (FHEO) is charged with enforcing many laws, including the Fair Housing Act, the Civil Rights Act, and the Americans with Disabilities Act. The FHEO is charged with the following responsibilities:

- Investigate fair housing complaints.
- Assist individuals with obtaining agreements to resolve complaints.
- Enforce fair housing laws.

Investigate Fair Housing Complaints. Complaints must be filed within one year of the alleged discrimination. FHEO will either investigate the complaint or refer the complaint to another agency to investigate. As part of HUD's Fair Housing Assistance Program, FHEO may refer a fair housing complaint to a state or local government agency for investigation.

When an individual reports possible discrimination, the FHEO may interview the individual to obtain additional information. If a formal complaint can be filed under one of the laws the FHEO enforces, the FHEO will draft a formal complaint. The person making the complaint reviews and signs the complaint. The FHEO then notifies all affected parties that a complaint has been filed.

After a formal complaint is filed, the FHEO investigates the allegations. The party against whom the complaint has been filed is given an opportunity to respond to the allegations. The investigator may interview the parties and witnesses, obtain documents, and inspect property. When the investigation is completed, FHEO prepares a written report of its findings. HUD will issue a determination as to whether reasonable cause exists to believe that discrimination has occurred. In the event a charge of discrimination is issued, the parties have 20 days after receiving notice to decide whether a party wants to have the case tried in federal court. If no one makes such request during the 20-day election period, the case is heard by a HUD administrative law judge (ALJ).

Agreements to Resolve Complaints. The Fair Housing Act requires HUD to bring the parties together to attempt conciliation. Throughout the investigation, both before and after a formal complaint is filed, the FHEO will attempt to assist the parties to resolve the complaint. The choice to conciliate the complaint is voluntary on the part of both parties. If the parties agree, the FHEO will mediate the complaint and have the parties sign a conciliation agreement. After both parties sign the agreement, the investigation is closed and the FHEO monitors compliance with the agreement. If either party breaches the agreement, FHEO can recommend that the U.S. Department of Justice (DOJ) file suit to enforce it.

Enforce Fair Housing Laws. The government may bring a fair housing case or other civil rights case based on the findings of the investigation. Cases before HUD ALJs are handled by HUD's Office of General Counsel, and civil trial cases in the federal courts are handled by the DOJ. The DOJ may initiate a suit in federal court if there is a breach in the conciliation agreement or there is a pattern of discrimination or if a number of persons have been injured. The Fair Housing Act allows for awards of compensatory (monetary) damages, equitable relief (such as requiring that housing be made available to the complainant), and punitive damages.

EXAMPLE: A charge of discrimination was issued by the county's Fair Housing Council and filed with HUD, alleging that Mr. Parker (Respondent) made a dwelling unavailable, imposed different terms and conditions in the rental of a dwelling, and made a discriminatory statement, based on familial status. The Regional Director of the Office of Fair Housing and Equal Opportunity (FHEO) determined that reasonable cause existed to believe that a discriminatory housing practice had occurred.

The subject property was an 18-unit property consisting of eight two-bedroom units and ten three-bedroom units. Respondent owned and managed the rental of the subject property. According to the Planning and Zoning Department, there were no applicable ordinances limiting the number of family members who may occupy a bedroom in a dwelling. (Note: Local occupancy ordinances that specify the number of persons per bedroom are enforceable.) At the time of the alleged discrimination, the Complainant, Ms. Brown had two children who were ages 8 and 17. Complainant called the phone number on the for-rent sign and heard the following voicemail recording:

Hi. This is Mike Parker of Parker Apartments in Richmond Hill. I have two- and three-bedroom units in the Richmond Height area. I require a 12-month lease and don't allow pets. No more than one child is allowed in a 2-bedroom or two children in a 3-bedroom. Non-smokers are preferred.

The voicemail recording demonstrates three violations of the Fair Housing Act (Act). The Respondent:

- Made housing unavailable based on familial status.
- Imposed different terms and conditions in connection with the rental of a dwelling based on familial status.
- Made a statement that indicated a preference, limitation, or discrimination based on familial status or an intention to make such a preference, limitation, or discrimination with respect to the sale or rental of a dwelling.

The Secretary of HUD, through the Office of the General Counsel, charged Respondents with discriminatory housing practices in violation of the Act and the following recommended order was issued:

- Award damages to fully compensate Complainant for the actual damages.
- Award a civil penalty against Respondent for each violation of the Act.
- Award additional relief as may be appropriate.
- Mandate Respondent, agents, and employees of the Respondent attend training that addresses the Act's prohibitions against familial status discrimination.
  Reference: *Brown v. Parker;* FHEO nos. 04-15-0533-8 and 04-15-0938-8.

WEBLINK @

For additional information regarding the complaint process, visit https://www.hud.gov/program_offices/fair_housing_equal_opp/complaint-process.

Florida Fair Housing Act

760.20, F.S.
760.37, F.S.

Florida Statute 760 contains the Florida Civil Rights Act and the Fair Housing Act. These state laws are similar in scope to the federal Civil Rights Act and the federal Fair Housing Act. Florida's Fair Housing Act prohibits discrimination in the following:

- Sale or rental of housing
- Brokerage services
- Financing of housing or in residential real estate transactions
- Land use decisions and in permitting of development

The Florida Commission on Human Relations enforces the Florida Fair Housing Act. The Commission on Human Relations works cooperatively with its federal counterpart (HUD). When a case of discrimination is filed with the Commission on Human Relations, it is usually also filed with HUD. As with federal complaints, complaints of housing discrimination submitted to the Commission on Human Relations must be filed in writing within one year of the alleged discrimination. If the Commission is unable to obtain voluntary compliance or it has reasonable cause to believe that a discriminatory practice has occurred, the Commission may institute an administrative proceeding under Chapter 120, F.S. The Commission on Human Relations may issue quantifiable damages and reasonable attorney's fees and costs to the aggrieved party. The parties also have the right to institute a civil action in state court.

Responsibility and Liability of Real Estate Licensees

Real estate licensees have a legal and ethical responsibility to ensure all customers have equal access to housing. Licensees should know the federal, state, and local governments' protected classes and who is not protected, such as smokers and illegal drug users. A real estate licensee should follow the fair housing laws in every aspect of their business, including advertising, written and verbal conversations, and social media. When discovered, licensees should report fair housing violations. The liability of violating such laws is significant. A fair housing violation could lead to HUD-imposed fines, restitution to the victims, FREC-imposed administrative fines, and even the revocation of one's real estate license. Remember, when advertising, always describe the property and *not* the potential buyer. It is acceptable to advertise that the licensee has a knowledge of languages other than English. When recently licensed sales associates are choosing a broker, sales associates should inquire of the real estate broker's fair housing policy and education program for associates and staff members to ensure the entire workforce understands what is expected of them when working with clients, future customers, and the public in general.

KEY POINTS OF CIVIL RIGHTS ACT OF 1866 AND FAIR HOUSING ACT, AS AMENDED

- *Jones v. Mayer* U.S. Supreme Court case upholds Civil Rights Act of 1866.
- Discrimination based on race is prohibited in ALL real estate transactions.
- Seven protected classes under Fair Housing Act, as amended.
- The Fair Housing poster must be displayed at real estate offices and businesses involved in the housing industry.
- Fair Housing Act applies to ONLY residential property (commercial property is not covered by the Act).
- Some real estate transactions are exempted under Fair Housing Act provided a real estate brokerage was not involved in the transaction; and no discriminatory advertising was used to market the property:
  - The sale or rental of a single-family residential property, provided the seller does not own more than three dwellings, and no more than one house is sold during a two-year period in which the owner was not the most recent resident.
  - Rental of multifamily residential property of four or fewer units and the owner resides in one of the units.
- Certain housing for older persons is exempt from the familial status protection.
- Religious organizations may restrict dwelling units they own or operate to members of their religion, provided the organization does not discriminate in accepting its membership.
- Private clubs may restrict rental units to its members.
- The Fair Housing Act prohibits certain activities including, steering, blockbusting, and redlining.

CASE STUDY

FAIR HOUSING CASE

U.S. Department of HUD, on behalf of Steve Times and Betty Brinson, Complainant v. Annette Banai, Janos Banai, Sylvia Arias, and Manhattan Group Real Estate, Inc., Respondents

What follows is information concerning federal case (HUDALJ 04-93-2060-8). The information has been summarized for education purposes.

In the aftermath of Hurricane Andrew, Steve Times and Betty Brinson (Complainants) sought to rent a place to live until repairs could be made to their home.

Janos and Annette Banai (Respondents) resided in New York. They owned a home in Hollywood, Florida, that they rented out on previous occasions using the services of a rental agent. Sylvia Arias was a licensed sales associate for Manhattan Group Real Estate, Inc. The Respondents listed their residence with the brokerage. The Respondents indicated that they wanted to rent the residence to hurricane disaster victims.

The Complainants responded to a newspaper advertisement placed by Arias and her brokerage firm on behalf of the owners. Arias showed the Complainants the house, and the Complainants indicated they wanted to rent the home. Before finalizing the rental, Arias called the Respondent to discuss the agreement. Arias told the Respondents that she had found "a very nice couple to rent the house." Ms. Banai (the Respondent) asked "what kind of people" they were. The conversation included, in part:

Respondent: "Are they Hispanic?"

Arias: "No."

Respondent: "Are they black?"

Arias: "Yes."

Respondent: "No, I cannot rent the house to black people because I live in part of the house and because of what the neighbors will say about something like that."

Arias: "We are not supposed to discriminate in that way."

Respondent: "Look for someone else."

Arias contacted the Complainants and told them, in part:

Arias: "I am very, very sorry to tell you that you are not going to be able to rent the house. I contacted the owners, and the owners said they did not want persons of color in their house."

Complainants: "What does that mean, because we're black?"

Arias: "Yes."

Arias showed the Complainants other rentals. Arias also reported the incident to her broker. The broker asked why Arias had identified the couple's race to the owners. Arias answered that the Respondents had asked her. The broker told Arias that she should have refused to respond to the question and that she should have stated that the race of the applicants is irrelevant to the transaction.

The broker sent a letter to the Respondents indicating that Manhattan Group could not be a party to any type of discriminatory practices and that the owners should rent to the couple. Further, if the owners refused to rent to the couple, Manhattan Group was withdrawing from the listing agreement with the owners.

Findings:

- A preponderance of evidence directly and unambiguously establishes that Banai refused to rent to Complainants solely because they were black.
- By answering the owner's inquiry concerning race, the sales associate violated fair housing law. Arias "facilitated and participated in Ms. Banai's refusal to rent to Complainants and thereby made a dwelling unavailable because of race [and] color."
- Because Arias was a sales associate for Manhattan Group Real Estate, Inc., at the time Arias violated the act, the brokerage is vicariously liable for Arias's actions.

Order:

- Respondents Annette and Janos Banai, Sylvia Arias, and Manhattan Group Real Estate, Inc., are permanently enjoined from discriminating with respect to housing because of race or color.
- The Banais were found guilty of discrimination and ordered to pay a $10,000 civil penalty to the secretary of HUD and compensatory damages of $35,000 each to Times and Brinson for emotional distress, inconvenience, and lost housing opportunity.
- Arias was fined $100 and required to attend fair housing training.

Appeal:

- Annette and Janos Banai appealed to the United States Court of Appeals, Eleventh Circuit (NO. 95-4377). The appeals court affirmed the $70,000 in compensatory damages to Steve Times and Betty Brinson.

To learn more about the Fair Housing Act, download the booklet *Equal Opportunity for All* at https://www.hud.gov/sites/documents/FHEO_BOOKLET_ENG.PDF (scan QR code).

Practice Questions

6. List the two categories of residential housing covered by the 1968 Fair Housing Act.
    1. ______________________________
    2. ______________________________
7. Lenders who deny loan applications in certain neighborhoods based on social or economic considerations of the geographic area are practicing ______________.
8. ______________ is the practice of channeling potential buyers to or away from a particular neighborhood because of their race, national origin, or other protected class.
9. Religious organizations may restrict dwelling units they own or operate to ______________ of their religion.

7.3 AMERICANS WITH DISABILITIES ACT OF 1990

The Americans with Disabilities Act (ADA) is a federal statute that protects employment and accessibility rights of individuals with mental and physical disabilities.

Access to Public Transportation, Public Accommodations, and Commercial Facilities. The act prohibits discrimination in places of public accommodations and in commercial facilities. **Public accommodations** are facilities open to the public, including sales and rental establishments, hotels, restaurants, and shopping centers. Individuals with disabilities may not be denied access to public transportation, public accommodations, and commercial facilities.

New Construction and Renovation. Public accommodations and commercial facilities must be newly constructed or renovated, if readily achievable, to meet accessibility standards. Criteria for determining whether a public accommodation or a commercial facility can be made accessible is set forth in the act. If readily achievable, structural, architectural, and communication barriers must be removed. Examples of alterations include widening doorways, making cuts in street curbs, lowering telephones, installing ramps, and providing ADA-compliant toilets and grab bars in restrooms.

ADA requirements also apply to private entities that own, lease, or operate commercial facilities, including real estate brokerage offices, even if the broker's office is located in a private residence. Buyers who purchase older homes with plans to turn the structures into offices may face costly unanticipated expenses to modify or upgrade the facility to ADA standards. If the broker's office is in a private residence, the accessibility standards apply to that portion of the home used exclusively as an office and to those portions of the house available to customers, including bathrooms. The accessibility standards do not apply to any portion of the home used exclusively as a personal residence.

553.503, F.S.

553.504, F.S.

Florida Americans With Disabilities Accessibility Implementation Act. This Florida statute adopts the federal standards for accessibility for disabled persons. The intent of the Florida law is to incorporate into state law the accessibility requirements of the Americans with Disabilities Act of 1990, as amended, and to obtain and maintain U.S. Department of Justice (DOJ) certification of the Florida Accessibility Code for Building Construction as equivalent to federal standards for accessibility of buildings, structures, and facilities to ensure certification of the state's construction standards and codes. Accessibility guidelines and specifications are available from local building inspectors and the DOJ. Local municipal or county governments are responsible for enforcing compliance with the codes.

WEBLINK

To learn about the ADA, visit https://www.ada.gov/#mainContent.

Practice Questions

10. __________ ________________ are facilities open to the public including sales and rental establishments, hotels, restaurants, and shopping centers.

11. Individuals with disabilities may not be denied ______________ to public ______________, public ______________, and ______________ facilities.

7.4 INTERSTATE LAND SALES FULL DISCLOSURE ACT (ILSA)

Title 15, Ch. 42, Sec. 1701-1720, USC

The advertising and sale or lease of real estate in one state to buyers in another state is subject to federal regulations. The Interstate Land Sales Full Disclosure Act (ILSA) is intended to prevent fraudulent marketing schemes when land is sold without being seen by purchasers. ILSA requires disclosure of full and accurate information regarding the property to prospective buyers before they decide to buy. ILSA is administered by the Consumer Financial Protection Bureau. Developers must register subdivisions of 100 or more lots with the bureau before they can offer unimproved lots in interstate commerce by telephone or through the mail.

Property Report. Developers of 25 or more lots must provide buyers with a **property report** prior to signing the sale contract. The property report contains important information about the property. Purchasers who timely receive the property report may cancel the contract up until midnight of the seventh day following signing the contract. Purchasers who were not given the property report before signing the contract may bring action to revoke the contract anytime within two years from the date of signing. The sale and purchase contract must clearly state the purchaser's right(s) to cancel. Developers who market subdivisions of fewer than 25 lots are exempt from registering under ILSA.

Practice Questions

12. Developers of 25 or more lots must provide buyers with a ____________ __________.

13. Prospective buyers who have received the property report before signing the sale contract may cancel the contract up until midnight of the ____________ day after signing the contract.

14. Subdivisions of no more than 24 lots are ______________ from registering under ILSA.

7.5 FLORIDA RESIDENTIAL LANDLORD AND TENANT ACT

The Landlord and Tenant Act applies to the rental of dwelling units (residential tenancies). Under Florida law, a person must be at least 18 years old to enter into a rental agreement.

83.49, F.S.

Deposits and Advance Rents. A security deposit is typically paid to guarantee that the property will be left in good condition. Rent in advance is also often paid (typically the last month's rent). The Landlord and Tenant Act mandates how landlords (not real estate brokers) must account for and handle tenants' deposits and advance rents. The landlord is typically the owner of a dwelling unit. When money is given to a landlord as a security deposit or advance rent, the landlord is obligated to account for such deposits in one of three ways:

1. Hold the money in a separate non-interest-bearing Florida bank account for the benefit of the tenant. The landlord may not commingle, hypothecate—that is, pledge as security for a debt—or use any such funds until the funds are due the landlord.
2. Hold the money in a separate interest-bearing Florida bank account for the benefit of the tenant. In this case, the landlord must pay the tenant at least 75% of the annualized average interest rate payable on the account or 5% per year, simple interest, whichever the landlord elects. The landlord must not commingle, hypothecate, or use any such funds until actually due the landlord.
3. Post a surety bond with the clerk of the circuit court in the county in which the rental property is located in the total amount of the security deposits and advance rents or $50,000, whichever is less. The landlord must pay the tenant interest on the security deposit or advance rent held on behalf of the tenant at the rate of 5% per year simple interest. Landlords who choose this method are not obligated to place the funds (deposits) into a separate account.

Landlords of five or more units must give tenants written notice of the advance rent or security deposit either in the lease agreement or within 30 days after receipt of advance rent or security deposit. The notice must be given in person or by mail to the tenant. The notice must indicate the name and address of the depository where the advance rent or security deposit is being held, or it must state that the landlord has posted a surety bond as provided by law. The notice must also indicate whether the tenant is entitled to interest on the deposit. The Act also requires that the notice include the following disclosure (see Figure 7.3).

FIGURE 7.3 ■ Residential Landlord and Tenant Act Disclosure

Your lease requires payment of certain deposits. The landlord may transfer advance rents to the landlord's account as they are due and without notice. When you move out, you must give the landlord your new address so that the landlord can send you notices regarding your deposit. The landlord must mail you notice, within 30 days after you move out, of the landlord's intent to impose a claim against the deposit. If you do not reply to the landlord stating your objection to the claim within 15 days after receipt of the landlord's notice, the landlord will collect the claim and must mail you the remaining deposit, if any.

If the landlord fails to timely mail you notice, the landlord must return the deposit but may later file a lawsuit against you for damages. If you fail to timely object to a claim, the landlord may collect from the deposit, but you may later file a lawsuit claiming a refund.

You should attempt to informally resolve any dispute before filing a lawsuit. Generally, the party in whose favor a judgment is rendered will be awarded costs and attorney fees payable by the losing party.

This disclosure is basic. Please refer to Part II of Chapter 83, Florida Statutes, to determine your legal rights and obligations.

475.25(1)(k), F.S.

Broker Property Management. Rental property is typically owned by absentee owners. Oftentimes, a real estate brokerage will contract to provide property management services on behalf of an offsite property owner. In such situations, the brokerage acts as an agent on behalf of the owner. Real estate brokers must abide by Chapter 475 with regard to handling deposits and advance rent. The deposits and advance rents are trust funds and, as such, must be deposited into the broker's escrow account by the end of the third business day after receipt of the trust funds. Brokers typically open a separate escrow account to handle rental property management; however, there is no requirement to keep the property management trust funds separate from sales trust funds. Brokers may keep up to $5,000 of the broker's personal funds or business funds in a property management escrow account for the purpose of maintaining the escrow account. Sales associates who collect rent from tenants do so for their employing broker. Sales associates who collect rent or deposits from a tenant must deliver the funds to their broker-employer no later than the end of the next business day. It is illegal for a sales associate or a broker associate to independently perform property management services for a property owner.

83.683, F.S.

Renting to Active Military Service Members. The Florida Residential Landlord and Tenant Act requires landlords to approve or deny the rental application of an active service member within seven days. The service member must be notified in writing whether the rental application has been approved. If the application is denied, the denial letter must include the reason for denial. If the application is not processed within seven days, the landlord must lease the rental unit to the service member, provided the member complied with all other terms of the application and lease. The timeframe to process an active service member's rental application also applies to condominium associations, cooperative associations, and homeowners' associations when the association requires prospective tenants to complete a rental application before residing in a rental unit.

83.49(7), F.S.

Selling Tenant-Occupied Homes. The sale of a property does not terminate a lease unless the lease specifically provides for its termination when title is transferred to a new owner. When a broker lists a rented property, it is important to determine whether the owner is selling the property subject to the lease. Typically, if the property is subject to an existing lease, the buyer would become the new landlord at title transfer. The lease should be reviewed to determine whether it includes a provision for the right to terminate the lease upon sale of the property. If the lease does provide for termination upon sale of the property, the buyer should decide whether the lease should be terminated. If the lease is to continue after the sale, arrangements need to be made regarding an assignment of the lease, transfer of the security deposits and advance rent, and an accounting of the tenant's funds. At closing, the Closing Disclosure should reflect the transfer of the security deposit and the advance rents to the buyer, and the prorated rent for the month of closing. The Florida Residential Landlord and Tenant Act requires that when a rental property is sold or in the event of a change in the designated rental agent who is holding deposits and advance rent, the tenants' funds must be transferred to the new owner or rental agent, together with any earned interest and a final accounting showing the amounts to be credited to each tenant's account.

CASE STUDY

FURLONG v. WINTER

What follows is information concerning an informal hearing (Case Number 2013-032956). The information has been summarized for educational purposes. Winter was licensed as a sales associate for approximately four months when the following events occurred.

Synopsis:

Winter (Respondent) was employed by a licensed real estate corporation (Broker).

Respondent intended to manage properties on behalf of a friend/investor (referenced as landlord in a lease entered as exhibit) in the case.

Respondent prepared a lease for the rental of the subject property. Respondent's employer (Broker) did not authorize Respondent to manage the subject property or prepare the lease for the subject property.

Respondent created a limited liability company (LLC). Respondent was the manager and registered agent for the LLC.

Respondent collected from the tenants a security deposit and pet deposit. The deposits were not collected in the name of the Respondent's employer (Broker) or with the consent of the Respondent's broker. Respondent deposited and held the security and pet deposits in a business account.

Relevant License Law:

Section 475.42(1)(b), F.S.: A person licensed as a sales associate may not operate as a broker or operate as a sales associate for any person not registered as her or his employer.

Section 475.42 (1)(d), F.S.: A sales associate may not collect any money in connection with any real estate brokerage transaction, whether as a commission, deposit, payment, rental, or otherwise, except in the name of the employer and with the express consent of the employer.

Rule 61J2-14.009, F.A.C.: Every sales associate who receives any deposit shall deliver the same to the associate's broker/employer no later than the end of the next business day following receipt of the item.

Conclusion:

An informal hearing was held before the Commission. The Respondent was found guilty and fined $1,000 plus costs of the investigation. The sales associate was further ordered to take 30 hours of education.

83.51, F.S.

Landlord's Obligation to Maintain Premises. A landlord's obligations to tenants include the following:

- Maintain the rented dwelling unit in a condition that meets all building, housing, and health codes in the community. If no codes have been established for the area, the law requires that the premises (rental unit) be maintained in "good repair and capable of resisting normal forces and loads."
- Provide extermination of rats, mice, roaches, ants, wood-destroying organisms, and bedbugs.
- Provide garbage receptacles and pickup.
- Provide working equipment for heat plus running hot water.

The landlord is allowed to charge tenants for services, provided the charges are included in the rental agreement. If the dwelling unit is a single-family home or a duplex, the landlord is required to install working smoke detectors before the beginning of the lease period, unless agreed to otherwise in writing.

Landlords may not be held responsible for conditions caused or created by negligent or wrongful acts of tenants or their guests. A landlord is not required to maintain a mobile home when a tenant is renting the landlord's lot.

83.52, F.S.

Tenant's Obligations. A tenant's obligations include the following:

- Comply with applicable building, housing, and health codes.
- Keep occupied premises, including the dwelling's plumbing fixtures, clean and sanitary.
- Use reasonable care in the operation of all plumbing, electrical, heating, and air-conditioning equipment.
- Behave, and make sure guests behave, so as not to disturb the peace of other tenants.

83.53, F.S.

Landlord's Access to Premises. A tenant may not unreasonably withhold consent for a landlord to enter rented premises from time to time to:

- inspect the premises;
- make necessary or agreed-on repairs, decorations, alterations, or improvements;
- supply agreed-on services; and
- exhibit or show the premises.

In case of emergency or when necessary to protect or preserve the premises, a landlord is entitled to enter a dwelling unit at any time. However, the law prohibits a landlord from abusing this right of access to harass a tenant. If the rent is current and the tenant notifies the landlord of an intended absence, the landlord may not enter the premises during the period of absence, except with the tenant's consent or in an emergency. Except in emergencies, landlords are obligated to enter rented premises at times reasonable and convenient for the tenant. The statute mandates that at least 24 hours is reasonable notice.

83.49(3), F.S.

83,491(2), F.S.

Vacating Premises. When a tenant vacates a rental unit at the end of a lease agreement, the landlord must abide by certain time restrictions as follows:

- The landlord has 15 days to return the security deposit and any accrued interest, if applicable, provided the landlord does not intend to make a claim on the security deposit.
- The landlord has 30 days to notify the tenant of intentions to impose a claim on the deposit.

The notification must be in writing and be sent by certified mail to the tenant's last-known mailing address. The notice must include the reason for the claim. Failure to give the required notice to the tenant within the 30-day period forfeits the right to claim part of the deposit. The landlord may not seek a setoff against the deposit. The landlord may file a separate court action for damages after return of the deposit (with any accrued interest, if applicable).

A tenant who is properly notified of the landlord's claim on the security deposit is allowed 15 days after receipt of the landlord's notice to file an objection. A tenant who fails to make a timely written objection does not waive the right of the tenant to seek damages in a separate court action.

The Florida Landlord and Tenant Act relieves brokers of the duty to notify the FREC of disputes regarding security deposits and advance rent. Section 83.49, F.S., provides that brokers holding security deposits and advance rent may disburse the funds from the rental escrow account without complying with the Commission's escrow dispute and notification procedures, provided the broker has fully complied with the Florida Landlord and Tenant Act.

TIME PERIODS REGARDING TENANT DEPOSITS

30 days	Landlords of five or more units must notify the tenant in writing of which method is used to hold the tenant's deposit: (1) non-interest-bearing Florida bank, (2) interest-bearing Florida bank, or (3) posted bond.
15 days	A landlord who does not intend to make a claim on the security deposit has 15 days to return the security deposit.
30 days	A landlord who is making a claim on the deposit has 30 days to notify the tenant of the claim.
15 days	After receiving written notification of landlord's claim on deposit, the tenant has 15 days to object in writing to the claim.

83.56 (1), F.S.

Termination of Rental Agreements by the Tenant. If a landlord fails to maintain rented premises or fails to comply with the terms and conditions of the rental agreement, a tenant may terminate the agreement by following this procedure:

1. The tenant first must give written notice to the landlord citing the noncompliance and stating the intent to cancel the agreement if the noncompliance is not corrected.
2. Thereafter, the landlord has seven days to correct the noncompliance and resolve the problem.
3. If the noncompliance is not corrected within seven days after delivery of the tenant's complaint to the landlord, the tenant is entitled to terminate the agreement.

In those cases in which a tenant does not desire to terminate the rental agreement but does want to correct a landlord's noncompliance, the law provides alternative courses of procedure:

- If the dwelling unit is habitable despite the landlord's failure to comply, the tenant may remain in occupancy of the premises, and the law states that the rent may be reduced by a court in proportion to the loss in rental value caused by the failure to comply.
- If the dwelling unit is rendered untenable (uninhabitable) owing to the landlord's failure, the tenant may not be liable for the rent during the period the premises remain untenable, if the court agrees with the tenant's assertions. This is a departure from the requirements of a nonresidential lease under which the landlord has no obligation to repair damaged premises unless the obligation is specifically contained in the lease agreement.

83.56 (2), F.S.

83.56(3), F.S.

Termination of Rental Agreements by the Landlord. If a tenant fails to comply with a lease or rental agreement, the landlord may terminate the agreement by following the three-step procedure previously mentioned. The same period of seven days is allowed for compliance by the tenant. However, if the tenant's noncompliance is failure to pay rent when due, the following procedure is required for a landlord to terminate the agreement:

1. The landlord must give the tenant written notice demanding either payment of rent within three business days or possession of the premises. The written notice can be mailed, personally delivered, or if the tenant is absent from the place of residence, attached to the door of the dwelling. It is always advisable to be accompanied by another person to witness delivery of the notice. The three-day time limit begins from the time the notice is posted by mail or delivered at the residence, not including weekends or holidays.
2. The tenant has three business days to either pay the rent or surrender the premises. If the tenant continues the default in payment of rent after the allotted days have lapsed, the landlord must resort to formal eviction to have the tenant removed.
3. If the tenant vacates the rented premises, the landlord then is required to give the tenant written notice by certified mail of any claim on the tenant's security deposit or advance rent held by the landlord, as described previously.

SUMMARY OF THE EVICTION PROCESS

The landlord serves the tenant a written notice allowing three business days (excluding weekends and legal holidays) for the tenant to pay the rent or to vacate the premises.

If the tenant does not pay the rent or moves, the landlord may begin legal action to evict by filing a *complaint for eviction* in county court.

If the court agrees with the landlord, the tenant is notified in writing. The tenant has five business days (excluding weekends and legal holidays) to respond in writing to the court.

If the tenant does not respond or if a judgment is entered against the tenant, the clerk of the county court issues a *writ of possession* to the sheriff.

The sheriff notifies the tenant that eviction will take place after a 24-hour notice has been posted.

Eviction Requirements. From time to time, a landlord has to evict tenants from rented dwelling units. In any eviction process, the landlord must adhere to the following procedure:

1. The tenant must be notified in writing that the landlord is demanding possession of the premises. The notice may be mailed to or served on the tenant or posted on the door of the tenant's residence. The landlord keeps a copy of the notice and notes the date mailed or delivered.

83.59, F.S.

2. If the tenant does not surrender the premises to the landlord within three business days after notification for nonpayment of rent (seven days for all other breaches of the rental agreement), the landlord must file a complaint for eviction in the court of the county where the dwelling is located. This complaint identifies the premises and cites the reasons that justify recovery of the property. The sheriff's department usually delivers the complaint to the tenant.

83.60, F.S.

3. The tenant is allowed five business days to file a reply in defense against the complaint. If the tenant decides to defend continued possession, the courts must decide the case.
4. If the tenant merely continues to occupy the premises without answering the complaint, the landlord must obtain a final judgment from the court. A landlord is entitled to have the motion for final judgment advanced on the court's calendar if the court approves the request.
5. After entry of judgment in favor of the landlord, the clerk of the court issues a writ to the sheriff to put the landlord in possession after a 24-hour notice has been posted on the premises.

83.62, F.S.

6. At the time the sheriff executes (signs) the writ of possession or anytime thereafter, the landlord or the landlord's agent may remove any personal property found on the premises. Subsequent to executing the writ of possession, the landlord may request that the sheriff stand by to keep the peace while the landlord changes the locks and removes the personal property from the premises.

When a tenant refuses to vacate and defends for continued possession, it sometimes takes one to two months to complete the entire eviction procedure. In the meantime, any unpaid rent creates a lien in favor of the landlord. That lien applies to all property of the tenant except beds, bedclothes, and wearing apparel, either on or off the rented premises. This general lien dates from the date a judgment is issued by a court in favor of the landlord. Any right or duty stated in Florida's Landlord Tenant Law is enforceable by civil action. This means that all legal remedies sought by either tenant or landlord under this statute are pursued through the civil courts.

WEBLINK @

You can learn more about Florida's Residential Landlord and Tenant Act. Visit https://www.fdacs.gov/Consumer-Resources/Landlord-Tenant-Law-in-Florida#, a Florida Department of Agriculture and Consumer Services site.

Practice Questions

15. A landlord who intends to make a damage claim against a security deposit must give the tenant written notice of the intent to make the claim within __________ days.

16. If a landlord holds security deposits and advance rent in an interest-bearing rental account, the tenant is entitled to at least ______________ of the annualized average interest rate payable on the account or ______________ simple interest, with disbursements at least once each year, whichever the landlord elects.

17. If a real estate brokerage provides property management services, the broker must place rental deposits and advance rent in an __________ account.

18. Brokers may keep up to ______________ of personal funds or business funds in a property management escrow account.

7.6 SUMMARY OF IMPORTANT POINTS

- The Civil Rights Act of 1866 prohibits racial discrimination in all real estate transactions without exception.
- The *Jones v. Mayer* case upheld the Civil Rights Act of 1866.
- The Civil Rights Act of 1968 (called the Fair Housing Act) and amendments, protects people from discrimination because of their race, color, religion, sex, disability, familial status, or national origin in the sale or rental of housing or residential lots. The Fair Housing Act does not protect individuals based on age, occupation, marital status, or sexual orientation.
- Several exemptions from the Fair Housing Act apply to individuals selling or renting their own property. However, if racial discrimination occurs, the individual is in violation of the Civil Rights Act of 1866. If a real estate licensee is involved in the transaction, the Fair Housing Act applies.
- Prohibited activities under the Fair Housing Act include refusing to rent to, sell to, negotiate with, or deal with a member of a protected class; quoting different terms or conditions for buying or renting; advertising that housing is available only to people of a certain race, color, religion, sex, national origin, disability, or familial status; denying membership in or use of any real estate brokerage services, brokers' organization, or MLS; and making false statements concerning the availability of housing for inspection, rent, or sale.
- The Fair Housing Act also prohibits blockbusting (inducing homeowners to sell their property by making misrepresentations regarding the entry of minority persons in order to cause a turnover of properties in the neighborhood); steering (channeling homeseekers to or away from particular neighborhoods because they are members of a protected class); and redlining (denying loans or insurance coverage or offering loans or insurance coverage with different terms or conditions for homes in certain neighborhoods).
- The Americans with Disabilities Act (ADA) prohibits discrimination in places of public accommodation and commercial facilities such as hotels and real estate offices.
- The Interstate Land Sales Full Disclosure Act allows a purchaser who received the required property report before signing the contract to cancel the contract within seven days. Developers must register subdivisions of 100 or more lots with the Consumer Financial Protection Bureau.
- The Florida Residential Landlord and Tenant Act requires landlords to (1) maintain security deposits and advance rent in a separate non-interest-bearing escrow account, (2) maintain security deposits and advance rent in a separate interest-bearing

account and pay the tenant at least 75% of the annualized average interest rate payable on the account, or 5% per year, simple interest, or (3) post a surety bond for the lesser of the amount of the funds or $50,000 and pay the tenant 5% interest. If a real estate broker holds the funds on behalf of the landlord, the broker must abide by real estate license law concerning escrow funds.

UNIT 7 EXAM

1. The federal statute that prohibits a private homeowner from discriminating strictly on the basis of race if selling, renting, or leasing is the
   a. 1968 Fair Housing Act.
   b. 1866 Civil Rights Act.
   c. 1934 National Housing Act.
   d. 1968 Interstate Land Sales Full Disclosure Act.
2. The law requiring developers with subdivisions of 100 or more lots to register with the Consumer Financial Protection Bureau is the
   a. Civil Rights Act of 1964.
   b. Federal Housing Act (FHA).
   c. Florida Deceptive and Unfair Trade Practices Act ("Little FTC Act").
   d. Interstate Land Sales Full Disclosure Act (ILSA).
3. The federal 1968 Fair Housing Act as amended prohibits discrimination based on
   a. race, color, religion, sex, national origin, familial status, or disability.
   b. race or age.
   c. religion, age, race, familial status, or disability.
   d. race, color, religion, age, or national origin.
4. A sales associate collects the rent for an absentee owner of a multifamily building. The sales associate must
   a. deposit the rent in the sales associate's escrow account.
   b. deliver the rent to the sales associate's broker no later than the end of the next business day after receipt.
   c. deposit the rent into the broker's business account.
   d. deliver the rent to the sales associate's broker no later than the third business day after receipt.
5. When security deposits or advance rents are required by a landlord in Florida, such funds
   a. must always be kept in a separate account.
   b. may be deposited in the landlord's account if a sufficient surety bond has been posted.
   c. must always be placed in an interest-bearing account.
   d. must bear interest at the rate of 7%.
6. Adam, an Asian man, meets with a sales associate to explain his housing needs and describe the desired area he is considering. The sales associate tells Adam they have a listing in an area that Adam will probably like better because there are "people like him there." Adam noticed when viewing the listing that the neighborhood looked primarily Asian. This is an example of
   a. steering.
   b. subordination.
   c. alienation.
   d. blockbusting.
7. A landlord who rents a duplex to two tenants is obligated to provide
   a. working equipment for air-conditioning.
   b. an operable washer and dryer.
   c. a designated parking space.
   d. working smoke detectors.
8. Which disclosure must be given to tenants in multifamily buildings of five or more units?
   a. No brokerage relationship notice
   b. Notice of where deposit is held within 30 days
   c. 15-day cancellation privilege
   d. Transaction broker notice

9. If a tenant vacates rented premises promptly when a lease or tenancy expires, the landlord must
   a. inform the tenant within 45 days if the landlord claims part of the security deposit.
   b. return the tenant's security deposit within 30 days or explain any exception.
   c. inform the tenant within 25 days if part of the tenant's deposit will be claimed.
   d. inform the tenant within 30 days if part of the tenant's deposit will be claimed.

10. The Fair Housing Act does NOT apply to which category?
    a. A property owner of a single-family home who owns two residential properties and is selling the single-family property as a for sale by owner
    b. Residential property owned by the county government
    c. Single-family home listed by a real estate sales associate
    d. 20-unit multifamily apartment building

11. If a tenant's rent is current and the tenant notifies the landlord of an intended absence, the landlord may
    a. not enter the tenant's rented premises without the tenant's consent, except in an emergency.
    b. enter only if accompanied by a second party.
    c. enter without any restriction.
    d. not enter the tenant's rented premises without first obtaining a sheriff's affidavit.

12. How long does a landlord have to correct a noncompliance after receiving written notice from a tenant?
    a. 7 days
    b. 10 days
    c. 2 weeks
    d. 30 days

13. An owner of a rental property decides to hire a different property management company. What are the requirements concerning the tenants' security deposits and advance rent if the current management company is holding the funds in its trust account?
    a. Reimburse the tenants within 30 days with a final accounting.
    b. Send a letter to the tenants requesting instructions to either refund the money to the tenant or to credit the funds on the tenant's behalf to the new property management company.
    c. Transfer the funds to the new property management company with a final accounting showing the amounts to be credited to each tenant's account.
    d. Transfer the funds directly to the owner of the property who must deposit the funds and then issue a check payable to the new property management company.

14. Which law prohibits hotels from discriminating against customers because of the customer's national origin?
    a. Civil Rights Act of 1866
    b. Civil Rights Act of 1964
    c. Fair Housing Act of 1964
    d. Americans with Disabilities Act

15. Which phrase may legally be included in an advertisement to sell real estate?
    a. "Cute cottage home, perfect for first-time buyer"
    b. "Beautiful neighborhood rich in ethnic heritage"
    c. "Spanish-speaking community"
    d. "Quiet neighborhood, no young children please"

UNIT 8

PROPERTY RIGHTS: ESTATES AND TENANCIES, CONDOMINIUMS, COOPERATIVES, AND TIME-SHARING

LEARNING OBJECTIVES

When you have completed this unit, you will be able to accomplish the following.

- Define real property based on the definition in Chapter 475, F.S., and explain the physical components of real property.
- Distinguish between real and personal property, and explain the four tests courts use to determine if an item is a fixture.
- Describe the bundle of legal rights associated with real property ownership.
- List the principal types of estates (tenancies), describe their characteristics, and describe the benefits and protections associated with the Florida homestead law.
- Distinguish among cooperatives, condominiums, and time-shares, and describe the main documents associated with condominiums.

KEY TERMS

bundle of legal rights
common elements
concurrent ownership
condominium
condominium documents
cooperative
declaration of condominium
estate for years
estate in severalty
fee simple estate
fixture
freehold estate
homestead
joint tenancy
land
leasehold estate
life estate
littoral rights
nonfreehold estate
personal property
proprietary lease
prospectus
real estate
real property
remainderman
right of survivorship
riparian rights
separate property
tenancy at sufferance
tenancy at will
tenancy by the entireties
tenancy in common
time-share
trade fixture
undivided interest

INTRODUCTION

This unit begins with a description of the physical components of real property. It goes on to discuss various types of estates and the rights that are included in each type of estate. It describes multiple ownership interests, as well as special ownership interests, including the constitutional homestead. The unit concludes with a thorough presentation of cooperatives, condominiums, and time-shares.

8.1 LAND, REAL ESTATE, AND REAL PROPERTY

Land refers to the *surface* of the earth and to everything attached to it by nature, such as trees and lakes. Land also includes products of nature beneath the surface, such as oil and limestone. Technically, land extends downward to the center of the earth and upward into the air to infinity.

Real estate refers to the land and all *human-made improvements* permanently attached to the land. Improvements are artificial (man-made) things attached to land, such as homes, factories, fences, streets, sewers, and other additions.

Real property includes all real estate plus the *bundle of legal rights* inherent in the ownership of real estate (the bundle of rights is explained in detail under "Basic Property Rights" later in this unit). The terms *real property* and *real estate* are often used interchangeably (see the definition of real property that follows). However, some references reserve the term *real property* to include the concept of a bundle of legal rights associated with ownership. Real property, therefore, includes not only the real estate (land plus improvements) but also the legal interests, rights, and privileges associated with the ownership of real estate.

DEFINITION OF REAL PROPERTY

Real property or real estate means any interest or estate in land and any interest in business enterprises or business opportunities, including any assignment, leasehold, subleasehold, or mineral right; however, the term does not include any cemetery lot or right of burial in any cemetery, nor does the term include the renting of a mobile home lot or recreational vehicle lot in a mobile home park or travel park.

Reference: Section 475.01(1)(i), F.S.

Physical Components of Land

An owner's rights to use the physical components of surface, subsurface, and air are called *surface rights*, *subsurface rights*, and *air rights* (see Figure 8.1).

FIGURE 8.1 ■ Physical Components of Land

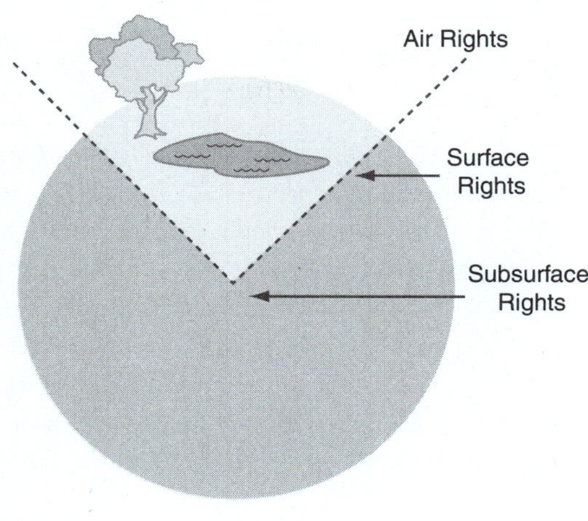

Land

Earth's surface—including trees and water, land and minerals—to the center of the earth and the airspace above.

Surface Rights. Surface rights include land and water rights. Two types of water rights are as follows:

- **Riparian rights** are associated with land abutting a flowing waterway, such as the banks of a river or stream. The property owner does not own the river or stream but has a right to use the water, such as for fishing and boating. The right is held in common with other riparian owners to make reasonable use of the waters that flow past, provided the use does not alter the flow of water or contaminate the water.
- **Littoral rights** are associated with land that abuts water that is nonflowing, including ponds and lakes. Littoral rights include ocean-front property and gulf-front property. The littoral owner's rights are the use and enjoyment of the shore and include ownership of the land adjacent to the water up to the average high-water mark.

TO REMEMBER: LITTORAL VS. RIPARIAN RIGHTS

Littoral	Lake, pond, ocean (nonflowing)
Riparian	River, stream (flowing)

DEFINITIONS ASSOCIATED WITH WATER RIGHTS

Accretion	The process of land buildup from water-borne rock, sand, and soil
Alluvion	New deposits of land as a result of accretion; alluvion deposits commonly occurring at the mouth of large rivers (The landowner is entitled to all new soil deposits.)
Erosion	Gradual loss of land due to natural forces (A landowner may lose land through the natural process of erosion.)
Reliction	Gradual receding of water, uncovering additional land (The new land usually belongs to the landowner of the area that was previously covered by water.)

Subsurface Rights. These consist of an owner's rights to underground minerals, petroleum, natural gas, and so forth, often called *mineral rights*.

Air Rights. Air rights involve that space above a tract, extending up to a height established by law (e.g., building rights, easements, aerial navigation).

Most real property transactions include all three physical components in the exchange of ownership rights. However, it is entirely possible for the seller to retain one or even two of the components if the buyer and the seller agree. For example, the MetLife Building in New York City was built by purchasing the air rights over Grand Central Terminal. The surface and subsurface components of that parcel continue to perform the same function as before construction of the MetLife Building. Another example of the separation of components of real estate occurred near Jay, Florida. Before the oil supply there was exhausted, owners often sold or leased the subsurface component, including oil rights, while retaining the surface and air rights.

Practice Questions

1. List three physical components of land.
    1. ______________________________
    2. ______________________________
    3. ______________________________
2. Reasonable use of waters that flow past an owner's property is called ______________ rights.
3. Littoral rights are associated with land that abuts ______________ water.
4. Land refers to the ______________ of the earth and to everything attached to it by ______________.
5. Real estate is defined as land plus all ______________ or ______________ improvements permanently attached to the land.

8.2 REAL PROPERTY VS. PERSONAL PROPERTY

The two basic types of property are real property and personal property (see Figure 8.2). Real property is basically land and improvements to the land. Property that is not real property is **personal property** (movable items or *chattel*). Personal property usually consists of items having a limited life that are easily movable from one place to another. Just as the term *realty* is used to denote real property, the term *personalty* is used to indicate personal property. It is important to distinguish between real property and personal property in a real estate transaction. All personal property included in the sale should be identified in the contract for sale, or the seller is entitled to remove the property.

FIGURE 8.2 ■ Real vs. Personal Property

Real Estate or Real Property
Land and anything permanently attached to it

Personal Property
Movable items not attached to real property; items removable without damaging real property

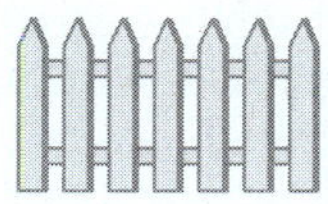

Fixture
Item of personal property converted to real property by attaching it to the real property with the intention that it become permanently a part thereof

Trade Fixture
Item of personal property attached to real property that is owned by a tenant and is used in a business; legally removable by tenant

Real property can become personal property by the *act of severance* (sever is to cut). For example, timber is real property, but when cut into logs, it becomes personal property by the act of severance. Vice versa, personal property can become real property by *attachment*.

Fixtures

A **fixture** is an item that was originally personal property that has been permanently attached to real estate in such a way that it is now legally part of the real property. A bathtub, for example, was personal property in its container in a warehouse, but once permanently attached in a home, it became real property. Some items, such as custom window treatments, ceiling fans, and chandeliers, are more difficult to classify. In those cases where contracting parties have not had the foresight to include such items in a real estate sale contract, the courts generally use the following set of legal tests to decide whether an item is a fixture.

Intent of the Parties. As in most points of law, intent of the party placing an article on or in real property is of primary importance. Statements made by an owner to witnesses may indicate the intent to make an item a fixture. For example, including a washer and dryer in a sale contract as part of the real property would remove any doubt about the owner's intention. If a dispute arises between a buyer and a seller or an owner and a tenant, the courts may be required to determine the original intent of the parties.

TO REMEMBER: LEGAL TEST FOR FIXTURES

I	**I**ntent of the parties
R	**R**elationship or agreement of the parties
M	**M**ethod or degree of attachment
A	**A**daptation of the item

Relationship or Agreement of the Parties. In this test, the courts seek to determine the exact nature of the relationship of the parties. Is it buyer and seller or landlord and tenant? Ordinarily, residential tenants are required to leave any item they have attached to the landlord's real property. However, if a building is leased as a retail store and the tenant has attached display racks to the walls, the courts would generally rule that the display racks are trade fixtures that may be removed by the tenant. A **trade fixture** is an item installed by a commercial tenant and used in the tenant's trade or business. Trade fixtures are legally considered personal property that are removable by the tenant, and the tenant would typically be responsible for necessary repairs associated with removal. For example, hydraulic car lifts installed by an auto repair shop are trade fixtures (see Figure 8.3).

Method or Degree of Attachment. The manner in which an article is attached to real property generally indicates whether it is a fixture or personal property. Normally, if removing the item would result in damage to real property, the article is classified as a fixture. A set of built-in storage cabinets in the utility room would usually be considered a fixture if removing it would damage the wall.

Adaptation of the Item. This test seeks to determine whether an item was designed for, or necessary to, the normal use of a specific property. If the item is adapted or custom built to fit the property, it will likely be considered a fixture even though it is movable. For example, hurricane shutters are considered fixtures because they are custom made to fit specific windows in a structure even though they are not on the windows at all times. The shutters are placed on the windows when a storm is approaching and removed when the danger has passed. Another example of a fixture is draperies that have been custom made using the same decorative pattern as the wallpaper.

Legal tests should not be necessary if all personal property to be sold with the real estate is listed in the sale contract. To avoid conflicts and misunderstandings between buyers and sellers, listing and sale contracts should clearly specify which items are considered part of the real property in a transaction and list any personal property that is to be included in the sale.

FIGURE 8.3 ■ Comparison of Fixtures and Trade Fixtures

	Fixture	Trade Fixture
Type of property	Real property	Personal property
Nature of property	Permanent	Removable
Use of property	Residential sale	Commercial lease
Sale contract	Included in sale	Not included in sale

Practice Questions

6. List the two basic types of property.
   1. ______________________________
   2. ______________________________

7. List the four legal tests that courts use to determine whether an item is a fixture.
   1. ______________________________
   2. ______________________________
   3. ______________________________
   4. ______________________________

8. An item that was personal property but has been permanently attached to real estate is called a ______________.

9. Movable items that are not attached to real property are called ____________ ____________.

10. Personal property, also called _______________ or _______________, consists of items having a _______________ life.

11. _________ ____________ are articles of _______________ property that are attached by a tenant and are a necessary part of the tenant's _______________ or _______________.

8.3 BASIC PROPERTY RIGHTS

Real property ownership rights are called a **bundle of legal rights**. The bundle of rights includes the following rights:

- *Disposition.* The right to sell, mortgage, dedicate, give away, or otherwise dispose of all or a portion of the property.
- *Enjoyment.* The right to enjoy and use the property without interference (the legal term is *quiet enjoyment*).
- *Exclusion.* The right to keep others from trespassing by entering or using the property without permission.
- *Possession.* The right to occupy the property in privacy. An owner acquires the right of possession of a property on the day the owner has legal title even though the owner may not have set foot on the land itself.
- *Control.* The right to uninterrupted use and control of the property consistent with local laws (for example, zoning).

TO REMEMBER: BUNDLE OF LEGAL RIGHTS

D	Disposition
E	Enjoyment
E	Exclusion
P	Possession
C	Control

Practice Questions

12. List the five real property ownership rights that are called a bundle of legal rights.
    1. ______________________________
    2. ______________________________
    3. ______________________________
    4. ______________________________
    5. ______________________________

8.4 ESTATES AND TENANCIES

An estate refers to the degree, quantity, nature, and extent of interest (ownership rights) a person can have in real property. The terms *estate* and *tenancy* are to be used interchangeably. Estates are divided into the following two general groups:

1. Freehold estates, which are for an indefinite length (of unknown duration) (see Figure 8.4)
2. Leasehold estates (also called *nonfreehold estates*), which are for a fixed term (known duration) (see Figure 8.5)

FIGURE 8.4 ■ Freehold Estates

Freehold estates are estates of ownership.

- *Fee simple* (absolute) is the most comprehensive estate and it is inheritable.
- *Life estate* is measured by a natural life span ("for the life of").
  - *Estate in reversion* occurs when property returns to the grantor.
  - *Remainder estate* occurs when property goes to a third party.

Freehold Estates

A **freehold estate** is an ownership interest for an indefinite period. That interest can be inherited (fee simple estate) or can be measured by the lifetime of an individual (life estate).

Fee Simple Estate. A **fee simple estate** is the largest bundle of legal rights. Fee, fee simple, and fee simple absolute are all used to describe the estate. All three terms identify an ownership interest with complete power to use, to dispose of, and to allow the property to descend to heirs. It is the highest type of real property interest recognized by law. Most title to property is held in fee simple.

Life Estate. Life estates are another type of freehold estate that can be created by the person who holds the fee simple title to real property. An estate in real property that is limited in duration to the life of its owner or the life of some other designated person is a **life estate**. During the time an owner enjoys a life estate, the owner must maintain the property and not permit *waste* (anything that reduces the value of property) to occur. The life estate owner also must pay the taxes and property insurance and keep current any mortgage(s) or lien(s) to preserve the property.

Because these life estates are created by agreement of the parties, they are *conventional life estates*. A conventional life estate can be created by a grantor who conveys a life estate to another individual.

EXAMPLE 1: Lucille has a fee simple estate in a home. She wants to provide for her brother, Andrew. Lucille executes a deed that transfers title to the home to Andrew for his lifetime. Lucille is the grantor who transfers a life estate to Andrew. The duration of the life estate is measured by Andrew's lifetime. The deed provides that upon Andrew's death, title will revert to Lucille (the original grantor).

A conventional life estate can also be formed by a grantor who reserves a life estate for the grantor's own use and transfers the remainder interest to another person (the grantee).

EXAMPLE 2: Lucille has a fee simple estate in a home. She wants to ensure that her brother Andrew will be able to continue to live in the home after her death. Lucille executes a deed that transfers title to the home upon her death to Andrew. Lucille is the grantor who reserves a life estate in the home for her lifetime and transfers the remainder interest to Andrew. The duration of the life estate is measured by Lucille's lifetime.

When a life estate is formed, two distinct ownership interests emerge from the original fee simple estate: the life estate and a remainder interest. Because these two parts are ownership interests, owners of either part can sell, mortgage, or gift their interest. The duration of a life estate is determined by the lifetime of a designated individual, so the deed creating the life estate must provide for transfer of title upon the designated person's death. At the end of the life estate, title reverts to the original grantor (estate in reversion) or conveys to a third party (remainder estate).

Estate in reversion. If the title will return to the original grantor (previous owner), an estate in reversion (reversion estate) is created. In Example 1, Lucille conveyed a life estate to Andrew. Because title to the property reverts to Lucille (the original grantor) upon Andrew's death, Lucille's interest in the home is an estate in reversion.

Remainder estate. If the title will be conveyed to a third party, called a **remainderman,** the remainderman owns a *remainder estate* while the life estate exists. The deed that established the life estate also designates the remainderman. When the life estate ends, the remainderman receives a fee simple estate. If there is only one remainderman, the grantee receives a fee simple estate in severalty.

In Example 2, Andrew is the remainderman. Andrew holds a remainder estate in the home while the life estate exists. When Lucille dies, Andrew receives fee simple estate in severalty. If there is more than one remainderman, the remaindermen receive a concurrent ownership. (Concurrent ownership is explained later in this unit.)

Life estates can also be created by law. These life estates are called legal life estates. For example, in Florida, if a homesteaded property is titled in one spouse's name only, by operation of law, the surviving spouse receives a life estate to the homesteaded property and the children receive a remainder estate.

Homestead. Homeowners (including single persons) in Florida may **homestead** their permanent (principal) residence. The Florida Constitution grants certain protections and benefits to the homestead:

196, F.S.
222, F.S.
Article X, Sec. 4, FL Constitution

- *Protection of the family.* If a married person dies and the family homestead was titled in that deceased person's name only (in severalty), by operation of law (even if a will states otherwise), the surviving spouse receives a legal life estate and the children (lineal descendants) receive a remainder estate. If there are no children, the surviving spouse receives a fee simple estate in the homestead. Signatures of both spouses are required on all contracts, mortgages, and deeds on homestead property, even if the homestead is titled in one spouse's name only. The purpose of the homestead law, therefore, is to protect the family and prevent the family from being displaced from the homestead.
- *Protection of the homestead.* Homestead property is protected from forced sale to satisfy judgment liens for debts owing to personal loans, credit card debt, and so forth. Homestead protection does not prevent foreclosure for nonpayment of property taxes, special assessments, mortgages, homeowners association fees, condominium association fees, vendors' liens, or construction liens secured with the homesteaded property.
- *Tax exemption.* Florida statute allows a tax exemption from assessed property value. The current homestead tax exemption is up to $50,000 for qualifying homesteads and is deducted from the assessed value when calculating taxable value (see "Homestead Tax Exemption," Unit 18).

- *Size of homestead*. The size of homestead property is restricted to 160 acres of contiguous land and improvements outside a municipality (city) or up to ½ acre of contiguous land and improvements if the property is located within the city.
- *Personal property*. Homestead protections include $1,000 of value of personal property.

FIGURE 8.5 ■ Nonfreehold or Leasehold Estates

Nonfreehold estates (leasehold) are estates of possession.

- *Estate for years* is a written lease agreement with a specific starting and ending date.
- *Tenancy at will* is either an oral agreement or one that has no specific ending date.
- *Tenancy at sufferance* occurs when the lease period has ended and the tenant is a holdover.

Nonfreehold or Leasehold Estates

Nonfreehold estates have a known duration and do not involve an ownership interest. *Nonfreehold* or *less-than-freehold* estates grant the right of quiet enjoyment (the right to use and possess but not own) real property. Nonfreehold estates are also called leasehold estates.

A **leasehold estate** (tenancy) is an interest in real property that a tenant possesses. Leasehold estates are measured in calendar time. Under a lease, the tenant possesses a leasehold estate and the landlord (property owner) possesses a reversion interest. At the end of the leasehold estate, the right of quiet enjoyment (use and possession) of the property reverts to the property owner. There are different types of leasehold estates: estate for years, tenancy at will, and tenancy at sufferance (see Figure 8.5).

Estate for Years. An **estate for years** (or tenancy for years) is a tenancy with a specific starting and ending date. It exists for a designated period, which may be any length of time from less than a year to a period of many years (such as a 99-year lease). An estate for years is a leasehold estate created by a written lease agreement. An estate for years establishes an interest in real property for the tenant (right of quiet enjoyment and exclusion) but does not convey actual title (or ownership) or the right of disposition (see "Basic Property Rights," in this unit).

83.46(2)(3), F.S.,

83.56(4), F.S.

83.57, F.S.

Tenancy at Will. A **tenancy at will** is a lease agreement that has no provision for the duration of tenancy. The payment of rent is determined by a period of time outlined in the lease agreement, such as a week-to-week or a month-to-month agreement. For example, assume Harry does not intend to use his lake cabin for a while, so Harry allows his friend Bill to live in the cabin for $100 per week. A tenancy at will has been created because Bill has been given permission to use the cabin and a rental rate has been agreed upon, but no ending date was established.

Florida statute calls this a *tenancy without specific term*. Tenancies at will may be written or oral agreements. All the duties and obligations of a landlord-tenant relationship exist in a tenancy at will, and notice of termination is required by either party. Notice for termination of tenancies at will is set in statute and is based on the time interval between rent payments:

- Week to week—7 days' notice
- Month to month—15 days' notice

Other actions that will terminate a tenancy at will include sale of the property or the death of the owner or the renter.

83.04, F.S.

Tenancy at Sufferance. A **tenancy at sufferance** occurs when a tenant stays in possession of the property beyond the ending date of a legal tenancy without the consent of the landlord. The tenant has no estate or title but only "naked" possession and is not entitled to notice to terminate. The payment and acceptance of rent alone must not be construed to be a renewal of the lease. However, if the tenant's *holding over* is continued with the written consent of the lessor, then the tenancy becomes a tenancy at will under Florida law.

Sole Ownership vs. Concurrent Ownership

61.075, F.S.

When title to property is held by one person, it creates an **estate in severalty** or sole ownership (to help you remember, think of this ownership interest as "severed" or cut away from any other ownership interest). **Separate property** is property that a spouse owns in the spouse's name only before marriage and property acquired by one spouse during the marriage by inheritance or gift.

Property acquired during marriage, except by inheritance or gift, is referred to as **marital assets**. For example, one spouse may purchase a property with her own savings and title the property in her name only. Unless the couple signed a prenuptial agreement, the property is legally a marital asset. If the couple later divorces the courts will divide marital property "equitably."

When working with sellers, it is important to know the existing form of ownership as it determines who must sign the various documents. Generally, if a property is owned as an estate in severalty, only the signature of the owner is required on the deed. However, if the property is homesteaded, regardless of whether both names or only one spouse's name is on the deed, both spouses must sign the deed.

FIGURE 8.6 Concurrent Ownership

Tenancy in Common	Tenancy by Entireties	Joint Tenancy
Two or more people	Married couple	Two or more people
Undivided possession	Undivided possession	Undivided possession
Equal or unequal percentage	Each spouse 100%	Equal percentage
Same or different time	Same time	Same time
Same or different title	Same title	Same title
No right of survivorship (Heirs inherit)	Right of survivorship (Surviving spouse inherits)	Right of survivorship (Surviving owner(s) inherit)

Ownership of property by two or more persons at the same time is called **concurrent ownership**. There are three types of estates (or tenancies) with concurrent owners: tenancy in common, tenancy by the entireties, and joint tenancy.

Tenancy in Common. When two or more persons wish to share the ownership of a single property, they may choose a tenancy in common. It is the most frequently used form of co-ownership, except for ownership by a married couple. A **tenancy in common** allows flexibility in how and when persons take title to property. For example, two or more owners may acquire title in any of the following combinations: same or different title (deed instruments); same or different time (date of execution), and hold an equal or unequal percentage of the ownership. Tenants in common own an undivided interest in the whole property. An **undivided interest** (also called undivided possession) is interest in the entire property rather than ownership of a particular portion of the property.

EXAMPLE: Sally and Kathy own a house as tenants in common. Sally holds two-thirds interest in the entire property, and Kathy owns one-third interest in the entire property. When Sally and Kathy die, their interest in the property will descend to their heirs. On Sally's death, for example, her two-thirds interest in the property will descend to her legal heirs (or as instructed in her will).

689.15, F.S.

Tenancy by the Entireties. A **tenancy by the entireties** is an estate that can only be created between a married couple. A tenancy by the entireties applies to all types of property purchased by a married couple. Residential, commercial, and industrial property purchased by a married couple together can be held as a tenancy by the entireties. The deed or other instrument of conveyance does not have to state expressly that a tenancy by the entireties exists. If the parties are truly married to each other, the estate is implied. While not mandatory, the deed should reflect a tenancy by the entireties to serve notice to others that such an estate exists. The deed, for example, typically would indicate John P. Smith and Sally R. Smith are a married couple.

With a tenancy by the entireties, each spouse has undivided possession of a 100% interest in the property. When one spouse dies, that individual's ownership interest automatically transfers to the surviving spouse by **right of survivorship**. This means that at the time of death of either spouse, the ownership interest automatically transfers to the surviving spouse. The surviving spouse immediately owns the property without it becoming a part of the decedent's estate. The surviving spouse will own the property in fee simple, and because the title conveys to the only surviving spouse, an estate in severalty (or sole ownership) exists. A tenancy by the entireties can only exist between a married couple; therefore, should the couple divorce, all property owned as a tenancy by the entireties will automatically become a tenancy in common, with each former spouse having undivided possession of an equal 50% share in the property.

When property is purchased by a married couple, unless provided otherwise, a tenancy by the entireties is created. If desired, a married couple could buy property together as a tenancy in common. In such a case, each would have 50% interest, they could own it 60%/40%, or something else, provided the deed specifically indicates each owner's percentage. One should not assume that simply because a couple is married, they want to purchase property as a tenancy by the entireties. The couple may choose instead to take title to the property as a tenancy in common. For example, a tenancy in common may be preferred if the married couple have children from a previous marriage. If the property is held as tenants in common, recall that each person's interest will descend to the tenant's heirs. Therefore, in this situation, a tenancy in common may be preferred so that a spouse can provide for their children from a previous marriage. The exception to a married couple choosing a tenancy in common is if the property is the couple's homestead (see "Homestead," earlier in this unit and Figure 8.7).

FIGURE 8.7 ■ Homestead Protection vs. Estate by the Entireties

Homestead	Tenancy by the Entireties
Protects the non-owning surviving spouse	Protects the owning surviving spouse
Protection applies to the principal residence	Protection applies to all types of property purchased by the married couple
If the owning spouse dies, the surviving spouse receives a life estate if there are children; if there are no children, the surviving spouse receives a fee simple estate in the homestead	At death of either spouse, ownership interest automatically transfers to the surviving spouse by right of survivorship
In the event of divorce, the non-owning spouse loses all protection in the homesteaded property	In event of divorce, by operation of law, the tenancy by entireties becomes a tenancy in common with each spouse having an equal share

Joint Tenancy. A **joint tenancy** features the right of survivorship, as does tenancy by the entireties. Recall that in a tenancy by the entireties, the right of survivorship meant that when one spouse (co-owner) died, the decedent's interest in the property automatically conveyed to the surviving spouse. In a joint tenancy, *right of survivorship* means that the share of a co-owner who has died goes to the surviving co-owner(s) and not to the deceased owner's heirs. Because a joint tenancy features the right of survivorship, for clarity, a true joint tenancy cannot be created unless specific wording in the deed provides for survivorship. Under present law, a deed conveying an estate in joint tenancy, to ensure the right of survivorship, must include wording similar to "as joint tenants with right of survivorship and not as tenants in common." The right of survivorship prevents disposition of the property by will or descent to heirs.

Joint tenants have undivided possession and an equal ownership interest in the real property. As joint tenants die, their shares are divided among the surviving tenants until only one owner is left. The sole survivor then has a fee simple estate in severalty.

> **EXAMPLE:** Bob, Bill, and Betty own 10 acres as joint tenants with right of survivorship, each owning a third share in the entire property. If Bob dies, Bill and Betty will remain as joint tenants, with each having a 50% share of ownership. If Bill dies later, Betty is the sole surviving joint tenant. At the time of Bill's death, Betty owns the property in severalty.

A joint tenant who wants to sell her share of a property may do so. However, the person who buys that share cannot be a joint tenant with the other original owners. This is because all of the joint tenants must acquire title together—that is, be named as grantee on the same deed instrument. Instead, the new owner will be a tenant in common without the right to receive any property on the death of one of the original joint tenants. The tenant in common's share can be disposed of by will, descent, or other arrangement.

> **EXAMPLE:** John, Jim, Jill, and Jane own an office building as joint tenants with right of survivorship. Each joint tenant has undivided possession with equal ownership interest. Jim sells his ownership interest (25%) to Sally. Sally is a tenant in common, while John, Jill, and Jane remain joint tenants. If John should die, his 25% interest will be divided between Jill and Jane. If Sally should die, her interest will go to her heirs or according to her will.

TO REMEMBER: FOUR UNITIES OF A JOINT TENANCY

P	Possession	Joint tenants have the same rights of undivided possession
I	Interest	Joint tenants have equal ownership interest
T	Title	Joint tenants acquire title on the same instrument (deed)
T	Time	Joint tenants acquire their interests in the property at the same time

Practice Questions

Andrew holds title to the property for his lifetime. The deed that Lucille executed states that upon Andrew's death, title to the property will transfer to her two children, Kathryn and Lynn.

13. Kathryn and Lynn hold a ______________ estate during Andrew's lifetime.

14. Andrew has a ______________ estate in the property.

15. List the four unities of a joint tenancy.

    1. ______________________________
    2. ______________________________
    3. ______________________________
    4. ______________________________

16. List the two types of estates that provide for right of survivorship.

    1. ______________________________
    2. ______________________________

17. List the number of days' notice to vacate that a tenant at will must be given, based on rent payment time intervals.

    1. Week to week: ______________
    2. Month to month: ______________

18. A freehold estate is an estate of ______________ for an ______________ period of time.

19. The most comprehensive estate with the largest bundle of legal rights is the __________ ______________ estate.

20. Leasehold estates are estates of ______________ and are also called ______________ estates.

21. Spouses who take ownership of property together create a tenancy _______ _______ ______________.

22. A tenancy for years must have a definite ______________ and ______________ date.

23. If title passes upon the death of a life tenant to someone other than the original grantor, the person receiving title is called a ______________.

24. A life estate created by the grantor is called a ______________ life estate; whereas a life estate created by law is called a ______________ life estate.

8.5 COOPERATIVES, CONDOMINIUMS, AND TIME-SHARING

Background

In Florida, the Cooperative Act (719, F.S.), the Condominium Act (718, F.S.), and the Florida Vacation Plan and Timesharing Act (721, F.S.) establish rights and obligations of the developer, the association, and unit owners and buyers. These statutes all require that, before the sale of developer residential shared housing, purchasers be provided with certain disclosure statements. These statements include, for example, property description, form of title-interest, description of common areas and amenities, existence of judgments or liens, management arrangements, escrow provisions for deposits, restrictions on the sale or transfer of units, apportionment of common expenses, construction completion date, estimated operating budget, estimated closing costs, and copies of key documents.

The Division of Florida Condominiums, Timeshares, and Mobile Homes of the Department of Business and Professional Regulation is the state agency charged with ensuring compliance with the laws regulating all three of these multiple-ownership forms. Because Florida is perhaps the most active of the states in producing and promoting multiple-ownership dwelling units, a complete description of cooperatives, condominiums, and time-sharing is appropriate here.

Cooperatives

719, F.S.

A **cooperative**, cooperative association, or co-op is a multiunit building that is owned by a corporation. The corporation holds title to the land and improvements. The unit owners purchase shares of stock in the corporation. Ownership of the stock entitles the purchaser to a **proprietary lease** and the right to occupy the unit.

The Cooperative Act stipulates that property taxes and special assessments be assessed against each cooperative unit (not against the corporation). The taxes and special assessments levied constitute a lien only on the individual unit. Shareholders pay a *pro rata* share of the property taxes, and the corporation pays the property tax bill. Owners-shareholders may deduct their real estate taxes and mortgage interest from taxable income. Shareholders also pay the corporation a monthly assessment based on a proportional share of the amount necessary for the payment of common expenses such as operating and maintenance expenses. Transfer of ownership of a cooperative unit is accomplished by sale of the stock.

719.503, F.S.

Disclosures and Cancellation Period. The developer is required to include a disclosure in the sale contract stating that the buyer of a residential cooperative unit may cancel the contract within 15 calendar days of signing the contract and receipt by the buyer of all items required by F.S. 719. The contract for resale of a residential cooperative unit must include a clause stating that the buyer acknowledges receipt of the articles of incorporation of the association, the bylaws and rules of the association, and the question and answer sheet at least three business days before signing the contract. If the buyer has not received these required documents before signing the contract, the contract for resale must include a clause stating that the buyer may cancel the contract within three business days of receipt of these required documents (see Figure 8.8). The buyer's right to cancel the contract terminates at closing. A contract for sale of a residential cooperative unit that does not include either disclosure is voidable by the buyer.

FIGURE 8.8 ■ Cooperative, Condominium, and Time-Share Rescission Periods

3 business days	Resale residential cooperative apartments and condominium units
10 calendar days	Time-shares sold by developer or resale
15 calendar days	Residential cooperative apartments and condominium units sold by developer

Condominiums

718, F.S.

A **condominium** consists of condominium units and common elements. Condominiums may look like apartment buildings, attached town houses, or freestanding houses; what makes the structures condominiums is how the developer organized the association. The Condominium Act provides that an association, usually a not-for-profit corporation, is responsible for operating the condominium. The condominium association is run by a board of directors, initially appointed by the developer, and subsequently turned over to elected directors.

A condo purchaser owns an individual unit in fee simple. The deed to the unit may be held by one or more persons in any type of estate or tenancy recognized by state law. The unit owner also owns an undivided fractional (proportionate) share of the common elements. **Common elements** are those portions of the condominium property that are not included in the units but are legally attached to each unit and are transferred with the unit when it is sold. A deed to a unit conveys the unit to the purchaser together with its proportionate ownership interest in the common elements. Property taxes are levied on individual units.

Condominium documents are a set of written instruments describing the condominium and the association. The four condominium documents in the following list are required to be given to buyers of residential units sold by the developer and to buyers of resale condominium units (see Figure 8.9).

1. *Declaration*. The **declaration of condominium** is an important condominium document because it is the document that creates the condominium. Creation of the condominium occurs when the declaration is recorded in the official records of the county where the property is located.
2. *Articles of incorporation*. The operation of a condominium is carried out through its association. The articles of incorporation create the corporate entity responsible for operating the condominium.
3. *Bylaws*. The bylaws describe the rules and regulations of the association. It provides for the administration of the association, including procedures for calling meetings, determining voting requirements, and so forth. Each purchaser, by accepting title to a unit, automatically becomes an association member and is bound by the association rules and regulations.
4. *Frequently asked questions and answers sheet (FAQ)*. The FAQ informs prospective purchasers about restrictions on the leasing of a unit, information concerning assessments, and whether and in what amount the unit owners or the association are obligated to pay rent or land use fees for recreational facilities.

Condominium Units Sold by a Developer. In addition to the four condominium documents listed previously, there are two additional disclosures required to be given to prospective buyers when purchasing residential units from a developer (see Figure 8.9).

1. *Prospectus*. The developer is required to provide a **prospectus** (offering circular) to purchasers if the condominium consists of more than 20 residential units. The prospectus summarizes some of the major points detailed in the condominium documents.
2. *Estimated operating budget*. The estimated operating budget provides detailed estimates of various common expenses that are to be shared by the unit owners.

718.503, F.S.

Buyers who are purchasing condominium units from the developer have a 15-day cancellation period. The developer must include a disclosure statement in the sale contract stating that the buyer has the right to cancel the agreement within 15 calendar days after the date of signing the contract and receipt of the condominium documents (6 documents in total listed previously). The developer will require buyers to sign a receipt for condominium documents. Buyers should verify that they have received all the documents listed on the receipt before signing.

718.504, F.S.

Resale Condominium Units Sold by Unit Owner. In addition to the four condominium documents previously discussed, unit owners of resale condominium units must give buyers three additional disclosures (see Figure 8.9).

1. *Most recent year-end financial report*.
2. *Rules of the association*.
3. *Governance form*. The governance form was developed by the Division of Florida Condominiums, Timeshares, and Mobile Homes to educate prospective purchasers on the rights and responsibilities of the condominium board and unit owners. The form was developed for use by condominium unit owners to give prospective buyers.

FIGURE 8.9 ■ Condominium Disclosures

	Developer (More than 20 New Residential Units)	Resale
Prospectus	✔	
Estimated operating budget	✔	
Most recent year-end financial report		✔
Rules of the association		✔
Governance form		✔
Declaration	✔	✔
Articles of incorporation	✔	✔
Bylaws	✔	✔
FAQ	✔	✔

The contract for resale of a residential condominium unit must include a rider stating that the buyer acknowledges receipt of the condominium documents and that the prospective buyer may cancel the contract within three business days after the date of execution of the contract and receipt by the buyer of the condominium documents. The cancellation period does not begin until the condominium documents have been delivered. A buyer should verify that all documents have been received before signing the receipt for delivery of the documents.

If a prospective buyer chooses to timely cancel the contract, a real estate broker may return the escrowed binder deposit to the prospective purchaser without first securing the seller's permission, provided the broker is notified in writing that the buyer is canceling the contract during the statutory cancellation period. Even if the seller objects, the real estate license law states that the broker may return the deposit to the purchaser without having to notify the Commission of conflicting demands.

The DBPR's Division of Florida Condominiums, Timeshares, and Mobile Homes "Condominium Governance Form," is available at http://www.myfloridalicense.com/dbpr/lsc/documents/CondominiumGovernanceForm.pdf.

WEBLINK

The Division of Florida Condominiums, Timeshares, and Mobile Homes publishes "A Guide to Purchasing a Condominium." It is available at www.myfloridalicense.com/dbpr/lsc/documents/purchasing_guide.pdf.

Time-Sharing

721, F.S.

Time-sharing evolved out of the vacation condominium concept. The property is first organized as a condominium. Each unit is divided into time intervals of ownership, usually 52 weeks. A deed or some evidence of share ownership or right of occupancy is prepared for each time interval. **Time-share** ownership involves an undivided interest in a living unit according to the number of weeks purchased. For example, if one week is purchased, the buyer owns a $1/52$ interest in the unit. Size, location, amenities, and time of year all affect the purchase price of the time-share unit.

Time-Share Act. Buyers of time-share units in Florida are protected by the Condominium Act and by the Florida Vacation Plan and Timesharing Act. Florida Statute Chapter 721 applies to time-share plans in Florida consisting of more than seven time-share periods over a span of at least three years.

475.011, F.S.

721.20, F.S.

Licensure Requirements and Exemptions. A real estate license is required to sell time-share plans unless specifically exempted. Owner-developers who develop and sell time-share units may hire unlicensed sales personnel, provided the salespeople are salaried employees who are not paid a commission and who do not receive compensation on a transaction basis, such as bonuses based on sales quotas. Owners of time-share periods who own the time-share for their own use and occupancy are exempt from licensure.

721.11, F.S.

Time-Share Disclosures. The Commission requires licensees who advertise, list, or sell time-share periods to provide disclosures in the listing agreement, advertisements, and sale contracts.

61J2-23.001, F.A.C.

61J2-23.002, F.A.C.

Time-Share Resale Listing Agreement Disclosures. FREC rules require that all agreements engaging the services of a broker in connection with the resale of a time-share period must contain the following disclosure, be included in conspicuous type, and located immediately above the space in the listing agreement reserved for the signature of the owner of the time-share period:

> **There is no guarantee that your time-share period can be sold at any particular price or within any particular period of time.**

Any written advertising material used by a broker or sales associate in connection with the solicitation of a listing agreement for the resale of a time-share period must also contain the disclosure statement in conspicuous type. It is unlawful for a real estate licensee to collect an advance fee for the listing of a time-share unit.

The listing agreement must also disclose

- fees, commissions, or other costs or compensation to be paid to the broker directly or indirectly;
- term of the agreement, a statement regarding the ability to extend the term of the agreement, and a description of all related costs and conditions under which the agreement may be extended;
- broker services under the agreement, the costs and obligations of each party regarding a resale purchase, and obligations regarding notification of the managing entity of the time-share plan and any exchange company;
- whether the agreement grants exclusive rights to the broker to locate a purchaser, to whom and when any proceeds from the sale of the time-share period will be disbursed, whether any party may terminate the agreement and the conditions for termination, and the broker compensation due from any party upon termination of the agreement before closing of the resale;
- whether the agreement allows the broker or other person to make use of the time-share period and a description of any such rights, including to whom any rents or profits generated from such use of the time-share period will be paid; and
- the existence of any judgments or pending litigation against the broker resulting from or alleging a violation of Chapter 475, 498, 718, or 721, F.S., or resulting from alleging consumer fraud.

Time-Share Resale Contract Disclosures. FREC rules require that a contract for resale of a time-share period used by a real estate licensee contain the following disclosure in at least 10-point, capitalized type located immediately above the purchaser's signature:

THE CURRENT YEAR'S ASSESSMENT FOR COMMON EXPENSES ALLOCABLE TO THE TIME-SHARE PERIOD YOU ARE PURCHASING IS _____. THIS ASSESSMENT, WHICH MAY BE INCREASED FROM TIME TO TIME BY THE MANAGING ENTITY OF THE TIME-SHARE PLAN, IS PAYABLE IN FULL EACH YEAR ON OR BEFORE _____. THIS ASSESSMENT (INCLUDES/DOES NOT INCLUDE) YEARLY AD VALOREM REAL ESTATE TAXES, WHICH (ARE/ARE NOT) BILLED AND COLLECTED SEPARATELY.

If ad valorem real property taxes are not included in the current year's assessment for common expenses, the following statement must be included:

THE MOST RECENT ANNUAL ASSESSMENT FOR AD VALOREM REAL ESTATE TAXES FOR THE TIME-SHARE PERIOD YOU ARE PURCHASING IS _____. EACH OWNER IS PERSONALLY LIABLE FOR THE PAYMENT OF HIS ASSESSMENTS FOR COMMON EXPENSES, AND/OR OWNERSHIP RIGHTS.

The broker may rely on information provided in writing by the managing entity of the time-share plan when making the required disclosures. The contract for purchase must also include the

- form of time-share ownership being purchased and a legally sufficient description of the time-share period being purchased;
- name and address of the managing entity of the time-share plan;
- terms and conditions of the purchase and closing, including the obligations of the seller or the purchaser regarding closing costs and title insurance; and
- existence of any mandatory exchange program membership included in the time-share plan.

Right to Cancel Purchase Agreement. The Florida Vacation Plan and Timesharing Act requires that purchasers be informed that they may cancel the contract within 10 calendar days of contract signing or receipt of the public offering statement, whichever is later (see Figure 8.8). The 10-calendar-day rescission period applies to time-share periods sold by the developer as well as resales.

Time-Share Ownership. The form of time-share ownership is normally divided into two types of legal formats:

1. *Interval ownership.* Interval ownership is a "deeded interest" time-share format that provides for fee simple ownership of each unit in specific time increments and allows the buyer to purchase a fractional interest in a unit. The owner has the right to sell, rent, will, or give away the fractional interest in the unit.
2. *Right to use.* The time-share purchaser receives the right to use the unit for a specified number of years, usually 20 to 40 years. At the end of the specified years, the usage rights revert to the developer-seller. The developer can increase or add fees and assessments, and sell the time-share to a third party. At the end of the specified years, the usage rights revert back to the developer-seller. Owners may lose their right to use if the developer goes bankrupt.

Practice Questions

25. Stock ownership in the corporation entitles the purchaser to the right of occupancy through a ______________ ________.

26. The shareholders pay a ______________ ______________ share of the property taxes to the corporation and the corporation pays the tax bill.

27. Transfer of ownership of a cooperative unit is accomplished by sale of ______________.

28. Condominium purchasers own an individual unit in _______ __________ in addition to an ______________ interest in the __________ ________.

29. Condominium property taxes are levied on ______________ ________.

30. Transfer of ownership of a condominium unit is accomplished by transfer by ______________.

31. Recording of the ______________ creates the condominium.

32. The "deeded interest" legal format of time-share ownership is called ___________ ____________.

8.6 SUMMARY OF IMPORTANT POINTS

- *Land* refers to the surface of the earth and everything attached to it by nature.
- *Real estate* refers to the land and improvements.
- *Real property* includes all real estate plus the bundle of rights.
- Physical components of land are surface rights, subsurface rights, and air rights.
- Any tangible asset that is not real property is personal property (movable items or chattel).

- The four tests regarding fixtures are (1) intent of the parties, (2) relationship or agreement of the parties, (3) method or degree of attachment, and (4) adaptation of the item.
- The bundle of legal rights consists of the following: right of disposition, right of enjoyment, right of exclusion, right of possession, and the right of control.
- A *freehold estate* is an ownership interest for an indefinite period. Fee simple is the most comprehensive freehold estate, and it is inheritable. A life estate is also a freehold estate, but it is measured by an individual's natural life span.
- A *leasehold estate*, or nonfreehold estate, is a tenant interest in real property measured in calendar time. The three types of leasehold estates are estate for years, tenancy at will, and tenancy at sufferance.
- An *estate for years* is a tenancy with a specific starting and ending date.
- A *tenancy at will* is a lease agreement that has a beginning date but no fixed termination date.
- A *tenancy at sufferance* occurs when a tenant retains possession of the property beyond the ending date of a legal tenancy without the consent of the landlord (tenant holds over).
- Sole ownership and concurrent ownership are ways that people hold freehold estates. An estate in severalty is created when title to property is in one person's name (sole owner). Ownership by two or more persons at the same time is concurrent ownership.
- The three types of concurrent ownership are (1) tenancy in common, (2) joint tenancy, and (3) tenancy by the entireties.
- Tenants in common have an undivided interest in the entire property. This interest can be left in a will or passed to heirs if there is no will.
- The four unities of a joint tenancy are (1) possession, (2) interest, (3) title, and (4) time. Joint tenancies are characterized by right of survivorship (when one co-owner dies, the deceased's share goes to the surviving co-owner).
- To create a tenancy by the entireties, the co-owners must be married to each other at the time they take title. The share of a deceased spouse automatically transfers to the surviving spouse by right of survivorship.
- The primary Florida residence of a homeowner qualifies for certain benefits and protections. These benefits include protection of the family, protection of the homestead, and a tax exemption from the assessed value.
- Purchasers of a unit in a cooperative buy shares of stock in a corporation. A proprietary lease entitles the purchaser to the right to occupy the unit.
- A *condominium* is real property consisting of condo units and common elements. A condominium is created by recording the declaration of condominium. The articles of incorporation create the corporate entity responsible for operating the condominium.
- Developers of more than 20 residential condo units must give purchasers a copy of the prospectus.
- There is a three-business-day cooling off period to cancel a condominium contract for sale from a property owner. There is a 15-calendar-day notice to cancel a condominium contract for sale from a developer.
- All listing agreements in connection with the resale of a time-share period must contain a disclosure stating that there are no guarantees regarding price or when the time-share unit may sell.

UNIT 8 EXAM

1. The MOST comprehensive interest in real property that an individual may possess is
   a. an estate for years.
   b. a life estate.
   c. a remainder estate.
   d. a fee simple estate.
2. Physical components of real property do NOT include
   a. surface.
   b. air space.
   c. equitable rights.
   d. subsurface.
3. Fixtures are items that
   a. are fixed, or attached, to real property.
   b. were once personal property but are now real property.
   c. have been incorporated as a part of real property.
   d. are all of these.
4. Which statement regarding cooperatives and condominiums is TRUE?
   a. The purchaser of a cooperative unit owns in fee simple; the purchaser of a condominium signs a proprietary lease.
   b. The buyer of a cooperative unit receives a deed, which includes the legal description of the cooperative and a fractional part of the common elements; the buyer of a condominium purchases shares of stock in the condominium corporation.
   c. Condominiums are regulated by the Division of Florida Condominiums, Timeshares, and Mobile Homes; cooperative units are regulated by the Division of Real Estate.
   d. Ad valorem taxes are assessed against each cooperative unit and each condominium unit.
5. The bundle of legal rights associated with real property does NOT include
   a. control.
   b. possession.
   c. disposition.
   d. utility.
6. A son gives his mother a conventional life estate for her lifetime. The deed states that upon her death, the property will transfer to her granddaughter. What type of estate does the granddaughter possess during the grandmother's lifetime?
   a. Remainder estate
   b. Life estate
   c. Estate in reversion
   d. Contingent estate
7. At the expiration of the lease period and before renegotiation of the lease, a tenant continued to occupy the apartment. The tenant's position is called
   a. a tenancy at will.
   b. a tenancy at sufferance.
   c. a freehold estate.
   d. an estate in reversion.
8. A family received a microwave as a housewarming gift. The microwave was installed above the range by screwing the unit to the kitchen cabinets and venting it through the attic. The microwave is considered
   a. a fixture.
   b. a trade fixture.
   c. separate property.
   d. personal property.
9. The homestead tax exemption is deducted from the
   a. market value of a property.
   b. assessed value of a property.
   c. sale price of a property.
   d. total cost, including all improvements.
10. A married couple own a homesteaded property with title in both names. They have one minor child and one adult son. One spouse dies. Which is MOST correct?
    a. The surviving spouse owns a life estate in the home.
    b. The property is split equally among the surviving spouse and the children.
    c. The surviving spouse owns the entire home through right of survivorship.
    d. The children own the home in fee simple.

11. The real estate protected by homestead rights is limited to
    a. 640 acres outside a city or town and 1 acre in town.
    b. 160 acres outside a city or town and 0.5 acres in town.
    c. 40 acres outside a city or town and 0.5 acres in town.
    d. 160 acres outside a city or town or 0.5 acres in town.

12. A constitutional homestead is owned by a man who is head of a family consisting of himself, his wife, and their three children. The man dies unexpectedly. After his death,
    a. the widow owns the homestead in fee simple.
    b. by operation of law, the widow owns a life estate in the homestead, and the children are vested remaindermen.
    c. the homestead will be distributed according to Florida's probate law.
    d. the homestead will descend to the man's heirs as specified in his will.

13. Which estate features right of survivorship?
    a. Leasehold estate
    b. Estate by the entireties
    c. Tenancy at will
    d. Tenancy in common

14. Chapter 475, F.S., defines real property as any interest or estate in
    a. land, improvements, leaseholds, subleaseholds, mineral rights, cemetery lots, or any assignment thereof.
    b. land, improvements, business enterprises and business opportunities, leaseholds, subleaseholds, mineral rights, mobile homes, or any assignment thereof.
    c. land, business enterprises and business opportunities, leaseholds, subleaseholds, mineral rights, cemetery lots, mobile home lots, or any assignment thereof.
    d. land, business enterprises and business opportunities, including any assignment, leasehold, subleasehold, or mineral rights.

15. In Florida, cooperatives and time-shares are regulated by the
    a. Division of Real Estate.
    b. Division of Florida Condominiums, Time-shares, and Mobile Homes.
    c. Department of Housing and Urban Development.
    d. Florida Real Estate Commission.

16. A condominium unit buyer has how long to cancel the purchase contract after signing an agreement with a developer?
    a. 3 days
    b. 10 days
    c. 15 days
    d. 20 days

17. Developers of condominium projects with more than 20 units must give buyers
    a. a copy of the prospectus.
    b. the names and business addresses of real estate sales associates assigned.
    c. the names of all current unit owners.
    d. the names of unit owners, unit numbers, and amounts due from unit owners delinquent in monthly assessment fees.

18. Which characteristic applies to condominium ownership?
    a. The corporation holds title to land and improvements.
    b. The purchaser receives shares of stock in the corporation.
    c. A proprietary lease entitles the purchaser to occupy a unit.
    d. The purchaser receives a deed to a particular unit.

19. All these apply to the constitutional homestead exemption EXCEPT
    a. protection from forced sale for nonpayment of certain debts.
    b. deduction of up to $50,000 from the assessed value of the homesteaded property, if claimed.
    c. claimants must hold title to the property and use the home as their principal residence.
    d. it automatically creates a tenancy by the entireties if the person filing for homestead is married.

20. A woman paid cash for a 60-acre lemon grove in Citrus County. The estate is for an indefinite period of time. The woman does NOT own which type of estate in the property?
    a. Fee simple estate
    b. Freehold estate
    c. Leasehold estate
    d. Estate in severalty

UNIT

9 TITLE, DEEDS, AND OWNERSHIP RESTRICTIONS

LEARNING OBJECTIVES

When you have completed this unit, you will be able to accomplish the following.

- Differentiate between voluntary and involuntary alienation, explain the various methods of acquiring title to real property, and describe the conditions necessary to acquire real property by adverse possession.
- Distinguish between actual notice and constructive notice.
- Distinguish between an abstract of title and a chain of title, and explain the different types of title insurance.
- Describe the parts of a deed and the requirements of a valid deed.
- List and describe the four types of statutory deeds and the legal requirements for deeds.
- List and describe the various types of governmental and private restrictions on ownership of real property and distinguish among the various types of leases and liens.

KEY TERMS

abstract of title
acknowledgment
actual notice
adverse possession
alienation
appurtenance
assignment
chain of title
condemnation
construction lien
constructive notice
deed
deed restrictions
easement
easement appurtenant
easement by necessity
easement by prescription
easement in gross
eminent domain
encroachment
equitable title
escheat
further assurance
general lien
general warranty deed
grantee
granting clause
grantor
gross lease
ground lease
habendum clause
intestate
involuntary alienation
junior lien
legal title
lender's policy
lien
mechanic's lien
net lease
opinion of title
owner's policy
percentage lease
police power
quiet enjoyment
quitclaim deed
restrictive covenants
seisin
specific lien
sublease
superior lien
testate
title
title insurance
variable lease
voluntary alienation
warranty forever

INTRODUCTION

This unit concerns the legal instruments and methods used to transfer title to real property. The unit also discusses the following concepts regarding title to real property: voluntary and involuntary alienation, title insurance, the two types of notice to title, the essential elements of a valid instrument of conveyance, certain covenants found in deeds, governmental and private restrictions on ownership, and the various types of leases.

9.1 LEGAL VS. EQUITABLE TITLE TO REAL PROPERTY

A person who holds ownership rights in property is said to have **title** to the property. **Legal title** is ownership of a freehold estate. Recall from Unit 8 that freehold estates include fee simple estates and life estates. Title to real property is a legal concept signifying ownership of the collection of rights called an estate.

Equitable title implies that an individual will receive legal title at a future date. When the buyer and seller execute the sale contract the buyer receives equitable title in the property. The law recognizes some ownership interest by the buyer even though the buyer is not yet the owner of record. For example, the buyer's equitable title means the seller cannot sell the property to someone else. The buyer will receive legal title when the deed is delivered to the buyer at the title closing.

ACQUIRING LEGAL TITLE

Alienation is the act of transferring ownership, title, or an interest in real property from one person to another. The alienation may be voluntary (with the owner's control and consent), or the transfer may be involuntary by operation of law (without control and consent of the owner).

Transfer by Voluntary Alienation

Voluntary alienation is the transfer of title with the owner's control and consent. There are two ways to transfer title by voluntary alienation: (1) by deed and (2) by will.

Deed. A *deed* is a written instrument used to convey an interest in real property. Thus, a deed conveys *legal title*. A deed is used to sell or gift real property to another person (or entity) during the owner's lifetime.

EXAMPLE 1: Mary and John Green sell their home to Lisa and Mike Smith. Title to the home is transferred from the Greens to the Smiths by deed.

EXAMPLE 2: Mary and John Green gift their home to The Arc as a residential home for persons with intellectual disabilities. Title to the home is transferred from the Greens to The Arc by deed.

732.501, F.S.

Will. A will is a legal instrument used to convey title to real and personal property after the person's death. To die **testate** indicates the *decedent* (deceased person) prepared a will before death. Conveyance of property according to a *last will and testament* is voluntary alienation because the person who left a will—the *testator* (male) or *testatrix* (female)—intended to gift property to a particular individual. A gift of real property is a *devise* and the recipient of the gift is the *devisee*. A gift of personal property is a *bequest* and the recipient is the *beneficiary* (see Figure 9.1).

FIGURE 9.1 ■ Parties to a Will

Deceased Creator of Will	Property Conveyed by Will	Recipient of Property by Will
Testator (male)	Devise (real property)	Devisee (real property)
Testatrix (female)	Bequest (personal property)	Beneficiary (personal property)

Transfer by Involuntary Alienation

732.101, F.S.

Title to property may be transferred without the owner's consent by **involuntary alienation**. Involuntary property transfers are usually carried out by operation of law.

Descent. When a person dies **intestate** (without leaving a will), all the property the deceased person owned at the time of death passes (descends) to the deceased person's legal descendants. The legal descendants are called *heirs*. Transfer of property by descent is a form of involuntary alienation because the state (not the deceased) determines the disposition of the property (see Figure 9.2).

FIGURE 9.2 ■ Involuntary Alienation

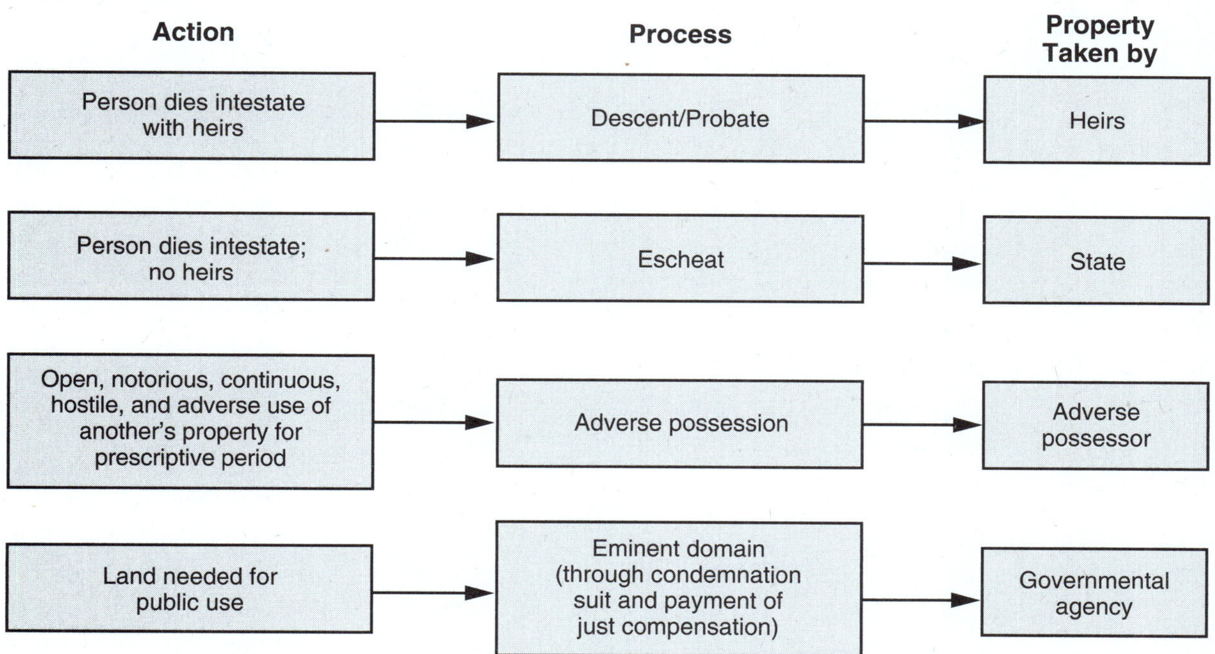

732.107, F.S.

Escheat to the State. **Escheat** provides for a government, normally a state government, to take the property of an owner who dies intestate and who has no known heirs entitled to receive the property. The power of escheat is a practical solution to ensure that property is always owned by someone.

95.18(1), F.S.

Adverse Possession. **Adverse possession** arises when the true owner of record fails to maintain possession and the property is seized by another. If the true owner "sleeps on his rights" and does not use the legal means available to remove a hostile trespasser, the owner will lose the right to the property after a period of time. In Florida, the person attempting to acquire property by adverse possession must comply with all the conditions listed in the text box below.

TO REMEMBER: CONDITIONS FOR ALIENATION BY ADVERSE POSSESSION

H	Hostile possession of the property (without owner's permission), to the exclusion of the true owner or any who may contest it
O	Open possession with no attempt to conceal occupancy
T	Taxes paid on the property by the adverse possessor during all the years of possession
C	Claim of title, even an imperfect one, exists (sometimes called color of title), thus creating a reasonable basis for the action
A	Adverse possession must continue for seven or more consecutive years without the consent of the owner
N	Notorious and flagrant public possession of the property

Always seek competent legal advice before acquiring real property if the title is based on adverse possession.

Eminent Domain. **Eminent domain** is the right of the local, state, and federal government to take private property for just compensation, provided the taking is for a public purpose. The government must pay a fair price for any land taken under eminent domain. **Condemnation** is the judicial or administrative proceeding to exercise the power of eminent domain. The appraised value of the property at the time of the appraisal is accepted by the courts as the valuation used to determine the amount of *just compensation*. The government may exercise this power (or delegate it to railroad and utility companies) regardless of whether the owner wants to part with the property. Therefore, it is a form of involuntary alienation.

Practice Questions

1. When the buyer and seller have signed a real estate sale contract, the buyer receives ______________ title to the property.
2. Legal title is the ownership of a ______________ estate.
3. Transfer by ______________ ______________ is accomplished with the owner's control and consent.
4. The instrument used to transfer title from one individual to another is a ______________.
5. A person who did not prepare a will before death died ______________.
6. Involuntary alienation is usually accomplished by ______________ of ______________.
7. Title by adverse possession may be obtained after ______________ or more consecutive years.

9.2 NOTICE TO LEGAL TITLE

In early English history, conveyances of title to real property did not depend on written instruments. Instead, the parties conducted their business on the land, and the townspeople assembled around them to witness the event. The seller verbally announced to the townspeople that he was transferring the land to the buyer. He symbolically "did the deed" by handing the buyer a twig or a clump of earth to give the world *actual notice* of the transfer of ownership rights. Today, there are two types of notice that have equal legal priority:

1. **Actual notice** is direct knowledge acquired in the course of a transaction. When the townspeople witnessed the transfer of earth or twig from one party to another, they witnessed the buyer's physical possession of the land. Actual notice was accomplished when the townspeople viewed the transfer of ownership rights. Assume that a seller verbally discloses to the buyer that there is a construction lien on his home for an unpaid pool repair job. The seller has given the buyer actual notice that there is a lien on the property.
2. **Constructive notice** (also called *legal notice*) is accomplished by recording a document in the public records. When the pool company records a construction lien on the property for the unpaid repair job, it gives the world constructive notice of the lien.

695.03, F.S.

Recording an instrument of conveyance puts the world on notice regarding an owner's interests in real property. Legal documents may be recorded in the public records of the county where the property is located. Recorded instruments are considered notice to the world. Actual notice and constructive notice have the same legal priority. In a court of law, it is easiest to prove constructive notice; therefore, constructive notice provides the best evidence of ownership.

People dealing with the real property are bound by all recorded documents. Recordation of a conveyance protects both the holder of the title and the public from fraud because the true ownership of real property is open to verification by the public. To be recorded, a deed must first be acknowledged by the grantor and the acknowledgment must be witnessed and certified by a notary public. **Acknowledgment** is the formal declaration before a notary public declaring that signing the document is a voluntary act. Other requirements for recording include the signatures of two witnesses. In Florida, the notary public taking the acknowledgment may be one of the witnesses (see Figure 9.4). (Note that Florida law does not require that documents be recorded.)

Practice Questions

8. List the two types of notice to legal title.

   1. ______________________________

   2. ______________________________

9. Recording a document in the public records provides ______________ notice.

10. ______________ is a formal declaration made before a notary public by a person signing a document declaring that the person signing the document is doing so voluntarily.

9.3 PROTECTION OF TITLE

Chain of Title. A **chain of title** is the complete successive record of a property's ownership. Beginning with the earliest owner, title may pass to many individuals. Each owner is "linked" to the next so that a "chain" is formed. A chain of title can be traced through linking conveyances from the present owner back to the earliest recorded owner.

Abstract of Title. An **abstract of title** is a search of the recorded documents concerning a parcel of real property. It is a condensed history that discloses those items about the property that are of public record. An abstract is conducted to determine the legal owner of the property and to reveal any mortgages, liens, judgments, or unpaid taxes that have not been satisfied to date. All recorded liens and encumbrances are included, along with their current status. The abstract of title does not guarantee or ensure the validity of the title of the property. The abstract of title does not reveal such items as encroachments or forgeries, or any interests or conveyances that have not been recorded.

Title Opinion. Some buyers will accept an **opinion of title** executed by an attorney who has studied the abstract of title. The opinion will list any defects or clouds on the title, such as liens, easements, or other encumbrances, and it will include the attorney's opinion of whether the seller has a *marketable title* (merchantable title). Most attorneys do not guarantee the opinion of title. It is an opinion only, backed by legal training and experience. If the opinion should prove to be in error, negligence must usually be proved for the attorney's client to receive reimbursement.

Title Insurance. The limited protection afforded buyers of real property by an opinion of title led to the need for title insurance. **Title insurance** is a contract that protects the policyholder from losses arising from defects in the title. Florida law does not require title insurance; however, it is a unique type of insurance because it protects a policyholder against loss from an occurrence that has happened in the past, such as a forged deed somewhere in the chain of title. Other insurable title defects include, for example, flaws due to incorrect marital status (failure to reveal a marriage where the spouse has a title interest), and incapacity of a grantor due to mental incompetence (see "Elements of a Deed," later in this unit). The title insurance company will defend a lawsuit based on an insurable defect, and it will pay claims up to the face amount of the policy if the title proves to be defective. Policies do not cover exceptions (exclusions) listed in the policy, such as an unrecorded easement or a lien arising after the policy was issued.

159, F.S.

Some buyers pay for the added protection of a municipal lien search. A municipal lien search is conducted to determine whether there are unrecorded special assessment liens, unrecorded liens existing by virtue of local ordinances, and unpaid waste fees payable to the county or municipality. A municipal lien search allows the title company to remove a standard exception in title insurance policies for special assessments, service changes, and waste fees.

There are two types of title insurance (see Figure 9.3):

1. **Owner's policy** is issued for the total purchase price of the property. It helps to protect the new owner (or the owner's heirs) against unexpected risks such as forged deed signatures and damages for any defect in the title (unless listed as an exception in the policy). A one-time premium is paid when the policy is issued. The policy is not transferable to another owner.
2. **Lender's policy** is issued for the unpaid mortgage amount. The lender policy (or *mortgagee policy*) protects the lender against title defects. Unlike the owner's title insurance, the lender's title insurance is transferable. If the mortgage lender sells the mortgage to another investor, the title insurance is *assignable* to the new lender. The lender policy will protect the new owner of the mortgage up to the unpaid balance of the mortgage loan. Most lenders require lender's title insurance as a condition of issuing a mortgage loan.

FIGURE 9.3 ■ Title Insurance Comparison

Owner Policy	Lender (Mortgagee) Policy
Issued for purchase price	Issued for loan amount
Claim will pay up to the purchase price	Claim will pay up to current loan balance
Benefits owner and owner's heirs	Benefits mortgage lender
Not transferable	Transferable (assignable)
Local custom determines who pays this closing expense	Buyer typically pays this closing expense
One-time premium	One-time premium

WEBLINK

Florida uses a standardized title insurance policy called the American Land Title Association (ALTA) form. ALTA provides a detailed explanation of the closing process, owner's title insurance, and lender's title insurance at http://www.homeclosing101.org.

475.25(1)(j), F.S.

61J2-24.001(3)(l), F.A.C.

Giving Opinions to Title. Brokers must handle statements regarding title to property with extreme caution. Real estate licensees are not qualified to render an opinion of title. Licensees must advise the buyer to either contact an attorney or a title insurance company to determine the condition of the seller's title. Florida law requires that when questions of title arise, licensees first must obtain a current opinion from an attorney before offering an opinion that title to a property is good or marketable. Real estate licensees are further required to advise prospective buyers to have their attorneys examine the abstract or to obtain a title insurance policy. In the event a licensee knows that the title to a property is not marketable or that liens exist, the licensee is required to inform prospective buyers of all such conditions.

Practice Questions

11. List the two types of title insurance policies.

    1. ______________________________

    2. ______________________________

12. An attorney's opinion of title is prepared after studying the ______________ of ______________.

13. The owner's policy is issued for the total ____________ _________.

14. Florida law does __________ require title insurance.

15. Real estate licensees must advise buyers to contact either an _______________ or a _________ _____________ company to determine the condition of the seller's title.

9.4 DEEDS

A **deed** is a written instrument that conveys legal title to real property. It is an instrument of conveyance whereby legal ownership to real property is transferred from one party to another. The two parties to a deed are the **grantor** (owner giving title) and the **grantee** (new owner receiving title). Title passes at the time of voluntary delivery and acceptance—when the grantor delivers a valid deed that is accepted by the grantee.

TO REMEMBER:

Important facts concerning the grantor include the following:

- The grantor must be *competent* (of sound mind and legal age).
- The grantor must sign the deed (if the property is homesteaded, the grantor's spouse must also sign the deed).
- Two witnesses must sign to attest that the grantor signed the deed.

Important facts concerning the grantee include the following:

- The grantee *does not have to be competent.*
- The grantee's name must be indicated on the deed.
- The grantee *does not sign* the deed (there is no signature line for the grantee).

Parts of a Deed Instrument

A deed must be in writing, and certain elements must be present in a deed to spell out clearly the necessary intent and the property to which it applies. The following items refer to the example of a general warranty deed (see Figure 9.4). The general warranty deed contains the most comprehensive collection of clauses. Other types of deeds will not include some of the clauses that are discussed as follows.

Premises. The premises section of the deed names the parties to the deed (grantor and grantee), marital status of the parties, address of the grantor and grantee, and the date of the deed. The date should be the date of execution by the grantor (see ①, Figure 9.4).

Consideration. The premises section of the deed also states the consideration that is given. Consideration is anything of value being given in exchange for title. The entire amount of the consideration need not be indicated. The wording "ten dollars and other good and valuable consideration" is common (see ②, Figure 9.4).

Granting Clause. The **granting clause** (also called words of conveyance) states the grantor's intention to transfer title to the grantee. Every deed must include a granting clause. The necessary words used to convey the property are *grants*, *bargains*, and *sells* or similar words (see ③, Figure 9.4).

Legal Description. A legal description of the property must be included in a deed to clearly identify the property being conveyed. A street address is insufficient because it may change over time and does not identify the exact boundaries of the property (see ④, Figure 9.4).

Appurtenances. An **appurtenance** is a right or privilege associated with the property. Typical appurtenances include parking spaces in multiunit buildings, easements, water rights, and other improvements. An appurtenance is connected to the property, and ownership of the appurtenance transfers to the grantee along with ownership of the property (see ⑤, Figure 9.4).

FIGURE 9.4 ■ Example of a Warranty Deed

Prepared by and return to:
Real Estate Law
Attorney at Law
Central Florida, P.A.
21 Center World Drive
Orlando, FL 32801
407-000-3333
File Number:

____________________[Space Above This Line For Recording Data]____________________

Warranty Deed

This Warranty Deed made this __ day of ______, **20__** between __________ whose post office address is ________________, grantor, and ___________________________ whose post office address is __________________, grantee: ①

(Whenever used herein the terms "grantor" and "grantee" include all the parties to this instrument and the heirs, legal representatives, and assigns of individuals, and the successors and assigns of corporations, trusts and trustees)

Witnesseth, that said grantor, for and in consideration of the sum of _______________________ ② ($____,000.00) and other good and valuable considerations to said grantor in hand paid by said grantee, the receipt whereof is hereby acknowledged, has granted, bargained, and sold to the said grantee, and grantee's heirs and assigns forever, the following described land, situate, lying and being in ________ County, **Florida** to-wit: ③

Lot ____ as recorded in Plat Book ____, Page _____, Public Records of ___ County, Florida.

Parcel Identification Number: _________________________________ ④

Together with all the tenements, hereditaments and appurtenances thereto belonging or in anywise appertaining. ⑤

To Have and to Hold, the same in fee simple forever. ⑥

And the grantor hereby covenants with said grantee that the grantor is lawfully seized ⑦ of said land in fee simple; that the grantor has good right and lawful authority to sell and convey said land; that the grantor hereby fully warrants the title to said land and will defend the same against the lawful claims of all persons whomsoever; ⑧ and that said land is free of all encumbrances, except taxes accruing subsequent to **December 31, 20__**. ⑨

In Witness Whereof, grantor has hereunto set grantor's hand and seal the day and year first above written.

Signed, sealed and delivered in our presence: Grantor

________________________________ ________________________ ⑩

Witness Name: ____________________

____

Witness Name: ____________________

State of Florida
County of _________

The foregoing instrument was acknowledged before me this ____ day of ___, 20__ by __________________. He/she [ ] is personally known to me or [ ] has produced a driver's license as identification.

[Notary Seal]

Notary Public

Printed Name: ______________________________

My Commission Expires: ____________________

Habendum Clause. The habendum clause defines the bundle of legal rights being conveyed to the grantee. The clause starts with the words *to have and to hold.* Then, the word *forever* usually follows if the estate is fee simple, or the words *for the life of the grantee* if it is a life estate (see ⑥, Figure 9.4).

Covenant of Seisin. The covenant of **seisin** (also called seizin) is a promise that the grantor owns the property and has the right to convey the property to the grantee (see ⑦, Figure 9.4).

Signature Lines. The deed must be signed by a competent (of sound mind and legal age) grantor and witnessed by two people. The grantee does not have to be competent to receive title to property. The grantee does not sign the deed (see ⑩, Figure 9.4).

Requirements of a Valid Deed

695, F.S.

A deed containing all the requirements of state law is said to be valid. A valid deed will be recognized by the courts. In Florida, for a deed to be valid, the following elements are required:

- In writing (statute of frauds)
- Names of the grantor and the grantee
- Grantor must be of legal capacity (competent and of legal age)
- Consideration must be described
- Granting clause (words of conveyance)
- Legal description
- Signed by the grantor and two witnesses (deeds do not have to be acknowledged, notarized, or recorded to be valid in Florida, but if the grantee wants to give constructive notice of ownership, the deed must be notarized before it can be recorded in public records)
- Voluntary delivery and voluntary acceptance of the deed

Practice Questions

16. Transfer of riparian rights or easements to the grantee are examples of ____________.

17. The deed must be signed by a ____________ ____________ and ______ ____________.

18. The words "to have and to hold for the life of the grantee" are found in the __________ clause and indicate that a __________ estate is being conveyed to the grantee.

19. Title to real property is transferred from the grantor to the grantee when the deed is voluntarily ____________ and ____________.

9.5 TYPES OF STATUTORY DEEDS

689, F.S.

A *statutory deed* is a deed whose format is defined by state law. Florida law provides for a short form of deed in which the covenants or warranties mentioned are implied to exist just as though they were written out in complete and detailed form. There are four types of statutory deeds: (1) quitclaim deed, (2) bargain and sale deed, (3) special warranty deed, and (4) general warranty deed.

Quitclaim Deed. A **quitclaim deed** provides the least protection to the grantee. A quitclaim deed contains a premises section with a granting clause that conveys what interest (if any) the grantor may have when the deed is delivered. The grantor makes no warranties about the quality or extent of the title being conveyed. Quitclaim deeds are used to clear existing or potential *clouds* on the title. To clear the title of possible trouble spots and defects, the grantor releases any claim or interest in the property. Words of conveyance used in a quitclaim deed are *remise*, *release*, and *quitclaim*.

Bargain and Sale Deed. A **bargain and sale deed** is similar to a quitclaim deed because the grantor makes no warranties about the quality or extent of the title being conveyed. Unlike the quitclaim deed, the bargain and sale deed contains a *seisin* clause indicating the grantor has title to the property; however, the grantor makes no express warranty against encumbrances. The granting clause in a bargain and sale deed uses the words *grants*, *bargains*, and *sells*. The bargain and sale deed is most often the deed that is transferred from a foreclosure or tax sale. In such cases, the grantor is a bank or tax authority, and therefore would not necessarily know of any encumbrances that may have been attached to the land by the previous owner. A bargain and sale deed is used when the grantor does not want to guarantee against any encumbrances. The bargain and sale deed includes a **habendum clause** (ownership interest) that declares the bundle of legal rights (estate) the grantor is transferring (see Figure 9.5).

Special Warranty Deed. A **special warranty deed** is similar to the bargain and sale deed because it contains a seisin clause indicating the grantor has title to the property. Like the bargain and sale deed, the special warranty deed uses the words *grants*, *bargains*, and *sells*. An important distinction between a bargain and sale deed and a special warranty deed is that the grantor in a special warranty deed guarantees the title against title defects arising during the period of the grantor's ownership of the property, but not against defects existing before that time. Like the bargain and sale deed, the special warranty deed includes a habendum clause (see Figure 9.5).

General Warranty Deed. The **general warranty deed** (or sometimes *warranty deed*) provides the greatest protection to the buyer because the general warranty deed contains all the covenants and warranties available to give the grantee every possible future guarantee to title protection. The general warranty deed is the most commonly used deed in Florida. If a real estate sale contract does not specify the type of deed to be delivered, a general warranty deed must be used. In addition to the granting clause and the habendum clause, the general warranty deed contains the following covenants:

- *Covenant of seisin*. The covenant of seisin (also *seizin*) is included in three of four types of statutory deeds; the covenant of seisin is not included in the quitclaim deed (see ⑦, Figure 9.4 and Figure 9.5).
- *Covenant against encumbrances*. The grantor warrants that the property is free from liens or other encumbrances, except as noted in the deed. This clause gives the grantee notice of all encumbrances (liens, restrictions, and so forth) associated with the property (see ⑨, Figure 9.4).
- *Covenant of* ***further assurance***. The grantor promises to sign and deliver any legal instrument in the future that might be required to make the title good.
- *Covenant of* ***quiet enjoyment***. The grantor guarantees peaceful possession undisturbed by hostile claims of title.
- *Covenant of* ***warranty forever***. The grantor guarantees to forever warrant and defend the grantee's title against all lawful claims (see ⑧, Figure 9.4 and Figure 9.5).

FIGURE 9.5 ■ Covenants in Four Types of Statutory Deeds

	Quitclaim Deed	Bargain and Sale Deed	Special Warranty Deed	General Warranty Deed
Features:	Grantor does not claim to hold title	Grantor does not promise to defend title	Grantor will only defend title during grantor's ownership	Grantor will defend title forever
Covenants/clauses:				
Granting	✓	✓	✓	✓
Habendum		✓	✓	✓
Seisin (seizin)		✓	✓	✓
Quiet enjoyment				✓
Further assurance				✓
Warranty forever				✓

Special Purpose Deeds

Legal problems may be encountered when property is being conveyed from one owner to another. Several types of deeds have evolved to provide solutions for these and other situations in which an owner cannot or refuses to sign a deed.

733.301, F.S.

475.011(1), F.S.

- *Personal representative's deed.* A *personal representative* is an individual either appointed by will or by order of a court to settle the estate of a deceased person. The testator typically identifies a trusted person to serve as personal representative who will be charged with carrying out the provisions of the will under the direction of the court in which the will was probated. If an owner should die without leaving a will, the probate court having jurisdiction will appoint a personal representative to settle the decedent's affairs. A personal representative's deed is used to formalize and record the transfer of title. It should show the full consideration paid for the property and contain a covenant of no encumbrances.
- *Guardian's deed.* A *guardian* acts on behalf of a minor (or other ward) and is also a fiduciary. Normally, the permission of a court is required for a guardian to sell or convey property belonging to the minor. When authorized by the courts, a guardian's deed legally conveys the minor's property.
- *Committee's deed.* One of the essentials of a valid deed is a competent grantor. When an owner is declared legally incompetent or is committed to an institution, a committee is often appointed by the court to administer the affairs of the incompetent. The committee functions under the direction of the court if conveying or disposing of the incompetent's estate. All members of a committee must sign the deed. A committee also must adhere to fiduciary disclosure requirements.
- *Tax deed.* The instrument used to convey title to property sold for nonpayment of taxes. No covenants are given, and the buyer assumes all risks for title defects. Extreme caution should be taken when purchasing property at a tax sale.

Practice Questions

20. List the five covenants contained in a general warranty deed.
    1. Covenant ______________________________
    2. Covenant ______________________________
    3. Covenant ______________________________
    4. Covenant ______________________________
    5. Covenant ______________________________
21. The deed that provides the greatest protection to the grantee is the __________ __________ deed.
22. The covenant in a general warranty deed guaranteeing that the grantee is receiving title free from hostile claims against the title is the covenant of __________ __________.

9.6 OWNERSHIP LIMITATIONS AND RESTRICTIONS

The two general categories of restrictions are government restrictions and private restrictions. Both have several subcategories of restrictions and limitations (see Figure 9.6).

FIGURE 9.6 ■ Ownership Restrictions

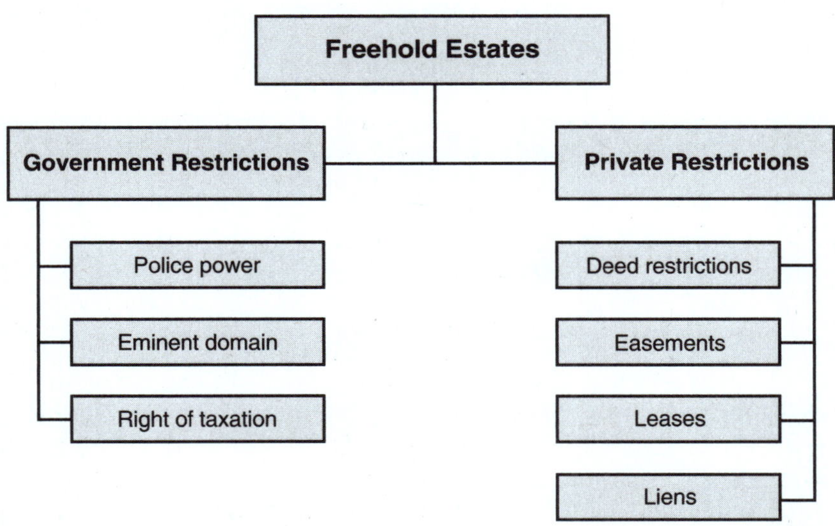

Government Restrictions on Ownership

The three most important subcategories of governmental limitations on ownership of real property are (1) police power, (2) eminent domain, and (3) taxation.

TO REMEMBER: GOVERNMENT RESTRICTIONS

P	**P**olice power
E	**E**minent domain
T	**T**axation

Police Power. The U.S. and state constitutions provide for the government to apply restrictions deemed necessary in the interest of the general health, welfare, or safety of its citizens. Under police power, the use of real property may be regulated. From these powers come the many ordinances and regulations governing zoning, building codes, health standards, city planning, and rent controls. **Police power** represents the broadest power of the government to limit or regulate the rights of property owners.

Eminent Domain. Eminent domain is also called a *taking for just compensation*. The constitutions of the U.S. government and state governments grant the power (right) to take private property for a public use (see "Transfer by Involuntary Alienation," earlier in this unit).

Property Taxation. This power was specifically limited to the various states by the U.S. Constitution. Citizens pay for the benefits and protection provided by the various levels of government. Property is usually the primary basis for local taxation. Local taxing authorities can foreclose on real property for nonpayment of taxes.

Private Restrictions on Ownership

Private limitations on ownership of real property usually include deed restrictions, easements, leases, and liens.

TO REMEMBER: PRIVATE RESTRICTIONS

D	**D**eed restrictions
E	**E**asements
L	**L**eases
L	**L**iens

Deed Restrictions. Deed restrictions are private restrictions placed in a deed that affect the use of a parcel of real property. Once placed in the deed by a previous owner, a deed restriction will limit the use of the property by the current owner and future owners. **Restrictive covenants** are recorded by the developer, along with the subdivision plat to maintain specific standards in the subdivision, such as requiring certain architectural or design specifications. Any restriction that does not discriminate against race, color, religion, sex, national origin, families with children, disability, or public policy may be included in a deed or in the restrictive covenants.

RESTRICTIVE COVENANTS AND DEED RESTRICTIONS

The terms *restrictive covenants* and *deed restrictions* are sometimes used interchangeably. However, deed restrictions refer to a single parcel of land, whereas restrictive covenants concern entire subdivisions.

Restrictive covenants impose limitations on the use of land in an entire subdivision. Examples of restrictive covenants that may affect a particular subdivision control such things as the minimum allowable square footage, whether the garage doors may face the street, or whether recreational vehicles and boats may be parked within view of the street.

Deed restrictions are placed by an owner who has created a restriction on future owners of the parcel of real estate. A deed restriction, for example, may prevent future landowners from selling alcoholic beverages on the site.

Easements. An **easement** is a right to use the land of another for a specific and limited purpose. Easements do not convey ownership (possession). Most commonly, an easement entails the right of a person (or the public) to use the land of another in a certain manner, such as utility easements, railroad rights-of-way, and ingress-egress easements.

An **easement appurtenant** involves two or more parcels of property and continues from owner to owner (the easement transfers with the title). An easement appurtenant allows an owner the use of an adjacent property.

EXAMPLE: The owner of a parcel of land subdivides the parcel into lots A and B (see Figure 9.7). The owner of lots A and B sells A and transfers with the title to A an easement appurtenant to cross B.

FIGURE 9.7 ■ **Easement Appurtenant and Easement in Gross**

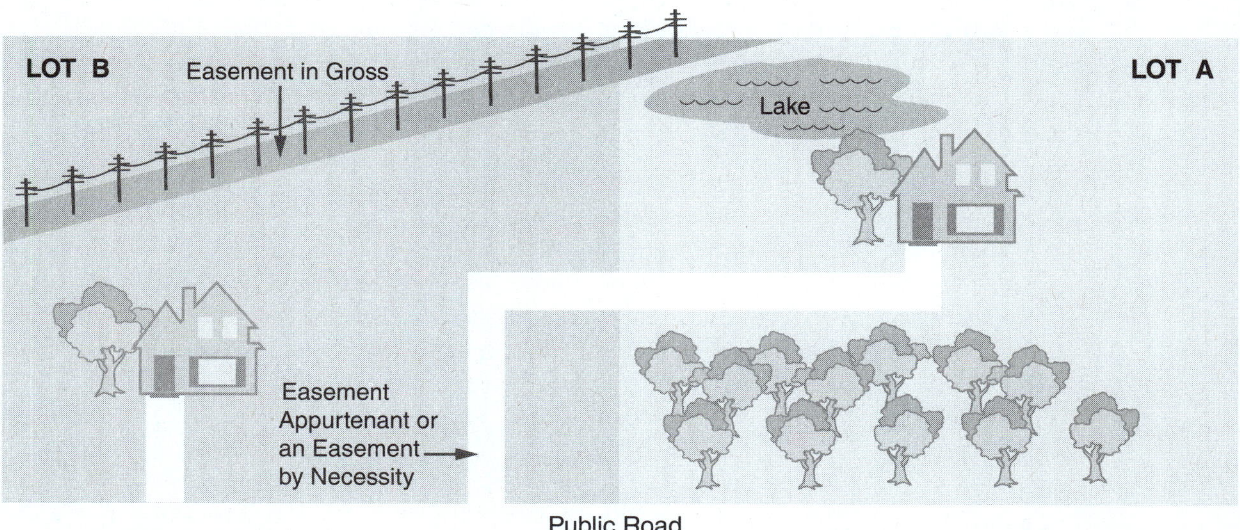

The owner of Lot A has the right to cross Lot B to access his property on Lot A. The right to the easement was granted by the owner of Lot B and created an easement appurtenant. If the property owner of Lot A had been given no such access and the home on Lot A was landlocked, the court would grant the owner of Lot A an easement by necessity. The utility company has an easement in gross across Lots A and B for its power lines.

An **easement in gross** does not benefit another specific parcel of land; the easement benefits the company that owns it.

EXAMPLE: There is a right-of-way utility easement across lots A and B in Figure 9.7 for power lines. The easement allows the utility company to access the land, trim trees, and so forth to maintain utility equipment. The easement in gross does not create a benefit to A over B or vice versa.

An **easement by prescription** is acquired by continually using another person's real property for the statutory period when such use is adverse to the owner's interest. The easement is created after 20 years of open, continuous, uninterrupted use. (Note the similarity to adverse possession; however, the adverse user in an easement by prescription acquires only an easement and not title.)

With an **easement by necessity**, if a landowner subdivides land, conveying part of it in a way that causes a parcel to be landlocked, the court may authorize creation of an easement by necessity to allow property owners to enter and exit their landlocked property.

EXAMPLE: The property owner of Lot A in Figure 9.7 has by court order been granted an easement by necessity to cross Lot B so that the property owner can reach his landlocked home. The property owner of A has been given the right of ingress (enter) and egress (exit). It is an easement by necessity rather than merely for convenience.

Unlike an easement, an **encroachment** is the unauthorized use of another's property. A fence or a garage located beyond a legitimate boundary without the owner's consent is an infringement or intrusion on property. An encroachment that has continued for more than seven years may create an *implied easement*. If encroachments are not known and a contract for sale is created before a survey reveals that one exists, the title might be unmarketable and the contract might be voidable.

Leases

A *lease* is an agreement between the landlord (lessor) and a renter (lessee) that grants the lessee the right of possession and use of the property (not ownership) for a specified time in return for compensation. Florida law requires that a lease of more than one year be in writing and be signed by the lessor, the lessee, and two witnesses to be enforceable. Leases for one year or less are enforceable, even when not in writing, if the terms can be verified and a termination date was agreed on.

Leases should be prepared by an attorney experienced in their preparation. Formats approved by the Florida Supreme Court for residential leases of one year or less may be completed by nonattorneys. Fill-in-the-blank lease forms approved by the court should be used by licensees. Leases of longer duration should be completed only by attorneys. Attorneys are authorized to draft leases on someone else's behalf. A property owner may draft a lease for a property that the owner owns in severalty (sole owner). Property owners may not delegate the authority to draft a lease to a nonattorney.

The major characteristics of five types of leases are described as follows (see Figure 9.8):

- In a **gross lease**, the tenant (lessee) pays a fixed (base) rent and the landlord (lessor) pays all expenses associated with the property, including taxes, utilities, insurance, and repairs. However, it is not uncommon for the tenant to pay unit-related utility costs. Most residential and office building leases are gross leases (also called *straight leases* or *flat leases*).
- In a **net lease**, the tenant (lessee) pays fixed rent plus property costs such as maintenance and operating expenses (taxes, insurance, and utilities). Net leases are typically used on commercial property. The terms *net*, *net-net*, and *triple-net* are often used in commercial real estate. The number of "nets" indicates that

the tenant is assuming more and more of the expenses. In a triple-net lease, the tenant pays all operating and other expenses in addition to the fixed rent. These expenses include taxes, insurance, assessments, maintenance, utilities, and other charges associated with the property.

- In a **percentage lease**, the tenant pays rent based on gross sales received by doing business on the leased property. Percentage leases are common with large retail stores, especially in shopping centers. A percentage lease can be either net or gross.
- In a **variable lease**, the tenant pays specified rent increases at set future dates. A variable lease is usually tied to an index, such as the consumer price index (CPI).
- In a **ground lease**, the tenant leases the land only and erects a building on the land. These leases are commonly used by government, commercial, or agricultural entities. Ground leases (or *land leases*) are long-term leases that will run for terms up to 99 years. Ground leases are characterized by separate ownership of the land and building(s). A land lease generally stipulates that the property owner will own the improvements and developments at the end of the lease unless otherwise specified.

FIGURE 9.8 ■ Types of Lease Agreements

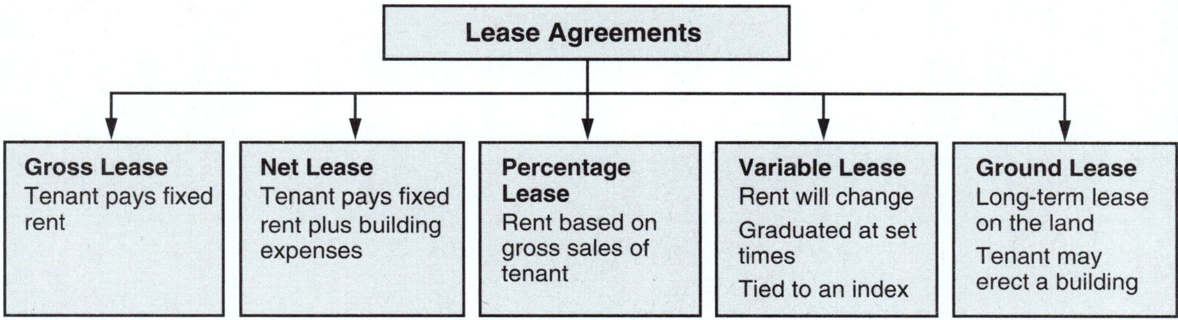

These five types of leases are not mutually exclusive. A triple-net lease, for example, can have its base rent increases tied to an index (a variable lease) and also require the tenant to pay a percentage of gross sales.

Calculating the Rent Owed for a Percentage Lease. Typically, percentage leases involve a base or minimum monthly rent plus a percentage of the gross sales in excess of an amount specified in the lease.

Formula: Percentage Lease

total gross sales – excess sales = sales subject to additional rent

sales subject to additional rent × percentage (%) charged = additional annual rent

additional annual rent + annual base rent = total annual rent

For example, assume that a lease calls for monthly minimum rent of $1,000 plus 3% of annual gross sales in excess of $325,000. What is the annual rent for the year if the annual gross sales were $450,700?

Step 1. Begin by determining how much of the gross sales are subject to the 3% charge.
$450,700 total gross sales – $325,000 = $125,700 subject to 3%

Step 2. Multiply the amount subject to the 3% charge.
$125,700 × .03 = $3,771 additional annual rent

Step 3. Add the additional annual rent to the base rent to determine total annual rent due.
$1,000 × 12 months = $12,000 annual base rent
$12,000 annual base rent + $3,771 additional rent = $15,771 total rent

Calculating Rent Owed for a Variable Lease. A variable lease features rent that changes at set times as specified in the lease agreement. A variable lease (or sometimes index lease) provides for adjustments of rent according to changes in a price index.

Formula: Variable (Index) Lease

$$\frac{\text{new index}}{\text{original index}} \times \text{original rental rate} = \text{new rental rate}$$

For example, assume that a building rents for $12 per square foot with an index of 1.5. The index increases to 1.8. What is the adjusted rental rate?

Step 1. Divide the new index by the original index.
1.8 ÷ 1.5 = 1.2

Step 2. Multiply the number from step one by the original rental rate.
1.2 × $12 = $14.40 new rental rate

Assignment and Sublease. A lease may be assigned to another party or a tenant (lessee) may choose to sublet the leased property.

- **Assignment** of a lease occurs when a lessee (tenant) assigns to another person all the leased property for the remainder of the lease.
- **Sublease** is used to give another person only part of an existing lease. This can occur in one of two ways:

1. A lessee (tenant) assigns only a portion of the leased property. For example, a college student who rents a three-bedroom home might sublet one of the bedrooms to another student.
2. A lessee (tenant) assigns all the property for a period that is less than the remaining term of the lease (such as for the summer only). Subleasing is also called *subrogation* and *subordination* of space. The original tenant remains obligated for the lease terms.

Liens

726.102(9), F.S.

A **lien** is a claim to have a debt or other obligation satisfied out of property belonging to another. Common examples are mortgage liens, construction liens, property tax liens, and judgment liens. Liens can entitle the holder (lienor) to have property sold, regardless of the desires of the owner (lienee).

Liens are usually recorded with the clerk of the circuit court in the county where the property is located. A lien is an encumbrance on the title to real property. However, not all encumbrances on property are liens. Encumbrances can also be easements, covenants, deed restrictions, encroachments, and governmental regulations.

Liens can be voluntary or involuntary (see Figure 9.9). *Voluntary liens* are ones the owner places against the property to secure payment of a long-term debt, such as a mortgage lien. *Involuntary liens* are created by law to protect interests of persons who have valid monetary claims against the owner of real property.

FIGURE 9.9 ■ Liens

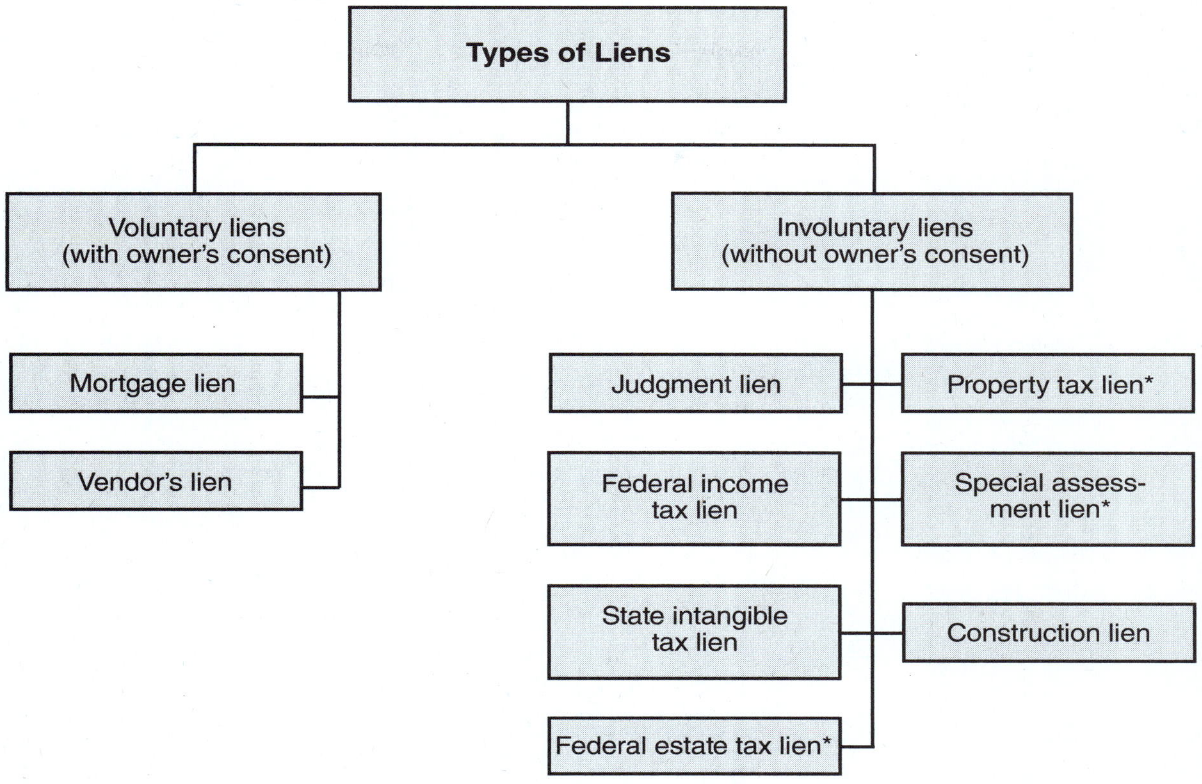

*Superior lien (ahead of other liens)

General and Specific Liens

Liens are divided into two major classifications: general liens and specific liens.

General Liens. A **general lien** is not restricted to one property but may affect all properties of a debtor. A general lien attaches to all of the lienee's (debtor's) real property located in the county where the lien is recorded. General liens include judgment liens, income tax liens, and estate tax liens.

- *Judgment lien.* A judgment lien is an involuntary lien attaching to real property when a judgment is obtained against the owner. A judgment lien is a general lien on all property of the debtor (unless specifically exempt by law) in the county where the judgment was recorded into the public records. In Florida, a judgment lien remains a lien on real property until it has been paid or expires by passage of time.
- *Income tax (IRS) lien.* Florida does not have a state income tax. However, failure to pay federal income taxes can result in a lien on property of the delinquent taxpayer. A federal tax lien, once filed, becomes a lien on all property owned by the taxpayer at the time of filing as well as on all future property acquired by the taxpayer until the lien is satisfied.
- *Estate tax lien.* Estate tax is a federal tax on a deceased person's taxable assets. Estate taxes are levied on the total value of a deceased person's money and property and are paid out of the decedent's assets before any distribution to beneficiaries. Estate tax liens are general liens because they attach to all the decedent's property. However, only the wealthiest estates pay federal estate tax.

Specific Liens. Liens classified as specific do not affect all of the debtor's property, applying only to certain specified property. **Specific liens** include the following:

- *Property tax and special assessment lien.* Municipal governments have been delegated the authority to levy real property taxes and special tax assessments. Unlike other debts and liens, property taxes and special assessments become liens as soon as the assessment is complete. The courts have ruled that special assessments may be levied only against properties that benefit by an increase in value. Special assessment liens are ahead of private liens in priority and second only to real property tax liens (property taxes and special assessments are discussed in greater detail in Unit 18).
- *Mortgage lien.* When a lender makes a loan using real estate as security, the property owner signs a mortgage document that creates a lien against the property. Mortgage liens are voluntary liens because they are made with the owner's consent. The date the mortgage is filed and recorded with the clerk of the circuit court establishes the priority of the lien against other claims on the property. If the borrower (mortgagor) defaults, the lender (mortgagee) can proceed to force sale of the property to satisfy the debt.
- *Vendor's lien.* If a buyer of property (vendee) is unable to make the full down payment required, a seller (vendor) frequently will allow a *purchase money mortgage* to make up the amount of money the buyer is unable to produce. Actually, any portion of the sale price remaining unpaid to the vendor creates a vendor's lien. This is an equitable lien of the grantor (seller) on the land conveyed in the amount of the unpaid purchase price. A vendor's lien is enforceable only against the party obtaining title from the vendor. It does not apply against later purchasers unless a written mortgage has been executed and placed in the public records. A valid vendor's lien is enforceable by foreclosure. Priority is established by the recording date of the purchase-money mortgage.
- *Construction lien.* This lien is based on the principle of law called *unjust enrichment.* Unjust enrichment means that property owners may not use the labor or material of another party to add value to their property without reimbursement to that party. A **construction lien** (or *mechanic's*, *materialman's*, or *laborer's lien*) is a statutory right of material suppliers or laborers to place a lien on property that has been improved by their supplies and/or labor. This lien must be filed with the clerk of the circuit court no later than 90 days after the last supplies are delivered or the last labor is performed in order to assume priority over any mortgage liens created after the first material/work appeared on the property affected. This, in effect, allows a construction lien filed after work is completed to become retroactive to the first delivery of material or first day of work. If a mortgage is placed on the property during the period when construction is in progress, a lien filed after construction is completed will precede the mortgage in priority. Once filed, a construction lien is effective for one year. The party who places the lien on the property must initiate court action to collect the debt during the lien's one-year life or forfeit the privilege. This lien may be discharged or canceled by expiration of time, payment of the debt, or court action through a suit.

Lien Priority

When there are two or more liens on a property, the *priority* of the liens determines the order in which the liens will be satisfied (paid off) if the property must be sold. Lien priority is important because the lienor (creditor) receives no compensation until all liens senior to the lienor's lien have been fully satisfied. Once a lien has been satisfied, a *release* or *satisfaction* of lien should be recorded to remove the lien.

197.122, F.S.

Superior Liens. **Superior liens** take priority over all other liens. They are automatically *superior* to any other lien. Three superior liens are as follows:

1. Real estate (property) tax liens, which become a lien January 1 each year
2. Special assessment liens
3. Federal estate tax lien (at time of death)

Junior Liens. The priority of **junior liens** is based on the date of recording in the public records. The priority of most liens is the date and time that the lien was recorded in the public records. Four important junior liens are the following:

1. Mortgage liens
2. Judgment liens
3. Vendor's liens
4. Income tax (IRS) liens

Construction Liens. Construction liens (also called **mechanics' liens**) are an exception to the priority rule regarding the recording date. A construction lien's priority in a foreclosure sale is retroactive to the date the work was first performed or materials were first delivered to the property.

Subordination Agreement. The priority of liens may be changed by a written agreement called a subordination agreement. Under a **subordination agreement**, the holder of a prior lien (lien with an earlier recording date) agrees to allow a junior lienholder's interest to move ahead of the prior lien.

Practice Questions

23. List three government restrictions on ownership.
    1. ____________________
    2. ____________________
    3. ____________________

24. List four types of private restrictions.
    1. ____________________
    2. ____________________
    3. ____________________
    4. ____________________

25. List three general liens.
    1. ____________________
    2. ____________________
    3. ____________________

26. An easement that attaches to the land and transfers from one owner to the next is an easement ______________.

27. An easement that does not benefit a specific property, such as easements for railroads, utility companies, and so forth, are easements ______ ______________.

28. A wooden fence that extends one foot into the neighbor's side yard is an ________________.

29. A ______________ lease agreement stipulates that the lessee will pay fixed rent plus certain expenses, such as the utilities.

30. Lien priority can be changed to allow a lien to move ahead in priority over a prior lien using a ______________ agreement.

31. A lease calls for a minimum rent of $2,800 per month plus 4% of annual gross sales in excess of $500,000. What is the annual rent if the annual gross sales were $725,500?

32. A tenant's lease requires a payment of $2,000 per month. The lease provides for an adjustment based on an index of 1.25. The index increases to 1.6. What is the new rent payment?

9.7 SUMMARY OF IMPORTANT POINTS

- *Alienation* is the act of transferring ownership, title, or an interest in real property from one person to another. Alienation may be voluntary (with the owner's control and consent) or involuntary (without control and consent).
- Voluntary alienation is accomplished using a deed or a will. Involuntary alienation occurs (1) when a person dies intestate (without leaving a will) and the property descends to the decedent's heirs, (2) when property transfers to the state through escheat because the owner died intestate and had no known heirs, (3) by adverse possession when the true owner fails to maintain possession and the property is seized by another, and (4) by eminent domain through a condemnation proceeding.
- *Actual notice* is direct knowledge acquired during a transaction; whereas, constructive notice is recording the information in the public record.
- A *chain of title* is the complete successive record of a property's ownership. An abstract of title is a summary report of what exists in the public record.
- The two types of title insurance are (1) owner policy, which is not transferrable and protects for the purchase price of the property and (2) lender (mortgagee) policy, which is transferable and protects for the balance of the mortgage loan.

- The two parties to a deed are the grantor (owner giving title) and the grantee (new owner receiving title). The deed must be signed by a competent grantor and witnessed by two people. The grantee does not sign the deed.
- The premises section of a deed names the parties to the deed and the date of the deed. The premises section contains the granting clause with the words used to convey the property. The habendum clause indicates the type of estate being conveyed. The seisin clause is a promise that the grantor has the legal right to convey title.
- The four types of statutory deeds are (1) quitclaim, (2) bargain and sale, (3) special warranty, and (4) general warranty. A general warranty deed provides the most comprehensive guarantee and contains three unique covenants: (1) quiet enjoyment, (2) further assurance, and (3) warranty forever.
- Public (government) restrictions on ownership include police power, eminent domain, and taxation. Private restrictions include deed restrictions, easements, leases, and liens.
- The five types of leases are (1) gross lease, (2) net lease, (3) percentage lease, (4) variable lease, and (5) ground lease.
- Assignment occurs when a tenant assigns to another all the leased property for the remainder of the lease. A sublease occurs when a tenant assigns only a portion of the leased property or the tenant assigns all the property for a portion of the remaining term of the lease.
- A general lien may affect all properties of a debtor. General liens include the following: judgment, income tax (IRS), and estate tax liens. A specific lien affects only a particular property. Specific liens include property tax and special assessment, mortgage, vendor, and construction liens.
- Lien priority of junior liens is the date and time a lien was recorded in the public records. However, property tax liens, special assessment liens, and federal estate tax liens are superior liens and take priority over all other liens (including IRS liens), regardless of recording date.

Note to Readers

A real estate broker or sales associate is allowed by Florida statutes to draw listing and sale contracts, but not deeds, unless conveying property in which the licensee owns an interest. In addition, only residential lease forms previously discussed may legally be completed by licensees. The drawing of any other lease or deed, or giving an opinion of title, may be construed as the unlicensed practice of law.

UNIT 9 EXAM

1. Which type of easement gives an electric company the authority to install and maintain electric power lines?
   a. In gross
   b. Prescription
   c. Appurtenant
   d. Implied

2. The government may take the property of an owner who has died without heirs through a process called
   a. condemnation.
   b. probate.
   c. escheat.
   d. adverse possession.

3. For a deed to be valid, a competent
   a. grantor, grantee, and two witnesses must sign the instrument.
   b. grantor and two witnesses must sign the instrument.
   c. grantee and two witnesses must sign the instrument.
   d. grantee only must sign the instrument.

4. The type or form of deed MOST commonly used to clear clouds on the title of real property is the
   a. general warranty deed.
   b. special warranty deed.
   c. bargain and sale deed.
   d. quitclaim deed.

5. If the sale contract does not specify the type of deed to be delivered, the seller is required to provide a
   a. general warranty deed.
   b. special warranty deed.
   c. bargain and sale deed.
   d. quitclaim deed.

6. The process of taking property under the power of eminent domain is called
   a. escheat.
   b. foreclosure.
   c. condemnation.
   d. voluntary alienation.

7. The type of deed in which the grantor does not warrant the title in any manner except against the grantor's acts or the acts of the grantor's representatives is called a
   a. general warranty deed.
   b. special warranty deed.
   c. bargain and sale deed.
   d. quitclaim deed.

8. The covenant against encumbrances in a deed is designed to guarantee that the
   a. grantor has not encumbered the property in any manner except as noted on the deed.
   b. grantee is responsible for any unpaid encumbrances.
   c. grantee has not encumbered the property.
   d. grantor will not encumber the property.

9. In answering questions pertaining to quality of title, real estate licensees are
   a. required to give opinions because of their role as experts.
   b. required to advise prospective buyers to have a lawyer render an opinion or obtain title insurance.
   c. allowed to give their opinions because of their role as experts.
   d. allowed to give their opinions only when specifically asked by the buyer.

10. The seisin clause in a deed specifies
    a. the type of estate being conveyed.
    b. the improvements being transferred with the land.
    c. the rights reserved by the grantor.
    d. that the grantor actually owns the property and has the right to sell it.

11. The provision in a deed that names the parties and contains the granting clause is the
    a. premises.
    b. encumbrance clause.
    c. habendum clause.
    d. seisin clause.

12. A developer states that homes in a specified development cannot be less than 1,800 square feet. This is an example of
    a. police power.
    b. a deed restriction.
    c. subdivision restrictive covenants.
    d. governmental restriction on ownership.

13. An example of an encumbrance on title to real property does NOT include
    a. an easement.
    b. a deed restriction.
    c. a lien.
    d. a premises clause in the deed.

14. The lender's title insurance policy is issued for
    a. an amount no greater than the purchase price and is not transferable.
    b. an amount no greater than the purchase price and is transferable.
    c. the loan balance and is transferable.
    d. the loan balance and is not transferable.

15. Which lien is first in priority?
    a. A property tax lien effective on January 1, 2023
    b. A special assessment lien certified on December 31, 2022
    c. A first mortgage lien filed on July 15, 2018
    d. A construction lien filed on November 30, 2017

16. A business has a five-year variable lease for a suite in an office park. The first year of the lease calls for rent of $21.50 a square foot based on a beginning index of 189. The index increases to 195 at the beginning of the second year. What is the new rental rate?
    a. $22.18
    b. $22.58
    c. $22.89
    d. $23.05

17. A married couple signed a contract to purchase a home in a residential subdivision. When the couple had the lot surveyed before closing, they discovered that the contractor had built the neighbor's garage three inches inside the west boundary of their lot. The garage in its present location is an example of
    a. a deed restriction.
    b. an easement by prescription.
    c. an implied easement.
    d. an encroachment.

18. When a pathway to a property has been used continuously and without interruption for more than 20 years, it creates an
    a. implied easement.
    b. encroachment.
    c. alienation by adverse possession.
    d. easement by prescription.

19. Soon after a man's death a deed was discovered in his desk. The deed is for the man's home and it deeded the property to a charitable organization. The man is survived by his son, who discovered the deed. The man died intestate. Based on this information, the house belongs to the
    a. state because the man died intestate.
    b. charitable organization because the deed conveyed ownership to it.
    c. legal heir because the deed was never voluntarily delivered and accepted.
    d. legal heir because the deed was not signed by the grantee.

20. A retail business rents a space in a mall. The lease calls for a base rent of $2,000 a month plus 5% of the annual gross sales that exceed $400,000. If the annual gross sales are $550,000, what is the total annual rent for the business?
    a. $20,600
    b. $24,000
    c. $27,500
    d. $31,500

UNIT

10

LEGAL DESCRIPTIONS

LEARNING OBJECTIVES

When you have completed this unit, you will be able to accomplish the following.

- Describe the purpose of legal descriptions and understand the licensee's role and responsibilities as it pertains to legal descriptions.
- Describe the process of creating a legal description using the metes-and-bounds method.
- Locate a township by township line and range.
- Locate a particular section within a township and understand how to subdivide a section.
- Calculate the number of acres in a parcel based on the legal description and convert acres to square feet.
- Explain the lot and block survey method and the use of assessor's parcel numbers.

KEY TERMS

base line
check
government survey system
legal description
lot and block
metes-and-bounds description
monument
point of beginning (POB)
principal meridian
range
section
survey
tier
township
township line

INTRODUCTION

This unit introduces the various methods used to locate and describe the boundaries of real property. Basic to the real estate business is a working knowledge of legal land descriptions.

10.1 PURPOSES OF LEGAL DESCRIPTIONS

The purpose of a **legal description** is to describe a parcel of land with sufficient detail that it will be accepted by a court of law. A legal description describes a particular piece of property in a way that uniquely identifies that parcel. A legal description is *legally sufficient* if it allows a surveyor to define the exact boundaries of the property. Purchasers (and title companies and lenders, if applicable) want documents such as deeds and mortgages to accurately identify the exact location, size, and shape of the property to be conveyed.

The description is based on information collected through a survey. A **survey** is a drawing of a parcel of land showing its boundary lines. The boundaries are measured by calculating the dimensions and areas to determine the exact location of a piece of land (see Figure 10.1).

There are five additional purposes of surveying property and developing legal descriptions for each parcel:

- Obtain current and accurate boundary information required to write a legal description
- Establish the exact quantity of area within a described tract, whether described in square miles, acres, or square feet
- Reestablish boundaries that may have become lost or obliterated
- Obtain data required to divide a large tract into smaller units for development and sale
- Identify and describe encroachments, if any

Licensee's Role and Responsibilities. Legal descriptions should be inserted into sale contracts with extreme care. Often, even punctuation is critical. Title problems can arise from an inaccurate legal description. Even if the contract can be corrected before the sale is closed, the real estate licensee risks losing a commission and may be held liable for damages suffered by an injured party because of an improperly worded legal description. Real estate professionals should refer to a reliable document, such as the deed that transferred the property to the current owner, or the tax roll/property appraiser's website for a full and accurate legal description.

Practice Questions

1. The purpose of a legal description is to describe a parcel of land with sufficient detail that it will be accepted by a ____________ of ____________.

2. A ______________ is a drawing of a parcel of land showing its boundary lines.

FIGURE 10.1 ■ Boundary Survey

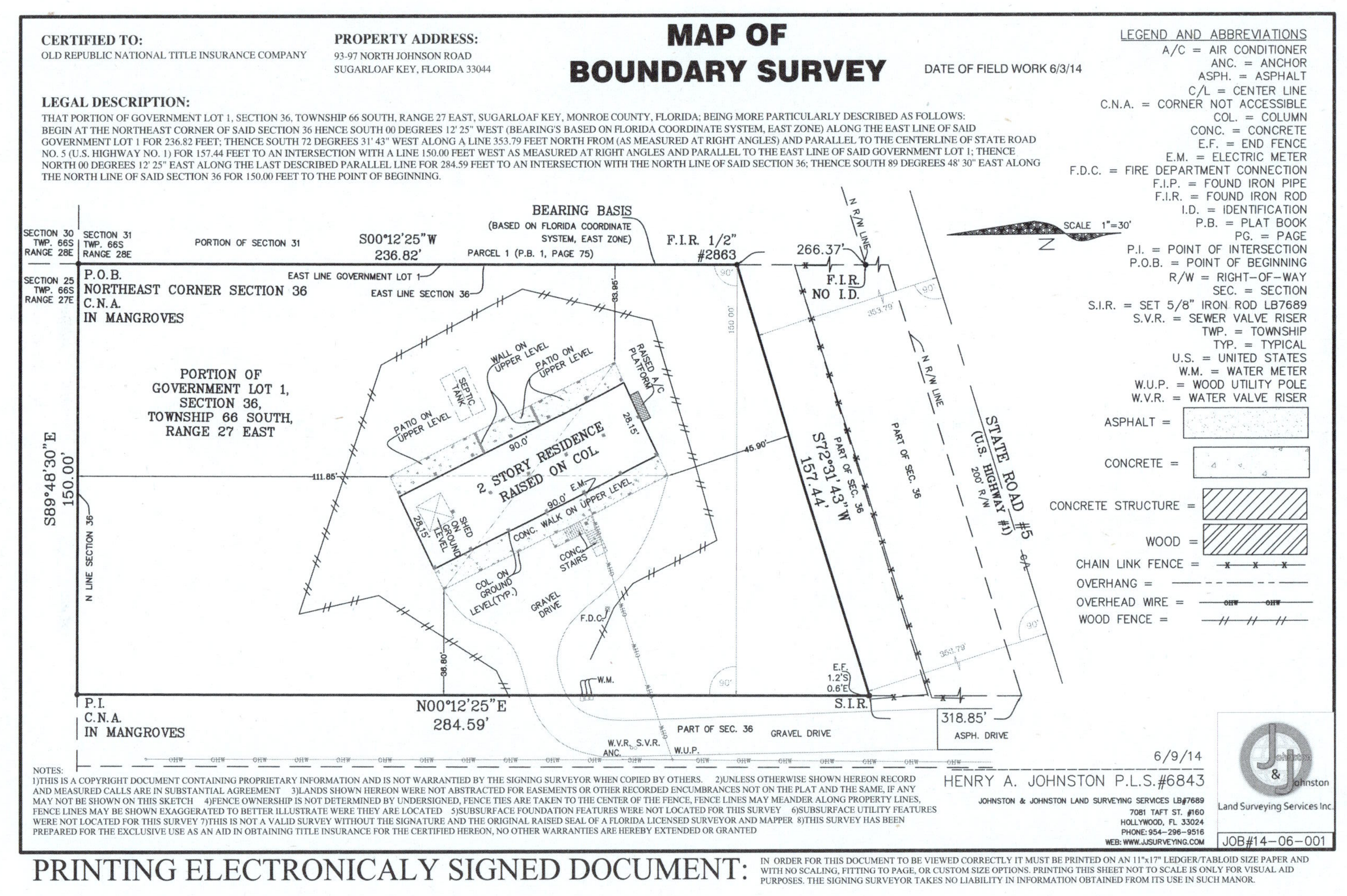

10.2 DESCRIPTION BY METES-AND-BOUNDS

There are three types of legal descriptions used today: (1) metes-and-bounds, (2) government survey system, and (3) lot and block descriptions.

The **metes-and-bounds description** is the oldest method of land description. Today, surveyors use computer software and laser equipment to create the most accurate surveys possible. The metes-and-bounds method is used for both regular and irregular shaped parcels. *Metes* refers to *distance* (measured in feet), and *bounds* refers to *direction*.

A metes-and-bounds description begins at an exact reference point, called a **point of beginning (POB)**. Starting at the POB, the first boundary is determined from the legal description that indicates the direction and the distance to the first corner of the parcel, followed by another direction and distance to a second corner, and so on, eventually returning to the POB so that the parcel is enclosed within its boundaries. The surveyor identifies each corner of the parcel with a visible marker called a **monument**. Monuments are fixed objects used to identify the POB, all corners of the parcel, and the location of intersecting boundaries. Monuments are made of concrete, iron, or brass, and they are carefully placed by the U.S. Army Corps of Engineers or trained private land surveyors.

Building Blocks of Metes-and-Bounds Descriptions. Compass bearings are used to describe the direction of a parcel's boundary lines. The POB and all turning points (corners of the parcel) should be regarded as being the exact center of a circle. Recall that a circle contains 360 degrees. A degree can be broken down into smaller units. To be more accurate, boundary directions are given in degrees (°), minutes ('), and seconds (").

EXAMPLE: N 45° 25' 20" E can also be written as North 45 degrees, 25 minutes, 20 seconds East.

Distances are measured in feet, usually to the nearest one-hundredth of a foot.

A compass has four primary directions: north, south, east, and west. If we draw a straight line connecting north and south, and a second line connecting east and west, the circle is divided into four quarters or *quadrants* (see drawing A in Figure 10.2). The line running north and south is the *primary reference line*. Metes-and-bounds descriptions will always begin with either north or south followed by a certain number of degrees, up to a maximum of 90 degrees. The direction that follows the number of degrees indicates whether the direction is east or west of due north or south.

FIGURE 10.2 ■ Compass Directions

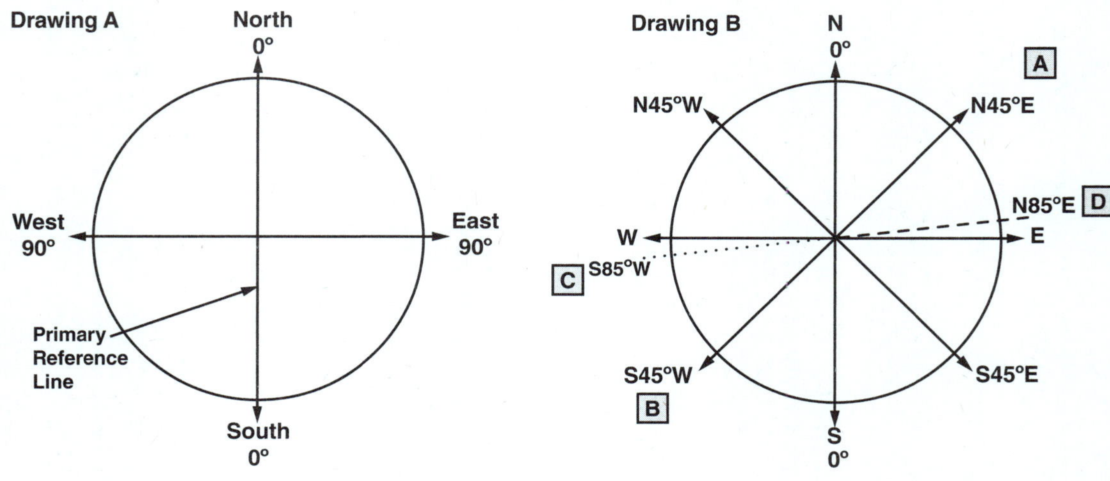

Let's begin by plotting *North 45 degrees East*. Using drawing B in Figure 10.2, place your pencil in a vertical (north-south) position over the circle. The first word in the description "North" indicates that we will begin with north as our primary direction, so our pencil lead should face upward (north). The second direction is "East," so rotate your pencil in an easterly direction (to the right on the drawing). How far is 45 degrees? It is halfway between zero degrees (due north) and 90 degrees (due east) (see line A on drawing B in Figure 10.2).

The reason why the number of degrees cannot exceed 90 is that one would pass the point midway between north and south and begin to move toward the other primary reference direction. For example, let's plot *South 85 degrees West*. Begin with your pencil in a vertical (north-south) direction with the pencil lead facing south (downward). Move 85 degrees to the west (to the left on the drawing). Because 85 degrees approaches 90, we can draw a line very close to due west (see line C on drawing B in Figure 10.2).

What would happen if you were to plot *North 95 degrees West*? I know—I just told you descriptions don't exceed 90 degrees, but let's see why. Again place your pencil in a vertical position, this time with the pencil lead facing upward (north). If you rotate the pencil 95 degrees to the west, notice that you pass due west (90°) and end up 5 degrees into the lower half of the circle. Therefore, the description should have begun with the primary reference direction of south. Let's rewrite the description properly as *South 85 degrees West*. Place your pencil in the vertical position with the pencil lead facing south. Rotate your pencil to the west 85 degrees, which is just 5 degrees shy of 90 degrees. We have confirmed that the line is correctly labeled as *South 85 degrees West* (see line C on drawing B in Figure 10.2).

Notice that the opposite of S 45° W (line B in Figure 10.2) is N 45° E (line A in Figure 10.2). The number of degrees does not change, only the compass directions. What is the opposite of S 85° W? It is N 85° E (see line D in Figure 10.2).

Practice Questions

3. The ______________ method is the oldest method of legal description.

4. *Metes* refers to ______________ and *bounds* refers to ______________.

5. A metes-and-bounds description begins and ends at the ____________ of ____________.

6. What is the opposite of N 45° W? To help you answer this question, refer to Figure 10.2, drawing B.

7. Without referring to Figure 10.2, what is the opposite of S 15° E? Hint: The number of degrees do not change, only the compass directions.

8. Write the following legal description in numbers and symbols: North 15 degrees 25 minutes 20 seconds West.

10.3 DESCRIPTION BY GOVERNMENT SURVEY

Following the Revolutionary War, the new federal government became the owner of all the land previously claimed by England. The government wanted an efficient way to survey all the newly acquired land. Congress chose a massive undertaking called the **government survey system**. The government survey system is based on the logic that you can identify a parcel by reference to two intersecting lines. By dividing the land into squares, the survey created land descriptions by identifying the square(s) in which the land was located. The process was to create a large grid with every square of the grid uniquely identified.

Principal Meridian and Base Line. A beginning reference was established in the center of the territory to be surveyed. The beginning reference is the intersection of a north-south line called a **principal meridian** and an east-west line called a **base line**. In all, 36 principal meridians and base lines were established and named in the United States. The Tallahassee Principal Meridian and base line are the reference lines used in surveys in Florida (see Figure 10.3).

FIGURE 10.3 ■ Map of Florida Showing Principal Meridian and Base Line

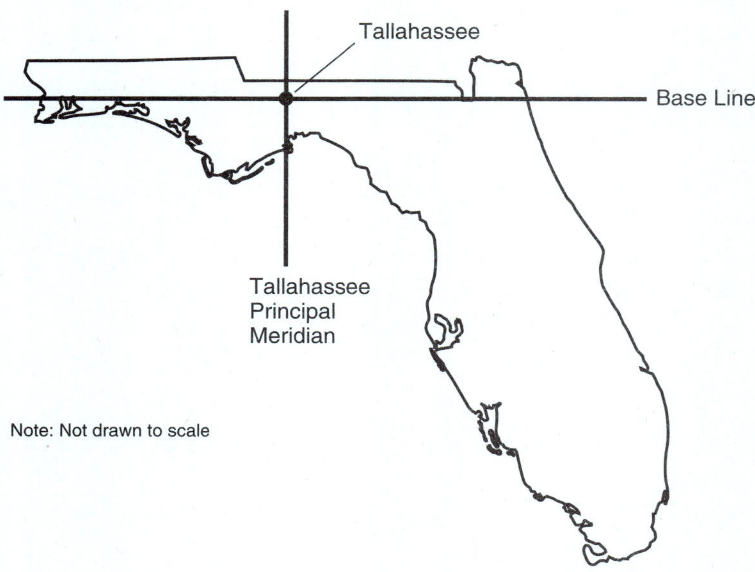

Range. To create the grid system, surveyors established vertical (north-south) *range lines* parallel to the principal meridian (PM) every six miles. This resulted in a series of lines six miles apart on either side of the PM. Each resulting six-mile-wide vertical (north-south) strip of land on either side of the PM is called a **range**.

Each range is numbered beginning at the PM. The first vertical (north-south) strip of land to the east of the PM is numbered Range 1 East or more concisely, R1E. The range numbers increase by 1 moving farther from the PM. For example, the next range east of the PM is R2E, then R3E, and so on. The numbering also begins with 1 to the west of the PM. The first range west of the PM is R1W, then R2W, and so on (see Figure 10.4).

FIGURE 10.4 ■ Map of Florida Showing Selected Range and Township Lines

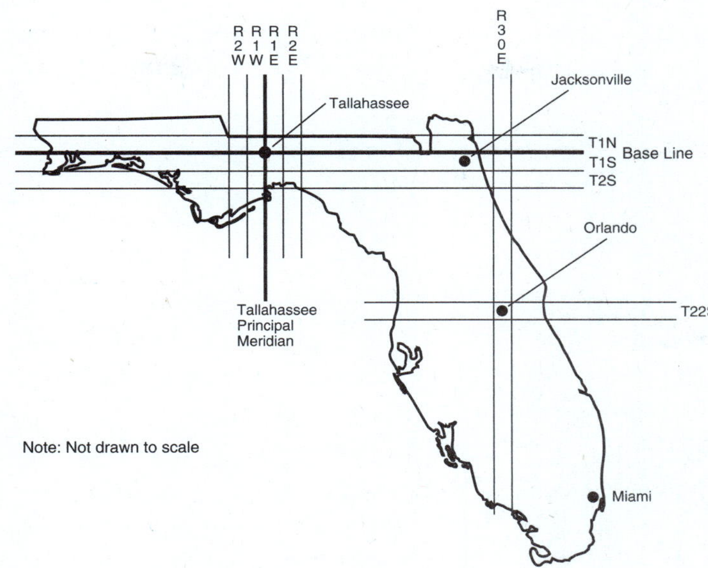

Tier or Township. The surveyors also established horizontal (east-west) **township lines** parallel to the base line (BL) every six miles. This resulted in a series of lines six miles apart on either side of the BL. Each resulting six-mile-wide horizontal (east-west) strip of land on either side of the BL is called a **tier** or simply *township*. To help remember that tiers are horizontal strips, think of the tiers of a wedding cake.

Each tier is numbered beginning at the BL. The first horizontal (east-west) strip of land above (north of) the base line is numbered Township 1 North, or more concisely, T1N. The township line numbers increase by 1 moving farther from the BL. For example, the next township tier north of the BL is T2N, then T3N, and so on. The numbering also begins with 1 below (south of) the base line. The first township tier south of the BL is T1S (the shaded row in Figure 10.5), then T2S, and so on (see Figure 10.5).

FIGURE 10.5 ■ T2S, R3E

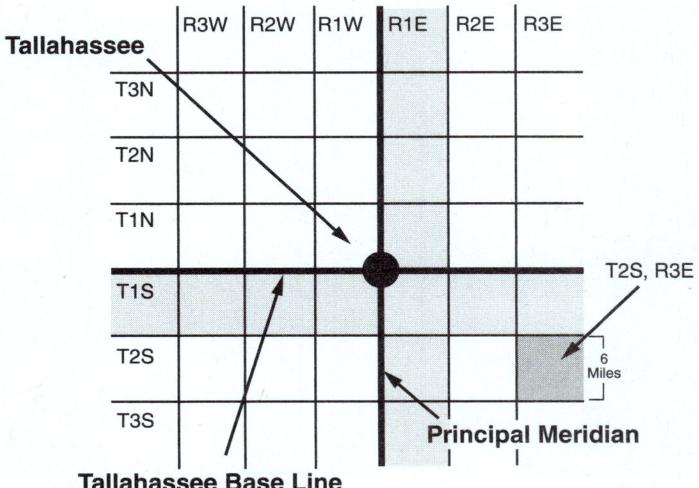

TO REMEMBER: TOWNSHIP AND RANGE LINES

The directions of township lines and range lines may be easily remembered by thinking of the words this way:

Township lines
Range lines

Townships. The grid pattern created by the intersection of two range lines and two township lines forms a 6-mile square called a **township**. A township contains 36 square miles (6 miles × 6 miles = 36 square miles).

Note that the term *township* has two meanings: In addition to an (east-west) strip of land north or south of a base line, the term also refers to the square formed by the intersection of two range lines and two township lines. Each 36-square-mile township (six miles on each side) is identified by the strip of townships (the tier) and the range in which it is located.

> **EXAMPLE:** T1S is the first tier south of the base line (refer to the shaded tier T1S in Figure 10.5). R1E is the first range east of the Tallahassee Principal Meridian (refer to the shaded range R1E in Figure 10.5).
>
> A particular township is identified by indicating the tier and range that intersect to form the 6-mile square. Township T2S, R3E is located in the second tier south of the base line and the third range east of the principal meridian (refer to the shaded township in Figure 10.5).

Practice Questions

9. Locate and mark the township numbered T2N, R2E on the following drawing.

10. Locate and mark the township numbered T3S, R1W on the following drawing.

	R3W	R2W	R1W	R1E	R2E	R3E
T3N						
T2N						
T1N						
T1S						
T2S						
T3S						

10.4 SECTIONS

Each township is further divided into 36 **sections**. Each section is one square mile or 640 acres. Sections are numbered in an S-pattern, beginning in the northeast (upper right) corner of the township with section number 1. The sections are numbered from 1 in the northeast corner and then consecutively to the west through section 6. The section numbers then wrap around in an S-pattern. The second horizontal row begins directly under section 6 and progresses west to east (left to right) from 7 to 12. Section 13 is directly under section 12, and one moves west (to the left) with section 18 last in that row. This method of numbering is repeated until section number 36 is reached in the southeast, or lower right, corner of every township. The numbering pattern of sections repeats itself inside each township (see Figure 10.6).

FIGURE 10.6 ■ Sections in a Township

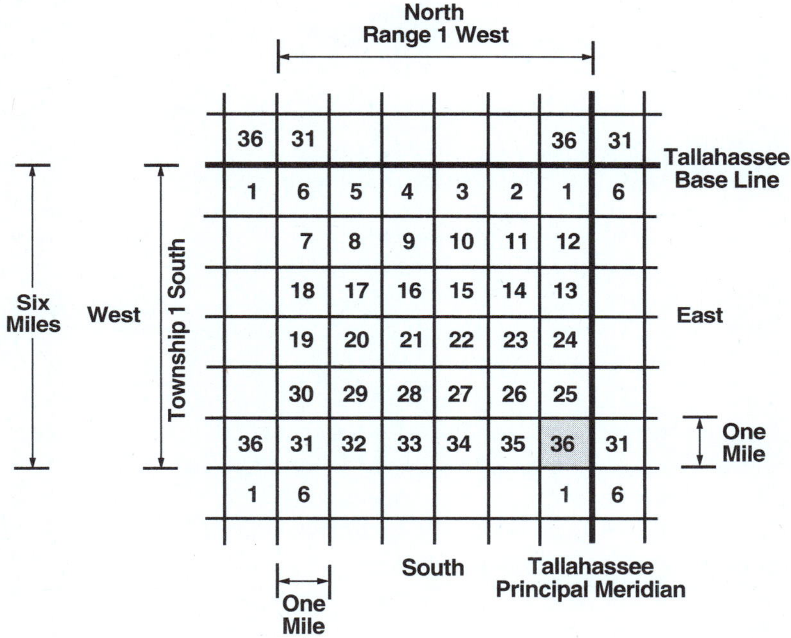

At first, this may seem odd to number sections this way; however, in the 1800s, surveyors measured the one-mile distances with metal chains and walked the sections on foot. Imagine surveyors departing the original 13 states and walking toward the west. This is why section 1 is located in the northeast corner of the township. Because of the primitive methods and tools they used at the time, surveyors found it more efficient and less tiring to measure the sections using this particular numbering sequence. To help remember the number system, think of the pattern people usually walk when doing their weekly grocery shopping at the supermarket as they go down one aisle and up another.

In writing a legal description of a section, it is customary to show the section number first, then the township tier number and direction, and last the range number and direction. For example, *Section 36, Township 1 South, Range 1 West of the Tallahassee principal meridian and base line* identifies Section 36 within the township that is located immediately southwest of the intersection of the principal meridian and base line. It is abbreviated to *Sec 36, T1S, R1W* (refer to the shaded Section 36 in Figure 10.6).

The survey presented in Figure 10.1 on page 229 is also identified as Government Lot 1, Section 36, Township 66 South, Range 27 East, Sugarloaf Key of Monroe County, Florida.

MEASURES AND TERMS ASSOCIATED WITH THE GOVERNMENT SURVEY SYSTEM

Check A square 24 miles on each side created by intersecting guide meridians and correction lines; used to adjust the grid pattern of squares because of the curvature of the earth. A check contains 16 townships.

Township A square 6 miles on each side (6 miles square) containing 36 square miles (36 sections); also an (east-west) strip of land north and south of a baseline (tier).

Section A square 1 mile on each side (1 mile square) containing 1 square mile (640 acres).

Quarter section 160 acres, measuring 2,640 feet by 2,640 feet. Historically, it was the area of land originally granted to a homesteader. Today, the 160 acres is still used to establish the limits of homesteaded property outside the boundaries of municipality.

Government lot Fractional pieces of land less than a full quarter section located along the banks of lakes and streams. Government lots were identified by a specific lot number, which became the legal description for that parcel.

How to Use the Government Survey System

Locating Sections. Suppose you want to locate a section of land in Florida, and this is the legal description given to you: "All of Section 36, Township 1 South, Range 1 West, Tallahassee principal meridian and base line." The numbers assigned to the township tier and range tell you immediately that you are dealing with property very near Tallahassee because the range (1 West) is the first six-mile segment immediately west of the principal meridian. The tier of townships (1 South) must be the first six-mile strip immediately south of the horizontal base line. Considering how sections are numbered, Section 36 cannot be anywhere except in the lower right corner of the township numbered T1S, R1W. Therefore, the section you seek begins five miles south of the intersection of the Tallahassee principal meridian and base line and immediately west of the Tallahassee principal meridian.

Practice Questions

11. Number the sections in the following township.

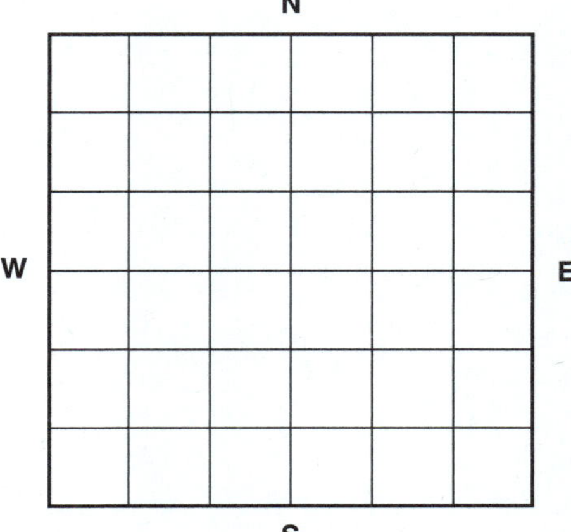

12. Using the completed township grid from question 11, fill in the blanks to complete the statements regarding sections.
    - The section number immediately north of section 36 is section ______________.
    - The section number immediately south of section 36 is section ______________.

10.5 SUBDIVIDING SECTIONS

Each section is theoretically a square, with all sides measuring one mile each and containing 640 acres within its boundaries. It is important to remember the exact number of acres in a section because 640 is used for many purposes. One reason is that the section is the basic reference when writing a legal description of land. It is also the reference when calculating acreage in subdivided tracts. Each section can easily be divided into halves, or into quarters, and so on, down into smaller divisions until the particular property one wants to locate or describe has been pinpointed.

Suppose you are interested in only a quarter section, 160 acres, of Section 36. First, divide the entire section into fourths by drawing a straight vertical line through the center of the section and a straight horizontal line through the center of the section. The two lines are perpendicular to each other and cross in the exact center of the section. The quarter section now situated in the upper right corner of the section is called the *Northeast Quarter*, the one in the lower right corner is the *Southeast Quarter*, and so on around the section (see Figure 10.7). Directions are always given in terms of the direction from the center of the section where the two dividing lines intersect.

FIGURE 10.7 ■ **Section 36**

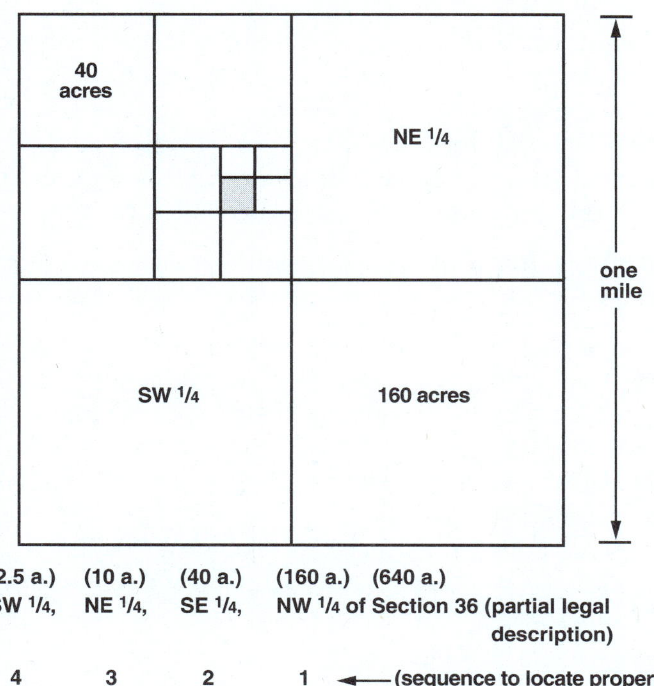

Quarter sections contain 160 acres. Suppose you are interested in a tract smaller than 160 acres. You can divide any quarter just as you did the section. Furthermore, you can keep on dividing the results until you find the tract in which you are interested.

Assume you need to find a 2.5-acre tract located somewhere near the center of Section 36. The legal description given to you is "SW¼ of the NE¼ of the SE¼ of the NW¼ of Section 36." Beginning with the section, divide it into quarters to start locating the property. In locating property from a legal description, it is necessary to start with the last part of the description and read from right to left. So, because you have located Section 36, move to the last fraction in the description (NW¼) and separate that quarter section from the whole. Move to the next fraction (SE¼), divide the previously located quarter section (NW¼) into four parts, and focus your attention on the resulting southeast quarter. Move to the next fraction (NE¼), divide the SE¼ of the NW¼ into four parts, and locate the northeast quarter of that division. You still have one more fraction (SW¼) remaining, so divide the last located parcel (NE¼) into fourths once more. When you find the southwest quarter of that division, you have located the tract described.

Calculating Size. To find the number of acres in a tract, two approaches are possible:

1. Take 640 (the number of acres in one section) and divide by the bottom number (the denominator) of each fraction in the legal description.

EXAMPLE 1: The SW¼, NE¼, SE¼, NW¼ of a certain section contains how many acres?

640 ÷ 4 = 160; 160 ÷ 4 = 40; 40 ÷ 4 = 10; 10 ÷ 4 = 2.5
or 640 ÷ 4 ÷ 4 ÷ 4 ÷ 4 = 2.5 acres

2. Multiply the denominators of each fraction together and then divide 640 by the result.

EXAMPLE 2: The SW¼, NE¼, SE¼, NW¼ of a certain section contains how many acres?

4 × 4 × 4 × 4 = 256
640 ÷ 256 = 2.5 acres

The previous exercise to determine the size of a given tract demonstrates, among other things, that generally the longer a legal description, the smaller the number of acres contained in the parcel described. With practice, one becomes familiar with the fact that a description containing four one-fourths will always result in a 2.5-acre tract. A description with only three one-fourths will result in a 10-acre parcel. If fractions other than fourths are used, the method for calculating acreage is the same.

***And* in a Legal Description.** You may be required to find the total acreage of a parcel with a legal description that contains the word *and* within the description.

EXAMPLE: The SE¼ of the NW¼ *and* NE¼ of the SW¼ of a certain section contain how many acres?

The acreage is calculated separately on either side of the word *and*. The acres are then added together to determine the total number of acres in the legal description.

Begin by dividing the denominators that immediately precede the *and*.

640 ÷ 4 ÷ 4 = 40 acres

Next, divide the denominators that follow the *and*.

640 ÷ 4 ÷ 4 = 40 acres

Finally, sum the two calculations to find the total acreage in the legal description.

40 + 40 = 80 acres

Calculating Square Feet and Cost Per Acre. Real estate professionals often describe vacant land by the number of acres in the parcel. When comparing parcels of land, cost per acre or cost per square foot are common units of measure. To be able to calculate the cost per square foot, it is necessary to memorize how many square feet are in an acre.

TO REMEMBER: NUMBER OF SQUARE FEET IN AN ACRE

4 people driving **35** mph in a **60-mph zone**

43,560 square feet in an acre

EXAMPLE 1: How many square feet are in 2.5 acres?

Multiply the number of acres in the parcel × 43,560 square feet per acre.

2.5 acres × 43,560 square feet = 108,900 total square feet

EXAMPLE 2: A 1-acre vacant parcel of land sold for $65,340. How much did the vacant parcel sell for per square foot?

Divide the selling price by 43,560 square feet per acre.

$65,340 ÷ 43,560 square feet = $1.50 per square foot

ADDITIONAL SURVEY MEASURES AND TERMINOLOGY

Acre	43,560 square feet
Benchmark	A permanent reference mark (PRM) affixed to an iron post or brass marker that is embedded in the sidewalk or street, used to establish elevations and altitudes above sea level on surveyed parcels

Practice Questions

13. A quarter of a section contains ___________ acres.

14. How many acres are there in a legal description S½ of the NE¼ of the SE¼ of the NW¼?

15. How many acres are there in the legal description N½ of the NE¼ of the SW¼ and the SE¼ of the NW¼?

16. How many square feet are in the parcel described in question 15?

17. A property costs $21,780 per acre. What is the cost per square foot of the property?

10.6 DESCRIPTION BY LOT AND BLOCK NUMBERS

Probably the most common type of legal description used for single-family dwellings located in developed subdivisions is the **lot and block** (recorded plat) method of land description. The lot and block method can be used only where plat maps, or simply *plats*, have been recorded in the public records. The platted subdivision is divided into large areas called *blocks*, and each block is subdivided into smaller areas called lots. The lots are usually numbered for convenience in identifying them. If the lots are numbered, the blocks may be assigned letters to eliminate confusing block numbers with lot numbers. For example, the shaded lot in Figure 10.8 is Lot 5, Block B of Glendale Estates Subdivision.

FIGURE 10.8 ■ Subdivision Plat Map

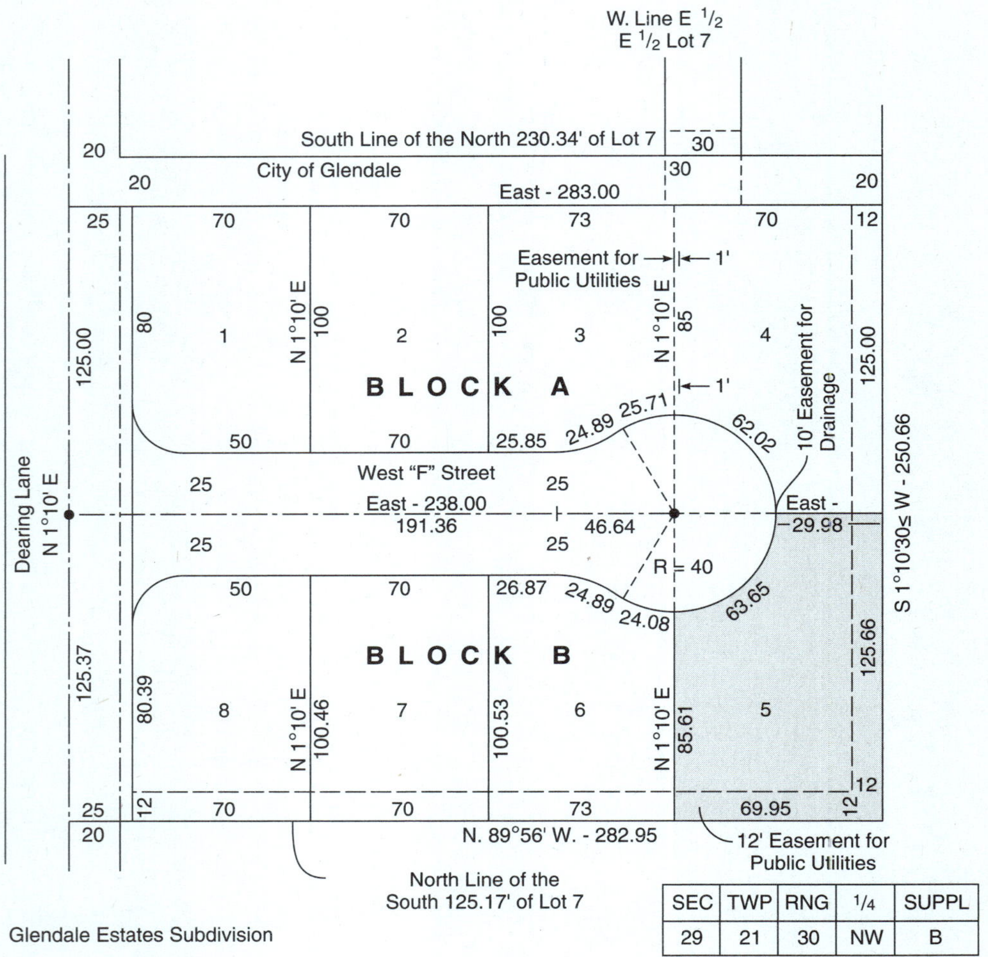

The plat map shows actual dimensions for lots, streets, and public utilities. The plat is recorded in the county courthouse under the subdivision name by book and page number and becomes the legal description for every lot in the subdivision.

Tax Maps. Every parcel of land within a tax district is assessed for tax purposes. To accomplish this task, each parcel is assigned a parcel ID (PID) number or *assessor's parcel number* by the county property appraiser's office. The parcel numbers are used to prepare tax maps, which are scaled drawings based on recorded plat maps of all real property within a tax district. Tax maps aid in the assessment of property for tax collection. The tax maps show the location of the property, dimensions, and the amount of the assessed value of each parcel. The information is used each year to prepare an assessment roll.

The assessment roll is public record of the assessed values of all lands and buildings within a county. The assessment roll lists every parcel in the county by the assessor's parcel number, owner's name and address of record, and the assessed value of land and structures.

Practice Questions

18. Platted subdivisions are divided into ______________ and ______________.

19. Tax maps are based on recorded __________ __________.

10.7 SUMMARY OF IMPORTANT POINTS

- The following three types of legal descriptions are used today: (1) metes-and-bounds, (2) government survey system, and (3) lot and block description.
- Metes-and-bounds is the most accurate method to describe both regularly and irregularly shaped parcels. The method is based on distances (metes) and directions (bounds). Metes-and-bounds descriptions begin and end with a starting point called a point of beginning (POB).
- Corners of parcels of land are identified using markers called monuments.
- The government survey system method of legal description relies on intersecting north-south and east-west lines that form a grid system.
- In Florida, the Tallahassee principal meridian and base line intersect in Tallahassee. The principal meridian runs north-south and the base line runs east-west. A series of lines parallel to the principal meridian were established every six miles forming six-mile-wide strips that run north and south and are called ranges. Parallel lines established every six miles on either side of the base line form east-west strips of land called tiers or townships.
- Township also describes a square that is six miles on each side (six miles square) and contains 36 square miles (36 sections).
- A section is a square that is one mile on each side (one mile square) and contains one square mile or 640 acres. Sections are numbered within a township in an S pattern, beginning at the top right corner and numbered right to left (sections one through six), then the next row of sections is numbered left to right (sections seven through 12), and so on.
- To calculate the acreage in a government survey legal description, multiply the denominators of each fraction together and then divide 640 by the result. If the word *and* appears in the description, calculate the acreage on each side of the word *and* separately and then add the two acreages together.
- Lot and block descriptions are used where plat maps of single-family subdivisions have been recorded in the public records. The platted subdivision is divided into blocks, and each parcel within the block is a lot.

UNIT 10 EXAM

1. The NW¼ of the NE¼ of the SW¼, Section 20, Township 4 South, Range 2 East describes a tract of
   a. .125 acre.
   b. .5 acre.
   c. 10 acres.
   d. 64 acres.

2. Which legal description consists of 120 acres?
   a. N½ of the NE¼ of the NW¼ of the NE¼ of Section 3
   b. S½ of the NE¼ of the SW¼
   c. NW¼ of the SW¼
   d. SW¼ of the S½ and the SE¼ of the SE¼

3. In the metes-and-bounds method of description,
   a. *metes* refers to direction and *bounds* refers to distance.
   b. *metes* refers to distance and *bounds* refers to direction.
   c. *metes* refers to distance and *bounds* refers to measurement.
   d. *metes* refers to metric and *bounds* refers to boundaries.

4. The government survey system is especially adapted to describing
   a. lots in platted subdivisions.
   b. odd-shaped tracts of land carved out of former land grants.
   c. land in concise symbols and words.
   d. parcels with man-made or natural physical features.

5. What is the designation of a township located three township tiers south of the base line and five ranges east of the principal meridian?
   a. R3S, T5E
   b. T3S, R5E
   c. R7E, T2S
   d. T3N, R5E

6. A check is a square with each side measuring
   a. 1 mile.
   b. 6 miles.
   c. 24 miles.
   d. 36 miles.

7. The tract of land located inside a square formed by intersecting range lines and township lines is called
   a. an acre.
   b. a check.
   c. a section.
   d. a township.

8. The vertical strip of land six miles wide beginning at the principal meridian and extending six miles east along the length of the principal meridian is called
   a. Range 1 East.
   b. Township 1 East.
   c. Tier 1 East.
   d. Section 6.

9. If you have located a township designated as T1N, R1E, the township due north of that township is
   a. T1N, R2E.
   b. T1S, R1E.
   c. T2N, R1E.
   d. T2N, R2E.

10. Which statement is FALSE concerning townships?
    a. A township contains 36 sections.
    b. A township contains 36 square miles.
    c. A township is 6 miles square.
    d. A township contains 36 acres.

11. In writing the legal description of a section, which is the standard sequence?
    a. Range number, township number, section number
    b. Section number, township number, range number
    c. Township number, range number, section number
    d. Section number, range number, township number

12. The north boundary of Section 36, Township 1 South, Range 1 West is located
    a. 6 miles south of the principal meridian.
    b. 35 miles west of the base line.
    c. 25 miles west of the principal meridian.
    d. 5 miles south of the base line.

13. A legal description that reads, in part, "the North one-half of the Northeast one-quarter of the Northwest one-quarter Section 12, Township 42 South, Range 12 East" describes a tract of
    a. 2.5 acres.
    b. 5 acres.
    c. 10 acres.
    d. 20 acres.

14. A man owned the NW¼ of a section. He sold the W½ of that NW¼. How many acres does the man still own?
    a. 40 acres.
    b. 80 acres.
    c. 160 acres.
    d. 640 acres.

15. Plat maps used in the lot and block method of legal description show
    a. the grid system of government squares.
    b. dimensions of streets and planned improvements.
    c. the numerical street address for each lot.
    d. distance and direction from the point of beginning.

UNIT

11

REAL ESTATE CONTRACTS

LEARNING OBJECTIVES

When you have completed this unit, you will be able to accomplish the following.

- List and describe the essentials of a contract, list the four types of contracts with which licensees may assist buyers and sellers, and describe the effect of the statute of frauds and the statute of limitations.
- Distinguish among formal, informal, bilateral, unilateral, implied, expressed, executory, and executed contracts.
- Describe the various ways an offer is terminated.
- Describe the various methods of terminating a contract and explain the remedies for breach of contract.
- Differentiate among the various types of listings.
- Describe the elements of an option contract.
- List and describe the information contained in a sale contract.
- Explain and describe the various disclosures required in a real estate sale contract.
- Recognize what constitutes fraud, misrepresentation, and culpable negligence.

KEY TERMS

assignment
attorney-in-fact
bilateral contract
competent
contract
enforceable contract
exclusive-agency listing
exclusive-right-of-sale listing
fraud
homeowners association (HOA)
liquidated damages
meeting of the minds
misrepresentation
net listing
novation
open listing
option contract
procuring cause
statute of frauds
statute of limitations
unenforceable contract
unilateral contract
valid contract
void contract
voidable contract

INTRODUCTION

Nearly every business transaction is based on an agreement.

11.1 CONTRACTS IN GENERAL

A **contract** defines the parties' legal relationship and spells out each party's rights and duties. It is a voluntary agreement or promise between legally competent parties, supported by legal consideration, to perform (or refrain from performing) some legal act.

Underlying every contract is the *promise*. In a real estate contract, the seller promises to convey title to the real estate, and the buyer promises to pay the purchase price. Contract promises are *enforceable* by law, provided the contract meets certain requirements.

PREPARATION OF CONTRACTS

454.23, F.S.

The drafting of legal documents or legal instruments for others is considered to be the practice of law. Unless they are attorneys, real estate brokers and associates may not prepare deeds, mortgages, promissory notes, or most other legal documents. Licensees who prepare such instruments are subject to discipline and could lose their licenses, even if the licensee did not receive compensation. Brokers and associates may also be charged with the unlicensed practice of law, a third-degree felony.

Authority of Real Estate Licensees to Prepare Contracts. Real estate licensees may not draft leases. However, licensees may fill in the blanks on residential lease instruments for lease periods that do not exceed one year, provided licensees use forms that have been preapproved by the Florida Supreme Court.

Real estate licensees may assist buyers and sellers with the completion of four types of contracts, as directed by the buyers and/or sellers:

1. *Listing agreement*. A listing agreement is an employment contract between a broker and a seller.
2. *Buyer brokerage agreement*. A buyer brokerage agreement is an employment contract between a broker and a buyer.
3. *Sale and purchase contract*. A sale and purchase contract is a contract between a buyer and a seller. If the licensee acts as agent or facilitator for one or both of the contracting parties, the licensee may prepare the sale and purchase contract.
4. *Option contract*. An option contract is an agreement between an owner of a property (the *optionor*) and a party interested in the property (the *optionee*) to keep open for a specified period of time an offer to sell or lease real property. In order to reduce liability, licensees are strongly advised to recommend that the buyer or the seller have a real estate attorney draft option contracts. Option contracts are explained in detail later in this unit.

Real estate brokerage offices typically use standardized listing agreements, buyer brokerage agreements, sale and purchase contracts, and option contracts. The Florida REALTORS® and other professional groups have developed standardized contracts for use by their members. This is desirable because the use of standardized contracts greatly reduces liability. Changing the preprinted words of any form contract by a nonlawyer can be viewed as the unlicensed practice of law. If more extensive language is needed in a contract beyond simply filling in the blanks, this language should be approved by an attorney before it is inserted.

ESSENTIAL ELEMENTS OF A CONTRACT

A **valid contract** is one that complies with the provisions of contract law and contains four essential elements:

- Contractual capacity of the parties (competent parties)
- Offer and acceptance (mutual assent)
- Legality of object (legal purpose)
- Consideration

Contractual Capacity of the Parties

Not all persons have the ability or capacity to make a valid contract. A person who is legally insane, intoxicated, suffering from dementia, or legally a minor may have only limited contractual capacity. The parties to a contract are **competent** if they have the *legal capacity to contract*, meaning they have no mental defects or insanity and are of legal age to contract.

Offer and Acceptance

One party (the *offeror*) makes an offer, and the other party (the *offeree*) accepts that offer. A contract is formed at the instant that acceptance of the offer is communicated to the offeror. A complete and mutual understanding must exist to produce a **meeting of the minds**.

Legality of Object

The agreements of a contract must be for a legal purpose.

EXAMPLE: Unbeknownst to the seller, a broker has an inactive real estate license at the time she takes a listing. At title closing, the seller discovers that the broker does not have a valid active real estate license, and the seller refuses to pay the commission. The listing agreement between the seller and the broker is void because the purpose of this employment contract is not legal. License law requires a valid active license to conduct real estate services for another for compensation, and the broker did not have an active license at the time the services were provided. A lawsuit for unpaid commission would be unenforceable in a court of law.

Consideration

Consideration is a thing of value given in exchange for some other value. People often think of consideration as the money exchanged by the parties. Legally, however, consideration is the *obligation* that each party makes to the other to make the contract enforceable. The parties to the contract must obligate themselves individually by placing some consideration in the agreement. A promise undertaken by one party must be supported by a promise undertaken by the other party. Mutual promises to perform or to forego some specific act are sufficient consideration, even if the benefit or sacrifice may not be equal. A common misconception is that the good-faith deposit (earnest money) in a real estate sale contract is the consideration. The good-faith deposit is made by a buyer to assure the seller that the buyer is serious about the transaction and the buyer intends to purchase the property. In real estate sale contracts, the seller normally promises to sell and convey, and the purchaser promises to pay for the property. There are two types of consideration:

- **Valuable consideration** is the money or a promise of something that can be measured in terms of money. Valuable consideration is used to support an arms-length transaction where the parties have conducted negotiations in their own best interest and money is paid.
- **Good consideration** is a promise that cannot be measured in terms of money, such as love and affection. Good consideration is used to support a gift, such as a father giving property to his daughter and the daughter either paying nothing or only token consideration for the property.

Either type of consideration is sufficient to enforce a contract. The law generally does not concern itself with the relative fairness of consideration. What is exchanged need not have the same measurable value. The law will accept that the parties thought the consideration to be fair because they freely agreed to the exchange.

STATUTE OF FRAUDS

725.01, F.S.

The **statute of frauds** requires that contracts *conveying an interest* in real property and all contracts that are not performed within one year from the date they become effective must be in writing and signed to be enforceable. An **enforceable contract** is a contract that the courts will recognize as legally binding. Contracts covered by Florida's statute of frauds include the following:

- Purchase and sale contracts
- Option contracts
- Deeds and mortgage instruments
- Lease agreements for a term longer than one year
- Listing agreements for a term longer than one year
- Buyer representation agreements for a term longer than one year

STATUTE OF LIMITATIONS

The **statute of limitations** is the period of time, set by statute, during which the terms of a contract may be enforced. It protects people from being compelled to perform or otherwise be sued after a period of time has expired. The times vary, depending on whether it is an oral contract or a written contract:

- Written contracts—five years
- Oral contracts—four years
- Partly written and partly oral—five years for the written portion and four years for the oral portion

TRANSFER OF REAL PROPERTY

Like all contracts, real estate purchase contracts must contain the four essential elements to be valid. Furthermore, to be enforceable in court, real estate purchase contracts must be in writing and signed by all parties who are bound by the agreement. Real estate purchase contracts are not required to be witnessed or notarized. Real estate contracts are not recorded.

TO REMEMBER: ELEMENTS OF A VALID AND ENFORCEABLE REAL ESTATE SALE CONTRACT

C	Competent parties
O	Offer and acceptance (meeting of the minds)
L	Legal purpose
I	In writing and signed (statute of frauds applies to real estate contracts)
C	Consideration (valuable or good)

The fact that a contract for the purchase and sale of real estate is oral does not automatically make the contract unenforceable. An oral real estate contract that contains all of the essential elements of a valid contract is valid and may be enforceable under certain circumstances. For example, if a buyer and a seller verbally agree to a purchase and sale of real estate, and the buyer pays part of the purchase price and takes possession of the property or has made improvements to the property, the courts will recognize the contract.

A contract does not have to be in any particular format to be valid, as long as it contains all the essential elements. The contract should have an unambiguous property identification. Because a contract is an agreement designed to clearly spell out the meeting of the minds between parties on a particular subject, it creates certain enforceable rights. It should also provide remedies for the affected parties if the contract is breached.

Void, Voidable, and Unenforceable Contracts

A **void contract** lacks one or more of the required elements of a valid contract and, therefore, has no legal effect. A contract that is void was never a legal contract. For example, the use of a forged name in a listing agreement would make the contract void.

A **voidable contract** allows one of the parties to potentially disavow contractual duties.

EXAMPLE 1: A contract in which one of the parties is an individual under the legal age to contract is voidable because the minor does not have capacity to contract—the minor does not meet the competent parties element of an enforceable contract.

EXAMPLE 2: A real estate contract that includes a home inspection contingency is voidable because if the contingency is not satisfied and released, the offer and acceptance (mutual assent) element of an enforceable contract is not met.

An **unenforceable contract** will not be enforced by a court of law. For example, a contract may be unenforceable because the statute of limitations has passed. Void contracts are also unenforceable contracts. An oral contract for sale and purchase of real estate may otherwise be valid but unenforceable because the statute of frauds requires such contracts to be in writing.

FIGURE 11.1 ■ Contracts in General

Valid	Contains all required essentials
Void	No contract; lacks one or more essentials
Voidable	May be made valid or void by one of the parties
Enforceable	Courts will enforce
Unenforceable	Courts will not enforce

Practice Questions

1. List the four types of contracts that may be prepared by a licensed real estate broker.
    1. ________________________________
    2. ________________________________
    3. ________________________________
    4. ________________________________
2. A contract for an illegal purpose, such as illegal gambling, is ______________.
3. A sane person contracting with an insane person produces a ____________ contract.
4. An oral real estate contract, with certain specific exceptions, is ______________.

11.2 CONTRACT CLASSIFICATIONS

Contracts can be classified by their method of formation, their content, or their legal effect.

Formal and Informal Contracts

Formal Contract. Historically, a formal contract was in written form and under seal. The seal has evolved from the old wax impression on a document to the word *seal* or the letters *L.S.* (*locus sigilli*, Latin for "the place of the seal") that appear after the signatures of parties signing the contract. The term *formal contract* also refers to a contract that depends on a particular form. For example, a negotiable instrument such as a promissory note is called a formal contract. A fill-in-the-blank contract on a preprinted form is also considered to be a formal contract. Today, the seal is not required for contracts to be valid.

Informal Contract. Informal contract refers to an oral contract as opposed to a written contract or specialty instrument. An oral agreement is also called a *parol contract*. Therefore, informal or parol contracts are verbal agreements as opposed to written or formal contracts.

Bilateral and Unilateral Contracts

The very name of the contract classification often indicates the way in which the contract was arranged, the requirements for its performance, or even the type of parties bound by the contract.

Bilateral Contract. A **bilateral contract** obligates both parties to perform in accordance with the terms of the contract. Both parties promise to do something; one promise is given in exchange for another.

> **EXAMPLE:** A sale contract is a bilateral contract because the buyer and the seller exchange reciprocal promises to buy and sell the property.

Unilateral Contract. A **unilateral contract** obligates only one party to an agreement. One party makes an obligation to perform without receiving in return any promise of performance from the other party. There is no obligation on the part of the other party involved.

EXAMPLE: A broker promises to pay a $1,000 bonus to the sales associate who gets the greatest number of new listings by the end of the month. The broker has promised to pay a bonus; however, the sales associates working for the broker are under no obligation to acquire new listings.

Express and Implied Contracts

A contract is classified as either express or implied according to how the contract is created.

Express Contract. An express contract is an actual agreement between the parties, the terms of which are declared orally or in writing, at the time of entering into the agreement. At the time parties enter into and communicate the terms of the agreement, an express contract is created. The primary requirements are mutual understanding and agreement. Real estate listing agreements and sale contracts are express contracts.

Implied Contract. An implied contract is inferred by the acts or conduct of the parties. The obligations and conditions of the contract are not stated in words but are implied by the acts of the parties. Every day, we enter into implied contracts. For example, if a person walks into a restaurant and orders dinner, an implied contract has been created. It is implied that the customer will pay for the service after enjoying the meal without actually discussing the actual payment or agreeing to pay for the meal until after the service has been rendered.

Executory and Executed Contracts

A contract is either executory or executed, depending on the extent to which the contract has been performed.

Executory Contract. An executory contract is an agreement between parties that involves promises to be completed at a future date. A purchase and sale real estate contract, between the time of signing the contract and the time that the title is conveyed from the grantor to the grantee, is an executory contract because the parties have not fully performed.

Executed Contract. An executed contract exists when both parties have performed their obligations. All of the parties to the contract have performed the promises stated in the contract. At title closing, a real estate sale contract is executed. A real estate sale contract becomes an executed contract when the title closing is completed and all the promises of both buyer and seller have been fulfilled (see Figure 11.2).

FIGURE 11.2 ■ **Contract Classifications**

Formal	In writing
Informal	Oral (Parol)
Bilateral	Both parties obligated
Unilateral	One party obligated
Express	In words
Implied	By acts and conduct
Executory	Not yet fully performed
Executed	Completed all terms and conditions

Executed Contract vs. Executing a Document. When people refer to executing a document, they mean the document has been signed by the parties to the contract. Real estate professionals who refer to an executed real estate contract typically mean that the document, whether a hard copy document or a digital contract, has been signed (executed) by the buyer and the seller. In this sense, the date of execution is the date on which the last of all parties' signatures are inscribed on the contract. Typically, this date is referred to as the effective date. Remember that when referring to contract classifications, an executory contract involves some future act that is yet to be accomplished (such as title closing). Thus, the term executed contract has two meanings. It can mean a signed document; however, when referring to an executed contract classification, it refers to a contract that is fully performed and nothing remains to be done by either party.

Practice Questions

5. A contract with an obligation by only one party is a ______________ contract.
6. A contract that is under seal is a ______________ contract.
7. A sale contract after the title closing is completed is an ____________ contract.

11.3 CONTRACT NEGOTIATION

An offer demonstrates an intention to enter into a contract. In the normal sequence of forming a contract, one party begins by making an *offer*. Assume that Rebecca is selling a parcel of land that she owns. Ken makes an *offer* to purchase the lot from Rebecca for $34,000. Ken is the *offeror* (the person making the offer) and Rebecca is the *offeree* (the person who receives the offer).

A common misconception is that the purchase contract form, when completed with the buyer's information, is a contract. In actuality, it is the buyer's offer; the buyer's criteria has been inserted in the blanks on the contract *form* to create the buyer's offer. It is not a contract until both parties have reached an agreement on the price, terms, and conditions.

Frequently, the offeree will make a *counteroffer* by altering the terms of the original offer. For example, if Rebecca decides to make a counteroffer of $35,500 and asks Ken to pay all the closing costs, Rebecca has replaced Ken's original offer with a counteroffer. A counteroffer nullifies the original offer and substitutes a new offer in its place.

When a counteroffer is made, the role of both parties also changes. Because Rebecca's counteroffer is based on new terms and conditions, she has "changed hats" and is now the offeror. Likewise, Ken is receiving the new terms and conditions, so he has become the offeree. It is not uncommon for a series of offers and counteroffers to take place before a meeting of the minds is accomplished. Once a meeting of the minds is reached—that is, when one party accepts the offer of the other party and communicates such acceptance—a contract has been formed. Both parties then are obligated to perform according to the contract.

An offer is terminated when any of the following happens:

- *Counteroffer*. A counteroffer indicates a willingness to contract, but on terms or conditions different from those contained in the original offer. It is not an acceptance because it indicates an unwillingness to agree to the terms of the original offer. The original offer is dead forever and cannot be later accepted. Each time a counteroffer is made, it nullifies the corresponding offer. The only offer that the offeree can consider is the one that is currently being made to the offeree.

475.5018, F.S.

- *Acceptance.* Communication of the acceptance of an offer creates a contract. An acceptance must be a mirror image of the terms of the offer. Letters and other written communications, including a signature, may be sent by electronic means or facsimile, and will be considered part of the contract. If Rebecca had accepted Ken's offer of $34,000 for her property instead of making a counteroffer, the offer would have become a contract on that acceptance and its communication.
- *Rejection.* To effectively terminate an offer, a rejection must be communicated by the offeree to the offeror. If Rebecca had chosen to reject Ken's offer, the offer would have terminated when Rebecca communicated the rejection to Ken.
- *Withdrawal by offeror.* An offeror may withdraw (or *revoke*) the offer at any time until notice of the offeree's acceptance is received by the offeror or the offeror's designated agent. Suppose, for example, that Rebecca decides to withdraw her counteroffer of $35,500. She may do so as long as her intention is communicated to Ken before he accepts her counteroffer.
- *Lapse of time.* Ordinarily, when an offer is made, a time limit for acceptance of the offer is specified. The offer terminates after expiration of that time. If no time limit for acceptance is specified, the offeree is considered to have a *reasonable length of time.* This time period is based on such considerations as the method of communication used, the location of the parties involved, and the terminology and nature of the offer.
- *Death or insanity.* The death or insanity of either the offeror or the offeree terminates the offer. An offer is not assignable (transferable); it may be accepted only by the person to whom it is made.
- *Destruction of the property.* Destruction of the subject matter terminates the offer.

TO REMEMBER: WAYS AN OFFER IS TERMINATED

W	Withdrawal by offeror
I	Insanity
L	Lapse of time
D	Death
C	Counteroffer
A	Acceptance
R	Rejection
D	Destruction of the property

Practice Questions

8. The person making an offer is the _______________.

9. A change in price or other terms by the seller to the buyer creates a _______________.

11.4 TERMINATION OF CONTRACTS

A contract is terminated when any of the following happens:

- *Performance*. When both parties have fully performed the terms and conditions of a contract, the purpose of the contract has been accomplished and the contract is terminated. The emphasis is on full performance of each and every contract term or condition. This is, of course, the desired outcome of any contract. However, sometimes contracts are terminated for other reasons.
- *Mutual rescission*. An agreement between the contracting parties to terminate their respective duties under the contract is called *mutual rescission* or *renunciation*. Both parties must mutually agree to discontinue the contract.
- *Impossibility of performance*. Performance may be impossible and beyond the control of the parties. For example, destruction of the physical improvements is a good excuse for impossibility of performance. The death of the buyer or the seller will usually be considered a reason for impossibility of performance, unless the real estate contract provides otherwise, such as binding the heirs of the deceased party.
- *Lapse of time*. Certain circumstances, such as lapse of time, will cause a contract to be terminated by operation of law. For example, a contract may be terminated as a result of the expiration of the statute of limitations. The words "time is of the essence" in a contract mean that dates and time limits in the contract must be complied with to avoid breach.
- *Breach*. A contract is breached when one of the parties fails to perform a valid obligation. The aggrieved party may sue over a breach of contract.

TO REMEMBER: WAYS TERMINATION OF CONTRACTS COULD OCCUR

B	Breach
L	Lapse of time
I	Impossibility of performance
M	Mutual rescission
P	Performance

Remedies for Breach

The Florida Real Estate Commission ordinarily has no authority or jurisdiction over breach-of-contract actions. Remedies for breach of contract are imposed by the court that considers the lawsuit. There are four legal remedies for breach of a contract:

1. *Specific performance*. If awards of money damages do not afford sufficient relief, the wronged party may sue for specific performance to have the courts force the other party to perform as the contract specifically states. This action is termed *relief in equity* because the party bringing the lawsuit is not seeking money damages. Instead, the party is asking the court for a remedy to create a fair outcome. If the party bringing the lawsuit is successful, the court will order the breaching party to do what the party promised to do in the contract. Typically, specific performance is sought by a buyer against a breaching seller.

2. *Liquidated damages*. Frequently the parties will stipulate an amount of money in the contract (usually the earnest money deposit) to be paid in the case of default by the buyer. This amount is called **liquidated damages** to the seller.
3. *Rescission*. To rescind is to cancel or annul the contract. If a court orders the parties placed back to their original positions as though the contract had never existed, both parties are relieved of their respective obligations under the contract. An injured buyer is entitled to the return of any earnest money, and the seller is obligated to return any earnest money or payment received.
4. *Compensatory damages*. Another remedy for breach of contract is a suit for damages. Usually the party bringing suit seeks an amount of money equal to the extent of loss suffered (*compensatory damages*). A wronged party may find that a certain property was misrepresented but decide to accept the property and, in addition, sue for damages. On the other hand, the buyer may decide to refuse the property and still sue for damages.

REMEDIES FOR BREACH OF CONTRACT

Specific performance	Court orders a party to perform according to the terms of the contract.
Liquidated damages	Amount of damages (usually the earnest money deposit) stipulated in the contract. If the buyer breaches the contract, typically the seller claims the earnest money deposit as liquidated damages.
Rescission	The contract is canceled and the parties are restored to their original positions.
Compensatory damages	This is the actual amount of the monetary loss to a party (also called *unliquidated* damages).

Assignment and Novation

A party may end involvement with a contract without actually terminating the contract. An **assignment** refers to the transfer of a person's rights and duties under a contract to another person. A contract is assignable (transferable) unless assignment is prohibited by the contract.

A person who assigns (transfers) legal rights in a contract is called the *assignor*. The person to whom legal rights in a contract are transferred (assigned) is called the *assignee*.

An assignor does not escape the obligation to perform the terms and conditions of the contract or to see that they are performed by the assignee, unless given a release from the other party to the original contract. The parties to a contract may agree to substitute another person's obligation to perform. A **novation** agreement is used to substitute a new party for the original one. The effect is to discharge the original party from the obligation.

Practice Questions

10. Damages specified in the contract are ________________ damages.
11. A ________________ agreement relieves the assignor from the liability to perform in a contract.

11.5 CONTRACTS IMPORTANT TO REAL ESTATE

Listing Agreements (Employment)

A listing agreement is an employment agreement between a property owner and a real estate broker authorizing the broker to find a buyer (or tenant) for a certain property. A listing agreement may be written, oral, or implied. However, listing agreements for a term longer than one year must be in writing to be enforceable under the statute of frauds.

Even though Florida law recognizes oral listing agreements, the prudent practice is to put listing agreements in writing. If litigation should result from some misunderstanding, default, or breach, it is easier to find a remedy by showing the written terms and conditions rather than trying to prove the terms or conditions of an oral listing.

A real estate sales associate's authority to provide real estate services originates with the broker. Even though the real estate sales associate may perform most, if not all, of the real estate services agreed to, the listing belongs to the broker. Sales associates are employed by the broker and are working on behalf of the broker when negotiating listing agreements. A sales associate cannot directly enter into a listing agreement with the owner.

Chapter 475, F.S., requires written listing agreements to include the following information:

- A definite expiration date
- Description of the property
- Listing price and terms
- Broker's compensation (fee or commission)
- Signature(s) of all owner(s) of record

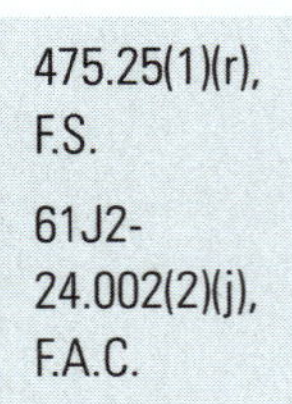

475.25(1)(r), F.S.

61J2-24.002(2)(j), F.A.C.

Florida law prohibits a provision in a listing agreement that requires the owner to notify the broker of the intent to cancel the listing once the listing has expired. A copy of the listing agreement must be given to the owner(s) within 24 hours of execution. Furthermore, the listing may not include an automatic renewal clause. Any extension of the listing agreement must be negotiated. The DBPR may issue a $200 citation for including a self-renewal clause in the listing or failure to timely deliver a copy of the listing to the owner.

COMPARISON OF LISTINGS

Type of Listing	Agent	Commission
Open	One or more brokers	Only to broker who sells property
Exclusive-agency	One broker	To listing broker if not sold by owner
Exclusive-right-of-sale	One broker	To listing broker no matter who sells

Types of Listings

The type of listing agreement used by the broker and owner determines the rights and obligations of the parties.

Open Listing. In an **open listing**, the owner reserves the right to sell the property and to list it with any number of brokers. The first broker to secure a buyer who is ready, willing, and able to purchase at the terms of the listing earns the commission. If the owner sells the property, no broker is entitled to a commission. Open listing agreements are unilateral contracts because the only promise made is that the seller will pay a commission if the broker causes a transaction to be consummated.

Exclusive-Agency Listing. A seller gives an **exclusive-agency listing** to one broker who handles the transaction. The seller reserves the right to sell the property without paying a commission, unless the buyer was introduced to the property by the broker or others acting under the broker. If the broker or another person acting under the broker's authority sells the property before the seller is able to do so, the broker is entitled to a commission. Exclusive-agency listings are bilateral contracts because both parties are obligated to perform.

Brokers rarely agree to this type of listing. When brokers and their associates market a property, they are expending resources up front in hopes that the listing sells and the expenses, plus a profit, are realized. There is too great a risk with an exclusive-agency listing that the seller will sell the property and the marketing expenses will go unreimbursed.

Exclusive Right-of-Sale Listing. The **exclusive right-of-sale listing** (or *exclusive-right-to-sell listing*) is the type of listing that gives the broker the greatest degree of protection. The seller gives the listing to a selected broker, who then becomes the exclusive real estate agent of the owner for the sale of the property during the time the listing agreement is in effect. The broker therefore is assured of a commission regardless of who sells the property. Even if the owner sells the property during the contract period, the broker is entitled to a commission. Exclusive right-of-sale listings are bilateral contracts because both parties are obligated to perform.

Net Listing. The amount of commission to be paid in a listing agreement is most often based on a percentage of the sale price. Alternatively, the commission can be paid on a *net* basis. An open listing, exclusive right-of-sale listing, or exclusive-agency listing can be structured as a net listing. A **net listing** is created when a seller agrees to sell a property for a stated acceptable minimum amount, called the *seller's net*. The broker retains the proceeds in excess of the seller's net as commission. The seller's net plus the broker's commission and closing costs equal the total sale price. Net listings are legal in Florida, however, the broker may not misrepresent the value of the property to gain a financial advantage. The broker and the seller jointly arrive at a listing price. The broker then retains, as commission, all proceeds of the sale after the costs of sale are paid and the seller receives the agreed-upon net amount.

Formula: Net Listing

100% – listing commission percentage = percentage for seller's net

total seller's net ÷ percentage for seller's net = desired sale price

EXAMPLE: Assume the property owner indicates to the sales associate that the owner wants to net $142,000 from the sale of the property. The sales associate must assist the property owner with a listing price that will cover the owner's estimated closing costs and provide the brokerage with a commission. The sales associate estimates that the seller's closing costs will be approximately $3,700.

$142,000 required net to seller + $3,700 closing costs = $145,700 total needed by seller

The broker's commission for this type of transaction is 6%.

100% – 6% commission rate = 94% remaining for seller

$145,700 ÷ .94 (94%) = $155,000 selling price

The property must sell for $155,000 to cover estimated closing costs of $3,700, to provide a commission of 6%, and for the seller to net $142,000.

Multiple Listing Service. A *multiple listing* refers to a service provided by brokers and not to a specific type of listing. It is created by a clause included in exclusive-right-of-sale and exclusive-agency listing agreements that allows the broker to convey listing information to a multiple listing service (MLS). An MLS serves as a clearinghouse for listings obtained by REALTOR® member brokers and then shared with other MLS member brokers through a published list of properties for sale. Any members of MLSs, regardless of the brokerage company they work for, can show their buyers the listings of other MLS members and receive compensation (part of the total commission) if the buyer purchases the property.

Buyer Brokerage Agreements

A *buyer brokerage agreement* is an employment contract with the buyer. The broker is presumed to be employed as the buyer's transaction broker. If the broker is to be employed as the buyer's single agent or have no brokerage relationship with the buyer, the broker must provide the required written disclosure. Buyer broker agreements typically include the following:

- The parties to and term of the agreement (beginning and ending dates)
- General characteristics of the property being sought by the buyer, including type of property, price range, and location
- Broker's obligations
- Buyer's obligations
- Retainer and compensation (either as a dollar amount or a percentage of purchase price)
- Protection period
- Early termination of the agreement and dispute resolution (buyer and broker agree to mediate first)
- Authorized brokerage relationship

WEBLINK

The National Association of REALTORS® Real Estate Buyer's Agent Council maintains a website at https://abr.realtor/.

To learn more about buyer brokers, visit the National Association of Exclusive Buyer Agents website at https://naeba.org/.

Broker's Compensation

Generally, the broker's compensation is specified in the listing or the buyer brokerage agreement. The compensation can be in the form of a commission or a brokerage fee. The compensation is computed as a percentage of the total sale price, a flat fee, or an hourly rate. The amount of a broker's commission is negotiable.

If the listing agreement requires the licensee to *find a purchaser*, the licensee must find a buyer who is ready, willing, and able to buy at a price and terms acceptable to the seller. A licensee who has performed these actions is entitled to a commission, even if a sale is not finalized (similar to earning a finder's fee). If required to *effect a sale*, the commission is earned only if the prospective buyer actually closes on the property.

475.42(1)(d), F.S.

The broker earns the commission. The broker then splits the commission with a cooperating broker (if applicable). The employing broker splits the commission with the sales associate involved with the sale. Sales associates must receive compensation from their employing brokers and not directly from the seller, the buyer, or other brokers. Some brokers have adopted a 100% commission plan. Sales associates in these offices pay the broker a monthly service fee for the use of office space, telephones, and clerical support. In return, associates receive 100% of the commissions from the sales transactions they negotiate for the broker.

The closing agent for a real estate transaction can legally prepare a check payable to a real estate sales associate for the sales associate's share of the commission. The check may be given to the associate at the closing, provided the broker has given the closing agent written authorization and instructions regarding the specific amount of commission the associate is to be paid for the particular transaction (a blanket authorization cannot be given to a closing agent).

To be paid a commission, the broker must:

- hold a current, active real estate license at the time the listing or buyer broker agreement is entered into and the real estate services are conducted;
- be employed by the seller and/or the buyer through a listing agreement or a buyer broker agreement; and
- be the procuring cause (note that payment could also result from a referral).

To be a **procuring cause**, the broker must have started the chain of events that resulted in a sale. The facts dictate who is the procuring cause. The person whose efforts cause the parties to enter into a contract is generally considered the procuring cause. The broker who has a current listing agreement with the seller is not necessarily the procuring cause. That broker may be entitled to a fee when another broker sells the property, but procuring cause goes to the broker who brings the buyer.

Procuring cause disputes between licensees are usually settled through an arbitration hearing. Disputes between a broker and a buyer or a seller may be litigated in court.

Practice Questions

12. A real estate licensee must give the owner a copy of a written listing agreement within ________ ______________.

13. An ____________ - ____________ listing is given to one broker; however, the seller reserves the right to sell the property without paying a commission.

11.6 OPTION CONTRACTS

An **option contract** is an agreement to keep open for a specified period of time an offer to sell or lease real property. The property owner (*optionor*) grants a prospective buyer or tenant (*optionee*) the exclusive right to buy or lease the owner's property for a specified price and terms within a certain period of time. Option contracts must be in writing and signed because they fall under the statute of frauds.

Unilateral Contract. In an option contract, the owner (optionor) is bound to perform the terms of the option if required to do so by the optionee. The optionee, however, may elect to walk away from the transaction because the option contract grants the optionee a right, not an obligation to buy the property. This makes the option a unilateral contract. The optionee can easily turn an option contract into a sale contract by notifying the optionor in writing that the option is being exercised. At that point, the option contract becomes a normal (bilateral) sale contract (see "Bilateral and Unilateral Contracts," earlier in this unit).

Consideration. The optionee pays a fee (valuable consideration) for the right to purchase the property for a specified price within a specified period of time. The option contract may provide that the money paid to purchase the option be applied as a part of the purchase price in the event the option is exercised. If the optionee does not exercise the option, the fee (consideration) is retained by the optionor.

Information Required. Options must contain all the terms and provisions required for a valid contract. The option must clearly specify the length of time the option is effective, the names of the contracting parties, the price of the property, a complete legal description, and the terms of the fee paid.

Options Assignable. Unless prohibited in the terms of the agreement, an option contract is assignable (transferable).

Licensee Requirements. Real estate licensees may draw option contracts. There is no case law indicating otherwise, and the legal counsel for the DBPR has indicated that licensees may draw options. However, because there isn't any case law that specifically addresses licensees and option contracts (only sale contracts), some attorneys disagree with this position. Licensees are encouraged to either fill in the blanks on standardized option contract forms or recommend to the buyer or the seller to have option contracts drawn by real estate attorneys. After all, you don't want to make your mark in real estate by being the subject of precedent-setting case law!

475.43, F.S.

Licensees who are really interested in obtaining an option on a property as a true optionee (not as a listing agent) must first divest themselves of their role as licensees. The licensee must give a valuable consideration (substantial and not nominal) for the option contract. They must inform the property owners that they are not functioning as real estate brokers or sales associates but are personally interested in acquiring an option on the property.

Practice Questions

14. The property owner in an option contract is the ______________.

15. The person asking for an option of real property is the ______________.

16. In an option contract, a __________ ________________ is paid for the right to purchase the property at a specified price within a specified period of time.

17. Licensees who are interested in obtaining an option on a property as a true optionee (not for a listing agent) must ______________ themselves of their role as licensee.

11.7 SALE AND PURCHASE CONTRACTS

The parties to a sale and purchase contract (sale contract) are the *vendor* (or seller) and the *vendee* (or buyer). Unlike the option contract, a real estate sale contract (also a *purchase agreement*) is a bilateral contract because it contains promises to perform by both parties.

Information Contained in Sale Contracts. Sale contracts must be in writing and signed and contain all the terms and provisions required for a valid contract. Although the Florida statute of frauds requires that sale contracts be in writing, courts have required that oral sale contracts be honored in some instances (see "Statute of Frauds" in this unit).

Information spelled out in the contract includes the following:

- Names of the vendor and vendee (or their legal representatives)
- Legal description (preferred) or street address of the property
- Consideration
- Purchase price
- Financing or cash terms
- Type of deed the seller will deliver (general warranty deed, unless agreed otherwise)
- Title evidence to be provided
- Terms of expenses and any prorations to be paid
- Personal property to be included with the real property
- Date, time, and place of closing
- When possession of the property will occur

The consideration in a sale contract is the promises the buyer and the seller make to each other. However, it is also a good idea to include a provision for an earnest money (binder) deposit and when it is to be paid. An earnest money deposit is valuable consideration given by the buyer to indicate serious intent to purchase the property under contract. Earnest money is not required to make the contract valid. However, it shows the buyer's intent to go through with the transaction. The contract usually states that the seller may retain the earnest money deposit as liquidated damages if the buyer breaches the contract.

Unless otherwise stated in the contract, the seller must convey a clear and merchantable title. Equitable title is the beneficial interest in real property that the buyer receives upon executing the contract and before title closing. Equitable title implies that the buyer will receive legal title at closing. Licensees may be guilty of fraud and subject to disciplinary action if they are aware of any title problem and do not inform the buyer before a contract is entered into or any part of the purchase price is paid. Most sale contracts require that the seller provide the buyer with an up-to-date abstract or a title insurance policy. If no such requirement is included in the sale contract, then the seller need not deliver either.

Spouse's Signature. When the property is co-owned by a married couple, or if it is the homestead and ownership is in only one spouse's name (*in severalty*), both spouses must sign the real estate sale contract. If the seller's spouse signs the sale contract, that spouse indicates a willingness to convey ownership rights and to relinquish homestead interest when the time comes to sign the deed that transfers title. If the buyer's spouse signs the sale contract, that spouse also becomes bound to purchase the property. Then, in the event of failure to perform, either party can be sued. If only one spouse signs a contract to purchase, only that spouse is accountable.

Power to Bind the Seller or the Buyer. A broker does not have the authority or power to sign a contract for the buyer or the seller or to bind the buyer or the seller to a contract unless the power to do so is specifically granted.

Power of attorney is a written legal document designating some other person as an **attorney-in-fact**. The attorney-in-fact then may sign for the person who granted the power of attorney, provided that power is specifically granted. A real estate licensee occasionally may come in contact with either a general power of attorney or a special power of attorney. The *general power of attorney* authorizes the attorney-in-fact to act generally for the principal in all matters. The *special power of attorney* limits the attorney-in-fact to one specified area of activity or one special act, such as signing a contract for sale or purchasing a designated property. When power of attorney is granted for acts related to title to real property, the instrument must be witnessed, acknowledged, and recorded in the public records. Licensees should consult an attorney before agreeing to be an attorney-in-fact for the buyer or seller whom they represent.

Practice Questions

18. When property is co-owned by a married couple, or if it is the homestead and ownership is in only one spouse's name, __________ __________ must sign the real estate sale contract.

19. The consideration in a sale contract is the __________ the buyer and the seller make to each other.

11.8 CONTRACT DISCLOSURES

Florida has enacted mandatory disclosure laws. These laws help consumers make informed decisions regarding real estate transactions. Most real estate contracts refer to the disclosures in the real estate contract, or the disclosures may be a separate form.

Material Defects Disclosure

Sellers of residential real property must disclose material defects concerning the property. *Johnson v. Davis*, a well-known legal case in Florida, set legal precedence concerning material defects. Mr. and Mrs. Davis entered into a contract to purchase a home from Mr. and Mrs. Johnson. Before the closing, Mrs. Davis asked about the peeling plaster around the corner of a window frame and stains on the ceilings. The sellers indicated that a minor problem with the window had been corrected a long time ago and that the stains on the ceiling resulted from wallpaper glue and ceiling beams being removed. Before closing, the buyers entered the then-vacant home following a downpour to find water "gushing" in from around the window frame and the ceiling of the family room. The Davises ordered a roof inspection and were informed that the roof was defective and would need to be replaced. The Davises sued to rescind the contract and to get a refund of their deposit. The Florida Supreme Court found in favor of the Davises and stated, "We hold that where the seller of a home knows of facts materially affecting the value of the property which are not readily observable and are not known to the buyer, the seller is under a duty to disclose them to the buyer."

The case is considered important because, before the *Johnson v. Davis* decision, the courts had favored the seller under the philosophy of *caveat emptor* (buyer beware). This court decision makes sellers accountable to truthfully disclose the condition of the property. A later case (*Rayner v. Wise Realty Co. of Tallahassee*) extended the duty to disclose material defects to real estate licensees. Although *Johnson v. Davis* concerned residential property, licensees are cautioned to always use sound ethical standards when dealing in all types of real property.

"As Is" Provision. The use of an "as is" provision in a contract for the sale of real property does not circumvent the duty to disclose all known material defects. The "as is" sale contract or addendum is typically used to remove the seller's obligation to make repairs for items not in working condition or for damage caused by wood destroying organisms. The terms and conditions of the contract typically require the buyer to perform any inspections or pursue whatever due diligence the buyer deems necessary to fully understand the condition and cost of repair of the known defects before becoming obligated to purchase the property.

Information That Is Not a Material Fact

689.25, F.S.

760.50, F.S.

Questions sometimes arise regarding whether certain information concerning the seller or previous occupants of a property must be disclosed to prospective buyers. Federal fair housing law and the Florida statutes specifically mandate that the fact that an occupant of real property is infected or has been infected with human immunodeficiency virus (HIV) or is diagnosed with acquired immune deficiency syndrome (AIDS) is not a material fact in a real estate transaction. This is personal medical information and must not be disclosed without prior authorization. Individuals inflicted with (or perceived to have) AIDS and HIV are entitled to the protections available to persons with disabilities, including fair housing protections.

Furthermore, Florida statute mandates that the fact that a property was, or was at any time suspected to have been, the site of a homicide, suicide, or death is not a material fact in a real estate transaction. A cause of action will not arise against a property owner or a real estate licensee for failure to disclosure information regarding HIV, AIDS, or that the property was the site of a homicide, suicide, or death.

Radon Gas Disclosure

404.056(5), F.S.

A radon disclosure statement on real estate sale and lease contracts is required on at least one document before or at the time of executing a sale contract or a rental agreement. At present, the disclosure consists only of what radon is; it does not require testing to disclose radon gas levels before a sale or lease.

RADON GAS DISCLOSURE

Notification shall be provided on at least one document, form, or application executed at the time to, or prior to, contract for sale and purchase of any building or execution of a rental agreement for any building. Such notification shall contain the following language:

> RADON GAS: Radon is a naturally occurring radioactive gas that, when it has accumulated in a building in sufficient quantities, may present health risks to persons who are exposed to it over time. Levels of radon that exceed federal and state guidelines have been found in buildings in Florida. Additional information regarding radon and radon testing may be obtained from your county health department.
>
> Reference: Section 404.056(5), F.S.

WEBLINK

The EPA offers the *Consumer's Guide to Radon Reduction* at www.epa.gov/radon. The EPA also provides a video concerning radon in real estate. The video *Breathing Easy: What Home Buyers and Sellers Should Know About Radon* is intended for consumers and real estate professionals. View it online at www.epa.gov/radon/radon-and-real-estate-resources#breath.

Lead-Based Paint Disclosure

When purchasing or renting pre-1978 housing, the Residential Lead-Based Paint Hazard Reduction Act requires that:

- sellers and landlords disclose to prospective buyers and tenants the presence of known lead-based paint in residential property built before 1978;
- sale contracts and leases include a disclosure about lead-based paint, either as a separate document, or the disclosure may be incorporated into the sale contract or lease;
- an EPA pamphlet regarding the danger of lead-based paint be given to buyers and tenants before the sale or lease of residential property built before 1978; and
- sellers allow homebuyers a 10-day period during which to conduct an inspection for the presence of lead-based paint (sellers are not required to pay the cost of the inspection).

Renovations and demolitions of properties built before 1978 can create harmful lead dust and chips. Because of this hazard and to prevent possible lead contamination, the Environmental Protection Agency (EPA) issued a rule that became effective in April 2010. The rule requires contractors who disturb paint in these properties to be certified and follow specific work practices. To become certified, a renovator must successfully complete an eight-hour training course offered by an accredited training provider.

When a real estate licensee lists pre-1978 property for sale, it becomes the responsibility of the licensee to make certain sellers comply with the law. The federal law does not require the testing or removal of lead-based paint. The focus of the law is disclosure of lead-based paint dangers and its presence. If a seller or landlord does not comply with the requirements of the lead-based paint law, a buyer or tenant who is harmed by the presence of lead-based paint may sue the seller or landlord.

WEBLINK @

Visit the EPA's Office of Pollution Prevention and Toxics website at www2.epa.gov/lead. The EPA also provides extensive ways to protect against lead at home at www2.epa.gov/lead/protect-your-family.

553.996, F.S.

Energy Efficiency Disclosure

The Florida legislature passed the Florida Building Energy-Efficiency Rating Act (Act) to provide for a statewide uniform system for rating the energy efficiency of new and existing buildings. The rating system applies to all public, commercial, and residential buildings. The Act requires that buyers, at the time of or before signing a sale contract, receive an information brochure notifying the purchaser of the option for an energy-efficiency rating on the building. The brochure contains a notice to residential purchasers that the energy-efficiency rating may qualify the purchaser for an energy-efficient mortgage from a lending institution.

WEBLINK

For helpful information concerning energy, visit the Florida Solar Energy Center at https://energyresearch.ucf.edu/.

720.401, F.S.

Homeowners Association Disclosure

A homeowners association is a Florida corporation responsible for the operation of a community or a mobile home subdivision. Voting membership is made up of parcel owners, and membership is a mandatory condition of parcel ownership. Homeowners associations may impose assessments that, if unpaid, may become a lien on the parcel. Florida Statute

720 requires sellers of property subject to a mandatory **homeowners association** to provide buyers with a disclosure summary regarding the association, the existence of restrictive covenants, and any assessments that the association imposes (see Figure 11.3). The disclosure summary must be supplied by the developer or by the current owner.

FIGURE 11.3 ■ Homeowners Association Disclosure Summary

1. As a purchaser of property in this community, you will be obligated to be a member of a homeowners association.
2. There have been or will be recorded restrictive covenants governing the use and occupancy of properties in this community.
3. You will be obligated to pay assessments to the association. Assessments may be subject to periodic change. If applicable, the current amount is $_____ per ______. You will also be obligated to pay any special assessments imposed by the association. Such special assessments may be subject to change. If applicable, the current amount is $_____ per ______.
4. You may be obligated to pay special assessments to the respective municipality, county, or special district. All assessments are subject to periodic change.
5. Your failure to pay special assessments or assessments levied by a mandatory homeowners association could result in a lien on your property.
6. There may be an obligation to pay rent or land-use fees for recreational or other commonly used facilities as an obligation of membership in the homeowners association. If applicable, the current amount is $______ per ______.
7. The developer may have the right to amend the restrictive covenants without the approval of the association membership or the approval of the parcel owners.
8. The statements contained in this disclosure form are only summary in nature, and as a prospective purchaser, you should refer to the covenants and the association governing documents before purchasing property.
9. These documents are either matters of public record and can be obtained from the record office in the county where the property is located, or if not recorded, can be obtained from the developer.

Purchaser's signature ______________________________

Date ______________________________

In addition to providing the Homeowners Association Disclosure Summary, the contract for sale and purchase must state that:

- the buyer should not sign (execute) the contract without first receiving and reading the homeowners disclosure summary;
- if the disclosure summary is not provided to the buyer before executing the contract for sale and purchase, the contract is voidable;
- to void the contract, the buyer must give the seller or the seller's agent written notice of the buyer's intention to cancel the contract within three calendar days after receipt of the disclosure summary or before closing, whichever occurs first; and
- the right to void the contract cannot be waived by the buyer. (The right terminates at closing.)

720.303, F.S.

Homeowners associations are required to register with the DBPR. Registration is accomplished online. Refer to the web link that follows.

WEBLINK @

For information about registering homeowners associations, visit http://www.myfloridalicense.com/DBPR/condos-timeshares-mobile-homes/homeowners-associations/.

689.261, F.S.

Property Tax Disclosure

Prospective buyers of residential property must be presented a disclosure summary concerning ad valorem taxes before or at the time of execution of the contract for sale. The purpose of the disclosure summary is to caution prospective buyers that they cannot rely on the amount of the seller's property taxes as an indication of the taxes purchasers will be required to pay in the year following purchase of the property.

The disclosure may be either attached to the contract for sale, or the wording may be inserted into the contract. If the disclosure is not inserted into the contract, the contract must refer to and incorporate by reference the disclosure summary. The reference to the disclosure must include, in prominent language, a statement that the potential purchaser should not execute the contract without first reading the required disclosure summary. The wording of the disclosure summary is presented in the text box.

PROPERTY TAX DISCLOSURE SUMMARY

Buyers should not rely on the seller's current property taxes as the amount of property taxes the buyers may be obligated to pay in the year subsequent to purchase. A change of ownership or property improvements triggers reassessments of the property that could result in higher property taxes. If you have questions concerning valuation, contact the county property appraiser's office for information.

WEBLINK

You can download the property tax disclosure summary contained in the Florida statute. The Florida statutes are available online at www.leg.state.fl.us/welcome/index.cfm. Under the Senate seal, select "Florida Statutes," then "Title XL Real and Personal Property," and then "Chapter 689." The summary is in section 689.261, F.S.

125.69(4) (d), F.S.

Building Code Violation Disclosure

A seller who has been cited for a building code violation and who is the subject of a pending enforcement proceeding must disclose in writing to the buyer that the property has been cited for a violation of the building code and that the buyer will be responsible for the violation after closing. The seller must give the buyer a copy of the pleadings, the code violation notice, and any other applicable documents received by the seller. The disclosure must inform the buyer that the buyer will be responsible for compliance with the applicable code and with the orders issued in the county court proceeding.

The statute does not require the seller to clear the violation before closing. The statute also does not address the liability of the seller regarding the costs associated with the code violation. Liability costs should be addressed and negotiated in the contract for sale and purchase. The seller must forward to the code enforcement agency the name and address of the new owner and a copy of the disclosures given to the buyer within five days after the title transfer.

190.048, F.S.

Community Development District

A *community development district (CDD)* is an independent special district created, pursuant to Florida law, to service the long-term specific needs of its community. A CDD constructs, operates, and maintains communitywide infrastructure and services for the benefit of its residents. CDDs provide an alternative way to fund and construct capital infrastructure to service projected growth without overburdening other governments and their taxpayers. The developer finances the construction of infrastructure by issuing bonds. Tax assessments are imposed on the homeowners to repay the bonds. The CDD tax assessments are in addition to county and city property taxes.

Initial contracts for sale of a parcel of real property and initial contracts for residential units within the CDD are required by law to include a disclosure to purchasers. The disclosure statement must appear immediately before the space reserved for the purchaser's signature and be written in boldfaced, conspicuous type that is larger than the type used in the rest of the contract:

> **The [name of district] community development district may impose and levy taxes or assessments, or both taxes and assessments, on this property. These taxes and assessments pay the construction, operation, and maintenance costs of certain public facilities and services of the district and are set annually by the governing board of the district. These taxes and assessments are in addition to county and other local governmental taxes and assessments and all other taxes and assessments provided for by law.**

Practice Questions

20. The Florida Supreme court case that obligates sellers to disclose to buyers all known defects that materially affect the value of residential property and that are not readily observable is ___________ *v.* ___________.

21. The *Rayner v. Wise Realty Company of Tallahassee* extended the duty to disclose material defects to real estate ______________.

22. The use of an "as is" provision in a contract for sale does ______________ eliminate the duty to disclose all known material defects.

23. Homeowners associations are required to register with the ______________.

11.9 MISREPRESENTATION AND FRAUD

The law allows real estate agents to enthusiastically describe the value of real estate and/or the potential of the property. Licensees may not, however, exaggerate, conceal, or misrepresent by making statements they know to be untrue. For example, the statement "The apartment has a fantastic view" is simply boasting about the property because the prospect is clearly able to assess the view, and the statement is the licensee's opinion. However, if the licensee had instead said, "The apartment has a fantastic view of the lake," when in fact the lake is not visible from the apartment, the statement is untrue and is illegal misrepresentation.

Misrepresentation is the misstatement of fact or the omission or concealment of a factual matter. Misrepresentation can lead to fraud. The elements of a cause of action for **fraud** are that the (1) licensee made a misstatement or failed to disclose a material fact, (2) licensee either knew or should have known that the statement was not accurate or that the undisclosed information should have been disclosed, (3) party to whom the statement was made relied on the misstatement, and (4) party to whom the statement was made was damaged as a result.

475.25(1)(b), F.S.

The law prohibits deceptive practices. For example, it is fraudulent and dishonest dealing by trick, scheme, or device for a licensee to:

- knowingly sell or offer for sale any property covered by a mortgage that also covers other property sold, unless the particular property sold or offered for sale may be released from the mortgage anytime before foreclosure sale on payment of an amount less than that remaining due from the purchaser after the sale (see "Blanket Mortgage," Unit 12);

- induce any person to buy property by promising that the licensee or the owner will resell or repurchase the property at any future time, unless there is proof that the guaranteed repurchase agreement has been approved by an agency of the State of Florida or there is evidence that the repurchase has been accomplished as promised;
- offer lotteries and schemes of sale involving the sale of chances or similar devices whereby it is represented that the purchaser is to receive property in an order to be determined by chance, whereby the price will depend on chance or the amount of sales made, or whereby the buyer may or may not receive any property; and
- invite the public to solve puzzles on the pretense of a drawing to receive property free, at a nominal price, or at cost.

Any representation made by a broker may later become the basis for charges of fraud, breach of contract, or breach of trust. In general, a purchaser has only a limited right to rely on the statements of a broker. However, if a broker invites trust and then betrays that trust, the broker is guilty of breach of trust. This legal concept brings to light an important ethical principle relating to those engaged in the sale of real estate: Whenever the trust or confidence of a buyer or a seller is invited, by actions or words, that trust or confidence, once given, must not be betrayed.

Ethical Practices. The real estate business is becoming increasingly complex, with rapid changes and constant pressures. A real estate brokerage firm is only as good as its reputation, and a good reputation can result only from a history of ethical business practices. Because just one dishonest or unethical person in a firm may destroy years of honest effort by others, ethical service is the only focal point around which a lasting reputation and career can be built.

The best policy is for the brokerage company to always instill ethical practices. When in doubt, always disclose to the parties facts material to the transaction. Document and communicate with the employing broker. A broker who does not give ordinary, careful attention to the brokerage or does not exercise reasonable control over sales associates can be charged with culpable negligence (see "Legal Terms to Know," Unit 6). Licensees must strive for individual ethical conduct and strive to maintain a high standard of ethical professionalism within the industry.

Practice Questions

24. ______________ is the misstatement of fact or the omission or concealment of a factual matter.

25. When in doubt, the best course of action is to ______________.

11.10 SUMMARY OF IMPORTANT POINTS

- Real estate licensees are allowed to assist buyers and sellers with the preparation of four types of contracts: (1) listing contracts, (2) buyer brokerage agreements, (3) option contracts, and (4) sale and purchase contracts.
- The statute of frauds requires that contracts conveying an interest in real property be in writing and signed to be enforceable. The statute of frauds applies to purchase-and-sale contracts, option contracts, and lease agreements and listing agreements of more than one year.

- The statute of limitations designates that written contracts are enforceable for five years. Oral (parol) contracts are enforceable for four years.
- A *valid contract* is one that complies with the provisions of contract law and contains four essential elements: (1) contractual capacity of the parties, (2) offer and acceptance, (3) legality, and (4) consideration.
- Real estate contracts must contain the four essential elements, be in writing, and be signed by all parties who are bound to the agreement. Real estate contracts are not required to be witnessed or notarized.
- *Valuable consideration* is the money or a promise of something that can be measured in terms of money. *Good consideration* is a promise that cannot be measured in terms of money.
- A bilateral contract obligates both parties to perform in accordance with the terms of the contract. A unilateral contract obligates only one party to an agreement.
- The *offeror* is the person who makes an offer. The *offeree* is the person who receives the offer.
- A contract is terminated when any of the following occurs: performance, mutual rescission, impossibility of performance, lapse of time, bankruptcy, and breach.
- The four legal remedies for breach of a contract are (1) specific performance, (2) liquidated damages, (3) rescission, and (4) compensatory damages.
- *Assignment* refers to a transfer (from assignor to a new assignee) of rights and duties under a contract.
- *Novation* is the substitution of a new party for the original one.
- Written listing agreements must include the following information: a definite expiration date, street address and legal description of the property, price and terms, fee or commission, and signature of the owner. A copy of the agreement must be given to the owner within 24 hours of execution. Listing agreements may not feature an automatic renewal clause.
- *Power of attorney* is a written legal document designating some other person as an attorney-in-fact. An attorney-in-fact is authorized to perform certain acts for another as authorized in the power of attorney.
- An *open listing* is given to one or more brokers. The seller reserves the right to sell the property and to list with other brokers. Only the broker who sells the property is entitled to commission.
- An *exclusive-agency listing* is given to one broker. The seller reserves the right to sell the property. The listing broker is entitled to commission unless the property is sold by the owner.
- An *exclusive-right-of-sale listing* is given to one broker who is assured of a commission regardless of who sells the property.
- A *net listing* is created when a seller agrees to sell a property for a stated acceptable minimum amount. The broker retains, as commission, all proceeds of the sale after the costs of the sale are paid and the seller receives the agreed-on net amount.
- A *buyer brokerage agreement* is an employment contract between a broker and a buyer.

- An *option contract* is a unilateral contract to keep open for a specified period of time an offer to sell or lease real property. The property owner (optionor) grants a prospective buyer (optionee) the exclusive right to buy the property within a specified period for a specified price and terms.
- The parties to a sale and purchase contract are the vendor (seller) and the vendee (buyer). Real estate sale contracts are bilateral contracts.
- Sellers must disclose material defects to a potential buyer even if selling the property "as is."
- A radon gas disclosure is required before or at the time of executing real estate sale and lease contracts. The disclosure explains what radon gas is and the possible health hazards associated with radon gas; however, it does not require a radon gas inspection.
- A lead-based paint disclosure must be given to buyers and renters of residential units built before 1978. Sellers must disclose the presence of any known lead-based paint, and buyers and renters must be given an EPA pamphlet.
- At the time of or prior to signing the sale contract, purchasers must receive an informational brochure about energy efficiency that informs them of the right to have an energy-efficiency rating performed on the structure.
- Florida law requires sellers of property subject to a mandatory homeowners association to provide buyers with a disclosure summary regarding the association, the existence of restrictive covenants, and any assessments that the association imposes.
- Purchasers must be given a property tax disclosure concerning ad valorem taxes before or at the time of executing the sale contract. The disclosure cautions buyers not to rely on the amount of the seller's property taxes as an indication of future property taxes the purchaser will pay.
- The seller must disclose to the buyer any pending building code violations.
- A community development district (CDD) is an independent special district created to service the long-term specific needs of its community.
- *Misrepresentation* is the misstatement of fact or the omission or concealment of a factual matter.

UNIT 11 EXAM

1. Which group of legal instruments may legally be prepared by a licensed real estate broker?
   a. Listing agreements, buyer brokerage agreements, commercial leases, and deeds
   b. Leases, option contracts, promissory notes, and buyer brokerage agreements
   c. Listing agreements, buyer brokerage agreements, sale contracts, and option contracts
   d. Mortgages, promissory notes, commercial leases, and option contracts

2. Failure to comply with the statute of frauds
   a. may not constitute an illegal act but would always invalidate a sale contract.
   b. would have to do with whether a contract is in writing.
   c. concerns adherence to prescribed time frames of enforcement.
   d. is prima facie evidence of the intent to commit fraud.

3. Which contract does NOT come under the jurisdiction of the statute of frauds?
   a. Lease agreements for one year or less
   b. Option contract
   c. Sale contract
   d. Listing agreement for more than one year

4. A valid real estate sale contract
   a. contains all the essential elements and is in writing.
   b. has been acknowledged.
   c. requires witnessing.
   d. transfers title to real property.

5. An adult contracting with a minor is an example of failure to meet which essential of a real estate contract?
   a. Legality of the object
   b. Offer and acceptance
   c. Meeting of the minds
   d. Competent parties

6. Canceling a daughter's property indebtedness in a contract because of love and affection is an example of
   a. good consideration.
   b. valuable consideration.
   c. insufficient consideration.
   d. inadequate consideration.

7. A contract that is NOT in writing is called
   a. a formal contract.
   b. a parol contract.
   c. a unilateral contract.
   d. an executory contract.

8. When a contract has been formed but an undertaking remains to be performed by one or both parties, it is an example of
   a. an implied contract.
   b. an express contract.
   c. an executory contract.
   d. a unilateral contract.

9. Which statement is FALSE regarding counteroffers?
   a. The original offer is terminated by the counteroffer.
   b. The original offeree becomes the offeror.
   c. A contract is created when the new offeree accepts the counteroffer and communicates the acceptance to the new offeror.
   d. The offeror and the offeree remain the same even though the terms are modified.

10. An offer is NOT terminated by
    a. a counteroffer.
    b. an acceptance.
    c. a rejection.
    d. an extension.

11. A closing is scheduled for next week. The broker would like the closing agent to prepare a check payable to the sales associate for the associate's share of the commission. Which statement is TRUE?
    a. The closing agent is required by law to make the check payable to the brokerage company.
    b. The broker may telephone the closing agent with instructions on how to disperse the escrow funds due the sales associate.
    c. The broker may enter into a written blanket authorization with the closing agent to always make the sales associates' commission payable to the associate.
    d. The broker must give specific written instructions to the closing agent regarding the exact amount of commission due the sales associate for next week's closing.

12. A woman gave an exclusive-right-of-sale listing to a broker to find a buyer for her residential lot. While the woman was vacationing with her family, a buyer signed an offer to purchase the woman's lot at the full price and terms of the listing agreement. Which statement is TRUE?
    a. Because this is an exclusive-right-of-sale listing, the broker is authorized to accept the offer on the woman's behalf.
    b. The broker may accept the offer on the woman's behalf, as long as she gets the woman's signature on the contract immediately upon the woman's return.
    c. The exclusive-right-of-sale listing does not give the broker the authority to accept the offer on the woman's behalf.
    d. The broker may accept the offer because it is a full-price offer.

13. A man and a woman enter into a written agreement. The man will mow the woman's lawn every week during the mowing season and every third week during the winter. In the middle of the summer, the man has back surgery. He hands over his lawn maintenance contracts to a friend, who assumes the responsibility for all of the man's customers for the remainder of the contract period. Which term describes this situation?
    a. Breach
    b. Assignment
    c. Specific performance
    d. Mutual rescission

14. Which applies to exclusive-right-of-sale listings?
    a. The broker is due a commission regardless of who finds the buyer.
    b. The listing may be submitted to the MLS by the listing broker.
    c. The seller must consent to the terms of the listing agreement.
    d. All of these apply.

15. Which disclosure regarding radon is required when purchasing or leasing real property in Florida?
    a. A disclosure statement in the contract indicating that the house has been tested for radon and that the test indicated a safe level of radon
    b. An estimate of the cost for a required radon test
    c. A disclosure statement in the contract indicating that the seller is required to have the property tested for radon at the seller's expense if requested by the buyer
    d. A disclosure statement in the contract explaining radon gas

16. A real estate sales associate must disclose to a prospective buyer that
    a. a former occupant of the property committed suicide in the home.
    b. the seller has been diagnosed with HIV.
    c. the family room addition does not comply with local building codes.
    d. families of other racial groups live in the immediate area.

17. Normally, a sale contract involving real property contains a provision that in case of breach by the buyer, the earnest money deposit will be regarded as
    a. compensatory damages to the seller.
    b. liquidated damages to the seller.
    c. compensatory damages to the broker.
    d. liquidated damages to be divided between seller and buyer.

18. The most advantageous type of listing from the broker's point of view is
    a. an open listing.
    b. an exclusive-agency listing.
    c. an exclusive-right-of-sale listing.
    d. a net listing.

19. Which statement is FALSE concerning Florida's building code violation disclosure?
    a. The seller is responsible for the costs associated with the code violation.
    b. The seller must inform the code enforcement agency regarding the name and address of the buyer within five days of the title closing.
    c. Copies of the pleadings and other documents concerning the code violation must be given to the buyer.
    d. The disclosure requires a statement that the buyer is responsible for compliance with the building code.

20. A couple have decided to make a written offer to purchase a home built in the 1950s. Which task is NOT required before signing the sale contract?
    a. The couple must be given a copy of the EPA pamphlet concerning lead-based paint hazards in the home.
    b. The seller must disclose any known presence of lead-based paint.
    c. The couple must have the home inspected for lead-based paint.
    d. The real estate sale contract must include a disclosure concerning lead-based paint.

UNIT

12

RESIDENTIAL MORTGAGES

LEARNING OBJECTIVES

When you have completed this unit, you will be able to accomplish the following.

- Describe the mortgage instrument and the promissory note.
- Distinguish between title theory and lien theory.
- Describe the essential elements of the mortgage instrument.
- Describe the various features of a mortgage, including down payment, loan-to-value ratio, equity, interest, loan servicing, escrow account, PITI, discount points, and loan origination fee.
- Calculate the loan-to-value ratio, explain the use of discount points, and calculate the approximate yield on a loan.
- Explain assignment of mortgage and the purpose of an estoppel certificate.
- Distinguish among the various methods of purchasing mortgaged property.
- Explain the foreclosure process, distinguish between judicial and nonjudicial foreclosure, and describe the mortgagor's and mortgagee's rights in a foreclosure.

KEY TERMS

acceleration clause
assignment of mortgage
assumption
blanket mortgage
buydown
contract for deed (land contract)
deed in lieu of foreclosure
default
defeasance clause
discount points
due-on-sale clause
equity
equity of redemption
escrow
estoppel certificate
first mortgage
foreclosure
hypothecation
interest
land development loan
lien theory
lis pendens
loan origination fee
loan servicing
loan-to-value ratio (LTV)
mortgage
mortgagee
mortgagor
note
novation agreement
partial release clause
PITI
prepayment clause
prepayment penalty
receivership clause
right to reinstate
satisfaction of mortgage
short sale
subject to
subordination agreement
takeout commitment
title theory

INTRODUCTION

This unit is an introduction to residential mortgages. Because most real property transactions involve some type of financing, real estate licensees must understand this aspect of the business.

12.1 LOAN INSTRUMENTS

An important part of purchasing a home is to find a lender that will finance the purchase. Some buyers are fortunate enough to pay cash for their purchase; however, the typical buyer must secure financing for the purchase. The lender will require the borrower to sign two legal documents: (1) a mortgage and (2) a promissory note.

Mortgage

A **mortgage** is an instrument that pledges the property as security (collateral) for the debt. It is the legal document that, when recorded, creates a lien on the real estate that secures the debt. A mortgage specifies the procedure that will be followed if the borrower doesn't repay the loan. For the lender, the property becomes security to ensure recovery of the loan. **Hypothecation** refers to the pledging of property as security for repayment of a loan without surrendering possession of the property. Mortgages identify the property being used to secure a loan and contain the borrower's promises to fulfill certain other obligations to the lender. A mortgage instrument must be in writing to be enforceable. The mortgage is recorded to establish constructive notice of the lien and to establish priority ahead of subsequent liens (see "Notice of Legal Title," Unit 9).

Parties to a Mortgage. There are two parties to a mortgage: (1) the **mortgagor**, or borrower (debtor), and (2) the **mortgagee**, or lender (creditor). The mortgagor owns the property, and the mortgagee owns the mortgage. A mortgage is regarded as an investment or chattel (personal property) by the mortgagee and, like other such investments, may be sold to another investor if desired (see Figure 12.1).

FIGURE 12.1 ■ Mortgage Financing

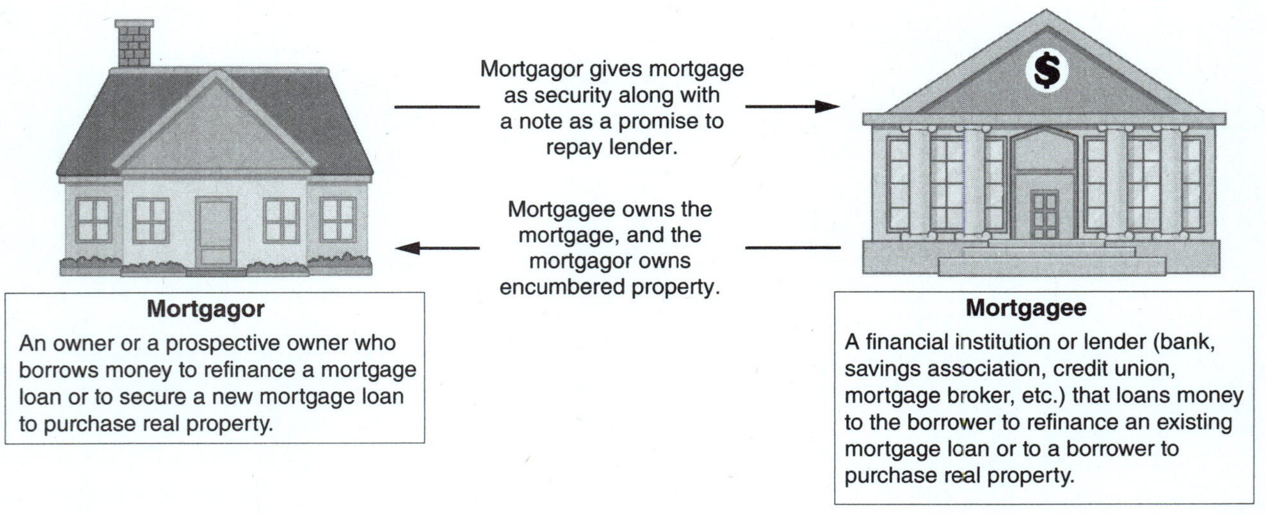

TO REMEMBER: MORTGAGOR VS. MORTGAGEE

Borrower (mortgagor) **receives** the money to finance the property.

Hint: There are two Os in borrower and mortgagor.

Lender (mortgagee) **provides the money**; the mortgage instrument, when recorded, creates a lien on the property.

Hint: There are two Es in lender and mortgagee.

Promissory Note

673.1041, F.S.

The second part of the home loan process involves the promissory note. A **note** is a legal instrument that serves as evidence of a debt. A note is a promise to repay the debt, and it makes the borrower personally liable for repayment of the obligation. Think of the note as an IOU for the money borrowed to purchase the home. Recall that the borrower has signed a mortgage instrument that is recorded by the lender to create a lien on the property. Because the buyer also signs a promissory note, if the collateral pledged in the mortgage is sold in foreclosure and the proceeds are not sufficient to cover all that is due from the borrower, the lender can sue the borrower for the remaining unpaid balance. The note is usually a separate legal instrument and must be signed by the borrower. The note is not witnessed nor is it usually recorded. A promissory note (or simply note) must accompany all mortgages in Florida.

Download the Fannie Mae/Freddie Mac Uniform Florida Fixed-Rate Note for single-family property at https://sf.freddiemac.com/tools-learning/uniform-instruments/2021-updated-instruments (scan QR code).

The note provides the financial details of the loan's repayment:

- **Amount of debt.** In return for the loan, the borrower promises to pay to the lender the amount of the loan, called the principal, plus interest.
- **Interest rate.** Interest is charged on the unpaid principal until the full amount of the principal has been repaid. Interest rates are stated as yearly (annual) rates.
- **Repayment method.** The amount of the monthly payment and the due date are indicated. The monthly payment consists of principal and interest (also called debt service). The payment is applied to interest before principal.
- **Term or time period to repay.** The date that the loan ends (has been fully repaid) is called the maturity date.
- **Borrower's failure to pay as required.** The borrower agrees to pay a late charge if the monthly payments are paid late. The lender also warns the borrower that if the payments are not paid in full each month on the due date, then the borrower will be in default. If the borrower defaults (violates the terms of the mortgage), the lender can *call* the loan (demand repayment of the entire loan before the end of the term).

Mortgage Lien Priority

When a mortgage loan is recorded in the public records, it becomes a lien on the real property. A lien is a right to have property sold to satisfy a debt. The mortgage lien is a *voluntary lien* created by the property owner in exchange for financing. Generally, the priority of a lien is determined by its recording date; however, there are a few exceptions. Property tax liens, for example, have automatic superiority over prior liens (see "Liens," Unit 9).

The first mortgage to be recorded is the **first mortgage**. The first mortgage is usually the loan used to purchase the property. If the property owner later executes another mortgage without paying off the first mortgage, the mortgage for the new financing becomes a second mortgage when it is recorded. The date and the time of day establishes the priority. Whether a recorded mortgage lien is a first mortgage, second mortgage, or third mortgage, and so on, it has priority over all subsequently recorded mortgages (mortgage instruments recorded at a later date).

When there is more than one lien on a property, the priority of liens determines the order in which the liens will be paid if the property is sold in a foreclosure sale, unless a higher priority lien is subordinated to subsequent liens. A separate **subordination agreement** (or subordination clause in a mortgage) is used when a mortgage that has been recorded earlier takes a lower lien priority to a mortgage that is recorded later.

EXAMPLE: Homeowners have a first mortgage on their home for $350,000 at 5% interest. The homeowners would like to refinance with a lower interest rate loan. They also have a second mortgage on their home for $50,000 that they used to remodel their kitchen. The homeowners would like to pay off the existing first mortgage of $350,000 with a new mortgage at 3% interest. Without a subordination agreement, the $50,000 second mortgage would now be in first position (a first mortgage). In the event of foreclosure, because the $50,000 loan was recorded at an earlier date than the new lower rate $350,000 mortgage loan, the $50,000 lien would take priority over the larger $350,000 mortgage lien. The lender that is refinancing the $350,000 loan would never agree to this arrangement. The only way to arrange refinancing is for the second mortgage holder to agree to *subordinate* the priority and allow the new lender to be in the first position. Because refinancing is common practice in the lending industry, most second mortgages (junior mortgages) will contain a *subordination clause*.

Satisfaction of Mortgage

701.04(2), F.S.

On that joyous occasion when the mortgagor pays the debt in full, the mortgagee executes a **satisfaction of mortgage** (or a *release of mortgage*). Florida statute requires that the mortgagee cancel the mortgage and send the recorded satisfaction to the mortgagor within 60 days. This document returns to the mortgagor all interest in the real property that had been conveyed to the mortgagee. Recording the satisfaction of mortgage in the public records shows that the mortgage lien has been removed.

Practice Questions

1. List the two parties to a mortgage, along with their common names.

   1. ______________________________

   2. ______________________________

2. The legal instrument that contains the amount of the debt, interest rate, and repayment provisions is called a ______________.

3. A mortgage is the instrument that pledges the property as ______________ for the debt.

4. The mortgagor gives a mortgage as security to the ______________.

12.2 MORTGAGE LAW

Lien Theory

697.02, F.S.

Today, most states, including Florida, are **lien theory** states. The *borrower* retains title to the property. The lender is protected with a lien on the real property to secure the payment of the mortgage debt. If the borrower defaults on the mortgage debt, the lender will foreclose to recover the money owed.

Title Theory

In some states, title to the mortgaged property is conveyed to the *lender* through a mortgage deed or to a trustee through a deed of trust. This mortgage theory is called **title theory**. If the borrower defaults, the lender may take possession of the property. The borrower retains equitable title to the property. Once the debt is paid in full, the lender conveys legal title to the borrower (see "Legal vs. Equitable Title to Real Property," Unit 9).

Practice Questions

5. In a ___________ theory state, the borrower or ______________ retains title to the property.

12.3 ESSENTIAL ELEMENTS OF THE MORTGAGE INSTRUMENT

Borrower's Covenants and Agreements

A mortgage is a contract between the mortgagor (borrower) and the mortgagee (lender). Because the mortgage instrument is a contract, it must contain the essential elements of a contract to be valid (see "Essential Elements of a Contract," Unit 11). Conventional mortgage lenders in Florida commonly use the Fannie Mae-Freddie Mac Single-Family Uniform Mortgage Instrument.

The first section of the Uniform Mortgage Instrument defines mortgage-related terms and indicates the date, name of the mortgagor, name of the mortgagee, mortgagee's address, and the property address. The mortgage instrument also references the promissory note and indicates the date the note was executed and the dollar amount of the note. The instrument provides for the borrower's signature and place for notarizing the instrument.

The next section of the uniform instrument contains *uniform covenants*. In this section, the borrower and the lender covenant (promise) and agree to certain conditions. An explanation of the most important covenants follows.

To download a copy of the mortgage instrument, go to https://sf.freddiemac.com/content/_assets/resources/doc/uniform-instruments/3010-floridamortgage.doc (scan QR code).

Promise to Repay. The borrower (mortgagor) promises to pay principal and interest according to the terms of the note. The mortgagor also agrees to pay escrowed items, prepayment charges, and late fees, if applicable.

Taxes and Liens. The borrower agrees to pay all taxes, assessments, and fines that could create a lien with superior priority over the mortgage (security) instrument. This clause also stipulates that the mortgagor will pay community association dues, if applicable.

Property Insurance. The mortgagor promises to keep the property insured against loss by fire and hazards included in an *extended coverage* policy. The lender may require the mortgagor to pay a one-time charge for flood zone determination and, if applicable, flood insurance coverage. If the borrower fails to maintain hazard insurance, the lender may obtain insurance coverage, at the lender's option, and charge the borrower for the expense.

Occupancy. The borrowers agree to use the property as their principal residence within 60 days after the execution of the mortgage instrument and shall continue to occupy the property as the borrower's principal residence for at least one year after the date of occupancy, unless the lender otherwise agrees in writing.

Maintenance and Covenant of Good Repair. The mortgagor promises to keep the property in good condition, maintain the property, and prevent waste. The lender is authorized to make reasonable inspections of the property.

Important Mortgage Provisions

Prepayment Clause. A **prepayment clause** allows the borrower to pay off part or all of the debt, without penalty or other fees, before maturity. In Florida, a borrower has the right to prepay a mortgage loan unless the mortgage instrument states otherwise. A prepayment clause typically stipulates conditions and terms under which the mortgage loan may be prepaid.

Prepayment Penalty Clause. The lender may choose to charge a **prepayment penalty** for early payment, if provided for in the mortgage instrument.

Acceleration Clause. The **acceleration clause** authorizes the lender (mortgagee) to accelerate or advance the due date of the entire unpaid balance if the mortgagor fails to fulfill any promises stated in the mortgage instrument. The acceleration clause gives the lender the power to declare the entire unpaid mortgage loan due and payable and to foreclose on the property if the mortgagor does not remedy the default. The foreclosure process cannot begin unless the entire debt is delinquent. Without the acceleration clause, the mortgagee could sue a delinquent mortgagor for only the monthly payments that are in arrears. The borrower is given 30 days from the date of the *notice of acceleration* to pay all sums secured by the mortgage instrument. If the borrower fails to pay the debt within the specified time period, the borrower is considered to be in default. The Fannie Mae-Freddie Mac Uniform Single-Family Mortgage Instrument includes in the acceleration clause the remedies for curing defaults.

Right to Reinstate. This clause provides for the mortgagor's **right to reinstate** the original repayment terms in the note after the mortgagee has initiated the acceleration clause. It gives the mortgagor the right to have foreclosure proceedings stopped before the foreclosure sale, provided the mortgagor pays all sums that would be due if no acceleration had occurred plus all expenses incurred by the mortgagee in enforcing the mortgage.

Due-on-Sale Clause. The **due-on-sale clause** allows the mortgagee (lender) to demand the outstanding loan balance plus accrued interest. If the property or any interest in the property is sold or transferred without the lender's prior written consent, the lender may require immediate payment in full.

Defeasance Clause. The **defeasance clause** is so named because it "defeats" the prior action when the borrower-mortgagor has made the final payment on the loan. Recall that in title theory states, the mortgaged property is conveyed to the lender through a mortgage deed. Therefore, in title theory states, the defeasance clause defeats the conveyance of legal title and returns the legal title to the borrower-mortgagor. In lien theory states, the lender is protected with a lien on the property that pledges the property as collateral until the debt is paid in full. Once the debt is repaid, the defeasance clause defeats the mortgage lien and the property is no longer pledged as collateral. Constructive notice that the mortgage is defeated is accomplished when the lender-mortgagee executes and records a satisfaction of mortgage (see "Mortgage Law" and "Satisfaction of Mortgage," earlier in this unit).

IMPORTANT MORTGAGE PROVISIONS

Acceleration	Upon default, accelerates the entire debt due and payable
Defeasance	In title theory states, requires the lender to convey legal title to the borrower once the debt is repaid; in lien theory states, requires the lender to release the mortgage lien when the debt is repaid
Due-on-sale	Upon sale (alienation), loan is due and payable
Prepayment	Conditions to repay debt in advance of due date
Prepayment penalty	Allows extra charge if any amount of the loan is paid off early
Right to reinstate	Mortgagor's right to reinstate the original repayment terms in the note after lender initiated acceleration clause

Practice Questions

6. If a borrower is in default, the ______________ clause allows the lender to call the entire loan balance due and payable.

7. The ____________ clause in a mortgage in Florida releases the mortgage lien once debt is paid in full.

12.4 MORTGAGE FEATURES

Down Payment. The down payment is the amount of cash a purchaser will pay at the time of purchase. Any earnest money pledged when the original offer to purchase was made is applied toward the total amount of cash down payment due at closing.

Loan-to-Value Ratio (LTV). The **loan-to-value ratio (LTV)** is the relationship between the amount borrowed and the appraised value (or purchase price) of a property. Lenders use this ratio as the measure of financial risk associated with lending and borrowing money. The higher the LTV (or the greater the loan compared with the property's value), the lower the lender's safety cushion should the borrower default.

Equity. An owner's **equity** in property is the monetary interest the owner has in property over and above the mortgage indebtedness. When purchasing a property, the owner's initial equity is the down payment. The greater an owner's equity, the less risk for the mortgagee.

Formula: Equity

current market value – mortgage debt = equity

EXAMPLE: The current market value of a home is $350,000. The owners have a mortgage loan with a principal balance of $280,900. How much equity do the homeowners have in their home?

$350,000 market value – $280,900 loan = $69,100 equity

Interest. **Interest** is the cost (rent paid) for the use of borrowed funds. A lender charges interest on the remaining principal balance (amount borrowed) over the life of the loan. Interest may be due at either the end of the payment period or at the beginning of each payment period. Payments made at the end of a payment period are called payments *in arrears*. This payment method is the general practice, and mortgages often call for end-of-period payments due on the first of the following month. Payments may also be made at the beginning of each period and are called payments *in advance*.

Loan Servicing. Some lenders handle the loan payment collection and recordkeeping for the mortgages they originate. **Loan servicing** is an additional source of income for lenders. *Servicing fees* typically range from ⅜ to ¾ of 1% of the unpaid balance of loans serviced. Lenders are generally willing to retain servicing of any loans sold to institutional investors.

Escrow (Impound) Account. Most lenders require borrowers to pay, in advance, monthly installments for property taxes and hazard insurance. The monthly escrow payment is one-twelfth of the estimated annual expense for property taxes and the hazard insurance premium. These payments are held in an **escrow** (impound) account for the borrower. When the taxes and insurance premiums become due, the lender pays the expenses out of the escrow account. Federal regulations limit the total amount of reserves that lenders may require. Holding funds in an escrow account to cover ongoing expenses associated with the property protects lenders from defaults, tax liens, and catastrophe.

PITI. The monthly mortgage payment paid by the borrower consists of principal and interest on the loan and the monthly reserve for property taxes and hazard insurance. The monthly principal, interest, taxes, and insurance payment is called **PITI**.

> **EXAMPLE:** A mortgage loan calls for monthly principal and interest payments of $2,186.25. The lender requires the borrowers to pay property taxes and hazard insurance in advance. Calculate the borrower's PITI based on estimated annual property taxes of $2,850 and annual hazard insurance of $1,680.
>
> The monthly escrow payment for is one-twelfth of the annual expense for property taxes and the hazard insurance premium. These payments are added to the monthly principal and interest payment to determine the monthly PITI.
>
> $2,850 annual property taxes ÷ 12 months = $237.50 monthly reserve property tax
> $1,680 annual hazard insurance ÷ 12 months = $140.00 monthly reserve insurance
> $2,186.25 monthly principal and interest + $237.50 + $140.00 = $2,563.75 PITI

Discount Points. **Discount points** are an added loan fee often charged by lenders to increase the yield on a lower-than-market-interest loan and to make the loan more competitive with higher-interest loans. Borrowers often pay discount points up front in order to gain a long-term, lower interest rate. The lower interest rate loan is advantageous to a homebuyer who plans to keep the loan for several years. This extra up-front fee is prepaid interest that increases the real yield, or annual percentage rate (APR), to the lender, making discount points advantageous for the lender (see "Discount Point Calculations" in this unit).

Loan Origination Fee. The processing of a mortgage application is called *loan origination*. Lenders typically charge the borrower a **loan origination fee**. Amounts vary, but the fee is typically 1% or 2% of the loan amount. The lender also charges the borrower all expenses encountered in obtaining credit reports, preparing loan documents, and processing a mortgage loan application.

> **EXAMPLE:** The lender is charging an origination fee of 1.5% on a new mortgage loan of $250,000. What is the cost of the fee?
>
> $250,000 × .015 (1.5%) = $3,750 cost of loan origination fee

Practice Questions

8. Discount points are charged by the lender to ______________ the ______________ on a mortgage loan.

9. Prepaid property taxes and hazard insurance costs are held by the lender in an ____________ ______________.

12.5 LOAN-TO-VALUE RATIO CALCULATION

The loan-to-value ratio (LTV) is calculated by dividing the mortgage loan amount by the property's sale price or appraised value (see the formula that follows).

Formula: Loan-to-Value Ratio (LTV)

loan amount ÷ sale price (or value) = loan-to-value ratio (LTV)

EXAMPLE 1: A purchaser secured a mortgage loan for $180,000. The home was purchased for $200,000. What is the LTV?

$180,000 loan amount ÷ $200,000 purchase price = .90 or 90% LTV

EXAMPLE 2: A home was purchased with a down payment of $60,000 and a loan of $240,000. What is the LTV?

Notice that this time the loan amount and down payment are given. Before the LTV ratio can be calculated, the purchase price must be determined:

$240,000 loan + $60,000 down payment = $300,000 total purchase price
$240,000 loan ÷ $300,000 purchase price = .80 or 80% LTV

EXAMPLE 3: A home was purchased with a down payment of $36,000 and a loan of $200,000 at 6.5% for 30 years. Monthly payments are $1,264.14. What is the LTV?

Notice that this time the monthly payment and loan term are given. This is extra information that is not needed to solve the question; however, it can make things seem more complicated. When solving a math question, always look for the key information *before* starting to do the calculation.

$200,000 loan + $36,000 down payment = $236,000 total purchase price
$200,000 loan amount ÷ $236,000 purchase price = .84745 or 85% LTV

Discount Point Calculations

Discount points are based on the loan amount, not on the selling price. When calculating the actual borrower's cost in dollars added by the discount points, each point is equal to 1% of the loan amount (1 point equals 1%). Discount points are charged as prepaid interest at the closing.

Formula: Cost of Discount Points

loan amount × discount points charged = cost of points (1 pt = .01 or 1%)

EXAMPLE 1: A lender charges 3 points on a $200,000 loan. Each discount point is equal to 1% of the loan amount. Therefore, 3 points is 3% of the loan amount. How much will the buyer pay for the discount points?

$200,000 loan amount × .03 = $6,000 cost of points

When the lender receives the $6,000, only $194,000 is needed from the lender's funds to make up the total $200,000 that is loaned to the borrower. However, the lender will receive interest based on the entire $200,000 during the full term of the loan. The *real yield* to a lender includes not only this interest but also the $6,000 paid as a mortgage discount.

EXAMPLE 2: Buyers purchased their home for $350,000. The buyers financed the purchase with an 80% conventional loan. The mortgagee charged 2.5 points. Calculate the actual cost in dollars of the points.

Discount points are paid on the loan amount; therefore, begin by calculating the amount of the loan. Each point is equivalent to 1% of the loan amount, so multiply the loan amount by 2.5% or .025.

$350,000 purchase price × .80 LTV = $280,000 loan amount

$280,000 × .025 = $7,000 cost of points

Lender's Effective Yield

Lenders use computers or prepared tables to determine the number of discount points that must be paid. However, as a general rule of thumb, each discount point paid to the lender will increase the lender's yield (rate of return) by approximately $^1/_8$ of 1% (.00125). When calculating yield, it is recommended to first convert from fractions to decimals so that the math can easily be solved with a calculator:

$^1/_8$ is the same as taking 1 ÷ 8 = .125

Multiply the number of discount points by .125 to determine the increase in yield.

Formula: Lender's Effective Yield

discount points × .125 = increase in yield

stated interest rate + increase in yield = effective yield

EXAMPLE: A buyer obtains a mortgage of $180,000, and the lender agrees to make the loan at 6% interest plus 2 points. How much will the 2 discount points increase the lender's yield?

2 points × .125 = .25%

Charging 2 discount points increases the lender's yield by .25%.

The approximate yield is also called the **effective yield**. The effective yield is based on the borrower paying the loan over the entire term of the loan. To calculate the effective yield, add the increased yield from the discount points (.25% in this case) to the stated interest rate of the loan (6%).

6% stated interest rate + .25% increase in yield from the discount points = 6.25% approximate (effective) yield

Frequently, a lender will state that mortgages are "going at" 98 or 97, for example. This is a different way of quoting discount points. It means that the lender is willing to lend only 98% or 97% of the face value of a mortgage loan. If the seller, the buyer, or a third party is willing to come up with the remaining 2% or 3%, then the lender will make the loan. It means exactly the same thing as quoting 2 points or 3 points. Regardless of the method used, the real interest rate earned for the lender will be increased approximately $^1/_8$ of 1% for each point charged up front.

Practice Questions

10. What is the loan-to-value ratio (LTV) for a home purchased for $315,000 with a loan of $283,500?

11. A borrower is getting a loan for $225,000 at 5% interest, and the lender is charging 2 points.
    a. What will the borrower pay for the points?

b. How much has the lender's yield increased?

12. The loan-to-value ratio is 80%. A buyer wants to acquire a property with a purchase price of $136,000. Calculate the required down payment.

12.6 ASSIGNMENT OF MORTGAGE

701.01, F.S.

When a homebuyer borrows money to purchase a home, the borrower (mortgagor) signs a promissory note and mortgage instrument. The mortgage and promissory note are the property of the mortgagee (lender). The mortgagee may choose to sell the negotiable instruments rather than continue to receive the monthly payments from the mortgagor.

When ownership of a mortgage is transferred from one company or individual to another, it is called an *assignment*. This process is accomplished by executing an **assignment of mortgage**. The assignment of mortgage is a legal instrument stating that the mortgagee assigns (transfers) the mortgage and promissory note to the purchaser. The assignment of mortgage is signed by the assignor (mortgagee) and delivered to the assignee (investor). The assignee becomes the new owner of the debt and security instrument.

Purpose of an Estoppel Certificate

718-720, F.S.

The purpose of an **estoppel certificate** is to stop a claim that the amount owed is different from the actual unpaid balance or that the interest rate is an amount other than the contracted rate. Estoppel certificates are used when the sale of property involves a condominium association or a homeowner's association, a mortgage lien on property, or a tenant occupied property.

EXAMPLE 1: When a company executes an assignment of mortgage, the company purchasing the mortgage instrument will receive an estoppel certificate (or estoppel letter) verifying the amount of the unpaid balance, the rate of interest, and the date to which interest has been paid before the assignment.

EXAMPLE 2: A title company, in preparation for the title closing, will order an estoppel certificate from the seller's mortgage lienholders. The title company will also order an estoppel certificate from the association if the property that is being purchased or refinanced is in a condominium, cooperative, or homeowners association.

WEBLINK

Download the Fannie Mae Assignment of Mortgage at https://singlefamily.fanniemae.com/media/6426/display. Note that this instrument indicates that the purchaser (assignee) is Fannie Mae.

Practice Questions

13. The parties to an assignment of mortgage are the seller/lender called the ______________ and the purchaser of the mortgage loan and promissory note called the ______________.

14. An ___________ ______________ verifies the unpaid loan balance, interest rate, and the date to which interest has been paid before the assignment of a mortgage instrument.

12.7 METHODS OF PURCHASING PROPERTY ENCUMBERED BY AN EXISTING MORTGAGE LOAN

A buyer may purchase mortgaged property in one of several ways. The most straightforward method is for the buyer to pay cash for the property. In this case, the seller's mortgage is paid in full from the sale proceeds, a satisfaction of mortgage is recorded by the mortgagee, and the property is delivered free and clear of the mortgage lien at the time of closing.

Often, the buyer either does not have sufficient funds to pay cash for the property or the buyer does not desire to use cash for the entire purchase. A buyer may choose to secure new financing to purchase the property. Any existing mortgage debt is paid off from the sale proceeds.

When purchasing property that is encumbered by an outstanding mortgage loan, a buyer may choose to purchase the property in one of two ways. The distinction between the two ways is important if the buyer defaults and the mortgage is foreclosed.

1. *Assumption of an existing mortgage*. When assuming an existing mortgage, the buyer is agreeing to assume the seller's debt. The **assumption** of the mortgage obligates the buyer to execute a promissory note and become primarily liable for the debt. However, unless there is an executed *novation agreement*, the seller is still liable for the debt on the original promissory note. In the event the buyer defaults, the lender can sue both the buyer and the seller for any deficiency outstanding from the foreclosure.

   If a seller wants to be completely free of the original mortgage loan obligation, the seller, the buyer, and the lender must execute a written **novation agreement**. The novation agreement makes the buyer solely responsible for any default on the mortgage loan. The original mortgagor (seller) is released as a party to the mortgage loan. In effect, an assumption with novation allows the buyer to assume the mortgage and assign personal liability for the balance of the loan to the buyer alone (see "Assignment and Novation," Unit 11).

   Lenders may want to prevent buyers from assuming an existing mortgage. Most lenders today include a *due-on-sale clause* in conventional mortgage loans. In effect, this clause prevents another party from assuming the mortgage and requires that the mortgage debt be paid in full when the property is sold.

2. *Subject to the mortgage*. When a property is sold **subject to** the mortgage, the buyer is not personally liable to the lender for payment of the mortgage debt. The buyer takes title to the property knowing that the seller is still legally responsible for the note even though the buyer will be making the mortgage payments. In the event of the buyer's default, the lender forecloses and the property is sold by court order to pay the debt. If the sale does not pay off the entire debt, the seller (not the purchaser) is liable for the difference. The mortgagee can sue the seller for the deficiency because the seller signed a promissory note at the time the mortgage was created.

Contract for Deed (Land Contract)

A **contract for deed** or **land contract**, is used to finance the sale of property when a buyer does not have sufficient cash to make a down payment large enough to secure traditional financing. The buyer agrees to the purchase price for the property, typically makes a small down payment, and pays monthly payments of principal and interest to the seller. The buyer takes possession of the property at closing, however, instead of receiving a deed, the purchaser receives a contract for deed, giving the buyer equitable title to the property. *Equitable title* entitles the buyer to homestead protection. The buyer is responsible for the expenses associated with ownership, including the real estate property taxes, property insurance, and upkeep. The seller retains *legal title* to the property until the debt is repaid. Once repaid, the seller delivers a deed and the legal title is conveyed to the buyer (see "Legal vs. Equitable Title," Unit 9).

This form of seller financing is advantageous to a buyer who has insufficient down payment or lacks credit history. There are also less closing costs compared with financing the purchase through a traditional lender. Because a contract for deed is seller financing, the parties to the agreement are referred to as vendor (seller) and vendee (buyer).

Only an attorney should prepare a contract for deed. In case of buyer default, regular foreclosure proceedings are required, just as though it were a seller-held mortgage.

LAND DEVELOPMENT LOANS AND CONSTRUCTION LOANS

Land Development Loans. Developers purchase raw land and use **land development loans** to finance the installation of the onsite and offsite improvements, including sewers, streets, and utilities.

Construction Loans. Developers secure construction loans to finance the construction of homes, apartments, office building, and so forth. The lender commits to the full amount of the loan but disburses the funds in payments called *draws* as the construction progresses. Construction loans are short-term financing. The borrower pays interest on the money as it is disbursed in draws on the loan.

Blanket Mortgage Loans. A **blanket mortgage** pledges several parcels, usually building lots, as security for the loan. The developer uses proceeds from the sale of individual lots to pay off the blanket mortgage loan. A **partial release clause**, commonly found in blanket mortgages, provides for the release of individual parcels from the blanket mortgage lien upon payment of a specified amount. The partial release clause stipulates the conditions under which the mortgagee will grant a release of lots, free and clear of the mortgage.

Takeout Commitment. The developer or contractor typically obtains a written commitment from a financial institution certifying that permanent financing will be provided when the project is completed. The financial institution is willing to become the permanent lender after construction is completed. The written commitment for permanent financing, called a **takeout commitment**, makes it easier to secure the construction loan. When the project is completed, the lender for the permanent loan advances the amount committed. The developer uses the funds to pay off the construction lender.

Buydown. In times of high interest rates, homebuyers may be reluctant to purchase or they may have difficulty qualifying for a mortgage loan. A **buydown** is a financing technique used to temporarily lower the interest rate on a mortgage loan. The developer or a seller pays an up-front fee to the lender. In exchange for the fee, the mortgagor's loan interest rate (and monthly mortgage payment) is reduced, generally for the first one to three years.

EXAMPLE: A builder agrees to buy down the interest rate for the first three years of a mortgage in a new subdivision. The borrower will pay 2% interest on the mortgage for the first year, 3% the second year, and 4% for the remaining years of the mortgage. The difference in the monthly payment in years 1 and 2 is made up by the buydown cash payment the builder gives the lender. If mortgage amount were $100,000 and the loan term 30 years, for the first year at 2%, the borrower's monthly principal and interest (PI) is $369.62. In the second year, at 3%, the borrower's monthly PI is $421.60. In years 3–30, the borrower's monthly PI is $477.42.

$477.42 – $369.62 = $107.80 (monthly differential year 1) × 12 monthly payments = $1,293.60

$477.42 – $421.60 = $55.82 (monthly differential year 2) × 12 months = $669.84

$1,293.60 + $669.84 = $1,963.44 amount of buydown

Each month the lender goes into the "buydown account" and takes out the amount necessary for the full monthly payment of 4%. A builder would rather make an additional cash payment to the lender than reduce the price on a home in a new development.

Practice Questions

15. When mortgaged property is sold ______________ to the mortgage, the buyer takes over the balance of the existing mortgage and the seller remains solely responsible for a deficiency judgment.

16. A seller who allows a purchaser to assume the existing mortgage should have the lender and the purchaser agree to execute a ______________ agreement.

17. The clause in a blanket mortgage that allows a parcel of property to be sold free and clear of the blanket mortgage upon payment of a specified amount is the __________ __________ clause.

12.8 DEFAULT

Foreclosure

The borrower is required to fulfill certain obligations agreed to in the promissory note. These obligations include repayment of the debt, payment of property taxes, maintenance and upkeep, and keeping the property insured. Failure to meet any of these obligations can result in a borrower's **default**. When default occurs, the lender has the right under the mortgage contract to pursue legal action against the borrower for payment of the debt.

In Florida, foreclosure is a judicial process that requires the mortgagee to file a foreclosure suit in court. **Foreclosure** is enforcement of the mortgage lien.

If default on the mortgage occurs, the mortgagee has two remedies:

1. *Initiate a suit on the promissory note*. The mortgagee may choose to sue on the note, obtain a judgment, and then execute the judgment against any real or personal property of the mortgagor. This judgment may be levied against any of the mortgagor's property except property that is specifically exempted (such as homestead property, unless it is the property on which the default is based).
2. *Initiate a foreclosure proceeding*. The mortgagee may foreclose on the property that is subject to the mortgage lien. The foreclosure process begins with the mortgagee accelerating the due date of all remaining payments and then filing a lawsuit to foreclose. On receiving final judgment, the sale is advertised (public notice of the sale), and the property is sold at public auction to the highest bidder.

Equity of redemption allows the mortgagor to prevent foreclosure from occurring by paying the mortgagee the principal and interest due plus any expenses the mortgagee has incurred in attempting to collect the debt and initiating foreclosure proceedings. In

Florida, the right of equity of redemption ends once the property has been sold at foreclosure sale.

Results of Foreclosure. If redemption is not made, on confirmation of the sale, the clerk files a certificate of title and title passes to the purchaser. There are no warranties; title passes "as is," although free of the former defaulted mortgage. The successful bidder obtains no better title than the mortgagor held. The doctrine of *caveat emptor* applies in foreclosure sales; that is, the purchaser is presumed to know that the purchase is subject to any prior liens of record or interests for which there is constructive notice.

The clerk then disburses the sale proceeds in accordance with the final decree. The difference between what is owed the mortgagee at foreclosure sale and the successful bid is called *surplus funds*. Any excess proceeds are paid to the mortgagor. If, however, the proceeds are not sufficient to satisfy the outstanding debt, the mortgagee may request that the court issue a *deficiency judgment* against the person(s) who signed the note. When granted, a deficiency decree can extend to include all real and personal property belonging to the maker of the note, except a homestead.

Short Sale

A **short sale** involves a real estate transaction where the net proceeds at closing will not satisfy the payoff amount of mortgages and other liens on the property. The deficiency in funds is because the seller is attempting to sell the home to the buyer for an amount less than the amount owed to the lender(s) and other lienholders (if any).

Sometimes, because of depressed market conditions, a mortgagee will allow a property secured by a mortgage loan to be sold for less money than what is owed the lender. The lender releases its mortgage so that the property can be sold free and clear to the new purchaser. The lender decides to cut its losses by agreeing to a negotiated sale rather than the delay and expense of a foreclosure action.

Deed in Lieu of Foreclosure

Sometimes the parties will agree to settle the default without going to court. This can be accomplished with a **deed in lieu of foreclosure**. The process is sometimes called a *friendly foreclosure* because it is a *nonjudicial* procedure (it does not involve a lawsuit). If the lender agrees, the borrower who is in default under the terms of the mortgage gives title (the deed) to the lender to avoid judicial foreclosure. The lender takes title to the property subject to existing liens.

Income Property

Mortgage loans on income-producing property typically include a receivership clause. If the borrower of income-producing property does not make timely payments on the mortgage loan, the lender wants the income from the property to be used to make the mortgage payments. A **receivership clause** allows a receiver to be appointed to collect income from the property and use the income to make mortgage payments in the event of default.

Lis Pendens

A **lis pendens** (Latin for *action pending*) is a notice recorded in the public records (constructive notice) of a pending legal action that involves real estate. The notice of pending legal action states the names of the parties, the object of the action, and a legal description of the property.

A lender initiating a lawsuit to foreclose on a mortgage will file a lis pendens in the county records where the property is located. The lis pendens informs the public that a legal action is pending against the property. If the owner attempts to sell the property and a title search is conducted by or on behalf of the prospective buyer, then the buyer will learn of the pending litigation.

Practice Questions

18. Any surplus funds remaining after all liens have been paid after a foreclosure sale belong to the ______________.

19. The right of a mortgagor in default to prevent foreclosure by paying all money owed, including principal, interest, and the expenses incurred in initiating a foreclosure proceeding, is called the ___________ of ______________.

20. A deed in lieu of foreclosure is a ______________ procedure because the defaulting mortgagor transfers the deed to the lender in lieu of a foreclosure process.

21. A _________ ________ involves a real estate transaction where the net proceeds at closing will not satisfy the payoff amount of mortgages and other liens on the property.

22. A ________ _____________ is constructive notice of pending legal action that involves a parcel of real estate.

12.9 SUMMARY OF IMPORTANT POINTS

- The two instruments created with a mortgage loan are (1) mortgage, which creates the lien interest and pledges the property as security for the debt; and (2) promissory note, the promise to repay and represents legal evidence of a debt.
- The two legal theories of mortgages are (1) title theory (title conveys to lender/mortgagee through a mortgage deed) and (2) lien theory (title remains with borrower/mortgagor and lender has a lien against property). Florida is a lien theory state.
- Once the borrower has repaid the mortgage loan in full, the mortgagee executes and records in the public record a satisfaction (release) of mortgage to remove the mortgage lien. Florida statute requires that the mortgagee send the recorded satisfaction to the mortgagor within 60 days.
- The priority of mortgage liens is determined by the recording date. The oldest recorded mortgage has the higher priority and is the first mortgage. Later recorded mortgages have lower priority and are called second mortgages or junior mortgages.
- The acceleration clause authorizes the mortgagee to accelerate the due date of the entire unpaid loan balance if the mortgagor fails to fulfill any promises stated in the mortgage instrument.
- The due-on-sale clause allows the mortgagee to call due the outstanding loan balance plus accrued interest. The clause prevents another party from assuming the mortgage.
- The defeasance clause, in title theory states, requires the lender to convey legal title to the borrower once the debt is repaid. In lien theory states, this clause requires the lender to release the mortgage lien when the debt is repaid.

- The amount of cash the buyer pays is called the down payment. The loan-to-value ratio is the percentage of the purchase price or the appraised value (whichever is lower) that the buyer has borrowed.
- The owner's equity is determined by subtracting the mortgage balance from the current market value of the property.
- Many lenders require the borrower to pay monthly installments of $\frac{1}{12}$ of the total estimated annual property taxes and hazard insurance premium. The lender holds the installments in an escrow account and pays the property taxes and insurance premium from the impound account.
- Discount points are an up-front charge paid at closing to increase the lender's yield. One discount point is equal to 1% of the loan amount. Each discount point increases the yield by about $\frac{1}{8}$ of 1%.
- Assignment of mortgage transfers ownership of a mortgage and note from one company or individual to another.
- A contract for deed is another type of financing arrangement. The buyer agrees to make payments to the seller over time, but unlike a mortgage, the seller retains legal title until all payments have been made.
- Equity of redemption allows the mortgagor to prevent foreclosure by paying the mortgagee the principal and interest due plus any expenses the mortgagee has incurred in attempting to collect the debt.
- A short sale occurs when the lienholders agree to allow the property to be sold for an amount less than what will satisfy the liens and agree to remove the liens from the property.
- A deed in lieu of foreclosure is a voluntary action when the mortgagor transfers title to the mortgagee to avoid a foreclosure proceeding.

UNIT 12 EXAM

1. In a mortgage transaction in Florida, the legal evidence of the personal debt is the
   a. property (collateral).
   b. note.
   c. mortgage instrument.
   d. borrower's credit history.

2. A type of seller financing in which the seller retains legal title until the buyer has repaid the debt is a
   a. balloon mortgage.
   b. purchase-money mortgage.
   c. contract for deed.
   d. blanket mortgage.

3. In title theory states, the mortgage clause that provides that the conveyance of title to the lender is defeated when all the terms of the agreement have been fulfilled is the
   a. penalty clause.
   b. release clause.
   c. defeasance clause.
   d. insurance clause.

4. A home was purchased with a down payment of $50,000 and a loan of $200,000 at 6% interest for 20 years. Monthly payments are $1,432.86. What is the loan-to-value ratio?
   a. 25%
   b. 70%
   c. 75%
   d. 80%

5. A borrower who is in default on a mortgage is allowed to prevent the lender from foreclosing on the property by paying the mortgagee the delinquent principal and interest, plus any expenses the mortgagee has incurred in attempting to collect the payments. This right is called
   a. novation.
   b. a satisfaction of mortgage.
   c. the equity of redemption.
   d. an acceleration clause.

6. A lender declares all the unpaid balance due and payable as a result of default. The lender is exercising the
   a. acceleration clause.
   b. due-on-sale clause.
   c. defeasance clause.
   d. right to reinstate clause.

7. The person who borrows money to help pay for the purchase of real property is called at various times the
   a. lender.
   b. mortgagee.
   c. lienor.
   d. mortgagor.

8. When a vendee buys "subject to the mortgage," the
   a. vendee becomes responsible for the note.
   b. original obligation is substituted with a new note by novation.
   c. vendor is relieved of the obligation for the promissory note.
   d. vendee is not responsible for the note.

9. A couple has just made the final mortgage payment on their home. What document must the mortgagee file on their behalf?
   a. Lis pendens
   b. Novation
   c. Satisfaction of mortgage
   d. Estoppel certificate

10. If a mortgagee does NOT want the mortgage to be paid ahead of schedule, the mortgage will normally contain
    a. a prepayment penalty clause.
    b. a redemption clause.
    c. a defeasance clause.
    d. an acceleration clause.

11. A buyer agrees to purchase a property with an existing mortgage lien. In which situation is the new buyer the only party responsible for the debt?
    a. Assumption of an existing mortgage
    b. Estoppel
    c. Assumption with novation
    d. Subject to the mortgage

12. The loan-to-value ratio is 80%. A buyer wants to acquire a property with a purchase price of $116,000. Calculate the required down payment.
    a. $20,000
    b. $23,200
    c. $32,800
    d. $92,800

13. The primary purpose of an estoppel certificate is to
    a. prevent foreclosure.
    b. relieve the mortgagor of personal liability for the debt.
    c. verify the loan balance.
    d. prevent transfer of title to the mortgagee.

14. When a lis pendens is filed properly with the county clerk, it becomes a type of
    a. attachment on the subject property.
    b. vendor's lien.
    c. constructive notice.
    d. easement by prescription.

15. A couple purchased their home for $125,000. They financed the purchase with an 80% conventional loan. The mortgagee charged 2.5 points. Calculate the actual cost of the points in dollars.
    a. $1,600
    b. $2,000
    c. $2,500
    d. $3,125

16. A mortgagor defaulted on a mortgage encumbering an apartment complex. Once the foreclosure proceedings were filed, the lender appealed to the courts to appoint
    a. a receiver.
    b. an onsite manager.
    c. an attorney to handle the case.
    d. an arbitrator.

17. The rule of thumb used to convert discount points to an annual percentage rate is that each discount point increases the yield by approximately
    a. ⅛ of 1%.
    b. ¼ of 1%.
    c. ½ of 1%.
    d. 1%.

18. A lender charged 7% plus 3 points. What is the approximate yield on this loan?
    a. 7.25%
    b. 7.375%
    c. 7.5%
    d. 7.75%

19. You have a loan with monthly principal and interest payments of $846.21. If the lender requires an impound account for taxes and insurance, what would the total payment amount be if your annual property taxes were $2,840 and your annual insurance cost was $1,570?
    a. $1,082.88
    b. $1,130.38
    c. $1,193.71
    d. $1,213.71

20. The market value of an apartment building is $350,000. The investor has mortgaged $300,000. What is the investor's equity in the property?
    a. $50,000
    b. $300,000
    c. $350,000
    d. $650,000

UNIT

13 TYPES OF MORTGAGES AND SOURCES OF FINANCING

LEARNING OBJECTIVES

When you have completed this unit, you will be able to accomplish the following.

- Explain the process of qualifying for a loan and calculate the qualifying ratios for different types of mortgage loan programs.
- Describe the features of conventional mortgages.
- Describe the features of an amortized mortgage and an adjustable-rate mortgage, including the components of an adjustable-rate mortgage.
- Describe the characteristics of FHA-insured mortgages and common FHA loan programs.
- Identify the guarantee feature of VA mortgage loans and the characteristics of VA loan programs.
- Distinguish among the various types of purpose-specific mortgage products.
- Distinguish among the primary sources of home financing.
- Describe the role of the secondary mortgage market and know the features of the major agencies active in the secondary market.
- Recognize and avoid mortgage fraud.
- Describe the major provisions of the federal laws regarding fair credit and lending.

KEY TERMS

adjustable-rate mortgage (ARM)
amortized mortgage
annual percentage rate (APR)
balloon payment
biweekly mortgage
Closing Disclosure
conforming loan
conventional loan
demand deposit
disintermediation
entitlement
home equity conversion mortgage (HECM)
home equity loan
housing expense ratio (HER)
index
intermediation
level-payment plan
lifetime cap
Loan Estimate
margin
mortgage broker
mortgage fraud
mortgage insurance premium (MIP)
mortgage lender
mortgage loan originator (MLO)
negative amortization
nonconforming loan
nonconventional loan
package mortgage
partially amortized mortgage
payment cap
periodic cap
primary mortgage market
principal
private mortgage insurance (PMI)
purchase money mortgage (PMM)
reverse mortgage
secondary mortgage market
teaser rate
total obligations ratio (TOR)
triggering terms
up-front mortgage insurance premium (UFMIP)

INTRODUCTION

This unit begins by discussing the process of qualifying for a mortgage loan and determining the qualifying ratios for different types of mortgage loan programs. Conforming and nonconforming loans are defined. Conventional fixed-rate amortized mortgages and conventional adjustable-rate mortgages are presented first, followed by nonconventional FHA-insured and VA-guaranteed mortgages. The unit also describes the role of the secondary mortgage market and the major provisions of federal laws regarding fair credit and lending procedures.

13.1 QUALIFYING FOR A LOAN

Loan Application Process

Lenders use the Uniform Residential Loan Application (URLA) form to qualify applicants (borrowers) applying for a one- to four-family residential property. The URLA requests general background information in addition to current and previous employment and monthly gross income (before deductions, including income tax and Medicare deductions). If the applicant has additional income from other sources that the applicant wants considered for the loan, the applicant can list the monthly income and income source. Assets and liabilities are also declared.

The applicant indicates the purpose of the loan and information about the property that the applicant is wanting to purchase or refinance, including whether the property will be used as a primary residence, second home, or as an income-producing property. The URLA also asks specific questions about the source of funding for the loan and past financial history, including, for example, whether the applicant is in default or delinquent on a federal debt, there are any outstanding judgments, or within the last seven years the applicant has had a property foreclosed upon or the applicant has declared bankruptcy.

WEBLINK

The Uniform Residential Loan Application (URLA) form can be downloaded at https://singlefamily.fanniemae.com/media/7896/display.

Credit Evaluation and Credit Scoring. Lenders review the applicant's credit history. A *credit report* is ordered to determine the applicant's debt and credit score. A *credit score* is a number that has been calculated based upon the borrower's repayment history, and the amount and types of debt, and it assists lenders with predicting whether an applicant is likely to make timely credit payments. Lenders use credit scores to measure potential risk of making a loan. Higher credit scores mean that an applicant is more likely to repay the loan and thus be approved and pay a lower interest rate for new credit.

WEBLINK

To learn more about credit scores, go to https://www.myfico.com/credit-education/credit-scores.

Qualifying Ratios. Lenders qualify applicants for a mortgage loan by reviewing how much debt the applicant has in relation to how much income the applicant earns. Lenders review the applicant's total monthly expenses in relation to the applicant's monthly gross income to determine what is called qualifying ratios. Qualifying ratios are important because borrowers who have high debt compared to gross income may run into trouble paying the mortgage payments if something unexpected should occur. Qualifying ratios will be discussed in detail later in this unit.

Qualifying the Property. The lender orders a property appraisal of the property that will be pledged as collateral for the loan. The appraiser estimates the property's value and, in the case of FHA and VA, determines if the overall condition of the structure meets the required minimum standards (FHA and VA mortgage loans are discussed in detail later in this unit).

Preapproval and Prequalification. Prequalifying is less formal. The lender asks the borrower questions concerning income and debt; however, a credit report is not pulled. Preapproval, however, is more detailed. The lender runs a credit report and verifies income and assets. The application is submitted for preliminary underwriting, and the prospective borrower is provided with a *preapproval letter* that defines the loan amount the buyer is approved to receive. Approval letters are usually valid for 120 days.

13.2 CONVENTIONAL VS. NONCONVENTIONAL MORTGAGE LOANS

Mortgage loans can be grouped into two general categories.

1. **Conventional loans** carry no government guarantee or government insurance for the lender if the borrower fails to repay the loan. The lender assumes the full risk of default in a conventional loan. To offset the lender's risk, borrowers are sometimes required to purchase insurance to protect the lender against the borrower's default. Qualifying for a conventional loan is generally more difficult than qualifying for a loan that is guaranteed or insured by a government agency.
2. **Nonconventional loans** are backed by the federal government. Nonconventional loans include FHA-insured and VA-guaranteed loans. Nonconventional loans offer more flexible options for borrowers.

Conventional Mortgage Loan Features

Interest Rate. Private lenders make conventional mortgage loans. Interest rates for conventional mortgages reflect market conditions and are negotiated between the lender and the borrower.

Assumption. Fixed-rate conventional loans include a due-on-sale clause that requires the loan balance to be paid in full when the property is sold, thereby preventing another person from assuming the mortgage loan. Adjustable-rate conventional loans are assumable (see "Adjustable-Rate Mortgage," in this unit).

Prepayment. Fixed-rate conventional mortgage loans contain a prepayment clause that allows borrowers to prepay the mortgage principal (see "Prepayment Clause," Unit 12).

Down Payment and Private Mortgage Insurance. Conventional loans typically require the borrower to make a larger down payment (equity) as compared with nonconventional loans. However, borrowers can make smaller down payments. **Private mortgage insurance (PMI)** is required for conventional loans that finance more than 80% of the purchase price. In other words, if the borrower makes a down payment of less than 20% of the purchase price, PMI is required. Private mortgage insurance protects lenders in case the borrower defaults.

Loan-to-Value Ratio. Recall that the loan-to-value (LTV) ratio is a financial term used by lenders to describe the ratio between the mortgage loan amount and the property's value. To calculate LTV, divide the loan amount by the property's purchase price (or the appraised value if it is less than the purchase price). As part of the lender's underwriting process, it will require that the borrower comply with a particular LTV.

The LTV ratio is also used to determine whether the borrower will have to purchase PMI. PMI is required if the LTV ratio is greater than 80%. The portion of the loan that exceeds 80% of the property's sale price (or appraised value) is insured with PMI. If the borrower defaults and the proceeds from the foreclosure sale are not sufficient to cover the amount that is due the lender, the mortgage insurance covers the difference. The borrower can request the PMI coverage to be cancelled once the outstanding balance of the mortgage drops to 80% of the original value of the home (.80 or 80% LTV).

Qualifying for a Conventional Mortgage Loan

Conventional loans have more stringent qualifying requirements compared with nonconventional loans. To qualify for a conventional loan, the borrower must have a good to excellent credit score and meet certain income requirements, work history, down payment, and qualifying ratios. These qualifying requirements are established by Fannie Mae and Freddie Mac guidelines (Fannie Mae and Freddie Mac are explained in detail later in this unit).

Qualifying Ratios. Lenders consider two qualifying ratios when borrowers apply for a conventional mortgage.

1. The **housing expense ratio (HER)** is calculated by taking the borrower's expected monthly housing expenses divided by monthly gross income. Housing expenses include principal, interest, property taxes, and hazard insurance (PITI) plus the monthly private mortgage insurance premium (PMI) for mortgage loans greater than 80% LTV. Homeowners association fees, condominium fees, and flood insurance, if applicable, are also considered housing expenses (see the following formula). The recommended HER for a conventional mortgage loan is 28%.

Formula: Housing Expense Ratio (HER)

monthly PITI + PMI ÷ monthly gross income = HER

2. The **total obligations ratio (TOR)** is a measure of a borrower's total monthly installment debt divided by monthly gross income. Monthly installment debt includes the expenses that appear on the borrower's credit report, such as credit card payments, auto payments, student loan payments, and child support payments, referred to as long-term obligations (LTO). The monthly installment debt also includes the monthly housing expense used in the HER (see the following formula). The recommended TOR for a conventional mortgage is 36%.

Formula: Total Obligations Ratio (TOR)

(PITI + PMI + LTO) ÷ monthly gross income = TOR

EXAMPLE: A couple has a combined monthly gross income of $6,737, a monthly mortgage payment of $1,420, a PMI premium of $96, and additional monthly obligations including the following:

- Car payment: $460
- Student loan: $200
- Credit card: $150

a. What is the couple's housing expense ratio?
b. What is the couple's total obligations ratio?
c. Does the couple qualify for a conventional mortgage?

Solution:

a. To determine the couple's HER, determine the total monthly housing expenses:
$1,420 PITI + $96 PMI = $1,516 total monthly housing expense
Next, divide the total monthly housing expenses by the monthly gross income:
$1,516 ÷ $6,737 monthly gross income = .2250 or 22.5% HER

b. To determine the couple's TOR, determine the total monthly obligations:
PITI + PMI + LTO = $1,516 + $460 car + $200 loan + $150 credit = $2,326
Next, divide the total monthly obligations by the monthly gross income:
$2,326 total monthly obligations ÷ $6,737 = .3452 or 34.5%

c. To qualify for a conventional mortgage loan, the borrower must have an HER that does not exceed 28%. The borrower's HER is 22.5%. So, 22.5% of the borrower's monthly gross income pays the borrower's monthly housing expenses. The borrower's HER is below the required threshold. The borrower meets the HER ratio requirement for a conventional mortgage.
To qualify for a conventional mortgage loan, the borrower's TOR must not exceed 36%. The borrower's TOR is 34.5%, which is less than 36%. The borrower meets the TOR ratio requirement for a conventional mortgage.

Practice Questions

1. _______________ loans are NOT insured or guaranteed by a government agency.

2. The total obligations ratio for a conventional mortgage loan may NOT exceed _______________.

3. A borrower has a combined monthly gross income of $5,900, PITI of $1,500, monthly PMI premium of $95, and additional monthly obligations including the following:

- Car payment: $260

- Student loan: $186
- Credit card: $260

a. What is the borrower's housing expense ratio?

b. What is the buyer's total obligations ratio?

c. Does the buyer qualify for a conventional mortgage?

13.3 COMMON TYPES OF MORTGAGES

The two most common types of conventional mortgage loans are fixed-rate amortized mortgage loans and adjustable-rate mortgage loans. The interest rate of a *fixed-rate* conventional mortgage loan is determined at the time that the loan is originated and does not change over the entire loan period, referred to as the *loan term*. With an *adjustable-rate* mortgage, the interest rate may go up or down during the loan term.

Amortized Mortgage

A fixed-rate **amortized mortgage** consists of a series of fixed, equal monthly payments over the loan *term*. Typical mortgage loan terms are 15-year and 30-year terms. At the end of the loan term, the loan is completely paid off. For example, a loan with a 30-year term will be paid in full in exactly 30 years (360 monthly payments). The monthly payments are constant (same monthly payment) each month for the loan term. Fixed-rate amortized mortgages are sometimes referred to as **level-payment plan** mortgages because the borrower pays the same mortgage payment each month.

Mortgage Amortization Table. An *amortization table* is a spreadsheet that lists each monthly payment for the entire loan term. An amortization schedule allocates each monthly payment into two components:

1. Interest paid. A portion of each monthly payment is applied to interest. Interest is the amount lender gets paid for making the loan to the borrower. The amount of the mortgage payment allocated to interest in the largest portion of the monthly payment in the early years of the loan term.
2. Principal paid. After the interest charges are allocated, the remainder of the monthly payment is applied to paying off the loan. This portion of the monthly payment is called **principal**. As the loan balance is gradually paid off, the amount allocated to interest gradually decreases, and the amount allocated to principal gradually increases.

The two components of the monthly mortgage payment, principal and interest, are referred to as PI. Recall from Unit 12 that, typically, borrowers also pay the property taxes and hazard insurance premiums as part of their monthly mortgage expense (PITI). One-twelfth of the annual property taxes and hazard insurance are added to the borrower's monthly payment. However, because these expenses are not part of the loan repayment, they are not included in the amortization table.

Amortization tables can be easily created from programmed software. There are three figures that must be inserted into the formula to create an amortization table:

- Loan amount

- Interest rate
- Loan term

Once these values are entered, the monthly PI payment and the amount applied to interest and principal is automatically calculated in the table. Portions of an amortization table for a $200,000 mortgage loan at 4% interest with a 30-year term are presented in Figure 13.1.

FIGURE 13.1 ■ Portions of an Amortization Schedule

Month	Monthly PI Payment	Interest Paid	Principal Paid	Balance
1	$954.83	$666.67	$288.16	$199,711.84
2	$954.83	$665.71	$289.12	$199,422.71
3	$954.83	$664.74	$290.09	$199,132.62
4	$954.83	$663.78	$291.06	$198,841.57
5	$954.83	$662.81	$292.03	$198,549.54
6	$954.83	$661.83	$293.00	$198,256.54
355	$954.83	$18.88	$935.95	$4,726.78
356	$954.83	$15.76	$939.07	$3,787.71
357	$954.83	$12.63	$942.20	$2,845.50
358	$954.83	$9.49	$945.35	$1,900.16
359	$954.83	$6.33	$948.50	$951.66
360	$954.83	$3.17	$948.49	$0.00

The first six monthly payments and the last 6 monthly payments are shown in Figure 13.1. The principal and interest payment (PI) is $954.83 every month for 360 payments. In months one through six, the amount allocated to interest is greater than the amount applied to principal reduction. However, in the last six months of the loan term, most of the monthly payments reduce principal and very little is applied to interest. The reduced amount allocated to interest is because most of the loan balance has been paid off in the last months of the loan term. In month 360 (12 monthly payments × 30-year term), the entire debt is paid in full.

Adjustable-Rate Mortgage

Unlike a **fixed-rate mortgage** that has an interest rate (and monthly payment) that does not change for the entire loan term, an **adjustable-rate mortgage (ARM)** is a loan that has an interest rate that can change at preset intervals, based on a predetermined index. Typically, ARMs feature an initial fixed-rate period for the first three to 10 years. The interest rate then may adjust each year thereafter once the initial fixed period ends. For example, a 5/1 ARM is a 30-year term loan. The first five years of the loan feature a fixed interest rate. Thereafter, the interest rate can adjust each year up or down based on the index. 3/1 ARMs and 5/1 ARMs often provide the lowest interest rates and monthly payments during the first three or five years, respectively. This type of loan can be advantageous for growing families who intend to move to a larger home in a few years. Also, conventional ARM loans do not have a due-on-sale clause and therefore are assumable. ARMs aren't for everyone. Many borrowers want the security of knowing that their interest rate (and their monthly mortgage payments) will remain the same for the entire loan term. ARMs also tend to be more popular when fixed-rate interest rates are high as borrowers are hoping to refinance their ARMs when fixed interest rates decline. The primary components of adjustable-rate mortgages are as follows.

Index. The **index** is an economic indicator that is used to adjust the interest rate in the loan. Lenders legally are allowed to link the interest rate of an ARM with any recognized index. Many indexes are tied to U.S. Treasury securities. The index moves up and down with fluctuations in the nation's economy. The index must not be controlled by the lender, and it must be verifiable by the borrower.

Margin. The **margin** (or *spread*) is the percentage added to the index. The margin represents the lender's cost of doing business plus profit. The margin percentage remains constant over the life of the loan.

Calculated Interest Rate. The calculated interest rate is arrived at by adding the index to the lender's margin.

Formula: Calculated Interest Rate

index + margin = calculated interest rate

EXAMPLE: Assume the borrower has an ARM tied to the one-year T-bill rate with a margin of 2.25. If the T-bill rate is 4%, the calculated interest rate is:

4% index + 2.25% margin = 6.25% calculated interest rate

Adjustment Interval. The interest rate on an ARM adjusts periodically based on the adjustment interval established in the mortgage loan documents. Some ARMs adjust annually based on the index. A hybrid ARM allows the borrower to lock in a fixed rate for a longer time than the usual one year before the adjustments begin. With a 5/1 hybrid, for example, the initial interest rate is fixed for the first five years and then beginning with year 6, the rate adjusts annually (pegged to the index) for the remaining term of the loan.

Interest Rate Caps. ARMs typically include rate caps to limit how much the interest rate may change per adjustment. Most ARMs have two types of rate caps—periodic cap and lifetime cap. A **periodic cap** limits the amount the interest rate may increase at any one time, usually a year. For example, the interest rate may be capped to not increase more than 2% during an annual adjustment interval. ARMs typically also feature a **lifetime cap** that caps the total amount the interest rate may increase over the life of the loan. For example, the loan might have a lifetime cap or ceiling of 6% over the life of the loan.

Payment Cap. A **payment cap** limits the amount the monthly payments can increase during any adjustment. The purpose of a payment cap is to protect the mortgagor from unaffordable high monthly payments. If interest rates rise sharply but the payments do not because of a payment cap, the unpaid interest is added to the loan balance. **Negative amortization** occurs when the mortgage payments are not large enough to cover the interest expense. The result is the mortgage loan balance increases (instead of decreasing). Negative amortization can result in a mortgagor owing the mortgagee more than the house is worth.

Teaser Rate. Sometimes a lender will offer borrowers an initial below-market interest rate called a **teaser rate**. The low rate is usually offered for the first year of the loan, with a sharp annual rate increase at the next rate-adjustment period to bring the loan in line with the agreed-upon index.

WEBLINK

The Federal Reserve Board's Consumer Handbook on Adjustable-Rate Mortgages is available at https://files.consumerfinance.gov/f/documents/cfpb_charm_booklet.pdf.

Practice Questions

4. In a fixed-rate amortized loan, the portion applied to principal gradually ______________ each month and the portion applied to interest gradually ______________ each month.

5. Another name for a fixed-rate amortized mortgage is a ________________ __________ mortgage.

6. An economic indicator used to adjust the interest rate on an ARM is called an ______________.

7. A mortgagee's costs of doing business plus profit is called the ______________.

8. The ____________ ________ limits the amount the interest rate may change at each adjustment interval.

9. If the monthly payment on the ARM is smaller than what is required to pay the principal and interest for the period, it will result in ___________ _______________.

13.4 GOVERNMENT-INSURED FHA PROGRAM

Recall that nonconventional loans are backed by the federal government. Nonconventional loans include FHA-insured loans.

Purpose of the FHA

The Federal Housing Administration (FHA) was created in 1934. The FHA is a government agency within the Department of Housing and Urban Development (HUD). Its mission is to stimulate homeownership. FHA loans are fully insured by the government to help increase the availability of affordable housing in the United States.

FHA loans are made by FHA-approved lenders. Lenders must meet certain criteria for their loans to be FHA-approved, after which the FHA insures the loans the lender issues against losses in the event that borrowers default on the loans. FHA loans protect lenders from financial risk. The cost of the mortgage insurance is paid by the borrower. The FHA does not make loans to borrowers, process loans, or build housing.

FHA loans are a good option for first-time homebuyers or for buyers who have challenges dealing with the more stringent requirements of conventional financing because they require a 3.5% down payment and have less stringent credit score requirements and other qualifying criteria compared with conventional loans. There are many types of FHA loan programs; however, the most popular loan program is a Section 203(b) loan, which is a fixed-rate mortgage loan for the purchase or construction of one- to four-family residential property. FHA-insured loan programs also are available for adjustable-rate mortgages and loans to finance the purchase of a condominium unit in condominium communities built to FHA standards. FHA-insured mortgage loans require that the borrower will use the home as a primary residence for at least the first year of ownership.

FHA Mortgage Loan Features

Interest Rate. The interest rate on FHA mortgages is not set by the FHA or HUD. The interest rate is allowed to fluctuate with the market and is negotiable between the lender and the borrower.

Discount Points. FHA-approved lenders may charge discount points on FHA-insured mortgage loans. Discount points may be paid by either the seller or the buyer (see "Discount Points," Unit 12).

Assumption. FHA mortgage loans do not have a due-on-sale clause in the mortgage. The FHA requires complete qualification of the buyer assuming the loan. All assumed loans (and new FHA loans) are for owner-occupied use only (no investor loans). The lender must release the original mortgagor from liability if the assuming mortgagor is found creditworthy and executes an agreement to assume and pay the mortgage debt. By law, FHA loans cannot charge prepayment penalties; the loan may be paid off early without penalty.

Down Payment. A major benefit of FHA-insured loans is that the down payment is much smaller than the amount required for most conventional mortgage loans. A borrower can obtain an FHA-insured loan with a down payment as low as 3.5% of the purchase price or the appraised value, whichever is less. FHA refers to the required down payment as the *minimum cash investment*. Closing costs may not be used to meet the minimum 3.5% down payment requirement. Borrowers must have a good credit history to qualify for maximum financing.

Loan Limit. Recall that FHA loans are a type of nonconventional loan because they are insured by the FHA. FHA sets limits on the amount that can be borrowed. The limits vary significantly, depending on the average cost of housing in different regions of the country. For example, the maximum FHA loan for a one-unit residence is greater in Fort Lauderdale and Miami than in Gainesville or Tallahassee because the average cost of housing is greater in the Fort Lauderdale and Miami markets. Lenders make FHA-insured loans in even $50 increments.

WEBLINK

A schedule of FHA mortgage limits by area is available at https://entp.hud.gov/idapp/html/hicostlook.cfm.

Loan Insurance Premium. FHA loans require two types of mortgage insurance. Borrowers are charged a one-time mortgage insurance fee at closing. This fee is called the **up-front mortgage insurance premium (UFMIP)**. The percentage of the UFMIP is based on the type (new or refinance) and term (15-year or 30-year) of the mortgage. The UFMIP is paid at closing and can be financed into the mortgage amount.

In addition to the UFMIP, the borrower is also charged an annual **mortgage insurance premium (MIP)**. The annual MIP is paid monthly (annual premium divided by 12) as part of the monthly mortgage payment. The MIP must be included in the proposed monthly expenses when calculating the buyer's qualifying ratios. The monthly MIP is paid for the life of the FHA loan when the borrower receives maximum financing. UFMIP and MIP go into an FHA fund for repaying lenders if borrowers default.

Qualifying Ratios. FHA lenders use two qualifying ratios for loan applicants. FHA requirements currently allow up to 31% for the housing expense ratio (HER) and up to 43% for the total obligations ratio (TOR).

EXAMPLE: A prospective borrower is applying for an FHA-insured loan. The borrower's gross monthly income is $3,500. The borrower's projected monthly PITI is $900, the MIP is $150, and based on a credit report, the borrower has the following long-term obligations:

- Car payment: $200
- Student loan: $150

a. What is the borrower's housing expense ratio?
b. What is the borrower's total obligations ratio?
c. Does the borrower qualify for an FHA mortgage?

Solution:

a. To determine the borrower's HER, determine the total monthly housing expenses:
$900 PITI + $150 MIP = $1,050 total monthly housing expense
Next, divide the total monthly housing expenses by the monthly gross income.
$1,050 ÷ $3,500 = .30 or 30% HER

b. To determine the borrower's TOR, determine the total monthly obligations:
PITI + MIP + LTO = $900 PITI + $150 MIP + $200 car + $150 loan = $1,400
Next, divide the total monthly obligations by the monthly gross income:
$1,400 ÷ $3,500 = .40 or 40%

c. To qualify for an FHA-insured mortgage loan, the borrower must have an HER that does not exceed 31%. The borrower's HER is 30%. So, 30% of the borrower's monthly gross income pays the borrower's monthly housing expenses. The borrower's HER is below the required threshold.
To qualify for an FHA-insured mortgage loan, the borrower's TOR must not exceed 43%. The borrower's TOR is 40%, which is less than the required threshold of 43%.

Appraisal. The home must be appraised by an FHA-approved appraiser. HUD requires the appraiser to confirm that the property meets HUD's minimum property standards. However, the FHA does not warrant the condition of the property. The FHA encourages buyers to have a home inspection conducted.

Insured Commitment. A developer will sometimes seek an FHA commitment to insure the mortgages on a planned project. The FHA gives a conditional commitment to insure the mortgage loans on the individual homes in the planned project that is dependent on the structures being completed according to verified FHA standards.

Practice Questions

10. List the two types of mortgage insurance charged on FHA mortgage loans.

    1. ______________________________

    2. ______________________________

11. List the two qualifying ratios used for FHA mortgage loans and their standard qualifying threshold.

    1. ______________________________

    2. ______________________________

12. An FHA borrower has monthly PITI of $2,276, MIP of $160, a car payment of $479, a revolving credit card minimum monthly payment of $165 per month, and a student loan of $200 per month. The borrower's gross monthly income is $8,000.

    a. What is the borrower's HER?

    b. What is the borrower's TOR?

    c. Does the borrower's financial ratios qualify for an FHA mortgage loan?

13.5 VA LOAN GUARANTEE PROGRAM

Recall that nonconventional loans are backed by the federal government. Nonconventional loans include VA-guaranteed loans.

A VA loan is a mortgage loan program established by the U.S. Department of Veterans Affairs (VA). VA loans assist service members, veterans, and eligible surviving spouses to become homeowners. The VA issues rules and regulations that set the qualifications and conditions for VA loans. The VA guarantees a portion of the loan referred to as a *partial guarantee*. The partial guarantee covers the top portion of the loan. VA home loans are provided by private lenders, such as banks and mortgage companies. The applicant must plan to use the home as a primary residence.

A major benefit of a VA purchase loan is that the VA does not require a down payment. However, a lender may require a down payment if the appraised value of the home is less than the sale price. Nearly 90% of all VA-guaranteed home loans are made with no down payment. The VA loan guarantee differs from the FHA program that insures loans; VA home loans do not charge a mortgage insurance premium.

VA Mortgage Loan Features

Qualifications for Program. Only veterans, unremarried surviving spouses of veterans, and active military personnel may apply for a VA loan.

Eligibility Requirements. Specific eligibility requirements are based on the period of active duty or the period of continuous service, as applicable. Real estate licensees should rely on a VA lender to determine an applicant's eligibility for a VA loan.

Lending Source and Eligible Property. VA loans are made by VA-approved lenders. However, the VA does have the power to make direct loans to veterans in areas where VA loans are not available. The VA loan program may be used to purchase, refinance, or construct one- to four-unit properties provided the veteran resides in one of the units. The lender, not the VA, sets the interest rate, discount points, and closing costs. The maximum loan term is 30 years. The interest rate on VA loans varies based on market conditions and is negotiated between the borrower and the lender.

Loan Guarantee and Entitlement. The VA establishes loan guarantee limits called the VA loan guarantee or the maximum entitlement. A veteran's **entitlement** is the maximum amount the government guarantees the lender will be paid in the event the borrower defaults. A veteran begins the loan process by applying to the VA for a certificate of eligibility. The *certificate of eligibility* states the amount of entitlement available to the veteran borrower.

Reusing Entitlement. A veteran who has used the entitlement in the past may only now be eligible for a portion of the entitlement. The unused portion is available to the veteran borrower up to the maximum guarantee. When a VA loan is paid off, the veteran's maximum entitlement is reinstated.

Loan Limits. The VA previously used Fannie Mae and Freddie Mac loan limits as the maximum guaranteed loan amount without a required down payment. Effective January 1, 2020, VA loan limits were eliminated for borrowers who have their full entitlement. The removal of loan limits does not mean that veterans have unlimited borrowing power without a down payment. The VA borrower must have sufficient income and meet the lender's credit requirements to qualify for the loan. Eligible military members and veterans can now use the loan amount they qualify for without making a down payment. This is good news for borrowers in high-priced parts of the country. Qualifying VA applicants can avoid significant out-of-pocket expense for a down payment under the new regulation (other closing costs still apply).

Down payments still apply to veterans who have one or more existing VA loans or have defaulted on a prior VA loan. VA borrowers are subject to the loan limits and will be required to make a down payment of 25% of the difference between the purchase price and the loan limit.

Loan Origination Fee. The VA borrower pays a loan origination fee to the lender. The VA allows a 1% origination fee to be charged to veteran borrowers.

VA Funding Fee. The veteran borrower pays a *funding fee* to the VA. The VA loan funding fee is on a sliding scale, with the lowest fees charged to first-time VA borrowers and higher fees for those VA borrowers who have previously used the VA loan program. Funding fee expenses may be added to the loan amount and financed over the life of the loan. If a veteran is a purple heart recipient or has a service-connected disability, the funding fee is waived. VA loans do not require mortgage insurance premiums (MIP).

Qualifying Ratio. To qualify loan applicants, the VA guidelines recommend a total obligations ratio (TOR) not to exceed 41% of the total monthly gross income (see Figure 13.2).

FIGURE 13.2 ■ **Comparison of Qualifying Ratios**

	Housing Expense Ratio (HER)	Total Obligations Ratio (TOR)
Conventional	28%	36%
FHA	31%	43%
VA		41%

Closing Costs. The lender may charge reasonable closing costs. The VA appraisal, credit report, state and local taxes, and recording fees may be paid by the purchaser, the seller, or shared. No commissions, brokerage fees, or buyer-broker fees may be charged to the veteran buyer.

Assumption. Because VA loans do not have a due-on-sale clause, they are assumable (even by nonveterans). Before assuming a VA mortgage loan, the buyer must be approved by the lender and the VA. The VA must also approve the assumption agreement. Processing fees and funding fees are charged on assumptions. Sellers who allow nonveterans to assume their VA loans will not have their VA eligibility restored until the assumer has paid off the VA loan, unless the assumer is also a veteran who agrees to substitute eligibility.

Prepayment. VA mortgage loans do not contain a prepayment penalty clause. Therefore, veterans may prepay all or a portion of the mortgage loan ahead of schedule without penalty. Figure 13.3 provides a comparison of FHA and VA mortgage loans.

FIGURE 13.3 ■ **FHA and VA Comparison**

	FHA Loan	**VA Loan**
Role of government	Fully government insured; does not originate loans	Partial government guarantee; can make direct loans if needed
Down payment	3.5% minimum investment	0%
Fees	UFMIP and MIP	Funding fee
Loan limit	Set by area	No established loan limit
Assumable	Yes	Yes
Due-on-sale clause	No	No

WEBLINK @

Visit the U.S. Department of Veterans Affairs Home Loan Guaranty program online at https://www.benefits.va.gov/homeloans/.

For additional information on VA loan limits go to https://www.va.gov/housing-assistance/home-loans/loan-limits/.

Practice Questions

13. A VA mortgage loan borrower's total obligations ratio (TOR) cannot exceed ________________.

14. The VA mortgage loan borrower pays a ________ ________________ fee to the lender and a ________________ fee to the VA.

13.6 PURPOSE-SPECIFIC MORTGAGE PRODUCTS

Biweekly Mortgage Loan

A **biweekly mortgage** loan is amortized the same way as fully amortized mortgage loans, except the borrower makes a payment every two weeks. The amount paid is equal to one-half the normal monthly payment. Because there are 52 weeks in the year, the borrower makes 26 biweekly payments. Therefore, the borrower makes the equivalent of an extra month's payment each year (26 half-size payments equal 13 full-month payments instead of 12). This saves the borrower considerable interest, and the loan is paid off sooner (see Figure 13.4).

FIGURE 13.4 ■ Purpose-Specific Mortgage Products

Type of Mortgage Loan	Description
Biweekly mortgage loan	26 payments per year
Partially amortized loan	Final balloon payment with monthly payments calculated as if the payments will be paid over a longer term
Purchase money mortgage (PMM)	Owner financing typically used to fill the gap between down payment and first mortgage
Home equity loan	Secured by primary residence and is usually a second mortgage
Package mortgage loan	Pledge both real and personal property as collateral
Reverse mortgage (HECM)	Uses homeowner's equity to provide monthly income for owners 62 and older

Partially Amortized Mortgage Loan

Recall that an amortized mortgage consists of a series of fixed, equal monthly payments and at the end of the loan term the loan is completely paid off. With a **partially amortized mortgage** (also called a balloon mortgage), the monthly payments are calculated for a 20-year or 30-year loan term; however, the payments are paid for a shorter period of time, such as five years. By amortizing the loan over 20 or 30 years, the fixed, monthly payments are smaller than if the loan were amortized over a five-year term. At the end of the stipulated period (in this example, five years), the remaining unpaid loan balance is due. A single large final payment (called a **balloon payment**) becomes due on the loan maturity date. In Florida, a partially amortized mortgage must be clearly identified as such on the face of the mortgage, with the amount of the final balloon payment disclosed (see Figure 13.4).

Purchase Money Mortgage (PMM)

A **purchase money mortgage (PMM)** is a mortgage in which payments are made to the seller (seller financing) rather than to a lending institution. It is typically used in lieu of a portion of a buyer's down payment when the buyer assumes an existing mortgage. The seller conveys legal title to the buyer at closing, and the seller retains a vendor's lien right as security for the debt.

EXAMPLE: The purchase price of a home is $200,000. The buyer is assuming the seller's FHA mortgage loan with an unpaid balance of $120,000.

$200,000 purchase price – $120,000 = $80,000 cash due at closing

The buyer asks the seller to accept $30,000 cash at closing and the remaining amount due to be paid to the seller over five years. The buyer is asking the seller to take back a purchase money mortgage at a specified interest rate and loan term in lieu of $50,000 cash at closing. This may be a good arrangement for both the buyer who does not have sufficient savings available for the entire amount of cash due at closing and the seller who can receive an income stream over time at a favorable interest rate. The buyer will sign a note and a mortgage with the seller. The assumed FHA mortgage was recorded as a first mortgage, so the PMM will be recorded as a second mortgage.

Home Equity Loan

Homeowners use **home equity loans** to finance consumer purchases; consolidate existing credit card debt; and pay for college tuition, medical expenses, or home improvements. If the home equity loan is used to make home improvements, the interest is tax deductible (certain limits exist).

The borrower (homeowner) may access the equity in the residence with a home equity loan or a home equity line of credit (HELOC). A home equity loan is a lump sum one-time equity draw. Home equity loans feature a fixed interest rate and equal monthly payments for the loan's term. A HELOC is a line of credit against the equity in the home, and the borrower accesses money from the line of credit as needed. HELOCs feature an adjustable interest rate. Borrowers only pay interest on the actual amount of money accessed from the line of credit. The LTV of both mortgages combined is typically limited to 80% of the property's value (see Figure 13.4).

Home Equity Conversion Mortgage (HECM) or Reverse Mortgage Loan

Homeowners age 62 and older who have paid off their mortgage or have only a small mortgage balance remaining are eligible to participate in HUD's **reverse mortgage** program. The only reverse mortgage insured by the federal government is called a **home equity conversion mortgage (HECM)** and is only available through an FHA-approved lender. The program allows homeowners to borrow against the equity in their homes. Homeowners can receive payments in a lump sum, on a monthly basis (for a fixed term or for as long as they live in the home), or on an occasional basis as a line of credit. The size of reverse mortgage loans is determined by the borrower's age, the interest rate, and the home's value.

Unlike ordinary home equity loans, a HUD reverse mortgage does not require repayment as long as the borrower lives in the home. Lenders recover the principal and interest when the home is sold. The remaining value of the home goes to the homeowner or to the homeowner's heirs. If the sale proceeds are insufficient to pay the amount owed, HUD will pay the lender the amount of the shortfall. The Federal Housing Administration (FHA), which is part of HUD, collects an insurance premium from the borrower to provide this coverage (see Figure 13.4).

WEBLINK @

The American Association of Retired Persons (AARP) offers comprehensive information about reverse mortgages at https://www.aarp.org/money/credit-loans-debt/reverse_mortgages/.

Package Mortgage Loan

A **package mortgage** loan includes both real and personal property as security for the debt. A buyer uses a package mortgage, for example, when purchasing a restaurant complete with cooking equipment and other personal property that serve as a part of the collateral for the debt (see Figure 13.4).

Practice Questions

15. The final large payment in a partially amortized mortgage loan is called a ___________ ___________.

16. A mortgage loan that pledges real and personal property as collateral is called a ______________ mortgage.

13.7 PRIMARY MORTGAGE MARKET

Depository Lenders

The **primary mortgage market** consists of lenders that originate new mortgage loans for borrowers. These lenders make money available directly to borrowers. Three major depository lenders originate mortgages (see Figure 13.5):

1. Savings associations (SAs) invest the bulk of assets in residential mortgages and home equity loans.
2. Commercial banks (CBs) specialize in construction loans for residential and commercial projects.
3. Credit unions (CUs) are nonprofit organizations that provide services to their members, providing financing for residential loans and home improvement loans.

SAs, CBs, and CUs are depository lenders, meaning that they accept savings deposits and **demand deposits** (checking accounts). These depository lenders are also called *portfolio lenders* because they can hold mortgage loans permanently in their portfolios.

EXAMPLE: A couple finances the purchase of their home by taking out a 30-year fixed-rate mortgage loan from their local credit union. The credit union is a portfolio lender because it will hold the mortgage and promissory note in its portfolio of investments.

The demand deposits and savings deposit accounts provide depository lenders with a relatively stable funding source. Lenders who accept deposits are called financial intermediaries because they make loans with the deposited funds. The flow of funds into deposits held by primary lenders, thereby increasing the mortgage money supply, is called **intermediation**.

FIGURE 13.5 ■ **Primary Mortgage Lenders**

Mortgage Lenders	Type of Primary Lender	Types of Loans Offered	Focus
Savings association	Depository	Prefer conventional residential and home equity loans Also offer FHA and VA	Historically, largest source of residential mortgage loans
Commercial banks	Depository	Conventional, FHA, and VA mortgage loans	Largest source of short-term commercial; construction loans
Credit unions	Depository	Conventional, FHA, and VA Home improvement loans	Largest source of short-term consumer loans Nonprofit organizations that offer loans to members only
Mortgage lenders	Non-depository	Residential and commercial mortgage loans	Primarily make FHA and VA loans

Nondepository Primary Lenders

Mortgage lenders are full-service mortgage companies that process, close, and sell the loans they originate. Mortgage lenders fund the loans they originate with either their own funds or borrowed capital. Mortgage lenders are non-depository primary lenders because they do not accept savings deposits and demand deposits. Mortgage lenders package loans they originate and sell them to institutional investors and to secondary-market participants. The principal activity of mortgage lenders is to originate and service loans for residential and income properties. They primarily make VA and FHA loans.

A **mortgage broker** license is required for an entity conducting loan originator activities through one or more licensed loan originators employed by the mortgage broker or as independent contractors to the mortgage broker. Mortgage brokers do not make loans. Instead, mortgage brokers arrange loans for prospective borrowers with various mortgage lenders. Mortgage brokers do not service loans.

A **mortgage loan originator (MLO)** is a person who holds a state MLO license for the purpose of soliciting mortgage loans, accepting mortgage loan applications, and negotiating the terms or conditions of new or existing mortgage loans on behalf of a borrower or a lender. MLOs process mortgage loan applications and negotiate the sale of existing mortgage loans to noninstitutional investors for compensation.

The Secure and Fair Enforcement for Mortgage Licensing Act (SAFE Act) sets minimum standards for licensing and registering of mortgage loan originators. The SAFE Act requires employees of commercial banks, savings associations, and credit unions that are regulated by a federal banking agency and who are engaged in residential mortgage loan origination, to register with the Nationwide Mortgage Licensing System (NMLS). Mortgage loan originators must submit fingerprints for a criminal background check.

Mortgage loan originators (MLOs) who are not employed by agency-regulated institutions are licensed by the states. Employees of mortgage lenders, including bank holding companies and their nonbank subsidiaries, who act as MLOs are subject to state licensure and state regulation, in addition to registration with the NMLS.

Practice Questions

17. List four major entities that originate mortgages.
    1. ______________________________
    2. ______________________________
    3. ______________________________
    4. ______________________________

18. The primary mortgage market is where loans are _______________.

19. Lenders that prefer to hold mortgages rather than sell them are called _____________ lenders.

20. The flow of funds into deposits held by primary lenders, increasing the mortgage money supply, is called _________________________.

13.8 SECONDARY MORTGAGE MARKET

Most lenders do not hold a mortgage that it originated for the entire loan term. It is common for a borrower's loan to be sold to one of the major mortgage investors within a few months of closing the loan. The **secondary mortgage market** is an investor market that buys and sells existing mortgages. The existence of a secondary mortgage market allows lenders to have stable cash flow so that they can originate more new loans. The borrower will continue to make monthly payments to the lender that originated the loan if the lender continues to service the loan.

The secondary mortgage market accomplishes two important objectives:

1. *Circulates the mortgage money supply*. The secondary mortgage market helps lenders raise capital to make additional mortgage loans. Prior to the existence of the secondary market, portfolio lenders had to rely on deposits flowing into their financial institutions. However, when depositors chose instead to invest their savings in other types of investments, such as the stock and bond markets, **disintermediation** led to a shortage of mortgage funds. With a secondary mortgage market, in times of disintermediation, lenders can sell more of their loans and use the cash to originate new mortgage loans.
2. *Standardized loan requirements*. The key to an efficient secondary market was the creation of standardized loan instruments. Standardized mortgage loan documents, appraisal forms, closing disclosures, and promissory notes make it possible for secondary market participants to better evaluate the mortgage loan packages being sold.

Fannie Mae and Freddie Mac

Fannie Mae and Freddie Mac are not government agencies. They are known as government sponsored enterprises (GSEs). GSEs are publicly traded corporations that are sponsored by the U.S. government. Fannie Mae and Freddie Mac are regulated under the conservatorship authority of the Federal Housing and Finance Agency (FHFA). Fannie Mae and Freddie Mac operate in the secondary mortgage market. They purchase about two-thirds of all U.S. mortgages. Fannie and Freddie set guidelines for the types of loans they will purchase. Mortgages that meet Fannie and Freddie guidelines are called **conforming loans**. Conforming loans meet, or conform to, loan amount limits set by the FHFA. Loans sold to Fannie and Freddie also must be written on uniform forms approved by Fannie and Freddie, including loan applications, appraisals, and mortgage instruments, in addition to meeting specific qualifying guidelines.

Loans that are for a larger loan amount that exceed the conforming loan limits are referred to as **nonconforming loans** or *jumbo* loans. Because Fannie Mae and Freddie Mac do not purchase nonconforming loans, these loans are more difficult to sell as investments, and lenders often have to hold these loans for long periods of time.

Fannie and Freddie buy conforming loans from local lenders and package them into mortgage-backed securities (MBS). MBSs are created by bundling thousands of mortgage loans together. The MBSs are sold worldwide to investors, providing funds to the financial institutions to make new consumer loans.

Fannie Mae. Fannie Mae (sometimes referred to as the Federal National Mortgage Association and FNMA) was created by Congress in 1938. It created the secondary market as a way to stimulate the housing market after the Great Depression. Fannie Mae and Freddie

Mac's guidelines vary somewhat from each other; however, both Fannie and Freddie have strict guidelines for the loans that they will purchase. For example, Fannie and Freddie limit the size of the individual mortgage loans they will purchase called the *loan limit*. Loan limits are subject to change annually and vary depending on the property's location.

Today, Fannie Mae purchases primarily conforming conventional mortgages from large commercial banks. Fannie Mae can also purchase FHA loans and VA-guaranteed mortgage loans. It is the largest secondary market participant (see Figure 13.6).

FIGURE 13.6 ■ Secondary Market

Fannie Mae	Not a government agency
	Buys conventional conforming loans from large commercial banks
	Purchases some government-insured and government-guaranteed loans
	Packages loans into mortgage-back securities and sells to investors
Freddie Mac	Not a government agency
	Buys conventional conforming loans from small banks, credit unions, and savings associations
	Packages loans into mortgage-back securities and sells to investors
Ginnie Mae	Government corporation under HUD
	Does not buy loans from lenders
	Guarantor of government-insured and government-guaranteed loans
	Has the full faith and credit guarantee of the federal government

Freddie Mac. Freddie Mac (sometimes referred to as the Federal Home Loan Mortgage Corporation and FHLMC) was created by Congress in 1970. Freddie Mac was originally created to provide competition to Fannie Mae. The goal was to reduce borrower's financing costs by providing more competition and liquidity. Freddie Mac provides a secondary market for conforming conventional mortgage loans purchased from smaller banks, credit unions, and savings associations (formerly called savings and loans). The loans are then pooled together and sold to investors as MBSs. Like Fannie, Freddie Mac purchases mortgages that meet their underwriting and product standards, package the mortgage loans into securities, and sell the securities to investors on Wall Street.

Ginnie Mae

Ginnie Mae (also referred to as Government National Mortgage Association and GNMA) provides a secondary market exclusively for government-insured and government-guaranteed loans, including FHA, VA, Rural Development, and American Native Indian Housing loans. Ginnie Mae, unlike Fannie and Freddie, is a government corporation housed within the Department of Housing and Urban Development (HUD). Ginnie's purpose is to provide liquidity for low- to moderate-income homebuyers. Ginnie is the only secondary participant backed by the *full faith and credit guarantee* of the federal government.

Unlike Fannie and Freddie, Ginnie Mae does not participate in determining eligibility for loans. Ginnie exists to solely guarantee the security of federally insured loans and federally guaranteed loans. Ginnie, unlike Fannie and Freddie, does not purchase mortgage loans from lenders. Once a lender makes a government-insured or government-guaranteed loan commitment to buyers, the lender obtains a guarantee from Ginnie. The lender pools similar mortgages together and delivers the pool of loans to a securities dealer. Securities dealers sell the Ginnie Mae guaranteed MBSs to investors. The securities dealers advise Ginnie Mae of the sales. The lender that originated the loans continues to service the loans and forwards the payments to Ginnie Mae. Ginnie disburses payments to investors. Ginnie's guarantee means that it makes the disbursements even if the payments have not been received from the borrower.

To learn more about the secondary mortgage market, visit these websites:

WEBLINK

- Fannie Mae: www.fanniemae.com
- Ginnie Mae: www.ginniemae.gov
- Freddie Mac: www.freddiemac.com

Practice Questions

21. List the two important objectives of the secondary mortgage market.
    1. ______________________________
    2. ______________________________

22. ______________ ______________ is the only secondary participant backed by the full faith and credit guarantee of the federal government.

13.9 FEDERAL REGULATORY BODIES AND MORTGAGE FRAUD

Federal Reserve System

The Federal Reserve System, also known as the Federal Reserve or just the Fed, is the central bank of the United States. It was established by Congress in 1913 to provide the nation with a safer and more stable monetary system. The Fed consists of a seven-member Board of Governors and 12 Reserve Banks located in major cities across the nation. The members of the Board of Governors are appointed by the president and confirmed by the U.S. Senate.

Today, the Fed's duties include (1) conducting the nation's monetary policy, (2) supervising and regulating banking institutions and protecting the credit rights of consumers, and (3) maintaining the stability of the financial system. *Monetary policy* refers to the actions undertaken by the Fed to influence the availability and cost of money and credit to promote national economic goals. The Fed is charged with the responsibility for setting monetary policy.

The Fed also has regulatory and supervisory responsibilities over banks that are members of the Fed. Additionally, the Board is responsible for the development and administration of regulations that implement major federal laws governing consumer credit, such as the Truth in Lending Act and the Equal Credit Opportunity Act.

Using a Straw Buyer

A *straw buyer* is someone whose credit is used to purchase a property and secure financing but who isn't actually going to own the property. Straw buyers never intend to live on the property and only lend their credit information for a fee. At other times, the straw buyer is a victim of identity theft. The victim's credit profile is stolen and used as a straw buyer. The true buyer cannot qualify for the mortgage, so someone (a straw buyer with better credit) fraudulently applies for the mortgage. The true buyer is deceiving the lender for the purpose of getting a better loan than the buyer would be able to obtain if the loan application contained accurate financial information.

Recall the elements for fraud: (1) a misstatement of facts or failure to disclose facts; (2) the individual who made the misstatement or omitted the true facts knows the facts to be untrue; (3) the lender relied on the facts and extended financing; and (4) the lender was damaged as a result. In many cases, the loans were not repaid and the properties were foreclosed. In other cases, the loans were sold on the secondary market and packaged in security instruments valued on erroneous risk characteristics (see "Misrepresentation and Fraud," Unit 11).

No Documentation Loans

No documentation loans were very popular before the mortgage crisis. Unlike the stated income/stated asset loan application process, this type of loan program allowed a borrower with a certain minimum credit score to qualify for a mortgage without disclosing employment information, income, and assets. The lender approved the loan application without verifying the borrower's financial information. It was convenient for borrowers who qualified for the loans they applied for; however, other borrowers lied about their income and assets to qualify for mortgage loans that they would not otherwise be able to obtain. As a result, many homeowners found themselves with mortgages they could not repay.

Red Flags

Another type of **mortgage fraud** involves inflating the appraised value of property for the purpose of obtaining more financing. Unscrupulous appraisers altered or fabricated information and/or used inappropriate comparable sales. Some cases of fraud involved using fake photos of the property under contract to substantiate a higher value. In other situations, real estate licensees entered inaccurate data into the MLS database. The appraiser did not verify the information (as required) through another independent source. The appraiser and licensee working in tandem created huge financial losses for lending institutions. For example, if the MLS erroneously indicated that a house closed for $100,000 in a neighborhood where the most recent sale was only $80,000 and the next buyers coming into the neighborhood saw the inflated closed sale price and thought they must pay the inflated price, it would cause all future sale prices in the neighborhood to artificially increase. The inflated contract prices resulted from inflated appraisals. The dollar amount difference between the inflated sale price and the actual property value was the money used to compensate the fraudulent activity.

Licensees should be aware of red flags that might indicate fraudulent activity. For example, if a sale contract states "owner of record" rather than identify the seller's name, it should be a red flag to the selling real estate agent that a property flip might be occurring and to be aware of other irregularities. A property flip is a transaction in which one party contracts to buy a property with the intention of quickly transferring (flipping) the property over to the ultimate buyer. Another red flag is when a seller has taken title to the property via a recently recorded quitclaim deed. A prudent sales associate who sees potential red flags should immediately present such concerns to the employing broker for guidance on how to deal with the issue before going any further.

817.545, F.S.

Ethical Practices. Florida law stipulates that committing mortgage fraud is a third-degree felony. The mortgage fraud increases to a second-degree felony when the stated value in the loan documents exceeds $100,000. Charges of mortgage fraud can extend to the borrower, mortgage loan originator, and the real estate licensee. If a real estate licensee obtains information that the buyer is less than truthful regarding intent to occupy the property, assets, or income, it is very important that the real estate licensee speak up and not become a participant in the fraud.

Practice Questions

23. A __________ __________ is someone whose credit is used to purchase a property and secure financing, but who isn't actually going to own the property.

24. ______ __________________ loans allowed a borrower with a certain minimum credit score to qualify for a mortgage without disclosing employment information, income, and assets.

13.10 CONSUMER CREDIT PROTECTION ACT

The Consumer Credit Protection Act (CCPA) is an encompassing law that contains several acts with more precise scopes. Among the specific federal laws under the CCPA are the Equal Credit Opportunity Act and the Truth in Lending Act. Each of these laws will be discussed in detail in this unit.

Equal Credit Opportunity Act (ECOA)

The Equal Credit Opportunity Act (ECOA), implemented by Regulation B, applies to all consumer and commercial credit, without regard to the nature or type of the credit or the creditor. Congress gave the Consumer Financial Protection Bureau (CFPB) the authority to supervise and enforce compliance with ECOA. If a transaction provides for the deferral of the payment of a debt, it is a form of credit covered by Regulation B.

The ECOA prohibits creditors from discriminating against a Regulation B protected class in any aspect of a credit transaction. Financial institutions and firms engaged in extending credit must make credit available with fairness and without discrimination on the basis of race, color, religion, national origin, sex, marital status, age, or receipt of income from public assistance programs (see Figure 13.7).

FIGURE 13.7 ■ Summary of Protected Classes

Law	Race	Color	Religion	Sex	Disability	Familial Status	National Origin	Marital Status	Age	Public Assistance Income
Civil Rights Act 1866	✔									
Fair Housing Act (as amended)	✔	✔	✔	✔	✔	✔	✔			
Equal Credit Opportunity Act (Lending)	✔	✔	✔	✔			✔	✔	✔	✔

Marital Status. A lender cannot require an applicant's spouse to join in (sign) a loan application.

Source of Income. The ECOA prohibits discriminatory treatment of income from alimony, child support, public assistance, or part-time employment.

Childbearing Plans. The ECOA prohibits inquiry about, or consideration of, childbearing plans or the potential for child bearing.

The ECOA also requires creditors to provide applicants with free copies of appraisals or other written valuations developed because of a credit application secured by a first lien (for example, a first mortgage) on a dwelling. Creditors must notify applicants in writing that copies of appraisals will be provided to them.

Truth in Lending Act

The Truth in Lending Act (TILA) is a federal law designed to promote the informed use of consumer credit. The TILA regulates what information lenders must make known to consumers about their products and services. It requires disclosures about its terms and costs and standardized the manner in which costs associated with borrowing are calculated and disclosed.

The TILA outlines rules that apply to closed-end credit, such as home loans and auto loans. Closed-end credit is a loan or type of credit where the funds are disbursed in full at closing and must be repaid in full, including the interest and finance charges, by the end of the loan term. The TILA also outlines rules that apply to open-end credit, including credit cards and home equity lines of credit (HELOCs). The TILA does not put restrictions on how much interest they may charge or whether they must grant a loan. It does not attempt to regulate interest rates. The rules are designed to make it easier for consumers to comparison shop when the want to borrow money.

Regulation Z is often used as another name for the TILA. While the two names are often used interchangeably, they are not the same thing. The TILA was enacted by Congress and is a federal law. Regulation Z is a Federal Reserve Board rule that implements how the TILA is applied. The Dodd-Frank Reform Act transferred the rule-making authority from the Federal Reserve Board to the Consumer Financial Protection Bureau (CFPB).

Required Credit Costs Disclosures Under TILA. The TILA required lenders to provide a Truth in Lending disclosure (TIL) to borrowers who made loan application and a final TIL disclosure statement prior to the loan closing. A major accomplishment of the TILA was to establish the requirement to disclose the **annual percentage rate (APR)**. The APR presents the annual cost of credit expressed as a rate. TILA also required disclosure of other facts about the full cost of the credit, including the total cost of the loan, the amount financed, and the total of payments.

Bait-and-Switch Advertising. TILA makes *bait-and-switch* advertising a federal offense. For example, if a subdivision developer advertises homes for sale with a down payment of $1,000, the seller must accept $1,000 as the complete down payment or be in violation of the law.

Triggering Terms. TILA is also concerned that consumers may be misled by being given truthful but inadequate information in advertising. While it does not require creditors to advertise credit terms, it does provide that if they advertise certain credit terms, called **triggering terms**, they must include additional disclosures. Trigger terms include the following:

- amount or percentage of any down payment,
- number of payments,
- period (term) of repayment,
- amount of any payment, and
- amount of any finance charge.

Advertisements containing any of the triggering terms must also disclose the following:

- Amount or percentage of down payment
- Terms of repayment
- Annual percentage rate, using that term, and if the rate may be increased in the future, that fact must also be disclosed

TILA allows general phrases such as "owner will finance" and "favorable financing terms available." Such expressions are too general to trigger additional disclosure requirements.

Right of Rescission. Consumers who are refinancing residential mortgage loans have the right of rescission, which is a cooling-off period of three business days during which they may cancel the loan without losing any money. The right of rescission applies to most consumer loans but does not apply to loans to purchase or construct a home. The three-business-day right of rescission applies to:

- home equity lines of credit,
- second mortgages, and
- refinance loans.

Real Estate Settlement Procedures Act (RESPA)

The Real Estate Settlement Procedures Act (RESPA) is a federal law administered by the Consumer Financial Protection Bureau (CFPB) and implemented by Regulation X. The law is designed to ensure that borrowers are informed regarding the amount and type of charges they will pay at closing. RESPA requires the lender to disclose to the borrower an advance estimate of closing costs and an information booklet. RESPA also attempts to eliminate kickbacks from vendors of closing-related service providers. The act applies to most closings that involve a "standard" home mortgage loan. Specifically, RESPA applies to closings where a federally related mortgage loan is secured by a one- to four-family residence.

Affiliated Business Relationships. Sometimes, several businesses that offer settlement (closing) services are owned or controlled by a common corporate parent. These businesses are called *affiliates*. When a lender, real estate broker, or other closing participant refers a borrower to an affiliate for a settlement service (for example, when a real estate broker refers a buyer to a mortgage broker affiliate), RESPA requires the referring party to give the borrower an affiliated business arrangement (AfBA) disclosure. This form explains to borrowers that they are not required, with certain exceptions, to use the affiliate and are free to shop for other providers. The AfBA must include an estimate of the affiliated business provider's charges. Except in cases where a lender refers a borrower to an attorney, credit reporting agency, or real estate appraiser to represent the lender's interest in the transaction, the referring party may not require the consumer to use the affiliated business.

Purchase of Title Insurance. RESPA prohibits a seller from requiring the homebuyer to use a particular title insurance company as a condition of sale. Generally, the lender will require title insurance. The borrower can shop for and choose a company. However, if the seller is paying for the owner's title insurance policy, the law does not prohibit the seller from choosing the title company.

Escrow for Taxes and Insurance. RESPA limits the amount that lenders can require borrowers to place in escrow for property taxes and hazard insurance. The lender must perform an annual escrow account analysis. An excess of $50 or more must be returned to the borrower.

Kickbacks, Fee-Splitting, and Unearned Fees. It is illegal under RESPA for anyone to pay or receive a fee, kickback, or anything of value in exchange for referring a settlement service business to a particular person or organization. For example, a mortgage lender may not pay a real estate broker a fee for referring a buyer to the lender. It is also illegal for anyone to accept a fee or part of a fee for services if that person has not actually performed settlement services for the fee. For example, a lender may not add to a third party's fee, such as an appraisal fee, and keep the difference. RESPA does not prevent title companies, mortgage loan originators, appraisers, attorneys, closing agents, and others who actually perform a service in connection with the mortgage loan or the closing from being paid for the reasonable value of their work.

It is a crime for someone to pay or receive an illegal referral fee. The penalty can be a fine, imprisonment, or both. The borrower may also be entitled to recover, by bringing a private lawsuit, three times the cost of charges for settlement services (also called triple or treble damages) that were illegally referred or charged with no actual service provided.

TILA-RESPA Integrated Disclosure Rule (TRID)

Over time, TILA and RESPA regulations were expanded to require four separate disclosures when a borrower sought a mortgage loan. Much of the information in the four disclosures was repetitive and confusing to borrowers. Therefore, in 2015, Congress directed the Consumer Financial Protection Bureau (CFPB) to publish an integrated disclosure for mortgage transactions, called the TILA-RESPA Integrated Disclosure rule (TRID). Under the new TRID rule, the mortgage disclosure requirements under the Truth in Lending Act and RESPA were condensed into two disclosure forms. The borrower receives a loan estimate disclosure form shortly after applying for a loan, and a closing disclosure is received shortly before closing (see Figure 13.8).

FIGURE 13.8 ■ Disclosure Documents Timing

Document	Timing Requirement
Loan Estimate	Delivered or placed in the mail no later than the third business day after receiving the borrower's loan application.
Closing Disclosure	Provided to the borrower at least three business days before the loan closing.

TRID applies to consumer loans secured by real property, including refinance loans. Most closed-end consumer mortgage loans to finance home construction secured by real property are also covered by TRID. Figure 13.9 features a list of the types of loans for which TRID rules apply and a list of TRID Exemptions.

FIGURE 13.9 ■ TRID Transactions and Exemptions

TRID Applies	TRID Exemptions
Consumer loans secured by real property	Commercial loans for building more than four units
Mortgage loans	Reverse mortgages
Refinance loans	Home equity line of credit (HELOCs)
Construction loans	Mobile home loans
Vacant land loans	Loans for dwellings not attached to real property
Loans secured by 25 or more acres	Loans for agricultural purposes

Loan Estimate. The **Loan Estimate** merged the Truth in Lending disclosure statement required under the TILA as well as the Good Faith Estimate form required under RESPA. The Loan Estimate clearly presents the information considered most important to consumers: the interest rate, monthly payment, total closing costs, and cash required to close. There is no obligation to work with a lender just because the prospective borrower submits a mortgage loan application. The borrower receives a Loan Estimate from each lender to whom the borrower submits a loan application, allowing the borrower to compare loan programs and find the lender that offers the lowest rates and best terms.

Under the TRID rule, the lender is prohibited from charging the borrower any fees until the borrower has received the Loan Estimate and indicated a desire to proceed with the loan. This prohibition includes fees for application, appraisal, and underwriting. The only fee that a lender may charge before issuing the Loan Estimate is a fee to obtain the borrower's credit report.

TRID replaced RESPA's requirement to give consumers a special information booklet with a smaller consumer-friendly booklet, *Your Home Loan Toolkit* (*Toolkit*). The *Toolkit* helps borrowers determine how much house they can afford, suggests questions to ask the lender, and features worksheets and checklists to fill out during the loan process. The booklet also describes the Loan Estimate and Closing Disclosure forms. Lenders are required to give borrowers the *Toolkit* within three business days of loan application.

WEBLINK

Download the information booklet, *Your Home Loan Toolkit*, at https://www.consumerfinance.gov/owning-a-home/explore/home-loan-toolkit/.

Closing Disclosure. Lenders are required to provide borrowers with a written Closing Disclosure at least three business days before closing the loan. The Closing Disclosure replaced the TILA's final Truth-in-Lending Disclosure and the HUD-1 Settlement Statement. The Closing Disclosure presents much of the same information as the Loan Estimate so that borrowers can compare the Loan Estimate with the Closing Disclosure. If the rates, fees, or principal amount changes drastically from the Loan Estimate, the *Toolkit* instructs borrowers to ask the lender to explain the discrepancies. The guidelines were designed to prevent lenders from attempting to use bait-and-switch schemes. A bait-and-switch scheme is a deceptive plan where a mortgage lender offers a borrower an attractive loan with low closing costs or interest rates, or a no-fee loan estimate and then switches their offer and presents the buyer with a different set of terms and conditions when it is time to close.

Important loan calculation information is presented in the Closing Disclosure. The first four calculations (total of payments, finance charge, amount financed, and annual percentage rate) are required by the TILA's Truth in Lending disclosure. TRID added a fifth calculation called total interest percentage (TIP). The five calculations and the explanation of each calculation is presented in Closing Disclosure Loan Calculation.

FIGURE 13.10 ■ Closing Disclosure Loan Calculation

The Closing Disclosure loan calculations are for a fixed-rate loan with a sale price of $180,000, loan amount of $162,000, 30-year loan term, and a fixed interest rate of 3.875%.

Total of payments. The total amount the borrower will have paid after making all scheduled payments of principal, interest, mortgage insurance, and loan costs.	$285,803.36
Finance charge. The amount financed expressed as the total dollar amount the loan will cost the borrower over the loan's term.	$118,830.27
Amount financed. The amount financed is expressed as the total amount of credit provided to the borrower.	$162,000.00
Annual percentage rate (APR). This includes the interest rate and other loan costs (e.g., origination fees, discount points, etc.) and represents the annual cost of credit expressed as a rate.	4.174%
Total interest percentage (TIP). The total amount of interest that the borrower will pay over the loan term as a percentage of the loan amount.	69.46%

Download the completed Closing Disclosure for a fixed-rate loan. The sale price, loan amount, loan term, and interest rate have not changed from the estimates provided on the Loan Estimate (see the Loan Estimate web link presented earlier in this unit) at https://files.consumerfinance.gov/f/201403_cfpb_closing-disclosure_cover-H25B.pdf (scan QR code).

FIGURE 13.11 ■ Comparison of Disclosures, Forms, and Prohibitions Under TILA, RESPA, and TRID

Truth in Lending Act (TILA)	RESPA	TRID
Truth in Lending Disclosure (TIL) and Final TIL Disclosure Statement	Good Faith Estimate (GFE) and HUD-1 Settlement Statement	Loan Estimate (replaced TIL and GFE) no later than third business day after receiving application Closing Disclosure (replaced HUD-1 and Final TIL) at least three business days before closing
TILA Credit Disclosures: 1. Total of payments 2. Finance charge 3. Amount financed 4. Annual percentage rate (APR)	Affiliated business relationship disclosure	Added fifth Credit Disclosure: 5. Total interest percentage (TIP)
Makes bait-and-switch advertising a federal offense	Prohibits kickbacks or referral fees for closing	Further prohibits lenders from using bait-and-switch loan schemes by comparing Loan Estimate with Closing Disclosure
Established triggering terms in advertising to require disclosure of: 1. Amount or percent of down payment 2. Terms of repayment 3. APR		
		Restricts lender from charging fees (except credit report) before borrower indicates desire to proceed with the loan
	Required special information booklet	Replaced special information booklet with *Your Home Loan Toolkit*
	Prohibits seller from requiring buyer to purchase title insurance from a particular company	
	Exempted construction-only loans secured by vacant land and loans secured by 25 or more acres	Removed exemption for construction loans and loans secured by 25 or more acres
	Limits amount lenders can require in escrow for taxes and insurance	
Three business day right of rescission for HELOCs second mortgages and refinance loans on a primary residence		

Practice Questions

25. TRID replaced HUD's special information booklet with a booklet titled __________ __________ ________ *Toolkit*.

26. TRID requires the lender to provide the Loan Estimate no later than the __________ ______________ ___________ after receiving the loan application.

27. Circle protected classes under the Equal Credit Opportunity Act (ECOA).

    a. Age

    b. Marital status

    c. Familial status

    d. National origin

28. The Equal Credit Opportunity Act prohibits discriminatory treatment of income from ________________, __________ ____________, __________ ___________________, or part-time employment.

13.11 SUMMARY OF IMPORTANT POINTS

- Conventional loans are written by private lenders and are not guaranteed or insured by the federal government. Conventional loans typically require a larger down payment, compared with FHA and VA loans, and therefore have a lower LTV. Borrowers must pay for private mortgage insurance (PMI) for the portion of the loan above 80% LTV. Fixed-rate conventional mortgage loans have a due-on-sale clause, so they are not assumable.
- The recommended maximum qualifying ratios for a conventional mortgage are 28% HER and 36% TOR.
- A *fixed-rate amortized mortgage* is one with regular payments each month of principal and interest. The monthly payment remains the same each month; however, the amount applied to principal increases each month, and the amount applied to interest decreases each month. Fixed-rate amortized mortgages are sometimes referred to as level-payment plan mortgages.
- A *purchase money mortgage* is a new mortgage accepted by the seller as part of the purchase price. The mortgage is taken back by a seller from a buyer.
- An *adjustable-rate mortgage (ARM)* is a loan that has an interest rate that can change at preset intervals based on a recognized and verifiable index. The margin is the percentage added to the index to cover the lender's costs plus profit. The index plus the margin equals the calculated interest rate.
- The Federal Housing Administration (FHA) is a government agency that insures mortgage loans made by approved lenders. FHA does not make loans nor does it regulate interest rates. Borrowers pay an up-front mortgage insurance premium (UFMIP) and an annual mortgage insurance premium (MIP). The annual premium is paid monthly as part of the monthly mortgage payment. Borrowers are required to make a down payment of at least 3.5%. The Section 203(b) FHA program insures fixed-rate loans on one- to four-family residences.
- The Department of Veterans Affairs (VA) partially guarantees mortgage loans. Private lenders provide VA loans to veterans, surviving spouses of veterans,

and active military personnel. The VA also has the power to make direct loans to veterans. A veteran's entitlement is the maximum amount the government guarantees the lender will be paid in the event the borrower defaults. A veteran's certificate of eligibility states the amount of entitlement available to the veteran borrower. Down payments are not required on VA loans if the borrower qualifies. The VA charges a funding (user) fee to help the government defray the cost of foreclosures. VA loans do not have due-on-sale clauses; therefore, they are assumable (even by nonveterans).

- With a *partially amortized mortgage*, the buyer makes regular payments smaller than what is required to completely pay off the loan by the date of termination. A single large final payment, called a balloon payment, of accrued interest and remaining unpaid principal is made at loan maturity.
- A *primary market* is the market where securities or goods are created. The primary mortgage market consists of lenders that originate new mortgage loans for borrowers.
- Mortgage loan originators (MLOs) do not make loans. They are middlemen (intermediaries) between borrowers and lenders. MLOs take loan information from a prospective borrower and "shop" for a lender offering the best rates and terms. Once a successful match is made and the loan is approved, the MLO earns a fee.
- A mortgage broker employs licensed loan originators. Mortgage brokers do not make or service loans. They work with lenders to arrange loans for prospective borrowers.
- A mortgage lender originates loans and packages them to investors. Mortgage lenders may use their own money or money borrowed from other lenders. Mortgage lenders also service loans.
- *Intermediation* is the process of consumers depositing funds into savings accounts at financial institutions. Lenders serve as intermediaries using borrowers' savings to provide funds to others for investment and borrowing.
- *Disintermediation* occurs when savers withdraw funds from intermediary financial institutions, bypassing them to invest elsewhere, thereby reducing the amount of funds available to the financial institutions.
- A *secondary mortgage market* is an investor market that buys and sells existing mortgages. Secondary market participants include Fannie Mae, Freddie Mac, and Ginnie Mae. Conforming loans are loans that meet Fannie Mae and Freddie Mac guidelines. Ginnie Mae is a government corporation under HUD. Ginnie Mae is a guarantor of government-insured and government-guaranteed loans and has the full faith and credit guarantee of the federal government.
- The Truth in Lending Act is implemented by the Federal Reserve's Regulation Z and requires lenders to disclose the annual percentage rate (APR) and all costs associated with credit. The law gives borrowers three business days to cancel most consumer loan contracts, except loans to purchase or construct a home.
- The Equal Credit Opportunity Act (ECOA) ensures that financial institutions make credit available without discrimination on the basis of race, color, religion, national origin, sex, marital status, age, or receipt of income from public assistance programs.
- The TILA-RESPA Integrated Disclosure Rule combined the TILA and RESPA disclosures into the Loan Estimate and the Closing Disclosure.

UNIT 13 EXAM

1. Which individual must be state licensed as a mortgage loan originator?
   a. Employee who processes loans for First National Bank of Orlando
   b. Employee of Bank of Florida who works as a bank teller
   c. Employee who works as a loan originator for a mortgage brokerage company that is not federally regulated
   d. Employee who works as a loan originator for First USA Credit Union

2. A commercial bank sold a group of 2,000 mortgages directly to Fannie Mae. This is an example of
   a. primary market activity.
   b. secondary market activity.
   c. loan correspondence.
   d. intermediation.

3. Which statement does NOT apply to Fannie Mae?
   a. Loans that meet Fannie Mae guidelines are called conforming loans.
   b. Fannie Mae purchases mortgages from local lenders and issues mortgage-backed securities.
   c. Fannie Mae is the largest participant in the secondary market.
   d. Fannie Mae is a government agency under HUD.

4. The market where mortgage loans are created, supplying funds to finance real estate purchases directly to borrowers, is called the
   a. primary market.
   b. secondary market.
   c. capital market.
   d. real estate market.

5. A home equity conversion mortgage (HECM) is also called a
   a. partially amortized mortgage.
   b. purchase money mortgage.
   c. reverse mortgage.
   d. home equity loan.

6. When investors bypass thrift institutions for direct investment elsewhere, the process is called
   a. loan correspondence.
   b. intermediation.
   c. disintermediation.
   d. capital-deficit area support.

7. Which set of maximum standard qualifying ratios is used to qualify a borrower for a VA mortgage loan?
   a. 28% HER; 36% TOR
   b. 30% HER; 36% TOR
   c. No HER; 41% TOR
   d. No HER; 43% TOR

8. An FHA loan is a
   a. government-insured loan.
   b. government-guaranteed loan.
   c. conventional loan that is insured with mortgage insurance.
   d. loan in which the mortgagor is protected against financial loss in the event of default.

9. A potential FHA borrower's monthly housing expense is $504, the total monthly gross income is $1,800, and the total monthly obligations are $648. What is the monthly housing expense ratio for the borrower?
   a. 28%
   b. 36%
   c. 38%
   d. 43%

10. In a fixed-rate amortized mortgage, the portion of the monthly payment that goes to reducing the principal
    a. remains constant throughout the loan term.
    b. gradually increases with each payment throughout the duration of the loan term.
    c. gradually decreases with each payment throughout the duration of the loan term.
    d. fluctuates based on the prevailing interest rates.

11. Which characteristic applies to both FHA and VA mortgage loans?
    a. Assumable
    b. Mortgage insurance required
    c. No established loan limits
    d. No down payment required

12. Which characteristic applies to VA loans?
    a. Government insured
    b. Minimum cash investment required
    c. Loan limit set by geographic area
    d. Funding fee charged

13. A man wants to buy a small restaurant and is considering financing the restaurant equipment in addition to the real estate. If the man pledges the personal property in addition to the real estate as collateral for the mortgage, the man's mortgage is
    a. an equipment mortgage.
    b. a package mortgage.
    c. an all-inclusive mortgage.
    d. a chattel mortgage.

14. A new mortgage accepted by the seller as part of the purchase price is
    a. a wraparound mortgage.
    b. an assumption of the mortgage.
    c. a chattel mortgage.
    d. a purchase-money mortgage.

15. Which protected class is covered under the Equal Credit Opportunity Act?
    a. Disability
    b. Familial status
    c. Occupation
    d. Marital status

16. The Truth in Lending Act (TILA)
    a. does not affect real estate financing credit.
    b. attempts to regulate maximum interest rates charged consumers.
    c. requires disclosure of finance charges, as well as annual percentage rates of interest.
    d. requires an affiliated business relationship disclosure.

17. Which regulation is NOT covered under RESPA?
    a. Prohibits the payment of a kickback in exchange for referring a settlement service business.
    b. Prohibits a seller from requiring the buyer to use a particular title insurance company as a condition of sale.
    c. Made bait-and-switch advertising a federal offense.
    d. Limits the amount lenders can require borrowers to escrow for property taxes and hazard insurance.

18. The TILA-RESPA Disclosure Rule requires that the borrower be provided with which item at LEAST three business days before closing?
    a. Closing Disclosure
    b. *Your Home Loan Toolkit*
    c. Guaranteed amount of settlement costs
    d. Loan Estimate

19. As part of the preparation for a closing, a listing broker referred a property owner to an appraiser. The appraiser completed the appraisal and charged the owner $250, which was entered on the Closing Disclosure. The appraiser gave the listing broker $50 for the referral, which the broker accepted. According to RESPA,
    a. the listing broker also must be licensed as an appraiser.
    b. the appraiser has not violated the law as long as the appraiser is state certified.
    c. both the broker and the appraiser have violated the law.
    d. the arrangement is entirely legal.

20. The Truth in Lending Act's right of rescission does NOT apply to which type of loan?
    a. Refinance loans
    b. Bank loan used to purchase a home
    c. Second mortgages
    d. Home equity line of credit (HELOC)

UNIT

14 REAL ESTATE–RELATED COMPUTATIONS AND CLOSING OF TRANSACTIONS

LEARNING OBJECTIVES

When you have completed this unit, you will be able to accomplish the following.

- Compute the sale commission.
- Calculate the percent of profit or loss, given the original cost of the investment, the sale price, and the dollar amount of profit or loss.
- Define settlement and title closing and list the preliminary steps to a closing.
- Prorate the buyer's and seller's expenses.
- Calculate the dollar amount of transfer taxes on deeds, mortgages, and notes and compute individual costs, allocating the transfer taxes and costs to the proper parties.
- Explain the rules of thumb for closing disclosure entries.

KEY TERMS

arrears	debit	profit
credit	preclosing inspection	proration

INTRODUCTION

Real estate brokers and sales associates must understand closing disclosures and should be capable of computing the various simple arithmetic problems to be solved in arriving at the figures entered on the closing disclosures provided to the contracting parties. Many adults have had little or no occasion to work with fractions, decimals, percentages, and the like for years.

14.1 WORKING WITH NUMBERS REVIEW

Fractions, Decimals, and Percentages

When a whole unit or number is divided into equal parts, each of the parts is a fraction (and a percentage) of the whole unit. For example, if a city block is divided into two equal parts, each of the parts is ½ (or 50%) of the city block.

Parts of a Fraction. When dealing with fractions, the number below the line is called the *denominator*. The denominator always indicates the total equal parts in a whole unit. In the example of the city block, each part was ½. The lower number indicates the total number of equal parts (two) in the entire city block. If the fraction ¼ had been used, the denominator would have indicated that the city block was divided into four equal parts.

The number in a fraction that appears above the line dividing the numbers is called the *numerator*. The numerator indicates how many of the equal parts of the whole unit are being counted. For example, in the fraction ¾, the top number indicates three equal parts are being counted, and the bottom number shows a total of four equal parts: therefore, you are talking about all but one equal part of something (all but ¼).

Changing Fractions to Decimals. The line separating the numerator from the denominator means division (the top number is divided by the bottom number). If you are dividing a fraction using a calculator, enter the numerator first, then press the division key, followed by the denominator. For example, in the fraction ½: press 1, followed by the division key, then press 2. Press the equal sign key (=) and the answer displayed is 0.5. You have now converted (changed) a fraction (½) into a decimal number (.5).

Changing Decimals to Percentages. To change a decimal number to a percentage, move the decimal point two places to the right and add the percent sign (%) (this is the same as multiplying the decimal number by 100). If only one decimal number is involved, add a zero to the right of the number.

EXAMPLES: .5 = .50 = 50%
1.5 = 1.50 = 150%

Changing Percentages to Decimals. To change any percentage to an equivalent decimal, simply place a decimal point two places to the left of the number and drop the percent sign (this is the same as dividing the percentage figure by 100).

EXAMPLES: 34% = .34
150% = 1.50

If only one number is involved, add a zero to the left to permit moving the decimal point two places to the left.

EXAMPLE: You want to calculate in dollars the 7.5% commission on a house sale price.
Convert the fractional part of the decimal number:
½% = 1 ÷ 2 = .5
Next, convert the entire commission percentage to a decimal number.
7½% = 7.5% = .075
Thus, the decimal number .075 is used to calculate the sale commission. Assume the sale price is $130,000. Calculate the commission.
$130,000 × .075 = $9,750

Decimal Place Values. A great deal of the basic arithmetic required to compute routine real estate problems involves decimal numbers. This review of decimals will be more meaningful if you refresh your memory of the decimal system of place values and the importance of the decimal point in separating whole numbers from fractional parts of whole numbers. The chart of decimal place values in Figure 14.1 should be memorized if you do not already know the place values. Notice that the *whole numbers* are to the left of the decimal point. The *decimal fractions* of a whole number are to the right of the decimal point.

FIGURE 14.1 ■ Decimal Place Values

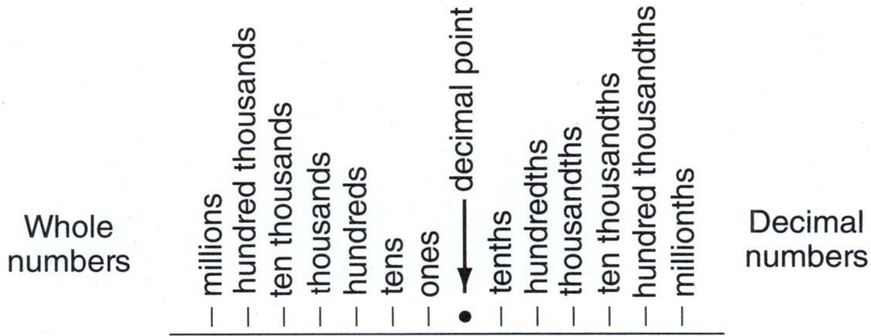

Working With Decimals. To divide a whole number by a decimal—for example, 41,500 divided by 1.85, first enter 41500 into your calculator, press the division key, then enter 1.85. When you press the equal sign key, the answer will appear in the display, as demonstrated in the illustration.

Calculator Method:

41,500 ÷ 1.85 =

Press	*Display*
[4] then [1] then [5] then [0] then [0]	41500
[÷] (the division key)	41500
[1] then [.] then [8] then [5]	1.85
[=] (equals sign)	22432.432

EQUIVALENT UNITS

Percentage	Fraction	Decimal
100%	100/100	1.00
50%	50/100	.50
6%	6/100	.06
½%	.5/100	.005
¼%	.25/100	.0025

SALE COMMISSIONS

If the broker has been hired to list and sell the property for the seller, the seller is usually responsible for paying the commission. If a buyer brokerage agreement exists, the buyer may be responsible for the commission. The commission is agreed to in the listing agreement and/or the buyer brokerage agreement.

Formula: Sale Commission

sale price × commission rate = total commission

total commission × percentage to listing brokerage = listing commission

listing commission × listing sales associate percentage = listing sales associate commission

total commission × percentage to selling brokerage = selling commission

selling commission × buyer's sales associate percentage = buyer's sales associate commission

Let's begin with an example of a commission calculation. In this example, the property is listed and sold by the same sales associate.

EXAMPLE: Suppose a broker's listing agreement specifies that a 6.5% commission is to be paid on the sale price. A sales associate for the firm lists and sells the property and is to receive 55% of the 6.5% sale commission. How much will the sales associate earn after selling the property for $62,000?

Step 1: Find the total sale commission.

$62,000 sale price × .065 rate = $4,030 total commission

Step 2: Find the sales associate's commission.

$4,030 total commission × .55 split = $2,216.50 sales associate's commission

More frequently, a property is listed with one brokerage company and sold by another brokerage through the MLS system. Members of the MLS make an offer of cooperation ("co-broke" or "co-op") when they place their listings in the MLS. When another brokerage sells the listing, it will receive the portion of the total commission that was specified by the listing brokerage.

EXAMPLE: A broker's listing agreement specifies that a 7% commission is to be paid on the sale price. The agreement specifies a 50-50 split between the listing and the selling offices. If the property sells for $100,000, how much commission is earned by the listing and the selling offices?

Step 1: Find the total sale commission.

$100,000 sale price × .07 rate = $7,000 total commission

Step 2: Find the selling and listing office's split.

$7,000 total commission × .50 split = $3,500 selling/listing office commission

The selling commission is typically shared between the broker of the selling office and the sales associate who works for the selling office that found a buyer for the property. The same is true for the listing office and the sales associate who listed the property for the brokerage company. The percentage that sales associates earn is negotiated between individual sales associates and their employing broker, taking into consideration each sales associate's experience and production.

EXAMPLE: Let's assume that the sales associate receives 60% of the total selling office commission. How much commission did the sales associate earn on the previous example? How much did the broker receive for the same transaction?

Step 1: Calculate the sales associate's split of the selling office commission.

$3,500 selling office commission × .60 split = $2,100 sales associate's commission

Step 2: Calculate the broker's split of the selling office commission.

$3,500 selling office commission × .40 split = $1,400 broker's commission

Today, 100% commission arrangements are popular. A sales associate in a 100% commission office receives the entire commission due the respective brokerage office. Instead of splitting the commission with the broker, the sales associate pays a specified share of office expenses plus a fixed monthly fee.

A broker who lists a property with higher-than-normal value may agree to a graduated (sliding scale) sale commission. This provides an incentive for the broker to get the seller the very best price possible.

EXAMPLE: The broker has a listing with a seller, and the parties agree to a graduated commission structure. The commission is 5% on the first $200,000 of sale price, 6.5% on the next $100,000 of sale price, and 8% on the amount over $300,000. What is the total commission if the property sells for $325,000?

Step 1: Calculate the first increment of commission.

$200,000 × .05 rate = $10,000 first increment commission

Step 2: Calculate the second increment of commission.

$100,000 × .065 rate = $6,500 second increment commission

Step 3: Calculate the third increment of commission.

$25,000 remaining portion of sale price × .08 rate = $2,000 third increment commission

Step 4: Add the commission increments to determine the total commission.

$10,000 + $6,500 + $2,000 = $18,500 total commission

Calculating Problems That Include Percent

Percent problems involve three elements. The three elements common to all percent calculations are

- part (of the total amount),
- rate (percent), and
- total (total amount).

We can use three simple formulas to assist with solving percent problems (see the following textbox).

Formula: Solving Percent Problems

part ÷ total = rate

part ÷ rate = total

total × rate = part

EXAMPLE 1: A property sold for $100,000. The commission was 7% of the sale price. What was the commission?

Rate = 7%

Total = $100,000

The formula indicates that to solve for the commission (part), we must multiply the total sale price by the rate:

total × rate = part

$100,000 × 7% = $7,000

EXAMPLE 2: A competing real estate company sold your neighbor's home for $200,000. The seller indicated that the commission on the sale was $13,000. What percentage of commission did the real estate company charge?

The formula indicates that to solve for the rate of commission (rate), we must divide the commission paid by the sale price:

part ÷ total = rate

$13,000 ÷ $200,000 = .065 or 6½%

EXAMPLE 3: Property taxes are $1,600 and are taxed at a rate of $2.50 for $100 of assessed value. What is the assessed value?

In this example, you must find the total assessed value. The part is the $1,600 property taxes. The rate is the $2.50 per $100. According to our memory device, we need to take the $1,600 (part) and divide by the rate ($2.50):

part ÷ rate = total

$1,600 ÷ $2.50 = 640

Because the rate was $2.50 per $100 of assessed value, if we multiply 640 by $100, the result is the amount of assessed value:

640 × $100 = $64,000

Practice Questions

1. A sales associate, while working for the broker, acquired a listing for $289,000 at a 6% commission rate. A second sales associate, who works for another brokerage office, found the buyer for the property. The listing and the selling brokers agree to a 50-50 split between the two offices. The property sold for the listed price. The selling broker kept 45% of the commission received by the selling office.
   - What was the total commission earned on the sale?
   - What was the selling office's split?
   - What was the sales associate's commission at the selling office?

2. What is the principal balance of a mortgage loan if the interest is $400 for one month at an annual rate of 4%?

3. A property sold for $115,900. The commission was 7% of the sale price. What was the commission?

4. A competing real estate company sold a residence for $350,000. The seller indicated that the commission on the sale was $25,375. What percentage of commission did the real estate company charge?

14.2 PERCENTAGE APPLIED TO SELLING PRICE, COST, AND PROFIT

Profit is how much you make over and above your cost. It may be expressed as the dollar amount of profit or as a percentage of profit.

EXAMPLE: Assume a buyer paid $100,000 for a lot and later sold the lot for $150,000. How much profit did the property owner make on the sale?

$150,000 sale price – $100,000 amount paid = $50,000 profit

Formula: Profit

amount made on sale ÷ amount paid = percentage profit

Hint: made ÷ paid

Refer to the previous example. We can take the amount the property owner made on the sale ($50,000 profit) and divide by the amount the property owner originally paid for the property ($100,000) to determine the percentage of profit made on the sale.

$50,000 amount made ÷ $100,000 amount paid = .50 or 50% profit

EXAMPLE: An investor purchased 4 acres of land for $150,000. The investor subdivided the land into two 2-acre lots and sold the lots for $90,000 each.

a. How much profit did the investor make on this investment?

$90,000 × 2 lots = $180,000
$180,000 sale price for the two lots – $150,000 paid = $30,000 profit

b. What was the investor's percentage of profit on the sale?

$30,000 made ÷ $150,000 paid = .20 or 20% profit

What if the investor purchases a property and, because of a prolonged economic recession, the investor must sell the property at a loss?

Formula: Loss

amount lost on sale ÷ total cost = percentage loss

Hint: lost ÷ cost

EXAMPLE 1: An investor purchased a lot for $100,000 and had to later sell the lot for $80,000, resulting in a $20,000 loss. What was the investor's percentage of loss?

$20,000 amount lost ÷ $100,000 amount cost = .20 or 20% loss

EXAMPLE 2: A lot sold for $6,000, making a 25% profit. What was the cost of the lot?

100% cost + 25% profit = $6,000
125% = $6,000 selling price
$6,000 selling price ÷ 1.25 = $4,800 cost

EXAMPLE 3: A lot sold for $10,000, representing a 20% loss. What was the cost of the lot?

100% – 20% = $10,000
80% = $10,000
$10,000 selling price ÷ .80 = $12,500 cost

Practice Questions

5. A lot that cost $45,000 sold for $54,000, yielding a profit of $9,000. What is the percentage of profit?

6. A lot that cost $50,000 sold for $47,000, resulting in a $3,000 loss. What is the percentage of loss?

7. A lot sold for $32,200, making a 15% profit. What was the cost of the lot?

8. A lot sold for $75,000, representing a 20% loss. What was the cost of the lot?

14.3 PRELIMINARY STEPS TO CLOSING

All real property sales or exchanges eventually conclude with a transfer of title. This occurs at the title closing (or settlement), when the seller delivers title to the buyer in exchange for the purchase price. The date and place of title closing should be specified in the sale contract. There are usually several things to accomplish between the time of signing the sale contract and the title closing. For example, some of the preliminary steps include the following.

Earnest Money Is Deposited. Sales associates must deliver the earnest money deposit (also called good-faith deposit, or escrow) to the broker by the end of the next business day. The broker must deposit the buyer's good-faith deposit into the escrow account no later than the end of the third business day after the brokerage company receives the funds. Some brokers do not maintain their own escrow accounts. If the earnest money deposit is placed with a title company or with an attorney, the sale contract must indicate the title company's or attorney's name, address, and telephone number. The broker must deliver the earnest money to the attorney or title company by the end of the third business day (see "Escrow or Trust Accounts," Unit 5).

Additional Deposit, if Required. If the sale contract requires the buyer to give additional funds as a good-faith deposit, the sales associate must keep track of when additional funds are due and document that the deposit was received, delivered to the escrow agent in a timely manner, and deposited into the escrow account.

Loan Application. If the buyers intend to finance the purchase, they will complete a mortgage application. The contract for sale specifies the number of days within which the buyer must submit a loan application. The listing and the selling licensees should monitor progress.

Contingencies. The licensee must keep track of any contingencies in the contract and follow up to ensure that the contingencies are cleared in writing in a timely manner.

Appraisal. Because the property is pledged as collateral for the mortgage loan, the lender will order an appraisal to determine whether the property's value is sufficient to ensure recovery of the loan amount should a default occur. The buyer also may want the property appraised to verify the property's value. The buyer is entitled to a copy of the appraisal no less than three business days prior to the closing.

Loan Approval. The lender's loan approval removes an important contingency. The seller should be notified once the buyer's financing has been approved.

Survey Is Ordered. A survey is required by the title company and the lender. The buyer will want to have the property surveyed to determine the exact location and size of the property and to make sure there are no encroachments, such as a neighbor's fence across the property line. See Unit 10 for or additional information regarding surveys.

Title Insurance. A search is made of the public records for condition of the title and existing liens, judgments, or other encumbrances. The seller is responsible for removing any encumbrances on the title. Typically, there is a simultaneous issue of the owner's policy and the lender's policy. See Unit 9 for complete details regarding title insurance.

Termite Inspection. A copy of the wood-destroying organisms (WDO) inspection report is given to the buyer, lender, and the title company. The WDO inspection is for termites and other WDOs (such as wood-boring beetles and fungi). The sale contract should specify the details should a termite treatment or repairs be required.

Required Repairs Are Ordered. Once the loan is approved, any required repairs should be ordered to remove these contingencies as soon as possible. The appropriate party should inspect the work to be sure the work has been done properly. The buyer and the seller should be notified once the work is complete.

Home Inspection. A home inspection is for the structural condition of the home (including electrical, HVAC, plumbing, etc.). Home inspectors cannot legally perform WDO inspections unless they work for a licensed pest control company.

Buyer Hazard Insurance. Buyers who are obtaining a mortgage must provide proof of homeowners insurance coverage at closing. The buyer should make a decision regarding the insurance company early in the transaction. If a tropical storm is named, the insurance company will suspend issuing homeowners insurance policies until the storm passes. Most insurance companies allow the buyer to purchase insurance up to 30 days in advance. As soon as the buyer's financing is approved, the buyer should have the insurance company "bind" the hazard insurance. Proof of hazard insurance coverage is forwarded to the closing agent.

Closing Documents Are Reviewed. The closing agent (title company or attorney) prepares the closing disclosure, warranty deed, and property tax proration agreement and the lender prepares the closing documents. The buyer and the seller are given the opportunity to review the closing documents before closing. It is important for sales associates to have an understanding of the closing documents. Sales associates should be able to explain and verify the entries on the closing documents. The day before the closing, licensees should examine and review the closing disclosure with the buyer or the seller to correct any errors and explain each entry. Sales associates usually attend the title closing with the buyer and the seller in case their knowledge of the transaction is needed to assist with answering any questions or concerns that may arise.

Preclosing Inspection Is Conducted. Before the title closing, the buyer makes a final **preclosing inspection** (*walk-through*) of the property with the sales associate. The purpose of the preclosing inspection is to verify that repairs have been completed and that the property has been left in good condition.

Buyer Is Informed of the Amount of Funds Needed to Close. The buyer is responsible for ensuring that the funds needed to close are delivered to the closing agent. The current industry practice for transmitting these funds is in the form of a certified check or wire transfer.

475.25(1)(d), F.S.

Earnest Money Is Transferred to the Closing Agent. When the earnest money has been held in the broker's escrow account, the sales associate is responsible for notifying the broker of the date that the earnest money is to be transferred to the closing agent. The sales associate should verify with the broker and the closing agent that the transfer has occurred. Florida real estate license law places the responsibility on the broker for an accurate accounting and delivery of all monies, deposits, drafts, mortgages, conveyances, leases, or other documents entrusted to the broker by the parties to the transaction.

Practice Questions

9. The purpose of a final ______________ ______________ is to verify that repairs have been completed and that the property has been left in good condition.

10. The buyer should arrange for hazard insurance early in the process because in the event of a named ____________ _________ insurance companies will suspend issuing homeowner policies.

14.4 CLOSING DISCLOSURES

The Closing Disclosure is a detailed accounting of funds in a real estate transaction. Some entries on the Closing Disclosure are shared between the buyer and the seller.

Prorated Expenses

The Closing Disclosure involves the division of financial responsibility between the buyer and the seller. Items that are to become a **credit** (reimbursed) or **debit** (charged) to either buyer or seller are *prorated* because the item applies to both the buyer and the seller. The various credits and debits are allocated between the buyer and the seller in the proportions or **prorations** specified in the contract.

Every sale contract should specify a date for prorating items. All prorations are calculated as of midnight: when one day ends and the new day begins. The closing day is allocated (belongs to) either the buyer or the seller as determined in the sale contract. It is customary when transferring title to have all prorated items determined as of midnight of the day before the closing date. This means that the seller's responsibility ends at midnight the day before the closing occurs and that the buyer is responsible for costs incurred from the closing date going forward. If the seller is being charged for the day of closing, simply add one extra day to the seller days.

Prorations are entered on the Closing Disclosure as double entries (one party is debited and the other party is credited). A single dollar amount is entered as a debit to one party and a credit to the other party.

365-Day and 360-Day Methods. There are two methods of calculating prorations:

1. The 365-day method is the most common and most accurate method. This method calculates the proration using the actual number of days in the proration period. The annual charge is divided by 365 (the number of days in a calendar year) to determine the daily rate. The actual number of days in the proration period is multiplied by the daily rate.

2. The 360-day method allocates 30 days to every month. In this method, the annual cost is divided by 360 to determine the daily rate. This method is not normally used for calculating prorations for closing disclosures.

County and/or City Property Taxes. Property taxes are paid once a year (on an annual basis). Property taxes become due on November 1 of each year, and the homeowner has through the end of March of the next year to pay the tax bill before the taxes becomes delinquent. Because the taxes are not due until late in the year, the buyer is credited at closing for the time the seller owned the property. The buyer will pay the tax bill at the end of the year when the entire tax bill becomes due (see "Property Tax Schedule," Figure 18.1).

Formula: Unpaid Property Taxes

property taxes for year ÷ 365 days = daily tax rate

daily tax rate × number of days seller owns property in year = proration amount (credit buyer, debit seller)

EXAMPLE 1: Closing date is July 23. The annual property taxes are $3,467.50 and have not yet been paid. How much is the seller to pay the buyer for the days the seller owned the property? The day of closing is charged to the buyer. (When doing calculations, use the 365-day method unless the 360-day method is specifically stated in the question.)

Step 1. Begin by dividing the annual property taxes by 365 to find the daily rate:

$3,467.50 ÷ 365 = $9.50 daily rate

Step 2. The seller will credit the buyer for January through June and through midnight the day before closing (midnight of July 22). Calculate the exact number of days in the months January 1 (when the tax year begins) through June and add 22 days for July.

January 31 + February 28 + March 31 + April 30 + May 31 + June 30 + 22 of July = 203 days

Step 3. Multiply the daily rate by the number of days the seller owes the buyer:

$9.50 daily rate × 203 days = $1,928.50

Step 4. Prorations are entered on the Closing Disclosure as double entries; a debit to one party and a credit to the other party. The dollar figure is identical for the debit and the credit.

The seller has not paid the property tax bill for the year because it won't become due until November 1. The seller owned the property for the tax year up until midnight of the day before closing. So the seller is charged (debited) $1,928.50 on the closing disclosure. The buyer is credited $1,928.50 on the Closing Disclosure. The buyer is credited $1,928.50 on the Closing Disclosure. When the tax bill becomes due later in the year, the buyer will pay the entire property tax bill of $3,467.50.

Closing Disclosure entry: $1,928.50 debit seller, $1,928.50 credit buyer

EXAMPLE 2: The closing date is April 15. The annual property taxes are $2,283.44. The day of closing is charged to the buyer. The proration is calculated as follows:

The daily rate of property tax is:

$2,283.44 ÷ 365 days = $6.256 daily rate

Taxes are paid in **arrears**, so the seller will owe the buyer for three months (January through March) and 14 days in April:

January 31 + February 28 + March 31 + April 14 = 104 days

$6.256 daily rate × 104 days = $650.624, rounded to $650.62 (debit seller, credit buyer)

If the closing occurs late in the year (November or December) and the seller has already paid the taxes for the year, the buyer will reimburse the seller for the remainder of the year. Thus the buyer will be charged a debit for taxes for the days remaining in the year, and the seller will receive a credit for the same amount.

PRORATING PROPERTY TAXES

- Property taxes (items paid in arrears) "seller days" are used to calculate the proration.
- Unpaid property taxes appear as a *credit* to the buyer and as a *debit* to the seller.
- Prorations always have the same dollar amount entered for the debit and the credit.

Prepaid Rent. Normally, any rental income collected in advance belongs to the new owner (buyer) as of the date of closing. In other words, the unused portion of advance rent belongs to the buyer. The total rent amount should be divided by the number of days involved in the rental period and allocated on a daily basis.

Formula: Prepaid Rent

rent paid for the closing month ÷ number of days in closing month = daily rental rate

daily rental rate × number of days buyer owns property in closing month = proration amount (credit buyer, debit seller)

EXAMPLE: Assume that a property rents for $1,245 per month. The closing date is on the 21st day of June. The seller (landlord) received the tenant's rent on the first of the month. Therefore, the buyer is entitled to the rent beginning with the day of closing through the remainder of June.

Step 1. Calculate the number of days owed the buyer.

30 days in June − 20 days seller owned property = 10 days rent due buyer

Step 2. Calculate the daily rate of rental income.

$1,245 ÷ 30 days in month = $41.50 daily rent

Step 3. Calculate the rent due the buyer.

$41.50 daily rent × 10 days due buyer = $415.00

Step 4. Prorations are entered on the closing disclosure as a double entry; the seller is debited (owes) $415.00 and the buyer is credited $415.00 for rental income beginning with the closing date through the remainder of the month.

Closing disclosure entry: $415.00 debit seller, $415.00 credit buyer

PRORATING ITEMS PAID IN ADVANCE

- When a prorated item is paid *in advance*, as is the case with rent, the "buyer days" are used to calculate the proration.
- Prepaid rent is entered as a *credit* to the buyer and a *debit* to the seller.
- If the rental property is a duplex, it has two units; a triplex has three units; and a fourplex has four units. For example, if the rent proration states the income property is a duplex, multiply the monthly rent per unit by 2.

Mortgage Interest on Assumed Mortgages. When a loan is assumed, the accrued interest for the month of closing must be prorated. Interest is paid in arrears, therefore, the monthly payment made on the first day of the month pays interest for the entire previous month. Interest is figured from the last date for which interest was paid. The exact number of days in each month is used, and interest is figured on a daily basis.

Formula: Interest on Assumed Mortgage

loan balance × interest rate = annual interest ÷ 365 days = daily interest rate

daily interest rate × number of days seller owns property in closing month = proration amount (credit buyer, debit seller)

EXAMPLE: A home is scheduled to close on May 8. The buyer is assuming the seller's loan. The loan has an interest rate of 4.5% and a monthly payment of $612.62 due on the first of each month. The loan balance on May 1 is $93,600. What is the proration?

Step 1. Find the daily rate of interest.

$93,600 loan balance × 4.5% interest = $4,212 annual interest

$4,212 ÷ 365 days = $11.539726 daily rate of interest

Step 2. Find the number of days of accrued interest the seller owes.

The seller owes the buyer interest for the period May 1 up until midnight of the day before closing, or seven days.

Step 3. Multiply the daily rate of interest by the days owed.

$11.539726 daily rate × 7 days owed = $80.778082 or $80.78

Closing Disclosure entry: $80.78 debit seller; $80.78 credit buyer

PRORATING MORTGAGE INTEREST ON ASSUMED MORTGAGES

- Interest on mortgage loans is paid *in arrears.*
- When prorating an item paid in arrears, use "seller days" to calculate the proration.
- Enter interest on an assumed mortgage as a *debit* to the seller and as a *credit* to the buyer.

FIGURE 14.2 ■ Proration Summary

Proration	Formula							Disclosure Entry*
Unpaid Property Tax	property taxes	÷	365 days	×	days seller owns property (1st part of year)	=	prorated amount	☹ seller ☺ buyer
Prepaid Rent	monthly rent	÷	days in closing month	×	days buyer owns property (2nd part of month)	=	prorated amount	☹ seller ☺ buyer
Interest on Assumed Mortgage	annual interest (loan × interest rate)	÷	365 days	×	days seller owns property in closing month (1st part of month)	=	prorated amount	☹ seller ☺ buyer

* In the column Disclosure Entry, if an individual receives money at the closing table, it is called a *credit,* which we can represent as a ☺ because credits make us happy. If the buyer or the seller must pay out money at the closing, it is called a *debit,* which we can represent as a ☹ because debits make us sad.

Practice Questions

11. The closing date is May 10, the annual property taxes are $3,011.25, and the tax bill has not yet been paid. The day of closing is charged to the buyer. How much is the seller to pay the buyer for the days the seller owned the property?

12. The closing date is April 14. The buyer is assuming the seller's mortgage loan that has a principal balance on April 1 of $200,500 at 4% interest. The day of closing is charged to the buyer. What is the proration and how is it entered on the Closing Disclosure?

13. The closing date is April 10, and the duplex rents for $1,200 per unit. The seller (landlord) received the rent from both tenants on the first of the month. What is the proration and how is it entered on the Closing Disclosure?

14.5 STATE TRANSFER TAXES

201.02, F.S.

Florida has three types of state taxes that apply to deeds, notes, or mortgages associated with the transfer of ownership of real property and financing.

State Documentary Stamp Tax on Deeds. Florida requires the payment of a tax on deeds and other conveyances. This state *documentary stamp tax on deeds* is assessed at the rate of $.70 ($.60 in Miami-Dade County) for each $100 of the full purchase price (or any fraction of $100). It makes no difference whether the purchase is all cash, all financed, or some combination of cash and financing because this tax is based on purchase price. This is a one-time tax and is not paid annually (see Figure 14.3).

Formula: Documentary Stamp Taxes on Deeds

purchase price ÷ $100 = taxable units; (if result is a decimal number, round to the next whole number)

number of taxable units × $.70* = cost of documentary stamp tax on deeds

* Rate is $.60 in Miami-Dade County

EXAMPLE 1: If a home sells for $171,200, the documentary stamp tax on the deed will be as follows:

$171,200 ÷ $100 = 1,712 taxable units
1,712 × $.70 = $1,198.40 documentary stamp tax on deed

EXAMPLE 2: Assume the purchase price in the previous example is $171,225. $171,225 divided by $100 is 1,712.25. The result is a decimal number, so round the taxable units to the next whole number of 1,713 before calculating the stamp tax due as follows:

$171,225 ÷ $100 = 1,712.25, round up to the next whole number = 1,713 taxable units
1,713 × $.70 = $1,199.10 documentary stamp tax on deed

EXAMPLE 3: A home sells for \$295,995. How much will the state charge for the documentary stamp tax on the deed?

\$295,995 ÷ \$100 = 2,959.95, round up to the next whole number = 2,960 taxable units
2,960 × \$.70 = \$2,072.00 documentary stamp tax on deed

The law requires that the seller deliver a recordable deed. Because a deed may not be recorded until the stamp tax has been paid, the seller is obligated to either deliver a deed having paid the stamp tax or negotiate with the buyer to assume the obligation. If the buyer does not agree to pay the stamp tax on the deed, the tax remains the seller's responsibility.

DOCUMENTARY STAMP TAX ON DEEDS

- Documentary stamp tax on deeds is charged at a rate of \$.70 (\$.60 in Miami-Dade County) for each \$100 of the full purchase price.
- Documentary tax is an expense. It is entered as a debit to the person paying the expense. Unlike a proration, there is no credit to the other party (expenses are single entries).
- On normal sales or exchanges, the documentary tax is shown as a debit to the seller on the Closing Disclosure.

201.08, F.S.

State Documentary Stamp Tax on Promissory Notes. Florida requires the payment of a documentary stamp tax on all new and assumed promissory notes. The tax rate is \$.35 per \$100, or fraction thereof, on the face value of the *promissory note*. This is an expense usually charged to the buyer. The tax is entered as a *debit* to the buyer on the Closing Disclosure (see Figure 14.3).

Formula: Documentary Stamp Taxes on Promissory Notes

promissory note ÷ \$100 = taxable units (if result is a decimal number, round up to the next whole number)

number of taxable units × \$.35 = cost of documentary stamp tax on promissory notes

EXAMPLE 1: A home sells for \$375,000. The buyer financed the purchase with a new 80% conventional loan and 20% cash. How much was the buyer charged for the documentary stamp tax on the promissory note?

\$375,000 purchase price × .80 = \$300,000 mortgage loan amount
\$300,000 ÷ \$100 = 3,000 taxable units
3,000 × \$.35 = \$1,050 documentary stamp tax on the promissory note

EXAMPLE 2: A home sold for \$90,000. The buyer paid \$10,000 cash, assumed a recorded mortgage of \$55,000, and created a new second mortgage in the amount of \$25,000. The documentary stamp tax on the promissory notes resulting from this transaction is as follows:

\$55,000 ÷ \$100 = 550 taxable units × \$.35 = \$192.50 (assumed)
\$25,000 ÷ \$100 = 250 taxable units × \$.35 = \$87.50 (new note)
\$192.50 + \$87.50 = \$280 (tax on notes)

CALCULATING DOCUMENTARY STAMP TAX ON PROMISSORY NOTES

- Documentary stamp tax on notes is charged at a rate of $.35 for each $100 of the promissory note.
- Documentary stamp tax is an *expense*. It is entered as a debit to the buyer (a buyer expense unless agreed to otherwise).

199.133, F.S.

State Intangible Tax on New Mortgages. Florida requires the payment of an *intangible tax* on *new* mortgages. (An assumed mortgage recorded previously is not to be taxed again; likewise, intangible tax is not charged on purchases subject to an existing mortgage.) The tax rate for the state intangible tax on new mortgages is two mills ($.002 or two-tenths of one cent) per dollar of debt (see Figure 14.3).

Formula: Intangible Tax on New Mortgages

new loan amount × $.002 = cost of intangible tax

EXAMPLE: Use the figures from the previous example. The intangible tax on the new second mortgage is as follows:

$25,000 new second mortgage × $.002 = $50 intangible tax on new second mortgage

This tax is usually shown as a debit to the buyer on the closing disclosure.

FIGURE 14.3 ■ **State Transfer Taxes**

Type of Tax	Rate	Charged On	Applies To
Doc Stamps on Deed	$.70 per $100 ($.60 per $100 Miami-Dade County)	Purchase Price	All Conveyances
Doc Stamps on Note	$.35 per $100	Promissory Note	New and Assumed Mortgage Loans
Intangible Tax	$.002	Mortgage Loan	New Financing

EXAMPLE: A property sold for $179,950. The buyer paid $25,000 cash down and arranged for a $154,950 mortgage loan. What are the state transfer taxes on this transaction?

Deed:
$179,950 ÷ $100 = 1,799.5, rounded up to 1,800 taxable units
1,800 taxable units × $.70 = $1,260 tax on deed
Intangible tax on new mortgage:
$154,950 × $.002 = $309.90 intangible tax on new mortgage
Note:
$154,950 ÷ $100 = 1,549.5, rounded up to 1,550 taxable units
1,550 taxable units × $.35 = $542.50 tax on promissory note
Total state transfer taxes:
$1,260 + $309.90 + $542.50 = $2,112.40

Other Charges

Preparation of Documents. The customary method of handling charges for preparation of documents is to require the person who must sign the document to pay the fee for its preparation. Therefore, the seller (grantor) pays for preparation of the deed, and the buyer (mortgagor) pays for preparation of the mortgage and note. The charges that result are shown as a *debit* on the Closing Disclosure of the person required to pay. Expenses are single entries (there is no corresponding credit).

Recording Fees. Several of the legal instruments signed at closing should be recorded to give constructive notice of new ownership and debt status. Charges associated with recording these documents are usually paid by the person who wants a particular document recorded. For example, the grantee (buyer) wants the deed recorded and pays for this service, even though the grantor (seller) pays for the deed to be prepared by an attorney. The various recording fees are shown as a debit to the appropriate party.

Broker's Commission. Normally, the person who employed the broker is required to pay the commission. The broker's commission is entered as a debit to the party charged with paying the commission.

Title Insurance. Legally, the seller of a property is not required to provide an abstract of title, title insurance, or an opinion of title without contractually agreeing to do so. However, title insurances are used to protect the lender and the buyer. Lenders usually will not accept abstracts of title but do demand up-to-date *lender's title insurance*. A buyer's representative should recommend that the buyer's interest be protected by obtaining *owner's title insurance*. Actually, these charges, like many, are negotiable regarding who pays what (see "Title Insurance," Unit 9).

Practice Questions

14. The documentary stamp tax on deeds is charged on the __________ __________.

15. The documentary stamp tax on deeds is charged at a rate of ______________ per ______________ unit.

16. The closing date is July 15. The purchase price is $250,575. The buyer obtained a new mortgage loan for 80% of the purchase price.

    - What is the charge for the documentary stamp tax on the deed, and how will the tax be entered on the Closing Disclosure?

    - What is the total charge for the state transfer taxes associated with the financing?

14.6 RULES OF THUMB

Recall that a Closing Disclosure is a detailed accounting of funds in a real estate transaction. The disclosure summarizes who is responsible for paying each item associated with the sale contract. You can think of the Closing Disclosure as a photograph of a special moment in time (the day of closing). Every entry on the Closing Disclosure concerns money on closing day (cash *today*). At the closing table, the buyer and the seller each have financial obligations to one another. If an individual receives money at the closing table, it is called a *credit*, which we can represent as a ☺ because credits make us happy. If the buyer or the seller must pay out money at the closing, it is called a *debit*, which we can represent as a ☹ because debits make us sad.

Purchase Price. The purchase price is *credited* ☺ to the seller because the seller is happy to be receiving money. The purchase price is entered on the disclosure as a *debit* ☹ to the buyer because the buyer is sad to be paying out money. Assuming a $200,000 purchase price, $200,000 will be *credited* to the seller (seller is receiving money), and the buyer is debited $200,000 (buyer is paying for the property).

Earnest Money Deposit. The initial earnest money deposit is typically paid at the time an offer is presented to the seller. Because the buyer has prepaid the deposit, the Closing Disclosure will indicate a *credit* ☺ on closing day. The buyer paid the deposit a month or so ago, so the buyer is happy on closing day that this has already been paid. If the buyer's earnest money deposit was $10,000, this is the amount of the *credit* ☺ to the buyer. No entry is made on the seller's side of the Closing Disclosure because the deposit was previously given to the broker or another escrow agent. On the day of closing, the escrow agent delivers the escrowed funds to the closing agent.

New Mortgage Loan. Very few buyers pay for a home with all cash. For example, this buyer received a 30-year, fixed-rate mortgage loan for 80% of the purchase price ($160,000 loan). Today, the lender is bringing $160,000 to the closing table on the buyer's behalf. That means that the buyer's lender, on closing day, is taking care of $160,000 of the purchase price. Therefore, the $160,000 is entered on the Closing Disclosure as a *credit* ☺ to the buyer. There is no entry on the seller's side of the disclosure because the $160,000 is transferred to the closing agent on the day of closing.

Purchase Money Mortgage. Sometimes, the buyer does not have sufficient cash to pay the entire down payment. If the same buyer mentioned previously secured a $160,000 loan, the buyer's equity is $40,000. The buyer has already paid an earnest money deposit of $10,000, leaving a $30,000 obligation for the down payment. If the buyer only has the ability to pay $20,000 cash toward the down payment, the seller may agree to financing a new purchase money mortgage in the amount of $10,000. The closing statement would indicate a *credit* ☺ to the buyer because the buyer does not have to produce the $10,000 cash at closing. The seller, however, is receiving $10,000 less cash at closing, so a *debit* ☹ of $10,000 is entered on the seller side of the Closing Disclosure.

Prorations. Recall that three types of prorations were discussed earlier in this unit: (1) property taxes, (2) rent, and (3) mortgage interest on an assumed mortgage. Prorations are *always* entered on the Closing Disclosure as double entries. This means that the proration is entered on both the buyer side and the seller side of the Closing Disclosure (a debit to one party and a credit to the other party) and the dollar amount of the debit and the credit is the same dollar figure.

1. *Property tax.* Property taxes are paid *in arrears*. This is because the homeowner does not receive the bill for the current year's taxes until November. Therefore, if the closing date is before November 30, the seller will give the buyer the seller's share of the property taxes at closing. The property taxes will be entered on the Closing Disclosure as a *debit* ☹ to the seller and the same amount will be *credited* ☺ to the buyer on the Closing Disclosure. When the buyer receives the property tax bill in November, the buyer will have already received the seller's portion of the tax obligation and the buyer (or the lender if the property taxes are escrowed) will pay the property tax bill for the year.

2. *Prepaid rent.* On the first of the month, assume the seller collected $1,000 in rent money from a tenant who occupies the property that is being sold. Midway through the month, on closing day, the seller will give the buyer a portion of the rent money. If the seller is giving money to the buyer on closing day, it is entered on the Closing Disclosure as a *debit* ☹ to the seller and as a *credit* ☺ to the buyer.

3. *Interest on an assumed mortgage.* Mortgage loan interest is paid *in arrears*. Therefore, when the borrower pays the February mortgage payment, the borrower is paying the principal for February and the interest charged for January. If the closing date is in January, this means that the buyer will make a mortgage payment on February 1 and the February payment will include interest due for the month of January. Because the seller only lived in the property for a portion of January, at closing, the seller will pay the buyer for the seller's portion of the January mortgage interest. The seller is giving money to the buyer, so the proration is entered as a *debit* ☹ to the seller and as a *credit* ☺ to the buyer. The buyer does not have to pay any interest on closing day.

Did you notice that in all three proration scenarios, the proration was entered on the Closing Disclosure as a *debit* ☹ to the seller and as a *credit* ☺ to the buyer? Typically, this will be the case. This rule will not hold in some cases, such as if the property taxes for the current year were paid before the closing day (perhaps a December closing), if the rent is not paid at the first of the month (closing date before the monthly rent was paid), and so forth. But for test purposes and for typical situations, the proration will be entered on the Closing Disclosure as a *debit* ☹ to the seller and as a *credit* ☺ to the buyer.

Expenses. Expenses are always entered on the Closing Disclosure as a *debit*. An expense means money is being paid at closing, so it is entered as a *debit* ☹ and is charged to the person paying the expense. The closing agent will look at the contract to determine who is responsible for paying the expense. An expense is normally a single-entry item because only one party is charged the expense, unless the contract states otherwise. There are some common practices regarding who is charged certain expenses:

- The documentary stamp tax on the deed is typically the responsibility of the seller and appears as a *debit* ☹ on the seller side of the Closing Disclosure. There is no entry on the buyer side of the Closing Disclosure because the buyer does not receive this money. The tax is paid to the state of Florida.
- Intangible tax on new mortgages is entered as a *debit* ☹ on the buyer side of the Closing Disclosure. Expenses associated with the buyer's financing are typically paid by the buyer.
- Documentary stamp taxes are paid on new and assumed notes. Because these expenses are associated with the buyer's financing, the expenses are typically entered as a *debit* ☹ to the buyer.

- Miscellaneous expenses that are entered on the Closing Disclosure include items such as the termite inspection, survey, broker's commission, and so forth. These expenses are entered as a *debit* ☹ to the party who agreed to pay the expenses.

Practice Questions

17. The earnest money deposit held in escrow by the broker is entered on the closing disclosure as a ______________ to the ______________.

18. Expenses are entered as ______________ on the closing disclosure.

19. Prorations are entered as ______________ entries on the closing disclosure.

14.7 SUMMARY OF IMPORTANT POINTS

- *Profit* is the amount you make over and above cost.
- A *preclosing inspection* is a final walk-through with the sales associate to verify that repairs have been completed and that the property is left in good condition.
- To *prorate* means to divide various debits (charges) and credits between buyer and seller. A *proration* is a shared expense between the buyer and the seller.
- Property taxes are paid in arrears and are prorated using a 365-day year (actual number of days in the proration period). Unpaid property taxes appear as a credit to the buyer and as a debit to the seller. Prorations have the same dollar amount in each entry. Seller days are used to prorate items paid in arrears.
- Rental income collected in advance belongs to the new owner as of the date of closing. Advance rental income appears as a credit to the buyer and a debit to the seller. Buyer days are used to prorate items paid in advance.
- Documentary stamp tax on deeds is paid on the full purchase price. The rate is $.70 ($.60 in Miami-Dade County) per $100, or fraction thereof.
- Documentary stamp tax on notes is paid on the amount of debt. This tax is paid on all new and assumed mortgage notes. The rate is $.35 per $100, or fraction thereof.
- Intangible tax is paid on new debt. The rate is $.002 per $1 of new debt.

UNIT 14 EXAM

This quiz is intended not only to help you review this unit but also to assist with the various computations in other units.

1. Change the percentages to decimals.
   a. 39½% _____
   b. 2% _____
   c. 75% _____
   d. 145% _____

2. Change the percentages to fractions.
   a. 50% _____
   b. 20% _____
   c. 25% _____
   d. 40% _____

3. Change the fractions to decimals.
   a. ⅛ _____
   b. ⅗ _____
   c. 1⁄16 _____
   d. 1⁄20 _____

4. Divide these numbers.
   a. 44,032 ÷ 1.72 _____
   b. 493.8 ÷ .60 _____
   c. 18,768 ÷ 25.5 _____
   d. 7,735 ÷ .17 _____

5. A broker lists a motel for $1,450,000. The listing agreement specifies a 6.5% sale commission for the first $600,000 of selling price, 7% for the next $800,000, and 8% commission on all of the actual sale price exceeding $1.4 million. The broker has agreed to a 45-55 split if the property is sold by one of the broker's sales associates. The property is sold "in house." The broker pays the sales associate involved in the transaction 55% of the total commission. What is the sales associate's commission if the associate sells the motel for the listed price?
   a. $44,550
   b. $54,450
   c. $95,000
   d. $99,000

6. A builder purchases a residential lot for $42,000 and constructs a new house at a cost of $178,000. The builder later sells the property for $187,000. What is the builder's percentage of loss on the sale?
   a. 13%
   b. 15%
   c. 20%
   d. 22%

7. You bought a house in Citrus County, Florida, for $130,000. You gave a deposit of $19,480, assumed a recorded mortgage of $90,520, and signed a new second mortgage and note for $20,000. What are the total state taxes due as a result of this transfer of property?
   a. $1,297.50
   b. $1,336.75
   c. $1,336.80
   d. $1,337.10

8. A broker lists a property, a 7% commission is agreed to, and the listing is placed in the MLS. The sale commission is to be split as follows: 45% to the listing broker and 55% to the selling broker. A sales associate who works for the selling broker sells the property for $160,000. The sales associate's agreement with her employer calls for a 60% share to her of all commissions she brings to the company. How much is due the sales associate?
   a. $2,016
   b. $2,464
   c. $3,024
   d. $3,696

9. A woman owned ⅜ of a property. She was paid $45,000 as her share of the proceeds from the sale of the property. What was the total selling price of the property?
   a. $61,875
   b. $72,000
   c. $90,000
   d. $120,000

10. A buyer has agreed to pay the state taxes associated with a new second mortgage loan of $31,000. What is the total cost?
    a. $62.00
    b. $108.50
    c. $170.50
    d. $217.00

11. A buyer is purchasing a house with a closing scheduled for April 22 (non-leap year). The annual property taxes are $2,652. The sale contract states that the day of closing belongs to the buyer. Calculate the property tax proration using the 365-day method.
    a. Credit seller $806.50, debit buyer $806.50
    b. Credit seller $1,854.50, debit buyer $1,854.50
    c. Credit buyer $806.50, debit seller $806.50
    d. Credit buyer $1,854.50, debit seller $1,854.50

12. A woman bought three 200-foot lots on a lake for $500 per front foot each. She then subdivided these lots into six lakefront lots, which she then sold for $62,500 each. What was her percentage of profit on the sales?
    a. 20%
    b. 25%
    c. 75%
    d. 80%

13. A warehouse measures 720 feet by 500 feet and rents for $118,000 a month. What is the rent per square foot per month?
    a. $.25
    b. $.33
    c. $3.05
    d. $3.96

14. A man incurred a 20% loss when he sold a 10-acre parcel (tract A) for $100,000. He also owns a 25-acre parcel (tract B) for which he paid $200,000. How much must he sell B for if he wishes not only to recover his loss from A but also to realize a 20% profit on his investment in B?
    a. $260,000
    b. $265,000
    c. $270,000
    d. $275,000

15. A couple is purchasing an apartment building. Each of the five apartments rents for $815 per month. The closing is scheduled for September 16, and the rents were collected on September 1. What is the rent proration for this transaction and to whom will the amount be credited? The day of closing belongs to the buyer.
    a. $407.50, credit buyer
    b. $1,901.67, credit seller
    c. $2,037.50, credit buyer
    d. $2,173.33, credit seller

16. A 28.5-acre parcel of land in Orange County sells for $4,100 per acre. What is the documentary stamp tax on the deed?
    a. $409.15
    b. $642.85
    c. $817.95
    d. $818.30

17. How is the buyer's binder deposit entered on the Closing Disclosure?
    a. Debit to buyer only
    b. Credit to buyer only
    c. Debit to seller and credit to buyer
    d. Debit to buyer and credit to seller

18. How is the purchase price entered on the Closing Disclosure?
    a. Credit to seller only
    b. Credit to buyer only
    c. Credit to seller and debit to buyer
    d. Credit to buyer and debit to seller

19. How are unpaid property taxes entered on the Closing Disclosure?
    a. Debit to seller only
    b. Debit to buyer only
    c. Credit to seller and debit to buyer
    d. Credit to buyer and debit to seller

20. The closing date is August 27. The buyer is assuming the seller's mortgage loan that has a principal balance of $242,500 at 4% interest. The day of closing is charged to the buyer. What is the proration and how is it entered on the Closing Disclosure?
    a. $132.88 debit seller; $132.88 credit buyer
    b. $132.88 debit seller; $690.96 credit buyer
    c. $690.96 credit seller; $690.96 debit buyer
    d. $690.96 debit seller; $690.96 credit buyer

UNIT

15 THE REAL ESTATE MARKET AND ANALYSIS

LEARNING OBJECTIVES

When you have completed this unit, you will be able to accomplish the following.

- Describe the physical and economic characteristics of real estate.
- Identify the factors that influence supply and demand for real estate.
- Distinguish among ways of interpreting market conditions and demonstrate understanding of the different market indicators.

KEY TERMS

buyer's market	seller's market	supply
demand	situs	vacancy rate
household		

INTRODUCTION

The word *market* has many meanings, depending on usage. It can mean a place where farmers and tradespeople display their produce and products for buyers. It can mean a place where securities are exchanged, such as the commodities market or the stock market. Regardless of difference in form, the basic principles of market operation hold true for all. A market can function only when sellers and buyers interact. Many markets use intermediaries to facilitate activity between seller and buyer, and the real estate market is one such market.

15.1 PHYSICAL AND ECONOMIC CHARACTERISTICS OF REAL ESTATE

There are physical and economic characteristics of the real estate market that set it apart from other markets.

Physical Characteristics of Real Estate

Immobility of Real Estate. The geographic location of real estate is fixed. Because of the immobility of real estate, location largely influences the value of real estate. Real estate value is heavily influenced by changes in the surrounding area.

Land Is Indestructible (Durable). Land's indestructibility refers to the durability of the land and its fixed location. Land cannot be destroyed. An appraiser, when applying the cost approach to valuation, does not depreciate the land; only the structure. The physical structures (improvements) on the land are relatively stable and long term; however, over time the improvements can become obsolete and deteriorate.

Land's indestructibility is the reason property insurance protects the owner's buildings and other man-made improvements; property insurance does not cover the land value—even in times of catastrophe the land will survive. Flood insurance is issued on the contents and the structure, not the land. Investments in real estate tend to be long term, primarily due to the immobility and indestructibility of the land.

Real Estate Is Unique. No two tracts of land are identical. Real estate is not standardized. Real estate, therefore, is unique or *nonhomogeneous* because even two lots side by side have different geographic locations.

Economic Characteristics of Real Estate

Government Controls Influence the Market. Government controls influence the market through zoning, building codes, taxes, monetary policy, and so forth.

Relationship Between Supply, Demand, and Price. In the real estate market, supply and demand interact to affect property prices. In any marketplace, supply and demand are continually adjusting; this causes changes in the price of real estate. When the supply increases relative to demand, prices go down. When demand increases relative to supply, prices go up.

The Market Is Slow to Respond to Change in Supply and Demand. Design, land acquisition, site preparation, and construction phases of real estate are time-consuming. For this reason, when the equilibrium between supply and demand is upset, it can be years before the imbalance is corrected.

Area Preference. Situs refers to prospective buyers' preference for certain area. Area preference, and therefore the property's location, is considered the most important economic characteristic of real estate. One of the top considerations of families with K–12 age children is school zones. Subdivisions in preferred school zones demand higher prices compared with other subdivisions. So goes the saying: location, location, location!

Practice Questions

1. List the physical characteristics of real estate.
    1. Land is ______________________________
    2. Land is ______________________________
    3. Land is ______________________________
2. When the supply increases relative to demand, prices go ______________.
3. When demand increases relative to supply, prices go ______________.
4. The premium paid for location preference is ______________.

15.2 SUPPLY AND DEMAND FACTORS

A study of markets and their operations reveals several factors that influence supply and demand.

Supply

Supply is the amount and type of real estate available for sale or rent at differing price levels in a given real estate market. The variables that influence supply are listed in the following text box.

VARIABLES THAT INFLUENCE SUPPLY

- Availability of skilled labor
- Availability of construction loans and financing
- Availability of land
- Availability of materials

Availability of Skilled Labor. Numerous skilled laborers, such as carpenters, roofers, and electricians, are required for construction. The availability and cost of labor depend on such things as unemployment rates, skill levels required, and the influence of foreign labor. When an area is growing rapidly, the growth usually is characterized by much construction with resulting high employment in the construction industry. These conditions cause competition for labor and its cost increases.

Availability of Construction Loans and Financing. New construction is directly related to the availability of construction loans and short-term financing. As money becomes more available and less expensive, more speculative homes will be built, increasing the available supply of housing. The same is true for commercial development.

Availability of Land. Although land seems physically plentiful, the supply of the type and location of land most in demand is always scarce. Two factors influence the availability of land: (1) the scarcity of readily usable land and (2) the regulations affecting its use and cost of development.

Availability of Materials. The availability of construction materials influences the supply of new housing. In the late 1970s and early 1980s, the construction industry nationwide was severely crippled by a shortage of drywall. Drywall couldn't be found anywhere. New construction was stalled, and construction costs spiraled.

Demand

Demand is the desire and ability to purchase or rent goods and services. In real estate, demand is the amount and type of real estate desired for purchase or rent in a given market at a given period of time. The variables that influence demand are listed in the text box that follows.

VARIABLES THAT INFLUENCE DEMAND

- Price of real estate
- Population numbers and household composition
- Income of consumers
- Availability of mortgage credit
- Consumer taste or preferences

Price of Real Estate. There is an inverse relationship between price and the demand for real estate. When prices rise, demand goes down. When prices decrease, demand goes up.

Population Numbers and Household Composition. The demand for dwelling space depends on both the population and composition of households in every market area. Mere population size does not provide sufficient information for accurately estimating the demand for dwelling space, nor does a count of households.

Modern lifestyles, changes in economic conditions, and reduced family size have caused the household to become the basis for most population analysis. A **household**, as defined by the U.S. Census Bureau, is any person or group of persons occupying a separate housing space. Thus, a household may be a single person living in a rented apartment, a married couple with four children living in their own home in the suburbs, or two unmarried adults living in a condominium near the city center. Each constitutes a household.

Just before the end of the 19th century, 100 dwelling units housed 490 people, due to the average size of households at that time (4.9 persons). The most recent census reveals that the decreased size of the average household (about 2.58 people per household) requires approximately 190 dwelling units to house 490 people. The change in average household size alone has therefore caused a 90% increase in demand. Those who study population trends believe that a further reduction in average household size will occur. This again will change the demand for housing, not only in numbers of units but also in size of dwellings. *Demographics* refers to the characteristics of the population: age distribution, family size, and population movements. Demographics affect not only the total demand for real estate but also the type of housing demanded.

WEBLINK

The 2020 U.S. Census is available at https://www.census.gov/programs-surveys/decennial-census/decade.2020.html.

For valuable information on economic indicators, visit https://www.census.gov/economic-indicators/. Data concerning construction spending, new home sales, and housing starts are updated regularly.

Income of Consumers. Whereas change in price is inversely related to change in demand, income is directly related to demand. As individual income increases, so does demand for dwelling space. Any change in local employment numbers or salary-wage levels causes a change in demand for dwelling space and related loan considerations.

Availability of Mortgage Credit. The availability and cost of mortgage credit has been called the barometer of the real estate market. Because the typical purchase of residential property involves two or three times the buyer's annual net income, it is easy to understand why a large number of homebuyers use credit to arrange the purchase. If a potential homebuyer can afford the monthly mortgage payments (principal and interest), plus property taxes and hazard insurance, the total cost of the house is of secondary importance.

The amortized (principal) portion of a monthly payment can be increased or decreased by (1) the amount of the down payment made on the property and (2) the term of the loan. Both of these have a direct bearing on demand for housing.

When a *tight money market* develops and interest rates rise, a corresponding drop is reflected in housing demand because the amount of money needed to make monthly mortgage payments increases. For example, a $90,000 mortgage loan at 7% interest for a period of 30 years requires a monthly payment of $598.77, not including taxes and insurance. The same amount of money for the same period of time but at 9% interest requires a monthly payment of $724.16, an additional $125.39 per month. An increase in mortgage interest rates of even 1% causes a definite drop in demand for housing.

Consumer Tastes or Preferences. Another factor related to demand concerns changing consumer tastes or preferences. Different architectural designs are sometimes introduced into the residential market and may enjoy brief periods of popularity. Generally speaking, however, enduring changes in consumer tastes occur slowly, over extended time periods. In recent years, the "green movement" has consumers preferring energy-efficient homes. Whatever style and type of house the buying public prefers at a given time is the type of dwelling that will be built more often than others, until a new demand creates a new preference.

Changes in demand for condominiums or second homes for vacation purposes also reflect changes in consumer preferences. For years, *empty nesters* (those parents whose children are grown and have moved away) continued to live in the same house where they had reared their children, although it was then entirely too large for their needs as a couple. The numerous chores of the homeowner related to maintenance, repairs, and grounds upkeep were often a joy but sometimes too physically demanding. The advent of condominiums and other forms of smaller, maintenance-free housing units offered a solution to these empty nesters and other small families.

Practice Questions

5. _______________ is the amount and type of real estate available for sale or rent at differing price levels in a given real estate market.

6. _______________ is the desire and ability to purchase or rent goods and services.

15.3 INTERPRETING MARKET CONDITIONS

Price Levels. The changes in price levels of home sales is an indicator of new housing supply and demand for certain price ranges.

Price and supply are inversely (oppositely) related: When supply goes down, prices go up (more buyers competing for fewer homes). The supply and demand equilibrium is upset by excess demand (more buyers than supply) and a **seller's market** develops.

When supply goes up, prices go down (fewer buyers are competing for a bigger supply of homes for sale). The supply and demand equilibrium is upset by excess supply (more houses for sale than potential buyers), and a **buyer's market** develops.

Market Indicators

Price Levels and Building Permits. Changes in price levels of home sales and the number of building permits issued for a given period of time are indicators of new housing supply and demand for certain price ranges.

Vacancy Rates. A **vacancy rate** is the percentage of rental units that are not occupied. Vacancy rates are one indicator of demand for housing in a certain market area. An increase in vacancy rates in rental housing indicates a surplus of housing space. A 5% vacancy rate (95% occupancy rate) is usually considered indicative of a healthy housing market. As the occupancy rate increases, rental rates tend to increase, and apartment dwellers who have been waiting to buy homes of their own start looking at houses for sale and moving out of apartments. This causes increased apartment vacancies and eventually a drop in rents, as well as a halt in construction of new apartments. One of the first indications of a revived real estate market is an increase in rental occupancies that cannot be attributed to reduced rents or giveaway programs. High occupancy rates lead to increased rents. Increased rents lead to new construction and a revived real estate market.

Sales Volume. Sales associates can collect information on the number and prices of homes sold during the recent past. Data on the number of houses sold and the sale price of each are available from county public records. From MLS data, licensees can extract information on how many sales occurred, the approximate sale prices, where the properties sold were located, and the types of houses.

A database system arranged by subdivision, by streets, or alphabetically can be of great value in building a current sales data file. A large-scale map of a town or those areas of a city where interest is high can become a valuable tool to pinpoint areas of greatest activity and to forecast direction of growth. When a sale is reported in a publication, a color-coded "pin" can be placed on the map in the database to indicate price range and location of property. A glance at such a map shows where most sales are occurring and the general price ranges. Direction and rate of growth also can be estimated from a sales data map.

Calculating Occupancy and Vacancy Rates

To calculate the occupancy rate, divide the number of occupied units by the total number of units in the building.

Formula: Occupancy Rate

occupied units ÷ total units = occupancy rate

EXAMPLE: Assume that 200 apartments are rented in a 250-unit apartment building. What is the building's occupancy rate?

200 rented units ÷ 250 total units = .80 or 80% occupancy rate

To calculate the vacancy rate, divide the number of vacant units by the total number of units in the building.

Formula: Vacancy Rate

vacant units ÷ total units = vacancy rate

EXAMPLE: What is the building's vacancy rate if 225 units are rented in a 300-unit apartment building?

300 total units – 225 rented units = 75 vacant units

75 vacant units ÷ 300 total units = .25 or 25% vacancy rate

Practice Questions

7. A ______________ market exists when demand exceeds supply.

8. Price and demand are ______________ related.

9. A 400-unit apartment building currently has 350 units occupied. What is the building's vacancy rate?

10. There are 180 apartments rented in a 225-unit apartment building. What is the building's occupancy rate?

15.4 SUMMARY OF IMPORTANT POINTS

- Physical characteristics of the real estate market are that (1) real estate is immobile; (2) land is indestructible (durable); and (3) real estate is unique (nonhomogeneous).
- Economic characteristics of real estate include (1) government controls influencing the market through zoning, building codes, and taxes; (2) the market's slow response to change in supply and demand; (3) area preference (situs) influencing the price buyers are willing to pay; and (4) supply and demand interacting to affect property prices.
- *Supply* is the amount and type of real estate available for sale or rent at differing price levels in a given real estate market. Variables that influence supply are availability of labor, availability of construction loans and financing, availability of land, and availability of materials.
- *Demand* is the desire and ability to purchase or rent goods and services. Variables that influence demand are price of real estate, population numbers and household composition, income of consumers, availability of mortgage credit, and consumer taste or preferences.
- *Situs* refers to prospective buyers' preference for a certain area.
- A buyer's market occurs when the supply and demand equilibrium is upset by excess supply (supply exceeds demand).
- A seller's market occurs when the supply and demand equilibrium is upset with excess demand (demand exceeds supply).
- A vacancy rate is the percentage of unoccupied rental units.

UNIT 15 EXAM

1. The economic characteristic that refers to preference for a certain location owing to various factors such as climate, employment outlook, public schools, and so forth is called
   a. highest and best use.
   b. vacancy rates.
   c. sales volume.
   d. situs.

2. Which characteristic does NOT describe the real estate market?
   a. Land is indestructible.
   b. The market is quick to respond to changes in supply and demand.
   c. Real estate is heterogeneous.
   d. Real estate is immobile.

3. Which statement is FALSE regarding the relationship between price and demand?
   a. An increase in price causes a decrease in demand.
   b. A decrease in price causes an increase in demand.
   c. There is an inverse relationship between price and demand.
   d. An increase in price causes an increase in demand.

4. Some 280 apartments are rented in a 350-unit apartment building. What is the building's occupancy rate?
   a. .20
   b. .70
   c. .80
   d. .85

5. Which statement is NOT associated with the economic concept of demand?
   a. Demand is the desire and ability to purchase or lease goods and services.
   b. Changes in price cause an inverse change in demand.
   c. Consumer preferences influence demand.
   d. The availability of building materials influences demand.

6. When the equilibrium of the real estate market is upset by an excess supply,
   a. builder activity increases in response to the need.
   b. a seller's market exists.
   c. a buyer's market exists.
   d. demand decreases.

7. One person or a group of persons occupying a separate housing space is technically defined as a
   a. unit.
   b. household.
   c. family.
   d. multiple ownership unit.

8. The uniqueness of real estate is also called land's
   a. immobility.
   b. nonhomogeneity.
   c. indestructibility.
   d. fixed location.

9. The durability of land refers to land's
   a. immobility.
   b. homogeneity.
   c. indestructibility.
   d. situs.

10. Factors affecting the supply side of the real estate market do NOT include the availability of
    a. land.
    b. skilled labor.
    c. material.
    d. mortgage credit.

UNIT

16

REAL ESTATE APPRAISAL

LEARNING OBJECTIVES

When you have completed this unit, you will be able to accomplish the following.

- Describe federal and state regulations pertaining to appraising, the appraiser's fiduciary relationship, and the *Uniform Standards of Professional Appraisal Practice (USPAP)*.
- Distinguish among value, price and cost; distinguish among the various types of value; define market value and describe its underlying assumptions; and describe the four characteristics of value.
- Distinguish among the principles of value.
- Differentiate among the three approaches to estimating the value of real property.
- Estimate the value of a subject property using the sales comparison approach.
- Estimate the value of a subject property using the cost-depreciation approach.
- Estimate the value of a subject property using the income approach.
- Reconcile the three approaches to establish the final value estimate.
- Calculate value using gross multiplier analysis.
- Explain how to prepare a comparative market analysis (CMA), comparing and contrasting with the sales comparison approach.

KEY TERMS

appraisal
assemblage
automated valuation model (AVM)
cost
cost approach
curable
depreciation
economic life
effective age
effective gross income (EGI)
federally related transaction
gross income multiplier (GIM)
gross rent multiplier (GRM)
highest and best use
income approach
incurable
investment value
market value
net operating income (NOI)
overimprovement
plottage
potential gross income (PGI)
price
principle of substitution
progression
reconciliation
regression
replacement cost
reproduction cost
sales comparison approach
subject property
Uniform Standards of Professional Appraisal Practice (USPAP)
vacancy and collection losses
value

INTRODUCTION

This unit will help students learn the basics of appraising required to develop and complete a comparative market analysis. It also will help to improve licensees' communications with professional appraisers.

Note that the examples of comparable sales used in this unit are hypothetical and offered for educational purposes only.

16.1 APPRAISAL REGULATION—FIRREA

475.612, F.S.

475.25, F.S.

The Appraisal Foundation. Title XI of the Financial Institutions Reform, Recovery, and Enforcement Act (FIRREA) brought the appraisal industry under federal oversight and mandated states to license and certify appraisers. FIRREA recognizes The Appraisal Foundation as the source for the promotion of professional standards and appraiser qualification. The Appraisal Foundation is a not-for-profit organization composed of representatives of the major appraisal organizations. The Foundation accomplishes its goals through the work of its two independent boards:

- *Appraiser Qualifications Board (AQB)*. The AQB establishes minimum criteria for state-certified appraisers and endorses uniform examinations for certification. The AQB establishes guidelines for the supervision of registered trainees, including education for new supervisors.
- *Appraisal Standards Board (ASB)*. The ASB sets minimum standards for appraisals performed for federally related transactions. The ASB develops, interprets, and amends the *Uniform Standards of Professional Appraisal Practice (USPAP)* on behalf of the appraisal industry.

Appraisal Subcommittee (ASC). The ASC maintains a national registry of state-certified and licensed appraisers who are eligible to perform appraisals in federally related transactions.

State-Certified Appraisers. Appraisers are certified according to state law that must conform to the criteria established by the AQB. FIRREA requires that property appraisals involved in federally related transactions be performed by certified appraisers. There are two categories of certified appraisers:

- *Certified residential appraiser.* Certified residential appraisers may issue appraisal reports for residential real property of one to four residential units.
- *Certified general appraiser.* Certified general appraisers may issue appraisal reports for any type of real property.

Federally Related Transactions. A **federally related transaction** is a real estate transaction involving the sale, lease, purchase, investment, or exchange in real property; or the refinancing of real property; or the use of real property as security for a loan; and the appraisal is being performed for a federal financial regulatory agency. A federally related transaction is any real estate–related financial transaction that a federal financial institutions regulatory agency has either contracted for, regulates, or requires the services of an appraiser. All appraisals for federally related transactions must be in writing and conform to *USPAP*. FIRREA also requires certified appraisals for all financial transactions involving Fannie Mae, Freddie Mac, FHA, and VA.

Uniform Standards of Professional Appraisal Practice (USPAP). FIRREA recognizes the ***Uniform Standards of Professional Appraisal Practice (USPAP)*** as the standard for valuing real property. *USPAP* is a set of guidelines (standards of practice) to follow when providing appraisal services. *USPAP* 's ethics rule concerns conduct, management, confidentiality, and recordkeeping. An appraiser must perform assignments with impartiality, objectivity, and independence, without personal interest. The appraiser must protect the confidential nature of the appraiser-client fiduciary relationship. It is unethical for an appraiser to accept compensation that is contingent on the value of the property.

WEBLINK

To order a current edition of the standards or to learn more about appraiser qualifications and licensure, visit www.appraisalfoundation.org.

Part I, Chapter 475, F.S., and Appraisal Services of Real Estate. Chapter 475, Part I, F.S., regulates real estate brokers, broker associates, and sales associates. Under Part I, appraising is included in the definition of real estate services. Therefore, real estate licensees may perform appraisals for compensation; however, the appraisal services must not involve federally related transactions. Real estate licensees may not represent themselves as certified or licensed appraisers (unless they also hold appraisal certifications under Chapter 475, Part II, F.S.). Real estate licensees may conduct appraisals of real property that do not require a state-certified or licensed appraiser. Real estate licensees, when performing appraisal services, must abide by *USPAP*. Real estate licensees who intend to provide appraisal services must be familiar with the *USPAP* standards. Failure to do so may subject a real estate licensee to discipline. Real estate licensees who are not state-certified appraisers are cautioned to get a statement in writing from the client that the appraisal is not associated with a federally related transaction and does not require the services of a state-certified appraiser before accepting the assignment.

Comparative Market Analyses (CMAs). Real estate sales associates typically prepare comparative market analyses (CMAs) to establish listing or offering prices. A real estate licensee who prepares CMAs is not required to comply with *USPAP* (see "Comparative Market Analysis and Broker's Price Opinion," Unit 1).

Broker's Price Opinions (BPOs). Real estate licensees are allowed to prepare and charge for BPOs, provided the BPO is not labeled as an appraisal. A real estate licensee who performs a BPO is not required to comply with *USPAP*.

Practice Questions

1. A ________ ___________ transaction is any real estate–related financial transaction that a federal financial institutions regulatory agency has either contracted for, regulates, or requires the services of an appraiser.

2. ______________ is a set of guidelines (standards of practice) to follow when providing appraisal services.

3. ______________ and ______________ are exempt from *USPAP* standards.

16.2 CONCEPT OF VALUE

Cost, Price, and Value

Cost is the total expenditure required to bring a new improvement into existence plus the cost of the land. A contractor will install site improvements (water, sewer, and so forth); acquire the necessary permits; secure the services of architects, engineers, surveyors, and other professionals; construct the building; landscape the site; market the property; and so forth. The total of these expenditures is called *cost*. A contractor wants the cost to be less than the *price* a consumer will pay—and the consumer will pay more than the cost only if the consumer perceives the property's *value* to exceed its cost. If there is no difference between the cost to build and the price a consumer pays, the contractor makes no profit.

Price refers to the amount of money actually paid in a transaction. Price and value are not necessarily equal. For example, you might purchase a computer for $2,000. Its price was $2,000. However, it may actually command less (or more) than $2,000 in exchange if you were to attempt to sell the computer.

Value is the monetary value of a good or a service to many buyers and sellers at a particular time. Value is what it is worth to the consumer.

TO REMEMBER: COST, PRICE, AND VALUE

Cost	Create	Expenditure to *create* an improvement, including, materials, labor, and land
Price	Paid	The amount *paid* in a particular transaction; the contract price
Value	Worth	The *worth* of something between many market participants

Types of Value

There are many types of value that an appraiser may be hired to estimate.

- *Assessed value* is the value used as a basis for property taxation. It is published on the property tax rolls and is sometimes confused with market value by buyers who are interested in a property.
- *Insurance value* is an estimate of the amount of money required to replace a structure in the event of some catastrophic event such as fire.

- *Investment value* is the price an investor would pay, given the investor's own financing requirements and income tax situation. This type of value is personal to a particular investor.
- *Liquidation value* is the amount a property most likely will bring at a forced or rapid sale. Liquidation value is used for businesses going out of business. It is sometimes used in valuing foreclosed properties and properties subject to tax liens.
- *Going-concern value* is the value of an income-producing property or business characterized by a significant operating history. It is the type of value estimated when the business will continue in operation but ownership is being transferred. Going-concern value includes intangible assets such as trademarks, patents, copyrights, and goodwill associated with the business's reputation, recognition of its name and franchise, and customer loyalty.
- *Salvage value* is the estimated amount for which improvements can be sold at the end of a structure's useful life.

Market Value

Market value is the most probable price a property should bring in a competitive and open market under all conditions requisite to a fair sale under certain guidelines published by Fannie Mae and Freddie Mac. Market value assumes that the buyer and the seller are each acting prudently and knowledgeably and that the price is not affected by undue stimulus. Market value assumes the consummation of a sale as of a specified date and the passing of title from seller to buyer under the following conditions:

- The buyer and the seller are typically motivated (neither party is under pressure to conclude the sale).
- Both parties are well-informed or well-advised, and each party is acting in what they consider to be their own best interest.
- The property is exposed on the open market for a reasonable time.
- Payment is made in terms of cash or in terms of comparable financial arrangements.
- The price represents normal valuable consideration for the property, unaffected by creative financing or sales concessions granted by anyone associated with the sale.

Characteristics of Value

To have value, goods or services must possess the following four traits:

- Demand
- Utility
- Scarcity
- Transferability

TO REMEMBER: CHARACTERISTICS OF VALUE

D	Demand
U	Utility
S	Scarcity
T	Transferability

Demand. In economics, demand is more than a desire or a need. Demand also implies the available means to obtain what is desired. Herders and farmers who live in the infertile desert lands of the world desire fertile land, but they do not have the financial means to obtain other, more expensive land. Consequently, their desires alone have no economic impact on the supply of fertile land or on the price of such lands. In contrast, look at Miami Beach, where people desire to live and have the money to acquire the use of part of the available supply. The need or desire combined with the economic means creates effective demand.

Utility. To be valuable, goods or services must be useful and able to fill a need. In real estate, *utility* means the ability to provide useful services and benefits to an owner or a tenant.

Scarcity. The availability of goods or services in relation to present or anticipated demand determines *scarcity*. If the supply exceeds demand, there is less scarcity and the value falls. If demand exceeds supply, more scarcity is created and value increases. When the number of available apartment units in an area exceeds the demand, apartment units are relatively less scarce and landlords must reduce rents or lose tenants. When apartments are scarce, landlords can increase rents and the excess demand will fill any resulting vacancies.

Transferability. The legal ability to convey title and possession of goods creates *transferability*. This is an unusually important factor in real estate. Value cannot exist in cases where rights in land and the use of property cannot be transferred.

Practice Questions

4. A property owner purchases a lot and builds a house for $270,000. Ten years later, the owner is thinking of selling the property and has the house appraised. The property is appraised at $525,000. Shortly before putting the property on the market, the owner's son graduates from law school and lands a position with a firm in the owner's hometown. The property owner decides to help the young lawyer and his family by selling the house to them for $450,000.
   - What is the cost of this home?
   - What is the price of this home?
   - What is the value of this home?
5. ____________ ____________ is the MOST probable price a property should bring in a competitive and open market under all conditions requisite to a fair sale.
6. ______________ value is the value associated with a rapid sale.
7. ______________ value is the value used as a basis for property taxation.

16.3 PRINCIPLES OF VALUE

Principle of Substitution

The **principle of substitution** states that the maximum value of a property tends to be set by the cost of acquiring an equally desirable substitute property through purchase or construction. This principle of value thus sets an upper limit of value for a property by establishing the cost of acquiring an equally desirable substitute property on the open market.

Highest and Best Use

The most profitable single use of a property is the property's **highest and best use**. The use must be:

- legally permissible (zoning),
- physically possible (soil type, the site's shape, size, and slope), and
- financially feasible (income generated considering cost of improvements).

The use that meets these three criteria and that yields the highest return to the land is the highest and best use. An appraiser estimates two types of highest and best use, which are described in the following paragraphs.

Highest and Best Use of the Land as Though Vacant. The appraiser considers the use that would yield the highest return to the land by taking into account the three elements previously described. If the site has existing improvements, the appraiser considers what type of use should be placed on the site if it were vacant.

Suppose there are three potential buyers for a site. The first buyer estimates the property would yield a net income of $6,000 per year. The second buyer estimates the property would yield $8,000 net income, and the third buyer estimates the property would yield $12,000 per year after expenses. Which buyer will offer the most for the land? Assume a 10% rate of return in all three cases. The use that produces $12,000 annually has a value of $120,000 compared to just $60,000 for the use that produces $6,000 annual net income. Therefore, assuming the three criteria (listed previously) have been met, the use that yields a net income of $12,000 per year is the site's highest and best use.

Highest and Best Use of a Property as Improved. The highest and best use of a property as improved pertains to how a property that already has improvements erected on the site can be best used. The appraiser considers whether (1) the improvements should continue as is, (2) the improvements should be renovated, or (3) the improvements should be demolished and new improvements erected. In each case, the appraiser must consider the costs associated with each option in relation to the income that will be generated. Therefore, highest and best use is a *residual* concept because it is concerned with value after expenses are deducted. Demolishing an existing structure and building a new apartment building may generate more monthly income than would remodeling the existing apartment building. But the highest and best use will be the use with the greatest yield after deducting the costs of renovation or the costs of demolition and new construction.

HIGHEST AND BEST USE

The *highest and best use* of land is the use that generates the most return (income) to the land and improvements when compared with alternative uses. Highest and best use is fundamentally determined by potential buyers bidding for a site in accordance with the locational and environmental value of the site in the various proposed uses. If the value of a site in its current use declines relative to competing uses, the highest and best use may change and land use transition will result.

In the Tampa Bay area, for example, there are mobile home parks located on waterfront or water-view sites. The land is attractive for other uses today, such as highrise waterfront condominiums or choice restaurant sites. Even though the property owners can get more money for their mobile home sites than their homes are worth, it is not sufficient compensation to warrant moving—the residents cannot "replace" the waterfront location they enjoy. So the highest and best use is for something other than mobile homes and the land use will eventually, over time, transition to another highest and best use.

Increasing and Decreasing Returns

Returns refers to the relationship between the cost of an improvement and the value it adds (its contribution) to the property. A certain number of improvements may add substantial value to the property (increasing return), but adding more than that number will add less value or no value (diminishing return). At some point, if a homeowner puts too many improvements into a home, the homeowner will not recover the capital investment. The home at that point is overimproved. An **overimprovement** occurs when an owner invests more money in a structure than the owner can reasonably expect to recapture.

Conformity

The appraisal principle of conformity is based on the concept that the more a property is in harmony with its surrounding properties, the greater the contributory value. In a single-family residential neighborhood, buildings should be similar in design, construction, size, and age.

Assemblage and Plottage

Assemblage is the combining of two or more adjoining properties into one tract; it is the process of consolidating properties. The purpose of assemblage is to increase the usability and value of the resulting consolidation. **Plottage** is the added value as a result of assembling (combining) two or more properties into one large parcel. For example, two adjacent lots, each valued at $35,000, might have a combined value of $90,000 if consolidated. The process of merging two separately owned lots under one owner is called assemblage. Plottage value is the increase in value that is realized through the act of assemblage.

Progression and Regression

Progression is the principle that the value of an inferior property is enhanced by its association with superior properties of the same type. In contrast, **regression** is the principle that the value of a superior property is adversely affected by its association with an inferior property of the same type.

Practice Questions

8. According to the principle of ______________, the maximum value of a property tends to be set by how much it would cost to purchase an equally desirable substitute property.
9. An ______________________ occurs when an owner invests more money in a structure than the owner can reasonably expect to recapture.
10. The combining of two or more adjoining properties into one larger tract is called ______________.

16.4 INTRODUCTION TO THE THREE APPROACHES TO VALUE

An **appraisal** is an opinion of value based on supportable evidence and approved methods.

There are three approaches to estimating real property value:

- Sales comparison approach (comparable sales method)

- Cost approach (cost method)
- Income approach (income method)

In theory, an appraisal report uses all three approaches to estimate the value of a property. If all the information used to prepare the appraisal were perfectly accurate, and if the real estate appraiser's judgment were perfect, the results from each of the three approaches theoretically would be the same.

However, in this imperfect world, most appraisers must *reconcile* the usually different results from each of the three approaches. Any detected errors are corrected and, based on the type of property, a degree of priority (importance) is assigned to each approach used.

Relevance of the Three Approaches to Value. If the property being appraised is a vacant lot in an established neighborhood, the sales comparison approach is considered the most relevant approach to value. The sales comparison approach is also the most relevant approach for estimating the value of single-family homes.

If the property is an income-producing property, the income approach usually is given the most importance.

The cost approach is considered the most significant for newly constructed homes and for cross-checking the other two approaches. The cost-depreciation approach is also considered the most relevant approach when appraising special-purpose properties such as hospitals, schools, or government buildings.

The remainder of this unit provides an introduction into the three approaches to value. Correct application of the information should help licensees produce reasonably accurate opinions of value and comparative market analyses. Much further study and experience is required before licensees should offer appraisal services.

Practice Questions

11. The ________ ______________ approach to value is the MOST relevant approach for estimating the value of a vacant lot.
12. The ______________ approach to value is the MOST relevant approach for estimating the value of special-purpose properties.
13. The ______________ approach to value is the MOST relevant approach for estimating the value of income-producing property.

16.5 SALES COMPARISON APPROACH

The **sales comparison approach** to value is based on the theory that a knowledgeable purchaser will pay no more for a property than the cost of acquiring an equally acceptable substitute property. The sales comparison approach (also called the *comparable sales approach*) is based on the premise that the value of a property can be estimated accurately by reviewing recent sales of properties (called *comparables* or *comps*) similar to the property being appraised (**subject property**) and comparing those properties with the subject property. Because time can affect property values, the sales used for comparison purposes must meet two qualifications:

- They must have occurred recently in the same market area where the subject property is located.
- The comparable properties selected must be similar to the subject property.

Because no two properties are exactly alike, adjustments must be made for any differences between the subject property and each of the comparable sale properties.

The Adjustment Process. Adjustments are made for transactional differences (changes in market conditions since date of sale, for example) and property differences (size, location, etc.). All adjustments necessary to achieve the maximum degree of similarity must be made to each comparable property, not to the subject property. The intent is to adjust the comparable property to make it as similar to the subject property as possible.

If a comparable property is *inferior* to the subject property on a given feature, an *upward* adjustment is made to that comparable property (add the value of the difference). If a comparable is *superior* on a given feature, a *downward* adjustment is made to the comparable property (subtract the value of the difference).

The process of comparison in the sales comparison approach is organized into an *adjustment grid*. The adjustment grid is used to ensure that no adjustment factor important to a value conclusion is overlooked.

TO REMEMBER: APPRAISAL ADJUSTMENTS

C	Comp	C	Comp
B	Better	I	Inferior
S	Subtract	A	Add

Adjustment Process Example. Figure 16.1 is an abbreviated adjustment grid example. The example illustrates the procedure for adjusting the sale prices of selected comparable properties to arrive at an approximate market value for the subject property.

FIGURE 16.1 ■ Adjustment Grid: Sales Comparison Approach

	Comparable 1	Comparable 2	Comparable 3
Address	3752 Shamrock Dr.	3748 Shamrock Dr.	3619 Shamrock Dr.
Date of sale	(6 months ago)	(3 months ago)	(0 months ago)
Sale price	$141,500	$136,000	$140,000
Financing	Conventional	Conventional	Conventional
Conditions of sale	Normal	Normal	Normal
Market conditions	+ $2,830	+ $1,360	Same as subject
Square footage	– $9,600	+ $1,200	Same as subject
Landscaping	Same as subject	Same as subject	– $1,000
Total Adjustments	–$ 6,770	+ $2,560	– $1,000
Adjusted Sale Price	$134,730	$138,560	$139,000
Reconciliation:	Comp 1: = $134,730 × .20	$26,946	
	Comp 2: = $138,560 × .30	$41,568	
	Comp 3: = $139,000 × .50	$69,500	
Indicated Value:		$138,014 or $138,000 (rounded)	

Adjustment Process Example. The appraiser prepares the adjustment grid by first entering the street address and sale price for each selected comparable. Adjustments for transactional differences such as conditions of sale, financing terms, and changes in market conditions since the date of sale are made first, followed by adjustments for property characteristics. Those adjustments include the following:

- *Financing terms*. Appraisers must confirm the financing associated with each sale because the sale price could reflect special financing terms, such as seller financing or seller-paid points. For purposes of the example presented in Figure 16.1, assume the financing associated with each of the sales was conventional financing and that it was typical financing for the market area.
- *Conditions of sale*. Appraisers must research the conditions of sale to determine whether the buyer or the seller was under abnormal pressure to buy or sell or if there was a special relationship between the parties to the transaction, such as between family members or business associates. In the example in Figure 16.1, the appraiser verified the conditions of sale for each of the sales and found them to be normal.
- *Market conditions*. A property that sold last month or last year may sell for more, or for less, today, even though the property itself has not physically changed. The criterion for making an adjustment for market conditions is whether the price paid for a comparable property, if that property were sold on today's market, would differ from the price paid during some other period of time. Referring to Figure 16.1, we see that the appraiser adjusted Comparable (Comp) 1 plus $2,830. Assume that Comp 1 sold six months ago and the appraiser has estimated a market conditions adjustment of 4% annually (or 2% for six months). The appraiser is adjusting the sale price of the comparable to estimate what the comp would have sold for under today's market conditions. Similarly, Comp 2 sold three months ago so the appraiser has entered a plus $1,360 adjustment (or 1%). Comp 3 sold very recently, so a market conditions adjustment was not needed.
- *Square footage*. Assume Comp 1 is 160 square feet larger than the subject property. Because Comp 1 is superior to the subject property with respect to square footage, a downward adjustment is needed. The appraiser has estimated $60 per square foot as an appropriate unit of comparison and has entered an adjustment of *minus* $9,600 (or 160 square feet × $60). Because Comp 2 is 20 square feet smaller than the subject, the appropriate upward adjustment is needed.
- *Landscaping*. Because Comp 3 has nicer landscaping, compared with the subject property, a downward adjustment is made to Comp 3.

Reconciliation. The process of analyzing and effectively weighing the various comps is called **reconciliation**. If the comparables are all equally suitable comparisons of the subject property, the appraiser may simply average the adjusted sale prices. On the other hand, if the appraiser considers one comparable to be a better indicator of the subject property's value than the others, the appraiser may "weigh" that comparable more heavily. This is entirely a matter of the appraiser's judgment.

Reconciling the Example. Note that, in the last row of Figure 16.1, the appraiser reconciled the three comps into a single indicated value. Because Comp 3 was considered most similar to the property being appraised, it received a reconciliation weight of 50%. This means that 50% of the appraised value of the subject property is going to be based on the adjusted sale price of Comp 3. Comp 2 was next in similarity and therefore was awarded a reconciliation weight of 30%. In each case, the adjusted sale price is multiplied by the reconciliation weight assigned, producing a part of the eventual reconciled value, which will be the estimated market value. The three reconciled values were added together to produce the sum of $138,014, which was then rounded to $138,000 indicated value.

Principle of Substitution at Work. The comparable sales approach is the real estate market "speaking" through past sales. By using only sales already transacted, the market tells us about that particular type of property. Regardless of what one might wish for a sale price, the market indicates what value buyers and sellers have already established for properties similar to the subject property. This is the theory behind the principle of substitution.

Valuing Vacant Property. The sales comparison approach is usually considered the most reliable approach in appraising single-family homes. The sales comparison approach is also effective for valuing vacant residential lots. The appraiser selects four to six lots most similar to the subject lot. Differences in size or shape are neutralized by using a common unit of comparison, such as front feet or square feet. Using the recent four to six sales selected as market indicators, one can find the price paid per square foot or front foot for each lot. The reconciled average of all comparable sales gives the approximate value per square foot or front foot of the subject lot. To calculate the average cost per square foot of any property, always divide dollars by square feet.

EXAMPLE: What is the estimated market value of a subject lot that is 110' × 120' (13,200 sq. ft.)?

Adjustment Analysis

Comparable Sales:

Sale 1: A lot 100' × 120' located across the street from the subject lot sold recently for $36,800.

Sale 2: A lot 110' × 120' in the same neighborhood as the subject lot sold recently for $37,000.

Sale 3: A lot 100' × 100' in a different but similar-quality neighborhood sold recently for $36,000.

Sale 4: A lot 130' × 150' located in a different but similar neighborhood but near a railroad sold recently for $39,800.

Solution:

Sale 1:	$36,800 ÷ 12,000 sq. ft. = $3.067 per sq. ft.
Sale 2:	$37,000 ÷ 13,200 sq. ft. = $2.803 per sq. ft.
Sale 3:	$36,000 ÷ 10,000 sq. ft. = $3.600 per sq. ft.
Sale 4:	$39,800 ÷ 19,500 sq. ft. = $2.041 per sq. ft.

Reconciliation:

Sale 1:	$3.067 × .35	= $1.073	
Sale 2:	$2.803 × .30	= $ .841	
Sale 3:	$3.600 × .20	= $ .720	
Sale 4:	$2.041 × .15	= $ .306	
	100%	= $2.940	= $2.94 per sq. ft.

$2.94 × 13,200 square feet = $38,808 or $38,800 is the estimated market value.

Note that in the reconciliation process, sale 3 was given less weight in the final analysis because it was in a different neighborhood, and sale 4 was given the least weight because of its proximity to a railroad track and its location in a different neighborhood.

If all the comparables had been considered good representations of the subject property, the appraiser would have given all four comparables equal weight and simply averaged them to arrive at a value per square foot.

Practice Questions

14. An appraiser is estimating the value of a single-family house. The house has three bedrooms, two bathrooms, and a pool. The appraiser has located one comparable that sold for $184,500. The comparable has four bedrooms and two bathrooms but does not have a pool. Based on the market in the neighborhood, the appraiser estimates that a fourth bedroom adds $6,000 of value and a pool adds $11,000. What is the adjusted sale price of the comparable?

15. The subject property is a vacant lot. It is located at the end of a cul-de-sac. A comparable lot in the same neighborhood recently sold for $27,000, but it is on an interior lot on a through-street (a less-desirable location). However, the comparable lot is larger than the subject. The difference in location is valued at $5,000, and the difference in size is valued at $4,000. What is the adjusted sale price of the comparable?

16. An appraiser has assigned weights to three adjusted sale prices (see the following table). Reconcile the adjusted sale prices using weighted averaging to determine the estimated market value.

Comparable	Adjusted Sale Price	Weight Assigned
Comp 1	$334,500	35%
Comp 2	$338,700	45%
Comp 3	$369,200	20%

16.6 COST APPROACH

The **cost approach** to value (also called the *cost-depreciation approach to value*) is based on the theory that a knowledgeable purchaser will pay no more for a property than the cost of acquiring a similar site and constructing an acceptable substitute structure. The maximum value of a property can be measured by determining the cost to acquire an equivalent site and to reproduce a structure as though new, and then subtracting accrued depreciation. There are four steps in the cost approach:

1. Estimate reproduction cost
2. Subtract accrued depreciation
3. Estimate the value of the land
4. Add the land value to derive indicated value of the property

Step 1: Estimate Reproduction Cost. The appraiser estimates the current cost to reproduce (or replace) the improvements as of the appraisal date. **Reproduction cost** is the amount of money required to build an exact duplicate of the structure. **Replacement cost** is the amount of money required to replace a structure having the same use and functional utility as the subject property, but using modern, available, or updated materials. Consider a historic bungalow home. The cost to duplicate the home in exact detail, including the hand-carved trim on the porch, is reproduction cost. However, if the home were to be reconstructed in the same bungalow style but with modern materials and techniques, this cost is replacement cost.

Formula: Cost Depreciation Approach

reproduction cost of the structure – accrued depreciation = depreciated value of the structure + estimated value of the site = indicated value of the property

The cost of reproducing a recently built structure similar in size and function to the subject structure is often used as a basis for estimating the reproduction cost. To reduce errors in this method, square-foot or cubic-foot costs are obtained for a standard (or *benchmark*) house of average size for the locality. Exterior walls are used for measurements. Adjustments are then made for quality, shape, and extra features. This method is the predominant costing method used for appraisal purposes. However, its use is limited to relatively small, uncomplicated structures such as single-family homes and small office buildings. Many cost-calculation publications and computer programs are available to assist appraisers in determining standard square-foot costs in different geographic regions. An abbreviated version of the comparative square-foot method is provided in Figure 16.2 to illustrate its use.

FIGURE 16.2 ■ **Comparative Square-Foot Method**

Estimated reproduction cost:		
Main dwelling:	2,110 sq. ft. @ $80 per =	$168,800
Utility room:	117 sq. ft. @ $52 per =	6,084
Entrance porch:	75 sq. ft. @ $32 per =	2,400
Garage:	412 sq. ft. @ $45 per =	+ 18,540
Total estimated reproduction cost of structure		$195,824
Less total accrued depreciation		– $13,055
Depreciated value of the structure		$182,769
Add value of land (sales comparison approach)		+ 36,000
Add value of improvements:		
Landscaping		$2,128
Driveway	300 sq. ft. @ $14 per sq. ft. =	+ 4,200
Indicated value of the property by cost approach		$225,097

Step 2: Subtract Accrued Depreciation. The appraiser begins with an estimate of what it would cost to reproduce the structure as though new today. But the subject property is usually not a brand new structure. The difference between the structure's reproduction (or replacement, if applicable) cost new and the perceived market value of the structure today in its actual condition is called *accrued depreciation*. **Depreciation** is the loss in value

caused by things such as wear and tear, poor design, or the structure's surroundings (proximity). *Accrued* depreciation is the total depreciation that has accumulated over the years.

Depreciation can be curable or incurable, depending on whether it can be corrected economically. **Curable** depreciation occurs when a building component has been added or repaired and the owners are able to get their money back in added value. For example, assume it costs $1,500 to repair and clean the screens in a screened-in porch. If potential buyers would pay at least $1,500 more for the home because of the condition of the porch, the depreciation is curable. **Incurable** depreciation occurs when a building component has been added or repaired but the owners are unable to get their money back in added value. For example, assume a home has five-year-old kitchen appliances in excellent working order. The owners purchase all new kitchen appliances for $20,000. If potential buyers are unwilling to pay an extra $20,000 for the home with new appliances, the depreciation (at least at the time of the appraisal) is incurable.

The appraiser estimates the amount of depreciation from all causes and deducts it from the reproduction (or replacement) cost. Generally, accrued depreciation is associated with a structure's age. As a building grows older, it loses value because of exposure to the sun and rain, as well as general usage. However, not all depreciation is associated with age. Depreciation in a structure can be attributed to three major causes:

1. *Physical deterioration.* Physical deterioration includes ordinary wear and tear caused by use, lack of maintenance, exposure to the elements, and physical damage. Brittle roof shingles or a worn-out central air-conditioning compressor are examples of physical deterioration.
2. *Functional obsolescence.* Anything that is inferior because of operational inadequacies, poor design, or changing tastes and preferences is functional obsolescence. Examples include a poor traffic pattern, too few bathrooms, or an inadequate amount of insulation. An overimprovement is also considered functional obsolescence.
3. *External obsolescence.* Any loss in value due to influences originating outside the boundaries of the property, such as an expressway adjacent to a residential subdivision or deterioration of the neighborhood, is external obsolescence. Because external obsolescence is normally beyond the control of the property owner, it is considered incurable.

Land is not depreciated in the cost-depreciation approach. Only the buildings or other improvements to land are subject to these three types of depreciation because the *site value* is estimated separately, typically using the sales comparison approach. Any adjustments to the site for size, location, and nonstructural improvements were already made when the appraiser applied the sales comparison approach to estimate the site value. When the cost to reproduce the improvements is determined, depreciation is applied only to that portion of the property. The appraiser estimates the total accrued depreciation from all causes (physical deterioration, functional obsolescence, and external obsolescence) and deducts it from the reproduction cost of the structure (or the replacement cost, if applicable). The result is the depreciated value of the structure.

Age-Life Method. Sometimes, appraisers estimate each category of depreciation separately. However, the vast majority of residential appraisals that employ the cost-depreciation approach use the age-life method to estimate accrued depreciation. The method is so named because it estimates a single value for accrued depreciation.

The age-life method is based on a ratio of a property's effective age to its economic life. **Effective age** is the age indicated by a structure's condition and utility. Chronologically, a home may be five years old. However, if the structure has been well maintained, its effective age may be only two years. There is no precise method for estimating effective age. The appraiser estimates a structure's effective age by observing the structure's current condition. A structure's total **economic life** (or useful life) is the total estimated number of years that the structure is expected to contribute to the property's value.

The appraiser divides the effective age of the structure by the total economic life of the structure. Refer to the following formula.

Formula: Accrued Depreciation

effective age ÷ total economic life × reproduction cost new = estimated total accrued depreciation

EXAMPLE: Suppose an appraiser estimates that the effective age of a 10-year-old building is four years. The appraiser estimates the cost to reproduce the structure as though new today is $225,000. If the total economic life is 60 years, what is the amount of accrued depreciation?

(4 years effective age ÷ 60 years economic life) × $225,000 reproduction cost new = $15,000 accrued depreciation

The age-life method of calculating depreciation assumes that a structure depreciates at a constant rate. For this reason, it is sometimes called straight-line depreciation (the same amount of depreciation each and every year).

EXAMPLE: To demonstrate this point, let's calculate the accrued depreciation in the previous example by first determining the amount of annual depreciation. Divide the reproduction cost by the economic life. The result is the annual depreciation. Multiply the annual depreciation by the effective age to derive the total accrued depreciation:

$225,000 reproduction cost new ÷ 60 years economic life = $3,750 annual depreciation × 4 years effective age = $15,000 accrued depreciation

Formula: Alternate Accrued Depreciation

reproduction cost new ÷ total economic life = annual depreciation × effective age = estimated total accrued depreciation

The value of the structure today, in its current condition, is estimated by subtracting the accrued depreciation from the reproduction cost new:

$225,000 reproduction cost new – $15,000 accrued depreciation = $210,000 depreciated value of the structure

Step 3: Estimate the Value of the Land. We have only been concerned with the structure thus far. Now the appraiser estimates the value of the site and nonstructural site improvements, assuming the site is vacant and will be put to its highest and best use. The value of land is normally determined by the sales comparison approach. For example, if neighboring comparable properties are selling for $5 per square foot and the lot on which the subject structure stands has an area of 11,000 square feet, the land value is estimated to be $55,000:

11,000 square feet × $5 per square foot = $55,000

Step 4: Add the Land Value to Derive Indicated Value of the Property. The appraiser adds the estimated value of the site, including site improvements, to the depreciated value of the structure. The estimated property value of the subject property is as follows:

$210,000 depreciated structure + $55,000 site value = $265,000 estimated value of subject property

Practice Questions

17. List the three types of depreciation used in the cost approach.
    1. ______________________________
    2. ______________________________
    3. ______________________________

18. ______________ cost is the current construction costs to produce improvements that are identical to the subject property.

19. ______________ is the loss in value caused by things such as wear and tear, poor design, or the structure's surroundings.

20. If the value added is greater than the cost to cure the defect, the depreciation is said to be ______________.

21. Total ____________ life (or useful life) is the total estimated number of years that the structure is expected to contribute to the property's value.

16.7 INCOME APPROACH

The object of the **income approach** is to measure a flow of income projected into the future. This method is a complete departure from the sales comparison and cost-depreciation approaches. The income approach develops an estimated market value based on the present worth of future income from the subject property. It is the primary approach for appraising income-producing property and for comparing possible investments.

Let's begin with an explanation of the various types of income.

Potential Gross Income. The total annual income a property would produce if it were fully rented and no collection losses were incurred is called **potential gross income (PGI)**.

Effective Gross Income. When **vacancy and collection losses** are *deducted* from annual PGI and any income from other sources (e.g., laundry, vending machines, parking) is *added*, the result is annual **effective gross income (EGI)**. *Vacancy and collection losses* consist of the expected income loss that will result from occasional turnover of renters and periodic vacancies, as well as the likelihood that not all rental income will be collected. Even when a property is 100% occupied, the probability of continuous total occupancy is unlikely. Therefore, some vacancy and collection losses always should be deducted from PGI.

Formula: Effective Gross Income (EGI)

potential gross income (PGI) – vacancy and collection losses + other income = effective gross income (EGI)

Net Operating Income. Net operating income (NOI) is the income remaining after subtracting all relevant operating expenses from EGI. Operating expenses are grouped into three separate categories:

1. Fixed expenses are costs that do not fluctuate with operations or occupancy level, for example, property taxes and hazard insurance.
2. Variable expenses fluctuate based on occupancy level, for example, utilities, maintenance, management, supplies, janitorial, and garbage collection.
3. Reserve for replacements. The term *reserve for replacements* refers to a reserve allowance that provides for the periodic replacement of building components, such as roof coverings and heating and air-conditioning equipment that wear out at a faster rate than structural components.

Formula: Net Operating Income (NOI)

effective gross income (EGI) – operating expenses = net operating income (NOI)

All costs of mortgage expense, depreciation, income taxes, capital improvements, personal expenses, and business-related expenses (such as payroll and advertising) that do not contribute to actual operation of the property are business expenses, not operating expenses. Depreciation does not involve an outlay of cash and is not used to calculate NOI.

NOI is the annual income (before mortgage or income tax payments) that may be expected to occur over the remaining economic life of a property. It is this income (NOI) that is capitalized into *present value*. To use the income approach, an appraiser must know the annual NOI produced by the property or be able to forecast the annual NOI based on reasonable estimates.

Licensees may have access to the accounts; may be provided the information required; or in the case of a vacant lot on which a business building will be constructed, may project a pro forma NOI statement from several existing similar properties.

EXAMPLE: Suppose your client is considering construction of a 10-unit apartment building. You are estimating the value of the vacant property zoned for apartments. Your survey of other apartment projects of similar size and quality in the market area reveals that each of the proposed new apartments could be competitive if rented at $665 per month. The survey also discloses that an annual vacancy and collection loss rate of 10% is typical for the area. By using normal costs of operation, a pro forma statement can be developed to indicate the probable annual NOI. Begin by estimating the potential gross income ($665 rent × 10 units × 12 months = PGI).

Solution:

Potential annual gross income	$79,800
Vacancy and collection losses (10%)	– 7,980
Effective annual gross income	$71,820

Expenses (per year):	
Taxes	$5,494
Insurance	996
Management	24,600
Repairs and maintenance	4,100
Reserve for replacements	+ 1,800
Total annual operating expenses	$36,990
Effective annual gross income	$71,820
Total annual operating expenses	– 36,990
NOI	$34,830

Once known or estimated, the NOI is usually divided by an *overall capitalization rate (OAR)*. The OAR normally is determined by using the sale prices and NOIs of similar properties in the market area. Dividing the NOI of a property by its current value or sale price produces an OAR.

Formula: Overall Capitalization Rate (OAR)

net operating income (NOI) ÷ value (sale price) = overall capitalization rate (OAR)

The components of this formula are said to be *market-driven*—that is, income figures and recorded sale prices represent the market in action. That is the reason most licensees, appraisers, and others prefer the OAR as a capitalization rate.

EXAMPLE: Sales data, income records, and expense records indicate the following:

Comparable Garden Apartment Complex	Annual NOI	÷	Sale Price	=	Indicated OAR
A	$31,400		$325,000		.097
B	$48,230		$450,000		.107
C	$39,600		$400,000		.099
D	$37,400		$395,000		.095
E	$44,700		$440,000		.102
	$201,330		$2,010,000		.500 ÷ 5 = .100

$201,330 ÷ $2,010,000 = .100 or 10% OAR

The same procedure could be used to determine the OAR for other types of income-producing properties. Once an appropriate capitalization rate and NOI are determined, the following formula is used to estimate the present value of income-producing properties.

Formula: Direct Capitalization

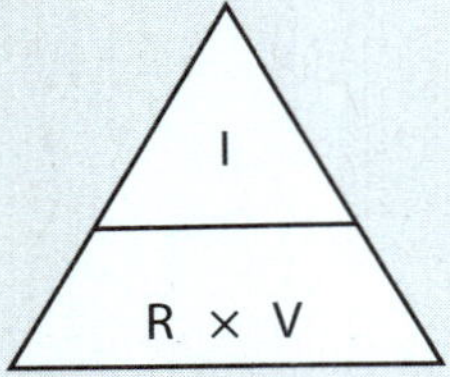

Income = Rate × Value
Rate = Income ÷ Value
Value = Income ÷ Rate

Where: I = Net operating income (NOI)
R = Capitalization rate
V = Value (or Sale price)

capitalization rate × value (or sale price) = net operating income (NOI)

net operating income (NOI) ÷ value (or sale price) = capitalization rate

net operating income (NOI) ÷ capitalization rate = value (or sale price)

For example, using the results of the pro forma statement in the earlier problem and the market area OAR of 10%, the estimated value of the property is calculated.

$34,830 (NOI) ÷ .10 rate = $348,300 estimated value

Investors, on the other hand, often prefer to specify a capitalization rate because investors are free to choose the acceptable rate of return they desire. When the type of estimated value is investor-driven, the minimum rate of return acceptable to the investor is frequently used as the capitalization rate. Net annual income is then divided by the specified capitalization rate to obtain the investment value of the property. It is important to mention, however, that this is not market value, but rather investment value. **Investment value** is the value of property to a particular investor based on the investor's desired rate of return, risk tolerance, and so forth. Market value is objective and impersonal; investment value is subjective and based on personal criteria.

EXAMPLE: A small income property produces an annual net income of $8,000. Your client wants you to tell her the amount of money that she may invest in the property to provide a return of 10% per year from the investment.

$8,000 NOI ÷ .10 rate = $80,000 value

So the investment value to this investor is $80,000 if a 10% rate of return is required from the subject property.

A definite relationship exists between present value, net income, and capitalization rate. If, for example, the rate (R) is increased and the net income (I) remains constant, the present value (V) will decrease. If the net income (I) goes up and the capitalization rate (R) remains constant, the present value (V) will be greater (see Figure 16.3).

FIGURE 16.3 ■ Effect of Change in Capitalization Rate or Expenses on Value

Value *decreases* when:	*Rate* increases NOI is unchanged
Value *decreases* when:	*Expenses* increase (NOI goes down) Rate is unchanged
Value *increases* when:	*Expenses* decrease (NOI goes up) Rate is unchanged
Value *increases* when:	*Rate* decreases Expenses are unchanged (NOI is unchanged)

EXAMPLE: To demonstrate the relationship between changes in the rate or NOI, let's take another look at the previous example. Suppose that the rate was increased from 10% to 12% but the NOI remained unchanged:

$8,000 NOI ÷ .12 rate = $66,666.67 value

We see that when the NOI was unchanged but the rate was increased, the value decreased.

EXAMPLE: This time, assume the rate remains unchanged at 10% in the original example, but decrease the NOI (more expenses results in smaller net income):

$7,000 NOI ÷ .10 rate = $70,000 value

When the NOI was decreased and the rate was unchanged, the value decreased.

Practice Questions

22. A property has a net income of $60,000 and sells for $400,000. What is the capitalization rate for this property?

23. An income property produces an annual net income of $75,000. Your client wants you to estimate what can be invested in the property to provide a 15% per year rate of return from the investment. What is the capitalization rate for this property?

24. The income approach is based on the ____________ __________ of ______________ income from the subject property.

25. ____________ __________ __________ is the total annual income of a property that is fully rented with no collection losses.

26. ___________ ______ ______________ ________ is the expected income loss that will result from occasional turnover of renters and periodic vacancies.

27. _______ _____________ __________ is the income remaining after subtracting all relevant expenses from the effective gross income.

16.8 RECONCILING THE VALUE INDICATIONS INTO A FINAL VALUE ESTIMATE

Reconciliation is the process of evaluating and weighting each value indication obtained from the three approaches to value. The appraiser will have three indicated values (one from each approach). The appraiser reconciles the three indicated values into a final estimate of value. The reconciliation process requires that the appraiser consider each approach's relative applicability and the source of the data collected in each approach. The appraiser evaluates the data's reliability and decides which approach is best suited to the specific appraisal assignment. The appraiser performs a weighted average from the alternative indications of value that best represents the subject property. The indicated value that best applies to the specific assignment is given the greatest percentage; the next best, the next highest percentage; and so on, so that the total assigned percentages in the weighted averages equal 100%.

EXAMPLE: Assume the appraiser has applied all three approaches to the appraisal of a two-year-old single-family home located in an established neighborhood. The appraiser was able to locate five recent comparable sales. The sales comparison approach is likely the most reliable indication of the subject property's worth because the comparables were actual sales in the same neighborhood. The indicated value using the sales comparison method is $160,000.

The appraiser also finds the cost approach reliable for valuing the subject property. The homes in the neighborhood are similar in style, construction, and age. The subject property is only two years old, so there is little accrued depreciation. The indicated value from the cost approach is $155,000.

The appraiser was able to apply the income approach using rental data obtained from two homes in the same neighborhood. However, the subject property is being sold as a single-family home that will be owner occupied (based on mortgage financing obtained for the purchase). Therefore, the appraiser decides that the sales comparison approach and the cost approach are the most relevant approaches for this assignment. The appraiser assigns 10% weight to the indicated value of $150,000 based on the income approach.

The appraiser reconciles the various data to obtain the final estimate of what the subject property is worth. In the final reconciliation, the appraiser used a weighted average, giving the most weight (55%) to the sales comparison approach, 35% weight to the cost approach, and just 10% weight to the income approach (see Figure 16.4).

FIGURE 16.4 ■ Final Reconciliation of the Three Approaches

Approach	Indicated Value		Weight		Weighted Value
Sales comparison	$160,000	×	55%	=	$88,000
Cost approach	$155,000	×	35%	=	$54,250
Income approach	$150,000	×	10%	=	+15,000
Final estimate					**$157,250**

Practice Questions

28. Using the information in the table, reconcile the three indicated values to estimate the value of the subject property.

Approach	Indicated Value	Weight
Sales comparison	$260,000	55%
Cost approach	$228,000	35%
Income approach	$220,000	10%

16.9 GROSS RENT MULTIPLIER (GRM)

A **gross rent multiplier (GRM)** relates sale price to monthly rental income. The GRM is a simple substitute for the income capitalization analysis for one- to four-unit residential rental properties. The GRM applies to rental income only. Use gross monthly rent when calculating a GRM. The GRM is found by dividing the sale price by the gross monthly rent:

Formula: Gross Rent Multiplier (GRM)

sale price ÷ gross monthly rent = gross rent multiplier (GRM)

EXAMPLE: A single-family property sold for $229,400. This residential investment property earns a monthly rental income of $1,850. What is the property's GRM?

$229,400 sale price ÷ $1,850 gross monthly rent = 124 GRM

Multipliers must be determined for each local area. A multiplier is market-derived by using comparable properties and averaging the results. To establish a market-derived GRM, an appraiser must locate recent sales and rental data from at least four rental properties that are comparable to the subject property. The sale price of each comparable rental property is divided by the property's gross rent to calculate each property's GRM. The individual GRMs are averaged to estimate a market area GRM. Then the market area GRM is used to estimate the subject property's market value:

Formula: Estimated Market Value

monthly rent × market area GRM = estimated market value

EXAMPLE 1: An appraiser has found five rental properties that are comparable to the subject property. The sale price and monthly rent for each of the five sales is listed in the table. What is the market area GRM?

Sale	Sale Price	÷	Monthly Rental	=	GRM
1	$98,000		$575		170.4
2	$96,600		$550		175.6
3	$99,900		$595		167.9
4	$92,500		$550		168.2
5	$98,000		$560		175.0
					857.1

857.1 (sum of GRMs) ÷ 5 comparable sales = 171.4 market area GRM

EXAMPLE 2: The appraiser has estimated the fair market rent for the subject property to be $560 per month. What is the estimated market value of the subject property using the market area GRM of 171.4?

$560 rental income × 171.4 GRM = $95,984 or $96,000 (rounded)

Gross Income Multiplier (GIM). The **gross income multiplier (GIM)** is used with small income-producing properties. Notice that the procedure for calculating a GIM is basically the same as for calculating a GRM. However, the GIM refers to all income a property may produce, while the GRM refers to rent only. The GIM uses annual income, whereas the GRM applies monthly rent.

Formula: Gross Income Multiplier (GIM)

sale price ÷ gross annual income = gross income multiplier (GIM)

gross annual income × market GIM = value

EXAMPLE 1: A commercial property produces $50,000 of annual gross income. The property recently sold for $400,000. What is the property's GIM?

$400,000 sale price ÷ $50,000 gross annual income = 8.0 GIM

EXAMPLE 2: The appraiser has projected that the subject property can generate a gross annual income of $58,000. What is the estimated market value of the subject property using the market area GIM 8.0?

$58,000 annual gross income × 8.0 GIM = $464,000

Practice Questions

29. What is the market value of a subject property using a market area GRM of 126.5 and gross monthly rent of $1,500?

30. What is the market value of a subject property using a market area GIM of 12.5 and gross annual income of $25,500?

31. What is the GIM of a small income-producing property that sells for $425,000 and has a projected gross annual income of $72,000?

16.10 COMPARATIVE MARKET ANALYSIS (CMA)

In the normal course of business, licensees typically prepare a comparative market analysis (CMA) for sellers or buyers as a means to help them make informed decisions on pricing a property. Although CMAs are a variation of the sales comparison approach, they are not appraisal reports. Appraisals employ all three approaches to value and must conform to the *Uniform Standards of Professional Appraisal Practice* (USPAP).

Preparation of a Comparative Market Analysis

Categories of Comparables. A CMA typically presents information concerning three major categories of properties:

- *Recently sold.* Studying the sale prices of similar properties in the same market area that have recently sold provides information concerning what buyers have been willing to pay for similar properties. The amount of recent sale activity and the average days on the market are also valuable information.

- *Currently on the market*. Studying the asking prices of properties in the market area provides important information concerning what the sellers of similar properties are asking in today's market. When properties with equally desirable characteristics are available, buyers normally choose the property with the lowest price. Therefore, the seller should price the property taking into consideration the average asking price of competing properties.
- *Recently expired listings*. Properties that were listed but failed to sell often were priced too high. This information helps explain to sellers the consequences of overpricing listings.

Common Elements of Comparison. It is important that all properties used in the CMA be similar to the subject property in size, age, amenities, and location. Adjustments should be made for important differences compared with the subject property, such as swimming pools, condition, style, and so forth. Examples of features that must be considered include location, size, and shape of the lot; landscaping; construction quality; style, design, and age of the structure; square feet; and number of rooms. Adjustments are made to the comps (comparables) using the same procedure as discussed in the sales comparison approach.

Computer-Generated CMAs. Software programs are available that will organize the data that sales associates gather into attractive presentations. Many MLS service providers offer software for REALTOR® members to download the comparable information directly into a listing presentation package.

Automated Valuation Models (AVMs)

The **automated valuation model (AVM)** is a data analysis that is compiled using a computer database of closed sales. AVMs are used by lenders in situations where the expense of an appraisal may not be warranted. For example, if a homeowner is applying for a home equity loan and the combined loan-to-value ratio of the first mortgage and the home equity loan are below certain risk levels, the lender may forgo a formal appraisal. AVMs are not appraisals and do not meet *USPAP* standards. They do not involve the inspection of the property, measurements, photographs, and so forth. AVMs work well in tract subdivisions where the homes are similar in condition, building materials, age, and square footage. However, AVMs are not as reliable when homes are unique or in areas with a mix of price ranges, and so forth. AVMs are available online at different real estate websites and are mostly free to customers. AVMs provide useful information to real estate associates and potential buyers and sellers.

Practice Questions

32. List the three major categories of property used in the preparation of CMAs.
    1. ______________________________
    2. ______________________________
    3. ______________________________

16.11 SUMMARY OF IMPORTANT POINTS

- Real estate licensees who conduct real estate appraisals are required to comply with USPAP. Appraisal reports involving a federally related transaction must be prepared by a state-certified or licensed appraiser.
- *Market value* is the most probable price that a property should bring in a competitive and open market under all conditions requisite to a fair sale, with the buyer and the seller each acting prudently and knowledgeably, and assuming the price is not affected by undue stimulus.
- *Value* is determined by what consumers are willing to pay in the marketplace. *Price* refers to the amount of money actually paid. *Cost* is the total expenditure to create the improvement.
- An *overimprovement* occurs when an owner invests more money in a structure than can reasonably be expected to be recaptured.
- To have value, goods and services must possess four traits: (1) demand, (2) utility, (3) scarcity, and (4) transferability.
- *Highest and best use* is the most profitable use of a property. The use must be legally permissible, physically possible, and financially feasible.
- The three approaches to estimating value are (1) sales comparison approach, (2) cost-depreciation approach, and (3) income approach. The principle of substitution is the basis for all three approaches.
- The *sales comparison approach* compares similar properties to the subject property. The comparable properties' sale prices are adjusted upward or downward to reflect differences between each comparable and the subject property. If a comparable is superior to the subject property on a given feature, a downward adjustment is made to the comp. If a comparable is inferior to the subject property, an upward adjustment is made to the comp. The adjusted sale prices of the comparables are reconciled using a weighted average to estimate the market value of the subject property.
- The *cost-depreciation approach* estimates the market value of a property based on the cost to buy an equivalent site and to reproduce the structure as if new, less depreciation. *Reproduction cost* is the amount of money required to build an exact duplicate of the structure. *Replacement cost* is the amount of money required to replace a structure having the same use and functional utility as the subject property but using modern, available, or updated materials.
- *Depreciation* is the loss in value. *Accrued depreciation* is the total depreciation that has accumulated over time. Depreciation is curable when a building component has been added or repaired and the owners are able to get their money back in added value. If the owners are not able to recoup the cost of the repaired or added item, it is said to be incurable depreciation. The three major causes of depreciation are (1) physical deterioration, (2) functional obsolescence, and (3) external obsolescence.
- The age-life method of estimating depreciation is based on a ratio of the property's effective age to its economic life. *Effective age* is the age indicated by a structure's condition and utility. *Total economic life* is the total estimated number of years that a structure is expected to contribute to the property's value.

- The *income approach* develops an estimated value based on the present worth of future income from the subject property. The approach capitalizes net operating income into value.
- *Potential gross income (PGI)* is the total annual income a property would produce if it were fully rented and no collection losses were incurred. *Effective gross income (EGI)* is calculated by subtracting vacancy and collection losses from the PGI. *Net operating income (NOI)* is the income remaining after subtracting operating expenses from EGI. The three categories of operating expenses are (1) fixed, (2) variable, and (3) reserve for replacements.
- The *gross rent multiplier (GRM)* is the ratio between a property's gross monthly rent and its selling price. The *gross income multiplier (GIM)* is the ratio between a property's gross annual income and its selling price.
- Automated valuation models are not appraisals. They do not conform to *USPAP* standards.

UNIT 16 EXAM

1. The total expenditure required to bring a new improvement into existence is called
   a. cost.
   b. price.
   c. market price.
   d. market value.

2. Which assumption does NOT apply to definition of market value?
   a. Payment is made in cash or its equivalent.
   b. Neither the buyer nor the seller is under any compulsion to act quickly.
   c. Market value is the median price a property will bring.
   d. Both buyer and seller are fully informed.

3. The approach to estimating value that is called "the real estate market speaking through past sales because it uses actual sales transactions" is the
   a. transactional comparison approach.
   b. economic indicator approach.
   c. sales comparison approach.
   d. sales transaction approach.

4. When more money is invested in a building than can reasonably be expected to be recaptured, it is called
   a. economic lack of utility.
   b. overimprovement.
   c. underimprovement.
   d. depreciation.

5. Loss of value for any reason is called
   a. transferability.
   b. substitution.
   c. depreciation.
   d. economic obsolescence.

6. All these characteristics are required to create value EXCEPT
   a. demand.
   b. supply.
   c. utility.
   d. transferability.

7. The approach to value MOST likely to be relevant for appraising a community college is the
   a. comparable sales approach.
   b. cost approach.
   c. income approach.
   d. straight-line approach.

8. The subject property has 200 less square feet of living area than a comparable. The market area value of 200 square feet is $20,000. Which adjustment should the appraiser make?
   a. Add $20,000 to the subject
   b. Add $20,000 to the comparable
   c. Subtract $20,000 from the subject
   d. Subtract $20,000 from the comparable

9. The MOST relevant approach to estimating the value of a vacant lot in a residential neighborhood usually is the
   a. square-foot approach.
   b. cost approach.
   c. unit-in-place method.
   d. sales comparison approach.

10. Which condition is considered external obsolescence?
    a. Peeling exterior paint
    b. One bathroom in a three-bedroom home
    c. Metal utility shed that is in poor condition located just inside the property line
    d. A residential property's proximity to an industrial area

11. Loss in value because of operational inadequacies, poor design, or changing tastes is called
    a. physical deterioration.
    b. functional obsolescence.
    c. external obsolescence.
    d. underimprovement.

12. The total estimated time in years that an improvement can be profitably useful is called
    a. effective age.
    b. economic life.
    c. accrued depreciation.
    d. chronological age of the improvement.

13. In the income approach, if the capitalization rate is increased and the net income is unchanged, the
    a. present value will be less.
    b. future value will be less.
    c. present value will be more.
    d. future value will be more.

14. A home has 1,800 square feet of living area and 200 square feet of garage. The reproduction cost new is $48 per square foot for living area and $28 per square foot for finished garage area. The site measures 75 feet wide by 110 feet deep and is valued at $3 per square foot. The economic life of the home is estimated to be 50 years. The house is 10 years old. The value of the property using the cost-depreciation approach is
    a. $73,600.
    b. $86,400.
    c. $92,000.
    d. $98,350.

15. A limited partnership wishes to purchase an apartment building that has a monthly net income of $4,000 and monthly expenses of $1,000. If the partnership is to get a 12% return on its investment, what should it pay for the property?
    a. $25,000
    b. $33,000
    c. $300,000
    d. $400,000

16. An income-producing property has a potential annual gross income of $81,420. Vacancy and collection losses are estimated at 10% of potential gross income. Expenses are estimated at $40,000. The estimated value of the property is $250,000. The capitalization rate for this property is
    a. 13.31%.
    b. 14.91%.
    c. 16.57%.
    d. 17.5%.

17. Effective gross income is
    a. net operating income divided by an appropriate capitalization rate.
    b. potential gross income minus vacancy and collection losses plus other income.
    c. net operating income minus annual mortgage expense.
    d. before-tax cash flow divided by equity invested.

18. You are preparing a CMA for a single-family home that has a two-car garage. You have located a comparable house that sold for $226,000, but it does not have a garage. If a two-car garage is valued at $18,000, which adjustment would you make?
    a. Add $18,000 to the comparable
    b. Subtract $18,000 from the comparable
    c. Add $18,000 to the subject
    d. Subtract $18,000 from the subject

19. A building is valued at $150,000 when NOI is capitalized at a rate of 8%. NOI is 40% of effective gross income. The effective gross income is
    a. $12,000.
    b. $22,000.
    c. $30,000.
    d. $32,000.

20. A commercial property has a potential gross income of $40,000. Vacancy and collection losses are 5% of PGI. Additional operating expenses total $12,920. The property has a first mortgage requiring payments of $1,070.75 per month. Using a capitalization rate of 12%, which amount is an accurate estimate of the property's value?
    a. $101,333
    b. $107,667
    c. $209,000
    d. $316,667

UNIT 17

REAL ESTATE INVESTMENTS AND BUSINESS OPPORTUNITY BROKERAGE

LEARNING OBJECTIVES

When you have completed this unit, you will be able to accomplish the following.

- Define key investment terms and distinguish among the different types of real estate investments.
- Identify the advantages and disadvantages of investing in real estate.
- Distinguish among the various types of risk.
- Describe the similarities and differences between real estate brokerage and business brokerage.
- Describe the types of expertise business brokerage requires and distinguish among the methods of appraising businesses.
- Describe the steps in the sale of a business.

KEY TERMS

appreciation
asset
basis
capital gain (or loss)
cash flow
equity
going-concern value
goodwill
leverage
liquidation analysis
liquidity
real estate investment trust (REIT)
risk
tax shelter

INTRODUCTION

This unit is an introduction to investment real estate. Investors consider different factors in their attempt to achieve various investment objectives according to their individual financial status, income tax bracket, motives for investing, and access to credit. Different types of real estate offer various abilities to meet investor objectives.

17.1 NEED FOR REAL ESTATE INVESTMENT ANALYSIS

Knowledge of real estate investment analysis is important to a licensee in Florida because a real estate licensee is allowed to sell investment property. The public regards a real estate broker or sales associate as an expert in all types of properties. While the rewards of negotiating the purchase or sale of investment property are often greater than they are for other types of real estate, so are the liabilities for untrained or unknowledgeable people. Cases have gone to court because real estate licensees either gave bad advice or did not properly analyze an investment before recommending a course of action that could have been avoided by a knowledgeable professional.

Real estate investment analysis is the process of determining the extent to which real estate investments achieve an investor's objectives. Potential investors go to real estate professionals for help and guidance. Licensees must be qualified to provide the needed expertise when they accept the trust and confidence of a client. At the beginning of this book, the point was made that real estate licensees have one major commodity to offer the public—expertise. But part of being a professional also includes knowing when to consult a specialist (e.g., an attorney or an accountant) and when to have one's seller or buyer consult a specialist. The purpose of this unit, therefore, is familiarization, a first step toward developing expertise in real estate investment matters.

INVESTMENT TERMINOLOGY AND TYPES OF REAL ESTATE INVESTMENTS

Appreciation is the increase in property value over a period of time due to economic causes.

Assets are the entire resources of a business, including tangibles and intangibles such as accounts and notes receivable (promissory notes), cash, inventory, equipment, real estate, and goodwill. The difference between assets and liabilities is net worth.

Cash flow is the total amount of spendable income generated from an investment. It is the total amount of money remaining after all expenditures have been paid. Expenses, for example, include property taxes, operating costs, and maintenance. The cash flow is determined by at least three important factors: the income received, operating expenses, and the method of debt repayment. Cash flow may be positive or negative.

EXAMPLE 1: A rental property has an annual income of $100,000 and operating expenses of $90,000. The property has a positive cash flow of $10,000.

EXAMPLE 2: A rental property has an annual income of $100,000 and operating expenses of $110,000. The property has a negative cash flow of $10,000.

Equity is the property's value minus mortgage debt. A property worth $500,000 has outstanding debt of $375,000. The investor's equity is $125,000.

$500,000 value – $375,000 mortgage debt = $125,000 equity

Leverage is the use of borrowed funds (often called *other people's money*) to finance an investment. Investors use leverage to increase purchasing power. An investor wants an investment property to produce cash flow in excess of the cost of borrowing the funds. Leverage can be positive or negative, based on whether or not the benefits from borrowing exceed the cost of borrowing. Generally, an investor can receive a maximum return from an initial investment by making a small down payment, paying a low interest rate, and spreading mortgage payments over a long period of time. Positive leverage occurs when the benefits from borrowing exceed the costs of borrowing. Negative leverage occurs when the borrowed funds cost more than they are producing.

EXAMPLE: Consider a property that costs $500,000 and produces a net income of $50,000 per year. If purchased for cash, the investor's annual rate of return on the equity invested is 10% ($50,000 income ÷ $500,000 equity). Assume that this investor leverages the purchase by borrowing $375,000 at 5% ($18,750 interest) annually and makes a down payment of $125,000. The $50,000 income earned from the investment is reduced by the cost of financing ($18,750). The income remaining after mortgage expense is $31,250. The resulting return on equity investment is an attractive 25%.

$31,250 income after financing costs ÷ $125,000 equity = .25 or 25% rate of return on equity

The investor made a greater return on equity investment by leveraging the investment. Positive leverage is the result.

Liquidity refers to the ability to sell an investment very quickly without loss of capital.

Basis is an investor's initial cost of the property. The basis is adjusted by adding any capital improvements made to the property and deducting depreciation expenses taken on tax returns during the years of ownership.

EXAMPLE: An investor purchases a property for $900,000. Improvements to the property during ownership total $100,000. During the ownership period, the investor took $125,000 in depreciation. The investor's adjusted basis is $875,000.

$900,000 cost + $100,000 capital improvements – $125,000 depreciation = $875,000 adjusted basis

Capital gain (or loss) is the difference between the adjusted basis of property and its net selling price. A capital gain or capital loss has tax consequences for the owner of investment property.

The term **tax shelter** describes the advantages of owning real estate investments. An investment is a tax shelter when it shields income from payment of income taxes.

Real estate investment trusts (REITs) offer investors the opportunity to invest in income-producing real estate properties. Individual REITs generally specialize in a particular type of property, such as multifamily communities, retail malls and shopping centers, office properties, and so forth. They provide a means for individuals to pool resources for investment in a professionally managed portfolio of real property and/or mortgages secured by real property. REITs are attractive because they offer diversification and liquidity, they are similar to mutual funds, and they offer the advantages of skilled centralized management and continuity of operation. REITs may be purchased through a stockbroker.

Risk is the chance of losing all or part of an investment. Generally, investors demand a higher return for higher investment risk.

Types of Real Estate Investments

Residential. Investments in residential properties include single-family homes, condominiums, apartments, and other multifamily complexes. Most experts agree that investing in an apartment project (or other income-producing property) is economically feasible when the projected future net income over a predetermined period will permit return of the investment (recover invested capital) and allow the investor an appropriate rate of return over the investment period.

In assessing the desirability of an apartment complex, several criteria should be considered, including the following: location, effective gross income, operating expenses, and property taxes. Existing properties should be inspected carefully, and repair and maintenance records should be studied to ensure that the property has been well maintained. A lack of proper maintenance is called *deferred maintenance*.

Commercial. This category includes retail and office properties. Retail properties include downtown commercial properties, shopping centers, and regional malls. A shopping center's economic characteristics depend on the nature of existing leases and on operating expenses. An investor should study all leases carefully to find out how much of the original term remains, whether investors participate in tenant income from sales, and whether the leases provide for appropriate costs to be shifted to tenants. Long-term leases and a tendency on the part of tenants to renew their leases are among the main attractions of investing in office properties.

Industrial. Industrial uses of real estate in urban areas generally involve manufacturing, assembly, and/or distribution. To be suitable for industrial use, a site should be located near transportation facilities such as railroad stations, expressways, and airports because of the need to receive and ship by rail, truck, and air.

Agricultural. Agricultural properties are often purchased by a farsighted investor-developer looking for large tracts of land that lie in the path of foreseeable urban growth. However, the holding period to realize such development potential may be many years.

Business Opportunities. One of the categories that Chapter 475, F.S., defines as real estate is "any interest in business enterprises or business opportunities." This category includes the sale or lease of a business and goodwill of an existing business, including business assets such as the stock of a corporation.

Practice Questions

1. The difference between assets and liabilities is _________ ___________.
2. ___________ _______________ is the type of real estate investment that involves the sale or lease of a business.
3. ___________ ___________ results when the cost of borrowed funds exceeds the rate of return on the investment.

17.2 REAL ESTATE AS AN INVESTMENT

Advantages of Real Estate as an Investment

Real estate investments have the following advantages (see Figure 17.1):

- *Rate of return.* Historically, real estate has produced an above-average rate of return for owner-investors compared with other types of investments.
- *Tax advantages.* Real estate investments receive certain tax benefits.
- *Hedge against inflation.* Historically, real estate prices have increased (property appreciation) at a faster pace than inflation. If a parcel of real property is acquired at market value or less, an owner will normally find that the sale price increases faster than other prices. This ability to maintain or increase purchasing power is one reason real estate is regarded as one of the best protections against inflation.
- *Leverage.* Real estate is typically highly leveraged. An investor can usually borrow 70% to 75% of the appraised value to finance a real estate investment. The goal of leveraging is to increase one's yield (return) on equity (investor's own capital) by using borrowed funds.
- *Equity buildup.* As a property appreciates in value and the mortgage debt is reduced, the investor's equity grows.

FIGURE 17.1 ■ **Advantages and Disadvantages of Real Estate Investments**

Advantages	Disadvantages
Usually above-average rate of return	Lack of liquidity (illiquid)
Tax advantages	More localized market
Hedge against inflation	Expenses associated with expertise
Leverage of borrowed money	Need for active management
Equity buildup	Relatively high degree of risk

Disadvantages of Investing in Real Estate

Following are some of the disadvantages of investing in real estate (see Figure 17.1):

- *Illiquidity*. Real estate is not considered a liquid investment over the short term. Therefore, it is said to be illiquid.
- *Market is local in nature*. The real estate market is more local in nature compared with other investments. An investor usually is interested in a particular property type and geographic area. Other types of investments, such as stocks, are bought and sold in an international marketplace.
- *Need for expert help*. Many expenses are associated with investing in real estate, including the need for property managers, financial consultants, and legal experts.
- *Need for active management*. Real estate requires active management. Properties must be cared for, rents collected, and so forth.
- *Risk*. An investor must weigh the chance of losing invested capital. Real estate investment involves a high degree of risk compared with other investments. Tenant turnover, increasing property taxes, and increased costs associated with operations are a few examples of the types of risk to which a real estate investor is exposed.

Practice Questions

4. One disadvantage of real estate as an investment is that it is _______________ in the short term.

5. An advantage of real estate investments is that they are a good _______________ against inflation.

17.3 ASSESSMENT OF RISKS

Investors have a target rate of return in mind when they invest in real estate. Factors out of the control of an investor, such as inflation, rising interest rates, and so forth, create uncertainty that the actual rate of return an investment will provide will meet the investor's target. This uncertainty is what we call risk. **Risk** is the chance of unfavorable events or outcomes. Some degree of risk is always associated with an investment.

Risks Associated With General Business Conditions

Business Risk. Business risk reflects the possible unsuccessful operation of a particular project. It is the probability that projected income will not be achieved or will not be adequate to meet operating expenses. This category of risk is associated with the degree of variance between projected income and expenses and actual income and expenses.

EXAMPLE: A regional shopping center that is fully rented under long-term net leases has less business risk than raw land to be developed into a hotel sometime in the future.

Financial Risk. Financial risk is the risk of defaulting on borrowed funds used to finance an investment. Financial risk is the potential inability of the investment's income to cover the required debt service. The more borrowed funds used to purchase an investment, the greater the financial risk.

Purchasing-Power Risk. Purchasing-power risk is inflation risk. Purchasing power risk reflects the fact that inflation may cause the investor to be paid back with less valuable dollars. If the rents are fixed by the lease, the gross income may not keep pace with inflation, while the operating expenses increase at the inflation rate.

EXAMPLE: A well-established restaurant with a loyal customer base that can adjust menu prices to cover increasing food costs during inflation has less purchasing-power risk than a warehouse leased for 20 years.

Interest-Rate Risk. Assume that the only change in a real estate investment is that the interest rate is raised by the lender. The property remains unchanged, the owners remain the same, and management remains in place. However, with the increase in interest rates, the value of the property as an investment goes down. That is interest-rate risk at work. Investments tied to a fixed-rate mortgage loan have less interest-rate risk than one leveraged with an adjustable rate mortgage.

Risks That Affect Return

Historically, businesses and individuals have put money in investments that offer the highest return commensurate with the liquidity and safety of the money.

Liquidity Risk. Real estate investments are particularly susceptible to liquidity risk. Liquidity risk is the risk that a quick sale will not be possible or that a significant price reduction will be required to achieve a quick sale.

Safety Risk. Safety risk is the possible loss of invested capital (return of investment) and/or expected earnings (return on investment). Safety risk is composed of market risk (possible loss of invested capital) and risk of default (possible loss of earnings):

- *Market risk* is the type of risk associated with a decrease in the market value of an investment as a result of increased interest rates (the interest-rate risk at work). Often, market risk is magnified by long periods of time. Investments that have earnings exposed to the cyclical gyrations of the money markets over extended periods experience increased market risk.
- *Risk of default* is the risk that the investment will not generate enough income to sustain itself.

Each investment opportunity has with it risks. Some types of risk are more likely with certain types of investments. If everything were equal, an investor would prefer a liquid, short-term investment because less risk would be involved. However, the possibility of a higher yield will induce some investors to commit funds to a less-liquid, long-term, riskier investment. It is a basic economic premise that risk and the desired rate of return are directly related (e.g., high risk, high return).

Practice Questions

6. Safety risk is composed of ______________ risk and risk of ______________.
7. ______________ risk is associated with the variance between ______________ income and expenses and ______________ income and expenses.
8. ___________ risk is risk of defaulting on borrowed funds to finance an investment.

17.4 BUSINESS BROKERAGE

Real estate licensees who engage in the sale, purchase, or lease of businesses are called business brokers. This real estate activity is sometimes called business opportunity brokerage. Business opportunity brokerage involves the sale or lease of existing businesses. In Florida, an active current real estate license is required to sell or lease business opportunities.

Similarities to Real Estate Brokerage

475.01, F.S.

Business brokerage almost always involves the sale of real property or an assignment of a long-term lease. Business brokerage activities require a real estate license under Chapter 475, Part I, F.S.

Differences From Real Estate Brokerage

Business brokerage differs from real estate brokerage in at least three ways (see Figure 17.2).

1. *Business brokerage assets often include personal property and goodwill.* **Goodwill** is attributed to a business's reputation and the expectation of continued customer loyalty. Goodwill is an intangible asset because goodwill does not have physical existence (it cannot be seen or touched) and yet it's "value" to a business opportunity is very real. The value of an intangible asset is in what it represents to the business, such as what the brand name "Kleenex" means to Kimberly-Clark. The value of goodwill is approximated by subtracting the value of tangible assets from the value of the business. Other intangible assets that add value include licenses, franchises, copyrights, and patents.
2. *The value of the business may differ from the value of the real estate.* In other words, the total **going-concern value** may be different from the real estate value. Going-concern value is the value of an established business property compared with the value of just the physical assets of a business that is not yet established.
3. *Markets for business enterprises are typically wider in geographic scope than markets for individual parcels of real estate.*

FIGURE 17.2 ■ Business Brokerage Compared With Real Estate Brokerage

Similarities	Differences
Sale of real property or assignment of a long-term lease	Assets include personal property and goodwill
Active real estate license required	Going-concern value may differ from real estate value
	Wider geographic market

Practice Questions

9. List two ways real estate brokerage and business brokerage are similar.

   1. ______________________________

   2. ______________________________

10. ______________ value is the value of an established business property compared with the value of the physical assets of a business that is not yet established.

11. An ______________ asset does not have physical existence, meaning it cannot be seen or touched.

17.5 EXPERTISE REQUIRED IN BUSINESS BROKERAGE

The expertise required in business brokerage includes the following:

- Corporate finance
- Business accounting
- Valuation of businesses

Corporate Finance

To become a reputable, successful business broker requires training and experience. People with corporate backgrounds or business education are able to draw upon those experiences. The business broker works in conjunction with CPAs and attorneys to provide the expertise required in the purchase and sale of businesses. Expertise in corporate finance includes knowledge of the following:

- *Classes and characteristics of corporate stock* [common (required of all corporations) and preferred]
- *Securities analysis and valuation*
- *Management of working capital* (the difference between total current assets and total current liabilities)
- *Budgeting* (an estimate of anticipated income and expenditures over a definite future period)

Business Accounting

Some areas important to business accounting are the following:

- *Income statement analysis.* The income statement is a concise summary of all income and expenses of a business for a *stated period of time*. It is designed to show the results of business operations over a specific period and to provide the basic data for analyzing the reasons for a firm's profits or losses.
- *Balance sheet analysis.* The balance sheet shows the company's financial position at a stated *moment in time*, the close of business on the date of the balance sheet. The balance sheet shows assets, liabilities, and owner's equity (net worth). It is customary to prepare an income statement and a balance sheet at the same time. This allows the net income or loss shown on the income statement for the prior period to be reflected on the balance sheet as of that particular moment.
- *Cash flow analysis.* Cash flow is the total amount of money generated from an investment after expenses have been paid. Operating expenses include reserves

for replacement and payment of mortgage principal and interest. Cash flow disregards depreciation because depreciation does not involve an outlay of cash.

- *Asset depreciation.* Business brokers must be able to separate the depreciable assets of a business into real property and personal property.
- *Taxation.* Anyone interested in buying or selling a business knows the critical role taxes play in the success or failure of that business. Business brokers must be alert to recommending that clients seek expert tax advice.

Valuation of Businesses

The methods used to estimate a business's value are similar to those used in appraising real property.

- *Comparable sales analysis.* Where records reveal previous sale prices for businesses with a high degree of similarity, the appraiser can use professional judgment to account for existing differences and to arrive at a close approximation of the market value of a business.
- *Cost approach.* This method is appropriate for estimating the value of improvements of any type. When reproduction cost is used as a basis, the appraiser calculates the amount required to duplicate exactly the business or building being appraised. When replacement cost is used, the appraiser calculates the cost that would result in a business's (or building's) having the same use and capabilities as the one being appraised, even though the new business/building might differ physically.
- *Income analysis.* Most income-producing properties derive a large portion of their value from their ability to produce an income stream. This method of appraising attempts to estimate accurately the present value of expected future benefits (earnings and appreciation of assets) by converting the anticipated income stream into a present value through the use of a capitalization rate. The income approach is the best approach for valuing a business.
- *Liquidation analysis.* The liquidation of a business may become necessary because of failure of a business, the death of a sole proprietor, the dissolution of a partnership, a court order, or any number of other reasons. In a **liquidation analysis**, business brokers and financial experts must consider such factors as the ability of the firm to pay off short-term obligations, the value of the inventory on hand, and the liquidation value of preferred stock.

In addition to all the activities mentioned, a business broker is required to observe the many regulatory provisions, including Chapter 475, F.S., and state and federal securities laws.

Practice Questions

12. The expertise required in business brokerage includes _______________ finance, ____________ _______________, and _______________ of businesses.

13. Working capital is the difference between total current _______________ and total current _______________.

14. The two types of corporate stock are _______________ and _______________ stock.

17.6 STEPS IN THE SALE OF A BUSINESS

The sale of a business generally can be described as a series of steps. In the case of an outright purchase (and sale), the following 12-step sequence usually occurs:

1. *The listing*. List the business for sale.
2. *Identify all assets of the business*.
3. *Valuation of the business*.
4. *Deduct liabilities*. Subtract the value of all short-term and long-term liabilities (including the value of preferred stock) from the value of the business.
5. *Valuation of stock*. If a corporation is being sold by transferring shares of stock, the share value must be determined. Divide the net value of the business by the number of common shares of stock outstanding. Most small businesses are sold as an asset sale even if the business is held as a corporation.
6. *Legal compliance with all pertinent laws*.
7. *Market (advertise) the business*.
8. *Secure a buyer*. Have the buyer sign a confidentiality (nondisclosure) agreement before releasing the name, location, and financial information regarding the business.
9. *Enter into a contract with both parties*.
10. *Due diligence period*. Buyer inspects the financials of the business.
11. *Closing preparation*. If real estate is not sold with the business, an assignment of the lease or a new lease from the landlord is prepared; if real estate is included in the sale, title work is ordered.
12. *Coordinate a date for closing the transaction*.

Practice Questions

15. Once all of the ______________ of a business are identified, the ______________ are deducted from the value of the business.

16. To protect a business's confidentiality regarding sale, the buyer should be required to sign a ____________________ agreement before releasing financial information regarding the business.

17. A ____________ ______________ period is established to allow the buyer to inspect the ______________ of the business.

17.7 SUMMARY OF IMPORTANT POINTS

- Real estate investment analysis is the process of determining the extent to which real estate investments achieve an investor's objectives.
- *Appreciation* is the increase in property value over a period of time due to economic causes.
- *Assets* are the entire resources of a business. An asset is anything of value. A tangible asset can be touched and has actual substance. An intangible asset has value but does not have physical substance, such as the goodwill of a business. The difference between assets and liabilities is net worth.

- *Cash flow* is the total amount of spendable income generated from an investment. It is the total amount of money remaining after all expenditures have been paid. Cash flow may be positive or negative.
- *Equity* is the property's value minus debt.
- *Leverage* is the use of borrowed funds to finance the purchase of an asset. Positive leverage occurs when the benefits exceed the cost of borrowing. Negative leverage occurs if the borrowed funds cost more than they are producing. *Liquidity* refers to the ability to sell an investment very quickly without loss of capital.
- *Basis* is an investor's initial cost of the property. The basis is adjusted by adding any capital improvements made to the property and deducting depreciation expenses taken on tax returns during the years of ownership.
- *Capital gain (or loss)* is the difference between the adjusted basis of property and its net selling price. A capital gain or capital loss has tax consequences to the owner of investment property.
- *Tax shelter* is the term used to describe advantages of owning real estate investments. An investment is a tax shelter when it shields income from payment of income taxes.
- Real estate investment trusts (REITs) offer investors the opportunity to invest in a pool of income-producing properties under professional management.
- Investors can choose from several types of real estate investments: residential, commercial, industrial, agricultural, and business opportunities.
- Advantages of real estate investment include the following: rate of return, tax advantages, hedge against inflation, leverage, and equity buildup.
- Disadvantages of investing in real estate include the following: illiquidity, local market, need for expert help, management requirements, and risk.
- *Risk* is the chance of losing all or part of an investment.
- Risk associated with general business conditions include the following: business risk, financial risk, purchasing-power risk, and interest-rate risk.
- Business brokerage and real estate brokerage similarities include (1) the sale of real property or assignment of a long-term lease may be involved, and (2) an active real estate license is required for business brokerage and real estate brokerage.
- Business brokerage differs from real estate brokerage in three ways. Business brokerage (1) may include personal property and goodwill assets; (2) the going-concern value may differ from real estate value; and (3) business brokerage may have a wider geographic market.
- *Going-concern value* is the value of an established business property compared with the value of just the physical assets of a business that is not yet established.
- An *income statement* is a concise summary of all income and expenses of a business for a stated period of time. A *balance sheet* shows the company's financial position at a stated moment in time.
- Expertise required in business brokerage includes corporate finance, business accounting, and valuation of businesses.
- The methods of appraising a business are comparable sales analysis, reproduction or replacement cost, income analysis, and liquidation analysis.

UNIT 17 EXAM

1. Investors who want to invest in office buildings and apartment complexes but want the advantages of liquidity and diversification often consider investing in
   a. a real estate investment trust.
   b. a large property management company.
   c. a mutual fund that invests in the broad stock market.
   d. none of these.

2. A case in which the interest paid for borrowed funds is less than the overall rate of return to an investor is an example of
   a. loan-to-value ratio.
   b. positive leverage.
   c. negative leverage.
   d. yield.

3. Business risk is chance of loss associated with the
   a. variance between projected and actual income and expenses.
   b. ability to pay all operating expenses from proceeds generated by the investment.
   c. increase in interest rates during the period of investment.
   d. effect of inflation on purchasing power.

4. Intangible assets of a business do NOT include
   a. goodwill.
   b. customer loyalty.
   c. trademarks.
   d. improvements.

5. A firm's working capital is customarily defined as the difference between the firm's total
   a. current assets and total current liabilities.
   b. current liabilities and total cash on hand.
   c. short-term liabilities and total cash on hand.
   d. long-term liabilities and total accounts receivable.

6. How does business brokerage differ from real estate brokerage?
   a. An appraisal is usually needed.
   b. An interest in real property is involved.
   c. Intangible assets must be considered.
   d. A real estate license is required.

7. The financial report that indicates a firm's financial position at a stated moment in time is the
   a. operating statement.
   b. balance sheet.
   c. working capital statement.
   d. statement of net earnings.

8. The value of an established business property, compared with the value of just the physical assets of a business that is NOT yet established, is called
   a. going-concern value.
   b. goodwill.
   c. business enterprise.
   d. tangible assets.

9. The advantages of real estate as an investment do NOT include
   a. a generally good rate of return compared with other types of investments.
   b. a hedge against inflation.
   c. income tax considerations.
   d. the need for active management.

10. A concise summary of all income and expenses of a business for a stated period of time is the
    a. balance sheet.
    b. income statement.
    c. cash flow statement.
    d. asset sheet.

11. All the resources of a business, including tangibles and intangibles, are called the
    a. net worth.
    b. capital.
    c. gross income.
    d. assets.

12. The market value of an apartment building is $975,900. The investor has leveraged $731,925. What is the investor's equity in the property?
    a. $178,925
    b. $197,759
    c. $243,975
    d. $731,925

UNIT

18 TAXES AFFECTING REAL ESTATE

LEARNING OBJECTIVES

When you have completed this unit, you will be able to accomplish the following.

- Discuss the city and county property taxation process and list the steps involved in the tax appeal procedure.
- Distinguish among immune, exempt, and partially exempt property and describe the various personal exemptions available to qualified owners of homestead property.
- Compute the property tax on a specific parcel, given the current tax rates, assessed value, eligible exemptions, and transfer of assessment limitation difference (save our homes portability) if applicable, and describe the purpose of Florida's Green Belt Law.
- Calculate the cost of a special assessment, given the conditions and amounts involved.
- Describe the tax advantages of home ownership.
- Explain how to determine taxable income of investment real estate and distinguish between installment sales and like-kind exchange.

KEY TERMS

adjusted basis
ad valorem
assessed value
assessment limitation (SOH benefit)
boot
capital gain
debt service
depreciation
exempt properties
Green Belt Law
immune properties
installment sale
just value
like-kind exchange
mill
special assessment
tax rate
taxable income
taxable value

INTRODUCTION

City, county, school board, and numerous special tax districts are empowered to impose taxes directly on real property in Florida as part of the powers delegated to them by the state government. The U.S. Constitution prohibits the federal government from taxing real property, passing that right on to the state and local governments. Florida is one of the states, however, that does not tax real estate at the state level.

18.1 CITY AND COUNTY PROPERTY TAXES

193, F.S.

Property taxes provide the bulk of local government revenues in Florida. They account for a large portion of the revenue needed to provide law enforcement, fire protection, and other services.

The Real Property Taxation Process

197.122, F.S.

193.023(2), F.S.

Real estate taxes (property taxes) are **ad valorem** taxes (based according to the value of the property). The county property appraiser assesses all properties within the county, called the **assessed value**. Florida law requires that the county property appraiser assess real property for all levels of government, thus avoiding duplication and possible controversy. All real property assessments must be updated annually.

Property taxes in Florida are levied on a calendar-year basis. Taxes are paid *in arrears* (at the end of the tax year) for the period of January 1 through December 31 each year (see Figure 18.1). Property taxes become a lien on all real estate in Florida on January 1 each year. This lien is legally superior to any other lien, regardless of date. Taxes are payable to the county tax collector on or after November 1 each year. Property owners may pay property taxes in four installments or in a single payment. A discount system permits property owners to realize a discount through prompt payment of taxes. All payments made on or after March 1 must be for the full amount of taxes levied. Property taxes for the previous year become delinquent on April 1.

FIGURE 18.1 ■ Property Tax Schedule

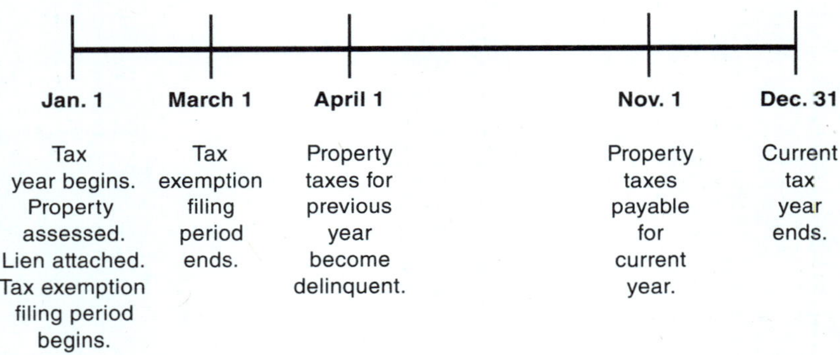

Determining Just Value

193.011, F.S.

Property taxes are levied against land and all improvements to the land. The assessed values of the land and improvements are arrived at separately and then combined to reflect a single assessed value. The state supreme court has interpreted Florida statutes as requiring that all real property be assessed at just value. **Just value** is the fair and reasonable value based on objective valuation methods. Just value has been interpreted by the Florida courts to represent market value. County property appraisers take into consideration property characteristics such as location, size, and condition of the property. The county property appraiser also considers the highest and best use of the property and, if income producing, the income generated from the property.

Property appraisers apply three approaches to value: the sales comparison approach, the cost approach, and the income approach. If the property is sold during the year, the sale price becomes a factor for consideration in assessing the value of the property, but it is not the controlling factor. Representatives of the property appraiser's office typically go into the community to assess property, collecting data using specific forms and recording procedures. The information obtained from field trips is then processed through a computer, using appropriate valuation formulas to render an objective estimate of assessed value.

Once an assessment has been placed on a property, the owner must be informed. A Notice of Proposed Property Taxes is mailed to the property owner at the address of record. The notice is also called a TRIM (truth in millage) notice. It is the responsibility of each property owner to see that a current mailing address is on file for all properties owned. Current addresses are needed to ensure that owners receive a notice of change in assessment before the time allowed for protest has expired.

Any property owner is entitled to protest a property assessment, but not every protest will be successful. For example, an owner of a home on a *standard lot* in a large, completely developed subdivision who complains that the assessment of the lot was too high will have little hope of getting the assessment changed. If the assessed value of the lot were changed, all the owners of similar lots could protest their assessments.

The same homeowner might have a better chance of obtaining a lowered assessment if the evidence indicates the *house* was assessed at a value greater than justified. The county property appraiser has fairly complete details on the square footage, construction materials, year built, and amount of estimated depreciation since the date of construction, as well as records showing the assessed values of similar structures in the neighborhood.

Protest Procedure

194.011, F.S.

When a Florida property owner feels the assessed value is inaccurate or does not reflect fair market value, the owner can use the following three-step protest (tax appeal) procedure.

Step 1. The first step is to seek an adjustment by contacting the county property appraiser or a representative of that office. If the arguments of the property owner are valid and have a basis in fact, the county property appraiser is authorized to make a change and to lower the assessed value.

194.015, F.S.

Step 2. If the property owner's request for an adjustment is rejected, the owner may file an appeal (petition) with the Value Adjustment Board. A property owner is allowed 25 days after the Notice of Proposed Property Taxes (TRIM notice) is mailed to file an assessment appeal. The board is composed of five members: two county commissioners, one school board member, and two citizen members. If the board agrees with the taxpayer that the assessed value of the property is too high, the board has the authority to change the assessment. If the board decides that the county property appraiser assigned the correct assessment value, the board will reject the taxpayer's request.

Step 3. The final step available to a property owner seeking a change in assessed value is litigation in the courts. The taxpayer may pay the taxes under protest and file a suit (a *certiorari proceeding*, meaning a review of the matter by the courts) against the county property appraiser and the county tax collector. The property owner's petition must be filed within the statutory period (Chapter 194, F.S.). The court may not arbitrarily assign an assessment value to a property. It may, however, specify the methods and procedures that the county property appraiser should use in reassessing the subject property. If the court judges the original assessed value to be just and equitable, the property owner has used all the steps available under the protest process, other than to appeal to a higher court.

PROTEST PROCEDURE WHEN A PROPERTY OWNER DISAGREES WITH THE ASSESSED VALUE

A	Appraiser (Contact the County Property Appraiser's Office)
B	Board (Value Adjustment Board)
C	Court (Litigation)

Practice Questions

1. Real estate property tax revenue is of primary importance to ______________ government.
2. A property owner has 25 days to protest the assessed value to the________ ______________ _________.
3. Real estate property taxes are _____ ___________ taxes.
4. The county property appraiser determines the ____________ value of the properties within the county.
5. The Florida courts have interpreted ______________ value to be ______________ value.

18.2 TAX DISTRICTS: BUDGETS AND TAX RATE LEVY

Every fiscal year, each of the primary tax districts (city, county, and school board) prepares an operating budget for the next fiscal year. Budgets are also prepared by numerous smaller special tax districts that provide services. These include fire control districts, water management districts, flood control districts, and so forth.

With a budget in hand, the tax district has a good estimate of expenses for the next year. The next issue is obtaining sufficient revenue (income) to pay the expenses. No elected official is eager to levy higher property taxes than are absolutely necessary to operate the tax district. So before a general real estate tax is calculated, an attempt is made to estimate the revenue that can reasonably be expected from all sources other than real property taxes. Each tax district may have different or unique sources of income, ranging from outright federal grants to profits resulting from municipal-owned utilities. Fines paid in courts, parking meter income, fees from occupational licenses, and tax funds returned by the state government are a few of the other sources of income. Estimating the amount of income from these nonproperty tax sources is made easier by records of preceding years, which indicate a predictable trend.

With a reasonable estimate in hand of the revenue expected from all nonproperty tax sources, the tax district is able to predict the amount of money needed from property taxes. The amount of property taxes paid to a tax district must come from its *tax base*. The tax base is the total assessed value of all taxable property in the tax district. The next component needed to compute a tax rate is the number and type of property tax exemptions granted.

Exemptions From Property Taxes

The owners of certain properties are relieved of the obligation to pay property taxes. Others are partially exempted.

Immune properties are city, county, state, and federal government properties. Examples of immune properties include county courthouses and military facilities. Immune properties also include special properties, such as municipal airports, that have been made immune by statute or ordinance. Immune properties are not subject to taxation.

Exempt properties include property belonging to eligible not-for-profit organizations that own and operate real estate for religious and charitable purposes. Exempt properties are subject to taxation, but the owner is released from the obligation.

Homestead Tax Exemption

196.031, F.S.

Florida residents who hold title to a home in Florida and use the home as their *permanent residence* may establish their residence as a homestead. Floridians who homestead their residence receive a homestead exemption, which reduces the amount of property taxes owed. A person who holds title to more than one residence in the state of Florida may homestead only one residence.

Applicants must reside in the home and have legal title to the property as of January 1 to be eligible to file for the homestead tax exemption. First-time applicants must file an application with the county property appraiser's office on or before March 1. Some counties allow homeowners to file the initial application throughout the year. However, if the application is filed after the March 1 deadline, the homestead exemption will not take effect until the following year.

The procedure for renewing the homestead exemption varies from county to county. In most counties, the property appraiser mails a renewal card on or before February 1 of each year. A county may choose to waive the requirement to renew the exemption each year once the initial application is made and the exemption is granted. However, if an individual no longer qualifies for the homestead exemption and fails to notify the county, the law provides for payment of penalties and interest.

Calculating Taxable Value. Owners of homesteaded property are granted a tax exemption, relieving the owners of a portion of the tax burden. Homesteaded properties are *partially exempted* from the total property tax burden the owners would have been charged if they had not homesteaded their residence. Homesteaded properties, therefore, are subject to taxation, but the owners are partially relieved of the property taxes. The **taxable value** of a homesteaded property is determined by subtracting all applicable exemptions from the assessed value.

Owners of property that make it a permanent residence for themselves or their dependents may be eligible to receive a homestead exemption up to $50,000, depending on the assessed value. The first $25,000 exemption applies to all property taxes, including school district taxes. The additional $25,000 exemption applies to assessed values over $50,000 but only goes toward city/county taxes. The maximum amount of exemptions for school district taxes is $25,000 (see Figure 18.2).

Formula: Taxable Value for Homesteads With Assessed Value up to $50,000

assessed value – base homestead exemption = taxable value

FIGURE 18.2 ■ Homestead Exemptions

Assessed Value of Home	City/County (Non-School Taxes)	School District (School Taxes)
Up to $50,000	Base $25,000 exemption	Base $25,000 exemption
Over $50,000	Base $25,000 + additional $25,000 = $50,000 exemption	Base $25,000 exemption

EXAMPLE: A homesteaded condominium unit has an assessed value of $49,000. What is the taxable value?

The assessed value of the homesteaded property is less than $50,000 but greater than $25,000 (refer to Figure 18.2), so the taxable value is as follows:

$49,000 assessed value – $25,000 base exemption only = $24,000 taxable value

The $24,000 taxable value is used to calculate the city, county, and school board property taxes.

Owners of homesteaded property with an assessed value that is greater than $50,000 are also entitled to the $25,000 base homestead exemption from city, county, and school board taxes. However, the owners of these homesteaded properties also qualify for an additional $25,000 exemption from the city and county taxes (but not school board taxes). Because the $25,000 base exemption only applies to school board taxes, when the assessed value exceeds $50,000, two taxable values must be calculated. One taxable value applies to school board taxes and a second taxable value is calculated for city and county property taxes.

Formula: Taxable Value for Properties With an Assessed Value That Exceeds $50,000

assessed value – $25,000 base exemption = taxable value for school board taxes

assessed value – ($25,000 base exemption + $25,000 additional exemption) = taxable value for city and county taxes or

assessed value – $50,000 exemption = taxable value for city and county taxes

EXAMPLE: A homesteaded single-family residence has an assessed value of $350,000. What is the taxable value of this property?

The assessed value of the homesteaded property is greater than $50,000, so the taxable value for school board taxes is calculated separately from the taxable value applied to city and county property taxes (refer to Figure 18.2).

$350,000 assessed value – $25,000 base exemption only = $325,000 taxable value for school board taxes

$350,000 assessed value – $50,000 exemption = $300,000 taxable value for city and county property taxes

196.101, F.S.

196.202, F.S.

Additional Homestead Tax Exemptions. Florida law provides certain additional exemptions from the assessed value of homesteaded property (see Figure 18.3). Florida statute dictates what proof must be submitted to qualify for the additional exemptions.

FIGURE 18.3 ■ Homesteaded Property Special Exemptions

Additional Exemption on Homestead	Additional Amount Deducted From Assessed Value
Surviving spouse who has not remarried	$5,000
Blind person	$5,000
Totally and permanently disabled nonveteran	$5,000
Totally and permanently disabled quadriplegic	Homestead property 100% tax exempt
Totally and permanently disabled first responder (applies also to surviving spouse)	Homestead property 100% tax exempt

Additional Homestead Tax Exemptions for Veterans. Florida law provides certain additional exemptions from the assessed value of homesteaded property for veterans and their surviving spouses (see Figure 18.4).

FIGURE 18.4 ■ Additional Homestead Exemptions for Veterans

Veteran Additional Exemptions	Additional Amount Deducted From Assessed Value
At least 10% disabled by misfortune or during wartime service (applies to surviving spouse who had been married to the veteran for at least five years on the date of death)	$5,000
Service-connected, totally disabled (applies also to surviving spouse)	Homestead property 100% tax exempt
Surviving spouse of veteran who died while on active duty	Homestead property 100% tax exempt

The Florida Department of Revenue has information concerning Florida property tax exemptions posted at https://floridarevenue.com/property/Pages/Taxpayers_Exemptions.*aspx* (scan QR code).

View the Department of Revenue's official application for filing homestead exemption at https://floridarevenue.com/property/Documents/dr501.pdf.

Cumulative Homestead Tax Exemptions. The taxable value of a homesteaded property is calculated by totaling all the tax exemptions that apply to the homeowners and deducting the applicable exemptions from the assessed value.

EXAMPLE 1: What is the total homestead exemption for a widower with an assessed value of more than $50,000 on a qualifying homesteaded property?

a. Eligible homestead exemptions for school board taxes are:

$25,000 base exemption + $5,000 surviving spouse = $30,000 total homestead exemption for school board taxes

b. Eligible homestead exemptions for city and county property taxes are:

$25,000 base exemption + $25,000 additional exemption for assessed values over $50,000 + $5,000 surviving spouse = $55,000 total homestead exemption for city and county taxes

EXAMPLE 2: A surviving spouse who is legally blind owns a home with an assessed value of $100,000. The owner is the primary resident of the property. What is the total homestead exemption the owner can receive?

a. $25,000 base exemption + $5,000 blind exemption + $5,000 surviving spouse exemption = $35,000 total homestead exemption for school board taxes

b. $25,000 base exemption + $25,000 additional exemption for assessed values over $50,000 + $5,000 blind exemption + $5,000 surviving spouse exemption = $60,000 total homestead exemption for city and county property taxes

Tax Rates

To calculate the dollar amount of property taxes owed, the taxable value of the property is multiplied by the appropriate **tax rate**. The taxable value is applied to the school board tax rate to calculate the taxes due for school property taxes. The taxable value for non-school taxes is applied to the city and/or county tax rates to calculate the non-school property taxes.

Understanding Tax Rates. The tax rate is expressed in mills. A **mill** is 1/1000 of a dollar ($.001). There are 10 mills in one penny. One penny (or one cent) is written as $.01, so 10 mills is $.010. Florida has legislated a cap (ceiling) that limits cities, counties, and school boards to a basic real property tax rate of no more than 10 mills each, except for voted levies. The maximum tax rate that can be charged on real property for county taxes (or city taxes or school board taxes) is 10 mills, which is equivalent to one cent per dollar of taxable value.

Tax rates expressed in mills must be converted to decimal values before calculating property taxes. To convert the tax rate to a decimal, simply move the decimal point three places (1,000th place) to the left. Add zeros as placeholders, if necessary. For example, 9 mills are expressed as .009 decimal and 25 mills are expressed as .025 decimal.

Formula: Annual Property Taxes Due

taxable value × tax rate = annual property taxes due

EXAMPLE: A home is assessed at $180,000. The owner has qualified for the homestead exemption. The county tax rate is 9.5 mills, the city tax rate is 8.0 mills, and the school district rate is 5.5 mills. How much will the property owner be charged for property taxes?

a. *Calculate school taxes.*

5.5 mills = .0055

$180,000 assessed value – $25,000 base exemption = $155,000 taxable value for school board taxes

$155,000 taxable value × .0055 = $852.50 school board taxes

b. *Calculate city and county (non-school) taxes.*

9.5 mills for county taxes + 8.0 mills for city taxes = 17.5 mills

17.5 mills = .0175

Because the assessed value exceeds $75,000, the total exemption is $50,000:

$180,000 assessed value – $50,000 homestead exemption = $130,000 taxable value for city and county property taxes

$130,000 taxable value for city and county property taxes × .0175 = $2,275 city and county property taxes

c. *Calculate total property taxes due.*

$852.50 school board taxes + $2,275.00 city and county taxes = $3,127.50 total property taxes due

Not all property owners are subject to the same tax rates. A homeowner living in a city pays city, county, and school board taxes. Perhaps additional taxes will be required as a result of bonds or other obligations approved by the voters. Usually, a homeowner living in the county but outside the city limits pays only county and school board taxes (plus any applicable special district rates). Often, additional taxes are required of county residents who are in special tax districts.

FACTS ABOUT CALCULATING PROPERTY TAXES

- Homestead exemptions are deducted from the assessed value to find the taxable value.
- On homesteaded property, the base $25,000 exemption is subtracted to calculate school board taxes.
- If the property is not homesteaded, the assessed value equals the taxable value.
- Taxable value is multiplied by the tax rate, in mills, to determine property taxes.

200.071, F.S.

200.081, F.S.

EXAMPLE: A homesteaded single-family residence has an assessed value of $350,000. The millage rate for the school district is 6 mills, city 7.1 mills, and county 8.2 mills. (a) How much is owed for school district taxes? (b) How much is owed for city and county taxes? (c) What is the total property tax bill for this property?

a. *Calculate school taxes.*

$350,000 assessed value – $25,000 base homestead exemption = $325,000 taxable value for school district taxes;

6 mills = .006;

$325,000 taxable value × .006 = $1,950 school district taxes

b. *Calculate city and county (non-school) taxes.*

Because the assessed value exceeds $50,000 the total exemption is $50,000:

$350,000 assessed value – $50,000 homestead exemption = $300,000 taxable value for city and county taxes;

7.1 city mills + 8.2 county mills = 15.3 mills = .0153;

$300,000 taxable value × .0153 = $4,590 city and county property taxes

c. *Calculate total property taxes due.*

$1,950 school taxes + $4,590 city and county taxes = $6,540 total property taxes due

Practice Questions

6. The assessed value of a homesteaded property is $395,000.
   - How much will the homeowner be charged for school property taxes?
   - How much will the homeowner be charged for city and county taxes?

7. _______________ properties are city, county, state, and federal government properties that are NOT subject to taxation.

8. _______________ properties include property belonging to religious organizations and nonprofit organizations.

9. The surviving spouse of a veteran who died while on active duty is entitled to a _______________ property tax deduction on homesteaded property.

10. A veteran who is at least 10% disabled by misfortune or during wartime service is entitled to an additional _______________ deduction from the assessed value of homesteaded property.

11. A homesteaded property is located in St. Petersburg, Florida, in Pinellas County. The city tax rate is 8.7 mills, the county tax rate is 9.2 mills, and the school district tax rate is 6 mills. The homeowner is blind and has qualified for homestead exemption. The home has been assessed at $165,000.

    a) How much is owed for school taxes?

    b) How much is owed for city and county taxes?

    c) What is the total property tax bill for this property?

18.3 FLORIDA STATUTES AFFECTING REAL PROPERTY

Save Our Homes and Portability

193.155, F.S.

The *Save Our Homes (SOH)* amendment to the Florida Constitution caps how much the assessed value of homesteaded property may increase in a given year. The just value of homesteaded property may be increased by the lesser of:

- 3% annually (based on the assessed value for the prior year); or
- the percentage change of the Consumer Price Index (CPI) for the preceding year.

The SOH benefit is the difference between the assessed value and the market value of a homesteaded property due to the annual limit on increases in assessed value.

EXAMPLE: Assume a homestead has a just value of $300,000, an accumulated $40,000 in SOH protections (called SOH **assessment limitation** or **SOH benefit**), and a homestead exemption of $25,000 plus the additional $25,000 exemption on nonschool taxes. What is the taxable value of this homestead?

$300,000 – $40,000 SOH benefit = $260,000 assessed value
$260,000 – $25,000 base homestead = $235,000 taxable value for school taxes
$260,000 – $50,000 total homestead = $210,000 taxable value for nonschool taxes

Save Our Homes Portability Transfer Eligible homestead owners may transfer their SOH benefit (up to $500,000) from their previous homestead to a new homestead. To be eligible, the homeowner must establish a homestead exemption for the new home within three tax years of January 1 of the last qualified homestead exemption (not three years after the sale). In effect, only one tax year with no homestead exemption is allowed to transfer the SOH benefit. Floridians who sell their homesteaded property and move into temporary housing while constructing a new home need to be especially mindful of the portability time clock.

> **EXAMPLE:** A married couple sells their homesteaded property in October 2022. The homestead exemption remains with the property until the end of the tax year, December 31, 2022. The last qualified homestead exemption for the property began on January 1, 2022, the beginning of the tax year. The homeowners have three tax years from the last qualified homestead exemption, until January 1, 2025, to transfer the SOH benefit to a new Florida homesteaded property.

689.261, F.S.

Discussing Property Taxes With Prospective Buyers. When homesteaded property is sold, it is assessed at just value as of January 1 of the year after a change in ownership. The assessed value of a homesteaded property may significantly increase after a change in ownership if the previous owners lived in the home for a number of years and the property in the area has experienced strong property appreciation.

Licensees should avoid estimating a buyer's property tax liability by referring to a seller's current taxes because the purchaser may be liable for substantially higher property taxes than the previous owner of the home. Prospective purchasers of residential property must be given a disclosure summary regarding property taxes. The disclosure summary informs purchasers that they cannot rely on the seller's current property taxes as the amount of property taxes the purchaser may be obligated to pay in the year following purchase of the property. The disclosure further explains that the sale of the property triggers a reassessment of the property's value (see "Property Tax Disclosure Summary," Unit 11). Buyers who have questions concerning the amount of property taxes they can expect to pay on the homes they are considering buying should be referred to the county property appraiser's office.

WEBLINK

The Department of Revenue has prepared a brochure about portability at https://floridarevenue.com/property/Documents/pt112.pdf.

Florida's Green Belt Law

193.461, F.S.

Florida law authorizes county property appraisers to assess agricultural land by a more favorable method than that used for other properties. If a taxpayer's land is so classified for assessment purposes, the county property appraiser must base the property tax assessment solely on the basis of the land's current character and use. The highest and best use of such land (such as commercial development) is not a factor in arriving at just value for agricultural purposes.

Florida's **Green Belt Law** was designed to protect farmers from having taxes increased just because the land might be in the path of urban growth and therefore well suited for development. An agricultural land classification results in a lower property assessment. Without such protection, a farmer's taxes could be raised to the point where it would no longer be economically feasible to continue the agricultural use. Because of lower taxes on agricultural land, speculators often have been attracted to such properties when they are located in the path of urban growth. In many instances, the law, which was intended to protect the farmer, has been used as a tax protection by speculators. To stop this practice, the Florida Green Belt Law was changed to require that all county property appraisers annually classify all lands within the county. Property owners desiring that their land be classified differently must request and rejustify such classification before March 1 each year. If the request is denied, these property owners may appeal the denial through the regular protest procedure used by other property owners.

Practice Questions

12. A homeowner has ______________ years from the last qualified homestead exemption to transfer the SOH benefit to a new Florida homesteaded property.

13. Florida's ______________ Law authorizes county property appraisers to assess land annually used for ______________ purposes to protect farmers from high property assessments based on potential development.

18.4 SPECIAL ASSESSMENTS

A **special assessment** is a tax levied on property to help pay for a public improvement that benefits the property. Laws require that to charge a special assessment, the property must benefit (increase in value) because of the improvement. Examples of special assessment taxes include paving streets that previously were unpaved, installing street lights, hooking up water and sewer services, installing sidewalks, and so forth.

Specific Superior Liens. Special assessment liens are *not* ad valorem tax liens. Ad valorem taxes are liens levied on property value to support the general functions of government, whereas special assessment tax liens are levied on property to pay the cost of a specific local improvement. Special assessment liens are a type of specific lien because the lien attaches to a specific property and not to all the assets of the property owner. Special assessment liens take priority over all other liens, except ad valorem tax liens. Recall that liens that take priority over other liens regardless of the recording date are called superior liens (see "Liens," Unit 9).

Street Paving Assessment. Street paving assessments are calculated on a front foot basis. Lot dimensions are written with the front footage first and then the depth of the lot. Front footage refers to the measurement along the street. Lot D (see Figure 18.5) has 130 front feet and the lot measures 130 feet by 100 feet.

FIGURE 18.5 ■ **Street Assessment**

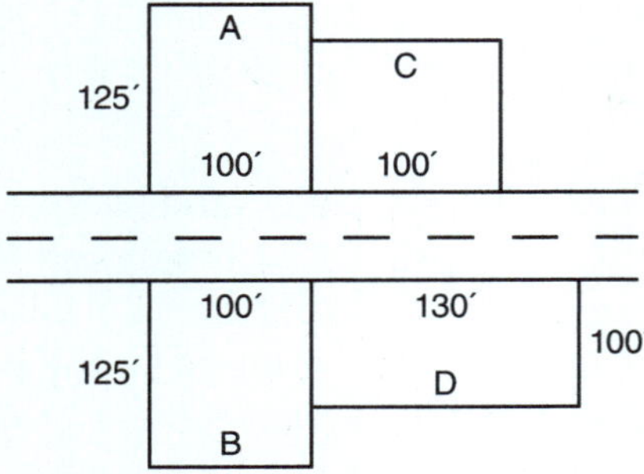

The local government typically bears a portion of the cost of the improvements; for example, the city may cover 40% of the total cost, leaving the remaining 60% to be paid by the property owners. When calculating a street paving assessment, it is important to remember that property owners are only charged to the middle of the street (or half of the total property owners' share). This is because the property owner across the street will also be charged a special assessment. The property owners of Lot A and Lot B in Figure 18.5 are across the street from one another. Each will pay half of the homeowner share of the street assessment. Notice that Lot C in Figure 18.5 also has front footage of 100 feet. The lot is not as deep compared with Lot A, but it will be charged the same street assessment as the adjoining Lot A because both Lot A and Lot C have the same front footage on the street. When calculating the special assessment for a property, the assessment is not affected by the dimensions of neighboring properties or how property across the street from the subject property is zoned (or utilized). For example, assume that the area to the east (right) of Lot C begins neighborhood common area. The common area has no effect on the special assessment of Lot D in Figure 18.5. The property owner of Lot D is only charged to the middle of the street.

Formula: Street Paving Assessment

front feet × cost per front foot = total cost

total cost × percentage paid by homeowners ÷ 2 (sides of street) = homeowner's cost of paving

EXAMPLE 1: The city is paving the streets in a neighborhood. The city will assume 30% of the expense. The city has approved a bid to pave the streets at a cost of $24 per front foot. How much is the special assessment for Lot A that measures 100 feet by 125 feet?

100 front feet × $24 per linear foot = $2,400
$2,400 × .70 (property owners' total share of cost is 100% – 30%) = $1,680
$1,680 ÷ 2 (one-half of the street paving cost) = $840

EXAMPLE 2: The city is paving the streets in a neighborhood. The city will assume 25% of the expense. The city has approved a bid to pave the streets at a cost of $28 per front foot. The subject lot measures 120 feet by 150 feet. Across the street is a neighborhood community center and pool. Calculate the subject lot's special assessment.

120 front feet × $28 per front foot = $3,360
$3,360 × .75 (property owners' total share of cost) = $2,520
$2,520 ÷ 2 = $1,260

Nonpayment of Real Property Taxes

Real estate taxes and non-ad valorem assessments are due each calendar year and are payable November 1. The taxes become delinquent April 1 of the following year. Property taxes constitute a lien superior to all other liens on real property. Special assessments are next in priority.

197, F.S.

Delinquent Real Estate Taxes. When a property owner fails to pay property taxes, the taxing authority must take steps to obtain the tax money needed to help pay for the cost of government. To do this, a property *tax certificate* is issued for each delinquent property. A list of all delinquent properties is published in a newspaper having general circulation throughout the county. The advertisement is printed weekly, three times prior to the tax certificate sale.

This publication gives all delinquent owners notice that tax certificates on their properties will be sold if the taxes are not paid before the date of sale. The published list of properties, including the amount of taxes in arrears, specifies a date, time, and place of the tax certificate sale. The county tax collector may conduct electronic online sales of tax certificates.

A property owner who pays the tax late in April or May is charged interest plus advertising cost.

Tax Certificate Auction. The tax collector is required to conduct a sale of tax certificates to collect the preceding year's unpaid real estate taxes. The sale begins on or before June 1. The delinquent tax amount (certificate's face amount) consists of the real estate tax and non-ad valorem assessment amount, interest for the months of April, May, and June, county tax collector's commission (5%), newspaper advertising charges, and internet tax certificate sale fees.

A tax certificate sale is not a sale of real property, nor does a tax certificate give the certificate holder a direct means to acquire a property. At the auction, any qualified person is entitled to bid for the tax certificate on any property. Instead of bidding in dollars, investors bid interest rates at the auction, starting at 18% and going down. The bidder who is willing to accept the lowest interest rate is issued the tax certificate. Once the certificate is sold, the bidder must pay the face amount of the certificate to the county (taxes, interest, and advertising cost).

Redemption of a Tax Certificate. The county tax collector issues a check or ACH transfer deposit to the certificate holder for the face amount of the certificate and the interest earnings when the property taxes are paid. For a certificate to be redeemed by the owner of the property, the tax collector must collect the face amount of the certificate plus all accrued interest. If the property owner does not pay the outstanding taxes and accrued interest within two years from the date the tax certificate was sold, the certificate holder can apply for a tax deed. The statute of limitation on a tax certificate is seven years from the date of issuance. If a tax deed has not been applied for within seven years and no other administrative or legal proceeding exists, the tax certificate is null and void by operation of law.

Tax Deed Process. The holder of the tax certificate may file a *tax deed application* anytime after two years has lapsed from the issuance of the tax certificate but before the expiration of seven years from the date of issuance. The certificate holder must pay the county tax collector all amounts required for redemption or purchase of all other outstanding tax certificates, any omitted taxes, current and delinquent taxes, plus interest and fees. The tax deed applicant is notified of the additional funds needed for advertising and other costs.

Anyone can bid at the foreclosure sale and the property will be sold to the highest bidder. If the property is purchased by someone other than the certificate holder, the tax certificate holder will be reimbursed all the sums paid plus accrued interest up to the date of sale. If there are no bidders, the holder of the certificate is issued a tax deed. Once the property is transferred by tax deed, all other liens against the property—including mortgages—are wiped out, with the exception of any government liens.

Practice Questions

14. __________ ______________ are one-time taxes levied on properties to help pay for some public improvement that benefits the property.

15. Special assessments are not _____ __________ taxes. Usually, special assessments are levied on a ______________ basis for items such as sidewalks and street paving.

16. The maximum rate of interest on a tax certificate is ______________.

17. A holder of a tax certificate that has not been redeemed may request a __________ __________ anytime after __________ years from the date the tax certificate was issued but no later than __________ years after the date the certificate was issued.

18. The city is petitioned to pave the streets in a neighborhood. The paving cost is $35 per foot, and the city is to pay 35% of the cost. There are homes on both sides of the streets to be paved. If the lot frontage on the street is 120 feet, what is the special assessment for the street paving for this homeowner?

18.5 FEDERAL INCOME TAXES

Principal Residence

Tax laws are designed to encourage homeownership and give preferred treatment to taxpayers who own their residences. The owner-occupied residence may be a house, a condominium, or a houseboat (note that the definition of residential property in Chapter 475 applies to brokerage relationships and does not apply for income tax purposes). The homeowner has certain income tax advantages. Homeowners who itemize deductions (rather than claim the standard deduction) on their annual federal income tax returns, may deduct mortgage interest and property taxes. Homeowners will want to compare the higher standard deduction to the amount paid for mortgage interest and property taxes. If the standard deduction exceeds the amount paid for mortgage interest and the property taxes, there is no added benefit to itemize deductions. Tax advantages of owning a principal residence are as follows:

- *Mortgage interest is deductible.* Interest paid on a mortgage loan on a principal and second home is deductible (certain limitations apply).
- *Property tax is deductible.* The annual property taxes paid on principal and second homes are deductible (up to $10,000).
- *IRA withdrawals for first-time homebuyers.* First-time homebuyers may make penalty-free (but not tax-free) withdrawals up to $10,000 from their tax-deferred individual retirement funds (IRAs) for a down payment. Different IRS rules apply to withdrawals from Roth IRAs.
- *Exclusion of gain from the sale of a principal residence.* Up to $250,000 of gain ($500,000 for married couples filing a joint return) realized on the sale or exchange of a principal residence may be excluded.

Additional tax benefits to homeowners are as follows:

- *Interest home equity loans is deductible.* The interest paid is deductible if the loan is used for improvements to the home. If the home equity loan is used to pay off personal expenses, such as paying off credit card debt, the interest would not be deductible.
- *Mortgage loan origination fees and points are deductible.* Loan origination fees and points paid on a mortgage loan to purchase or construct a principal residence are deductible in the year they are paid. Points paid on a refinance loan must be amortized over the life of the loan. Points charged to finance a second home must be deducted over the life of the loan.

Sale of Real Property

Federal income tax laws classify real property as a *capital asset*. **Capital gain** income is profit from the sale of a principal residence, an investment property, a property used in a trade or business, or an income-producing property, and it must be reported for tax purposes. The taxable gain on real estate is determined by two factors:

1. **Adjusted basis** is the original purchase price, plus expenses associated with the purchase and any capital improvements.
2. Amount realized from the sale is the sale price less the expenses associated with the sale.

EXAMPLE: A homeowner originally purchased a new home for $190,000. During the period of ownership, the homeowner spent $15,000 in capital improvements. The homeowner sold the home 10 years later for $265,000. The homeowners paid a brokerage fee of $13,250 and closing costs of $1,155. What is the capital gain from the sale?

Step 1: Calculate the adjusted basis.

$190,000 original purchase price + $15,000 capital improvements = $205,000 adjusted basis

Step 2: Calculate the amount realized from the sale.

$265,000 sale price – $13,250 commission – $1,155 closing costs = $250,595 amount realized

The capital gain (or loss) is the amount realized from the sale less the adjusted basis.

$250,595 amount realized from sale – $205,000 adjusted basis = $45,595 capital gain

Exclusion of Gain From the Sale of a Principal Residence. The IRS allows homeowners to exclude up to $250,000 of gain ($500,000 for married couples filing a joint return) realized on the sale of a principal residence. Any gain above the exclusion is taxed at the applicable capital gains rate. The exclusion is allowed each time taxpayers sell a principal residence, as long as the homeowners have occupied the property as their residence for at least two years during the five-year period ending on the date of the sale.

The taxpayer is not required to reinvest the sale proceeds in a new residence to claim the exclusion. The exclusion of gain is generally allowed only once every two years. However, homeowners who do not meet the two-year requirement because of a change in health, job transfer, or other allowable reasons may be eligible for a prorated exclusion of gain.

Disposition of Real Property From Foreign Sellers. Real estate licensees need to be aware of federal regulations regarding the purchase of real property in the United States from foreign sellers. The sale of real property by a foreign person is subject to the Foreign Investment in Real Property Tax Act (FIRPTA) income tax withholding. FIRPTA requires a buyer of property owned by a foreign investor to withhold 15% of the amount realized on the sale. The sale of a personal residence is exempt if the amount realized is not greater than $300,000. All licensees should encourage their buyers and sellers to consult the IRS or a tax specialist regarding the application of this rule. It is always wise to retain professional counsel regarding tax situations.

WEBLINK @

For additional information regarding FIRPTA withholding, go to https://www.irs.gov/individuals/international-taxpayers/firpta-withholding.

Download the IRS Form 8288 instructions at https://www.irs.gov/pub/irs-pdf/f8288.pdf.

Practice Questions

19. List the tax advantages of homeownership.

    1. ______________________________
    2. ______________________________
    3. ______________________________
    4. ______________________________

20. The exclusion of gain from the sale of a principal residence is up to ______________ of gain, or up to ______________ of gain for married couples filing a joint return, provided the taxpayer-homeowner had occupied the residence for at least two of the last five years.

21. A homeowner originally purchased a new home for $250,000. During the period of ownership, the homeowner spent $28,000 in capital improvements. The homeowner sold the home 15 years later for $339,900. The homeowner paid a brokerage fee of 6% of the sale price and paid out-of-pocket closing costs totaling $2,500. What is the homeowner's capital gain from the sale?

18.6 INVESTMENT PROPERTY

Federal income tax laws encourage real estate investment. Buyers and sellers should always seek competent tax advice to ensure the most favorable tax treatment in a real estate transaction. Advance planning is necessary if an investor's after-tax return on investment is to be maximized.

Types of Income. Recall from Unit 16 the types of income:

- Effective gross income (EGI)
- Net operating income (NOI)

Formula: Effective Gross Income (EGI)

potential gross income (PGI) – vacancy and collection losses + other income = effective gross income (EGI)

Formula: Net Operating Income (NOI)

effective gross income (EGI) – operating expenses = net operating income (NOI)

Determining Taxable Income. An investor's appropriate tax rate is applied to a taxpayer's taxable income. **Taxable income** is the amount of income that remains after all applicable deductions and adjustments to income are applied.

Operating expenses are those cash outlays necessary for running and maintaining the property. Certain operating expenses are deductible from taxable income in the year paid. Property taxes are a fixed operating expense and are deductible from gross income for tax purposes.

The cash "reserve" for replacements is not deductible for tax purposes. Think of reserve for replacements as an emergency savings account. When calculating taxable income, the money held in the savings account would be part of the taxable income. However, any *replacement expenses* actually paid during the tax year are deducted.

EXAMPLE: An investor maintains a reserve in the operating budget of an apartment complex for replacement of items such as carpet, kitchen appliances, and roof shingles. The reserve account totals $180,000. The $180,000 may not be deducted to calculate taxable income. During the tax year, the investor replaced the carpet in 10 of the units at a cost of $20,000. The investor may reduce the taxable income by the $20,000 carpet expense.

Debt service is the amount of money needed to meet the periodic payments of principal and interest on a loan that is being amortized. Investors may deduct the interest paid on the mortgage loan, as well as the costs of obtaining borrowed money. Mortgage interest is deductible in the year paid. Loan origination fees and points are only deductible if charged as a percentage of the loan amount. These fees and points must be amortized over the life of the loan.

Depreciation is a means of deducting the costs of improvements to land over a specified period. The land itself is not depreciable. Depreciation (or cost recovery) allows taxpayers to recover the cost of depreciable property by paying less tax than they would otherwise have to pay.

Under present tax law, the depreciation deduction usually bears little relationship to actual changes in property value. Depreciation is used to stimulate economic expansion by making certain types of real property more attractive to investors. Depreciation is allowed only for business property and income-producing property (which includes investment property). It is not allowed for inventory property or for a personal residence.

Depreciation Components. The *depreciable basis* of the property is the amount that may be depreciated. For real property, it is generally the initial cost of the asset plus acquisition costs minus the value of the land. Acquisition costs generally include such items as the buyer's attorney's fees, appraisal fees, survey fees, and title insurance costs. Because land is not depreciable, this basis (total cost) must be allocated between the improvements (buildings, etc.) and the land, based on the respective values of each.

Straight-Line Method. Depreciation is calculated using the straight-line method. An equal amount of depreciation is taken annually over the useful life of the asset. The Internal Revenue Service (IRS) has currently established useful asset life as 27.5 years for residential rental property and 39 years for nonresidential income-producing property.

Residential rental property can be single-family homes, condominiums, apartments, townhomes, or other types of residential structures. If a property owner purchases a duplex and lives in one of the units and rents the other to tenants, the IRS classifies the unit the property owner lives in as the owner's primary residence and the other unit is classified as residential rental property. Nonresidential income-producing property includes industrial and commercial investment property, such as offices, restaurants, retail stores, warehouses, and so forth.

Formula: Straight-Line Method

total cost to acquire property – value of the land = depreciable basis

depreciable basis ÷ useful life (27.5 or 39 years) = annual IRS depreciation deduction

EXAMPLE 1: In 2019, a duplex classified as a residential real estate investment property was purchased for $250,000, with a land value of $50,000. The depreciable basis is $200,000 ($250,000 sale price less the land value). What is the amount of the yearly depreciation deduction?

$200,000 depreciable basis ÷ 27.5 years = $7,273 annual depreciation deduction

EXAMPLE 2: In 2019, a nonresidential real estate investment property was purchased for $2,350,000, with a land value of $250,000. What is the amount of the yearly depreciation deduction?

$2,350,000 – $250,000 land value = $2,100,000 depreciable basis

$2,100,000 ÷ 39 years = $53,846 annual depreciation deduction (rounded to nearest dollar)

Depreciation provides favorable tax relief as an allowable deduction that requires no current outlay of cash, as is necessary to deduct other expenses (such as property taxes and mortgage interest). In addition, depreciation is based on the total cost of improvements, including that portion paid with borrowed funds (the leveraged portion). An investment is a tax shelter when it shields income or gain from payment of income taxes. One of the features of a tax-sheltered real estate investment is depreciation. Depreciation protects at least a portion of income from tax and also may produce a tax loss, thus possibly creating additional tax sheltering of other income.

Sound real estate investments depend primarily on the inherent productivity of a property, not on its tax aspects. A good real estate investment always combines positive cash flow (if income-producing property) with appreciation of property value. If a property declines in value in an amount equal to or greater than the depreciation deduction allowable for tax purposes, that property is not a tax shelter.

Capital Gains and Capital Losses. Capital gain income results from the sale of capital assets. Capital gains (and losses) are either short term (the asset is held for less than 12 months) or long term (the asset is held for more than 12 months). Capital gains are taxed at the applicable capital gains rate.

A capital gain from the sale of real estate investment property can be used to offset a capital loss from the sale of other investment property. Furthermore, if an investor's capital loss exceeds capital gains, the investor may deduct up to $3,000 in losses in a given year. Assume, for example, an investor has two investment properties. One earns a capital gain of $10,000, and the other has a capital loss of $15,000. The investor can offset the $10,000 gain with $10,000 of the loss. This leaves a net $5,000 loss of which the investor can deduct $3,000. The investor must carry forward the remaining $2,000 loss to the next year. A loss from the sale of your personal residence is not deductible.

Tax on Gain at Time of Sale. In general, when income property is sold for cash, all gain or loss must be recognized (reported) immediately for income tax purposes. The total realized gain is the difference between the net sale price (selling price less selling expenses) and the depreciated basis of the property. The seller pays tax on the gain from the sale of real estate in the year the gain is collected. Because of the tax consequences of the immediate recognition of gain, the installment sale method or a like-kind exchange may provide beneficial tax results.

Installment Sale Method. Under the **installment sale** method, the gain is received over a number of years and the seller recognizes the gain for tax purposes over the same period. The installment sale method relieves the seller of paying tax on gain not yet collected. Generally, it calls for the gain to be reported only as payments are actually received, with each payment treated as part profit and part recovery of investment in the property sold. If an installment sale results in a loss, however, the seller may not use the installment sale method to report the loss over a period of years for tax purposes. A qualified loss must be recognized (reported) in the year of sale. Because the IRS requirements regarding the installment sale method are complex, early tax counsel is mandatory.

Like-Kind Exchange. Real estate investors can defer paying taxes by exchanging real property. The income tax is deferred, not eliminated. A **like-kind exchange** enables a taxpayer-investor to realize the benefits of investment and property appreciation immediately while paying taxes later. When the investor sells the new property (acquired in the exchange), the capital gain will be taxed.

To qualify as a tax-deferred exchange under Section 1031 of the Internal Revenue Code, real property must be exchanged for other real property (hence the term *like-kind*). However, it may be a different type of real property. For example, a multifamily complex can be exchanged for an office complex. Any additional capital or personal property included with the transaction to even out the value of the exchange is called **boot**. The IRS requires tax on the boot to be paid at the time of the exchange by the party who receives it. Because exchanges are subject to a number of IRS rules that must be strictly adhered to, the transactions must be carefully structured, with early tax counsel mandatory. Personal residences and foreign property do not qualify.

Practice Questions

22. __________ income is the amount of income that remains after all applicable deductions and adjustments to income have been applied.

23. _______ ___________ is the amount of money needed to meet the periodic payments of principal and interest on a loan that is being amortized.

18.7 SUMMARY OF IMPORTANT POINTS

- Property taxes are payable for the current year on or after November 1. Unpaid property taxes become delinquent on April 1 of the following year.
- *Assessed value* is the value of a property established for property tax purposes. Property owners use a three-step procedure to protest the assigned assessed value: (1) contact the county property appraiser, (2) appeal to the Value Adjustment Board, and (3) file a suit in court (certiorari proceeding).
- The Value Adjustment Board is made up of five members: two county commissioners, one school board member, and two citizen members.

- Immune properties consist of city, county, state, and federal government properties. Immune properties are not assessed and are not subject to taxation.
- Exempt properties include property belonging to churches and nonprofit organizations. Exempt properties are subject to taxation, but the owner is released from the obligation.
- Partially exempt property is subject to taxation, but the owner is partially relieved of the burden. Taxable value is determined by beginning with assessed value and subtracting appropriate exemptions.
- Florida residents who hold title to a home in Florida and use the home as their permanent residence may homestead the property. Homeowners are entitled to a $25,000 homestead exemption from the assessed value of the home for city, county, and school board taxes. Homesteaded properties with an assessed value greater than $50,000 are entitled to an additional $25,000 homestead exemption from city and county taxes (but not school board taxes).
- An additional $5,000 exemption from the assessed value of homesteaded property is available to widows and widowers, legally blind persons, and nonveterans who are totally and permanently disabled. An additional $5,000 exemption is available to veterans who are at least 10% disabled by military service–connected misfortune.
- Florida's Green Belt Law shields agricultural property from higher tax assessments.
- The Save Our Homes amendment caps how much the assessed value of homesteaded property may increase each year to 3% annually or the CPI, whichever is less.
- The Save Our Homes (SOH) benefit is portable. The homeowner must transfer the homestead exemption for the new home within three tax years of the last qualified homestead exemption.
- A *mill* is one one-thousandth of a dollar or one-tenth of a cent. Cities, counties, and school boards are capped at a basic real property tax rate of no more than 10 mills each.
- *Special assessments* are one-time taxes levied on properties to help pay for a public improvement that benefits the property. A special assessment becomes a lien on the property.
- Property taxes constitute a lien superior to all other liens on real property. Property taxes become a lien on January 1 of each year.
- Property owners who itemize deductions may deduct interest and property taxes. Loan origination fees and points are deductible in the year paid on a loan to finance a principal residence. Points charged to finance a second home must be paid over the life of the loan.
- Deductions from taxable income on investment property include operating expenses (but not reserve for replacements), financing expense, and depreciation.
- *Depreciation* is a means of deducting the cost of improvements to land over a specified time. The land itself is not depreciable. Depreciation is calculated using the straight-line method; an equal amount is taken annually over the useful life of the asset. The IRS has established the useful life of 27.5 years for residential rental property and 39 years for nonresidential income-producing property.

- Under the installment sale method, the gain is received over a number of years and the seller recognizes the gain for income tax purposes over the same period. The installment sale method relieves the seller of paying income tax on gain not yet collected.
- A like-kind exchange enables a taxpayer-investor to realize the benefits of investment and property appreciation immediately while paying taxes later.

UNIT 18 EXAM

1. An investor purchased an apartment building in January for $975,000. The contract specified that 90% of the purchase price was allocated to the building and 10% of the purchase price was for the land. The investor made a down payment of $97,500 and financed the remainder of the purchase. What is the annual IRS depreciation allowance for the property? (Round to nearest dollar.)
   a. $22,500
   b. $31,909
   c. $25,000
   d. $35,455

2. Each year in Florida, property taxes for the previous year become delinquent on
   a. January 1.
   b. April 1.
   c. November 1.
   d. December 31.

3. The first step in protesting the assessed value of real property is to
   a. contact the county property appraiser or a representative.
   b. contact the county tax collector or a representative.
   c. contact the Value Adjustment Board.
   d. file suit against the Value Adjustment Board.

4. The Value Adjustment Board is composed of
   a. the city manager, property appraiser, and three other elected officials.
   b. three school board members and two county commissioners.
   c. one school board member, two county commissioners, and two citizen members.
   d. five school board members and two county commissioners.

5. A 25% service-disabled veteran, who is 75 years old, has been granted a homestead exemption on his $270,000 residence. How much is his total homestead exemption for county taxes?
   a. $25,500
   b. $30,000
   c. $55,000
   d. Totally tax exempt

6. Which statement is FALSE concerning Florida's Green Belt Law?
   a. The law is intended to protect owners of agricultural property.
   b. Farmers' lands are shielded from excessive taxation.
   c. The law has been strengthened by qualifying agricultural land annually.
   d. The law is intended to promote open green spaces along our nation's interstates.

7. If a lot frontage is 100 feet, street paving costs are $40 per running foot, and the city will pay 25% of paving costs, what will be the assessment to the property owner?
   a. $1,000
   b. $1,500
   c. $3,000
   d. $4,000

8. A widow owns a home in Gainesville, Florida, in Alachua County. The city tax rate is 9.3 mills, the county rate is 9.7 mills, and the school district tax rate is 6 mills. The woman has homesteaded her principal residence. Her home has been assessed at $178,000. The amount of total property taxes owed after all allowable tax exemptions is
   a. $3,187.50.
   b. $3,225.00.
   c. $3,344.00.
   d. $3,347.00.

9. Current state law allows the buyer of property tax certificates to collect interest up to a maximum of
   a. 12%.
   b. 18%.
   c. the tax rate in each county.
   d. allowable interest voted by the residents of each county.

10. If a married couple who files jointly realizes a profit from the sale of their home that exceeds $500,000, what is the result?
    a. The homeowners will not pay capital gains tax if at least one of them is older than 55.
    b. Up to $125,000 of the excess profit will be taxed as a capital gain.
    c. The excess gain will be taxed at the current applicable capital gains rate.
    d. The excess gain will be taxed at the homeowner's income tax rate.

11. The maximum amount of profit that may be excluded from taxation on the sale of a home for a qualifying couple, filing separately, is
    a. $125,000.
    b. $150,000.
    c. $250,000.
    d. $500,000.

12. Tax advantages of homeownership do NOT include
    a. a tax deduction of property taxes paid.
    b. penalty-free withdrawal from an IRA if used as a down payment on a personal residence for first-time homebuyers.
    c. exclusion of gain from the sale of a principal residence up to $500,000 for married couples filing a joint return.
    d. a tax deduction of the cost of homeowners hazard insurance.

13. For tax purposes, when the installment sale method is used, gain
    a. is reported as payments are received.
    b. or loss is reported as payments are received.
    c. must be deferred.
    d. or loss must be deferred.

14. Which item is NOT a deductible expense for an income-producing property?
    a. Depreciation
    b. Reserve for replacement
    c. Hazard insurance
    d. Mortgage interest

15. A tax-sheltering real estate investment is one in which the
    a. debt service is greater than net operating income.
    b. secondary purpose is the productivity of the property.
    c. primary purpose is reduction of personal taxable income.
    d. amount of depreciation taken for tax purposes is greater than the actual depreciation of the property.

UNIT

19

PLANNING, ZONING, AND ENVIRONMENTAL HAZARDS

LEARNING OBJECTIVES

When you have completed this unit, you will be able to accomplish the following.

- Describe the composition and authority of the local planning agency and the purpose of land-use controls and the role of zoning ordinances.
- Calculate the number of lots available for development, given the total number of acres contained in a parcel, the percentage of land reserved for streets and other facilities, and the minimum number of square feet per lot.
- Distinguish among the five general zoning classifications, zoning ordinances, building codes, and health ordinances.
- Explain the purpose of a variance, a special exception, and a nonconforming use and describe the characteristics of planned unit developments.
- Understand the basic provisions of the national flood insurance program.
- Explain the various environmental hazards associated with real estate.

KEY TERMS

asbestos
buffer zone
building codes
building inspection
building permit
certificate of occupancy
concurrency
environmental impact statement (EIS)
health ordinance
nonconforming use
planned unit development (PUD)
special exception
special flood hazard area (SFHA)
special purpose property
variance
zoning ordinance

INTRODUCTION

In a residential community located in a fashionable area, homes are meticulously landscaped with rose bushes and beautiful fountains. It is a neighborhood of executives and their families. Across the street from one of the fashionable homes is a small candy factory, and farther down the street is a soft-drink bottling company. This is just one example of what happens when community planning and land-use control are absent.

19.1 HISTORY OF PLANNING AND ZONING

Before the Industrial Revolution, the United States was primarily an agrarian society. Industrialization brought about urbanization as field workers moved to the cities to find factory work. The philosophy of *laissez-faire* prevailed among business and political leaders. Laissez-faire, a philosophy of noninterference by the government in private business affairs, advocated letting the owners of land and business fix the rules of competition. Planning and growth management were largely ignored. Property owners used their land to produce the greatest private gain without regard for the impact on the community. Unorganized growth resulted.

In 1916, the first serious efforts were made to create and enforce zoning ordinances. The garment industry in New York City was about to expand into the exclusive Fifth Avenue district. A zoning ordinance was enacted to protect Fifth Avenue property values by prohibiting all but specified property uses in that district. Other cities began to adopt zoning ordinances to create or protect local property values.

In 1926, the U.S. Supreme Court ruled that legally enacted zoning laws were constitutional. This ruling gave powers of enforcement to municipalities that had enacted zoning laws for the purpose of regulating future growth and to protect residential property. These controls gave rise to city planning and growth management all across the nation.

Florida's Growth Policy and Community Planning Act

163.2514, F.S.

163.3161, F.S.

163.3180, F.S.

Florida's Growth Policy Act requires on a statewide basis that a **concurrency** provision mandating infrastructure for sanitary sewers, potable (drinking) water, and waste treatment facilities be in place before new development is allowed. Many communities have experienced complete curtailment of new construction because of a building moratorium until a new sewage treatment plant, for example, is completed.

Florida's Community Planning Act (CPA) placed growth decisions in the hands of local government while the state's role is to focus designated areas of critical concern. Regulation was shifted from state oversight to local government control of the planning and growth management process. State's role is to focus on protecting the functions of important state resources and facilities. The purpose of the CPA is to manage future development consistent with the role of local government by recognizing and protecting the traditional economic base of the state (agriculture, tourism, and military presence) while also encouraging economic diversification, workforce development, and community planning.

Under the CPA, state-mandated concurrency is not required for transportation, schools, and parks. Local governments have been delegated the discretion to implement as optional elements, or delete existing regulations through a plan amendment. The CPA significantly downsized state growth planning and created the Department of Economic Opportunity (DEO).

Local governments, municipalities, and counties establish development goals by creating a *comprehensive plan*. The comprehensive plan is not a regulatory document. It is a guide that attempts to anticipate changing needs within the community. The plan is a long-term strategic plan that anticipates future growth and services to meet the growth.

Planning Goals

City planning attempts to achieve the following basic goals:

- *Save tax money by preventing sprawl.* Urban sprawl is characterized by low density, automobile-dependent development with either a single use or multiple uses that are not functionally related, requiring the extension of public facilities and services in an inefficient manner, and failing to provide a clear separation between urban and rural uses.
- *Provide adequate provision of services.*
- *Provide for road right-of-ways and setbacks.* Setback provisions are designed to keep buildings away from streets and to ensure that occupants have more light and air and less noise, smoke, dust, danger of spread of fire, and in some cases, a better view at street intersections.
- *Protect against costly drainage, flooding, and environmental problems.*
- *Reduce problems associated with political and equity issues caused by existing landfills, prisons, and so forth.*

LOCAL PLANNING AGENCY

Composition

163.2514, F.S.

163.3180, F.S.

Planning commissions are most effective when composed of members who represent all walks of life. Members most often are not trained professional planners. The overriding goal is to have representatives from a cross section of interests. A planning commission composed entirely of developers, for example, could not possibly speak for all the people. The homes, desires, and goals of all residents should be considered.

Members of the planning commission are usually appointed (not elected) and serve in a voluntary, unpaid capacity. The primary legislative body of the city or the county is the appointing authority, usually a city council or a county commission. Planning commissions vary in size, and the terms for which planning commissioners are appointed may vary from the terms of their colleagues. This ensures a staggered rate of replacement and is designed to prevent any one appointing authority from selecting an entire planning commission. Planning commissioners are usually appointed for terms longer than the term of the appointing authority to reduce the commissioners' obligation to any single political body. This minimizes political influence within the planning body.

The planning commission or board serves as an advisory body to the elected city or county government. As important as the planning function may be to the future welfare of a community, the commission is not the final authority in matters related to planning. The commission is responsible for planning, just as the police department is responsible for law enforcement, but the elected government must make the final decisions based on recommendations from subordinate agencies.

Authority

Three areas of responsibility for which city planning commissions are commonly delegated final authority are (1) subdivision plat approval, (2) site plan approval, and (3) sign control.

Subdivision Plat Approval. A developer planning to create a subdivision must submit a *subdivision plat* to the planning commission for approval (also see Unit 1). A developer is not issued a building permit until final approval is granted by the planning commission. When approval is received, the developer may proceed to record the plat in the public records and receive a building permit.

Site Plan Approval. The *site plan* serves the same function that a subdivision plat serves for a subdivision. It is a detailed plan of how the project is to be developed, how traffic and parking will be dealt with, and what impact on neighboring properties may be expected. This is an area in which the expertise of the planning commission's support staff can be of great assistance. Reviewing and checking site plan proposals requires painstaking attention to detail and a well-rounded background of information. This ensures compliance with all physical, economic, and environmental requirements.

Sign Control. More and more cities are exercising control over signs. The primary aims of sign control are to minimize distraction to motorists and to eliminate actual safety hazards created by signs at blind corners, lighted signs that glare into the eyes of drivers at night, and the like. Any aesthetic improvement resulting from sign control is a welcomed by-product.

Support Staff

While appointed members of the commission may be experts in their own fields, they often are not urban planning experts. The planning commission's function is to make policy recommendations regarding the type of city it feels that citizens want in the future. It sets goals and provides residents with a number of feasible alternative plans for achieving those goals. The job of collecting, sorting, analyzing, and reporting is handled by the staff of the planning commission.

The planning commission support staff is composed of full-time city or county employees. Staff members are normally college- or university-trained planners. They have learned how to evaluate the economic base of a city. They know the most productive sources of information regarding population, proper land uses, and support requirements for future growth. The planning support staff collects and refines the raw data to produce the basic studies needed to develop a flexible, comprehensive plan for future growth.

Practice Questions

1. List the three areas of final authority of local planning commissions.

    1. ______________________________

    2. ______________________________

    3. ______________________________

2. The philosophy of noninterference by the government with regard to land use is ______________.

3. One of the goals of city planning is to prevent ____________ ____________.

19.2 CALCULATING LOTS PER ACRE

Assume that a particular residential zone—for example, R-1A—requires that all lots in that subcategory contain at least 9,000 square feet of land. This automatically restricts the number of lots a developer can create from each acre in a subdivision. Every acre of land contains 43,560 square feet. With this information, we can calculate the number of lots available for development. In the process of turning raw land into a subdivision, between 20% and 25% of the land is commonly used for streets and open space. Wider streets and open green space add quality but reduce the amount of land available for lots.

Formula: Buildable Lots in a Tract

43,560 square feet per acre × percent available for lots = square feet available for lots per acre

Square feet available for lots per acre × number of acres in tract = total available square feet

Total available square feet ÷ minimum square feet per lot = number of buildable lots in tract

EXAMPLE 1: A tract of 100 acres is being developed. The applicable zoning requires a minimum of 9,000 square feet per residential lot. The developer must set aside 25% of the acreage for streets, sidewalks and so forth. How many buildable lots are in the tract?

43,560 square feet per acre × .75 available for lots = 32,670 square feet available for lots per acre

32,670 × 100 acres in tract = 3,267,000 total available square feet

3,267,000 ÷ 9,000 minimum square feet per lot = 363 buildable lots

EXAMPLE 2: A tract of 20 acres is being developed. The county requires that the subdivision reserve 10% of the tract for common space. The developer is also planning for an entry road that will be 500 feet long by 30 feet wide. The county requires a minimum of 12,000 square feet per residential lot. How many buildable lots are in the tract?

In this example, there is an extra step to subtract the square footage allocated for the entry road. Proceed with the first two steps in the formula for buildable lots in a tract.

43,560 square feet per acre × .90 = 39,204 square feet available after allowing for common space

39,204 square feet available per acre × 20 acres = 784,080 total available square feet (before allowing for the road)

Now, calculate the square footage allocated to the entry road and subtract that value to determine the total buildable square footage in tract.

500 × 30 = 15,000 square feet for road

784,080 – 15,000 = 769,080 total buildable square feet in tract

769,080 ÷ 12,000 minimum square feet per lot = 64 buildable lots

Practice Questions

4. A residential zoning category requires at least 10,000 square feet per lot. The developer is reserving 30% of the land to streets, sidewalks, and a community center. The tract of land for development consists of 125 acres. How many residential lots are available for development?

19.3 ZONING, LAND USE RESTRICTIONS, AND BUILDING CODES

Zoning Ordinances

Zoning ordinances are local laws that implement the comprehensive plan. Local government exercises *police power* by regulating and controlling the use of land and structures within designated land-use districts or zones. Each zone is assigned a specific land-use classification. No other land-use controls affect all properties in a community to a greater degree than zoning ordinances. Zoning regulations control types of structures allowed, lot sizes, building heights, setbacks (distance from the lot line to the building line), and density. Used in conjunction with building codes, they are effective in protecting property values.

Zoning Classifications

Residential. Residential zoning controls *density*, or the number of homes per acre. The zoning classification for residential typically begins with "R." Residential zoning regulates minimum lot size, setback requirements (distance from the lot line to the building line), and lot coverage. The residential zoning classification is usually further divided into subcategories that establish different minimum sizes for lots. For example, in the same county, residential zoning subcategory R-1AA may require one-acre lots, while R-1B may require only a minimum of 8,000 square feet per lot. Zoning authorities may create as many zoning subcategories as needed.

Commercial. The purpose of commercial zoning is to regulate *intensity* of use. Commercial zoning regulates parking requirements and building height and size limitations. Zoning ordinances often create a buffer zone between residential and commercial zones. A **buffer zone** is a strip of land separating one land use from another. Frequently, the buffer zone will allow multifamily zoning (for example, apartments) next to single-family residential areas, then a professional business zone, then higher intensity commercial zones.

Industrial. Industrial zoning controls emissions and effluents. Industrial zoning controls industry's by-products, such as noise, odor, smoke congestion, and chemicals.

Agricultural. The agricultural zoning classification is an all-inclusive category; it is not divided into subcategories. If the existing use of the property is for some type of agriculture, no zoning controls will attempt to regulate the type of agriculture permitted. If the use fails to qualify for an agricultural classification, the property then can be rezoned into another zoning category.

Special Use. Most zoning authorities consider all property owned by all levels of government as a type of special use property. Special use zoning includes, for example, city parks, county courthouses, and federal post office buildings. This zoning category is exempt from local zoning regulation.

Building Codes

553.72(2), F.S.

Building codes protect the public health and safety from inferior construction practices. Building codes set minimum standards for materials and quality of workmanship, sanitary equipment, electrical wiring, fire prevention, and so forth. Florida has a statewide building code called the *Florida Building Code (Code)*. The Florida Building Commission is responsible for the Florida Building Code. The Code incorporates building, electric, plumbing, mechanical and administrative codes, including accessibility, energy, coastal, manufactured, and state agency codes. Included in the Code is Florida's energy code. It is a minimum standard for energy use in buildings. The energy code sets minimum *R-values* for walls, ceilings, and floors. R-value refers to the effectiveness of insulation and is measured by its resistance to heat flow. The higher the R-value, the better the energy efficiency. The energy code also sets standards for overall energy efficiency of residential structures, called the building envelope.

The Florida Building Code also includes wind-speed maps. Coastal areas of Florida must meet higher *wind load* requirements compared with interior counties. The Florida Building Code requires that new construction and structural renovations to existing structures be engineered to withstand high winds. Wind load (not wind speed alone) controls design requirements for construction. Implementation of the Code requires many design considerations to be taken into account to properly determine a structure's wind load design.

553.72(2), F.S.

Local government enforces building codes. The process begins by issuing a **building permit** after review of the architectural and engineering drawings. Part of the building permit process is the energy code compliance certification. A code official must review the plans and specifications and the energy calculations and sign off on the building permit that the project is in compliance with the Florida Energy Code. Also included in the permit process is determining whether the plans and specifications meet wind load requirements for roofs, doors, windows, shutters, and so forth.

Inspectors visit each job site and conduct **building inspections** at various phases of construction. The inspections must pass before the next phase of construction can proceed. A final **certificate of occupancy** is issued once construction is completed and the municipal building inspector agrees that the structure conforms to code.

WEBLINK

To learn more about the Florida building code, visit https://www.floridabuilding.org/dca/dca_fbc_default.aspx.

Health Ordinances

Health ordinances control maintenance and sanitation of public spaces. The local health department inspects and enforces sanitary standards in a community's food and drinking establishments.

Practice Questions

5. List five major zoning classifications.

   1. ____________________
   2. ____________________
   3. ____________________
   4. ____________________
   5. ____________________

6. ________ ____________ are local laws that implement the comprehensive plan.

7. Residential zoning controls ____________ by regulating minimum ________ ________, ____________ requirements, and ______ __________.

8. A ________ ________ is a strip of land separating one land use from another.

19.4 APPEALS AND EXCEPTIONS

Zoning Board of Adjustment

Owners of real estate may appeal enforcement of zoning restrictions in cases where strict compliance would cause undue hardship or reduce property values. To handle appeals and requests for relief, most zoning authorities have established a semijudicial body called the zoning board of adjustment or, simply, board of adjustment. The primary function of the zoning board of adjustment is to provide property owners some degree of relief from otherwise rigid zoning codes. The board must take all possible precautions to render objective, unbiased decisions because its quasi-judicial powers give it some of the characteristics of a court. Once the zoning board of adjustment renders a decision, most zoning laws will allow a property owner only one additional avenue of appeal, litigation in the courts.

Variances. A **variance** allows a property owner to *vary* from strict compliance with all or part of a zoning code because to comply would force an undue hardship on the property owner. Two conditions must be met before a property owner may be granted a variance from existing zoning requirements:

- The property owner must show that a *hardship* exists or will be created by strict compliance with zoning requirements and that the owner did nothing to cause the hardship. This will prevent a property owner or developer from taking some action designed for private benefit with the expectation that the zoning board of adjustment will accept or approve the situation the property owner or developer created.
- The zoning board of adjustment must use the same established criteria to judge the validity of all requests for a variance. This ensures fair and impartial treatment for each property owner requesting a variance.

Many people have trouble with the word *hardship*. It has nothing to do with economic or personal hardships. It involves land *use*, and the hardship must relate to the use of the property. For example, suppose you bought a nice lot on a river where zoning restrictions require "setback" distances of 25 feet from the front of the lot and 30 feet from the river or rear of the lot. Imagine you are about to start construction of a new house designed to fit precisely according to the setback requirements when a survey reveals that erosion by the river over time has carried away 10 feet from the river side of your lot. The maximum setback distance possible is now only 20 feet. Because zoning restrictions require 30 feet, you will be in violation if you go ahead with construction. Violation of zoning laws can cause removal of the offending structure. To prevent potential trouble, you request a variance. The hardship exists, and you did nothing to cause the hardship. You would have met the hardship requirement for a variance (the first condition in the preceding list).

Special Exceptions. The zoning board of adjustment is authorized to issue **special exceptions** for controlling the location of particular land uses. A dentist's office might be granted a special exception in an area located near a large mobile home community. Another example is an adult day care facility in a residential area composed primarily of retirees. A special exception grants a specific use of a particular parcel. Special exceptions are a departure from the zoning ordinance, generally permitted in cases where it is determined that the surrounding area would be better served by allowing the special exception. Most communities require public hearings before a special exception is granted so that property owners of surrounding parcels have an opportunity to provide input in the decision process. **Special purpose property** refers to a combination of land and improvements with only one economically feasible use because of some special design, such as a place of worship, nursing home, school, post office, or hospital.

Legally Nonconforming Uses. If a property's use was lawfully established but no longer conforms to the use regulations of the zone in which it is located because of the enactment of a new zoning ordinance, the use is allowed to continue as a **nonconforming use**. For example, a small neighborhood gas station might have located in an area that was later zoned residential. The gas station is *grandfathered* as a nonconforming use.

The U.S. Constitution prohibits depriving a person of property without due process or fair compensation. Local governments may not employ eminent domain powers to correct nonconforming uses unless the property is taken for a public use. The methods used to correct a nonconforming use vary around the state. Most zoning authorities allow a time period long enough for nonconforming property owners to recapture their investment in the property. After the expiration of this designated period, the property owner must convert the use of the property to that use for which the area is zoned. If, during the designated period, the structure on the property is damaged or more than 50% destroyed, the property must be converted to a use that conforms to area zoning. Other communities allow a legal nonconforming use to continue until ownership changes. Nonconforming-use properties usually are not permitted to be increased in size or to undergo structural changes. Most zoning authorities restrict repairs and maintenance of such properties to those needed for sanitation and safety purposes. These procedures are designed to result in all properties eventually becoming conforming-use properties (see Figure 19.1).

FIGURE 19.1 ■ Government Land-Use Controls

Method	Function
Building code	Controls construction and materials
Zoning ordinance	Controls use
Health ordinance	Controls maintenance and sanitation
Variance	Permission to build or use to relieve a hardship not caused by owner
Special exception	Permission to build or use in apparent conflict with existing zoning ordinance
Nonconforming use	Permission to continue to use in spite of enacted zoning ordinance

Developments of Regional Impact

380.06, F.S.

Florida statute defines *developments of regional impact (DRIs)* as any development that, because of its character, size, or location, will have a substantial effect on the health, safety, or welfare of citizens of more than one county in the state. Statewide guidelines and standards, along with numerical "thresholds" (limits), are used to determine whether particular developments must undergo DRI review. DRIs include projects such as shopping centers and malls, and attraction and sports facilities.

Guidelines and standards considered when evaluating DRI proposals include the following:

- Extent to which the development would create or alleviate environmental problems, including air, water pollution, or noise
- Amount of pedestrian or vehicular traffic likely to be generated
- Number of persons likely to be residents, employees, or otherwise present
- Size of the site to be occupied
- Likelihood that additional or subsidiary development will be generated

- Extent to which the development would create an additional demand for, or additional use of, energy, including the energy requirements of subsidiary developments
- Unique qualities of particular areas of the state

Planned Unit Development

A **planned unit development (PUD)** is a type of special land use allowed under most local zoning ordinances. The developer clusters residential units on smaller lots to create maximum open spaces. The open spaces are typically developed into parks and recreation areas. The dwelling lots and structures are individually owned. A nonprofit community association is organized to provide for maintenance of the common areas. The special characteristics of PUDs are summarized in the paragraphs that follow.

Clustered Homes. Clustering homes together on smaller lots allows for large open green spaces. Clustering results in the same overall density as in a conventional development; however, the clustered improvements result in more open common areas.

Mixed Land Use. A variety of types of housing may include single-family detached homes in addition to, for example, town houses and garden apartments. Some PUDs incorporate shopping, restaurant, and entertainment facilities into the development to create a sense of community. *Mixed land use* is the use of real property for more than one use, such as a condominium that has residential and commercial units. It could, for example, combine residential units with a neighborhood restaurant and office space.

Practice Questions

9. A property owner may qualify for a ______________ if the owner can prove a hardship exists.

10. Legal permission to change the use of a property in apparent conflict with a zoning classification requires the owner to seek a __________ ______________.

19.5 ENVIRONMENTAL REQUIREMENTS AND LEGISLATION

Environmental Impact Statement

When a large project is proposed, an environmental impact study is conducted to analyze the long-term impact the project will have on the quality of the surrounding environment. The study must estimate the impact on waste-disposal systems, air quality, traffic, local employment, and so forth. An **environmental impact statement (EIS)** summarizes into a single document the long-term effect the proposed project will have on the surrounding environment. The EIS provides local government agencies and the public with important information regarding the environmental impact that can be expected from proposed development.

National Flood Insurance Program (NFIP)

Qualifying for the Flood Insurance. Congress created the National Flood Insurance Program (NFIP) to help provide property owners with coverage against losses due to flooding. The NFIP offers flood insurance to homeowners, renters, and business owners if their community participates in the NFIP. Participating communities agree to adopt and enforce ordinances that meet or exceed Federal Emergency Management Agency (FEMA) requirements to reduce the risk of flooding. FEMA administers the flood program. Flood insurance can be purchased through insurance agencies for property located in communities participating in the NFIP. More than 40% of purchasers of flood insurance are Floridians.

Flood Insurance Rate Maps (FIRMs). FEMA prepares Flood Insurance Rate Maps (FIRMs) for every city and county in the United States. Flood maps identify flood zones, which are geographic areas that FEMA has defined according to varying levels of flood risk and type of flooding. The zones are depicted on the FIRM. Zones are categorized as low-risk, moderate-risk, and high-risk areas.

Special Flood Hazard Areas. High-risk flood hazard areas are identified on the FIRM as **special flood hazard areas (SFHAs)**. SFHAs are located in a base flood area (100-year floodplain) and are areas that have a 1% or greater chance of being inundated by a flood event in a given year, which is equivalent to a 26% chance of flooding over the life of a 30-year mortgage. Floodplain areas located in SFHAs are identified on the FIRM as A zones.

High-Risk Coastal Areas. Coastal land located in SFHAs is identified on the FIRM as V zones. High-risk coastal areas have a 1% or greater chance of flooding and an additional hazard associated with storm waves. In communities that participate in the NFIP, mandatory flood insurance purchase requirements apply to high-risk coastal areas (Zone V).

Development Within SFHAs. Because of their coastal location, buildings in V zones are subject to a greater hazard than buildings built in floodplain A zones. NFIP regulations require coastal communities to ensure that buildings built in V zones are anchored to protect against the impact of waves, hurricane-force winds, and erosion acting simultaneously. The NFIP requires that all new and substantially improved residential structures in V zones be elevated to or above the base flood elevation (BFE), on open foundations (such as pilings) that allow floodwaters and waves to pass beneath the elevated structures. Nonresidential structures must meet the residential requirement or be watertight below the BFE.

Mortgage Loan Requirements. For every mortgage transaction involving a structure in the United States, lenders review the current FIRM, for the community in which the property is located, to determine its location relative to the Special Flood Hazard Area (SFHA). Structures located in an SFHA (A zones and V zones) that are financed with mortgage loans from federally regulated or insured lenders are required to have flood insurance. Flood insurance is available, but not mandatory, for property located in low-risk and moderate-risk areas in communities that participate in the NFIP.

Cost of Flood Insurance. Recent changes have been made to funding of the NFIP. These changes may result in substantial increases in the flood insurance premiums a new owner will be required to pay. Licensees should advise buyers to research the cost of flood insurance premiums for a property located in an SFHA.

WEBLINK

For additional information regarding flood insurance, visit www.floodsmart.gov and www.fema.gov/national-flood-insurance-program/.

Practice Questions

11. Land located in a base flood area (100-year floodplain) is called a ___________ __________ ___________ _________.

19.6 ENVIRONMENTAL HAZARDS ASSOCIATED WITH REAL ESTATE

Asbestos

Asbestos is a mineral fiber in common use until 1978 in a variety of building construction materials for insulation and as a fire retardant. These products include, for example, pipe insulation wrapping; furnace encasements; shingles, siding, and roofing; resilient floor tiles; the backing on vinyl sheet flooring; and stove and oven door gaskets. Any products manufactured today that contain asbestos must be labeled clearly. Asbestos fibers become dangerous when they are disturbed or removed improperly, causing the fibers to become airborne. Inhaling microscopic asbestos fibers can result in respiratory diseases, including lung scarring, lung cancer, and cancer of the chest cavity.

Not all asbestos-containing material poses a hazard. It is best not to disturb asbestos material that is in good condition. Generally, material in good condition does not release asbestos fibers. Care should be taken to prevent the material from being damaged, disturbed, or touched. The danger escalates when the fibers become fragile or exposed to the air. An alternative to removing the asbestos is to encapsulate (seal off) disintegrating asbestos. A Phase I environmental assessment should include an asbestos inspection in any structure built before 1978. The EPA recommends periodic inspection of known asbestos-containing material for signs of damage or deterioration. An owner who is considering renovating or remodeling a structure containing asbestos materials should consult an asbestos specialist.

Radon

You cannot see, smell, or taste radon, yet it is all around us—even in the fresh air we breathe. Outdoors, radon is not a problem because the surrounding air and natural breezes allow the gas to dissipate into the atmosphere. However, when radon gas accumulates in high concentrations within buildings, it is known to cause lung cancer. Well-insulated, energy-efficient homes especially tend to trap radon gas. Decaying uranium in the soil produces radon gas, which can seep into homes and accumulate. Radon typically moves up through the ground to the air above and into a home through cracks in the foundation, utility conduits, spaces around the plumbing, basement floors and walls, and crawl spaces.

Chapter 404, F.S., mandates radon disclosure at the time or before a person enters into a contract for sale and purchase or a rental agreement. Florida law does not require testing to determine radon levels before sale or lease of any building (see "Disclosures," Unit 11).

Lead-Based Paint

It is estimated that 75% of the nation's housing stock built before 1978 (about 64 million dwellings) contains lead-based paint, and the vast majority of homes built before 1950 contain substantial amounts of lead-based paint. The federal government has determined that as many as 3 million children younger than age six in this country have low-level lead poisoning. The ingestion of household dust containing lead from deteriorating lead-based paint is the most common cause of lead poisoning in children. At low levels, lead poisoning in children causes intelligence quotient deficiencies, reading and learning disabilities, impaired hearing, reduced attention span, hyperactivity, and behavior problems.

Congress passed the Residential Lead-Based Paint Hazard Reduction Act in 1992. The law requires the disclosure of known information on lead-based paint and lead-based paint hazards before the sale or lease of most housing built before 1978. Lead-based paint hazards are any conditions that expose people to lead from lead-contaminated dust, lead-contaminated soil, or lead-contaminated paint that has deteriorated or is present in accessible surfaces, such as window sills. When listing a pre-1978 property for sale, the licensee is responsible for making certain that sellers comply with the law. The law pertains only to housing built before 1978 because the Consumer Product Safety Commission banned the use of lead-based paint for residential use in that year (see "Disclosures," Unit 11).

Mold

Molds reproduce by means of tiny spores; the spores are invisible to the naked eye and float through outdoor and indoor air. Mold may begin growing indoors when mold spores land on wet surfaces. There are many types of mold, and none of them will grow without water or moisture.

482.071, F.S.

Molds have the potential to cause health problems. Molds produce allergens (substances that can cause allergic reactions), irritants, and in some cases, potentially toxic substances. Inhaling or touching mold or mold spores may cause allergic reactions in sensitive individuals. Allergic responses include hay-fever-like symptoms, such as sneezing, runny nose, red eyes, and skin rash (dermatitis). Allergic reactions to mold are common. They can be immediate or delayed. Molds can also cause asthma attacks in people with asthma who are allergic to mold. In addition, mold exposure can irritate the eyes, skin, nose, throat, and lungs of both mold-allergic and non-allergic people. Symptoms other than the allergic and irritant types are not commonly reported as being related to inhaling mold. Research on mold and health effects is ongoing.

468.84, F.S.

The DBPR licenses mold assessors and remediators. Florida law prohibits anyone from performing or offering to perform mold remediation to a structure if that mold assessor or the mold assessor's company provided a mold assessment within the past 12 months. It is a violation to accept compensation, inducement, or reward from a mold assessor or mold assessor's company for the referral of business from the mold assessor or the mold assessor's company or to offer compensation, inducement, or reward to a mold assessor or mold assessor's company for the referral of business from the mold assessor or the mold assessor's company.

If a real estate licensee suspects that mold is present in a home, the licensee should ask questions about leaks, floods, and prior damage and remind the sellers to disclose any insurance claims regarding mold or other water issues.

Water Supply

Groundwater is below the earth's surface and forms the water table, the natural level at which the ground is saturated. The underground water can be contaminated from leaking underground storage tanks (USTs), septic systems, storm drains, herbicides, and other sources. Contamination can threaten private wells and public water supplies. The Safe Drinking Water Act regulates the public drinking water supply. On transfer of ownership, any water source other than a municipal supply should be tested, as should septic systems.

Wood-Destroying Organisms

The Florida Department of Agriculture and Consumer Services licenses individuals and businesses engaged in the pest control business, including termites and other wood-destroying organisms. When an inspection for wood-destroying organisms is made by a pest-control-licensed company for purposes of a real estate transaction and either a fee is charged for the inspection or a written report is requested by the customer, a wood-destroying organism inspection report must be provided by the licensed company. The inspection must be made in accordance with standards established by rule and must include inspection for all wood-destroying organisms. The inspection findings must be reported to the person requesting the inspection.

The inspection report must include the date of the inspection; disclosure of any visible accessible areas that were not inspected and the reasons for not inspecting them; description of the areas of the structure that were inaccessible; any visible evidence of previous treatments for, or infestations of, wood-destroying organisms; the identity of any wood-destroying organisms present; and any visible damage caused.

If any pest control treatment is provided at the time of the inspection, the inspection report must also provide the name of each of the wood-destroying organisms for which treatment was provided, the name of the pesticide used, and all conditions and terms associated with that treatment. The inspection report must also include a statement certifying that the inspector has no financial interest in the property and the inspector is not associated in any way with a party to the transaction other than for inspection purposes.

The inspector must post the inspection notice immediately adjacent to the access to the attic or crawl area or other readily accessible area of the property inspected. It is a violation for anyone other than the property owner to remove the notice. A copy of the inspection report must be retained by the pest control company for three years.

Practice Questions

12. ______________ is a mineral fiber that was used in a variety of building construction materials for insulation and as a fire retardant.

13. Florida law requires radon ______________ at the time of or before entering into a contract for sale or rental.

14. Florida law does __________ require testing to determine radon levels before sale or lease of real property.

15. When a real estate licensee lists pre-1978 property for sale, it becomes the responsibility of the ______________ to make certain ______________ comply with the lead-based paint law.

19.7 SUMMARY OF IMPORTANT POINTS

- City planning commissions are delegated final authority for subdivision plat approval, site plan approval, and sign control.
- Zoning ordinances authorize the segmentation (dividing) of a community into districts or zones in keeping with the character of the land and structures and their suitability for particular uses to protect against uses that might reduce the value of neighboring properties.
- Building codes protect the public health and safety from inferior construction practices. The Florida Building Code is a statewide building code.
- Residential zoning regulates density, meaning the number of homes per acre. Commercial zoning regulates intensity of use, such as vehicular traffic generated by a commercial enterprise.
- A *buffer zone* is a strip of land separating one land use from another.

- The zoning board of adjustment handles appeals and requests from property owners for zoning changes.
- Variances allow property owners to vary from strict compliance with all or part of a zoning code because to comply would force an undue hardship on the property owner.
- *Special exception* is permission to build or to use property in apparent conflict with existing zoning ordinances.
- *Nonconforming use* is continuing land use that is not in compliance with a newly enacted zoning ordinance.
- A *planned unit development (PUD)* is a self-contained development planned under special zoning ordinances that allow maximum use of open space by reducing lot sizes and street sizes.
- Environmental impact statements summarize the effect that proposed development will have on the surroundings.
- Congress created the National Flood Insurance Program (NFIP) to help provide property owners with coverage against losses due to flooding. The NFIP offers flood insurance to homeowners, renters, and business owners if their community participates in the NFIP.
- Asbestos is a mineral fiber that was used in a variety of building construction materials for insulation and as a fire retardant.
- Florida law requires radon disclosure at the time of or before entering into a contract for sale or rental. The law does not require testing to determine radon levels.
- Sellers and landlords must disclose the presence of lead-based paint in homes built before 1978.

UNIT 19 EXAM

1. One of the major reasons for the lack of emphasis on city planning prior to the 1900s was the
   a. focus on identifying and locating rural tracts for farming using a new method of describing real property.
   b. philosophy of laissez-faire.
   c. reduction in university course offerings in real estate and urban development.
   d. exodus from the farms to the cities for jobs.

2. The section in Florida's Growth Policy that requires that sewers and drinking water be available before new development is allowed is called the
   a. utilities provision.
   b. infrastructure provision.
   c. concurrency provision.
   d. level of service provision.

3. A planning commission is usually composed of
   a. trained professional planners.
   b. elected officials.
   c. appointed unpaid members.
   d. members of the primary legislative city or county body.

4. The BEST composition of a planning commission is generally thought to be one with representation from
   a. each licensed professional occupation.
   b. senior adult homeowners because of their experience.
   c. real estate and mortgage lending firms.
   d. a cross section of interests.

5. Florida law requires disclosure of which environmental hazard before or at the time of entering into all residential sale or lease contracts?
   a. Radon gas
   b. Lead-based paint hazard
   c. Mold
   d. Erosion

6. The primary function of a planning commission is to
   a. make policy recommendations to the elected government body.
   b. make policy recommendations to the trained professional staff.
   c. advise the next higher planning board (county, regional, etc.) of its recommendations and actions.
   d. collect, refine, and produce the basic studies needed to develop a comprehensive plan for future growth.

7. A strip of land that separates one land use from another is called
   a. an easement.
   b. an egress.
   c. a buffer zone.
   d. a median.

8. Minimum standards for quality of workmanship, electrical wiring, and fire prevention are found in Florida's
   a. building code.
   b. concurrency provision.
   c. comprehensive plan.
   d. health ordinance.

9. To be granted a variance, a property owner must provide evidence that
   a. the same treatment has been afforded other owners.
   b. a hardship related to land use exists.
   c. the variance, if granted, will be for the owner's use only.
   d. the land use existed before passage of zoning laws.

10. Residential zoning is designed to regulate
    a. intensity.
    b. frequency.
    c. density.
    d. all of these.

11. Commercial zoning is designed to regulate
    a. intensity.
    b. frequency.
    c. density.
    d. all of these.

12. A small general store that existed before a change to residential zoning is an example of a
    a. special exception.
    b. variance.
    c. PUD.
    d. nonconforming use.

13. The legal right to enact zoning laws is derived from
    a. police powers.
    b. public policy.
    c. property taxation.
    d. all of these.

14. Zoning ordinances regulate
    a. the firewall rating of a wall located between the kitchen and dining areas of a restaurant.
    b. the setback requirements of a building from the property lines.
    c. the electrical rating of the wiring in a residential home.
    d. all of these.

15. A parcel of land contains 75 acres. A developer has reserved 25% of the land for streets and green space. Applicable zoning regulations require a minimum of 9,500 square feet per residential lot. The number of permissible lots is
    a. 86.
    b. 232.
    c. 257.
    d. 260.

APPENDIX A: PRACTICE END-OF-COURSE EXAM

This practice exam consists of 100 multiple-choice questions. While a student who achieves a score of at least 80% without using any reference material should be in a strong position relative to subsequent examinations, it is important to note that the experience will likely be different from practice exam to final exam to licensing exam. Because there are more testable topics than there are questions on the licensing exam, the licensing exam experience is different from one attempt to the next. It is recommended that at least two hours of uninterrupted time be budgeted to take this exam.

1. A licensed real estate broker has been hired by a lender to appraise a home for a buyer who has applied for an FHA loan. Which statement is TRUE regarding this situation?
   a. The broker's license entitles him to appraise this property.
   b. The broker may not charge for this assignment.
   c. The broker is required to be a state-certified appraiser to perform this appraisal assignment.
   d. The broker may not accept this appraisal assignment because to do so is a conflict of interest.

2. Which disclosure must be given to the buyer of both new and resale residential condominium units?
   a. Prospectus
   b. Governance form
   c. Estimated operating budget
   d. Declaration

3. An individual who typically finds a tenant for property and collects a fee is referred to as
   a. an absentee owner.
   b. a property manager.
   c. a community association manager.
   d. a rental agent.

4. Failure to comply with the statute of frauds will result in
   a. a charge of fraud.
   b. an illegal contract.
   c. an unenforceable contract.
   d. a revocation of licensure.

5. Which property is NOT covered under the Fair Housing Act?
   a. Multifamily housing of five or more units
   b. Commercial property
   c. Government-owned residential property
   d. Privately owned residential property listed by a broker

6. A broker received a $5,000 deposit from a buyer on Tuesday at 1:00 pm. The seller will not be available until Monday. The broker's normal banking day is Monday. The broker is required to deposit the $5,000 before the end of
   a. the next business day.
   b. business on Wednesday.
   c. business on Thursday.
   d. business on Friday.

7. Which expense is subtracted to derive NOI?
   a. Vacancy and collection losses
   b. Mortgage payments
   c. Income taxes
   d. Depreciation

8. An investor wanted to build a motel. A broker showed him three choice sites zoned hotel-motel. The investor promised to decide on a site in three weeks, so the broker took a two-week vacation. When the broker returned, the investor bought one of these sites. The broker sold the site, not knowing that the zoning on that site had been changed to industrial. Which is correct?
   a. The broker is guilty of culpable negligence.
   b. The broker is not guilty of wrongdoing.
   c. The property owner is guilty of fraud.
   d. The broker is guilty of fraud.

9. Which clause is included in a mortgage to prevent a subsequent buyer from assuming an existing mortgage loan?
   a. Acceleration clause
   b. Defeasance clause
   c. Due-on-sale clause
   d. Prepayment penalty clause

10. Within what period of time must landlords of five or more units notify tenants in writing of the method used to hold security deposits?
    a. 3 business days
    b. 15 days
    c. 21 days
    d. 30 days

11. The seller instructs the listing broker not to show his home to members of a protected class. The broker informs the seller that this is a violation of fair housing laws, but the seller is insistent. Which choice is the broker's best course of action under these circumstances?
    a. Report the incident to the Fair Housing Administration
    b. Report the seller to the DBPR
    c. Withdraw from the listing agreement
    d. Follow the seller's instructions because to do otherwise would violate the broker's fiduciary duties to the seller

12. A buyer or seller must be given a brokerage relationship disclosure for which transaction?
    a. Purchaser of an auctioned residential property
    b. Owner who lists a 10-unit townhouse property
    c. Purchaser of 15 acres of land zoned for 15 residential homes
    d. Purchaser of a single-family home working with a single agent buyer's broker

13. A woman has homesteaded her residence. Her home has an assessed value of $279,000. She is a nonveteran who is totally and permanently disabled as a result of a serious car accident. She is also legally blind. What is her cumulative county tax exemption on her homesteaded residence?
    a. $26,000
    b. $55,000
    c. $60,000
    d. $65,000

14. The duties of a real estate licensee, owed to a buyer or a seller who engages the real estate licensee as a single agent, do NOT include
    a. dealing honestly and fairly.
    b. limited confidentiality, unless waived in writing by a party.
    c. presenting all offers and counteroffers in a timely manner, unless previously directed otherwise in writing.
    d. loyalty.

15. Which entity is a primary mortgage lender that does NOT accept demand deposits?
    a. Commercial banks
    b. Mortgage lenders
    c. Savings associations
    d. Credit unions

16. A sales associate who is employed by an owner-developer who owns properties in the name of various entities may be issued
    a. multiple licenses.
    b. a group license.
    c. a commercial license.
    d. a branch office license.

17. A tenant signed a 10-year lease requiring a monthly base rent of $1,900, plus 2% of all monthly gross sales volume over $95,000. The tenant also must pay all property taxes, insurance, and other costs normally considered property owner's costs. This is a
    a. gross lease.
    b. fixed lease.
    c. variable sale lease.
    d. net lease.

18. A real estate license may be revoked without prejudice for which action?
    a. Culpable negligence
    b. Failure to account or deliver escrow funds
    c. Issuance of a license by mistake of the Commission
    d. Conversion

19. A licensee with an economic hardship discovers seven months after their last license renewal that the license has gone to a null and void status. To operate again as an active licensee, they must
   a. complete 28 hours of continuing education and pass the continuing education course exam.
   b. complete post-licensing education course(s) and 28 hours of continuing education and pass the state's licensing exam.
   c. reapply and requalify for licensure, including retaking and passing the state license exam.
   d. request and receive an economic hardship extension for license renewal from the Florida Real Estate Commission.

20. Which individual must hold an active real estate license?
   a. A salaried employee of an oil company who buys and sells land on behalf of the company
   b. A person who sells time-share periods for customers
   c. An executor of a will who is selling the real property of a deceased individual
   d. A person employed by Meadow Hills Cemetery to sell cemetery lots

21. Which statement concerning characteristics of the real estate market is FALSE?
   a. Real estate is immobile.
   b. The market is slow to respond to changes in supply and demand.
   c. The real estate market is organized and controlled centrally.
   d. Land is indestructible.

22. A comparable property has one more bedroom ($8,000) and is on a slightly larger lot ($2,000) than the subject property. The comparative market analysis requires a net adjustment of
   a. minus $8,000 to the comparable property.
   b. plus $2,000 to the subject property.
   c. plus $10,000 to the subject property.
   d. minus $10,000 to the comparable property.

23. Which entity may NOT be registered as a real estate brokerage?
   a. Corporation for profit
   b. Corporation sole
   c. Partnership
   d. Sole proprietorship

24. The formula to calculate the overall capitalization rate is
   a. NOI ÷ value (or price).
   b. NOI × value (or price).
   c. debt service × value (or price).
   d. NOI ÷ owner's equity.

25. Which action is NOT a requirement under the TILA-RESPA Integrated Disclosure Rule (TRID)?
   a. Give mortgage applicants the Closing Disclosure at least three business days before closing
   b. Require that mortgage applicants receive the information booklet, *Your Home Loan Toolkit*, within three business days of loan application
   c. Give mortgage applicants a list of competing lenders so they can comparison shop for the best rate
   d. Give mortgage applicants the loan estimate within three business days of receiving the loan application

26. A transaction broker does NOT have which duty?
   a. Duty of using skill, care, and diligence in the transaction
   b. Duty of accounting for all funds
   c. Duty to disclose all known facts that materially affect the value of residential real property and are not readily observable to the buyer
   d. Full fiduciary duties to both the buyer and the seller

27. Which governmental entity must be informed when the FREC takes disciplinary action against one of their licensees?
   a. Division of Firearms and Tobacco
   b. Division of Florida Condominiums, Timeshares, and Mobile Homes
   c. Florida Department of Administrative Law
   d. County courthouse where the licensee resides

28. A real estate brokerage company is a transaction broker for a buyer. The buyer wants to purchase a new home so the sales associate takes him to three model centers listed by three competing real estate companies. The sales associate must give a written no brokerage relationship notice to
   a. the buyer.
   b. the model home employees at each model center.
   c. no one.
   d. the owner-developer of each new homes subdivision.

29. Title to real property is technically conveyed when the deed is
   a. recorded in the public records.
   b. voluntarily delivered and voluntarily accepted.
   c. signed and witnessed.
   d. acknowledged.

30. Which variable does NOT influence demand?
   a. Availability of mortgage credit
   b. Availability of construction loans
   c. Income of consumers
   d. Consumer tastes and preferences

31. A seller transfers title to a buyer with a general warranty deed. In which clause of the deed does the seller define the quality of ownership interest conveyed to the buyer?
   a. Covenant of further assurance
   b. Covenant of quiet enjoyment
   c. Habendum
   d. Seisin

32. A single agent broker received an offer on a listed property at the seller's price and terms. Before informing the seller, the broker received a higher offer. The broker submitted only the first offer, and the seller, his principal, accepted it. The broker
   a. has violated his fiduciary duty to his principal.
   b. is guilty of conversion.
   c. has fulfilled his duty to the seller because the offer was for the seller's full price and terms.
   d. is not required to submit the second offer.

33. A man earned a $7,500 commission by selling a coin-operated laundry business, which has six more years before the expiration of its present lease. The man
   a. must be registered with the Florida Retail Commission as a business broker.
   b. must be registered with the Florida Real Estate Commission as a business broker.
   c. must be registered with the Florida Real Estate Commission as a real estate licensee.
   d. need not be registered with any state agency in the given situation.

34. Three claimants are requesting relief from the Real Estate Recovery Fund. All three claimants were named in a single judgment (the same real estate transaction). What is the maximum payment from the Recovery Fund for this claim?
   a. $50,000
   b. $75,000
   c. $150,000
   d. $1,000,000

35. Which federal law made bait and switch advertising a federal offense?
   a. Real Estate Settlement Procedures Act (RESPA)
   b. Truth in Lending Act (TILA)
   c. Equal Credit Opportunity Act (ECOA)
   d. Federal Reserve System (FRS)

36. Local government exercises its greatest effect on the real estate business by
   a. creating tax shelters for those developing low-income housing.
   b. using zoning, taxation, and the planning process.
   c. providing financing where justified.
   d. supervising contractors and their on-the-job performance.

37. Which information must be disclosed to all prospective buyers?
   a. The seller's brother was murdered in the residence.
   b. A previous occupant was infected with HIV.
   c. The home is situated in a flood-prone area.
   d. The neighborhood residents are Hispanic.

38. Which statement does NOT describe a planned unit development?
    a. A variety of types of housing may be used.
    b. Dwelling units are typically clustered, with planned green space areas between clusters.
    c. Industrial parks are a welcomed offshoot of the PUD concept.
    d. The open space areas are maintained by a community association.

39. A real estate broker is accused of taking money from the company escrow account to pay personal expenses. The broker decides that she does not want to go through the hearing process so the broker turns over her real estate license to the DBPR. What term describes this situation?
    a. Emergency suspension
    b. Voluntary relinquishment for permanent revocation
    c. Revocation
    d. Suspension

40. A licensee makes a statement that is material to the transaction as though it were a fact when the licensee does not know whether the statement is true or false, and the buyer relies on the statement. As a result of the statement made by the licensee, the buyer suffers damages. This situation constitutes
    a. culpable negligence.
    b. fraud.
    c. breach of trust.
    d. deceptive services.

41. The DRE may issue which penalty for an initial offense of a minor violation by a licensee?
    a. Notice of noncompliance
    b. Subpoena to appear
    c. Notice of assignment
    d. Final order

42. A man owns a farm in fee simple. He deeds the farm to a friend until the friend dies, at which time a woman will acquire a fee simple title to the farm. The woman's interest in the farm is a
    a. life estate.
    b. fee simple estate.
    c. reversion estate.
    d. remainder estate.

43. Business brokers appraise businesses using appraisal methods similar to real estate appraisal EXCEPT
    a. stock, bond, and debenture analysis.
    b. asset appreciation analysis.
    c. working capital analysis.
    d. liquidation analysis.

44. What authority originates from the U.S. Constitution and relates to protection of health and welfare of citizens at local levels?
    a. Escheat
    b. Situs
    c. Police power
    d. Community protection power

45. Which element is NOT essential in a valid real estate sale contract?
    a. A legal objective or purpose
    b. Competent parties
    c. An earnest money deposit
    d. The vendor's signature

46. A provision in all mortgages that allows the delinquent mortgagor to avoid foreclosure by paying all the back mortgage payments, late penalties, and costs of collection up until the time of foreclosure sale is the
    a. equity of redemption.
    b. due-on-sale clause.
    c. acceleration clause.
    d. defeasance clause.

47. The statute of limitations is the authority that outlines the
    a. requirement that real estate sale contracts be in writing.
    b. essential elements of a contract.
    c. remedies available in case of breach.
    d. period of time during which a contract may be enforced.

48. When the parties to a contract state the terms of the contract and show their intentions in words, either orally or in writing, what type of contract classification has been created?
    a. Parol
    b. Implied
    c. Express
    d. Executed

49. Which item is entered on the Closing Disclosure as a credit to the seller and as a debit to the buyer?
    a. Prorated property taxes that have not been paid before closing
    b. Seller's mortgage paid off at closing
    c. Prepaid rent on rental property
    d. Purchase price

50. Which statement concerning tenancy by the entireties is FALSE?
    a. It is a form of concurrent ownership.
    b. The estate includes right of survivorship.
    c. The property must be owned by a married couple.
    d. The deed must specifically state intent to create such a tenancy.

51. The financial term applied to the use of borrowed funds to finance the purchase of an office building is
    a. leverage.
    b. liquidity.
    c. intermediation.
    d. disintermediation.

52. A mortgage in which changes in the interest rate may cause changes in the monthly payment amount is called
    a. a partially amortized mortgage.
    b. an adjustable-rate mortgage.
    c. a graduated-payment mortgage.
    d. an escalator mortgage.

53. Depreciation (cost recovery)
    a. may be taken on a principal residence.
    b. includes the cost of land in the amount to be depreciated.
    c. is an allowable deduction on investment property that requires no current outlay of cash.
    d. does not include the mortgaged portion of an apartment building in the amount to be depreciated.

54. Constructive notice is
    a. information learned by reading, seeing, or hearing.
    b. information advertised in the newspaper.
    c. provided by recording in the public records.
    d. notarizing a conveyance.

55. In a deed, the warranty of quiet enjoyment pertains to
    a. peace and tranquility on and around the property.
    b. peaceful possession undisturbed by others' claims of title.
    c. guaranteed satisfaction with the property.
    d. property that is completely vacated.

56. The original law requiring that the annual percentage rate be disclosed to consumers was the
    a. Real Estate Settlement Procedures Act.
    b. Equal Credit Opportunity Act.
    c. Truth in Lending Act.
    d. Florida "Little FTC Act."

57. Eligible homestead owners may transfer up to what amount of their Save Our Homes (SOH) benefit from their previous homestead to a new homestead?
    a. $50,000
    b. $100,000
    c. $225,000
    d. $500,000

58. Which survey term is associated with a metes-and-bounds description?
    a. Range
    b. Township
    c. Point of beginning
    d. Section

59. A buyer who obtains a mortgage loan that covers the purchase of a condominium plus furniture, appliances, and other personal property, such as towels and kitchen utensils, has a
    a. blanket mortgage.
    b. personal mortgage.
    c. wraparound mortgage.
    d. package mortgage on investment property.

60. The bundle of legal rights associated with real property ownership does NOT include the right of
    a. control.
    b. intent.
    c. possession.
    d. disposition.

61. Which estate includes the right of survivorship?
    a. Joint tenancy
    b. Fee simple estate
    c. Tenancy in common
    d. Tenancy for years

62. A title theory state is one in which a mortgage
    a. transfers title to the lender or escrow agent until the loan is paid.
    b. creates only an encumbrance on title to a property.
    c. creates a tenancy in common until the loan is paid.
    d. creates a joint tenancy for the lender until the loan is paid.

63. Which term refers to a situation where, during the early years of a loan, the principal balance increases?
    a. Graduated payments
    b. Positive leverage
    c. Negative amortization
    d. Reverse annuity

64. Which statement is TRUE regarding the monthly payments on a 30-year, fully amortized loan?
    a. Initially, interest is the smallest portion of the payment.
    b. Initially, principal and interest are approximately equal.
    c. Initially, interest is the larger portion of the payment.
    d. Level monthly payments means the same amount of principal is paid each month.

65. Which secondary market participant is a guarantor of government-insured and government-guaranteed loans?
    a. HUD
    b. Freddie Mac
    c. Fannie Mae
    d. Ginnie Mae

66. A real estate brokerage offers property management and the selling of real property. They use a single escrow account to hold sales escrow funds and property management escrow funds. What is the maximum amount of brokerage funds allowed to be placed in the account?
    a. None
    b. $1,000
    c. $5,000
    d. $6,000

67. An example of an ad valorem tax is
    a. a special assessment.
    b. a property tax.
    c. an income tax.
    d. a zoning tax.

68. Which individual is exempt from the continuing education requirement?
    a. Out-of-state Florida licensee
    b. Real estate licensee who earned a four-year degree or higher in real estate
    c. Real estate licensee who is also a Florida attorney in good standing with the Florida bar
    d. Real estate licensee who holds a voluntary inactive license

69. A developer who wants to develop a new subdivision must submit
    a. a subdivision plat map to the planning commission.
    b. a site plan to the zoning board of adjustment.
    c. an existing land-use study to the planning commission.
    d. a thoroughfare study to the Department of Transportation.

70. You have been hired to appraise the local public library building. The approach that is likely to be the MOST relevant is the
    a. comparable sales approach.
    b. cost approach.
    c. public land and property approach.
    d. income approach.

71. The owner of a hardware store has filed for bankruptcy, and the real estate is up for sale. The money that the property will bring at auction is BEST described as which type of value?
    a. Going-concern value
    b. Salvage value
    c. Liquidation value
    d. Investment value

72. The purchase price of a business minus the value of the tangible assets of that business equals the intangible assets of the business. This includes
    a. personal property.
    b. real property.
    c. common stock.
    d. goodwill.

73. A sales associate received a $5,000 earnest money deposit from a buyer. She immediately delivered the deposit to her broker. The broker deposited the check on the third business day into his general operating account.
    a. This is the proper procedure for handling earnest money deposits.
    b. This is an example of commingling of escrow funds.
    c. The broker is guilty of dishonest dealing by trick, scheme, or devise.
    d. This is the proper procedure, provided the broker uses a title company that has trust powers.

74. Sales associate Terry Stoufer may have which information entered on his license, if applicable?
    a. Terry's Real Estate Services
    b. Terry Stoufer, LLC
    c. Terry Stoufer Enterprises, LLC
    d. Best Homes, Inc.

75. Which statement is FALSE regarding advertising?
    a. All advertisements must include the name of the brokerage firm.
    b. Advertising includes flyers and promotional materials.
    c. The brokerage firm's address is required in all advertising.
    d. Licensees may insert their personal names in ads provided they include their last name as registered.

76. Which statement is FALSE regarding a corporation for profit that is doing business as a real estate broker?
    a. The broker must file the articles of incorporation with the Florida Department of State.
    b. There must be at least one officer who is an active real estate broker.
    c. The corporation must be registered with the FREC.
    d. All stockholders must be registered with the FREC as inactive brokers.

77. A broker who changes the business address must notify the Commission of the address change within how many days?
    a. 5
    b. 10
    c. 30
    d. 60

78. In relation to section 1 of a township, section 12 is due
    a. north.
    b. east.
    c. west.
    d. south.

79. A man is a 72-year-old retired college professor. The local lender to whom the man applied for a 30-year mortgage denied the man's loan application, even though he has sufficient income from his pension plan and an excellent credit history.
    a. This is a violation of fair housing laws.
    b. The lender's actions are legal because it is unlikely that the man will survive the term of the loan.
    c. This is an example of redlining.
    d. The lender's actions violate the Equal Credit Opportunity Act.

80. Requirements of a valid deed do NOT include
    a. voluntary delivery and acceptance.
    b. good or valuable consideration.
    c. signature of two witnesses.
    d. signature of a competent grantee.

81. An honorably discharged veteran who applies for a real estate license within 60 months of discharge is exempt from which fee?
    a. Application fee
    b. License exam fee
    c. Fingerprint processing fee
    d. Real estate recovery fund fee (if collected in license period)

82. Individuals who solicit mortgage loans, accept applications for mortgage loans, and negotiate the terms of new mortgage loans on behalf of a borrower are called mortgage
    a. lenders.
    b. finders.
    c. loan originators.
    d. agents.

83. The Florida Real Estate Commission is empowered by law to
    a. levy fines up to, but not exceeding, $500.
    b. impose prison sentences up to 60 days.
    c. assess damages resulting from breach-of-contract suits.
    d. reprimand, fine, or otherwise discipline licensees.

84. If a seller refuses to pay a broker her sales commission after the residential property is sold, the broker may
    a. file a vendor's lien on the owner's property.
    b. file a suit in the courts for her commission.
    c. refuse to permit the closing to occur.
    d. keep the binder deposit as just compensation.

85. If you have located a township numbered T2S, R4E, the township due south of that township is
    a. T2N, R1E.
    b. T2S, R5E.
    c. T3S, R4E.
    d. T2S, R3E.

86. In Florida, real property is assessed on January 1 of each year, and property taxes become a lien on the property on
    a. January 1, the same year.
    b. April 1, the next year.
    c. November 1, the same year.
    d. December 31, the same year.

87. Which valuation assignment is exempt from *USPAP* requirements?
    a. Appraisal for the purpose of refinancing the first mortgage loan
    b. Appraisal report prepared by a certified appraiser
    c. Appraisal assignment conducted by a real estate broker for the purpose of an estate sale
    d. Broker's price opinion prepared for a lender concerning a short sale

88. For application and licensing purposes, a Florida resident is a person who has resided in Florida continuously in
    a. an apartment in Florida for four weeks.
    b. a Florida hotel for six weeks.
    c. a Florida residence for two months.
    d. a recreational vehicle for four months.

89. A broker who holds funds belonging to customers or clients may NOT use an account established with
    a. a Florida commercial bank.
    b. a community bank in North Carolina.
    c. a savings and loan association in Florida.
    d. a Florida credit union.

90. A real estate company represents a motel owner who wishes to list one of his motels for sale. The owner has told the listing agent that he does not want to sell the motel to any racial minorities. Which statement is TRUE?
    a. Because this is not a sale of a residential dwelling under the Fair Housing Act, the listing agent may honor the owner's instructions.
    b. The listing agent may not refuse to show or sell the motel to a minority buyer; however, the owner may refuse to sell to certain individuals if he sells the property "for sale by owner."
    c. It is a violation of the Fair Housing Act to abide by the owner's wishes.
    d. To refuse to sell or lease any real property based on a party's race is a violation of the federal Civil Rights Act of 1866.

91. A property closes on June 10, with the day of closing charged to the buyer. The buyer is assuming the seller's mortgage loan with its principal balance of $227,500 at 4.5% interest. Which entry will appear on the Closing Disclosure?
    a. Debit to seller and credit to buyer in the amount of $589.01
    b. Credit to seller and debit to buyer in the amount of $589.01
    c. Debit to seller and credit to buyer in the amount of $252.43
    d. Credit to seller and debit to buyer in the amount of $252.43

92. The following taxes were paid at the closing of a new home: $1,540 state documentary stamp tax on the deed, $693 state documentary stamp tax on the note, and $396 state intangible tax on the mortgage. What was the purchase price of the home?
   a. $198,000
   b. $220,000
   c. $346,500
   d. $440,000

93. A residential zone requires at least 7,500 square feet per lot. The developer is reserving 25 percent of the land for streets, sidewalks, and a community center. The tract of land for the development consists of 175 acres. How many residential lots are available for development?
   a. 254
   b. 762
   c. 813
   d. 1,106

94. A prospective borrower is applying for a conventional fixed-rate loan. The borrower's monthly gross income is $6,500. The borrower's projected monthly PITI is $1,372, the PMI is $150, and, based on a credit report, the borrower has the following long-term obligations:
   - Car payment: $400
   - Student loan: $390
   - Credit cards: $250

   What is the borrower's total obligations ratio, and does it meet the lender's required threshold for a conventional mortgage loan?
   a. .2341 or 23.4% TOR is less than the TOR threshold for a conventional loan
   b. .3941 or 39.4% TOR is greater than the TOR threshold for a conventional loan
   c. .3710 or 37.1% TOR is greater than the TOR threshold for a conventional loan
   d. .3941 or 39.4% TOR is less than the TOR threshold for a conventional loan

95. You are appraising a five-year-old, single-family home. The livable area is 60 feet by 50 feet. The garage is 24 feet by 20 feet. According to figures obtained from a cost-estimating service, the base construction cost per square foot of livable area is $103 and $92 per square foot for the garage. Calculate the reproduction cost new of the structure.
   a. $303,720
   b. $345,440
   c. $353,160
   d. $358,440

96. A homeowner originally purchased a new home for $244,900. During the period of ownership, the homeowner spent $27,000 in capital improvements. The homeowner sold the home 16 years later for $329,900. The homeowner paid a brokerage fee of 6% of the sale price and paid other closing costs totaling $2,750. What was the homeowner's capital gain from the sale?
   a. $35,510
   b. $35,456
   c. $62,456
   d. $85,000

97. A homesteaded property is located in Jupiter, Florida, in Palm Beach County. The property has been assessed at $185,000. The city tax rate is 8.8 mills, the county tax rate is 9.3 mills, and the school board levy is 6.5 mills. The owner is a widow and has qualified for and received homestead tax exemption. How much will the owner pay in property taxes?
   a. $3,308.70
   b. $3,360.50
   c. $3,483.50
   d. $3,923.70

98. A developer purchased three oceanfront lots, each measuring 75 by 110 feet, for $20 per square foot. The developer later sold the lots for $200,000 each. What was the developer's percentage of profit on the sale of the three lots? (Round to nearest percentage.)
   a. 2%
   b. 18%
   c. 21%
   d. 25%

99. A seller listed a home for $200,000 and agreed to pay a commission rate of 5%. The listing agreement required the listing office and the selling office to share the commission on a 50-50 basis. The home was sold four weeks later for 90% of the list price. The listing broker paid the listing sales associate 50% of the listing office's commission. The selling broker paid the selling associate 60% of the selling office's commission. How much commission did the selling sales associate receive?
    a. $2,700
    b. $3,000
    c. $4,500
    d. $5,400

100. An appraiser has assigned the following weights to three adjusted sale prices:
    - Comparable 1: $322,500, 40% weight
    - Comparable 2: $319,000, 35% weight
    - Comparable 3: $312,000, 25% weight

    What is the estimated market value of the subject property?
    a. $270,275
    b. $286,225
    c. $317,425
    d. $318,650

APPENDIX B: LIST OF ACRONYMS

A BAR SALE	Real estate services (Unit 2)
ADD	Three duties required in all brokerage relationships (Unit 4)
BLIMP	Ways termination of contracts occurs (Unit 11)
CBS and CIA	Appraisal adjustments (Unit 16)
COLD	Four unique duties of a single agent (Unit 4)
COLIC	Elements of a valid and enforceable real estate sale contract (Unit 11)
CPV	Cost to create, price paid, and value or worth (Unit 16)
DEEP C	Bundle of legal rights (Unit 8)
DELL	Private restrictions (Unit 9)
DUST	Characteristics of value (Unit 16)
HOT CAN	Conditions for alienation by adverse possession (Unit 9)
IRMA	Legal test for fixtures (Unit 8)
MALE	Four settlement procedures (Unit 5)
PET	Government restrictions (Unit 9)
PITT	Four unities of a joint tenancy (Unit 8)
WILD CARD	Ways an offer is terminated (Unit 11)

APPENDIX C: KNOW YOUR -ORS AND -EES

assignor: person who transfers a legal right to another (e.g., mortgagee selling mortgages and notes; a buyer transferring rights to another person in a sale contract)

assignee: person to whom a legal right is transferred (e.g., Fannie Mae buying mortgages and notes in the second mortgage market)

grantor: party giving the deed that conveys title (e.g., seller in a sale contract)

grantee: party receiving the deed and acquiring title (e.g., buyer in a sale contract)

lessor: landlord who gives lease

lessee: tenant who receives lease

lienor: person who has a claim on another's property

lienee: person whose property is subject to a claim or charge by another

mortgagor: borrower who gives note and mortgage to obtain a loan

mortgagee: lender who receives note and mortgage

offeror: buyer making an offer to purchase

offeree: seller receiving an offer to purchase and who accepts, counters, or rejects the offer

optionor: owner who gives an option to a buyer

optionee: buyer who receives an option contract

vendor: seller in a sale contract

vendee: buyer in a sale contract

APPENDIX D: MATH FORMULAS

Unit 9: Title, Deeds, and Ownership Restrictions

- Percentage lease
  total gross sales – excess sales = sales subject to additional rent; sales subject to additional rent × percentage (%) charged = additional annual rent; additional annual rent + annual base rent = total annual rent
- Variable (index) lease
  (new index / original index) × original rental rate = new rental rate

Unit 11: Real Estate Contracts

- Net listing
  100% – listing commission percentage = percentage for seller's net
  total seller's net ÷ percentage for seller's net = desired sales price

Unit 12: Residential Mortgages

- Equity
  current market value – mortgage debt = equity
- Loan-to-value ratio (LTV)
  loan amount ÷ sale price (or value) = loan-to-value ratio (LTV)
- Cost of discount points
  loan amount × discount points (1 pt = 1%) = cost of points
- Increased yield
  Convert ⅛ of 1% increase in yield for each discount point
  1 ÷ 8 = .125
  .125 × number of points = increased yield
- Lender's effective yield
  discount points × .125 = increase in yield
  stated interest rate + increase in yield = effective yield

Unit 13: Types of Mortgages and Sources of Financing

- Total obligations ratio (TOR) for conventional mortgage loan
  total monthly obligations (PITI + PMI + LTO) ÷ monthly gross income = total obligations ratio (TOR)
- Calculated interest rate
  index + margin = calculated interest rate
- Housing expense ratio (HER)
  monthly housing expenses (PITI + MIP) ÷ monthly gross income = housing expense ratio (HER)
- Total obligations ratio (TOR) for FHA
  total monthly obligations (PITI + MIP + LTO) ÷ monthly gross income = total obligations ratio (TOR)

Unit 14: Real Estate–Related Computations and Closing of Transactions

- Sales commission
  sale price × commission rate = total commission
  total commission × percentage to listing brokerage = listing commission
  listing commission × listing sales associate percentage = listing sales associate commission
  total commission × percentage to selling brokerage = selling commission
  selling commission × buyer's sales associate percentage = buyer's sales associate commission
- Solving percent problems
  part ÷ total = rate
  part ÷ rate = total
  total × rate = part
- Profit
  amount made on sale ÷ total cost = percentage profit
- Loss
  amount lost on sale ÷ total cost = percentage loss
- Unpaid property taxes
  property taxes for year ÷ 365 days = daily tax rate
  daily tax rate × number of days seller owns property in year = proration amount (credit buyer, debit seller)
- Prepaid rent
  rent paid for the closing month ÷ number of days in closing month = daily rental rate
  daily rental rate × number of days buyer owns property in closing month = proration amount (credit buyer, debit seller)
- Interest on assumed mortgage
  loan balance × interest rate = annual interest ÷ 365 days = daily interest rate
  daily interest rate × number of days seller owns property in closing month = proration amount (credit buyer, debit seller)
- Documentary stamp taxes on deeds
  Purchase price ÷ $100 = taxable units (if result is a decimal number, round to the next whole number)
  Number of taxable units × $.70* = cost of documentary stamp tax on deeds
  * Rate is $.60 in Miami-Dade County
- Documentary stamp taxes on promissory notes
  Promissory note ÷ $100 = taxable units (if result is a decimal number, round *up* to the next whole number)
  Number of taxable units × $.35 = cost of documentary stamp tax on promissory notes
- Intangible tax on new mortgages
  new loan amount × $.002 = cost of intangible tax

Unit 15: The Real Estate Market and Analysis

- Calculating occupancy rate
  occupied units ÷ total number of units = occupancy rate
- Calculating vacancy rate
  vacant units ÷ total number of units = vacancy rate

Unit 16: Real Estate Appraisal

- Cost depreciation approach
  reproduction cost of the structure – accrued depreciation = depreciated value of the structure + estimated value of the site = indicated value of the property
- Accrued depreciation
  effective age ÷ total economic life × reproduction cost new = estimated total accrued depreciation

  Or

  reproduction cost new ÷ total economic life = annual depreciation × effective age = estimated total accrued depreciation
- Effective gross income (EGI)
  potential gross income (PGI) – vacancy and collection losses + other income = effective gross income (EGI)
- Net operating income (NOI)
  effective gross income (EGI) – operating expenses = net operating income (NOI)
- Overall capitalization rate (OAR)
  net operating income (NOI) ÷ value (sale price) = overall capitalization rate (OAR)
- Direct capitalization
  capitalization rate × value (or sale price) = net operating income (NOI)
  net operating income (NOI) ÷ value (or sale price) = capitalization rate
  net operating income (NOI) ÷ capitalization rate = value (or sale price)
- Gross rent multiplier (GRM)
  sale price ÷ gross monthly rent = gross rent multiplier (GRM)
- Estimated market value
  rental income × market area GRM = estimated market value
- Gross income multiplier (GIM)
  sale price ÷ gross annual income = gross income multiplier (GIM)
  gross annual income × market GIM = value

Unit 17: Real Estate Investments and Business Opportunity Brokerage

- Equity
  property value – mortgage debt = equity

Unit 18: Taxes Affecting Real Estate

- Taxable value for homesteads with assessed value up to $50,000
  assessed value – $25,000 base homestead exemption = taxable value (city/county and school board taxes)
- Taxable value for properties with an assessed value that exceeds $50,000
  assessed value – $25,000 base exemption = taxable value for school board taxes
  assessed value – $50,000 exemption = taxable value for city and county taxes
- Annual property taxes due
  taxable value × tax rate = annual property taxes due
- Street paving assessment
  front feet × cost per front foot = total cost
  total cost × percentage paid by homeowners ÷ 2 (sides of street) = homeowner's cost of paving

- Effective gross income (EGI)
  potential gross income (PGI) – vacancy and collection losses + other income = effective gross income (EGI)
- Net operating income (NOI)
  effective gross income (EGI) – operating expenses = net operating income (NOI)
- Straight-line method
  total cost to acquire property – value of the land = depreciable basis
  depreciable basis ÷ useful life (27.5 or 39 years) = annual IRS depreciation deduction

Unit 19: Planning, Zoning, and Environmental Hazards

- Buildable lots in a tract
  43,560 square feet per acre × percent available for lots = square feet available for lots per acre
  Square feet available for lots per acre × number of acres in tract = total available square feet
  Total available square feet ÷ minimum square feet per lot = number of buildable lots in tract

APPENDIX E: LIST OF QR CODES

Unit 2:

2.1 A Historical Perspective of Florida Real Estate License Law

FL Statutes

61J2 Administrative Rules

Candidate Booklet

2.3 Application Requirements

Apply for license

Application Requirements

Unit 3:

3.4 License Renewal and License Statuses

DBPR License Portal

Unit 7:

7.1 Federal Fair Housing Law

FHEO Outreach Materials

7.2 Provisions of the Fair Housing Act as Amended

FHEO Booklet

Unit 12:

12.1 Loan Instruments

Uniform Florida Fixed-Rate for SFP

12.3 Essential Elements of the Mortgage Instrument

Fannie Mae/Freddiemac - mortgage instrument

Unit 13:

13.10 Consumer Credit Protection Act

Closing Disclosure

Unit 18:

18.2 Tax Districts: Budgets and Tax Rate Levy

FL Dept. of Revenue website, Homestead Exemption Information page

GLOSSARY

A

abandonment A surrender of rights; point when a broker makes no effort to service or sell listed property; failure to perform.

absentee owner A property holder who does not reside on the property and who usually relies on a property manager to supervise the investment.

abstract of title Condensed history of title to real property consisting of a summary of the links in the "chain of title" extracted from documents bearing on the title status.

acceleration clause Stipulation in a mortgage that the entire unpaid balance of the debt may become due and payable if a default of expressed conditions should occur.

acceptance Voluntary receipt of an item offered by another.

accretion Gradual addition of land caused by natural forces, such as wind, tide, flood, or watercourse deposits.

acknowledgment Formal declaration before an authorized official, by the person who executed the instrument, that it is a free act.

acre 43,560 square feet.

active license A current, valid license registered with the DBPR. The status required to actively engage in the real estate business.

actual notice Information a person has actually learned by reading, seeing, or hearing.

ad valorem According to the value; in proportion to worth.

adjustable-rate mortgage (ARM) A financing technique in which the lender can raise or lower the interest rate according to a set index.

adjusted basis The owner's original cost plus buying expenses plus capital improvements.

administrative law The body of law created by administrative agencies in the form of rules, regulations, orders, and decisions.

administrative law judge An attorney employed by the Division of Administrative Hearings, Department of Administration, to hear complaints and issue recommended orders.

advance fee A commission or partial compensation received by a broker before completing the real estate service.

adverse interest A purpose in opposition to the interest of another party (as, for example, with a buyer and a seller).

adverse possession A method of obtaining title to real property by occupying it in an open and hostile manner contrary to the interests of the owner.

affidavit A sworn statement written down before a notary or public official.

affiliated business relationship An arrangement in which (a) a person who is in a position to refer business incident to or a part of a real estate settlement service involving a federally related mortgage loan, or an associate of such person, has either an affiliate relationship with or a direct or beneficial ownership interest of more than 1% in a provider of settlement services; and (b) either of such persons directly or indirectly refers such business to that provider or affirmatively influences the selection of that provider.

agency Express or implied authorization for one person to act for another.

agent A representative; one who is authorized to act on behalf of another.

air rights The freedom to use the open space above a property.

alienation The act of transferring ownership, title, or an interest or estate in real property.

alluvion (alluvium) The increase of land by the gradual and imperceptible action of natural forces (e.g., deposits of sand and mud on a riverbank).

amortized mortgage A loan characterized by payment of a debt by regular installment payments.

anniversary date Recurring each year; the date an insurance policy must be renewed to continue in effect.

annual debt service The amount of money required each year for the payment of all mortgage interest and principal.

annual percentage rate (APR) Total yearly cost of credit.

antitrust laws State and federal laws designed to maintain and preserve business competition.

appeal A request to some authority for a decision or judgment.

applicant A person who applies for something; a candidate.

appraisal The process of developing and communicating an opinion of a property's value based on supportable evidence and approved methods as of a certain date.

appraised value Estimated worth of a property determined by someone qualified in valuation.

appraiser One who is registered, licensed, or certified by the DBPR and provides an estimate of value.

appreciation An increase in value.

appurtenance A right or privilege associated with the property, such as a parking space in a multiunit building.

arbitration The act of having a third party render a binding decision in a dispute between two parties.

arrears The state of being behind in the discharge of an obligation; paid at the end of the period for which something is due (the opposite of in advance).

asbestos A mineral fiber used until 1978 in a variety of building construction materials for insulation and as a fire retardant.

assemblage The combining of two or more adjoining properties into one tract.

assessed value Worth established for each unit of real property for tax purposes by a county property appraiser.

assessment The imposition of a tax or charge according to a preset rate; the allocation of the proportionate individual share of a common expense in a condo or co-op building.

assessment limitation (SOH benefit) The accumulated difference between the assessed value and the market value of a homesteaded property due to limit on increases in the assessed value.

assessor's parcel number A numerical ID assigned to each parcel of land within a tax district used to prepare tax maps.

asset Anything of value.

assignee Person to whom a right or interest is transferred.

assignment Written instrument that serves to transfer the rights or interests of one person to another.

assignment of mortgage A legal instrument stating that the mortgagee assigns (transfers) the mortgage and promissory note to the purchaser.

assignor Person who gives legal rights or interests to another person.

assumption The buyer of real property that is already mortgaged assumes liability for the mortgage payments of the original loan that remains on the property.

at arm's length Conducting negotiations on one's own behalf without being subject to the other party's control or influence.

attachment A legal writ obtained to prevent removal of property that is expected to be used to satisfy a judgment.

attorney-in-fact One who is authorized to perform certain acts for another under a power of attorney.

automated valuation model (AVM) A data analysis compiled from a computer database of closed sales used by lenders when an appraisal is not warranted.

B

balance sheet A financial report that shows the company's financial position at a stated moment in time.

balloon payment A single, large payment made at maturity of a partially amortized mortgage to pay off the debt in full.

bargain and sale deed A type of deed in which title is transferred and a limited number of warranties are made respecting title to or use of the property.

base line Imaginary lines running east and west and crossing a principal meridian at a definite point; used by surveyors for reference in locating and describing land under the government survey system.

basis The initial cost of an investor's property.

before-tax cash flow The resulting amount when annual debt service is subtracted from net operating income. Also called *cash throwoff* or *gross spendable income*.

biennium (biennial) A period of two years.

bilateral contract An agreement wherein both parties are legally obligated to each other to perform.

binder A memorandum given subject to the writing of a formal contract for sale, usually acknowledging receipt of a portion of the down payment for purchase of real property.

biweekly mortgage A mortgage loan amortized the same way as other loans with monthly payments, except that the borrower makes a payment every two weeks.

blanket mortgage One debt instrument covering two or more parcels.

blind advertisement An advertisement that provides only a telephone number, a post office box, and/or an address without the licensed name of the brokerage firm.

blockbusting The illegal practice of inducing homeowners to sell their property by making misrepresentations regarding the entry or prospective entry of minority persons in order to cause a turnover of properties in the neighborhood; discriminatory acts against sellers.

bona fide Without deceit or fraud; genuine; in good faith.

boot Money or other property that is not like-kind, which is given to make up any difference in value or equity between exchanged properties.

borrower The mortgagor; one who gives a mortgage as security for a debt. Also called a *debtor*.

branch office A business location other than the real estate broker's principal place of business.

breach of trust Failure to do or perform what has been promised.

broker An individual or business entity licensed by the DBPR to perform services of real estate for others for compensation.

broker associate An individual who is qualified to be issued a broker's license but who operates as a sales associate in the employ of another.

broker's price opinion (BPO) A written opinion of the value of real property. Florida real estate licensees are allowed to prepare and charge for BPOs provided the BPO is not called an appraisal. Price opinions are often requested by relocation companies and lenders involved in short sales of distressed properties.

buffer zone A strip of land separating one land use from another.

building codes Government ordinances regulating construction practices and materials.

building inspection A procedure conducted during construction to check that workmanship conforms to building code.

building permit A document issued after the local government has reviewed the architectural and engineering drawings and signed off on the energy calculations.

bundle of legal rights An ownership concept describing all the legal rights that attach to the ownership of real property, including disposition, enjoyment, exclusion, possession, and control.

business broker Real estate licensees who engage in the sale, purchase, or lease of businesses.

business opportunity The real estate activity dealing in the sale, purchase, or lease of businesses.

buydown A financing technique in which points are paid to the lender by the seller or the builder that lowers (buys down) the effective interest rate paid by the buyer/borrower, thus reducing the amount of the monthly payment for a set period of time.

buyer brokerage agreement An employment contract with a purchaser.

buyer's market The supply of available properties exceeds the demand.

bylaws Rules that govern the administration of the condominium.

C

cancel A license ceases to exist, effective as of the date approved by the Commission, and does not involve disciplinary action.

capital The collective wealth (money and property) of a person or business; the investment in a property. *See also* equity.

capital asset Certain property held by a taxpayer, not including inventory for sale to customers.

capital-deficit area A region where the total amount of local savings is not sufficient to finance economic development already under way in that area.

capital gain (or loss) The profit (or loss) from the sale of an asset, including real property.

capitalization rate The relationship between the net income from a real estate investment and the present value.

cash flow The resulting amount when annual debt service, tax liability, and capital improvement costs are subtracted from net operating income.

caveat emptor Latin for "let the buyer beware."

cease and desist order An action by a government agency to require a person or business to stop an illegal or unfair practice.

cease to be in force A licensee cannot perform real estate services because certain events occur, such as when a broker changes business address.

certificate of occupancy An occupancy permit issued by the local government after construction is completed and the final inspection is approved.

certificate of title opinion A document signed by a title examiner (attorney or title company agent) stating the judgment that, based on an examination of the public records, the seller has good title to the property being conveyed to the buyer (not to be confused with title insurance). Also called an *opinion of title*.

chain of title A successive listing of all previous holders of title (owners) back to an acceptable starting point.

chattel Any item of personal property. *See also* personal property.

check A square measuring 24 miles on each side and representing the largest unit of measure in the government survey system.

citation Statements of alleged violations and the penalties to be imposed.

Civil Rights Act of 1866 A federal act that prohibits any type of discrimination based on race in any real estate transaction (sale or rental) without exception.

closing Final settlement between the buyer and the seller; the date on which title passes from the seller to the buyer.

Closing Disclosure A form that must be provided to the borrower at least three business days before closing; replaced the Settlement Statement (HUD-1).

cloud on title Any defect, valid claim, or encumbrance that serves to impair the title or curtail an owner's rights.

co-ownership Title to real property held by two or more persons at the same time. Also called *concurrent ownership* or *multiple ownership*.

collateral Real or personal property pledged as security on a debt.

collusion Two or more parties jointly attempting to defraud a third party.

color of title A condition in which ownership of real property appears to be good but is not good because of a defect.

commercial A classification of real estate that includes income-producing properties such as office buildings, gasoline stations, restaurants, shopping centers, hotels and motels, and parking lots. Commercial property usually must be zoned for business purposes.

commingle To mix together money or a deposit with personal funds; combine; intermingle.

commission Compensation paid to a broker or sales associate for successfully concluding a real estate transaction.

Commission Short for the Florida Real Estate Commission (FREC).

common elements The parts of a multiple-ownership property not included in the units; those parts in which each unit owner holds an undivided interest.

common law Judge-made law manifested in decrees and judgments of the courts (case law), as opposed to statutory law.

community association manager (CAM) A person who holds a CAM license to manage community associations of more than 10 units and associations with annual budgets in excess of $100,000.

community development district (CDD) An independent special district created pursuant to Florida law to service the long-term specific needs of its community. A CDD constructs, operates, and maintains communitywide infrastructure and services for the benefit of its residents. CDDs provide an alternative way to fund and construct capital infrastructure to service projected growth.

community property Real property acquired during a marriage (Florida is not a community property state).

comparable property A recently sold property similar to one being evaluated. Also called a *comparable* or *comp*.

comparative market analysis (CMA) An informal estimate of market value performed by a real estate licensee for the seller to assist in arriving at an appropriate listing price, or if working with the buyer, an informal estimate of market value to assist the buyer in arriving at an appropriate offering price.

compensation Anything of value or a valuable consideration, directly or indirectly paid, promised, or expected to be paid or received.

competent A party to a contract who possesses the legal capacity to enter into a binding contract.

complaint Formal allegation or charge.

comprehensive plan A statement of policies for the future physical development of an area (e.g., city, county, region). Also called a *master plan*.

concealment The act of keeping from sight or keeping secret.

concurrency A provision in Florida's Growth Policy Act that requires water and waste treatment facilities needed to support additional population to be in place before new development is allowed.

concurrent ownership When two or more persons own property at the same time, such as joint tenants, tenants by the entirety, or tenants in common.

condemnation The taking of private real property for a public purpose under the right of eminent domain for a fair price.

condominium A multiunit project consisting of individual ownership of a dwelling unit and undivided ownership of common areas.

condominium documents A set of papers describing the condominium and the association.

conflicting demands When different parties each make claims that are inconsistent with one another.

conforming loan A standardized conventional loan written on uniform documents that meets the purchase requirements of Fannie Mae and Freddie Mac.

consent to transition A written agreement to gain the principal's permission to a change in brokerage relationship.

consideration Inducement offered to conclude a contract.

construction lien A claim based on the principle of "unjust enrichment"; favors parties who have performed labor or delivered materials or supplies for the repair or building of an improvement to real property.

constructive notice The recording of a document or an instrument in the public records designed to give adequate notice to all.

consumer member A member of the Florida Real Estate Commission who does not hold a real estate license.

Consumer Price Index (CPI) A measurement of average price changes of goods and services using a base period.

contract An agreement between two or more competent parties to do, or not do, some legal act for a legal consideration.

contract for deed (land contract) A financing technique wherein the seller agrees to deliver the deed at some future date and the buyer takes possession while paying the agreed amount. Also called an *installment sale contract* or *agreement for deed.*

conventional loan A real estate loan that is neither FHA-insured nor VA-guaranteed.

conversion Unauthorized use or retention of money or property that rightfully belongs to another person.

convertible mortgage A financing instrument allowing a change from an adjustable-rate to a fixed-rate mortgage.

conveyance Written instrument that serves to transfer an interest in real property from one party to another.

cooperative A multiunit project consisting of individual dwelling units owned by the corporation in which the individual apartment tenants own stock rather than owning their respective units.

corporation An artificial or fictitious person formed to conduct specified types of business activities.

corporation not for profit An artificial or fictitious person organized for business purposes and similar to a corporation for profit.

corporation sole An artificial or fictitious person formed by a nonprofit religious organization.

cost The amount to produce or acquire something.

cost approach A method for estimating the market value of a property based on the cost to buy the site and to construct a new building on the site, less depreciation.

counteroffer A rejection of the original offer by proposing a new offer, thereby terminating the original offer.

covenant A warranty, guarantee, or promise formally given in a legal document.

credit As a verb, to make an entry on the right or credit side of an account; as a noun, payment or value received.

creditor A lender; person or business entity to whom a debt is owed.

culpable negligence Inadequate attention to duties and obligations by those who know, or should know, what is required of them.

curable When the correction of a defect results in as much added value as the cost to correct the defect.

current mailing address The residential address a licensee uses to receive mail through the U.S. Postal Service.

current status Indicates a licensee is up to date with respect to the DBPR's licensure requirements.

customer One with whom the broker or sales associate hopes to be successful in accomplishing the purpose of employment. Per Section 475.01, F.S., a member of the public who is or may be a buyer or a seller of real property and may or may not be represented by a real estate licensee in an authorized brokerage relationship.

D

damages Losses incurred as a result of a breach of contract or some other cause. *See also* liquidated damages and unliquidated damages.

debit As a verb, to make an entry on the left or charge side of an account; as a noun, a charge or expense.

debt service The amount of money needed to meet the periodic payments of principal and interest on a loan that is being amortized.

decedent A deceased person, usually one who has recently died.

declaration of condominium The legal document that the developer of a condominium must file and record in order to create a condominium under state law.

declaratory judgment A course of action declaring rights claimed under a contract or statute intended to prevent loss or to guide performance by the party or parties affected.

dedication An offer of land for some public use, by an owner, together with acceptance by or on behalf of the public.

deed A type of conveyance; a written instrument to transfer title to real property from one party to another.

deed in lieu of foreclosure A friendly foreclosure (nonjudicial procedure) in which the mortgagor gives title to the mortgagee.

deed restrictions Provision placed in deeds to control future uses of the property.

default Failure to comply with the terms of an agreement or to meet an obligation when due.

defeasance clause A provision in a mortgage that specifies the terms and conditions to be met in order to avoid default and thereby defeat the mortgage.

defendant The person or party being sued or charged.

deficiency decree Judgment brought when a mortgage is foreclosed and the sale proceeds fail to cover the costs of the sale, taxes, and the unpaid mortgage balance.

demand The quantity of goods or services wanted by consumers.

demand deposit Checking accounts; payable on demand by holder.

denial A refusal or rejection.

density The number of homes or lots per acre.

Department of Veterans Affairs (VA) Guarantees mortgage loans to encourage private lending agencies to give liberal mortgages to veterans and their spouses.

deposit Earnest money or some other valuable consideration given as evidence of good faith to accompany an offer to purchase or rent. *See also* binder and earnest money.

deposition Written testimony of a witness under oath.

depreciation A loss in value for any reason; a deduction for tax purposes.

descent The passage of title to real property upon the death of the owner to the legal descendants.

designated sales associates Two real estate licensees designated to represent the buyer and the seller as single agents in a nonresidential transaction. The buyer and the seller must have assets of $1 million or more and sign disclosures stating that their assets meet the required threshold.

development of regional impact (DRI) Any development that because of its character, magnitude, or location could have a substantial effect on the health, safety, and welfare of citizens of more than one county.

devise A gift of real property by a will.

devisee One who receives real property under a will.

devisor One who gives real property through a will.

disability A protected class as defined in the Fair Housing Act and the Americans with Disabilities Act consisting of a physical or mental impairment that substantially limits one or more major life activities.

discount points A method for increasing a lender's yield. *See also* mortgage discount point.

discount rate The amount of interest the Federal Reserve charges to lend money to its eligible banks.

disintermediation A disengagement process when depositors withdraw money from savings for direct investment in stocks, money market funds, and other securities.

Division of Administrative Hearings (DOAH) The governmental entity that hears all formal hearings resulting from an administrative complaint against a licensee.

doc stamps An abbreviated term for documentary stamp tax.

down payment A portion of a purchase price paid before closing the transaction. Earnest money may be part of or the entire down payment.

dual agency Representing both principals in a transaction (not a legal agency relationship in Florida).

due-on-sale clause A provision in a conventional mortgage that entitles the lender to require the entire loan balance to be paid in full if the property is sold.

E

earnest money A type of money that a broker may handle for others in the ordinary course of business; also called a good-faith deposit or binder deposit.

easement A right, privilege, or interest in real property that one individual has in lands belonging to another; a legal right to trespass; right-of-way authorizing access to or over land.

easement appurtenant An easement that runs with the land and benefits an adjacent parcel of land.

easement by necessity An easement created by a court of law in cases where justice and necessity dictate it, such as when property is landlocked.

easement by prescription A right acquired by an adverse user to use the land of another, created through a court of law after long and uninterrupted use.

easement in gross A type of easement that benefits an individual or business entity and is not related to a specific adjacent parcel, for example, utility easements.

economic life The period of time a property may be expected to be profitable or productive; useful life.

effect a sale A provision in a listing agreement requiring the broker to obtain a signed contract from a ready, willing, and able buyer on the terms specified.

effective age The age indicated by a structure's condition and utility.

effective gross income (EGI) The resulting amount when vacancy and collection losses are subtracted from potential gross income. *See also* vacancy and collection losses.

eminent domain The constitutional right given to a unit of government to take private property involuntarily, if taken for public use and a fair price is paid to the owner.

employer The individual who hires the services of another.

encroachment Unauthorized use of another person's property.

encumbrance Any lien, claim, or liability affecting the title or attaching to real property.

encumbrance clause A provision in a deed to real property warranting that no liens, claims, or liabilities exist on the property being conveyed, except as specified.

enforceable contract A legally binding contract that the law will recognize.

entitlement That portion of a VA-guaranteed loan that protects the lender if the borrower defaults.

environmental impact statement (EIS) A document that summarizes the effect proposed development will have on the surroundings.

equitable title The beneficial interest in real estate that implies that an individual will receive legal title at a future date.

equity The market value of a property less any debt against it; in a business entity, assets minus liabilities equals capital (owner's equity); a system of legal rules administered by a court of chancery.

equity of redemption The right of a mortgagor, before a foreclosure sale, to reclaim forfeited property by paying the entire indebtedness.

erosion Gradual loss of land due to water or other natural causes.

estate for years A tenancy measured from a starting date to a termination date (may be for a few days or longer than any natural life; e.g., a leasehold is an estate for years).

escheat Reversion of property to the state when an owner dies without leaving a will or any known heirs.

escrow An impound account required by most lenders that require borrowers to pay in advance monthly installments for property taxes and hazard insurance. The monthly escrow payment is one-twelfth of the estimated annual expense for property taxes and the hazard insurance premium.

escrow account An account in a bank, title company, credit union, savings association, or trust company used solely for safekeeping customer funds and not for deposit of personal funds; impound account or trust account.

escrow disbursement order (EDO) A course of action for determining the disposition of a contested deposit.

estate Tenancy; the interest one holds in real property; the total of one's property and possessions.

estate by the entireties A tenancy created by a married couple jointly owning real property with complete right of survivorship.

estate in reversion An estate that comes back to the original grantor.

estate in severalty Ownership of property vested in one person alone, also called sole ownership.

estate of remainder An estate that can become effective only after another estate has terminated.

estoppel A principle of law that prohibits (stops) people from defending themselves against their own acts or lack of action.

estoppel certificate A written statement that bars the signer from making a claim inconsistent with the instrument (commonly used with a mortgage assumption).

evidence Any proof that may legally be admitted in settlement of an issue.

exclusion The right of an owner to control entry onto the property.

exclusive-agency listing Employment contract given to one real estate broker as the sole agent for the sale of an owner's property.

exclusive-right-of-sale listing An employment contract given to one real estate broker as the sole agent for the sale of an owner's property, with the commission going to that broker regardless of who actually sells the property during the employment contract period.

executed contract An agreement in which the terms have been fully performed by all parties; a signed document.

executive Duties related to the education of licensees, the regulating of professional practices, and the publishing of materials.

executory contract An agreement containing some act or condition that remains to be completed.

exempt properties Properties that have been decreed to be excluded from taxation or claim by others.

express contract An agreement wherein the terms are specifically stated by the parties, either orally, in writing, or by a combination of the two.

expungement A process by which the record of a criminal conviction is destroyed or sealed after expiration of time.

F

failure to account or deliver The act of failing to pay money to a person entitled to receive it.

Fair Housing Act An act contained in Title VIII of the Civil Rights Act of 1968 that created protected classes of people and prohibits discrimination when selling or renting residential property when based on race, color, religion, sex, national origin, familial status, or disability.

familial status A protected class as defined in the Fair Housing Act, consisting of one or more individuals under age 18 living with a parent or legal guardian and pregnant women.

Fannie Mae An institution in the secondary mortgage market that buys and sells mortgages.

farm area A selected geographical area or a group of people from which to solicit real estate business and to which a real estate licensee devotes special attention and study.

Federal Deposit Insurance Corporation (FDIC) A federal agency that insures deposits of member banks and savings associations.

Federal Housing Administration (FHA) Insures mortgage loans made by FHA-approved lenders on homes that meet FHA standards in order to make mortgages more desirable investments for lenders.

Federal Reserve System (the Fed) A central banking authority that influences the cost, availability, and supply of money.

Federal Trade Commission (FTC) A federal agency that investigates and eliminates unfair and deceptive trade practices.

federally related transaction Any sale transaction that ultimately involves a federal agency in either the primary or secondary mortgage market. Under FIRREA, state-certified or state-licensed appraisers must be used for certain loans in federally related transactions.

fee simple estate The most comprehensive and complete interest one can hold in real property; freehold estate. Also called *fee* or *fee simple absolute*.

fiduciary A person in a position of trust and confidence with respect to another person.

fiduciary relationship An alliance of trust and confidence that creates a moral and legal obligation when extended by one person and accepted by another.

final order A decision rendered by the FREC.

find a purchaser A provision in a listing agreement requiring a broker to produce a ready, willing, and able buyer or offer on the terms specified.

first mortgage A mortgage on property that is superior in right to any other mortgage.

fixture An object that was once considered personal property but has become real property because of attachment to, or use in, improvements to real property.

Florida resident For application and licensing purposes, a person who has resided in Florida continuously for four calendar months or more within the preceding year.

follow-up What a sales associate does after a sale to maintain customer contact and goodwill.

foreclosure A legal procedure whereby property used as security for a debt is sold to satisfy the debt owing to default in payment of the mortgage note or default of other terms in the mortgage document.

formal (administrative) complaint An outline of the charges against a licensee that must be answered within the statutory time limit.

formal contract Any agreement that contains all the essentials of a contract, including that it is in writing and under seal; a contract dependent on a particular form.

formal hearing A session in which testimony and arguments are presented, especially before an official.

fraud The intent to misrepresent a material fact or to deceive in order to gain an unfair advantage or to harm another person.

Freddie Mac Formerly called the Federal Home Loan Mortgage Corporation (FHLMC). A secondary mortgage market institution that buys and sells conventional, FHA, and VA loans.

free and clear Title to real property that is absolute and unencumbered.

freehold estate A tenancy in real property with no set termination date that can be measured by the lifetime of an individual or can be inherited by heirs.

further assurance A provision in a deed containing a covenant or warranty to perform any further acts the grantee (buyer) might require to perfect title to the property.

G

general agent A representative authorized by the principal to perform only acts related to a business or to employment of a particular nature.

general lien A claim that may affect all the properties of a debtor.

general partnership An association of two or more persons for the purpose of jointly conducting a business, each being responsible for all the debts incurred in the conducting of that business.

general warranty deed An instrument of conveyance containing the strongest and most comprehensive promises of further assurance possible for a grantor (seller) to convey to a grantee (buyer).

Ginnie Mae A federal agency that is part of the Department of Housing and Urban Development (HUD). Ginnie Mae plays an important role in achieving the HUD's goal of providing low-cost mortgage credit to traditionally underserved sectors of the housing market.

going-concern value The worth of a business, including real estate, goodwill, and earning capacity.

good consideration A promise that cannot be measured in terms of money, such as love and affection.

good-faith doubt A broker's uncertainty as to which party should receive the escrowed property.

goodwill An intangible asset (value) of a business.

government lot Fractional piece of land of less than a quarter section, resulting from geographical features (e.g., lakes, streams) interfering with land surveying.

government survey system A type of land description, developed by the federal government for subdividing lands using surveying lines.

grantee Party who receives a deed or grant; buyer.

granting clause The provision in a deed that specifies the names of the parties involved, the words of conveyance, and a description of the property.

grantor Party who signs and gives a deed; seller.

Green Belt Law Legislation that authorizes county property appraisers to assess land used for agricultural purposes according to its current value as agricultural land.

gross income multiplier (GIM) A rule of thumb for estimating the market value of commercial and industrial properties; the ratio to convert annual income into market value.

gross lease An agreement for the tenant to pay a fixed (base) rent with the landlord paying all the expenses associated with the property.

gross rent multiplier (GRM) A rule of thumb for estimating the market value of income-producing residential property; the ratio to convert rental income into market value.

ground lease An agreement for the tenant to lease the land only and erect a building on the land.

group license A right granted a sales associate or broker associate to work various properties owned by affiliated entities under one owner developer.

H

habendum clause A provision in a deed to real property that stipulates the estate or interest the grantee is to receive and the type of title conveyed.

hazard insurance Coverage by contract whereby one party undertakes to guarantee another party against loss resulting from physical damage to real property.

health ordinance Local codes that regulate maintenance and sanitation of public spaces.

highest and best use A principle of value that focuses on the most profitable legal use to which a property can be put.

home equity conversion mortgage (HECM) The only reverse mortgage program insured by the federal government that allows homeowners to borrow against the equity in their home.

home equity loan A mortgage secured by a personal residence. It provides a line of credit available for draws when needed by the homeowner. It is sometimes used as a home improvement loan.

homeowners association (HOA) A Florida corporation responsible for the operation of a community or a mobile home subdivision in which the voting membership is made up of parcel owners and membership in the HOA is a mandatory condition of parcel ownership. An HOA is authorized to impose assessments that, if unpaid, may become a lien on the parcel.

homestead Term used to describe three separate but related situations: (1) a tax exemption, (2) a tract of land limited in size, and (3) a statutory condition designed to protect the interests of a spouse and lineal descendants.

household One individual, or a group of individuals, living in one dwelling unit.

hypothecation To pledge real or personal property as security for a debt or obligation without giving up possession of the property.

I

immediately The time period during which a broker must deposit escrow funds; no later than the end of the third business day after the broker's sales associate or an employee has received the funds.

immune properties Real property that is owned by a unit of government and is not subject to taxation.

implied Expressed indirectly (e.g., an implied contract).

implied contract An agreement wherein the terms are not stated but are inferred from the conduct of the parties.

implied listing An employment contract that arises from the conduct of the broker and the seller and may be enforceable even though not clearly spelled out in words.

improvement Addition that increases the value of real property (not repairs).

income Amount earned or gained, not return of capital.

income approach A method for estimating the market value of a property based on the present and future income the property can be expected to generate.

income statement A summary of all income and expenses of a business for a stated period of time.

incurable When the cost to correct a defect is greater than the value added by the cure.

index The variable component that is added to the margin to calculate the interest rate in an adjustable-rate mortgage.

informal hearing A respondent who does not dispute allegations of material fact in the administrative complaint may request an informal hearing before the FREC for final action on the complaint.

injunction A writ or order by a court forbidding a party from doing something.

installment sale The seller receives the proceeds from the sale in periodic payments over time.

instrument Any legal or formal writing, such as a will, option, lease, contract, or deed.

insurance clause A provision in a mortgage that requires the mortgagor to obtain and keep current a hazard insurance policy.

intangible asset Something of value lacking physical substance; existing only in connection with something else (e.g., the goodwill of a business).

intensity The concentration of activity (pedestrian and vehicular traffic) used as a means of designating land for commercial zones.

interest The price paid for the use of borrowed money; estate.

interest rate The percentage charged for the use of borrowed money.

intermediation The process whereby financial middlemen consolidate many small savings accounts belonging to individual depositors and invest those funds in large, diversified projects.

interpleader A course of action when two contesting parties cannot reach an arbitrated agreement; a legal proceeding whereby the broker, having no financial interest in the disputed funds, deposits with the court the disputed escrow deposit so that the court can determine who is the rightful claimant.

interval ownership Fee simple possession, for the limited time purchased (one or more weeks), of a time-share unit, complete with deed, title, and equity.

intestate Without a will.

investment value The worth of a property to a particular investor based on the investor's desired rate of return, risk tolerance, etc.

involuntary alienation When a person dies intestate and the property either descends to the decedent's heirs or transfers to the state through escheat.

involuntary inactive The license status that results when a license is not renewed at the end of the license period.

involuntary liens Claims imposed against real property without the consent of the owner (e.g., taxes, special assessments).

J

joint tenancy An estate or interest owned by more than one person, each having equal rights to possession and enjoyment; the interest a deceased tenant conveys to surviving tenants by specific wording in the deed establishing the joint tenancy.

joint venture Two or more parties in an arrangement confined to only one or a limited number of business deals. Also called a *joint adventure*.

judgment Decree of a court that not only declares that one party owes another party a debt but also fixes the debt amount.

judicial review The power of a court to reexamine statutes or administrative acts and to determine their validity; a rehearing or appeal to a higher court.

junior lien Priority is based on the date of recording in the public records.

junior mortgage A mortgage, such as a second mortgage, that is subordinate in right or lien priority to an existing mortgage on the same real property.

just value The fair market value.

K

kickback Payment of money from someone other than the buyer or the seller associated with real estate business.

L

laissez-faire Allow to act; noninterference by government in trade, industry, and individual action generally.

land The surface of the earth and everything attached to it by nature.

land description A definite and positive written identification of a specific parcel of land and its location without additional oral testimony. Also called a *legal description*.

land development loan Financing instrument for the installation of on- and offsite improvements to the land, including sewers, streets, and utilities.

lay member One not belonging to or connected with a particular profession.

lease An estate for years; an agreement that does not convey ownership but does convey possession and use for a period of time and for compensation.

leasehold estate A tenancy in real property held under a lease arrangement for a definite number of years; nonfreehold.

legal description A series of boundary lines on the earth's surface.

legally sufficient A complaint that contains facts indicating that a violation of a Florida statute, a DBPR rule, or a FREC rule has occurred.

lender's policy Title insurance issued for the unpaid mortgage amount to protect the lender against title defects.

lessee A tenant or leaseholder; party given a lease.

lessor The landlord or owner; party granting a lease.

level-payment plan A method for amortizing a mortgage whereby the borrower pays the same amount each month.

leverage The use of borrowed funds to finance the purchase of an asset; the use of another's money to make more money.

liabilities Debts; financial obligations; drawbacks.

license A privilege granted by the state to operate as a real estate broker, broker associate, or sales associate; a type of time-share interest.

license by endorsement qualifications met by a licensee from one state that will be accepted by another state regardless of if an agreement between the states exists.

licensee An individual who has qualified for, and been registered as, a real estate broker, broker associate, or sales associate.

licensure Certification as a licensee; the granting by the state of a license to practice real estate.

lien A claim on property for payment of some obligation or debt.

lien theory Legal concept that regards a mortgage as a just claim on specific property pledged as security for a mortgage debt.

lienee One whose property is subject to a claim or charge by another.

lienor One who has a claim or charge on the property of another.

life estate Tenancies whose durations are limited to the life of some person; freehold.

lifetime cap Limits the total amount the interest rate may increase over the life of an adjustable-rate mortgage loan.

like-kind exchange An exchange of real property held for investment for another property held for investment that qualifies for deferment of takes from gain on the sale.

limited liability company (LLC) An alternative, hybrid business entity with the combined characteristics and benefits of both limited partnerships and S corporations.

limited liability partnership (LLP) A business entity that features protection from personal liability but with fewer legal restrictions compared with other business entities.

limited partnership A business entity consisting of one or more general partners and one or more limited partners.

limited representation Transaction brokers provide a limited form of nonfiduciary representation to a buyer, a seller, or both in a real estate transaction.

lineal Descended in a direct family line; relating to or derived from ancestors.

liquidated damages The amount of valuable consideration specified in an agreement as a penalty for default. *See also* damages.

liquidation The process of determining liabilities and apportioning the assets in order to discharge the indebtedness of a business to be sold.

liquidation analysis An appraiser's methodology and estimate of the value of a business that is being liquidated. An assessment of such factors as the ability of the firm to pay off short-term obligations, the value of the inventory on hand, and the liquidation value of preferred stock.

liquidity The ability to convert noncash assets into cash quickly; refers to a firm's cash position and its ability to meet obligations.

lis pendens A pending legal action.

listing Oral or written employment agreement between a broker (or a sales associate employed by a broker) and the property owner; authorization to sell, rent, or exchange.

litigation A lawsuit; the act of carrying on a lawsuit; a case before a court of law.

littoral rights Legal rights related to land abutting an ocean, sea, or lake, usually extending to the high-water mark.

Loan Estimate A disclosure form with good-faith estimates of credit costs and transactions terms that must the given to the borrower no later than the third business day after receiving the loan application.

loan origination fee A charge by a lender for taking a mortgage in exchange for a loan.

loan servicing An additional source of income for lenders. Servicing fees typically range from ⅜ to ¾ of 1% of the unpaid balance of loans serviced.

loan-to-value ratio (LTV) Relationship between amount borrowed and appraised value (or sale price) of a property.

lot and block A type of legal description of land.

M

maintenance clause A provision in a mortgage agreement that requires mortgagors (borrowers) to maintain mortgaged property in good condition.

majority A person having attained 18 years of age, or having married, or by court order; no longer a minor; a number greater than half the total.

margin The fixed component that is added to the index to calculate the interest rate in an adjustable rate mortgage.

marital assets Real and personal property acquired during marriage.

market allocation An agreement between brokers to split up competitive market areas among themselves and not compete in each other's areas.

market value The most probable price a property will bring from a fully informed buyer, willing but not compelled to buy, and the lowest price a fully informed seller will accept if not compelled to sell.

marketable title Rights to real property that are so clear that a buyer may have peaceful and quiet enjoyment of the property free of litigation. Also called *merchantable title*.

material fact A piece of information that affects the value of real property and is relevant to a person making a decision about that property.

mechanic's lien *See* construction lien.

mediation The act of having a third party attempt to reconcile a dispute between two parties.

meeting of the minds The point when two people, thinking of the same thing, reach an agreement through an offer and acceptance.

meridian Any of the imaginary lines of longitude on the earth's surface; in land description, the vertical lines running in a north-south direction parallel to the principal (prime) meridian and separating the various ranges.

metes-and-bounds description A method of legal description that identifies a property by specifying the shape and boundary dimensions of the parcel. A metes-and-bounds description starts at the point of beginning and follows the boundaries of the land by compass direction and linear measurements and returns to the point of beginning.

mill A unit of money used to specify a property tax rate ($1 for each $1,000 of taxable value).

millage A tax rate, expressed as the number of mills to be applied.

ministerial duties The duties of the Division of Real Estate that involve recordkeeping.

misdemeanor Any crime punishable by fine or imprisonment other than in a penitentiary.

misrepresentation A false or misleading statement of a material fact; concealment of a material fact.

mixed land use More than one type of zoning, such as a condominium that has residential and commercial units.

monetary policy The actions undertaken by the Fed to influence the availability and cost of money and credit.

monument Man-made or natural object used to establish boundaries of land.

moral turpitude An act of corruption, vileness, or moral depravity; a disgraceful action or deed.

mortgage A written agreement that pledges property as security for payment of a debt.

mortgage broker A business entity that conducts loan originator activities. Mortgage brokers can employ mortgage loan originators. Mortgage brokers do not make loans or service loans—they arrange loans.

mortgage discount point A charge of 1% of the mortgage value; assessment by a lender to increase the interest yield to compete with the interest yield from other types of investments. *See also* discount point.

mortgage fraud A crime in which the intent is to materially misrepresent or omit information on a *mortgage* loan application to obtain a loan or to obtain a larger loan than would have not been obtained had the lender or borrower known the truth.

mortgage insurance premium (MIP) Fee paid by FHA borrowers to obtain a loan (up-front and annual).

mortgage lender A business entity that originates, sells, and then services mortgage loans. Mortgage lenders are not depository institutions. They originate loans and then package the loans together and sell the entire package.

mortgage loan originator (MLO) One who finds a lender for a potential borrower, and vice versa.

mortgagee A lender who holds a mortgage on specific property as security for the money loaned to the borrower.

mortgagor A borrower who gives a mortgage on the borrower's property in order to obtain a loan from a lender.

multiple licenses Licenses held by a broker in two or more real estate brokerage firms.

multiple listing service (MLS) An arrangement among members of a real estate board or exchange that allows each member broker to share listings with other members so that greater exposure is obtained and a greater chance of sale will result.

mutual assent The making and acceptance of an offer.

mutual recognition agreement A transactional agreement between Florida and another state that provides for the two states to recognize each other's real estate license education.

N

negative amortization A financing arrangement whereby monthly mortgage payments are less than required to pay both interest and principal. The unpaid amount is added to the loan balance.

negative leverage Borrowed funds cost more than the income the funds generate.

net income Profit from property or business after expenses have been deducted; effective gross income less operating expenses.

net lease An agreement for the tenant to pay fixed rent plus property costs, such as taxes, insurance, and utilities.

net listing An agreement or contract to sell or rent a property for a specified minimum net amount for the owner.

net operating income (NOI) The resulting amount when all operating expenses are subtracted from effective gross income.

no brokerage relationship The broker doesn't represent the customer (the customer may be the buyer or the seller). *See also* nonrepresentation.

nolo contendere/no contest A pleading of no contest by a defendant; a plea in a criminal action not admitting guilt but subjecting the defendant to punishment as though it were a guilty plea.

nonconforming loan A residential mortgage loan that exceeds the loan amount acceptable for sale to Fannie Mae.

nonconforming use Continuing land use that is not in compliance with zoning ordinances.

nonconventional loan A mortgage loan that is insured or guaranteed by the federal government (FHA or VA).

nonfreehold estate An estate in real property in which ownership is for a determinable time period, as in a lease.

nonrepresentation A no-brokerage relationship.

note Legal evidence of a debt that must accompany a mortgage in Florida; a legally executed pledge to pay a stipulated sum of money. *See also* promissory note.

notice of noncompliance Issued by the DBPR in the case of a minor rule violation that does not endanger the public health, safety, and welfare.

novation The substitution of a new party and/or new terms to an existing obligation.

null and void The license status when a sales associate has failed to successfully complete post-license education prior to the first renewal of the license or when a licensee has failed to renew two or more renewal cycles; the license status has been involuntary inactive for more than 24 months.

O

obligee A lender or mortgagee.

obligor A borrower or mortgagor.

obsolescence A cause of loss in value. *See also* depreciation.

occupancy rate The percentage of occupied rental units.

offer An intentional proposal or promise made by one party to act or perform, provided the other party acts or performs in the manner requested.

offeree One who receives an offer, usually the seller.

offeror One who makes an offer, usually the buyer.

open listing An employment contract given to any number of brokers who work simultaneously to sell the owner's property.

open-market operations Purchase and sale of U.S. Treasury and federal agency securities.

opinion of title A formal statement by an attorney regarding the status of a title after examination of the chain of title.

opinion of value An estimate of a property's worth given by a licensee for the purpose of a prospective sale.

option contract A right or privilege to purchase or lease real property at a specified price during a designated period based on a sufficient consideration.

optionee The party who takes an option and pays a consideration.

optionor The party who gives an option and receives a consideration.

ostensible partnership One or more parties cause a third party to be deceived into believing that a business relationship exists when no such arrangement exists.

overage Retaining more than the agreed amount of sales commission, without the express knowledge and consent of the parties involved; a form of fraud. Also called *secret profit* or *secret commission*.

overall capitalization rate (OAR) The relationship between annual net operating income and the value or sale price of a property.

overimprovement An addition or change to property not in line with its highest and best use, or a betterment that exceeds that justified by local conditions.

owner-developer An unlicensed entity that sells, exchanges, or leases its own property.

owner's policy Title insurance issued for the total purchase price of the property to protect the new owner against unexpected risks.

P

package mortgage A loan covering both real and personal property.

parol contract An agreement that is not in writing; oral agreement.

partial release clause Stipulates the conditions under which the mortgagee will grant freeing building lots from a mortgage lien upon payment of a certain amount of money.

partially amortized mortgage The buyer makes regular payments smaller than what is required to completely pay off the loan (payments do not fully amortize the loan) resulting in a larger balloon payment to pay off the remaining amount due.

partnership Two or more competent individuals, each of whom agrees to share in the profits and losses of the business.

pass-through securities Certificates pledging a group (pool) of existing government-backed mortgages used for the purpose of channeling funds into housing markets.

payment cap Limits the amount the monthly payments of an adjustable-rate loan can increase during any adjustment.

penalty clause A provision in a mortgage that requires the borrower to pay a penalty in money if the mortgage payments are made in advance of the normal due date or if the mortgage is paid in full ahead of schedule.

per diem By the day; per day; an allowance for daily expenses.

percentage lease An agreement for the tenant to pay rent based on the gross sales received by doing business on the leased property.

performance Point when a party or parties to a contract fulfill the promises or obligations in the contract.

periodic cap Limits the amount the interest rate of an adjustable-rate loan may increase at any one time (usually a year).

personal assistant An individual hired by a licensee to perform administrative tasks associated with real estate transactions. Whether a personal assistant must be a real estate licensee is determined by the tasks the assistant performs.

personal property Tangible and movable property (transferred by bill of sale); property not classified as real property. Also called personalty or chattel.

personal representative Administrator of a deceased person's estate.

petition for review A request to a court of appeal (appellate court) asking it to examine the record of the proceedings in a specific case. *See also* judicial review.

PITI Principal, interest, taxes, and insurance payment on a mortgage loan.

plaintiff The person or party bringing suit or charges; the complaining party; complainant.

planned unit development (PUD) A residential project with mixed land uses and high residential density.

planning commission An official agency, usually made up of appointed lay citizens, that directs and controls the use, design, and development of land in a city, county, or region. Also called a *planning board*.

plottage The added value as a result of combining two or more properties into one large parcel.

point of beginning (POB) The starting (and ending) place in a land survey using the metes-and-bounds method of property description.

point of contact information Any means by which to contact the brokerage firm or individual licensee, including mailing address(es), physical street address(es), email address(es), telephone number(s), or facsimile telephone number(s).

police power The authority of government to protect the property, life, health, and welfare of its citizens.

positive leverage The benefits from borrowing funds exceed the costs of borrowing.

potential gross income (PGI) The total annual income a property would produce with 100% occupancy and no collection or vacancy losses.

power of attorney Designation of another person to act for a principal who may not be present.

preclosing inspection A final walk-through with the sales associate to verify that repairs have been completed and that the property is left in good condition.

prepayment clause A provision in a mortgage that allows the mortgagor to pay the mortgage debt ahead of schedule without penalty.

prepayment penalty The amount set by the creditor that the debtor is charged for retiring the debt early.

present value The worth of all future benefits of an investment in terms of today's dollars.

price The amount paid for something.

price-fixing Competing brokers conspire to establish a standard commission rate rather than let the rate be set by the open market.

prima facie evidence Requiring no further proof; acceptable on the face of.

primary lender Financial institution that makes mortgage loans directly to borrowers (e.g., savings association, bank).

primary mortgage market A source for the purchase of a mortgage loan by a borrower.

principal The party employing the services of a real estate broker; amount of money borrowed in a mortgage loan, excluding interest and other charges.

principal meridian Imaginary lines running north and south and crossing a base line at a definite point; used by surveyors for reference in locating and describing land under the government survey system.

principle of substitution An economic law of value: No prudent buyer will pay more for a property than the cost of an equally desirable replacement property.

private mortgage insurance (PMI) Needed to insure all of the mortgage representing more than 80% of appraised value or purchase price.

pro forma statement An estimate of the economic results of a proposed project; a projected income statement.

probable cause Reasonable grounds or justification for prosecuting.

probation An administrative penalty imposed by the FREC that allows the licensee to continue to practice real estate under the guidance of the FREC for a period of time while completing conditions specified by the FREC.

procuring cause The person whose efforts are the cause of an executed sale contract, regardless of who actually writes the contract.

professional association (PA) A business corporation consisting of one or more individuals engaged in a primary business that provides a professional service (e.g., lawyer, doctor).

professional member A member of the FREC who holds either an active broker license or an active sales associate license.

profit The amount one makes over and above one's cost.

progression The principle that states that the value of an inferior property is enhanced by its association with superior properties of the same type.

promissory note A written promise to pay a specific amount. *See also* note.

promulgates The formal act of announcing a statute or an administrative rule. To publish and officially announce a new or amended rule or statute. The FREC may promulgate rules and regulations.

property A bundle of legal rights.

property management The leasing, managing, marketing, and overall maintenance of property for others.

property manager A person who manages properties for various owners. A property manager's primary duties are to secure and keep tenants, to provide financial records and accounts, and to provide upkeep and maintenance of the properties.

property report A disclosure document required under the federal Interstate Land Sales Full Disclosure Act.

proprietary lease A written agreement between the owner-corporation and the tenant-stockholder in a cooperative apartment.

proration To divide or assess proportionate shares of charges and credits between the buyer and the seller according to their individual period of ownership.

prospectus A document prepared by a developer of more than 20 new condominium units that summarizes some of the major points contained in the condominium documents.

public accommodations Private entities that own, lease, lease to, or operate facilities such as restaurants, retail stores, hotels, movie theaters, private schools, convention centers, doctors' offices, homeless shelters, transportation depots, zoos, funeral homes, day care centers, and recreation facilities, including sports stadiums and fitness clubs.

purchase money mortgage (PMM) Any new mortgage taken as part of the purchase price of real property by the seller.

Q

quadrant Quarter; any of the four quarters into which something is divided.

qualification The process of reviewing before approval (of a buyer's housing needs and financial abilities, of a borrower's mortgage loan application, or of an application for licensure). *See also* underwriting.

quasi-judicial Powers delegated to the FREC to discipline real estate licensees for violations of real estate license law and FREC administrative rules.

quasi-legislative Powers delegated to the FREC to enact rules and regulations, decide questions of practice, and validate records (imprint with FREC's seal).

quiet enjoyment A provision in a deed guaranteeing that the buyer may enjoy possession of the property in peace and without disturbance by reason of other claims on the title by the seller or anyone else.

quiet title A suit or action in a court to remove a defect, cloud, or claim against the title to real property.

quitclaim deed A type of deed that will effectively convey any present interest, claim, or title to real property that the seller (grantor) may own.

quorum The minimum number of persons who may lawfully transact the business of a meeting (51% or four of the members of the Florida Real Estate Commission).

R

R-value Resistance to heat flow. The measure of the energy-effectiveness of insulation.

range In the government survey system of land description, a vertical strip of land six miles wide located between two consecutive submeridians or range lines.

range lines The surveyed north-south lines running every six miles east and west of the principal meridian. Also called *submeridians*.

ratio The relationship in quantity, size, or amount between two things; proportion.

ready, willing, and able "Ready" indicates the buyer is in a position and of a mind to complete the transaction; "willing" implies that the buyer desires to do so at the price and terms agreed; "able" refers to the buyer's financial ability to produce the required money when necessary.

real estate Land, including the air above and the earth below, plus any permanent improvements affecting the utility of the land; real property; property that is not personal property.

real estate brokerage A part of the real estate business that is concerned with bringing together buyers and sellers and owners and renters and completing a real estate transaction.

real estate business A commercial activity in which the sale, purchase, leasing, rental, exchange, or management of real property is conducted by qualified and licensed parties acting either for themselves or for others for compensation.

real estate investment trust (REIT) A method of pooling investment money using the trust form of ownership.

real estate profession A profession requiring knowledge of real estate values, experience in dealing with the public, plus exceptional personal integrity and character as qualifications to act as advisors and agents for members of the public.

Real Estate Recovery Fund A state-regulated account to cover claims of aggrieved parties who have suffered monetary losses from licensee's actions.

real estate services Real estate activities involving compensation for performing the activities for another.

real property Any interest or estate in land, including leaseholds, subleaseholds, business opportunities and enterprises, and mineral rights; real estate.

REALTOR® A real estate broker who is a member of a local board of REALTORS® and is affiliated with the state association (Florida Realtors®) and the National Association of REALTORS®. The term is not synonymous with "real estate agent."

realty A synonym for real estate and real property.

reasonable time A variable period of time, which may be affected by market conditions, desires of the owner, supply and demand, fluctuations of values, or an official decision.

receiver An independent party appointed by a court to impartially preserve and manage property that is involved in litigation, pending final disposition of the matter before the court.

receivership clause A provision in a mortgage, related to income-producing property, that is designed to require that income derived be used to make mortgage payments in the event the mortgagor (borrower) defaults.

reciprocity The practice of mutual exchanges of privileges. Some states have reciprocal arrangements for recognizing and granting licenses to licensed real estate professionals from other states.

recommended order A determination by an administrative law judge that includes findings and conclusions, as well as other information required by law or agency rule to be in a final order.

reconciliation The process of weighting the estimates of value derived from the sales comparison, cost, and income approaches to arrive at a final estimate of market value.

record To place any document or instrument affecting title or an interest in real property in the public records of the county in which the property is located.

recovery period The assigned time over which property is depreciated for tax purposes.

redemption To repurchase, to buy back, to recover property used as security for a mortgage by paying the debt. *See also* equity of redemption.

redlining Discriminatory financing by a lending institution.

registration Authorization by the state to place an applicant on the register (record) of officially recognized individuals and businesses.

regression The principle stating that the value of a superior property is adversely affected by its association with an inferior property of the same type.

release clause A provision in a blanket mortgage covering more than one unit of real property that provides for the mortgagor to obtain freedom from the mortgage for each unit when a designated amount has been paid to the mortgagee for each unit.

reliction Gradual receding of water and resulting permanent increase in land once covered.

remainderman The party designated to receive an estate at the end of a life estate.

rental agent A person who, for a fee, acts as an intermediary between a person seeking to lease a housing accommodation and a property owner seeking to acquire a lease for a housing accommodation. Rental agents who are paid on a transaction basis must be licensed real estate agents. Salaried employees who work in an onsite rental office in a leasing capacity are exempt from a real estate license, provided they are not paid on a transactional basis.

renunciation To abandon an acquired right without transferring that right to another.

replacement cost The expenditure of constructing a building with +current materials and techniques that has the same functional utility as the structure being appraised.

replacement reserves A portion of the annual income set aside for covering the cost of major components (e.g., air-conditioning) that wear out faster than the building itself. Also called a *reserve for replacements*.

reprimand An official act of oral and/or written criticism with a formal warning included.

reproduction cost Amount required to duplicate the property exactly.

rescind To annul, cancel, repeal, or terminate.

reserve requirements The amount of funds that an institution must hold in reserve against deposit liabilities.

residential sale The sale of improved residential property of four or fewer units, the sale of unimproved residential property intended for use as four or fewer units, or the sale of agricultural property of 10 or fewer acres.

respondent A person who answers to an informal complaint proceeding prior to being adjudged innocent or being named as a defendant.

restriction Any device or action that controls or limits the use of real property.

restrictive covenants Conditions placed by developers that affect how the land can be used in an entire subdivision.

reverse mortgage A form of mortgage that enables elderly homeowners to borrow against the equity in their homes so they can receive monthly payments needed to help meet living expenses.

reversion That portion of the net proceeds from the sale of property that represents the return of the investor's capital.

revocation To cancel, rescind, annul, or make void; the permanent cancellation of a person's license.

right of survivorship A legal concept whereby the surviving owners of a joint interest in real property are entitled to the interest formerly owned by one or more deceased owners without the need for probate proceedings.

right to reinstate A mortgage clause based on the equity of redemption. The mortgagor's right to reinstate the original repayment terms in the note after the mortgagee has initiated the acceleration clause.

right-to-use A leasehold interest in a time-share unit based on the limited time (one or more weeks) specified in the agreement.

riparian rights Private ownership rights extending to the normal high-water mark along a river or stream and including access rights to water, boating, bathing, and dockage in accordance with state and federal statutes.

risk The chance of losing all or a part of an investment; the uncertainty of financial loss.

S

sale and leaseback A financing arrangement in which an investor buys property owned and used by a business accompanied by a simultaneous leasing back of the property to the business by the buyer-investor.

sale contract An agreement whereby one party agrees to sell and the other party agrees to buy according to the terms set forth. Also called a *deposit receipt contract, purchase agreement*, or *contract for sale and purchase*.

sales associate A licensed individual who, for compensation, is employed by a broker or owner-developer.

sales comparison approach A method for estimating the market value of a property by comparing similar properties to the subject property.

satisfaction of mortgage A certificate issued by the lender when the debt obligation is paid in full.

seal A mark, emblem, or impression on a document used to authenticate the document or a signature.

sealed Statutes in some states permit a person's criminal record to be sealed, and thereafter such records cannot be examined except by order of the court or by designated officials.

second mortgage A loan that is junior or subordinate to a first mortgage, normally taken out when the borrower needs more money. Also called *secondary financing*.

secondary lender Agency or financial institution that buys mortgage loans previously made by primary lenders.

secondary mortgage market A source for the purchase and sale of existing mortgages.

section One of the primary units of measurement in the government survey system of land description. A section is one mile square and contains 640 acres.

Secure and Fair Enforcement of Mortgage Licensing Act (SAFE Act) The SAFE Act sets a minimum standard for licensing and registering mortgage loan originators. (MLOs were previously licensed as mortgage brokers.)

security Evidence of a debt or of ownership.

seisin A covenant in a deed that warrants that the grantor (seller) holds the property by virtue of a fee simple title and has a complete right to dispose of same. Also called a seizin clause.

seller's market The demand for available properties exceeds the supply.

separate property Real property owned by a spouse before the marriage with the spouse having no present rights in such property; property owned individually.

setback Restrictions established by zoning or deed on the space required between lot lines and building lines.

severalty Sole ownership of real property ("severed" from all others).

severance The act of removing something attached to the land (e.g., fruit, timber, fence).

short sale A sale of secured real property that produces less money than is owed the lender. The lender releases its mortgage so that the property can be sold free and clear to the new purchaser.

single agent Per Section 475.01, F.S., a broker who represents, as a fiduciary, either the buyer or the seller but not both in the same transaction.

site plan A document that indicates the improvement details for a project of greater-than-average size.

situs Relationships and influences created by location of a property that affect value (e.g., accessibility, personal preference).

sole proprietorship Dealing as an individual in business.

special agent One authorized by a principal to perform a particular act or transaction, without contemplation of continuity of service as with a general agent.

special assessment Taxes levied against properties to pay for all, or part of, improvements that will benefit the properties being assessed.

special exception An individual ruling in which a property owner is granted the right to a use otherwise contrary to law.

special flood hazard area (SFHA) Defined by FEMA as the area that will be inundated by the flood event having a 1% chance of being equaled or exceeded in any given year. The 1% annual chance flood is also called the base flood or 100-year flood.

special information booklet A booklet containing consumer information regarding closing costs the borrower may incur at closing. RESPA requires lenders to give the booklet to loan applicants.

special purpose property A combination of land and improvements with only one economically feasible use because of some special design.

specific lien Claims that affect only the property designated in the lien instruments or agreements.

specific performance A remedy for an injured party obtained through a court of equity, which requires specific accomplishment of the contract terms by a defendant.

state-certified appraiser A person verified by the DBPR as qualified to issue state-certified real property appraisals.

state documentary stamp tax on deeds Tax required on all deeds or other documents used as conveyances. The charge is based on the total purchase price.

state documentary stamp tax on notes Tax required on all promissory notes. The cost is based on the face value of the note.

state intangible tax on mortgages Tax required before a mortgage is recorded. The cost is based on the face value of the mortgage.

statute An established rule or law passed by a legislative body.

statute of frauds An act requiring that certain real estate instruments and contracts affecting title to real property be in writing in order to be enforceable.

statute of limitations An act that prescribes specific time restrictions for enforcement of rights by action of law.

statutory law Law created by the enactment of legislation, as opposed to law created by judicial decisions (common law).

statutory month method A proration method in which each month is considered to have 30 days.

statutory redemption period In some states (not Florida), the period of time after a judicial foreclosure proceeding during which a person has the right to redeem (buy back) a property lost in a judicial foreclosure.

stay Delay temporarily; stop for a limited time.

steering Discriminatory acts against buyers.

stipulation An agreement as to the penalty reached between the attorneys for the DRE and the licensee or licensee's attorney.

subagent A person authorized to assist and represent the agent and whose duties are delegated by the original agent.

subdivide To segment large, acquired tracts of real property in order to create small tracts for the purpose of resale.

subdivision plat map A plan of a tract of land subdivided into lots and showing required or planned amenities.

subject property The real property under discussion or appraisal.

subject to A buyer makes regular periodic payments on the mortgage but does not assume responsibility for the mortgage.

sublease A lessee leasing a property to a third party for a period of time less than the original lease. Also called *subletting*.

subordination agreement A written agreement between holders of liens on a property that changes the priority of mortgage, judgment, or other liens under certain circumstances.

subordination clause A provision in a mortgage in which the lender voluntarily permits a prior or subsequent mortgage to take priority over the lender's otherwise superior mortgage; the act of yielding priority.

subpoena A writ or order commanding the person named to appear and testify in a legal proceeding.

suit An act of suing; an action in a court of law for the recovery of a right or claim.

summary (emergency) suspension order Emergency or immediate action taken by the secretary of the DBPR against a license to protect the public.

superior lien A lien that takes priority over all other liens.

supply The quantity of goods or services offered for sale to consumers.

survey The procedure used to measure and describe a specific tract of real property for the purpose of determining exact boundaries and the area contained therein.

suspension To cause to cease operating for a period of time; the temporary withholding of a person's license, rendering it ineffective; a period of enforced inactivity.

T

takeout commitment A written commitment from a financial institution certifying that permanent financing will be provided when the project is completed.

tangible asset Anything of substance; personal and real property (e.g., cash, building, equipment, land).

target market A specific group of prospects chosen because of its demographic, financial, and lifestyle characteristics.

tax certificate A document sold by a local tax authority granting the certificate buyer the right to receive delinquent taxes plus interest when paid by the legal property owner.

tax deed A type of deed used to convey title after real property is sold at auction by public authority for nonpayment of taxes.

tax district An authority, such as a city, county, school board, or special levy area (e.g., water district), with the power to assess property owners annually in order to meet its expenditures for the public good.

tax lien A claim against real property arising out of nonpayment of the property taxes.

tax rate The percentage of value that is used to determine the amount of tax to be levied against each individual unit of property; ad valorem (according to the value).

tax shelter An investment that shields items of income or gain from payment of income taxes; a term used to describe some tax advantages of owning real property (or other investments), including postponement or even elimination of certain taxes.

taxable income Gross income minus tax deductions; net operating income plus reserve for replacements minus financing costs and allowable depreciation.

taxable value The assessed value less allowable exemptions resulting in an amount to which the tax rate is applied to determine property taxes due.

team advertising The name or logo used by one or more licensees who represent themselves to the public as a team (or group).

teaser rate A below-market interest rate usually offered for the first year on some adjustable-rate mortgages.

telephone solicitation The initiation of a telephone call for the purpose of encouraging the purchase of, or investment in, property, goods, or services.

tenancy The estate or rights of a tenant. *See also* estate.

tenancy at sufferance An estate lawfully acquired for a temporary period of time but retained after a period of lawful possession has expired; nonfreehold estate.

tenancy at will An estate that may be terminated by either party at any time upon proper notice; nonfreehold estate.

tenancy by the entireties An estate created by spouses jointly owning real property with instant and complete right of survivorship.

tenant A person or party with rights of occupancy or possession of real property.

tenants in common A form of ownership by two or more persons each having an equal or unequal interest and passing the interest to heirs, not to surviving tenants.

term mortgage A nonamortizing loan that normally calls for repayment of the principal in full at the end of the loan term.

testate Having left a will.

testator A person who makes a will. A female testator is called a testatrix.

third party Generally, a member of the public; not the principal or agent in a transaction.

tier An east-west row of townships (as used in the government survey method of land description).

time is of the essence A phrase in a contract making failure to perform by a specified date a breach or violation of the agreement.

time-share An individual interest in a real property unit together with a right of exclusive use for a specified number of days or weeks per year.

title Evidence of ownership of real property, such as a deed.

title closing The consummation of a real estate transaction, when the seller delivers title to the buyer in exchange for payment from the buyer of the purchase price.

title insurance A policy of insurance that protects the holder from any loss resulting from defects in the title.

title search An examination of all the public records to determine whether any defects exist in the chain of title.

title theory Legal concept that vests title to mortgaged property in the mortgagee (lender) or a third party.

topography Surface features (natural and manufactured) of land (e.g., lakes, mountains, roads).

township A square tract of land measuring six miles on each side and including 36 sections (formed by the crossing of range and township lines).

township line The east-west survey lines located every six miles north and south of the primary base line. Also called a *subbaseline*.

trade fixture An article that is attached by a commercial tenant as a necessary part of the tenant's business and is personal property.

trade name Any adopted or fictitious name used to designate a business concern.

transaction broker A broker who provides limited representation to a buyer, a seller, or both in a real estate transaction, but does not represent either in a fiduciary capacity or as a single agent.

transaction value The loan amount in most appraisal assignments.

triggering terms The Truth in Lending Act requires creditors to disclose certain information if certain credit terms, called triggering terms, are included in the advertisement. Triggering terms include the amount or percentage of down payment, number of payments, period (term) of repayment, amount of any payment, and the amount of any finance charges.

trust A right of property, either real or personal, held by one party for the benefit of another.

trust funds Cash, checks, money orders, and items that can be converted into cash, such as deeds and personal property, that a person (broker) holds in trust for another person.

trustee A person or party, either appointed or required by law to administer or manage another's property. Also called an *escrow agent*.

Truth in Lending Act (TILA) A body of federal law that is part of the Consumer Credit Protection Act and implemented by the Federal Reserve Board's Regulation Z. The main purpose of the act is to ensure that borrowers and customers of consumer credit are given meaningful information with respect to the cost of credit so that consumers can compare the various credit terms available.

U

underwriting The analysis of the extent of risk assumed by a lender in connection with a proposed mortgage loan. Also called *loan qualification* or *risk analysis*.

undivided interest An interest in the entire property, rather than ownership of a particular part of the property.

unenforceable contract A contract that was valid when made but either cannot be proved or will not be upheld by a court.

Uniform Standards of Professional Appraisal Practice (USPAP) The set of standards that must be followed when performing appraisal services.

unilateral contract An agreement in which only one party promises to perform without receiving a reciprocal promise to perform from the other party.

unities Individual prerequisites required to constitute a single joint tenancy. Also called the *four unities*.

universal agent A representative authorized by the principal to perform all acts that the principal can personally perform and that may be lawfully delegated to another.

unliquidated damages The amount of valuable consideration awarded by a court to an injured party as a result of default. *See also* damages.

up-front mortgage insurance premium (UFMIP) A one-time mortgage insurance premium on FHA mortgage loans that is paid at closing.

V

vacancy and collection losses A deduction from potential gross income for (1) current or expected future space not rented as a result of tenant turnover and (2) loss from uncollected rent due from delinquent tenants.

vacancy rate The percentage of rental units that are not occupied.

vacate To set aside, cancel, or annul; to leave empty.

valid Sufficient to be legally binding; enforceable.

valid contract An agreement binding on both parties and legally enforceable against all parties to the agreement.

valuable consideration The money or a promise of something that can be measured in terms of money.

value The worth of something.

variable lease An agreement for the tenant to pay specified rent increases based on a predetermined index (CPI) at set future dates.

variance An exception to zoning regulations or ordinances granted to relieve a hardship.

vendee The buyer or purchaser of real property under an agreement of sale.

vendor The seller of real property in an agreement of sale.

vendor's lien A claim against property giving the seller the right to hold the property as security for any unpaid purchase money.

void contract An agreement that does not meet all the required elements of a valid contract and has no legal effect.

voidable contract A contract that because of the manner or method in which it was brought about, one of the parties is allowed to avoid contractual duties.

voluntarily relinquish The licensee requests that the DBPR cancel the license. The DBPR will accept a licensee's request to voluntarily relinquish a license, provided there is no investigation or discipline pending against the licensee. The licensee sends written communication to the DBPR indicating that the licensee is retiring or no longer desires to be licensed.

voluntary alienation The transfer of title is accomplished with the owner's control and consent.

voluntary inactive The license status that results when a licensee has met all the requirements for licensure, yet the licensee chooses not to engage in the real estate business and has requested that the license be placed in this status.

voluntary liens Claims imposed against real property with the consent of the owner.

voluntary relinquishment for permanent revocation A licensee-respondent may choose to avoid a disciplinary hearing and relinquish the real estate license in lieu of discipline, permanently revoking the license.

W

warranty forever A provision in a deed guaranteeing that the seller will for all time defend the title and possession for the buyer.

waste An improper use or abuse of property by one who holds less than the fee simple ownership of it.

will A written document legally executed by which an individual disposes of an estate, effective after death.

withhold adjudication When the court determines that a defendant is not likely to again engage in a criminal act and that the ends of justice and the welfare of society do not require that the defendant suffer the penalty imposed by law, the court may withhold adjudication of guilt, stay (stop) the imposition of the sentence, and place the defendant on probation.

witness A person who gives testimony; one who observes and attests to the signing or executing of a document.

writ of certiorari An order to bring from a lower court to an appellate court an action or record of proceedings in a case.

writ of mandamus An order of a superior court directing a lower court or body to do some specified act.

writ of supersedeas A stay of enforcement; temporary stop in a legal proceeding; restraining order.

Y

yield The rate of return; the return on an investment or the amount of profit stated as a percentage of the amount invested; the ratio of the annual net income from a property to the cost or market value of the property.

Z

zoning ordinance Classification of real property for various purposes; the governmental power to control and supervise the use of privately owned real property (actually, the exercise of police powers).

ANSWER KEY

Unit 1 Practice Questions Answers

1. expert information
2. property transfer, market conditions, how to market real estate and businesses
3. Residential, commercial, industrial, agricultural, businesses
4. farm area
5. Target marketing
6. absentee owner
7. rental agents, property managers
8. return, investment
9. management agreement
10. federally related
11. broker, directly
12. USPAP
13. mortgage loan originator
14. counseling
15. Land acquisition, subdividing and development, recording the subdivision plat map
16. Dedication
17. Speculative (spec) homes, custom homes, tract homes
18. buyer, speculation
19. REALTOR®
20. multiple listing

Unit 1 Exam Answers

1. b (1.8)
2. d (1.2)
3. a (1.4)
4. c (1.3)
5. a (1.4)
6. a (1.4)
7. b (1.2)
8. b (1.3)
9. c (1.7)
10. a (1.6)
11. c (1.2)
12. c (1.2)
13. d (1.3)
14. c (1.2)
15. b (1.4)

Unit 2 Practice Questions Answers

1. 61J2
2. 20
3. broker associate
4. salary, commission
5. c, d
6. 30
7. 90
8. four
9. 40, 75%
10. c, d, e
11. Attorneys, Florida Bar
12. a, c
13. two
14. two
15. 21
16. two
17. core law
18. three
19. 45
20. 24 months, five years
21. 60, first renewal
22. prima facie
23. a, b, c, d, e, g
24. Advertise real estate services, buy, appraise (non-federally related transactions), rent or provide rental information or lists, sell, auction, lease, exchange
25. a, c, d

Unit 2 Practice Exercise: When a Real Estate License Is (or Is Not) Required

1. *License is required.* Chris performed real estate services (buying and selling activities) by giving suggestive information about the property that was not presented in pre-printed materials. This is a violation of Chapter 475.

2. *License is not required.* Court-appointed individuals acting within the limitations of their duties are exempt from real estate licensure. Matthew may sell the property in accordance with the instructions of the court. Compensation is usually paid from the assets of the estate.

3. *License is not required.* Property owners do not need a real estate license to sell their own property. They may split the proceeds of the sale based on their percentage share of ownership. If an unlicensed individual receives more than their ownership share, a license would be required. It would be a violation of license law.

4. *License is required.* The sales staff of an owner-developer is exempt from a real estate license if the staff is paid strictly on a salaried basis. In this case, a commission is paid (compensation on a transactional basis), so an active license is required. Sally should have been registered with an active license status under her employer (the developer) for this to be in accordance with Chapter 475.

5. *License is not required.* A sales associate or broker associate must be registered under a broker or an owner-developer to be paid a commission. The associate can also work as a rental agent, provided the associate is paid a salary. Salaried individuals who work in a leasing capacity and who do not receive compensation on a transactional basis are exempt from a real estate license under 475.011, F.S. Therefore, it is not a violation of license law for Teresa to work as an agent of her broker and to receive a salary from another employer for working in a leasing capacity.

Unit 2 Exam Answers

1. b (2.1)
2. c (2.5)
3. d (2.7)
4. c (2.8)
5. b (2.3)
6. a (2.2)
7. d (2.3)
8. c (2.3)
9. b (2.3)
10. a (2.4)
11. a (2.6)
12. b (2.9)
13. d (2.8)
14. b (2.6)
15. c (2.9)
16. d (2.9)
17. d (2.9)
18. d (2.9)
19. d (2.9)
20. a (2.3)

Unit 3 Practice Questions Answers

1. Tallahassee
2. governor, senate
3. Orlando
4. recordkeeping
5. secretary
6. FREC
7. five
8. two

9. one
10. unlicensed
11. Executive, quasi-legislative, quasi-judicial
12. quasi-legislative
13. quasi-judicial
14. executive
15. prima facie
16. promulgates
17. involuntary inactive
18. expiration
19. two years
20. two years, null, void
21. 12, 24, 28
22. 10
23. cease to be in force
24. immediately
25. 60
26. group
27. Multiple licenses

Unit 3 Exam Answers

1. c (3.2)
2. d (3.2)
3. c (3.3)
4. d (3.4)
5. b (3.2)
6. c (3.2)
7. d (3.3)
8. c (3.3)
9. d (3.2)
10. c (3.1)
11. b (3.1)
12. a (3.4)
13. a (3.2)
14. a (3.4)
15. a (3.4)
16. d (3.4)
17. a (3.5)
18. a (3.4)
19. b (3.5)
20. d (3.4)

Unit 4 Practice Questions Answers

1. principal
2. agent

3. at arm's length
4. unwritten law
5. statutory law
6. general
7. No brokerage relationship, single agent, transaction broker
8. Account for all funds, deal honestly and fairly, disclose all known facts that affect value of residential property
9. customer
10. confidentiality
11. obedience
12. loyalty
13. Full disclosure
14. transaction broker
15. limited
16. fiduciary
17. consent, transition
18. a.) No, transaction broker relationship duties include the duty to disclose all known facts that affect value of residential property. The fact that a transaction broker relationship existed did not relieve Harbor Realty from the duty to disclose the air-conditioning compressor's condition.

    b.) Yes, Merissa can be charged with violating Section 475.278, F.S.: failure to disclose facts that materially affect the value of property.

    c.) Yes, the broker for Harbor Realty, in addition to the sales associate, can be disciplined for not disclosing the air-conditioning compressor's condition.
19. four
20. b, c
21. showing of property
22. duties, customer
23. listing agreement, showing
24. five
25. nonresidential
26. designated sales associates

27. single agents
28. single agent
29. Fulfillment, Mutual agreement, Destruction, Death, Bankruptcy

Unit 4 Exam Answers

1. d (4.6)
2. b (4.7)
3. a (4.4)
4. b (4.5)
5. c (4.3)
6. b (4.3)
7. d (4.5)
8. d (4.5)
9. b (4.1)
10. d (4.1)
11. b (4.3)
12. a (4.8)
13. b (4.1)
14. d (4.9)
15. c (4.3)

Unit 5 Practice Questions Answers

1. one, privacy
2. zoning, sign
3. not, location
4. not, employer
5. Trade name (if one is used), broker's name, licensed (lic.) real estate broker
6. exterior, interior
7. brokerage firm
8. c
9. a, b, d, e, f
10. second
11. name, point of contact
12. false advertising
13. Telephone Consumer Protection
14. 8:00 am, 9:00 pm
15. Friday, Tuesday
16. signatory
17. title company, attorney's trust account
18. next business day
19. third business day
20. commingling

21. account, deliver
22. Mediation, arbitration, litigation, escrow disbursement order (EDO)
23. writing, 15 business
24. 30 business, received
25. disclosed
26. net proceeds, commercial
27. a, d, e
28. 14, temporary, 60
29. a, c

Unit 5 Exam Answers

1. c (5.7)
2. c (5.4)
3. b (5.4)
4. c (5.4)
5. c (5.5)
6. d (5.4)
7. c (5.7)
8. b (5.3)
9. d (5.7)
10. d (5.6)
11. b (5.7)
12. c (5.7)
13. d (5.2)
14. c (5.7)
15. c (5.5)
16. b (5.6)
17. b (5.7)
18. d (5.6)
19. a (5.6)
20. c (5.7)

Unit 6 Practice Questions Answers

1. The licensee concealed that the licensee had signed the buyer's signature on the contract for sale.
2. material
3. legally sufficient
4. confidential, 10
5. one, current
6. formal complaint
7. not, prohibited
8. stipulation
9. informal
10. administrative law judge
11. recommended order
12. 30

13. a, d
14. deficient
15. prejudice
16. 10
17. reprimand
18. permanent
19. first-time
20. citation
21. Falsifying a license application, Unlicensed activity, Theft or reproduction of a license exam
22. first
23. second
24. Attorney's fees, Court costs, Actual damages
25. $50,000
26. $150,000
27. treble (triple) interest
28. suspended, reimburses
29. $10,000
30. $28,000

Unit 6 Exam Answers

1. a (6.8)
2. d (6.3)
3. c (6.6)
4. a (6.7)
5. b (6.4)
6. c (6.2)
7. b (6.8)
8. a (6.2)
9. a (6.5)
10. b (6.4)
11. a (6.6)
12. c (6.8)
13. c (6.7)
14. a (6.6)
15. b (6.8)

Unit 7 Practice Questions Answers

1. a, c, e
2. offices, housing
3. race, any
4. race, residential, commercial

5. Civil Rights Act, 1968
6. Single-family, multifamily
7. redlining
8. Steering
9. members
10. Public accommodations
11. access, transportation, accommodations, commercial
12. property report
13. seventh
14. exempt
15. 30
16. 75%, 5%
17. escrow
18. $5,000

Unit 7 Exam Answers

1. b (7.1)	6. a (7.2)	11. a (7.5)
2. d (7.4)	7. d (7.5)	12. a (7.5)
3. a (7.1)	8. b (7.5)	13. c (7.5)
4. b (7.5)	9. d (7.5)	14. b (7.1)
5. b (7.5)	10. a (7.1)	15. a (7.2)

Unit 8 Practice Questions Answers

1. Surface, subsurface, air
2. riparian
3. nonflowing
4. surface, nature
5. human-made, man-made
6. Real property, personal property
7. Intent of the parties, relationship of the parties, method or degree of attachment, adaptation of the item
8. fixture

9. personal property
10. chattel (movable items), personalty, limited
11. Trade fixtures, personal, trade, business
12. Disposition, enjoyment, exclusion, possession, control
13. remainder
14. life
15. Possession, interest, time, title
16. Joint tenancy, Tenancy by the entireties
17. 7 days, 15 days
18. ownership, indefinite
19. fee simple
20. possession, nonfreehold
21. by the entireties
22. starting, ending
23. remainderman
24. conventional, legal
25. proprietary lease
26. pro rata
27. stock
28. fee simple, undivided, common elements
29. individual units
30. deed
31. declaration
32. interval ownership

Unit 8 Exam Answers

1. d (8.4)
2. c (8.1)
3. d (8.2)
4. d (8.5)
5. d (8.3)
6. a (8.4)
7. b (8.4)
8. a (8.2)
9. b (8.4)
10. c (8.4)
11. d (8.4)
12. b (8.4)
13. b (8.4)
14. d (8.1)
15. b (8.5)
16. c (8.5)
17. a (8.5)
18. d (8.5)
19. d (8.4)
20. c (8.4)

Unit 9 Practice Questions Answers

1. equitable
2. freehold
3. voluntary alienation
4. deed
5. intestate
6. operation, law
7. seven
8. Actual notice, constructive notice
9. constructive
10. Acknowledgment
11. Owner's policy, lender's policy
12. abstract, title
13. purchase price
14. not
15. attorney, title insurance
16. appurtenances
17. competent grantor, two witnesses
18. habendum, life
19. delivered, accepted
20. of seisin, against encumbrances, of further assurance, of quiet enjoyment, of warranty forever
21. general warranty

22. quiet enjoyment
23. Police power, eminent domain, taxation
24. Deed restrictions, easements, leases, liens
25. Judgment lien, income tax lien, federal estate tax lien (Note: Florida does not have an estate tax)
26. appurtenant
27. in gross
28. encroachment
29. net
30. subordination
31. $725,500 total gross sales – $500,000 = $225,500 subject to 4%. $225,500 × .04 = $9,020 additional annual rent. $2,800 × 12 months = $33,600 annual base rent. $33,600 annual base rent + $9,020 additional rent = $42,620.
32. 1.6 new rate ÷ 1.25 original rate = 1.28. $2,000 × 1.28 = $2,560 new rent payment.

Unit 9 Exam Answers

1. a (9.6)
2. c (9.1)
3. b (9.4)
4. d (9.5)
5. a (9.5)
6. c (9.1)
7. b (9.5)
8. a (9.4)
9. b (9.3)
10. d (9.4)
11. a (9.4)
12. c (9.6)
13. d (9.3)
14. c (9.3)
15. a (9.6)
16. a (9.6)
17. d (9.6)
18. d (9.6)
19. c (9.1)
20. d (9.6)

Unit 10 Practice Questions Answers

1. court, law
2. survey
3. metes-and-bounds
4. distance, direction
5. point, beginning
6. S 45° E
7. N 15° W
8. N 15° 25' 20" W

9. and 10.

	R3W	R2W	R1W	R1E	R2E	R3E
T3N						
T2N					#9	
T1N						
T1S						
T2S						
T3S			#10			

11.

N

W / E

6	5	4	3	2	1
7	8	9	10	11	12
18	17	16	15	14	13
19	20	21	22	23	24
30	29	28	27	26	25
31	32	33	34	35	36

S

12. 25, 1

13. 160

14. 640 ÷ 2 ÷ 4 ÷ 4 ÷ 4 = 5 acres or 640 ÷ 128 = 5 acres

15. 640 ÷ 2 ÷ 4 ÷ 4 = 20 acres
640 ÷ 4 ÷ 4 = 40 acres
20 + 40 = 60 acres

16. 60 acres × 43,560 square feet per acre = 2,613,600 square feet

17. An acre contains 43,560 square feet.
Cost divided by square feet in an acre = cost per square foot.
$21,780 ÷ 43,560 = $.50 per square foot

18. lots, blocks

19. plat maps

Unit 10 Exam Answers

1. c (10.5)
2. d (10.5)
3. b (10.2)
4. c (10.3)
5. b (10.3)
6. c (10.4)
7. d (10.3)
8. a (10.3)
9. c (10.3)
10. d (10.3)
11. b (10.2)
12. d (10.4)
13. d (10.5)
14. b (10.5)
15. b (10.6)

Unit 11 Practice Questions Answers

1. Listing agreement, buyer brokerage agreement, sale contract, option contract
2. void
3. voidable
4. unenforceable
5. unilateral
6. formal
7. executed
8. offeror
9. counteroffer
10. liquidated
11. novation
12. 24 hours
13. exclusive-agency
14. optionor
15. optionee
16. valuable consideration
17. divest
18. both spouses
19. promises
20. *Johnson*, *Davis*
21. licensees
22. not
23. DBPR

24. Misrepresentation
25. disclose

Unit 11 Exam Answers

1. c (11.1)	8. c (11.2)	15. d (11.8)
2. b (11.1)	9. d (11.3)	16. c (11.8)
3. a (11.1)	10. d (11.4)	17. b (11.7)
4. a (11.1)	11. d (11.5)	18. c (11.5)
5. d (11.1)	12. c (11.5)	19. a (11.8)
6. a (11.1)	13. b (11.6)	20. c (11.8)
7. b (11.1)	14. d (11.5)	

Unit 12 Practice Questions Answers

1. Mortgagor (borrower), mortgagee (lender)
2. note
3. security
4. mortgagee
5. lien, mortgagor
6. acceleration
7. defeasance
8. increase, yield
9. escrow account
10. \$283,500 loan amount ÷ \$315,000 purchase price = .9 or 90% LTV
11. (a) \$225,000 loan amount × .02 = \$4,500 cost of points
    (b) 2 points × 0.125 = .25%; 5% interest + .25% = 5.25% effective yield
12. The loan amount represents 80% of the purchase price. Therefore, the down payment is 20% of the purchase price. \$136,000 purchase price × .20 = \$27,200 down payment.
13. assignor, assignee
14. estoppel certificate
15. subject
16. novation
17. partial release

18. mortgagor
19. equity, redemption
20. nonjudicial
21. short sale
22. lis pendens

Unit 12 Exam Answers

1. b (12.1)	8. d (12.7)	15. c (12.5)
2. c (12.7)	9. c (12.1)	16. a (12.8)
3. c (12.2)	10. a (12.3)	17. a (12.5)
4. d (12.5)	11. c (12.7)	18. b (12.5)
5. c (12.8)	12. b (12.5)	19. d (12.4)
6. a (12.3)	13. c (12.6)	20. a (12.4)
7. d (12.1)	14. c (12.8)	

Unit 13 Practice Questions Answers

1. Conventional
2. 36%
3. \$1,500 PITI + \$95 PMI = \$1,595 total housing expense

   \$1,595 housing expense + \$260 car + \$186 loan + \$260 credit = \$2,301 total monthly obligations

   a. \$1,595 total housing expense ÷ \$5,900 monthly gross income = .270 or 27% HER

   b. \$2,301 total monthly obligations ÷ \$5,900 = .39 or 39% TOR

   c. The borrower's HER is below the required threshold of 28%; however, the borrower's monthly debt is too high in comparison to monthly gross income. The borrower's TOR of 39% is above the required threshold of 36% standard TOR for a conventional mortgage.
4. increases, decreases
5. level-payment plan
6. index
7. margin
8. periodic cap
9. negative amortization
10. up-front mortgage insurance premium (UFMIP), mortgage insurance premium (MIP)

11. housing expense ratio (HER): 31%, total obligations ratio (TOR): 43%
12.
    a. $2,276 + $160 = $2,436 monthly housing expense ÷ $8,000 gross monthly income = .3045 or 30% HER.
    b. $2,276 + $160 + $479 + $165 + $200 = $3,280 housing and recurring obligations ÷ $8,000 = .41 or 41% TOR.
    c. Yes, both the HER and TOR are within FHA qualifying ratio guidelines.
13. 41%
14. loan origination, funding
15. balloon payment
16. package
17. savings associations, commercial banks, credit unions, mortgage lenders
18. originated
19. portfolio
20. intermediation
21. circulate the mortgage money supply, standardized loan requirements
22. Ginnie Mae
23. straw buyer
24. No documentation
25. *Your Home Loan*
26. third business day
27. a, b, d
28. alimony, child support, public assistance

Unit 13 Exam Answers

1. c (13.7)
2. b (13.8)
3. d (13.8)
4. a (13.7)
5. c (13.6)
6. c (13.8)
7. c (13.5)
8. a (13.4)
9. a (13.4)
10. b (13.3)
11. a (13.5)
12. d (13.5)
13. b (13.6)
14. d (13.6)
15. d (13.10)
16. c (13.10)
17. c (13.10)
18. a (13.10)
19. c (13.9)
20. b (13.10)

Unit 14 Practice Questions Answers

1. \$289,000 sale price × .06 rate = \$17,340 total commission. \$17,340 total commission × .50 split = \$8,670 selling office's split. 100% – 45% = 55% selling office sales associate's split; \$8,670 × .55 = \$4,768.50 sales associate's commission at selling office.
2. Part ÷ rate = total. \$400 × 12 months = \$4,800 part. \$4,800 ÷ .04 = \$120,000 principal due on mortgage loan
3. Total × rate = part. \$115,900 × 7% = \$8,113
4. Part ÷ Total = Rate

   \$25,375 ÷ \$350,000 = .0725 or 7¼%
5. \$9,000 profit ÷ \$45,000 cost = .20 or 20% profit
6. \$3,000 loss ÷ 50,000 cost = .06 or 6% loss
7. 100% cost + 15% profit = \$32,200. 115% = \$32,200 selling price. \$32,200 selling price ÷ 1.15 = \$28,000 cost.
8. 100% – 20% = \$75,000. 80% = \$75,000. \$75,000 selling price ÷ .80 = \$93,750 cost.
9. preclosing inspection
10. tropical storm
11. \$3,011.25 ÷ 365 = \$8.25 daily rate. January 31 + February 28 + March 31 + April 30 + May 9 = 129 days. \$8.25 × 129 days = \$1,064.25 debit seller; \$1,064.25 credit buyer.
12. \$200,500 mortgage loan × .04 = \$8,020 annual interest. \$8,020 ÷ 365 = \$21.9726 daily rate of interest. \$21.9726 × 13 days = \$285.64 debit seller; \$285.64 credit buyer.
13. 30 days in April – 9 days seller owned property = 21 days rent due buyer. \$1,200 × 2 units = \$2,400 total rent for month of April. \$2,400 ÷ 30 days in month = \$80 daily rent. \$80 × 21 days due buyer = \$1,680 debit seller; \$1,680 credit buyer.
14. purchase price
15. \$.70, \$100
16. \$250,575 purchase price ÷ \$100 = 2,505.75, rounded up to 2,506 taxable increments. 2,506 taxable increments × \$.70 = \$1,754.20 tax on deed debit seller. \$250,575 purchase price × .80 = \$200,460 mortgage loan amount. \$200,460 new mortgage × \$.002 = \$400.92 intangible tax on new mortgage. \$200,460 ÷ \$100 increments = 2,004.6 rounded up to 2,005 taxable increments. 2,005 taxable increments × \$.35 = \$701.75 tax on promissory note. \$701.75 + \$400.92 = \$1,102.67 state transfer taxes associated with financing.
17. credit, buyer
18. debits
19. double

Unit 14 Exam Answers

1. (a) .395; (b) .02; (c) .75; (d) 1.45 (14.1)
2. (a) ½; (b) ⅕; (c) ¼; (d) ⅖ (14.1)
3. (a) .125; (b) .6; (c) .0625; (d) .05 (14.1)
4. (a) 25,600; (b) 823; (c) 736; (d) 45,500 (14.1)

5. b (14.1)
6. b (14.2)
7. d (14.5)
8. d (14.1)
9. d (14.1)
10. c (14.5)
11. c (14.4)
12. b (14.2)
13. b (14.4)
14. b (14.2)
15. c (14.4)
16. d (14.5)
17. b (14.6)
18. c (14.6)
19. d (14.6)
20. d (14.4)

Unit 15 Practice Questions Answers

1. Land is immobile (fixed) in its location, land is indestructible (durable), land is unique (nonhomogeneous)
2. down
3. up
4. situs
5. Supply
6. Demand
7. seller's
8. inversely
9. 400 – 350 = 50 vacant units. 50 ÷ 400 = .125 or 12.5%.
10. 180 ÷ 225 = .80 or 80%

Unit 15 Exam Answers

1. d (15.1)
2. b (15.1)
3. d (15.2)
4. c (15.3)
5. d (15.2)
6. c (15.2)
7. b (15.2)
8. b (15.1)
9. c (15.1)
10. d (15.2)

Unit 16 Practice Questions Answers

1. federally related
2. *USPAP*

3. CMAs, BPOs
4. $270,000, $450,000, $525,000
5. Market value
6. Liquidation
7. Assessed
8. substitution
9. overimprovement
10. assemblage
11. sales comparison
12. cost-depreciation
13. income
14. $184,500 comp sale price – $6,000 for fourth bedroom (comp is better; subtract) + $11,000 for pool (comp is inferior; add) = $189,500 adjusted sale price
15. $27,000 comp sale price + $5,000 for location (comp is inferior; add) – $4,000 for lot size (comp is better; subtract) = $28,000 adjusted sale price
16. Comp 1: $334,500 × .35 = $117,075. Comp 2: $338,700 × .45 = $152,415. Comp 3: $369,200 × .20 = $73,840. $117,075 + $152,415 + $73,840 = $343,330 estimated market value
17. Physical deterioration, functional obsolescence, external obsolescence
18. Reproduction
19. Depreciation
20. curable
21. economic
22. $60,000 net income ÷ $400,000 sale price = .15 or 15% capitalization rate
23. $75,000 NOI ÷ .15 rate = $500,000 investment; an investment of $500,000 with an annual net income of $75,000 will produce a capitalization rate of 15%.
24. present value, future
25. Potential gross income
26. Vacancy and collection loss
27. Net operating income
28. $260,000 × .55 = $143,000. $228,000 × .35 = $79,800. $220,000 × .10 = $22,000. $143,000 + $79,800 + $22,000 = $244,800 estimated value.
29. $1,500 monthly rental income × 126.5 GRM = $189,750 market value.

30. $25,500 gross annual income × 12.5 GIM = $318,750
31. $425,000 sale price ÷ $72,000 gross annual income = 5.90 (rounded) GIM
32. Recently sold, currently on the market, recently expired listings

Unit 16 Exam Answers

1. a (16.2)
2. c (16.2)
3. c (16.5)
4. b (16.3)
5. c (16.6)
6. b (16.2)
7. b (16.6)
8. d (16.5)
9. d (16.5)
10. d (16.6)
11. b (16.6)
12. b (16.6)
13. a (16.7)
14. d (16.7)
15. d (16.9)
16. a (16.7)
17. b (16.7)
18. a (16.5)
19. c (16.7)
20. c (16.7)

Unit 17 Practice Questions Answers

1. net worth
2. Business opportunities
3. Negative leverage
4. illiquid
5. hedge
6. market, default
7. Business, projected, actual
8. Financial
9. Sale of real property or assignment of a long-term lease is involved, active real estate license is required
10. Going-concern
11. intangible
12. corporate, business accounting, valuation
13. assets, liabilities
14. common, preferred
15. assets, liabilities
16. confidentiality
17. due diligence, financials

Unit 17 Exam Answers

1. a (17.1)
2. b (17.1)
3. a (17.3)
4. d (17.4)
5. a (17.1)
6. c (17.4)
7. b (17.5)
8. a (17.4)
9. d (17.2)
10. b (17.5)
11. d (17.1)
12. c (17.1)

Unit 18 Practice Questions Answers

1. local
2. Value Adjustment Board
3. ad valorem
4. assessed
5. just, market
6. $395,000 assessed value – $25,000 base homestead exemption = $370,000 taxable value for school taxes only. $395,000 assessed value – $50,000 homestead exemption = $345,000 taxable value for city and county taxes (non-school taxes).
7. Immune
8. Exempt
9. 100%
10. $5,000
11. a) $165,000 assessed value − $25,000 base homestead exemption − $5,000 blind exemption = $135,000 taxable value for school taxes; $135,000 taxable value × .006 = $810 school taxes owed. b) $165,000 assessed value − $50,000 homestead exemption − $5,000 blind exemption = $110,000 taxable value for city and county taxes; 8.7 mills city + 9.2 mills county = 17.9 mills = .0179. $110,000 taxable value × .0179 = $1,969 city and county taxes owed. c) $810 school taxes + $1,969 city/county taxes = $2,779 total taxes due.
12. three, tax
13. Green Belt, agricultural
14. Special assessments
15. ad valorem, front-foot
16. 18%
17. tax deed, two, seven
18. 120 front feet × $35 per foot = $4,200. $4,200 × .65 (owner's share of cost is 100% – 35%) = $2,730. $2,730 ÷ 2 (one-half of the street paving cost) = $1,365.
19. Mortgage interest is deductible, property tax is deductible, IRA withdrawal for first-time homebuyers, exclusion of gain from sale of principal residence

20. $250,000, $500,000

21. $339,900 ×.06 = $20,394 broker commission. $339,900 – $20,394 – $2,500 closing costs = $317,006 amount realized from sale. $250,000 purchase price + $28,000 capital improvements = $278,000 adjusted basis. $317,006 – $278,000 = $39,006 capital gain.

22. Taxable

23. Debt service

Unit 18 Exam Answers

1. b (18.6)	6. d (18.3)	11. c (18.5)
2. b (18.1)	7. b (18.4)	12. d (18.5)
3. a (18.1)	8. b (18.3)	13. a (18.6)
4. c (18.1)	9. b (18.4)	14. b (18.6)
5. c (18.2)	10. c (18.5)	15. d (18.6)

Unit 19 Practice Questions Answers

1. Subdivision plat approval, site plan approval, sign control

2. laissez-faire

3. urban sprawl

4. 43,560 square feet per acre ×.70 land available for lots = 30,492 square feet available per acre. 30,492 ÷ 10,000 minimum square feet per lot = 3.0492 lots per acre. 3.0492 × 125 acres = 381.15 or 381 total subdivision lots.

5. Residential, commercial, industrial, agricultural, special use

6. Zoning ordinances

7. density, lot size, setback, lot coverage

8. buffer zone

9. variance

10. special exception

11. special flood hazard area

12. Asbestos

13. disclosure

14. not

15. licensee, sellers

Unit 19 Exam Answers

1. b (19.1)	6. a (19.1)	11. a (19.3)
2. c (19.1)	7. c (19.3)	12. d (19.4)
3. c (19.1)	8. a (19.3)	13. a (19.3)
4. d (19.1)	9. b (19.4)	14. b (19.4)
5. a (19.6)	10. c (19.3)	15. c (19.2)

Answer Key for Practice End-of-Course Exam

The answer key includes in parentheses the unit number and section where the question's content is located.

1.	c	(16.1)	21.	c	(15.1)	41.	a	(6.6)	61.	a	(8.4)	81.	a	(2.3)
2.	d	(8.5)	22.	d	(16.5)	42.	d	(8.4)	62.	a	(12.2)	82.	c	(13.7)
3.	d	(1.3)	23.	b	(5.7)	43.	d	(17.5)	63.	c	(13.3)	83.	d	(3.3, 6.5)
4.	c	(11.1)	24.	a	(16.7)	44.	c	(9.6)	64.	c	(13.3)	84.	b	(5.6)
5.	b	(7.1)	25.	c	(13.10)	45.	c	(11.1)	65.	d	(13.8)	85.	c	(10.3)
6.	d	(5.4)	26.	d	(4.5)	46.	a	(12.8)	66.	c	(5.4)	86.	a	(18.1)
7.	a	(16.7)	27.	b	(3.3)	47.	d	(11.1)	67.	b	(18.1)	87.	d	(1.4)
8.	a	(6.1)	28.	c	(4.5)	48.	c	(11.2)	68.	c	(2.6)	88.	d	(2.4)
9.	c	(12.3)	29.	b	(9.4)	49.	d	(14.6)	69.	a	(19.1)	89.	b	(5.4)
10.	d	(7.5)	30.	b	(15.2)	50.	d	(8.4)	70.	b	(16.6)	90.	d	(7.1)
11.	c	(4.4, 7.1)	31.	c	(9.4)	51.	a	(17.1)	71.	c	(16.2)	91.	c	(14.4)
12.	d	(4.4)	32.	a	(4.4)	52.	b	(13.3)	72.	d	(17.4)	92.	b	(14.5)
13.	c	(18.2)	33.	c	(2.9)	53.	c	(18.6)	73.	b	(5.4)	93.	b	(19.2)
14.	b	(4.4)	34.	a	(6.8)	54.	c	(9.2)	74.	b	(5.7)	94.	b	(13.2)
15.	b	(13.7)	35.	b	(13.10)	55.	b	(9.5)	75.	c	(5.3)	95.	c	(16.6)
16.	b	(3.5)	36.	b	(19.3)	56.	c	(13.10)	76.	d	(5.7)	96.	b	(18.5)
17.	d	(9.6)	37.	c	(11.8)	57.	d	(18.3)	77.	b	(3.4)	97.	b	(18.3)
18.	c	(6.6)	38.	c	(19.4)	58.	c	(10.2)	78.	d	(10.4)	98.	c	(14.2)
19.	c	(3.4)	39.	b	(6.4)	59.	d	(13.6)	79.	d	(13.10)	99.	a	(14.1)
20.	b	(2.9)	40.	b	(6.1)	60.	b	(8.3)	80.	d	(9.4)	100.	d	(16.8)

INDEX